eBay® Business
ALL-IN-ONE

FOR
DUMMIES®
A Wiley Brand
3RD EDITION

by Marsha Collier

FOR
DUMMIES®
A Wiley Brand

eBay® Business All-in-One For Dummies®, 3rd Edition

Published by:
John Wiley & Sons, Inc.
111 River Street
Hoboken, NJ 07030-5774
www.wiley.com

Copyright © 2013 by John Wiley & Sons, Inc., Hoboken, New Jersey

Published simultaneously in Canada

For general information on our other products and services, please contact our Customer Care Department within the U.S. at 877-762-2974, outside the U.S. at 317-572-3993, or fax 317-572-4002. For technical support, please visit www.wiley.com/techsupport.

Wiley publishes in a variety of print and electronic formats and by print-on-demand. Some material included with standard print versions of this book may not be included in e-books or in print-on-demand. If this book refers to media such as a CD or DVD that is not included in the version you purchased, you may download this material at http://booksupport.wiley.com. For more information about Wiley products, visit www.wiley.com.

Library of Congress Control Number: 2013937654

ISBN 978-1-118-40166-8 (pbk); ISBN 978-1-118-40169-9 (ebk); ISBN 978-1-118-40167-5 (ebk); ISBN 978-1-118-40168-2 (ebk)

Manufactured in the United States of America

10 9 8 7 6 5 4 3 2 1

Contents at a Glance

Table of Contents

Book III: Selling Like a Pro 261

Introduction

It seems that I'm always writing about eBay and how to do business online. That's because the Internet changes from year to year (as does the e-commerce market), and I am obsessive about keeping my advice for small businesses updated.

My books about eBay don't just give you the information you can find in help pages; they give you the ins and outs of selling and connecting online, based on my daily experience and research. I also stay on top of the current trends in online and social marketing, test them out, and pass the results back to you. This book gives you more information than even many long-time sellers know.

I am lucky enough to have been selling on eBay since 1996, a charter member of the PowerSeller program and now a Top Rated Plus Seller. Running a business online has given me the opportunity to spend more time with my loved ones and have better control of my life. I can make my own schedule and enjoy what I'm doing because my business is making a profit. Owning a small business can be empowering.

But those of us who run a small business always seem to be doing *something*. Buying, selling, and communicating — even when going on a vacation, our businesses keep humming. There's no 9-to-5 schedule, no regular weekends or holidays. Our stores on eBay are always open for business — making sales and making us money.

Alas, all that success and freedom takes some work. That's why you have this book.

About This Book

This book will give you the basics, the hows and whys of setting up a home-based business on eBay and on your own website. I've authored several best-selling books about running a business on eBay. This book gives you the information you need to get started in one nifty (albeit heavy) volume. You can get the info found in several books about eBay all in one place. Here are some good-to-know features of this All-in-One:

✦ There's no need to read straight through all the chapters and minibooks in order. Use the Table of Contents to find information you want to learn. When you have a question, use the Index to find your answer, as you might do with a Google search.

✦ Within this book, you may note that some printed web addresses break across two lines of text. If you're reading this book in print and want to visit one of these web pages, simply type in the web address exactly as it's noted in the text, pretending as though the line break doesn't exist. If you're reading this as an e-book, you've got it easy — just click the web address to be taken directly to the web page.

✦ When instructions in the book tell you exactly what to type on your keyboard, you'll see those letters, numbers, and symbols in **boldface** type. Of course, if the instruction itself is boldface, **you'll see what to type in** non-bold **type**.

✦ I occasionally give you key combinations to use as keyboard shortcuts. For example, when you see something like *Ctrl+S*, that means to hold down the *Ctrl* key and press *S*.

Foolish Assumptions

While writing this book, I've made a few assumptions about you. Because you bought this book, naturally I assume you're an intelligent person with refined tastes. Kidding aside, that may well be true — but the main assumption I've really made about you is that you want to find out more about eBay and selling online.

I assume also that you

✦ Have a computer and an Internet connection

✦ Are comfortable browsing the Internet

✦ Are familiar with e-mail

✦ Are looking for a way to make some extra money

✦ Have checked out eBay and perhaps bought a few items

You've probably also sold a few items and made a couple of dollars. Maybe you think eBay just might be a good place to earn a regular stream of extra income. It also helps if you've read my current edition of *eBay For Dummies* where you get familiar with the basics of eBay.

If you can accept that nothing comes without a bit of effort, you might just be on the track of a new career.

Icons Used in This Book

I've written quite a few books in the *For Dummies* series, and all the books have cute little icons to draw your attention to special comments. Following are the ones I use, along with what they mean.

This icon indicates a story about a real event. The story may come from one of my dealings or from a fellow eBay user. I hope you find the stories interesting and learn from another user's mistake (or dumb luck).

When you see this icon, it's a friendly reminder to keep in mind the short fact that follows. No doubt it will come up again, and you'll be ahead of the game if you remember it.

Here are a few words from me to you, to help you do things the easy way. I've made the mistakes, but you don't have to make them too.

This little bomb of a fact will keep you out of trouble. Often these facts are not generally known. Be sure to read them to avoid common pitfalls.

Also, you will see sidebars (with light gray behind the text), these are important things that I like to emphasize — so don't forget to read them.

Beyond the Book

Here, in one volume, are nine individual minibooks related to becoming an expert on eBay and online sales. Each book is broken down into individual chapters to give you more in-depth information on the subject at hand.

You will notice title pages at the beginning of each minibook (we call them *parts pages*) where you see what's included in the associated minibook, and where you can go online to find more information (for example, `www.dummies.com/extras/ebaybusinessaio`).

And don't forget the book's related Cheat Sheet, which is another source of quick reference information. Find it online at `www.dummies.com/cheatsheet/ebaybusinessaio`.

Where to Go from Here

It's time to open the book and dive in. For ongoing eBay-related adventures in cyberspace (the latest frontier), here are some handy destinations:

✦ You can find current editions of my *For Dummies* books at `www.dummies.com`.

✦ For updates on the topics I cover in this book, be sure to visit my website, `http://www.coolebaytools.com`. You'll find articles about things going on at eBay, online business, and social media.

✦ For time-sensitive and possibly silly posts, I have a blog at `http://mcollier.blogspot.com`.

If you'd like to ask me questions personally, you can find me on the following social media sites:

✦ **Twitter**: `@MarshaCollier`

`https://twitter.com/MarshaCollier`

✦ **Facebook**: `Marsha Collier`

`https://www.facebook.com/MarshaCollierFanPage`

✦ **Google+**: `Marsha Collier` Circle me and join me for a hangout?

`https://plus.google.com/101540468776840533944`

✦ **YouTube**: DealingDiva (don't judge — I opened that account a long time ago). I post videos to answer many questions I receive.

`http://www.youtube.com/user/dealingdiva`

You can contact me directly from the Contact page on my website. I read all e-mails and try to answer as many as I can. But please remember that I'm just me. No giant staff, no big offices. I write books, research new products to help online citizens, consult with eBay sellers just like you, run an eBay business, and try to have a life.

Thank you for buying this book. Please e-mail me and let me know about your eBay successes.

eBay Basics

getting started
with an
eBay
business

Visit http://www.dummies.com/extras/ebaybusinessaio and find an
article defining the buying and selling vocabulary used on eBay.

Contents at a Glance

Chapter 1: Hooking Up with Online Technology

In This Chapter

✔ **Setting up your hardware**

✔ **Going online without your own computer**

✔ **Choosing your Internet service provider**

✔ **Getting e-mail**

✔ **Getting friendly with your browser**

*1*f the whole idea of *technology* gives you the creeps, don't back out now. I feel your pain. Every tech-oriented bit of knowledge that's entered my pea-sized brain has penetrated only after a great deal of mental whining. I suffered the pain so that you wouldn't have to.

Better yet, you don't need to know much technology (in the true sense of the word) to run a successful online business. Most online sellers have about as much knowledge as you will after you read this chapter.

Starting with the Right Computer

You don't have to know a lot of fancy computer mumbo-jumbo to do well on eBay, but you must *have* a computer. If you're in the market for a computer, you can buy a new, used, or refurbished system, depending on your computing needs.

The absolute necessities

Although the following list is geared mainly toward the purchase of new PCs (which you can get for considerably under a thousand bucks), you should read this info even if you're thinking of buying a used computer:

✦ **Look for a computer with a good memory.** Remember that 1960s classic movie *The Time Machine?* The more time you spend using your computer, the more stuff you want to save on your hard drive. The more stuffed your hard drive, the farther back in time it goes. I recommend that you buy the biggest hard drive your budget affords you — because no matter how large your hard drive is, you'll find a way to fill it up.

✦ **Consider a backup drive as large as 1.5 TB (that's *terabytes*, which equals 1,048,576 megabytes).** Backing up your data on a regular basis can help save you from the many disasters that sometimes befall a computer that's active on the Internet. You can find new 1TB drives for sale on eBay for under $75.

✦ **Make sure you have a top-quality modem.** Your modem connects your computer to the Internet using a telephone line or broadband cable. Even if you have a high-speed connection (see later in this chapter), you will need a modem that connects you to the Internet. (A modem transfers data at many thousands of bits per second, or *bps*). A 56Kbps modem is the old-school standard; these days you can easily expect 1Gbps from a wired high-speed connection. Speed is important when you plan on using a lot of digital images (photographs) to help sell your items.

✦ **Get a big screen.** An LCD or LED monitor that has at least a 23-inch screen and a resolution of at least 1920 x 1080 pixels can make a huge difference after several hours of rabid listing, bidding, or proofreading your item descriptions. If your monitor is smaller, you may have a hard time actually seeing the listings and images.

✦ **Make sure the computer's central processing unit (CPU) is fast.** A CPU (also known as a "chip") is your computer's brain. It should be the fastest you can afford. You can always opt for the top of the line, but even a slower 2 GHz (gigahertz) processor could suffice. One of my computers is an antique slowpoke, but it's still fast enough that it won't choke when I ask it to do some minor multitasking. If you want lightning-fast speed (imagine a Daytona 500 race car with jet assist), you have to move up to at least a 3.2 GHz quad-core processor.

✦ **Include an optical drive.** A disc burner is no longer standard equipment. You may use the drive to load new software programs into your computer from DVD discs. You can also use the discs for your backups. Most models play and record DVD movies on your computer, but I think you'll be so entertained by eBay that you can skip the frills and save the bucks.

✦ **You must have a keyboard.** No keyboard, no typing. The basic keyboard is fine. They do make funky ergonomic models, but if the good old standard keyboard feels comfortable to you, stick with it.

Different keyboards have different feels. I like a keyboard with "clicky" keys, because their action lets my fingers know that the letters I type actually appear. Test out several keyboards and see which one suits your typing style.

✦ **You need a pointing device, usually a mouse.** Some laptops come with touchpads or trackballs designed to do the same thing — give you a quick way to move the pointer around the screen so you can select options by clicking.

Buying a used computer

If you don't have a computer yet and don't have much money to spend, you might want to investigate the used market. Thousands of perfectly good used machines are floating around looking for a caring home. You can pick up a model that's a few years old for a couple of hundred dollars, and it will serve your budding eBay needs just fine. The same holds true for used Macs. Make sure a monitor is included in the purchase price. eBay's sellers sell their old computers when they upgrade. You can get some great deals.

Buying a refurbished computer

If you don't feel comfortable buying a used machine, you may want to consider a factory-refurbished model. These are new machines that were returned to the manufacturer for one reason or another. The factory fixes them so they're nice and spiffy and then sweetens the deal with a warranty. Some companies even offer optional, extended, on-site repairs. What you're getting is a new computer at a deep discount because the machine can't be resold legally as new.

For the most part, refurbished computers are defined as returns, units with blemishes (scratches, dents, and so on), or evaluation units. The factories rebuild them to the original working condition, using new parts (or sometimes used parts that meet or exceed performance specs for new parts). They come with 60- to 90-day warranties that cover repairs and returns. Warranty information is available on the manufacturers' websites. Be sure to read it before you purchase a refurbished computer.

Major computer manufacturers such as Dell, IBM, Sony, Hewlett-Packard, and Apple provide refurbished computers. Check whether their websites have outlet stores (which may reside in eBay Stores). For example, I visit www.hp.com/go/refurbished, sony.com (click the Shop Now button and then select Outlet from the Shop All drop-down menu), and www.dell.com/outlet, and check the sites for closeouts and refurbished goods all the time — I've never been burned!

Because the inventory of refurbished computers changes daily (as do the prices), there's no way of telling exactly how much money you can save by buying refurbished instead of new. I suggest that you find a new computer system you like (and can afford) in a store or a catalog and then compare it with refurbished systems. If you're thinking about buying from the web or a catalog, don't forget to include the cost of shipping in the total price. Even with shipping costs, however, a refurbished computer may save you between 30 and 60 percent, depending on the deal you find.

Upgrading your system with the help of eBay

You may think I'm putting the cart before the horse with this suggestion, but you can get a new or used computer system at a great price by signing on to eBay *before* you buy your computer. You can get online at a local library or ask to borrow a friend's computer. I've seen eBay listings for workable, "vintage" PCs (a few years old), fully outfitted, for $200. Often such systems also come loaded with software. And when you have your new system in shape, why not auction off your old system on eBay?

You can also find on eBay all the bits and pieces you need to upgrade your computing system. The items you may find most useful include

- ✦ Digital cameras and scanners
- ✦ DVD drives and flash memory cards
- ✦ Monitors
- ✦ Printers

Home wireless networks are becoming *de rigueur*; many people have them set up even if they don't have a business at home. I have an HP LaserJet Pro Wi-Fi printer/scanner combination that allows me to send scans and print jobs through my network from my computer to a device located elsewhere in my home.

You may have to keep checking in and monitoring the different listings that eBay has going on; they change daily. Go put in your best auction bid, and check back later to see whether you've won! (If you want to find out about the fine art of sniping — bidding at the last minute — skip to Chapter 6 in this minibook. I won't be insulted if you leave me in Chapter 1 for a while now. Honest.)

Connecting to eBay without a Computer

Yes, sometimes life is a Catch-22 situation. Say your goal is to make some money on eBay so you can afford to buy a computer. Because you can't log on to eBay *without* a computer, you can't make money, right? Well, not exactly. Here's how you can start selling and bringing in some cold, hard cash for that shiny new (or not-so-shiny used) hardware.

Libraries: from Dewey Decimal to eBay

If you haven't been to your local library lately, you may be surprised to find that most libraries are fully wired with computers that connect to the Internet. The card catalog has been replaced by computers that keep the Dewey Decimal System (DDS) alive and connected to libraries all over the world. For example, you'll find this book classified in 381.17, with the subject heading "Auctions — computer network resources."

Free Wi-Fi at Starbucks and more!

If you love Starbucks already, you're going to love it even more now that you can buy a cuppa joe and get free Wi-Fi all day. Other business locations like Barnes & Noble, McDonalds, Peet's Coffee, and Panera Bread Company also graciously provide free Wi-Fi for customers.

Check out the site www.wififreespot. com to find a free Wi-Fi hotspot close to you

---

Some libraries don't even require you to have a library card if you want to use a computer. Others limit the amount of time you can spend online and the sites you can log on to (often only adult sites are blocked). eBay is considered fair game, and exploring it is even considered research.

The upside of using the library's computer is that it's free. The downside is that you may have to wait for some kid to finish doing research for a term paper on the ceremonial use of yak milk.

Commercial cyber-outlets and cafés

If you strike out at the public library (or you're tired of the librarian shushing you as you cheer your winning bids), your friend throws you out of the house, and your boss watches you like a hawk, you can use a commercial outlet to kick off your eBay career. There's also the option of finding Internet cafés that have computers ready and waiting to use.

National chains such as FedEx Kinko's — or, with any luck, your favorite local cybercafé — offer computer usage at an hourly rate. FedEx Kinko's offers computers (both PCs and Macs loaded with all the software you need) that can get you online for around on a cost-per-minute basis. No restrictions apply: You get full access to the Internet and can enjoy all the elements of eBay. You can conduct your business by posting your listings and checking back regularly. You can also watch for great computer deals that you may want to bid on.

Cybercafés can be another way to go. If you live near a college, you'll probably find some. Hourly rates are much cheaper because you end up ordering a cup of joe or a soda. I once checked on my auctions from a cybercafé in Peru; they charged only $1.50 an hour — what a deal!

Hooking up from work

If you get a long lunch at work or have to kill time waiting for clients to call back, you may want to get started on eBay from your work computer. But give it a lot of thought before you do. Pink slips can come unbidden to those who run auctions on company time.

Choosing an ISP

Okay, so you bought (or found a way to access) a computer, and you're ready to surf eBay. Hold on a minute — before you start surfing, you need *access* to the Internet. (Details, details. . . .) The way to access the Internet is through an ISP, or *Internet service provider*, such as Earthlink, Comcast, or RoadRunner. If you don't already belong to one of these, don't worry; joining is easy.

When you go to a computer store or buy a computer, you're hit with all kinds of free trial offers that beg you to "Sign up now, first month free!" You can find free introductory deals everywhere! (They used to just come on CDs. I have a friend who painted all her free CDs and hung them on her Christmas tree. Another sawed them in half and made a very unattractive cyberbelt.) If you're new to the Internet and not sure which ISP to go with, your best bet may be to start with DSL Extreme. This ISP has been around since the 90s and offers DSL connections for as low as $12.95 a month.

If you have a need for speed, and your time is worth a bit more than an increase in ISP cost, you may want to look into getting a broadband connection. The quality of the different types of broadband (DSL and cable) can vary greatly from area to area, even from street to street.

Before you decide what kind of broadband connection you want, go to the following site, shown in Figure 1-1:

```
www.broadbandreports.com
```

Type your ZIP code in the appropriate text box under the Review Finder, and click the Go button. From the resulting list, read the reports from other users in your area. You can also click the Reviews in Detail link to see which broadband service provider is doing the best job. You can e-mail, post questions, and get all the information you need to decide what kind of high-speed connection will work best for you.

Broadband (high-speed) connections can be a boon to your eBay business. Here's the skinny on the different types:

✦ **DSL:** Short for *Digital Subscriber Line.* For as little as $12.95 a month, you can move quickly over regular copper phone lines and always be connected to the Internet. A DSL line can move data as fast as six megabits per second (6 Mbps) — that's six *million* bits per second, or 140 times as fast as a 56Kbps modem. At that speed, a DSL connection can greatly enhance your eBay and Internet experiences. For more information about what DSL is and how to get it, visit `www.dslreports.com`.

Book I
Chapter 1

Hooking Up with
Online Technology

✦ **Cable:** An Internet cable connection is a reliable method for Internet access if you have digital cable TV. Your Internet connection runs through your television cable and is regulated by your cable TV provider. With the advent of digital cable, this reliable and speedy Internet connection is an excellent alternative. (See my speed report from my wireless network in Figure 1-2.) Most cable accounts include several e-mail addresses and space to store your images.

Figure 1-1: The Broadband Reports website has handy tools to help you select an ISP in your area.

Figure 1-2: Notice the comparison of connection speeds on my test results.

Accessing E-Mail

After you have access to the Internet, you need access to e-mail. If you have your own computer and an ISP, you probably have e-mail access automatically. But if you're logging on to the Internet away from home, you might want to look into setting up a free e-mail provider.

Most ISPs will allow you to check your e-mail from their websites, but commonly, you'll want to check your e-mail through another platform, perhaps Windows Live Mail which can be downloaded at `essentials-home`.

Google Gmail and Yahoo! Mail are popular web-based, free e-mail providers. (You also can forward your ISP mail to them.) They are free and secure, and signing up is a snap. I like them because they have apps, which allow you to read your Gmail or Yahoo! Mail on your smartphone. You can join Gmail at `www.gmail.com` or Yahoo! Mail at `www.yahoo.com`.

Some common sense rules can help you protect your account:

+ **Select a password that's difficult to guess.** Use letter-and-number combinations or nonsensical words that nobody else knows. Don't use common names or words relating to you (such as the name of your street).

+ **Keep passwords secret.** If someone asks for your password online, you can bet it's a scam. *Never* give out your password.

+ **Use two-step authentication when available**. Gmail offers an option to authenticate any device that attempts to sign on to your account. After you set up this option (in Settings), Google will send a code to your smartphone each time you sign on from a new device or an updated browser. You type in this code, along with your password, to sign on.

+ **Don't open an e-mail with an attachment from an unknown person.** The attachment (another file attached to your e-mail message) could contain a virus.

+ **Don't respond to spam e-mail.** *Spam* is online slang for harassing, offensive, or useless-but-widely-distributed messages or advertisements. If you ignore and delete such junk without even opening it, the senders will probably just go look for somebody else to bother.

Browsing for a Browser

When you get a computer, you get an Internet browser for free. A *browser* is the software program that lets your computer talk to the Internet. It's like having your own private cyberchauffeur. Type the address (also known as the *URL*, for *Uniform Resource Locator*) of the website you want to visit, and boom, you're there. For example, to get to eBay's home page, type **www.ebay.com** and press Enter. (It's sort of a low-tech version of "Beam me up, Scotty!" — and almost as fast.)

The most popular browsers are Firefox and Google Chrome (available both for Mac and the PC), with Microsoft Internet Explorer still hanging in there with Windows users. All three programs are powerful and user-friendly. Figures 1-3 and 1-4 show you these browsers and how they show pages in the same way. (Sit, browser! Now shake! *Good* browser!) The one you choose is a matter of preference — I use them all!

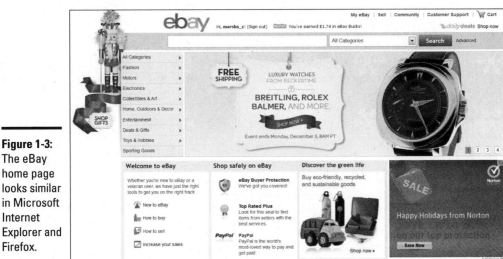

Figure 1-3:
The eBay home page looks similar in Microsoft Internet Explorer and Firefox.

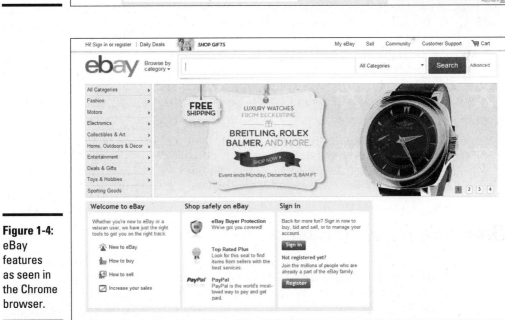

Figure 1-4:
eBay features as seen in the Chrome browser.

eBay also offers apps (called *extensions* or *add-ons*), which integrate into the browser of your choice. The app gives you a mini version of eBay (shown in the Chrome webstore in Figure 1-5) to keep at your fingertips at all times. Download an app for your browser at `http://anywhere.ebay.com/browser/`.

Figure 1-5:
The Chrome webstore offers the eBay browser extension.

You can get Microsoft Internet Explorer, Chrome, or Firefox for free. To find out more information (or to make sure you're using the most up-to-date version of the software):

✦ Go to `www.google.com/chrome` for Google's Chrome browser.

✦ Go to `www.microsoft.com/en-us/download` for Microsoft Internet Explorer.

✦ Go to `www.mozilla.com/firefox` for Firefox.

Have you ever wondered what all those buttons and drop-down lists at the top of your browser do? In the following sections, I explain Explorer and Firefox in more depth. According to recent statistics, from StatCounter, 34.77 percent of Internet users are using Chrome to surf the web, 32.08 percent Internet Explorer, 33.32 percent Firefox, and 7.81 percent use Apple's Safari. Read on while we browse together.

Perusing the menus

At the top of almost all Microsoft-enabled programs are standard drop-down lists that invoke various programs, except for Google's Chrome. Chrome has shortcuts, which I outline in the next section. Who'd ever think you'd need to use menus, given all the colorful icons that Internet Explorer provides?

Well, the drop-down lists give you more in-depth access to the program's capabilities. Tables 1-1 and 1-2 give you an overview of the various tasks you can perform from the menus.

Table 1-1	Internet Explorer Menus
Menu	*What You Can Do*
File	Open, print, save, and send HTML web pages
Edit	Select, cut, copy, paste, and find text on the currently displayed page
View	Change the way Explorer displays Internet pages
Favorites	Save your favorite pages in the Favorites file
Tools	Enable pop-up blockers, add filters, and clear your history of websites visited
Help	Find help

Table 1-2	Firefox Menus
Menu	*What You Can Do*
File	Open, print, save, and send HTML web pages
Edit	Select, cut, copy, paste, and find text on the currently displayed page
View	Change the way Firefox displays Internet pages
History	See and navigate back and forth in your current session sites visited
Bookmarks	Bookmark a page or access your saved bookmarks (same as favorites)
Tools	Enable features, add add-ons, clear Private Data, and set browser options
Help	Find help

Dabbling with the toolbar

Being a graphical interface, Internet Explorer (IE) presents you with lots of colorful icons that allow you to invoke programs or tasks with a click of the mouse. If your version of IE doesn't show these icons, right-click in the upper area of your browser where you normally see icons. A menu appears, as shown in Figure 1-6. Place check marks next to Menu Bar, Favorites Bar, Status Bar, and so on to see all the IE visual clues.

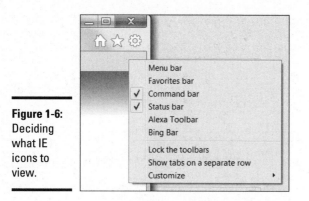

Figure 1-6:
Deciding
what IE
icons to
view.

Table 1-3 gives you an introduction to these icons, as they appear in Internet Explorer 9. You can customize which ones you view from the Tools menu, or you can choose just to see words.

Table 1-3		**Internet Explorer Icons**
Button	*Name*	*What It Does*
	Back	Moves back to the previously viewed web page
	Forward	Moves ahead to the page you moved back from
	Stop	Stops the web-page loading process
	Refresh	Reloads the current web page
	Home	Brings you to your preselected home page
	Search	Opens a box on the side of your browser to perform a specialized search on the web
	Favorites	Opens a Favorites box that allows you to easily add to or organize your existing favorite web pages
	Mail	Opens your default e-mail program
	Print	Prints the page you're viewing

Expert keyboard shortcuts

I'm all about using keystrokes instead of clicking! I also love the controls available on my mouse. Table 1-4, 1-5, and 1-6 give you a list of all the shortcuts I could find. You'll see that Microsoft Internet Explorer and Firefox share many of the same shortcut keys — Chrome lives in a special world all its own. I hope these tips help cut down your desk time.

Table 1-4	Internet Explorer Shortcuts
Press This	*Explorer Will*
F1	Open a help window
Ctrl+F	Open the Search box so you can perform search on the current page for a word
F4	Open your URL list so you can click back to a site that you just visited
F5	Refresh the current page
F11	Display full screen, reducing the number of icons and amount of stuff displayed
Esc	Stop loading the current page
Home	Go back to the top of the web page
End	Jump to the bottom of the current page
Backspace	Go back to the last-viewed web page
Ctrl and mouse wheel	Enlarge or reduce the text on the screen
Ctrl+D	Add the current page to your favorites list. (don't forget to organize this list once in a while)

Table 1-5	Firefox Shortcuts
Press This	*Firefox Will*
Backspace	Go to the previous page you've viewed
Ctrl+O	Open a window to open files from your computer
Ctrl+F5	Refresh current page
Ctrl+B	View or search your bookmarks
Ctrl+U	View Page source (to study HTML)
F11	Display full-screen, reducing the amount of icons and stuff displayed
Esc	Stop loading the current page

(continued)

Table 1-5 *(continued)*

Press This	Firefox Will
Ctrl+P	Print the page
Ctrl+S	Save the current page to a file on your computer
Backspace	Go back to the last viewed web page
Ctrl++ or Ctrl+-	Enlarge or reduce the text on the screen
Ctrl+F	Find a word on the current web page

Table 1-6   Chrome Hot Keys

Press This	Chrome Will
Alt+Home	Open a homepage that shows either a preset homepage or thumbnails of the sites visited most often from that computer
Ctrl+O	Open a window to open files from your computer
F5	Refresh current page
Ctrl+U	View page source (to study HTML)
F11	Display full screen, reducing the amount of icons and stuff displayed
Esc	Stop loading the current page
Ctrl+1 through Ctrl+8	Switch to the tab at the specified position number
Ctrl+9	Switch to the last tab that is open in your browser
Ctrl+Shit+T	Reopen the last closed tab
Ctrl+P	Print the page
Ctrl+D	Bookmark the current page
Ctrl+S	Save the current page to a file on your computer
Backspace	Go back to the last viewed web page
Ctrl+Shift+N	New Incognito window;; websites you browse in this tab will not be recorded in your Internet history
Ctrl+T	Opens a new Tab; when you want to visit another web page and want to leave the current one open
Ctrl++ or Ctrl+-	Enlarge or reduce the text on the screen
Ctrl+F	Find a word on the current web page

Chapter 2: Navigating through eBay

In This Chapter

↵ **Homing in on the front page**

↵ **Going places lightning-fast with the navigation bar**

↵ **Browsing categories**

↵ **Using the home-page quick search**

As I've said before, the writer Thomas Wolfe was wrong: You *can* go home again — and again. At least with eBay you can! Day after day, millions of people land at eBay's home page without wearing out the welcome mat. The eBay home page is the front door to the most popular e-tailing site on the Internet.

Everything you need to know about navigating eBay begins right here. In this chapter, I give you the grand tour of the areas you can reach right from the home page with the help of links.

Homing In on the Home Page

The eBay home page is shown in Figure 2-1. It includes several key areas:

✦ A navigation bar at the top of the page with eBay links that can zip you straight to any of the many eBay areas

✦ An important link to your eBay shopping cart

✦ A list of links to auction categories

✦ Links to other eBay companies, and the 45 international eBay sites

At the top of almost every eBay page is a search box that helps you find items by keywords.

Figure 2-1:
My very
favorite
home page
(other than
my own).

Do not adjust your computer monitor. You're not going crazy. You may notice that a link was on the eBay home page one minute but gone the next minute. The links on the eBay home page change to reflect what's going on — not just on the site but also in the world.

Home-page links, the next generation

If you look carefully on the home page, you can see several other links that give you express service to several key parts of the site. Here are the highlights:

✦ **eBay Daily Deals:** Click the link on the home page (it's the same as `http://deals.ebay.com`) to visit the featured items near the bottom of the page. Here at eBay, deals are the draw, so a Top Rated seller can deeply discount an item, offer free shipping, and get eBay to feature his or her listing on the home page. eBay rotates six featured items each day; during that timeframe, these items are replaced with other items only when the inventory of a featured item has been fully depleted. When you click one of the featured items, you're instantly beamed to the eBay deal's featured items page, as shown in Figure 2-2. You can also access this page directly by typing `http://deals.ebay.com/` into your web browser.

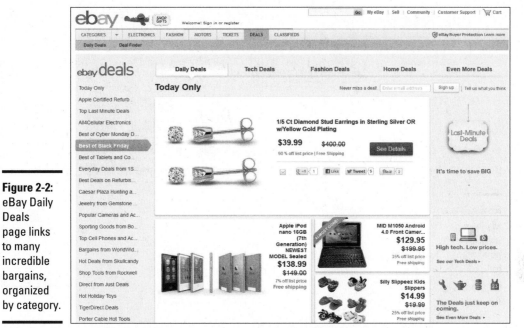

Figure 2-2:
eBay Daily
Deals
page links
to many
incredible
bargains,
organized
by category.

You can find everything from jewelry to stores built by major brands to sell their items on eBay. Featured Items are not for mere mortal sellers. They've been lifted to that exalted status because sellers met eBay's stringent requirements for Top Rated Sellers and have assured eBay that they have enough stock to fulfill a huge swath of orders.

Buying Daily Deal items works the same way as buying any other item on the site.

✦ **eBay Companies:** If you click the Legal & More tab at the bottom of the page, you will find links to the ever-growing family of eBay — other eBay-owned companies. Clicking *See all* at the bottom of the list reveals even more. Currently the list includes

 • **Bill Me Later:** With this service, you can Buy Now and Pay Later. Bill Me Later (a PayPal service) is an online reusable credit line that's yours without carrying a card.

 • **eBay Classified:** Free Classifieds? How cool is that? Visit `http://ebayclassifieds.com` for a website full of local classified ads. These ads are like the ads that appear in the newspapers, but in this case, they're online. You can see the Los Angeles area site in Figure 2-3.

Figure 2-3:
eBay
Classified
home page
for the Los
Angeles
area.

- **Half.com:** `Half.com` is a long-standing Internet site where sellers offer items at fixed prices. These items have a UPC, ISBN, or SKU number. They are not collectible items. The items sold on Half.com are books, textbooks, music, movies, video games, and video game consoles. You can also find Half.com by going to `http://www.half.ebay.com/`.

- **MicroPlace:** "Invest wisely. End poverty." This is something unique — a website of "microfinance" (`www.microplace.com`) where you can invest in very small businesses from every corner of the world. And you actually have the potential to earn interest.

- **PayPal:** PayPal's no secret; its home page is at `www.paypal.com/home`. Visit Books II, III, and VI for the lowdown on the Internet's leading payment processor for small business.

- **ProStores:** An eBay company (at `www.prostores.com`) that will help you set up your own business on the web. The stores are integrated with eBay — although you can also make a similar connection with a regular hosted e-store.

- **Shopping.com:** As a web-based price-comparison service, `Shopping.com` has features to help shoppers make informed shopping decisions. This site also has extensive product reviews and ratings from across the web.

- **StubHub:** At `www.stubhub.com` you'll find a service that acts as an online marketplace for buyers and sellers of tickets for sports, concerts, theater, and other live entertainment events. StubHub takes a 15-percent commission of the total amount of the sale.

✦ **eBay sites:** Links you to eBay's international ecommerce sites. From a pop-up menu, you may enter eBay Argentina, Austria, Australia, Belgium, Brazil, Canada, China, Czech Republic, Denmark, Finland, France, Germany, Greece, Hong Kong, Hungary, India, Ireland, Italy, Korea, Malaysia, Mexico, Netherlands, New Zealand, Norway, Philippines, Poland, Portugal, Russia, Singapore, Spain, Sweden, Switzerland, Taiwan, Thailand, Turkey, United Kingdom, and (whew) Vietnam. The international sites are in the country's native language. It might be a good place to practice your third-year French — or maybe not! Remember that after you leave eBay USA, you're subject to the contractual and privacy laws of the country you're visiting.

You may notice that the graphic links on the home page change from day to day — and even hour to hour. If you're interested in the featured areas of the site, visit this page several times a day to see the entire array of special happenings on eBay.

---

eBay's Center Square: The promotion du jour

The eBay community is constantly changing. To help you get into the swing of things right away, eBay provides a box, smack dab in the middle of the home page, packed with links that take you to the latest eBay special deal events.

Even if the main promotion box doesn't appeal to you, usually you can find some interesting links dotted around the home page without a headline. Also take a look at the small promotion boxes below the featured items.

You *can* get there from here — lots of places, in fact:

- ✔ A rotating list of special-interest links changes at least once a day. (Half the fun is getting a closer look at pages you haven't seen.)

- ✔ Special money-saving offers from third-party vendors can be a boon if you're on the lookout for a bargain.

Bottoming out

At the very bottom of the home page, nested into category titles, is an unassuming group of hierarchical links to some seriously handy pages. Here's a guide to a few of the links you'll find:

✦ **Tools:** A link to delve into the depths of eBay technology. There are links to eBay software downloads and tools. (See Book II for more on these super tools.) If you have a hankering to create some eBay-compatible software, there's a link to the developers' network. You can also visit the Security Center from here. This link takes you to a page where concerns about fraud and safety are addressed. Before buying or selling, it's a good idea to check out the Security Center in Chapter 3 of this minibook.

Clicking the eBay Site Map link provides you with a bird's-eye view of the eBay world. Every top-level (or main) link available on eBay is listed on the Site Map page. If you're ever confused about finding a specific area, try the site map first. If a top-level link isn't listed here, it's not on eBay — yet. When you get lost on eBay (it happens), the Site Map page will generally get you going in the right direction.

✦ **Gift Center:** Send an eBay gift certificate or gift card for any special occasion. You can print it yourself, or eBay will send it to any mail or e-mail address you provide. The gift certificate is good for any item on the site.

✦ **About eBay:** This is always a fun place to visit. You can get company info, investor information, company history, and more. Figure 2-4 shows you a very special portion (to me) of eBay history. If you think you might want to work *for* eBay instead of *through* eBay, there's a link to jobs available all over the globe.

Figure 2-4: My *eBay For Dummies* book is pictured as a pivotal point in eBay history.

The link to contact eBay often seems elusive just when you really need it. You will find a Contact Us link at the bottom of the About eBay category heading. You will also find the Policies link, the place to go to brush up on the site's policies and guidelines.

eBay invites their sellers to get active in the politics of online selling and buying through their Government Relations group. Join in, share your views, and send letters to congresspeople — make a difference!

✦ **Affiliates:** If you have your own website and want to make a few bucks, click this link. If you sign up for the program and put a link to eBay on your web page, eBay pays you for new users who sign up directly from your website (plus other bonuses). Click the link for the current details.

✦ **Community:** When you want to know about new features on eBay or about any late-breaking news, look here. You will also see links to preview eBay's latest innovations.

On other eBay pages, the bottom navigation bar looks different. You can access these special, categorized links only on the eBay home page.

Navigating eBay the Easy Way

The navigation bar is at the top of the eBay home page and lists five eBay links that take you directly to different eBay areas. Using the navigation bar is kind of like doing one-stop clicking. You can find this bar at the top of every page on eBay. Hovering over some of the links reveals a subnavigation list with links to other, related (and important) places.

Think of links as expressways to specific destinations. Click a link and, the next thing you know, you're right where you want to be. You don't even have to answer that annoying old question, "When are we gonna get there?" from the kids in the backseat.

Links to main areas

Here, without further ado, are the links on the navigation bar — and where they take you:

✦ **My eBay:** Clicking the top level, the My eBay link, may bring you to different places. If you are new to the site, it will bring you to your personal My eBay transactions page. This is where you keep track of all your buying and selling activities and account information.

If you've been selling on the site and are using Selling Manager, clicking this link will take you to those pages. (Find the pertinent details on this area in Book II, Chapter 5.)

By mousing over (and not clicking) the My eBay link, you make a drop-down menu appear with additional links:

- **Summary:** Clicking here takes you to your eBay Summary page or your Selling Manager, based on how you've been using the site.

- **Bids/Offers:** Clicking here takes you to a page that tracks any bids you've placed on items up for auction. It also shows any fixed-price listing in which you've placed an offer. (For more about how to make an offer on a fixed-price item, see Chapter 6 in this minibook.)

- **Watch List:** Every eBay item has a link you can click to Watch that item. Doing so gives you the opportunity to bookmark an item for possible future purchase, or to keep an eye on bidding in an auction. Any item you've marked to Watch will be listed on this page.

- **Wish List:** Here you can add eBay items to a wish list that you can share with friends who may feel the need to send you a gift. It is a very handy tool for birthdays, holidays, and major family events.

- **All Lists:** This page duplicates the listing of items you are watching, along with any other lists you've set up.

- **Purchase History:** If you buy on eBay, the site keeps an online record of every purchase you make. Clicking, and going to the Purchase History page, allows you to view all your purchases as far back as three years ago.

- **Selling:** Here you'll find an interactive list of all the items you currently have up for sale on eBay.

- **Saved Searches:** If (like me) you have many different things you search for, eBay gives you a tool for saving certain searches you make. (Book II, Chapter 5 gives you more info on this.) On the Saved Searches page, you can view, edit, or add product searches.

- **Messages:** Click this link and you'll be brought to the eBay message area. When someone wants to contact you regarding an eBay item, that person's e-mail will appear here. You'll also find messages from eBay — which it also sends to your registered eBay e-mail address.

   This is eBay's private e-mail system where you can reply without exposing your personal e-mail address.

✦ **Sell:** Takes you to the start of the Sell an Item form, which you must fill out to start your sale. I explain how to navigate this form in Book III, Chapter 3. The Sell drop-down menu also gives you these options through convenient links:

- **Sell an Item:** Here's your direct link to the Sell an Item form. Try to remember to click here directly when you want to list an item for sale — one step is easier than two, especially when the first step has promotional information.

- **Check for Instant Offers:** This option is eBay's little known recycling service for small electronics like phones or iPods. If you don't want to put something up for sale and will accept quick cash, you can input the item here. You will find out how much eBay is willing to pay you before you complete the transaction (**Hint:** You'll probably get more for the item if you put it up for sale on eBay. Just do the research by searching the site.)

- **Sell It For Me:** If you're new to eBay and think you'd much rather have someone else do the work for you, by clicking here you'll be brought to eBay's Trading Assistant page. Since you're reading this book, I suspect you might be more interested in becoming a Trading Assistant. If that's the case, Book IV, Chapter 3 will give you the information you need.

- **Seller Information Center:** On this hub page, you'll find tips on how to sell. (Let's just say that whoever wrote these tips must have read an earlier edition of this book.) You'll also find links to eBay resources for sellers. Read this book, and you'll be ten steps ahead.

  Keep in mind that all informational links provided to you by eBay in these drop-down menus are just that: from eBay. They may be influenced by sponsorship deals or alliances with providers . . . get the drift? Don't ever consider the information you get on eBay as unbiased. This book is unbiased — I have no sponsors or advertisers to please.

✦ **Community:** The drop-down menu you'll find here gives you four options. Clicking the various options takes you to pages where you can find the latest eBay news and announcements, chat with fellow traders in the eBay community, try out new features, and find out more about eBay.

✦ **Customer Support:** Mousing over this link gives you several options in which you can find answers to your questions about eBay. The most important is the Resolution Center. Here you can file cases with eBay regarding problematic transactions.

✦ **Cart:** When you're in a shopping frenzy on eBay, you'll see your cart fill up. Click here to check out and pay for your items.

Links to register, sign in, or shop

On the eBay navigation bar (next to the Sign In link) is a link to eBay's Daily Deals (if you're not an eBay member, you may see and invitation to register). It's clear they don't want you to miss the deals, so click the link to see the discounts! To the left, on the same line is the Sign In/Sign Out link. It toggles between Sign In and Sign Out depending on your current status. Your browser (and eBay) remember you and whether you're signed in or out; this link may also read *Hi,* followed by your user ID.

You'll also find a big honking search bar which enables you to perform a quick search site-wide or directly within a category selectable from a drop down menu. (Find more on searching in the section "Exploring Home Page Search Options" later in this chapter.)

To the left of the center square are tabs (shown in Figure 2-5) that represent the main top-level categories on eBay.

Figure 2-5: Click a category from the drop-down menu.

In similar fashion, a drop-down menu, to the right of the eBay logo, beckons you to Shop by Category. Clicking any of the links in these two areas will bring you to the hub page for the category. This page lists the main subcategories of that category. Click your desired department, and you arrive at the subcategory page, where you see sort links at the top of the listings.

✦ **Active Listings:** This is the default setting for the page. This option delivers on its promise — you see all items, including auctions and those items that can be purchased immediately using Buy It Now.

✦ **Sold Listings:** Here you find items in the category that have ended and have been sold.

✦ **Completed Listings:** Any item that has been up for sale and has closed (sold or not) appears here.

To the left of the items, you'll find a way to just see the different formats of listing.

✦ Put a check in the box next to **Auction** to see only the items that are up for auction.

✦ Clicking the **Buy It Now** box isolates a view of all items listed as fixed price or with the Buy It Now feature where the item is up for immediate sale.

Getting around on a catalog page

Searching eBay with a product code will bring you to an item-specific eBay catalog page. Items are listed based on their universal SKU (Stock Keeping Unit) number and assigned eBay product ID (EPID). When you see the specific product you are looking for, click the title to be brought to a page the gives you information about the item, user reviews, and a list of how many of the item are for sale and whether they are auctions or fixed-price listings. A Top Pick will appear at the top; this is the item for sale at the lowest price by one of eBay's Top Rated Sellers. An example product page is pictured in Figure 2-6.

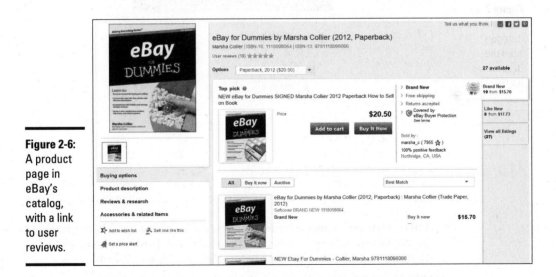

Figure 2-6:
A product page in eBay's catalog, with a link to user reviews.

Also, just below the tabs and above the listings is a drop-down menu of options (see Figure 2-6) that allows you to sort your category results. You can sort from an initial search in these ways:

✦ **Best Match** is the default search option; it sorts the listings you see by their relevance. A listing's relevance is based, in part, on past successful buyer behavior for similar items. The added reasoning behind this sort order is to identify sellers who provide great buying experiences and sellers who don't, all gauged by the use of Detailed Seller Ratings and feedback ratings.

✦ **Time: ending soonest** allows you to view the category listings in time order, with the soonest to end on top. (This is the way I always sort when I'm browsing.)

✦ **Time: newly listed** shows the items that have recently been listed in the category.

✦ **Time: new today** is where you can get the jump on other bargain hunters and see the full listing of items launched within the past 24 hours.

✦ **Price + Shipping: Lowest first** sorting can be deceiving. Many sellers list their items at an extremely low starting price to attract bidders. You may have to wade through 20 pages of 99-cent items before you reach the dollar ones — a huge waste of time.

✦ **Price: Highest first and Price + Shipping: Highest first** are good choices if you're looking for high-ticket items in a category.

✦ **Distance: nearest firs**t is used if you want to buy a large item (sofa? refrigerator? car?) and would rather save on shipping or want to drop by to inspect the item, this is the best search for you.

You can also search through the category. Type some keywords in the search box to find, for example, a particular book. Because more than 20 million items are up for auction at any given time, finding just one (say, a book on antique Vermont milk cans) is no easy task.

Maneuvering the Categories

So how does eBay keep track of the millions of items up for sale at any given moment? The brilliant minds at eBay decided to group items into nice, neat little storage systems called *categories*. The home page lists most of the main categories, but eBay also lists tens of thousands of subcategories, ranging from Antiques to Weird Stuff. And don't ask how many sub-subcategories (categories within categories) eBay has — I can't count that high.

Well, okay, I *could* list all the categories and subcategories currently available on eBay — if you wouldn't mind squinting at a dozen pages of really small, eye-burning text. But a category browse is an adventure that's unique for each individual, and I wouldn't think of depriving you of it. Suffice it to say that if you like to hunt around for that perfect something, you're in browsing heaven now.

Here's how to navigate around the categories:

1. From the drop-down menu on the home page next to the eBay logo, click the category that interests you, such as Entertainment.

You're transported to that category's page. You see categories and sub-categories listed next to each heading. Happy hunting.

If you don't find a category that interests you among those on the initial drop-down menu, simply click See All Categories at the bottom of the menu, and you'll see the main categories.

If you really and truly want to see a list of all categories and subcategories click the See Item Counts link at the bottom of the main category list. Or, if you want to make it easy on yourself, go directly to the following link (see Figure 2-7):

```
http://listings.ebay.com/ListingCategoryList
```

All Categories

[Search titles & descriptions]   [Search]

Browse Categories

Category	Format	Listings	Location	
All Categories ▾	All Items ▾	All Active ▾	Available on: eBay.com ▾	Show

◉ Show number of items in category   ○ Show category numbers

Antiques (566131)
Antiquities (15127)
Architectural & Garden (28704)
Asian Antiques (81205)
Books & Manuscripts (15825)
Decorative Arts (79513)
Ethnographic (8830)
Furniture (23304)
Home & Hearth (4345)
Linens & Textiles (Pre-1930) (24580)
Maps, Atlases & Globes (49795)
Maritime (6947)
Mercantile, Trades & Factories (3981)
Musical Instruments (Pre-1930) (736)
Periods & Styles (17733)
Primitives (23548)
Restoration & Care (163)
Rugs & Carpets (20625)
Science & Medicine (Pre-1930) (5533)
Sewing (Pre-1930) (6658)
Silver (121570)
Reproduction Antiques (16739)
Other (10670)
See all Antiques categories...

Art (743505)
Direct from the Artist (114988)
Art from Dealers & Resellers (619004)
Wholesale Lots (9513)
See all Art categories...

Computers/Tablets & Networking (1959305)
iPads, Tablets & eBook Readers (13682)
iPad/Tablet/eBook Accessories (117591)
Laptops & Netbooks (28355)
Desktops & All-in-Ones (19935)
Laptop & Desktop Accessories (450638)
Cables & Connectors (108163)
Computer Components & Parts (460887)
Drives, Storage & Blank Media (104249)
Enterprise Networking, Servers (170274)
Home Networking & Connectivity (36980)
Keyboards, Mice & Pointing (55929)
Monitors, Projectors & Accs (23174)
Power Protection, Distribution (9074)
Printers, Scanners & Supplies (211040)
Software (42310)
Manuals & Resources (1271)
Vintage Computing (18967)
Wholesale Lots (2412)
Other (84374)
See all Computers/Tablets & Networking categories...

Consumer Electronics (959199)
Portable Audio & Headphones (120703)
TV, Video & Home Audio (276266)
Vehicle Electronics & GPS (144635)
Home Automation (6002)
Home Surveillance (40778)
Home Telephones (37537)
Multipurpose Batteries & Power (65325)
Radio Communication (48841)

Musical Instruments & Gear (502261)
Accordion & Concertina (1873)
Brass (6021)
Electronic Instruments (10091)
Equipment (7510)
Guitar (145346)
Harmonica (3466)
Instruction Books, CDs & Video (26636)
Karaoke Entertainment (7565)
Percussion (37623)
Piano & Organ (9020)
Pro Audio Equipment (74658)
Sheet Music & Song Books (107769)
Stage Lighting & Effects (11424)
String (24752)
Woodwind (16593)
Wholesale Lots (237)
Other (11677)
See all Musical Instruments & Gear categories...

Pet Supplies (336088)
Aquarium & Fish (34872)
Bird Supplies (7753)
Cat Supplies (15055)
Dog Supplies (243567)
Horse Supplies (19129)
Reptile Supplies (3053)
Small Animal Supplies (4087)
Wholesale Lots (521)
Other (8051)
See all Pet Supplies categories...

Figure 2-7: The numbers next to the categories signify the number of listings. Holy cow!

2. After the category page appears, find a subcategory below the main category title that interests you. Click the subcategory, and keep digging through the sub-subcategories until you find what you want.

For example, if you're looking for items honoring your favorite television show, click the Entertainment Memorabilia category or the DVDs & Movies category. Note that the Entertainment Memorabilia category has many links, including the Television Memorabilia subcategory. Below the Television Memorabilia link, you'll see links to these subcategories:

Autographs-Original, Autographs-Reprints, Movie Memorabilia, Music Memorabilia, Television Memorabilia, Theater Memorabilia, Video Game Memorabilia, and Other. Click the link that appeals to you and you're off on a shopping spree.

3. **When you find an item that interests you, click the item and the full listing page pops up on your screen.**

Congratulations — you've just navigated through several million items to find that *one* collectible item that caught your attention. (Pardon me while I bid on that Justin Bieber signed picture.) You can instantly return to the home page by clicking its link at the top of the page (or return to the listings page by repeatedly clicking the Back button at the top of your browser).

Near the bottom of every subcategory or search-results page, you can see a list of numbers. The numbers are page numbers, and you can use them to fast-forward through all the items in that subcategory. So, if you feel like browsing around page 8 without going through eight pages individually, just click number 8; you're presented with the items on that page (their listings, actually). Happy browsing.

If you're a bargain hunter by habit, you may find some pretty weird stuff while browsing the categories and subcategories of items at eBay — some of it super-cheap and some of it just cheap. There's even a Weird Stuff category (under Everything Else)! Remember that (as with any marketplace) you're responsible for finding out as much as possible about an item before you buy — and definitely before you bid. So if you're the type who sometimes can't resist a good deal, ask yourself what you plan to *do* with the pile of stuff you can get for 15 cents — and ask yourself *now,* before it arrives on your doorstep. (Book I, Chapter 6 offers more information on savvy bidding techniques.)

Exploring Home Page Search Options

There's an old Chinese expression that says, "Every journey begins with the first eBay search." Okay, so I updated the quote. They're very wise words nonetheless. You can start a search from the home page in one of two ways:

✦ **Use the search box.** It's right there at the top of the home page (and most eBay pages), and it's a fast way of finding item listings.

✦ **Use the Advanced link (which is next to the search box).** This link will take you to the sophisticated Advanced Search area (explained in Book II, Chapter 1), where you can do all kinds of specialized searches.

To launch a title search from the home page, follow these steps:

1. **In the search box, type no more than a few keywords that describe the item you're looking for.**

   Refer to Figure 2-1 to see the search box.

2. **Click the Search button.**

   The results of your search appear in a matter of seconds.

You can type just about anything in the search box and get some information. Say you're looking for *Star Trek* memorabilia. If so, you're not alone. The original television show premiered on September 8, 1966, and even though it was canceled in 1969 because of low ratings, *Star Trek* has become one of the most successful science-fiction franchises in history. You can use the search box on the eBay home page to find all sorts of *Star Trek* stuff. I just ran a search and found around 168,848 items in numerous categories on eBay with *Star Trek* in their titles.

When you search for popular items at eBay (a classic example is *Star Trek* memorabilia), you may get inundated with thousands of auctions that match your search criteria. Even if you're traveling at warp speed, you could spend hours checking each item individually. ("Scotty, we need more power *now!*") If you're pressed for time like the rest of us, eBay has not-so-mysterious ways for you to narrow down your search to make finding a specific item much more manageable. Turn to Chapter 4 for insider techniques that can help you slim down those searches and beef up those results.

Chapter 3: Signing Up and Getting Started

In This Chapter

✔ **Registering with eBay**

✔ **Choosing a password**

✔ **Selecting a user ID**

✔ **Signing in**

✔ **Following eBay's rules**

*T*he prospect of getting started on eBay is exciting — and daunting. Perhaps you've visited the eBay website once or twice with the idea that you might buy something. Maybe you've heard your friends talk about the things they've bought. Did you look up something simple, such as a golf club? Did eBay come up with several thousand listings? Or maybe you figured you'd get smart and narrow the search down to a 3 iron, but you still got more than a thousand listings?

Did you consider buying something and then just left the site, for fear you'd get ripped off? eBay works much better for me than any quasi-convenient TV shopping channel because there's no overly made-up huckster telling me how great I'd look in the outfit on the screen (displayed on a size-4 model). On eBay, you have the opportunity to give an item a leisurely once-over, read the description and terms, and click a link to ask the seller a question *before* you bid or buy. eBay's as simple as that. If you don't like the seller's response, you can just go on to the next seller. That's the great thing about eBay: There's always another seller — and always another item.

Registering on eBay

You can browse eBay all you want without registering, but before you transact any sort of business on eBay, you must register. I recommend registering right now — while you're reading this book.

You don't have to be a rocket scientist to become a member on eBay. The only hard-and-fast rule is that you have to be 18 or older. Don't worry; the Age Police won't come to your house to card you — they have other ways to discreetly ensure that you're at least 18 years old. (***Hint:*** Credit cards do more than satisfy account charges.)

If you're having a momentary brain cramp and you've forgotten your age, just think back to your childhood. If your first memory is watching *Saved by the Bell* on TV, you're in. Head to the eBay home page and register. The entire process takes only a few minutes.

During the early days of online trading, I was selling *Star Trek* memorabilia on Auction Web (the original eBay site) and doing quite well. I ran into William Shatner (Captain Kirk of *Star Trek* fame) at a marketing meeting in mid-1997. Anxious to let him know how well I was doing with my merchandise online, I tried to explain Auction Web (soon to become the awesome eBay). Shatner scoffed, "No one will ever make any money on the Internet." (Really, I have witnesses — remember, this is the future Mr. Priceline.com.) Ah, well. The future is full of surprises.

Before you can sign up, you have to be connected to the web, so now's the time to fire up your computer. After you open your Internet browser, you're ready to sign up. In the address box of your browser, type www.ebay.com and press Enter.

Your next stop is the eBay home page. Right there, where you can't miss it, is the Hi! Sign In or Register set of links. Click the word *register* and let the sign-up process begin.

When you're at the Registration form, you go through a three-step process. Here's an overview:

1. **Enter the basic required info.**

2. **Read and accept the User Agreement.**

3. **Confirm your e-mail address.**

The following sections fill you in on all the details.

You register on eBay through an encrypted (supersecret) connection called SSL (Secure Sockets Layer). You can tell because the normal http at the beginning of the web address is now https.

The SSL certificate verification (in a lower corner of the Get Started on eBay page) means that eBay has moved you to a secure place on their site that is safe from unauthorized people seeing or receiving your information. Your information is treated with the highest security, and you can fill out these forms with the utmost level of confidence. I could tell you how SSL works, but instead I'll just give you the bottom line: It *does* work, so trust me and use it. The more precautions eBay (and you) take, the harder it is for some hyper-caffeinated high-school kid to get into your data.

Filling in required information

After you click the Register link, you go to the first registration page. At the top of the page, you will see that you are creating a personal account. If you'd prefer to start a business account, click the appropriate link. Why not start with a personal account — just to get your feet wet. eBay asks you to fill in some required information (see Figure 3-1).

You can change your personal eBay account into a business account when and if you decide it's time. A quick link to that page is

```
https://scgi.ebay.com/ws/eBayISAPI.dll?ChangeRegistration
    AccountType
```

Get started with eBay

Create your personal account or start a business account.

First name   Last name

Email address

eBay user ID ?

Password   Strength

Confirm password

By clicking "Submit" I agree that:
• I have read and accepted the User Agreement and Privacy Policy.
• I may receive communications from eBay and can change my notification preferences in My eBay.
• I am at least 18 years old.

Figure 3-1: Required information for your eBay registration.

To get started, follow these steps:

1. **eBay needs to know stuff about you. Enter the following information:**

   • Your full name.

   • Your e-mail address (*yourname@myISP.com*).

If you register with an *anonymous e-mail service* such as Yahoo!, Gmail, or Outlook, you go to a page that requires additional information for authentication. You must provide valid credit card information for identification purposes. Your information is protected by eBay's privacy policy, and your credit card won't be charged.

After you input your personal information, you're ready to create your eBay persona.

2. **Type in your new eBay user ID.**

   Your user ID is the name that will be shown to other users when you bid, buy, or sell. But don't strain your brain too much right now over your choice of user ID. You can change your user ID once every 30 days. (See "Selecting Your User ID," later in this chapter, for some tips on making your selection.) If your chosen ID is already taken, eBay has a handy tool to help you select another one, as shown in Figure 3-2.

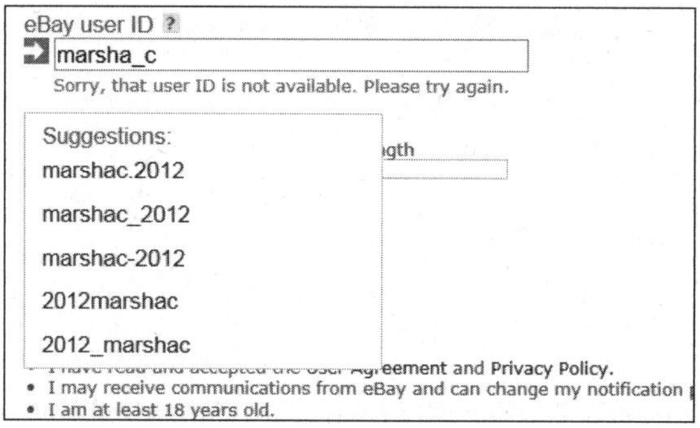

eBay user ID ?
➡ marsha_c
   Sorry, that user ID is not available. Please try again.

   Suggestions: gth
   marshac.2012

   marshac_2012

   marshac-2012

   2012marshac

   2012_marshac

   • I have read and accepted the User Agreement and Privacy Policy.
   • I may receive communications from eBay and can change my notification
   • I am at least 18 years old.

Figure 3-2:
eBay's
instant
user-ID
suggestion
form.

3. **Choose a password, enter it in the Password box, and then type it a second time in the Confirm Password box to confirm it.**

   The best passwords for eBay or any website are more than six characters long and include a combination of letters (upper- and lowercase) and numbers. Never use your user ID, name, pet's name, address, birthdate, or anything that may be easily known by others. C'mon, get a little cagey. For more information on choosing your password, see "Picking a Pickproof Password," later in this chapter.

4. **Read the not-so-fine print and click the Submit button.**

At this point, eBay tells you that they will send an e-mail to your e-mail address for confirmation (see Figure 3-3). If that's OK, click the Yes, Continue button. If you'd prefer the e-mail be sent to a different e-mail address, click the No, Please Send to Another Email Address link. eBay will prompt you to type the alternate e-mail address in the original Email Address text box. So give them the right one, the first time.

The upcoming section will tip you in on what to expect in the "fine print."

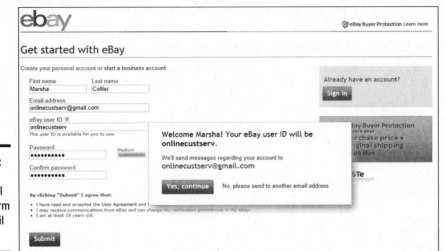

Figure 3-3:
Clicking
Submit will
help confirm
your e-mail
address.

It's safe to use your personal e-mail address for eBay registration. You will not be put on any spurious e-mail lists.

If you change your user ID, an icon of a little blue character changing into a gold one appears next to your user ID. This icon stays next to your user ID for 30 days. Double-check when you see others with this icon. The world being what it is, they may have just changed their user IDs to mask a bad reputation. They can't hide it completely, though. You can find the dirt on anyone on eBay by reading his or her feedback profile. (For more information on feedback, see Chapter 5 in this minibook.)

Do you solemnly swear?

After you fill in your required information and scroll down, you should click the links to see the eBay User Agreement and Privacy Policy. At this page, you take an oath to keep eBay safe for democracy and commerce. You promise to play well with others, to not cheat, and to follow the golden rule. No, you're not auditioning for a superhero club, but don't ever forget that eBay takes this stuff seriously. You can be kicked off eBay or worse. (Can you say, "Federal investigation"?)

Be sure to read the User Agreement thoroughly when you register. So that you don't have to put down this riveting book to read the legalese right this minute, I provide the nuts and bolts here:

✦ You understand that every transaction is a legally binding contract. (Click the User Agreement link at the bottom of any eBay page for the current eBay rules and regulations.)

✦ You agree that you can pay for the items you buy and the eBay fees that you incur.

✦ You understand that you're responsible for paying any taxes.

✦ You're aware that if you sell prohibited items, eBay can forward your personal information to law enforcement for further investigation.

✦ eBay makes clear that it is just a *venue,* which means it's a place where people with similar interests can meet, greet, and do business.

When everything goes well, the eBay website is like a school gym that opens for Saturday swap meets. At the gym, if you don't play by the rules, you can get tossed out. But if you don't play by the rules at eBay, the venue gets un-gymlike in a hurry. But fair's fair; eBay keeps you posted by e-mail of any updates in the User Agreement.

If you're a stickler for fine print, head to `pages.ebay.com/help/policies/overview.html` for all the *Ps* and *Qs* of the latest policies.

It must be true if you have it in writing

After you click Submit, the screen notifies you that an e-mail has been sent to the e-mail address you supplied during your registration. It takes eBay less than a minute to e-mail you a confirmation notice. When you receive the confirmation e-mail, you'll be heartily congratulated, as shown in Figure 3-4.

Figure 3-4:
This e-mail lets you know it's time to start dealing!

Your license to deal (almost)

You are now officially a *newbie,* or eBay rookie, licensed to shop to your heart's content on the site. The only problem is that you're still at the window-shopping level. If you're ready to go from window shopper to item seller, just click the Sell button in the navigation bar. You'll have to fill out a few more forms, shown in Figure 3-5, and before you know it, you can start running your own sales on eBay.

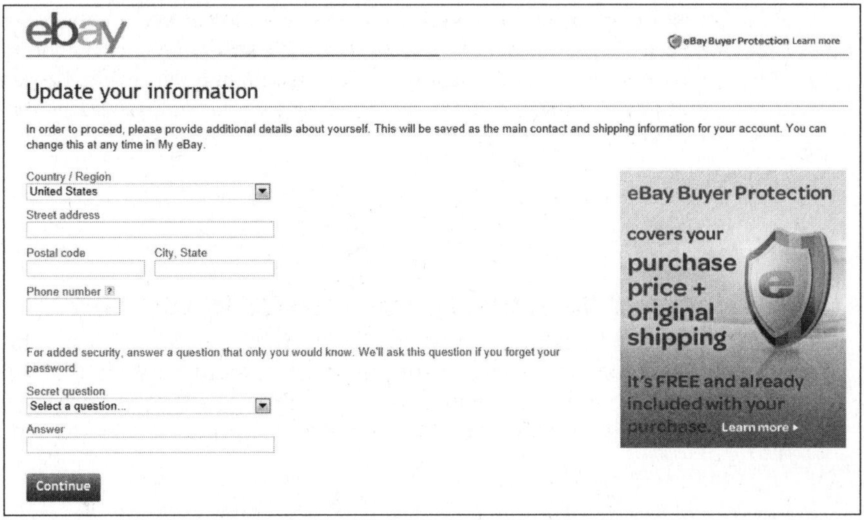

Figure 3-5:
Fill out more details to register to sell on the site.

 eBay will ask for your business address and phone number, and ask you to create your secret question and input the answer. Once you've filled that out, click Continue. You're brought to the Sell Your Item page.

eBay uses the secret question you select here as a security test should you need help to remember your password. There are six choices. I suggest you do not select the "What is your mother's maiden name?" question because banks and financial institutions often use this question for identification. Guard your mother's maiden name and don't give it out to anyone blithely. Select one of the other questions and fill in the answer. For more info on secret questions and their power, visit Book IX, Chapter 4.

Until you've been a member of eBay for 30 days, a picture of a beaming, golden, cartoonlike icon is next to your user ID wherever it appears on the site. This doesn't mean you've been converted into a golden robot; the icon merely indicates to other eBay users that you're new to eBay.

Don't tell anyone, but your info is safe on eBay

eBay keeps most personal information secret. The basics (your name, phone number, city, and state) go out only to answer the specific request of another registered eBay user (if you are involved in a transaction with that person), law enforcement, or members of the eBay Verified Rights Owner program (eBay's copyright-watchdog program). Other users may need your basic access info for several reasons — a seller may want to verify your location, get your phone number to call you regarding your auction, or double-check who you are. If somebody does request your info, you get an e-mail from eBay giving you the name, phone number, city, and state of the person making the request. Just one more reason you need to keep the information on your My eBay page up to date. If you don't, you risk being banished from the site.

Picking a Pickproof Password

Choosing a good password is not as easy (but is twice as important) as it may seem. Whoever has your password can (in effect) "be you" at eBay — running auctions, bidding on auctions, and leaving possibly-litigious feedback for others. Basically, such an impostor can ruin your eBay career — and possibly cause you serious financial grief.

Many passwords can be cracked by the right person in a matter of seconds. Your goal is to set a password that takes too much of the hackers' time. With the number of available users on eBay or PayPal, odds are they'll go to the next potential victim's password rather than spend too many minutes (or even hours) trying to crack yours.

As with any online password, you should follow these commonsense rules to protect your privacy:

✦ **Don't** choose anything too obvious, such as your birthday, your first name, or (*never* use this) your Social Security number. (***Hint:*** If it's too easy to remember, it's probably too easy to crack.)

✦ **Do** make things tough on the bad guys — combine numbers and letters (use uppercase and lowercase) or create nonsensical words.

✦ **Don't** give out your password to anyone — it's like giving away the keys to the front door of your house.

✦ **Do** change your password *immediately* if you ever suspect someone has it. You can change your password, by going to the Account Information area of your My eBay page or to the following address:

```
signin.ebay.com/ws/eBayISAPI.
    dll?ChangePasswordAndCreateHint
```

✦ **Do** change your password every few months just to be on the safe side.

For more information on passwords and other security stuff, check out Book IX.

Selecting Your User ID

Making up a user ID is always a pleasant chore. If you've never liked your real name or never had a nickname, here's your chance to correct that situation. Choose an ID that tells a little about you. Of course, if your interests change, you may regret too narrow a user ID.

You can call yourself just about anything, but remember that this ID is how other eBay users will know you. Here are some guidelines:

✦ **Don't** use a name that would embarrass your mother.

✦ **Don't** use a name with a negative connotation, such as *scam-guy*. If people don't trust you, they won't buy from you.

✦ **Don't** use a name that's too weird, you know, something like *baby-vampire-penguin*. People may chuckle, but they may also question your sanity.

✦ **Remember** that eBay doesn't allow spaces in user IDs, so make sure that the ID makes sense when putting two or more words together. A friend of mine intended to register as "gang of one." She forgot the hyphens, so her ID reads *gangofone*.

If you're dying to have several short words as your user ID, you can use underscores or hyphens to separate them, as in *super-shop-a-holic*. And if you sign in to eBay for the whole day, you won't have to worry about repeatedly typing a complicated ID.

You can change your user ID once every 30 days if you want to, but I don't recommend it because people come to know you by your user ID. If you change your ID, your past does play tagalong and attaches itself to the new ID. But if you change your user ID too many times, people may think you're trying to hide something.

Nevertheless, to change your user ID, click the My eBay link, which appears at the top of most eBay pages. From your My eBay Summary page, click the My Account: Personal Information link, scroll to the User ID area, and click the Change link. Fill in the boxes, and then click the Change User ID button. You now have a new eBay identity.

eBay also has some user ID rules to live by:

✦ No offensive names (such as &*#@guy).

✦ No names with *eBay* in them. (It makes you look like you work for eBay, and eBay takes a dim view of that.)

✦ No names with & (even if you *do* have both looks&brains).

✦ No names with @ (such as @Aboy).

✦ No symbols, such as the greater than or less than symbol (> <), and no consecutive underscores (__).

✦ No IDs that begin with an *e* followed by numbers, an underscore, a hyphen, a period, or *dot* (as in dot.com).

✦ No names of one letter (such as Q from *Star Trek*).

When you choose your user ID, make sure that it *isn't* a good clue for guessing your password. For example, if you use *Natasha* as your user ID, don't choose *Boris* as your password. Even Bullwinkle could figure that one out.

Signing In to Deal

You don't have to wear one of those tacky "Hello, my name is" stickers on your shirt, but you and several million other folks will be roaming around eBay's online treasure trove. eBay needs to know who's who when we're browsing. So, keeping that in mind, sign in when you first go on to the eBay website, please! By clicking Sign In on the eBay home page, you're ready to shop or sell.

If you're the only one who uses your computer, be sure to select the check box that says "Stay signed in." This way, you're signed in to eBay every time you go to the site. The sign-in process places a *cookie* (a techno-related piece-of-code thingy) on your computer that remains a part of your browser until you sign out. If you don't select the check box, you will be signed in only while you're on the site. If you do select it, your password will be saved in the browser until you sign out, even if you disconnect from the Internet, close your browser, or turn off your computer.

Here's how to get to the eBay Sign In page and sign in:

1. **Click the Sign In link near the eBay logo on the eBay home page.**

2. **Enter your user ID and password.**

3. **Click the Sign In button.**

You're now signed in to eBay and can travel the site with ease. You may go to your My eBay page's eBay Preferences to tell eBay where you want to land after you sign in.

eBay's Trust & Safety Is Watching

The Security Center is where eBay's Trust & Safety gurus focus on protecting the website from members who aren't playing by the rules. Through this department, eBay issues warnings and policy changes — and in some cases, it gives eBay bad guys the old heave-ho.

You can find eBay's Security Center by clicking the Security Center link at the bottom of most eBay pages. Trust & Safety's Security Center page is more than just a link to policies and information. It also connects you with a group of eBay staffers who handle complaints, field incoming tips about possible infractions, investigate infractions, and dole out warnings and suspensions via e-mail in response to the tips.

To go directly to the Trust & Safety (SafeHarbor) question and answer boards, visit

```
answercenter.ebay.com/support-forum/Trust-Safety-
    Safeharbor/2
```

eBay staffers look at complaints on a case-by-case basis, in the order they receive them. Most complaints they receive are about these problems:

✦ Shill bidders (see the section on "Selling abuses" in this chapter)

✦ Feedback issues and abuses (see the section on "Feedback abuses" in this chapter)

Keep in mind that eBay is a community of people, most of whom have never met each other. No matter what you buy or sell on eBay, don't expect eBay transactions to be any safer than buying or selling from a complete stranger. If you go in with this attitude and stay personable-but-vigilant, you won't be disappointed.

Staying Notified about the Rules

For an up-close online look at eBay's rules and regulations, click the Policies link (which is at the bottom of most eBay pages) and then read the User Agreement. (The agreement is revised regularly, so check it often.)

To visit the User Agreement page, go to

```
http://pages.ebay.com/help/policies/user-agreement.html
```

If you plan on being an active eBay member, it's probably worth your while to regularly check eBay's announcements. (Find the Announcement link under the Community drop-down in the navigation bar.). You can also find links in the footer of eBay pages.

Abuses You Might Report to Trust & Safety

Before you even consider blowing the whistle by reporting someone who (gasp!) gave you negative feedback to Trust & Safety, make sure that what you're encountering is *actually* a misuse of eBay. Some behavior isn't nice (no argument there), but it *also* isn't a violation of eBay rules — in which case, eBay can't do much about it. The following sections list the primary reasons you may start Trust & Safety investigations.

Selling abuses

If you're on eBay long enough, you're bound to find an abuse of the service. It may happen on an auction you're bidding on, or it may be one of the sellers who compete with your auctions. Be a good community member and be on the lookout for the following:

✦ **Shill bidding:** A seller uses multiple user IDs to bid, or has accomplices place bids to boost the price of his or her auction items. eBay investigators look for six telltale signs, including a single bidder putting in a really high bid, a bidder with really low feedback but a really high number of bids on items, a bidder with low feedback who has been an eBay member for a while but who's never won an auction, or excessive bids between two users.

✦ **Auction interception:** An unscrupulous user, pretending to be the actual seller, contacts the winner to set up terms of payment and shipping in an effort to make off with the buyer's payment. This violation can be easily avoided by paying with PayPal directly through the eBay site.

✦ **Fee avoidance:** A user reports a lower-than-actual final price or illegally submits a Final Value Fee credit. (I explain Final Value Fees in Book III, Chapter 1.)

✦ **Bid manipulation:** A user, with the help of accomplices, enters dozens of phony bids to make the auction appear to have a lot of bidding action. Let the experts at eBay decide on this one; but you may wonder if loads of bids come in rapid succession but the price moves very little.

To report issues with individual eBay listings, look for the *Report Item* link on the far right of the *Description* and *Shipping and Payments* tabs on the item page.

Bidding abuses

If you want to know more about bidding in general, see Chapter 6. Here's a list of bidding abuses that eBay wants to know about:

✦ **Bid shielding:** Two users work in tandem. User A, with the help of accomplices, intentionally bids an unreasonably high amount and then retracts the bid in the closing moments of the auction — leaving a lower bid (which the offender or an accomplice places) as the winning bid.

✦ **Bid siphoning:** Users send e-mail to bidders of a current auction to offer the same merchandise for a lower price elsewhere.

✦ **Auction interference:** Users warn other bidders through e-mail to stay clear of a seller *during a current auction*, presumably to decrease the number of bids and keep the prices low.

✦ **Bid manipulation (or invalid bid retraction):** A user bids a ridiculously high amount, raising the next highest bidder to the maximum bid. The manipulator then retracts the bid and rebids *slightly* over the previous high bidder's maximum.

✦ **Unpaid item (nonpaying bidder):** No matter how eBay chooses to couch it by fancy verbiage, I call these bidders deadbeats. The bottom line is that these people win auctions but never pay.

✦ **Unwelcome bidder:** A user bids on a specific seller's auction despite the seller's warning that he or she won't accept that user's bid (as in the case of not selling internationally and receiving international bids). This practice is impolite and obnoxious. If you want to ban specific bidders from your auctions, you can exclude them in your My eBay area links.

Feedback abuses

All you have at eBay is your reputation, and that reputation is made up of your feedback history. eBay takes any violation of its feedback system seriously.

Because eBay's feedback is transaction related, unscrupulous eBay members find that manipulating the system is much harder. Here's a checklist of feedback abuses that you should report to Trust & Safety:

✦ **Feedback extortion:** A member threatens to post negative feedback if another eBay member doesn't follow through on some unwarranted demand.

✦ **Personal exposure:** A member leaves feedback for a user that exposes personal information that doesn't relate to transactions on eBay.

✦ **–4.3 feedback:** Any user reaching a net feedback score of –4.3 is subject to suspension.

Identity abuses

Who you are on eBay is as important as what you sell (or buy). eBay monitors the identities of its members closely — and asks that you report any great pretenders in this area to Trust & Safety. Here's a checklist of identity abuses:

✦ **Identity misrepresentation:** A user claims to be an eBay staff member or another eBay user, or registers under the name of another user.

✦ **False or missing contact information:** A user deliberately registers with false contact information or an invalid e-mail address.

✦ **Underage:** A user falsely claims to be 18 or older. (You must be at least 18 to enter into a legally binding contract.)

✦ **Dead or invalid e-mail address:** When e-mails bounce repeatedly from a user's registered e-mail address, chances are good that the address is dead. Usually return e-mail indicates that the address is unknown.

✦ **Contact information:** One user publishes another user's contact information on the eBay site.

Operational abuses

If you see someone trying to interfere with eBay's operation, eBay staffers want you to tell them about it. Here are two roguish operational abuses:

✦ **Hacking:** A user purposely interferes with eBay's computer operations (for example, by breaking into unauthorized files).

✦ **Spamming:** The user sends unsolicited commercial e-mail to eBay users.

Miscellaneous abuses

The following are additional problems that you should alert eBay about:

✦ A user is threatening physical harm to another eBay member.

✦ A person uses racist, obscene, or harassing language in a public area of eBay.

For a complete list of offenses and how eBay runs each investigation, go to the following address:

    pages.ebay.com/help/buy/report-trading.html

See the next section for information on how to report violators to eBay.

Reporting Abuses

If you suspect someone of abusing eBay's rules and regulations, click Customer Service in the main navigation bar. You are presented with self-service tools, as shown in Figure 3-6. From this page, you can search eBay for policy related to your issue.

Figure 3-6:
The customer support area allows you to search policies.

If you are sure you have a security issue, click the Contact eBay tab. Mousing over the three buttons on this tab reveals a flyout menu with related options. Clicking any of the resulting links takes you to the appropriate page, whether to open a case or clarify the situation. The Contact eBay page consists of three areas:

✦ **Buying:** Any issue you may have relating to the purchase of an item; from initial bids to receiving an item "not as described."

✦ **Selling:** These links connect to Seller's problems that may arise while dealing on the site. Clicking the appropriate topic allows you to open a case when necessary.

✦ **Account:** Any situation that might arise that involves your account, from forgetting your user ID to reporting another member will be available here.

If you file a report, make your message clear and concise by including everything that happened, but don't editorialize. (Calling someone a "lowdown mud-sucking cretin" doesn't provide any useful info to anyone who can help you — and doesn't reflect well on you, either.) Keep your comments businesslike — just the facts, ma'am. Be sure that the subject line of your report precisely names the violation and that you include all pertinent documentation.

Here's a checklist of backup documentation you may need for your Trust & Safety report:

✦ **A copy of the facts you recorded on your report:** And remember to stick to *only* the facts as you know them.

✦ **E-mail correspondence:** Although eBay can access e-mails sent through eBay Messages, you may have had correspondence outside of eBay from your personal e-mail account. Keep any pertinent e-mails with complete headers should eBay request them during their investigation. (*Headers* are all the information found at the top of an e-mail message.) Trust & Safety uses the headers to verify how the e-mail was sent and to follow the trail back to the author.

✦ **Receipts and cancelled checks:** These help verify that a transaction took place, and when.

eBay's response may vary

If your complaint doesn't warrant an investigation by the folks at Trust & Safety, they pass it along to someone from the overworked customer-support staff, who then contacts you. (Don't bawl out the person if the attention you get is tardy.)

Depending on the outcome of the probe, eBay may contact you with the results. If your problem becomes a legal matter, eBay may not let you know what's going on. The only indication you may get that some action was taken is that the eBay member you reported is suspended, or turns out to be NARU (Not A Registered User).

Unfortunately, NARU members can show up again on the eBay site. Typically, nefarious sorts such as these just use different names. In fact, this practice is common, so beware! If you suspect that someone who broke the rules once is back under another user ID, alert Trust & Safety. If you're a seller, you can refuse to accept bids from that person. If the person persists, alert customer support by e-mail.

Make sure that you don't violate any eBay rules by sharing any member's contact information as you share your story in a chat room. In addition, make sure that you don't threaten or libel (that is, say untrue things or spread rumors about) the person in your posting.

Speeding up a response (or not)

As eBay has grown, so has the number of complaints about slow response from customer support. I don't doubt that eBay staffers are doing their best. Although slow response can get frustrating, *avoid* the temptation to initiate a reporting blitzkrieg by sending reports over and over until eBay can't ignore you. This practice is inconsiderate at best and risky at worst, and it just slows down the process for everyone — and won't endear the e-mail bombardier to the folks who could help.

If you need immediate help, the Contact eBay page (shown in Figure 3-7) often leads to a Call Us link. This link assigns you a code number to identify you when you make the call to the number you're given. You may get a link to send a report to an agent via a Report a Problem form. This form will vary, based on the issue you present.

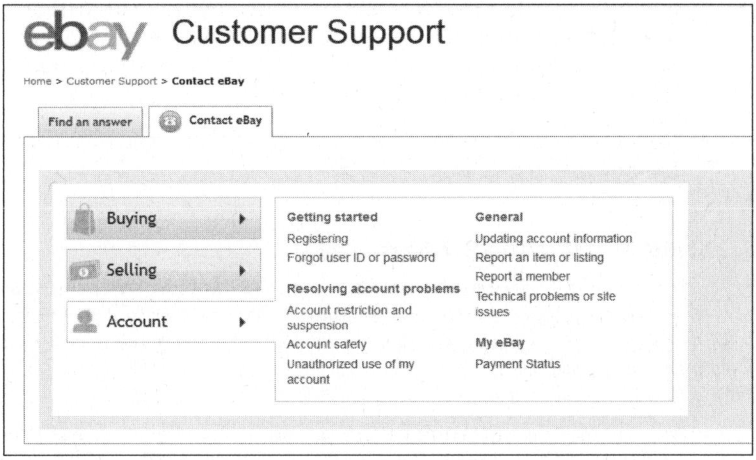

Figure 3-7:
Clicking here will get you in contact with eBay posthaste!

ebay **Customer Support**

Home > Customer Support > **Contact eBay**

| Find an answer | Contact eBay |

Buying ▶

Selling ▶

Account ▶

Getting started
Registering
Forgot user ID or password

Resolving account problems
Account restriction and suspension
Account safety
Unauthorized use of my account

General
Updating account information
Report an item or listing
Report a member
Technical problems or site issues

My eBay
Payment Status

If you don't think your issue requires speaking to a live human at that very minute, I suggest you visit the eBay Answer Center (found under Community in the Navigation bar at the top of every page). This is an area where other eBay members answer your questions.

Don't Get Caught in a Trading Violation

Playing by eBay's rules keeps you off the Trust & Safety radar screen. If you start violating eBay policies, the company's going to keep a close eye on you. Depending on the infraction, eBay may be all over you like jelly on peanut butter. Or you may safely lurk in the fringes until your feedback rating is lower than the temperature in Nome in November.

Here's the docket of eBay no-no's that can get members flogged and keel-hauled — or at least suspended:

- ✦ Feedback rating of –4.3
- ✦ Three instances of deadbeat bidding
- ✦ Repeated warning for the same infraction
- ✦ Feedback extortion
- ✦ Bid shielding
- ✦ Unwelcome bidding after a warning from the seller
- ✦ Shill bidding
- ✦ Auction interception
- ✦ Fee avoidance
- ✦ Fraudulent selling
- ✦ Identity misrepresentation
- ✦ Bidding when younger than age 18
- ✦ Hacking
- ✦ Physical threats

If you get a suspension but think you're innocent, respond directly to the person who suspended you to plead your case. Reversals do occur. But *don't* broadcast your suspicions on chat boards. If you're wrong, you may regret it. Even if you're right, it's oh-so-gauche.

Be careful about accusing members of cheating. Unless you're involved in a transaction, you don't know all the facts. Perry Mason moments are great on television, but they're fictional for a reason. In real life, drawing yourself into a possible confrontation is senseless. Start the complaint process, keep it businesslike, and let eBay's staff figure out what's going on.

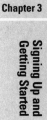

**Book I
Chapter 3**

**Signing Up and
Getting Started**

Chapter 4: Knowing eBay Sales

In This Chapter

✓ **Checking out a listing page**

✓ **Bidding on an auction or buying something right now**

✓ **Visiting eBay's specialty sites**

Sometimes, when you know exactly what you want to buy, you find not one but many auctions and fixed-price listings with that same item for sale. In this situation, knowing the different eBay sales formats is important. In this chapter, I go over the various types of sales and show you the ways to use each type to your advantage.

Checking Out the Listing Page

All item pages on eBay — whether auctions, fixed-price items, or Buy It Now items — look about the same. Figure 4-1 shows a conventional auction-item page. If you were viewing this auction page on the screen, you could scroll down and see a complete description of the item, along with shipping information.

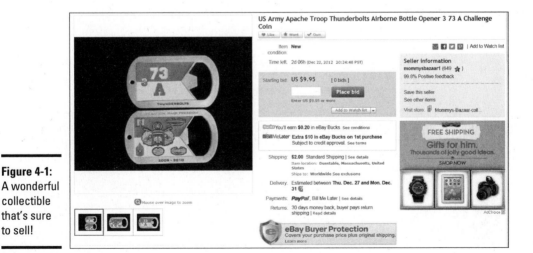

Figure 4-1:
A wonderful collectible that's sure to sell!

eBay auction listings have some subtle differences. (With a venue as big as eBay, you gotta have some flexibility.) You may see the words *Bill Me Later* (which indicates you can use PayPal's payment plan) or *Add Warranty* (where the seller offers a warranty from Square Trade). Most listings also have preset item specifics that appear above the description written by the seller. If you're looking at an item in a fixed-price sale, you'll see the words *Buy It Now*, as shown in Figure 4-2.

Figure 4-2:
Bypass the bidding and buy on the spot for $78.99.

Examining listing info

Here's a list of stuff you see as you scroll down a typical item page:

✦ **Item category:** Located just above the item title, you can click the category listing and do some comparison shopping. (Book II, Chapter 1 offers some more searching strategies.)

✦ **Item title and number:** The title and number identify the item. Keep track of this info for inquiries later. You will find the item number cleverly hidden at the top left of the Description tab, just above Item Specifics. Some sellers also use a subtitle to pass on more information about their items.

If you're interested in a particular type of item, take note of the keywords used in the title (you're likely to see them again in future titles). Doing so helps you narrow down your searches.

✦ **Add to Watch List:** Click this link, and the item is magically added to the Watching list on your My eBay Lists page so you can keep an eye on the progress of an auction — without actually bidding. If you haven't signed in, you have to type your user ID and password before you can save a listing to your My eBay page.

✦ **Email, Facebook, Twitter, and Pinterest icons:** Next to the *Add to Watch list*, you see four social sharing icons. Clicking any one of these opens a share window that allows you to post a link to the listing for all your social media friends to see. If the listing is an auction, this may not be in your best interest. The less competition you have, the lower your win price will be.

✦ **Time left:** Although the clock never stops ticking on eBay, you must continue to refresh your browser to see the time remaining on the *official* clock. When the item gets down to the last hour of the auction, you'll see the time expressed in minutes and seconds. You'll also see the date and time that the listing will close.

Timing is the key in an eBay bidding strategy (covered in Chapter 6), so don't forget that eBay uses Pacific Standard Time (PST) or Pacific Daylight Time (PDT) as the standard, depending on the season.

✦ **Quantity:** This field appears only when multiple items are available. If it's a multiple-item, fixed-price sale, you have no opportunity to bid — you use Buy It Now to purchase whatever quantity of the item you want. You'll be prompted for a quantity when you buy.

✦ **Seller information:** This area, on the right side of the page, gives you information about the seller. *Know thy seller* ranks right after *caveat emptor* as a phrase that pays at eBay. As I tell you nearly a million times in this book, *read the feedback rating!* (Okay, maybe not a million — it would drive the editors bonkers.) Like any community, eBay has its share of good folks and bad folks. Your chance for a flawless transaction is to read the seller's feedback. You'll see several things in the Seller Information box (as shown in Figure 4-3).

Figure 4-3:
Lots of
data on the
seller is
accessible
here.

> **Seller information**
> **marsha_c** (7966 ⭐) m🔲
> 100% Positive feedback
>
> Top Rated Plus
>
> ┈┈┈┈┈┈┈┈┈┈┈┈┈┈┈
> Save this seller
> See other items
> Visit store: 🔲 Marsha Collier's F...

- **Seller icons:** Various icons that show the status of the seller. A varicolored star reflects the feedback level of the seller. If the seller is a Top Rated, you see the Top Rated icon. The *me* icon links to a seller's About Me page to find out more about the person or business behind the sale (not every seller sets one up). Click the blue-and-red *me* icon.

- **Feedback rating:** This number is also to the right of the seller's name in parentheses. Click the number next to the seller's ID to view his or her Feedback profile and entire feedback history. Read as much of the feedback you want to ensure you feel comfortable doing business with this person.

  Keep in mind that no matter what the seller's rating is, your purchase is covered under eBay's Buyer protection to be exactly as described.

- **Positive feedback percentage:** The eBay computers calculate this figure. It's derived from all the positive and negative feedback that a user receives.

✦ **Starting bid or Current bid:** In an auction listing, this is the dollar amount that the bidding has reached. The amount changes throughout the auction as people place bids. If no bids have been placed on the item, it will read *Starting bid.*

Sometimes, next to the current dollar amount, you see *Reserve not met* or *Reserve met.* This means the seller has set a *reserve price* for the item — a secret price that must be reached before the seller will sell the item. Most auctions do not have reserve prices.

✦ **Buy It Now price:** If you want an item immediately and the price listed in this area is okay with you, click Buy It Now. You will be taken to a page where you can complete your purchase. Buy It Now is an option in auctions and does not appear in all listings.

✦ **Number of bids:** Clicking this number takes you to a page that shows you the bids that have been placed. The starting bid is listed on this page as well, in light gray, below the list of bids. When the listing is live, you can click the number of bids to find out who is bidding and when bids were placed. (Only the seller can view the true user IDs of the bidders.)

When you're bidding, eBay hides your bidder ID by using anonymous names. Your actual user ID is shown to the seller of this item only. Bidders are assigned anonymous names, such as a***k.

You can click the number of bids to see how the bidding action is going, but you won't be able to see the high bidder's proxy bid (more about proxy bids later in this chapter).

Sometimes an item has no bids because everyone is waiting until the last minute. Then you see a flurry of activity as bidders try to outbid each other (called *sniping,* which Chapter 6 in this minibook explains). It's all part of the fun of eBay.

✦ **Shipping:** If the seller is willing to ship the item anywhere in the country for free (or for a flat rate), you'll see that here. This area may also link to eBay's shipping calculator if the seller customizes the shipping expense according to weight and distance.

✦ **Item location:** This field tells you, at the very least, the country where the seller is located. You may also see more specific info, such as the seller's city and geographic area. (What you see depends on how detailed the seller chooses to be.) The item location is handy if you'd like to go pick up the item — but e-mail the seller first to see whether he or she would be willing to meet you at (say) a local Starbucks to complete the transaction.

✦ **Ships to:** If the seller ships to only the United States, it will state so here. If the seller ships to any other countries, this is where they will be listed.

Moving on to the tabs

If you scroll on down the listing page, you see tabs that give you even more detailed information about the item that's for sale or auction, as follows. When you click the Description tab, you find the item description, which will state "revised" if the seller has made any revisions to the description during the run of the listing. Read all this information carefully before buying or bidding:

✦ **Item Specifics:** At the top of the Description tab, you will see a box containing specific descriptors about the item for sale. The seller generally adds the information you see here, but often, information is pulled from eBay's product catalog (based on a product's SKU, UPC, or ISBN).

✦ **Detailed item info:** Depending on the type of item, this box may just contain a few lines — or, in the case of media or electronics, a bucketload of data (as shown in Figure 4-4). This type of information is also supplied from eBay's catalog.

Detailed item info

Synopsis
The unparalleled guide to successfully buying and selling on eBay, fully revised and updated eBay is the world's #1 shopping and selling site, where millions find bargains and make money with their own sales. Marsha Collier is the #1 eBay expert and bestselling author, with more than a million copies of her books in print. And eBay For Dummies has been the bestselling book on eBay since the original edition in 1999. Thoroughly updated to cover all the changes in the eBay site, eBay For Dummies, 7th Edition is an easy-to-follow path for new users to get from registration through making purchases to making sales. Ultimate eBay authority Marsha Collier gets you started with information about signing up, navigating the site, and using the My eBay page to track you activity. She then shows you how to find the best bargains, make a winning bid, and complete your purchase securely. While she guides you into becoming a successful eBay seller, she also shows you how you can pick up extra money in a tight economy with eBay sales. Walks you through listing an item, shoot and post a photo, communicate with bidders, safely ship a sold item, and securely collect your money Shows you how to set up a seller account, list items, offer customer service, ship merchandise, and receive payment securely Highlights expanded guidance on selling on eBay, which is the process that sparks the most demand for outside help Explores eBay's special features, showing you how to work within the rules, use the community, and even set up a charity auction Shares tips for managing multiple auctions, creating a store, troubleshooting, maintaining privacy, and reporting abuses eBay For Dummies, 7th Edition prepares you to save money on your purchases and make money on your sales, all from the comfort of your home.

Product Identifiers
ISBN-10	1118098064
ISBN-13	9781118098066

Key Details
Author	Marsha Collier
Number Of Pages	408 pages
Format	Trade Paper
Publication Date	2012-01-10
Language	English
Publisher	Wiley & Sons, Incorporated, John

Additional Details
Edition Number	7
Copyright Date	2011
Illustrated	Yes

Dimensions
Weight	20.8 Oz
Height	0.9 In.
Width	7.4 In.
Length	9.3 In.

Target Audience
Group	Trade

Classification Method
LC Classification Number	HF5478
Dewey Decimal	381/.17/02854678
Dewey Edition	21

Certain data records © 2012 Bowker. Rights in cover images reserved by owners.

Figure 4-4: Catalog details on the item for sale in a standardized format.

By clicking the Shipping and Payments tab, you'll find some other important data on the typical listing page, as shown in Figures 4-5 and 4-6.

Description	**Shipping and payments**				Print	Report item

Seller assumes all responsibility for this listing.

Shipping and handling

Item location: Northridge, California, United States

Shipping to: United States

Quantity: 1   Change country: United States   ZIP Code: 91325   Get Rates

Shipping and handling	Each additional item	To	Service	Delivery*
Free shipping	Free	United States	Economy Shipping (USPS Media Mail™)	Estimated between **Mon. Dec. 24** and **Wed. Jan. 2**
US $2.99	US $2.50	United States	Expedited Shipping (USPS Priority Mail®)	Estimated between **Mon. Dec. 24** and **Wed. Dec. 26**
US $18.00	US $18.00	United States	One-day Shipping (USPS Express Mail®)	Estimated by **Sat. Dec. 22**

* Estimated delivery dates include seller's handling time, and will depend on shipping service selected and receipt of **cleared payment**. Delivery times may vary, especially during peak periods.

Handling time	Estimated sales tax
Will usually ship within 1 business day of receiving cleared payment.	Seller charges sales tax for items shipped to: CA*(8.75%). * Tax applies to subtotal + S&H for these states only

Get It Fast This seller offers expedited shipping services and will ship your item within one business day of receiving your payment. To receive the item as soon as possible, please pay immediately using a fast and reliable payment method such as PayPal. Seller is not liable for normal variability of shipping services.

Figure 4-5: The shipping and handling details for the item listing.

✦ Who pays

✦ Whether the seller is charging flat-rate shipping or is offering more than one shipping option through a shipping calculator

✦ The estimated delivery date

✦ Which states have to pay sales tax (if any) and the sales tax rate

✦ Whether the seller is willing to ship to your area

Sometimes sellers won't ship internationally; if that's the case, they'll let you know here. Be sure to also check the item description for other shipping information and terms.

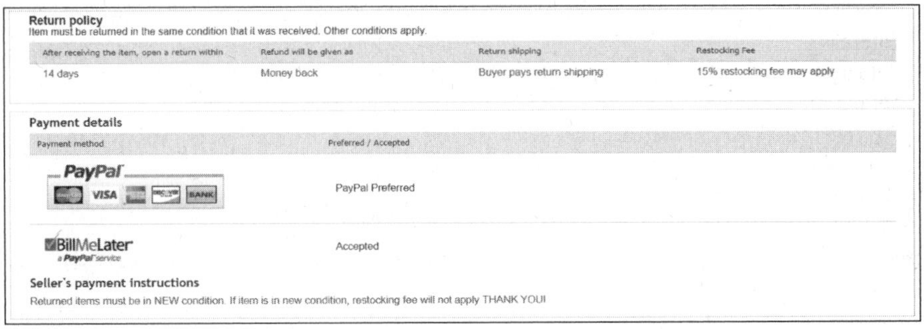

Return policy
Item must be returned in the same condition that it was received. Other conditions apply.

After receiving the item, open a return within	Refund will be given as	Return shipping	Restocking Fee
14 days	Money back	Buyer pays return shipping	15% restocking fee may apply

Payment details

Payment method	Preferred / Accepted
PayPal VISA	PayPal Preferred
BillMeLater a *PayPal* service	Accepted

Seller's payment instructions
Returned items must be in NEW condition. If item is in new condition, restocking fee will not apply THANK YOU!

Figure 4-6:
The seller's return policy.

If the item doesn't have flat-rate shipping, the seller may have conveniently included eBay's shipping calculator in this area. eBay knows your ZIP code, so you're presented with the shipping cost to your location.

The seller's return policy will be listed here too, so if you want the option to return an item (if it doesn't fit?) you'd better check here first.

The Payment details area tells you the payment methods that the seller accepts: PayPal, Paymate, Propay, or their own merchant credit card service. Often, you are directed to read the item description for more details.

Be sure to use the Watch This Item feature when shopping around. Organization is the name of the game on eBay, especially if you plan to bid on multiple auctions or compare pricing in fixed-price listings. I figure you're in the bidding game to win, so start keeping track of items now.

Getting even more info (if you want to)

Links in the Seller Information area and on the item's Description tab give you access to details about the seller as well as enable you to contact the seller. For example, you can find the date the seller joined eBay and the country in which he or she registered by clicking the Feedback number link to the right of the seller's user ID.

Clicking the Ask a Question link (scroll down to find it at the bottom of the Description tab) hooks you up with eBay's e-mail system so you can ask the seller a question regarding the item.

To ask a seller a question, follow these steps:

1. **Scroll all the way to the bottom of the Description tab and click the Ask a Question link.**

   You're presented with the Find Answers form.

2. **Select a topic from the drop-down list that most closely matches your query.**

   The seller may have posted common answers to questions. If you haven't found your answer, click other, and a Continue button will appear.

3. **Click the Continue button to get an e-mail form.**

4. **Fill in the topic and the message area; then click Send Message.**

   Expect to hear back from the seller within a day. If it takes the seller more than a day to respond (unless it's over the weekend — eBay sellers are entitled to a little rest), and you get no explanation for the delay, consider buying from someone else.

Also in the Seller Information area is a See Other Items link. This link takes you to a page that lists all the seller's current auctions and fixed-price sales. If the seller has an eBay Store, a link to it appears in the Seller Information area as well. I tell you about eBay Stores in the later section "Shopping eBay Stores."

Bidding on Auctions

To give you a sense of the auction process, here's a real-world example of my addictions put to the eBay test. I searched and found an item that I wanted, "Home-baked Snickerdoodle cookies." (Yes, you can find real food in the Home and Garden⇨Food and Wine category!) After reading the seller's feedback (and skipping lunch), I wanted the item even more! None of this seller's previous buyers were unhappy with the product. As a matter of fact, no one seems able to say enough good things about the quality of their food. Yum! (If I buy cookies for research for this book, it makes my baked goods a tax write-off, no?)

For a dozen cookies, the starting bid is $6.95, and the auction ends in over four days. So I need to observe several things about the auction. How many more are up for sale on the eBay site? A simple search shows that only one is up for auction. What did they sell for in the past? I run a Completed Listings search and see that they've sold in both auctions and fixed-price listings for up to $20. (Shipping is free.)

You have to make some decisions and observations as a buyer, even if all you're after is yummy snacks. I have observed that these cookie auctions have an active bidding pattern, so at this early stage I bid the minimum amount just to get the item to show up as one of the items in the My eBay page⇨Buy⇨Bids/Offers area.

Bidding can be like a game of poker. If you want to win a one-of-a-kind item, don't show your hand to other bidders. Simply mark the auction to watch. Note, however, that this strategy isn't necessary for an item that will be sure to be listed again (like those Snickerdoodle cookies).

When it comes to auctions, the highest bid wins. *Remember this, please.* People are constantly boo-hooing because they've been outbid at the last minute (or *sniped,* as I explain in Chapter 6). You can't be outbid if you're the high bidder!

Automatic bidding

Bidding on eBay goes up by a *prescribed bid increment,* which is the minimum amount by which your bid can be raised. But what if you're not able to sit in on an auction 24 hours a day, 7 days a week, upping your bid every time someone bids against you? (You mean you have a life?)

You do receive e-mail messages from eBay (or notifications on your smartphone app) to let you know that you've been outbid, but you may busy doing other things and you might not get the notice in time to place a new competitive bid.

If you're interested in an item but you don't have the time to follow it closely from the beginning of the auction to its conclusion, you can place a *proxy bid* using eBay's automatic bidding system to place your bid for the highest amount you're willing to pay for an item — without spending your valuable time constantly following the auction. eBay will increase your bid automatically on your behalf (using the prescribed bid increment) up to your maximum bid — to maintain your position as the high bidder or to meet the item's reserve price.

Instead of waiting it out with eBay's automatic bidding, you can also go to the seller's eBay Store to see whether a duplicate item is for sale at a fixed price. Or, if the seller has set a Buy It Now price and (again) you're too impatient to wait until the end of the auction to win, click Buy It Now and go from there.

Before you place your proxy bid, you should give serious thought to how much you want to pay for the item. When you place an automatic bid (a proxy bid) on eBay, eBay's bidding engine places only enough of your bid to outbid the previous bidder. If there are no previous bidders and the seller has not entered a reserve price, your bid appears as the minimum auction bid until someone bids against you. Your bid increases incrementally in response to other bids against yours. Table 4-1 lists eBay's bidding increments.

Table 4-1	eBay's Bidding Increments
Current High Bid ($)	*Next Bid Increased By ($)*
0.01–0.99	0.05
1.00–4.99	0.25
5.00–24.99	0.50
25.00–99.99	1.00
100.00–249.99	2.50
250.00–499.99	5.00
500.00–999.99	10.00
1000.00–2499.99	25.00
2500.00–4999.99	50.00
5000.00 and up	100.00

No one will know how much your proxy bid is — unless someone outbids you and becomes the high bidder. To place a proxy bid in an auction, follow these steps:

1. **Type your maximum bid in the appropriate box, or click the Place Bid button.**

   A confirmation page appears, and you have one last chance to back out.

2. **If everything is in order, click Confirm Bid, as shown in Figure 4-7. Or, if you get cold feet, click Change bid.**

   After you've placed your bid, the next page lets you know whether you're the high bidder.

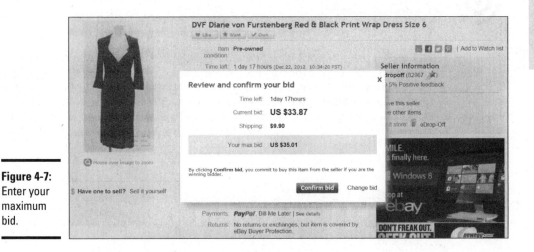

Figure 4-7:
Enter your maximum bid.

3. **The confirmation page tells you if you are the high bidder. If you're not the high bidder (as shown in Figure 4-8), just click the Increase max bid button and place another bid.**

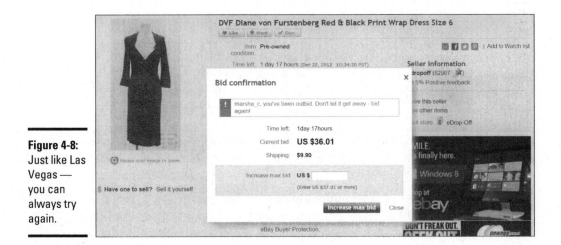

Figure 4-8:
Just like Las Vegas — you can always try again.

You'll often come across auctions that have the words *Reserve not met* next to the bid amount. By placing a reserve price on the auction, the seller ensures that the item will not sell until the bidding reaches that mysterious reserve figure.

Private auctions

Private auctions are handled in the same way as plain vanilla auctions, except only the buyer and seller know who the winner is. As a matter of fact, all bidders' names are hidden from anyone other than the seller.

After you've been on eBay for a while, you might see the same group of names bidding on the same auctions as you. I like bidding in private auctions because they're handy for snaring items secretly, without my regular competitors knowing that I'm bidding on the item. (See Book 1, Chapter 6 for more about bidding strategies.)

Buying an Item Outright

Although eBay's success was built on auctions, eBay also allows sellers to handle outright sales. You can make a direct purchase

+ By using the Buy It Now feature in an eBay auction
+ In a fixed-price sale
+ In one of eBay's stores

Buy It Now

You may have already looked at auctions and seen a Buy It Now price located below the minimum or starting bid amount. That little indicator means that if you want the item badly enough, and the Buy It Now price is within your budget, you can end the auction right then and there by buying the item for the stated amount.

Before using the Buy It Now option (because you think you've hit upon a bargain), be sure to check the seller's shipping charges. Many sellers set a low Buy It Now price but place a high shipping amount on the item to make up their missing profits. A Buy It Now transaction is *final;* you can't withdraw your commitment to buy. It's best to know what you're getting into beforehand.

If you decide that you want to buy, scroll down to the bottom of the page and click the Buy It Now button. An eBay confirmation page appears. If you still want to make the purchase, you can click Confirm to tell eBay that you're willing to pay the purchase price. Then all you have to do is go through the checkout process and pay the seller.

You can still place a bid on an auction that has a Buy It Now option. When you do, the option to immediately buy disappears and the item goes into auction mode. If the item has a reserve, the Buy It Now option doesn't disappear until the bidding surpasses the reserve amount.

Fixed-price sales

eBay also offers items for sale without the option to bid. These fixed-price listings may be for a single item or for multiple items. When multiple items are offered, you can buy as many as you like. Just backspace over the default 1 in the Quantity box, and type in the number of items you want to buy (see Figure 4-9).

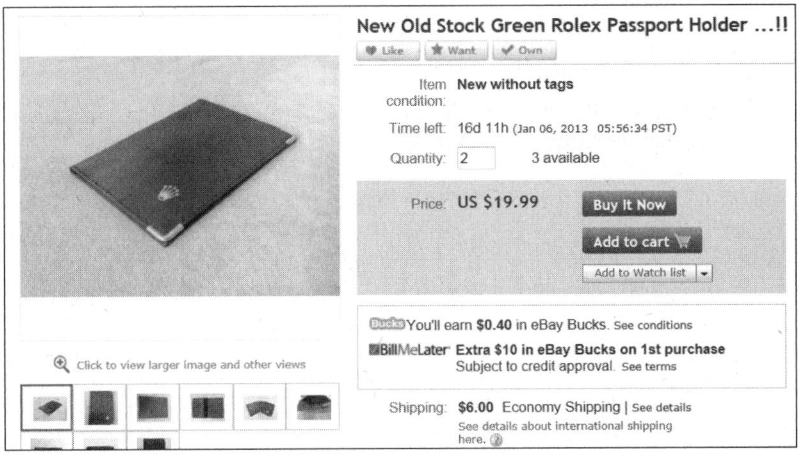

Figure 4-9:
Buy one
or up to
three of this
item in one
transaction.

New Old Stock Green Rolex Passport Holder ...!!

Item condition:	**New without tags**
Time left:	16d 11h (Jan 06, 2013 05:56:34 PST)
Quantity:	2 3 available
Price:	**US $19.99**

Buy It Now
Add to cart
Add to Watch list

Bucks You'll earn **$0.40** in eBay Bucks. See conditions
BillMeLater Extra **$10** in eBay Bucks on 1st purchase
Subject to credit approval. See terms

Shipping: **$6.00** Economy Shipping | See details
See details about international shipping here.

Click to view larger image and other views

Add to cart

Just like having a shopping cart at the market, eBay has its own version. When you click the Add to Cart button, the item is added to your shopping cart. When you put an item in your shopping cart, just as in real life, you haven't bought it yet. Only when you check out is the purchase transaction completed.

If the seller has only one of the item you put in your cart for sale, it behooves you to check out swiftly. The item is not yours until you confirm the purchase.

Shopping eBay Stores

eBay Stores are the secret weapon for knowledgeable eBay shoppers. First, of course, you can consistently find great deals. But you can also help small businesses make it against the behemoths. Sellers open eBay Stores to make searching merchandise easier for buyers; these stores also help save sellers money because sellers don't need to set up private e-commerce websites. Translation? Sellers can list items in their eBay Stores for even lower fees, passing their savings on to you, the savvy bargain hunter.

Before you buy any item from a listing on eBay, check to see whether the seller has the small, red *stores* icon next to his or her user ID. If so, be sure to click the icon *before* you bid on the item. Most sellers run auctions for items to draw people into their eBay Stores, where you may be able to find more interesting merchandise you can buy, have the seller put it in the same crate along with your auction item, and save on shipping.

You can get to the eBay Stores hub by typing the following web address:

```
http://stores.ebay.com
```

At the center of the eBay Stores hub page, as shown in Figure 4-10, you see a small group of store logos. These logos change every few minutes as eBay rotates its *anchor stores* through the area. Store owners pay a considerable amount to have their stores listed as anchor stores.

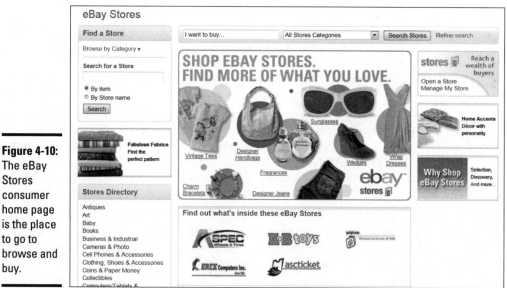

Figure 4-10: The eBay Stores consumer home page is the place to go to browse and buy.

Strolling through an eBay Store

When you finally arrive at the eBay Store of your choice, you see a page that looks similar to the one in Figure 4-11. An eBay Store displays every active auction or Buy It Now item the seller has placed on the eBay site.

Figure 4-11:
The home page for my eBay Store.

Most eBay Stores have a column on the left side of the home page that displays the following:

✦ **Store Search:** Below the store name banner is a column topped by a search box that allows you to search all the items this seller has for sale.

✦ **Store Categories:** eBay Store owners may assign their own custom categories to the items they sell to better organize things within the store. You may click individual categories to see items in that classification from that seller.

✦ **Display:** You can decide how you'd like to view the items in the seller's store. Figure 4-11 shows you the store in gallery view and the remaining time before the auction ends.

✦ **Store Pages:** This area includes links to Store Policies (the terms and conditions of the seller's auctions) as well as the About the Seller area (which offers an About Me page).

At the top and bottom of the store home page, you'll see a variety of things:

✦ **The store name:** This is the name the store owner has chosen for the store. Each eBay Store has its own address that ends in the eBay Store's name, like this: `www.stores.ebay.com/`*insertstorename*`. For example, my store's URL is

`http://stores.ebay.com/Marsha-Colliers-Fabulous-Finds`

✦ **Seller's user ID and feedback rating:** Some stores choose to put this on the home page; others replace it with graphics. Next to *Maintained by* are the seller's user ID and the ubiquitous feedback rating.

✦ **Save the Seller:** If you click this link, the store is added to the Saved Sellers list in your My eBay area.

✦ **Store logo and description:** In the middle of the page is the store's graphic logo, and to the right of that is the seller's description of the store. (This is the area that is searched when you search Stores by store name *and* description.)

Supercategories and Specialties

Aside from owning PayPal (the world's largest online payment service), eBay runs some special categories that make up a good deal of the business on eBay.

Real estate

Since the founding of our country, land has been valued as a great commodity; passed from generation to generation. As Gerald O'Hara so eloquently put it, "it's the only thing that lasts." (Remember that scene from *Gone with the Wind?*) People buy land for investment, vacations, or retirement. It's no longer common for a family to spend their entire life in one home. Real estate, although a major purchase, is becoming more and more an everyday transaction.

The smart people at eBay are sly trend-spotters, so they opened an official category for real estate transactions in the fall of 2000. You can access eBay's Real Estate category through the category link (on the left side of the home page) or by going directly to

`http://realestate.shop.ebay.com/`

Because substantial legal restrictions are involved in real estate transactions, sellers can choose to list their properties either as auctions or in the form of classified advertisements, depending on the laws in their areas. The categories in eBay Real Estate are varied, as shown in Figure 4-12.

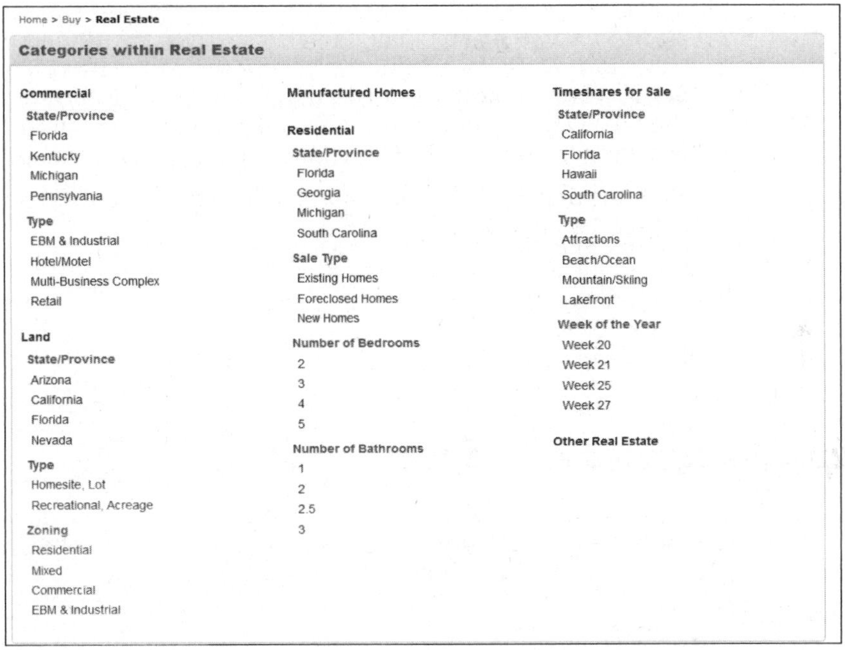

Home > Buy > **Real Estate**

Categories within Real Estate

Commercial
State/Province
  Florida
  Kentucky
  Michigan
  Pennsylvania
Type
  EBM & Industrial
  Hotel/Motel
  Multi-Business Complex
  Retail
Land
State/Province
  Arizona
  California
  Florida
  Nevada
Type
  Homesite, Lot
  Recreational, Acreage
Zoning
  Residential
  Mixed
  Commercial
  EBM & Industrial

Manufactured Homes

Residential
State/Province
  Florida
  Georgia
  Michigan
  South Carolina
Sale Type
  Existing Homes
  Foreclosed Homes
  New Homes
Number of Bedrooms
  2
  3
  4
  5
Number of Bathrooms
  1
  2
  2.5
  3

Timeshares for Sale
State/Province
  California
  Florida
  Hawaii
  South Carolina
Type
  Attractions
  Beach/Ocean
  Mountain/Skiing
  Lakefront
Week of the Year
  Week 20
  Week 21
  Week 25
  Week 27

Other Real Estate

Figure 4-12: Stake your claim on some real estate.

When you participate in a listing that is in an ad format, you do not place bids. At the bottom of the item's description page is a form for you to fill out that's sent to the seller. After the seller receives this information, he or she can contact you, and the two of you may negotiate privately. When you browse the Residential Homes category, such listings will have the words Classified Ad next to the title. Many residential home sales are handled in this manner. Land and timeshares are typically sold in the auction format.

Because of a wide variety of laws governing the intricacies and legalities in real estate transactions, the auction format may be nonbinding. Before getting involved in any real estate transactions on eBay, I suggest you read the official rules, which you can find on the following page:

        http://pages.ebay.com/help/policies/real-estate.html

Cruising eBay Motors

Buying a car — that's one purchase I don't enjoy making. Please don't misunderstand. I love cars and have had a personal attachment to every car I've owned. It's just that each time I'm approached by a car salesperson, I get intimidated. The minute the salesperson says "I've got to check with my sales manager to see if I can do that," I know I'm a goner. And when I've finally decided on the car model I want, I still have to face *the deal,* when the finance manager tries to sell me warranties, alarms, and extras that I never wanted or needed. I feel the need to run out of the dealership — and I usually do.

If this feeling is familiar to you, I would like to introduce you to the sweetest deal of the 21st century, eBay Motors (see Figure 4-13). eBay Motors is the largest auto mall in the universe and is consistently ranked the number-one automotive site on the web by Nielsen/NetRatings.

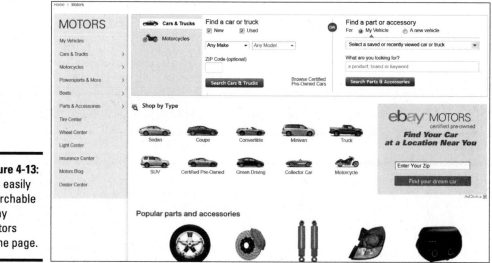

Figure 4-13: The easily searchable eBay Motors home page.

For some of us, eBay Motors is a magnificent fantasy site. I have a friend who browses the Volkswagen bus category; his eyes glaze over with hope and awe as he reads each listing. I'm sure he's reliving his hippie days of the late '60s. Another friend reads the Ferrari and Lamborghini listings; he pooh-poohs all the aftermarket changes to the classics. My best friend checks out the vintage Thunderbirds and pictures herself as Suzanne Somers flirting with the guys in *American Graffiti.* Then of course there's my fantasy car — the buttercup-yellow Rolls-Royce Corniche convertible driven by Teensy in *Ya-Ya Sisterhood.* (I've yet to find one on eBay in that color — but then again, some things are best kept a fantasy.)

Finding more than cars

The truly amazing part about eBay Motors is that it has more than just the usual cars and vans. In fact, the rule seems to be that if it has an engine, you'll find it here. Here's a description of the Other Vehicles categories:

✔ **ATVs:** Within the ATV subcategory of Powersports, you'll find a wide selection of new and used 4x4s and 2x4s, three-wheelers and four-wheelers. I even found a few six-wheel amphibious vehicles! Bidding in this category is active, and the items move quickly.

✔ **Aircraft:** Anything that flies can be found here, from hot-air balloons to military trainer jets. Browsing this category is amazing (found under "other vehicles"). Who could imagine that with a click of your mouse (and enough money) you could own your own Bell helicopter or Gulfstream jet? If you've ever dreamt of taking up flying, this might be the category to get your hobby started!

✔ **Boats:** This category was so full that I got seasick just browsing! It has its own sub-categories of Fishing Boats, Personal Watercraft (Sea-Doo, Yamaha, Kawasaki, and so on), Powerboats, Sailboats, and Other (kayaks, canoes, pontoons, tenders, and dinghies). I know boats, and I saw some great deals in this category. There were some beautiful Bass boats and Boston Whalers at incredible prices. A dozen or so Bayliners caught my eye, especially the 47-foot Pilot House Motoryacht with a starting bid of $290,000.00 (sigh). It was also nice to see a wide selection of prices for sailboats. With some time spent shopping in this category, you can find just about anything you want within your price range.

✔ **Buses:** No kidding. You want to start your own bus line? Here's the place to find the buses — and it seems that plenty of people are interested in them! There's active bidding on old school buses in this category. (And I thought the American family was getting smaller!)

✔ **Commercial trucks:** Since commercial trucks are something I know jack about, I went to some experts who browsed the site and examined the deals. Here's their review for those in the know. The items are good quality and of the type they'd like to find at commercial truck auctions. They tell me the prices are bargains and that they'll be visiting the site regularly from now on — sounds like a good recommendation to me!

✔ **Scooters and minibikes:** Aside from what you'd expect to find here, this is the home for beautiful vintage and new Vespa motor scooters.

✔ **Snowmobiles:** I've never lived in a snowy part of the country, so I can only imagine how much fun these bad boys are. You'll see everything from top-of-the-line new ones to gently used private sales.

✔ **Other:** How about a 1947 Coca-Cola vending truck — complete with fountain, cotton-candy machine, and propane-powered hot-dog cooker! Sounds like a carnival on wheels! Okay, it doesn't run, but hey — it's only $3000! There's also a Shelby Cobra kit, with no motor or tranny, but you need a hobby, don't you? I also found a Think Neighbor electric vehicle; a sandrail dune buggy four-seater; go-karts, and car haulers. There's nothing you can't find on eBay!

Many of the cars on eBay Motors are private-party sales, bank cars (repossessions), and cars that have been cherry-picked by wholesalers and dealer overstocks. In addition, professional car dealers sell rare, hard-to-find cars to a marketplace that draws between 4 and 5 million visitors per month. You can't get that many people through the door at a local dealership! Dealers put up the rare colors and limited-edition vehicles because this *is* an auction site — the rarer an item, the more likely bidders are to get excited. The more excited bidders are, the more they lose their heads — and the higher the price goes.

With an average of seven to eight bids per sale, eBay Motors is a competitive environment for the most desirable cars. Dealers can sell cars for less on eBay because it costs them less to sell. (They don't have to pay the finance manager to twist your arm to buy the extras.)

You can enter the eBay Motors site in two ways. Click the Motors link on the left of the home page, or go to

```
www.ebay.com/motors
```

For more on eBay Motors auction bidding strategies, check out Chapter 6 in this minibook.

Supercategories

When it comes to unique shopping, there are some supercategories worth taking a look at. On the eBay home page, take a look at the major category list of links on the left. By poking around the major category-listing links, you'll find links to unique eBay areas.

eBay gurus outlined these specialized categories to reflect interests that cover more than one category. Some interesting (and popular) supercategories to check out are

✦ Business & Industrial

✦ Collectibles

✦ Giving Works (Charity)

These supercategories come in handy when you're looking for cross-category merchandise.

Business & Industrial

If you're looking for anything to outfit a business, the Business & Industrial category is the place to go. Shown in Figure 4-14, it covers everything from tractor parts to welding equipment to computers. You can browse the sub-category of your choice and see what's available.

However, if you need a particular brand name or item, you may find it easier through eBay's search. For professional tips on eBay's search, check out Chapter 6.

Giving Works: Giving back to nonprofits

Many charitable organizations are selling their wares on eBay to raise money for their fine work (see Figure 4-15). You can get some rare and unusual items here, such as the annual NBC *Today Show* Green Room autograph book. This one-of-a-kind book has signatures and notes from the famous guests of the *Today Show*. One of these Green Room books sold for $87,500! The super-hottest auction is the annual lunch with Warren Buffet (the CEO of Berkshire Hathaway); in 2012 it raised $3,456,789 — bidding almost tripled in the last seconds!

eBay partnered with a leader in online charitable auctions, MissionFish, which has been helping organizations turn donations into cash through online auctions since 2000. MissionFish works with eBay sellers to raise money for nonprofit organizations.

Figure 4-14: The Business & Industrial category covers a varied group of items.

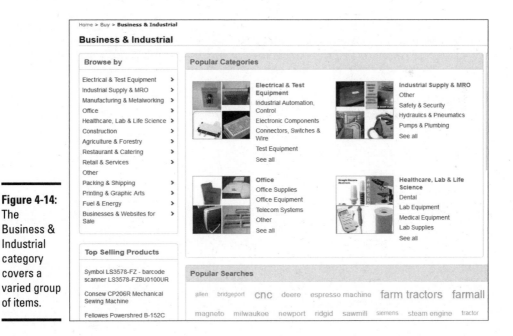

Figure 4-15:
Do a little shopping while doing some good.

When you list an item on eBay, you can choose a nonprofit from a certified list and designate a percentage of the proceeds (from 20 to 100%) to donate. The item appears in the search results with a Charity Auction icon. When you go to the item page, you'll see the name of the nonprofit, some information about it, and the percentage of the final bid that the seller is donating. You can search eBay for your favorite nonprofits by name.

Chapter 5: Checking Out the Seller and Leaving Feedback

In This Chapter

✔ Giving feedback

✔ Reading eBay's DSR System

✔ Viewing the seller's profile

✔ Comparing items

✔ Playing it safe with buyer-protection programs

When you're shopping on eBay, you're faced with hundreds of items, perhaps even hundreds of listings for the same item. How do you decide where to place your order or your bid? In this chapter, I show you the tools on eBay that guide you to a safe and positive transaction.

Understanding and Giving Feedback

One of eBay's strong suits is a sense of community formed through its use of announcements and feedback. Many experts say the reason eBay originally succeeded where dozens of other dot-com auction sites failed is that eBay paid close attention to the needs of its users.

In the early days, the concept was clear. Pierre and his employees figured that if users complained openly (for all other members to see), feedback would be more genuine — not so much *flaming* as *constructive*. "Do unto others as you'd have them do" prevailed as a philosophy; above all else, Pierre encouraged buyers and sellers to give each other the benefit of the doubt and to conduct themselves professionally.

It soon became clear to eBay's three employees that they did not have time to adjudicate member disputes. Thus the feedback system was born. But the *pièce de résistance* of feedback policy, the part that makes eBay work, is the fact that Pierre and his staff encouraged users to give *positive* feedback as often as they give negative or neutral feedback.

The benefits of the feedback policy are immediately clear. Before even placing a bid with a seller, a buyer (you) can check the experience other eBay buyers have had doing business with this seller. You can see whether items in a seller's previous auctions shipped quickly, whether items were packed carefully, whether communication was clear and frequent, and so on. You now have more information about an eBay seller then you have when you walk into a new store in your neighborhood!

The types of feedback

Every eBay member has a feedback rating. Buyers rate sellers (more on that below), and sellers rate buyers — no one is immune. Although sellers can no longer leave negative or neutral feedback for a buyer, a seller still might comment on how quickly you paid for an item, how well you communicated, or how you reacted to a problem.

Leaving feedback for the seller comes in three exciting flavors:

✦ **Positive feedback:** Someone once said, "All you have is your reputation." Reputation is what makes eBay function. If the transaction works well, you get positive feedback — and whenever it's warranted, you should give it right back.

✦ **Negative feedback:** If there's a glitch (for instance, it takes six months to get your *Charlie's Angels* lunchbox, or the seller substitutes a rusty Thermos for the one you bid on, or you never get the item), you have the right — some would say *obligation* — to leave the seller negative feedback.

✦ **Neutral feedback:** You can leave neutral feedback if you feel so-so about a specific transaction. It's the middle-of-the-road comment that's useful when, for example, you bought an item that has a little more wear and tear on it than the seller indicated, but you still like it and want to keep it.

Keep in mind that neutral feedback will affect the seller's feedback percentage (and reputation). The feedback percentage (next to the feedback number) is calculated based on the total number of feedback ratings received in the last 12 months. This does *not* include repeat feedback from the same buyer in the same week.

Leaving feedback for a buyer isn't quite as colorful. A seller can leave only positive feedback for a transaction — or none at all. If I've dealt with a particularly difficult buyer, there is a good chance that I won't leave any feedback at all.

You're not required to leave feedback, but because it's the benchmark by which all eBay users are judged, you should *always* leave feedback comments whether you're buying or selling. Every time you complete a transaction — the minute the package arrives safely and you've checked the contents, whether you're a seller or a buyer — you should go to eBay and post your feedback.

The magic feedback number

You know how they say you are what you eat? At eBay, you are only as good as your feedback says you are. Your feedback is made up of comments — good, bad, or neutral — that people leave about you (and you leave about others). In effect, people are commenting on your overall professionalism. (Even if you're an eBay hobbyist with no thought of using eBay professionally, a little businesslike courtesy can ease your transactions with everyone.) These comments are the basis for your eBay reputation. You wouldn't be caught dead in a store that has a lousy reputation, so why on Earth would you want to do business on the Internet with someone who has a lousy reputation?

When you get your first feedback, the number that appears next to your user ID is your feedback rating, which follows you everywhere you go on eBay, even if you change your user ID or e-mail address. It sticks to you like glue.

Click the number next to any user ID and get a complete look at the user's feedback profile. When you do, here are some points to recognize about the user's magic feedback number:

✦ **This number is a *net figure*** of the positive and negative comments that were left for that eBay user. For example, if you get 50 positive comments and 49 negative comments, your feedback rating is 1.

For every positive comment you receive, you get a plus 1. For every negative comment, you get a minus 1. Negative comments deduct from your total of positive comments, thereby lowering the number beside your user ID. Theoretically, if you play nice, your feedback rating grows as you spend more time using eBay.

Anyone with a −4.3 rating has his or her eBay membership terminated. And don't make automatic assumptions just because someone has a high feedback rating. You should always click the number after the name to double-check the person's eBay feedback profile. Even if someone has a total of 1,000 feedback messages, 250 of them *could* be negative.

✦ **This number shows more than how good a customer or seller you are.** As it grows, the feedback number also tells how experienced you are at doing business on the site.

✦ **This number ignores neutral comments.** A neutral comment is neither negative nor positive; it doesn't change the number that appears after your user ID. Neutral comments are used most often when buyers may not be completely happy with transactions, but not so unhappy that they choose to destroy someone's reputation over the situation.

eBay riddle: When is more than 1 still 1? Gotcha, huh? The answer is, when you get more than one feedback message from the same person in the same week. Confused? This example should help: You can sell one person 100 different items, but even if the buyer gives you a glowing review 100 times, your feedback rating doesn't increase by 100. In this case, the other 99 feedback comments appear in your feedback profile, but your rating increases by only 1. There's something else: Say you sell to the same eBay user twice. The user can give you positive feedback in one case and negative feedback in another case — neutralizing your feedback by netting you a 0 feedback rating from that person. eBay set up the system this way to keep things honest.

Members may affect your score by one point per week. If they leave you great feedback for multiple transactions spread from one week to another — you will get credit (hopefully) for two positives. To get credit for selling multiple items to one bidder, the bidder must leave feedback. For feedback purposes, eBay defines a week as Monday through Sunday, Pacific Time.

Giving Detailed Star Ratings Properly

In addition to a feedback comment and rating (positive, negative, or neutral), buyers can leave detailed seller ratings, too. After the buyer types a comment, he or she is prompted to rate the seller with one to five stars on four different factors of the transaction. Figure 5-1 shows the specific rating factors, and Table 5-1 outlines what the stars mean.

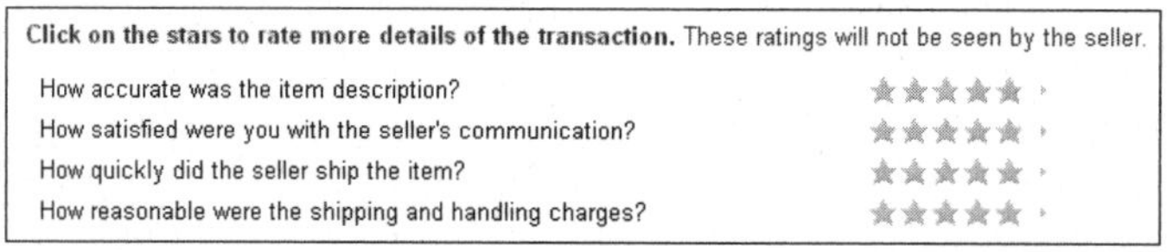

Figure 5-1:
eBay
Detailed
Star Rating
system.

Click on the stars to rate more details of the transaction. These ratings will not be seen by the seller.	
How accurate was the item description?	★ ★ ★ ★ ★
How satisfied were you with the seller's communication?	★ ★ ★ ★ ★
How quickly did the seller ship the item?	★ ★ ★ ★ ★
How reasonable were the shipping and handling charges?	★ ★ ★ ★ ★

In some cases, Detailed Star Ratings (DSRs) are grayed out when you attempt to leave feedback. This situation occurs under three circumstances:

✦ **Communication:** If you haven't sent any messages to the seller via eBay's message system, the seller specifies one-day handling time and uploads tracking information by the end of the next business day there will be no option to rate the seller.

✦ **Shipping quickly:** When the seller posts tracking numbers to eBay for your shipment within the time frame promised in the listing and the package arrives within four days, eBay automatically gives the seller a five-star rating.

✦ **Shipping charges:** If the seller provided free shipping, he or she automatically receives a five-star rating.

Table 5-1	What the DSR Stars Mean	
Rating Question	*# of Stars = Meaning*	*In the Real World*
How accurate was the item description?	1 = Very inaccurate 2 = Inaccurate 3 = Neither inaccurate or accurate 4 = Accurate 5 = Very accurate	In Marsha's world, the item was either described right or wrong — to me, there is no in-between. So when I rate a seller, the item is either is as advertised, or it isn't.
How satisfied were you with the seller's communication?	1 = Very unsatisfied 2 = Unsatisfied 3 = Neither unsatisfied or satisfied 4 = Satisfied 5 = Very satisfied	As I buyer, I lean toward being very satisfied that I got enough communication from the seller if I get a question answered, and at least get a tracking number notification, I'm satisfied. But if I haven't heard from a seller until the item reaches my door, I'm definitely rating in the two-star range.
How quickly did the seller ship the item?	1 = Very slowly 2 = Slowly 3 = Neither slowly or quickly 4 = Quickly 5 = Very quickly	As a buyer, you need to check the postmark on the package you receive. If the seller ships the next day or the next day after that, it's fair to click 5 (Very quickly), no matter how long the postal service took to get it to you.
How reasonable were the shipping and handling charges?	1 = Very unreasonable 2 = Unreasonable 3 = Neither unreasonable or reasonable 4 = Reasonable 5 = Very reasonable	When I purchase an item, I know what the shipping cost will be. The only surprise here is when you get an item in a small envelope and you've paid $9.00 for shipping — or if you paid for Priority Mail and it comes in another class of service. This is, to me, pretty black-and-white. It's either going to be reasonable or not.

Here are some other items to keep in mind when you're deciding on the Detailed Star Ratings for sellers:

✦ **Shipping takes time:** In most cases, as a buyer, it is your choice whether an item is to be shipped via Ground or Priority Mail. You've got to realize that Ground shipping can take up to 10 days. This isn't the seller's fault. So before leaving this rating, make sure that you always check the postmark or the date on the shipping label.

✦ **Shipping costs money:** Sellers have to add a little charge to cover the costs of tape, boxes, and packing materials. As a buyer, you've got to keep that in mind. If you are unfamiliar with postage rates, you should also know that a package costs a lot more to ship across the country than to ship to the next state. So do a little homework and evaluate shipping costs before you buy. If the shipping is too high, go to another seller.

✦ **Ratings affect the seller's costs:** If your seller is a Top-Rated Seller, you should also know that your star ratings affect the fees he or she pays to eBay. Being a good seller (with high DSRs) can save 20 percent on Final Values Fees, so your rating is a very serious matter. Visit Book VIII, Chapter 3 for the lowdown on how these ratings affect the Top Rated Seller's pocketbook.

Becoming a Star

Yes, eBay *loves* the stars. When you first join eBay, it seems like everyone on eBay has a star next to the user ID except for you. It's so unfair isn't it? Well, not really. The stars of many colors are awarded based on the amount of your feedback rating. When you receive a feedback rating of 10, you get a bright new gold star (just like in school).

You may notice stars of other colors — even shooting stars; Table 5-2 gives you the lowdown on what each star color represents.

Table 5-2	Star Colors Reflect Feedback Rating
Star	*Feedback Rating*
Gold star	10 to 49
Blue star	50 to 99
Turquoise star	100 to 499
Purple star	500 to 999
Red star	1000 to 4999
Green star	5000 to 9999
Gold shooting star	10,000 to 24,999
Turquoise shooting star	25,000 to 49,999
Purple shooting star	50,000 to 99,999
Red shooting star	100,000 and higher

Fetching feedback facts

How to get positive feedback

If you're selling, here's how to get a good reputation:

- Answer any questions you receive through eBay Messages as quickly as possible.

- After you've received payment, send out the item quickly.

- Make sure that your item is exactly the way you described it.

- Package the item well and ship it with care.

- React quickly and appropriately to problems — for example, if the item's lost or damaged in the mail or the buyer is slow in paying.

If you're buying, try these good-rep tips:

- Read the entire item description before you buy.

- Send your payment fast.

- Work with the seller to resolve any problems in a courteous manner.

How to get negative feedback:

If you're selling, here's what to do to tarnish your name big time:

- Tell a major fib in the item description. (Defend truth, justice, and legitimate creative writing — see Book III.)

- Take the money but take your time shipping the item.

- Package the item poorly so that it ends up smashed, squashed, or vaporized during shipping. (To avoid this pathetic fate, see Book VII.)

If you're buying, here's how to make your status a serious mess:

- Bid on an item, win the auction, and never respond to the seller.

- String the seller out with constant claims of "I will go to PayPal when I get my paycheck."

- Ask the seller for a refund because you changed your mind.

After you have a star and you reach a higher level, I assure you that you will get a silly tingly feeling of accomplishment. Very silly, yes, but it's all part of being an active member of the eBay community.

Leaving Feedback with Finesse

Writing feedback well takes some practice. It isn't a matter of saying things; it's a matter of saying *only the appropriate things.* Think carefully about what you want to say — because after you submit feedback, it stays with the person for the duration of his or her eBay career. I think you should always leave feedback, especially at the end of a transaction, although doing so isn't mandatory. Think of leaving feedback as voting in an election: If you don't leave feedback, you can't complain about lousy service.

eBay recommends that you make feedback "factual and emotionless." You won't go wrong if you comment on the details (either good or bad) of the transaction. If you have any questions about what eBay says about feedback, click the Community link in the navigation bar and on the resulting page click the Feedback Forum link at the end of the navigation links on the left side of the page.

In the Feedback Forum, you can perform the following feedback-related tasks:

✦ **Leave Feedback:** Here you see all pending feedback for all transactions within the past 90 days — the ones for which you haven't left feedback. Fill them in, one at a time. Then, with one click, you can leave as many as 25 feedback comments at once.

✦ **View a Feedback Profile:** Clicking here allows you to type any eBay member's ID to see that person's feedback profile (the same as if you clicked the number next to the member's name).

✦ **Reply to Feedback received:** If you've received feedback that you'd like to respond to, click this link. This comes in handy when a buyer leaves what you feel is an unwarranted negative; you can briefly state your case.

✦ **Follow up to Feedback left:** Here you may also leave follow-up feedback after the initial feedback should situations change.

✦ **Request Feedback revision:** This is possible, but before you do it, review this chapter — in particular, the "eBay will consider removing feedback if . . ." sidebar and the next section's links to current feedback policy.

✦ **Make Feedback public or private:** This is where you can decide to show your feedback profile to the public or keep it to yourself.

If you make your feedback profile private, you will hinder your future business on eBay.

✦ **Report buyer problems:** If you feel you are having a problem with a transaction, click the link and go to the Report a Buyer form in the Resolution Center. To report a buyer, follow these steps:

1. *Select the recent transaction in question by clicking the option button next to the buyer's ID, or type the item number in the text box.*

2. *Click Continue and select the appropriate situation from the Next, Tell Us What Happened section, as shown in Figure 5-2.*

3. *Click the Submit button to send your complaint to eBay Trust and Safety.*

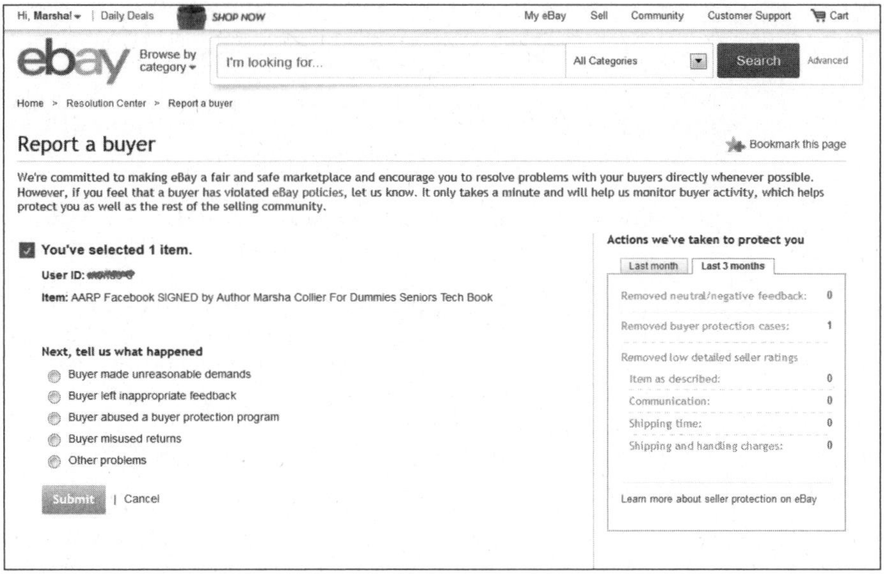

Figure 5-2:
Select
the buyer
problem that
matches
your issue.

On this page, you also have more links that explain the ins and out of the eBay feedback system. Here are the details on a few:

✦ **All About Feedback:** This link takes you to an exclusive help area for feedback questions.

   `http://pages.ebay.com/help/feedback/allaboutfeedback.html`

✦ **Feedback Policies:** Learn about Feedback policies and the various forms of Feedback Abuse — and how eBay deals with them.

   `http://pages.ebay.com/help/policies/feedback-ov.html`

✦ **Feedback FAQs:** Here you find answers to frequently asked questions about how to handle feedback — and how buyers can rephrase their knee-jerk negative or neutral feedback entries to something more accurate after sober reflection. (Only the verbiage can be changed; the rating will stay.)

   `http://pages.ebay.com/services/forum/changes.html`

In the real world (at least in the modern American version of it), anybody can sue anybody else for slander or libel; this fact holds true on the Internet, too. Be careful not to make any comments that could be libelous or slanderous. eBay is not responsible for your actions, so if you're sued because of posting slanderous feedback (or anything else you've written), you're on your own. The best way to keep yourself safe is to stick to the facts and don't get personal.

Mincing words: The at-a-glance guide to keeping feedback short

It is best to keep things simple. If you want to compliment, complain, or take the middle road, you have to do it in 80 characters or less. That means your comment needs to be short and sweet. If you have a lot to say but you're stumped about how to say it, here are a few examples for any occasion. String them together or mix and match!

Positive feedback:

✔ Very professional

✔ Quick e-mail response

✔ Fast service

✔ A+++

✔ Good communication

✔ Exactly as described

✔ Highly recommended

✔ Smooth transaction

✔ Would deal with again

✔ An asset to eBay

✔ I'll be back!

Negative feedback:

✔ Never responded

✔ Never paid for item

✔ Beware track record

✔ Item not as described

Neutral feedback:

✔ Slow to ship but item as described

✔ Item not as described but seller made good

✔ Poor communication but item came OK

If you're angry, take a huge breather *before* you type your complaints and click the Leave Comment button. If you're convinced that negative feedback is necessary, try a cooling-off period before you send comments. Wait an hour — or a day — and then see whether you feel the same. Nasty feedback based on emotion can make you look vindictive, even if what you're saying is true.

Safety tips for giving feedback

And speaking of safety features you should know about feedback, you may want to study up on these:

✦ **Remember that feedback, whether good or bad, is *sticky*.** eBay won't remove your feedback comment if you change your mind later. Be sure of your facts and carefully consider what you want to say.

✦ **Before you leave feedback, read what other people had to say about that person.** See whether what you're thinking is in line with the comments others have left.

✦ **You can leave feedback comments as long as the transaction remains on the eBay server.** This is usually within 60 days of the end of the auction. After 60 days have passed, you may still be able to leave feedback if you have the transaction number.

✦ **Your comment can be a maximum of 80 letters.** Okay, that's really short when you have a lot to say. Before you start typing, organize your thoughts and use common abbreviations to save precious space.

✦ **Before posting negative feedback, try to resolve the problem by eBay messages or telephone.** You may discover that your reaction to the transaction is based on a misunderstanding that can be easily resolved.

✦ **Use negative feedback only as a last, desperate resort.** It's worth remembering that eBay members generally want to make each other happy.

If, as a buyer, you leave a negative or neutral comment that you later regret, you can change your words but not the rating. You can go back to follow up and leave an explanation or a more positive comment and change the initial feedback. If you write a nice message to the other person in the transaction and are able to solve a problem, make the change. See the "eBay will consider removing feedback if . . ." sidebar.

The ways to leave feedback

Several ways are available to leave feedback comments:

✦ If you're on the transaction page, click the Leave Feedback link; the Leave Feedback page appears.

✦ In the Purchase History area of your My eBay page, click the Leave Feedback link next to the transaction.

✦ In the Feedback Forum, click the Leave Feedback link to see a list of all your completed auctions from the last 60 days for which you haven't left feedback.

✦ On your My eBay page, scroll down and on the left side you will see the Shortcuts heading. You will see a Leave Feedback link, which will take you to your pending Feedback list.

✦ Click the Community⇨Announcements link, in the main navigation bar, and then click eBay Feedback Forum. On the next page that appears, click the Leave Feedback link.

To leave feedback for a seller, follow these steps:

1. **Enter the required information.**

   Note that your item number is usually filled in, but if you're placing feedback from the user's feedback page, you need to have the number at hand.

2. **Choose whether you want your feedback to be positive, negative, or neutral.**

3. **Type your feedback comment.**

4. **Fill in your star ratings by clicking the stars next to the questions (as I discuss in the earlier section, "Giving Detailed Star Ratings Properly").**

   If you decide that the seller's description was inaccurate, you will have to explain why by clicking next to the explanations that appear (shown in Figure 5-3).

5. **Click the Leave Feedback button.**

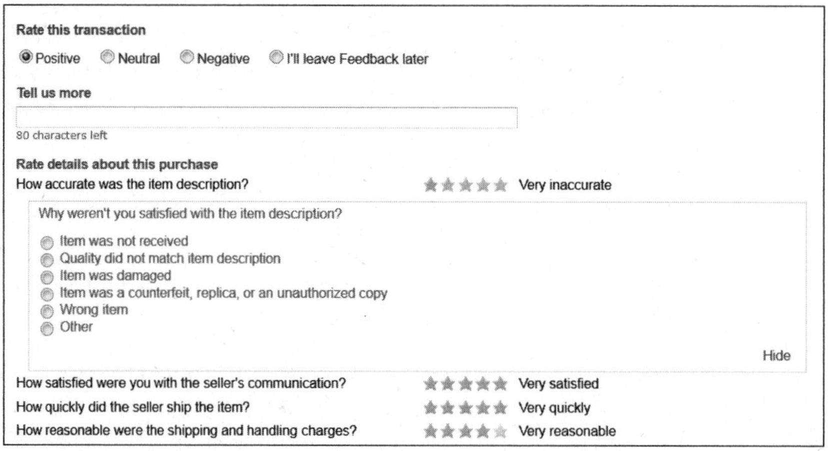

Figure 5-3: Be sure to select the proper reason you are giving a seller low ratings.

eBay will consider removing feedback if . . .

Only under certain, special circumstances will eBay remove feedback:

✔ eBay is served with a court order stating that the feedback in question is slanderous, libelous, defamatory, or otherwise illegal. eBay will also accept a settlement agreement from a resolved lawsuit submitted by both attorneys and signed by both parties.

✔ The feedback in question has no relation to eBay — such as comments about transactions outside eBay or personal comments about users.

✔ The feedback contains a link to another page, picture, or a script.

✔ The feedback comprises inappropriate comments. For eBay's policy on what it deems inappropriate, visit `http://pages. ebay.com/help/policies/ inappropriate-feedback-comments.html`.

✔ The feedback contains any personal identifying information about a user.

✔ The feedback is left by a user who supplied invalid contact information and couldn't be contacted.

✔ The feedback is intended for another user, when eBay has been informed of the situation and the same feedback has been left for the appropriate user.

eBay used to permit buyers and sellers to mutually withdraw feedback after they agreed that the transaction went OK. This is no longer the policy. To check on the current feedback removal policies, go to

```
http://pages.ebay.com/help/
policies/feedback-removal.
html
```

and

```
http://pages.ebay.com/help/
policies/inappropriate-
feedback-comments.html
```

You Have the Last Word — Responding to Feedback

After reading feedback you've received from others, you may feel compelled to respond. If the feedback is negative, you may want to defend yourself. If it's positive, you may want to say thank you.

Do not confuse *responding* to feedback with *leaving* feedback. Responding does not change the other user's feedback rating; it merely adds your response below the feedback comment in your own feedback profile.

To respond to feedback, follow these steps:

1. **Click the Leave Feedback link of your My eBay page, scroll to the bottom of the next page, and click the Feedback Forum link.**

   You're transported to the Feedback Forum page.

2. **Click the Reply to Feedback Received link.**

3. **When you find the feedback you want to respond to, click the Reply link.**

4. **Type your response.**

Checking Out a Seller's Reputation

You've finally found an item you'd like to buy. Don't place that bid just yet! Taking a look at the seller's feedback will supply you with a good deal of information about the reputation of your potential trading partner.

Although eBay Buyer Protection covers your transaction in almost any way, it will not cover you if the seller takes a long time to ship. By looking at the seller's feedback, you can tell whether you'll get the birthday gift you bought for your sister in time for the celebration.

Always look for the Top Rated Seller or Top Rated Seller Plus icon (shown in Figure 5-4) when you are buying an expensive or time-sensitive item. eBay bestows this appellation on only the best sellers.

Figure 5-4: Top Rated Seller Plus icon shows the sellers with the best customer service.

When you consider buying a more expensive item, be sure to click the seller's feedback number when you visit the item page. Clicking the number will show you the *member profile*: the Feedback Summary and the DSR ratings, as shown in Figure 5-5. After you click the feedback number, you should examine some important details if you want to be a savvy, security-minded shopper.

AUCTION ANECDOTE

Privacy in feedback may not be a good thing

I believe in the adage, "Keep your business private," except when it refers to feedback. In your eBay dealings, you may come upon a buyer with private or hidden feedback. Most users show their comments, and eBay's default setting is for public viewing of feedback. This way, everyone at eBay can read all about you as a member of the community.

If you want to make your feedback a private matter, you need to go to the Feedback Forum. On the resulting page, click the Make Your Feedback Profile Public or Private link, and you see the page shown here.

Make Your Feedback Profile Public or Private

Your Feedback Profile is a valuable asset that helps you earn the trust of other eBay members.

⦿ **Make your Feedback Profile public**
Keeping your Feedback Profile public increases the likelihood that members will trade with you.

⦾ **Make your Feedback Profile private**
If you make your Feedback Profile private, your Feedback comments will be hidden from other users. This may decrease the chance that other members will want to do business with you.
Note: If you choose to make your Feedback Profile private, you will not be able to sell items.

[Save] Cancel

Feedback Forum   Discussion Boards   Groups   Answer Center   Chat Rooms   Community Values

---

Hiding your feedback comments is a bad idea. You want people to know that you're trustworthy; being honest and up-front is the way to go. If you hide your feedback, people may suspect that you're covering up bad things. It's in your best interest to let the spotlight shine on your feedback history.

Your feedback is your reputation, your money, and your experience as an eBay member. Keep in mind that all three are always linked.

Feedback profile

Report a buyer

marsha_c (7972 ☆) me 🔲   [Top Rated: Seller with highest buyer ratings ?]

Positive Feedback (last 12 months): 100%
[How is Feedback percentage calculated?]
Member since: Jan-04-97 in United States

View your Seller Dashboard
View items for sale
View seller's Store
View ID history
Add to favorite sellers
View eBay My World
View reviews & guides
View About Me page

Recent Feedback ratings (last 12 months)   ?

	1 month	6 months	12 months
⊕ Positive	50	185	404
⊖ Neutral	0	0	0
⊝ Negative	0	0	0

Detailed seller ratings (last 12 months)   ?

Criteria	Average rating	Number of ratings
Item as described	★★★★★	310
Communication	★★★★★	336
Shipping time	★★★★★	337
Shipping and handling charges	★★★★★	356

eBay Buyer Protection
Covers your purchase price + original shipping
Learn more

Figure 5-5:
A sample member profile.

Check the seller's About Me page

If you notice that the seller has a small Me icon next to his or her user ID, click the icon to learn more about the seller. Every eBay member may have his or her own home page on eBay called the About Me page (you can have one, too). The About Me page is where members talk about themselves, their businesses, and their collections. For example, you can find my About Me page at

```
http://members.ebay.com/
aboutme/marsha_c
```

I came across the About Me page in the figure when I was looking at an auction for a Limoges plate. This is a great example of how eBay members show their personalities and build trustworthy person-to-person (rather than computer-to-computer) relationships with other members of the eBay community.

Hello! Thanks for checking out...

Bella Boutique

specializing in new and gently-used quality children's clothing

Welcome! My name is Christine, and I'm mom to 3 great kids. I have a full-time job and ventured into selling on eBay part-time, where I specialize in quality, name-brand children's clothing, from gently-used to Brand New! I have to admit...I'm quite the "shop-a-holic", and having a 3-year-old little girl only justifies my condition! My older two are out of the stage where *I* can still dress them, so I'm having a blast with my youngest! I have so many clothes, it's like having my own little boutique! I have also come to admire the talent and uniqueness of the many great children's clothing designers right here on eBay!

My number one priority is making sure each transaction goes smoothly. If there are ever any questions or concerns, please e-mail me and I'll be happy to work with you. *I'll also have other great items to offer, so please check back often!*

Thanks for visiting!

If a new seller (without a lot of feedback) does the smart thing — puts up an About Me page and talks about his or her eBay goals and business — you may feel more comfortable about doing business with that person.

On the left side of the page you see Recent Feedback Ratings; on the right, the Detailed Seller Ratings. You also see the counts of feedback comments divided by time periods: 1 month, 6 months, and 12 months. Note the following significant entries:

✦ **Positive Feedback comments:** You may notice that the *actual* number of positive comments is higher than the positive figure. This is because every eBay community member can comment only once a week on another member and have it count in the feedback rating. (The net rating was previously based on comments from *unique* users.) All feedback entries count as long as they're left in different weeks.

✦ **Neutral comments:** Neutral comments are usually left when a party wasn't thrilled with the transaction but nothing happened that was bad enough to leave a dreaded, reputation-ruining negative comment. You may also notice that some long-time eBay users have neutral comments, converted previously, from users no longer registered.

✦ **Negative comments:** The number of negative comments may also vary, just as the positives do, for the same reason.

This feedback page is where all those little stars you place when leaving Feedback show up. You'll be able to see how many ratings have been left for each category and where the Average Rating lies.

Examining the Member Profile

Also part of this comprehensive feedback page is the eBay member profile, which carries historic information about the member: Think of your feedback profile as an eBay report card. Your goal is to get straight As — in this case, all positive feedback. Here's what you find on it:

✦ **User ID:** The eBay member's nickname appears, followed by a number in parentheses — the net number of the positive feedback comments the person has received, minus any negative feedback comments.

✦ **Member links:** Next to the seller's picture you'll see the date the person signed up as a member of the eBay community and the country from which the seller is registered. You find these links on the right: the member's eBay Store (if the seller has one, of course), his or her other items for sale (which show whether the seller is experienced in selling the type of item you're looking to buy), his or her ID history (the seller's past user IDs, if any), and the seller's About Me page.

✦ **Contact member:** Click the Contact Member button to view an e-mail form allowing you to send an e-mail to the member through eBay's e-mail system.

✦ **Bid retractions:** By clicking the Feedback as a buyer tab, you can see how often a buyer has retracted bids in auctions. A history of bidding on items and then changing one's mind is a danger signal — more for sellers than for buyers. As a buyer, you may, under certain circumstances, retract your bid (see Chapter 6). Just keep in mind that each time you retract your bid from an auction, the retraction shows up in this area. Sellers often check this area to determine a bidder's reliability.

Be careful when you retract a bid. All bids on eBay are binding, but under what eBay calls exceptional circumstances, you may retract bids — sparingly. Here are the circumstances in which it's okay to retract a bid:

✦ If you've mistakenly put in the wrong bid amount — say, $100 instead of $10

✦ If the seller adds to his or her description after you've placed your bid, and the change considerably affects the item

✦ If you can't authenticate the seller's identity by reaching him or her by phone or by e-mail

You can't retract a bid just because you found the item elsewhere for less, or you changed your mind, or you decided that you can't afford the item.

Reading feedback reviews

Scrolling down the feedback history page, you'll be able to read the actual reviews left by other eBay members. In Figure 5-6, you'll see a sample of my feedback. You see each the member's user ID, along with his or her feedback rating and comment.

6,816 Feedback received (viewing 1-25)

Feedback	From / Price	Date / Time
Good buyer, prompt payment, valued customer, highly recommended.	Seller: ▨▨▨ (10 ☆)	Jul-31-08 20:33
-- (#160264595963)	--	View Item
Arrived as described....thanks....	Buyer: ▨▨▨ (850 ★)	Jul-31-08 10:30
Museum Putty QUAKE HOLD Wax Quakehold Earthquake LARGE (#110257294053)	US $6.90	View Item
item as described; fast delivery	Buyer: ▨▨▨ (1010 ★)	Jul-30-08 15:51
Museum Putty QUAKE HOLD Wax Quakehold Earthquake LARGE (#110257294053)	US $6.90	View Item
great book and very quick shipment	Buyer: b▨▨▨ (99 ★)	Jul-30-08 07:02
eBay For Dummies 5 Book MARSHA COLLIER SIGND FREE Bonus (#110272136332)	US $16.55	View Item
super fast shipment/ excellent product!! A+A+ seller	Buyer: ▨▨▨ (380 ☆)	Jul-29-08 08:28
Portable PHOTO WINGS Lighting Diffuse Soft Box Umbrella (#120148378419)	US $28.99	View Item
best ebayer ever! easy to work with! great communication! love to do business w/	Seller: q▨▨▨ (6132 ☆)	Jul-29-08 00:06
-- (#200216200013)	--	View Item
AAAAA+++++ Excellent transaction! Fantastic seller, super fast shipping!	Buyer: ▨▨▨ (3119 ★)	Jul-28-08 18:57
Museum Putty QUAKE HOLD Wax Quakehold Earthquake LARGE (#110257294053)	US $6.90	View Item
great, thanks	Buyer: c▨▨▨ (15577 ☆)	Jul-28-08 10:54
eBay For Canadians For Dummies CANADA Selling COLLIER (#350055229722)	US $21.99	View Item
As described. Arrived super quickly. Thanks.	Buyer: j▨▨▨ (419 ☆)	Jul-26-08 07:01
Museum Putty QUAKE HOLD Wax Quakehold Earthquake LARGE (#110257294053)	US $6.90	View Item
Fantastic Kayak!! Very Smooth Transaction!! Love to Do Business With Again!!!	Buyer: ▨▨▨ (235 ☆)	Jul-25-08 17:09
OCEAN KAYAK MALIBU TWO with 2 paddles tandem FUCSHIA (#350081557090)	US $300.00	View Item

Figure 5-6: Feedback comment page.

By default, you see the All Feedback Received tab. You may use the other tabs at the top of the page to sort the comments as follows:

✦ **Feedback as a Seller:** These are comments from people who bought something from this seller.

✦ **Feedback as a Buyer:** When you buy and play by the rules, you get some positive feedback.

✦ **All Feedback:** A conglomeration of all feedback left for the particular member, regardless of whether that person was a buyer or a seller in a transaction.

✦ **Feedback Left for Others:** Checking the type of feedback someone leaves about others can give you an insight into his or her personality. When considering making a big purchase, I always check this area; it helps me know the type of person I'm dealing with. When you read feedback that makes nasty slams at the other person, or if the person uses rude words or phrases when leaving feedback, it's a clue that you may be dealing with a loose cannon.

Here's what else you see:

✦ The date the feedback was left, along with the transaction number. If the transaction is 90 days old or less, you can click the View Item link to get a closer look at the transaction.

✦ Seller or Buyer on the right side of each comment. Seller means that the feedback was left by the seller in the transaction, and Buyer means it was left by a buyer.

Many independent eBay sellers are experienced buyers as well as sellers — they have an excellent grasp of how eBay feels from a customer's point of view, and know how to handle any of your concerns.

Here are some tips for assessing feedback, depending on the situation:

✦ When buying from a seller who sells the same item repeatedly, use the clickable links to past transactions to see whether *other* buyers of the same item were pleased with their purchases.

✦ When you come across neutral or negative feedback, look for the seller's response. A seller or a buyer may respond to the feedback by clicking the Reply to Feedback Received link at the bottom of the Feedback page.

The feedback system relies on the expectation that members give each other the benefit of the doubt. When you come across negative (or neutral) feedback about a seller, look for the seller's response and see whether the problem was resolved before making your final judgment.

You may even see a follow-up feedback comment from the buyer saying that everything has been settled.

Comparing Items Before Buying

By examining the results of your eBay search, you can get some useful information as to which item is the best deal.

In Figure 5-7, I performed a search for the Poodle Hat CD from Weird Al Yankovic. (This CD features his famous "eBay Song," a parody of the Backstreet Boys hit "I Want It That Way.").

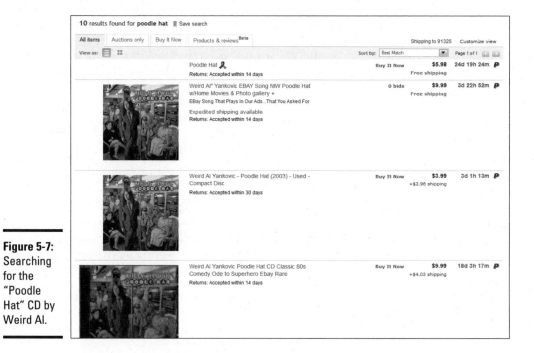

Figure 5-7: Searching for the "Poodle Hat" CD by Weird Al.

By looking at the result I can identify certain facts about each listing:

✦ **Item title:** A clickable link to the listing and a link to watch this item.

✦ **Price:** The current bid or the Buy It Now price.

✦ **Shipping cost:** The seller's shipping cost to your ZIP code is posted for comparison, provided the seller input the flat shipping fee when the item was posted for auction or sale. If you don't see a shipping cost, you have to click the title to read the description.

✦ **All Items, Auctions Only or Buy it Now:** See the number of bids that have been placed on an item or if the item is available for a flat sales price. This information gives you a quick snapshot of the costs for the item you're searching for.

✦ **Time Left:** The countdown to the end of the auction or fixed-price sale listing.

Getting Protection on eBay

One thing's for sure in this world: Nothing is for sure. That's why insurance companies exist. Several forms of protection are available for eBay users:

✦ eBay Buyer Protection

✦ eBay Motors Vehicle Purchase Protection

✦ PayPal buyer protection

✦ Verified Rights Owner program

For more information on how to acquire various protections for your buyers, see Book VIII, Chapter 4.

eBay Motors Vehicle Purchase Protection

A major benefit of buying a car on eBay is that you are covered against certain losses associated with some types of fraud. To qualify (this is the easy part), you simply need to purchase the car on eBay. (See? I told you it was simple.)

The Protection Plan gives you some pretty specific protections against conditions such as these that may result in losses:

✦ You pay for a vehicle and never receive it.

✦ You send a refundable deposit for a vehicle and never receive it.

✦ You pay for a vehicle and receive it but suffer losses because

• The vehicle was determined by a law enforcement agency to have been stolen at the time the listing ended.

• The vehicle has an undisclosed or unknown lien against its title.

• The vehicle make, model, or year is different from what was described in the seller's listing at the time you placed your bid or offer.

- A title is required for the vehicle by your state and the seller's state but you did not receive a title from the seller and it is not possible to obtain a title from the appropriate DMV.

- The vehicle has a title with an undisclosed salvage, rebuilt/rebuild-able, unrebuildable, reconstructed, scrapped/destroyed, junk, lemon, manufacturer-buyback, or water-damage brand at the time the listing ended. (This protection is not available for vehicles listed in the Dune Buggies, Race Cars, or Trailers categories.)

- The vehicle is less than 20 years old and has more than a 5,000-mile odometer discrepancy from the mileage as stated in the seller's listing. (This protection is only available for vehicles listed in the Cars & Trucks and RVs & Campers categories.)

- The vehicle had undisclosed engine, body, transmission, and/or frame damage at the time of purchase that will cost more than $1,000 to repair. The cost of repair to any one of those components must exceed $1,000. For vehicles in the Boats (engine and hull only), Buses, Commercial Trucks, and RVs & Campers categories, the cost of the undisclosed engine, body, transmission, or frame damage must exceed $1,500. Vehicles in the Race Cars category are not eligible for this protection (gee, I wonder why).

Learn more about this protection and any current updates at

```
pages.ebay.com/ebaymotors/buy/purchase-protection/
index.html
```

PayPal purchase protection

Aside from safety, PayPal offers an even better reason to pay when you shop online through their service. If you've purchased your item through a PayPal-verified seller, and something goes awry, you may be fully covered for your loss.

This protection covers you only for nondelivery of tangible items and tangible items that are received but are significantly not as described — it does not cover items that you are simply disappointed with.

If you've paid with a credit card through PayPal, be sure to make a claim with PayPal first. Do *not* make a claim with your credit card company. PayPal protection is for PayPal purchases and you are not covered if you've made a claim with your credit card company.

For the latest information on this program, go to

```
https://cms.paypal.com/cgi-bin/us/?cmd=_render-
content&content_ID=security/buyer_protection
```

or

```
https://www.paypal.com/us/webapps/mpp/security/safe-
online-shopping
```

Verified Rights Owner program

eBay is a *venue* — a place where sellers sell their wares to smart shoppers like you. No one at eBay owns the items, and no one at eBay can guarantee that any item is as described in auction listings. That means you could, theoretically, buy a "genuine" Kate Spade purse on eBay for $24, and immediately realize when it arrives that the purse is counterfeit. That's *not* eBay's fault. (Shame on you for thinking you could get that kind of deal on a new Kate Spade purse — but if you can, for real, e-mail me and let me know where.)

Just because eBay doesn't take the blame for its fraudulent sellers' handiwork doesn't mean that eBay doesn't care if you get duped. Their VeRO (Verified Rights Owner) program connects eBay with companies or persons who care to protect their intellectual property rights (such as a copyright, trademark, or patent) against possible infringements in eBay listings. VeRO members send proof to eBay that they own the specified intellectual property. In return, they can report infringements to eBay — and eBay's listing police will end the counterfeit listings. This is not an automatic service, however, and the property owners are responsible for finding their own infringements on the site.

Many VeRO members have their own About Me pages. To see a list of links to these pages, go to

```
http://pages.ebay.com/help/community/vero-aboutme.html
```

Chapter 6: Bidding to Win

In This Chapter

✔ **Placing bids**

✔ **Timing your bid**

✔ **Bidding strategies you don't want to miss**

✔ **Becoming an expert at sniping!**

✔ **Retracting a bid in an emergency**

Quite a few years ago, on the day after Christmas, I was on *The Today Show* with Matt Lauer talking about post-holiday bargains on eBay. This wasn't the first time I'd been on the show with him; but this time Matt seemed very interested in getting a deal on a child's lamp that I happened to be selling. He and his wife had just had a baby, and everyone likes a bargain.

If everyone likes a bargain, then I'm not like everyone — because I *love* bargains! When I was teaching classes at eBay's own eBay University (yes, there really was one), my favorite class to teach was Buying and Browsing, because I love the thrill of the chase and the acquisition of a good deal without all the haggling.

Often, the first thing that people ask me is how they can stop getting outbid at the last minute of an auction. I always say the same thing — become an expert *sniper* and bid higher than the other guy!

Okay, but how? In this chapter, I give you my tips and a few I picked up from other wise shoppers along the way.

eBay treats every bid — other than bids on some real estate sales or incorrectly placed bids — as binding. If you win an auction or buy an item and do not go through with your commitment by purchasing, the seller will file an Unpaid Item Case on you. If you establish a history as a nonpaying bidder with eBay (that is, you repeatedly back out of purchasing what you bid on), you have a strong chance of getting suspended from the community.

How much an item sells for depends on how many people see the item and how badly others want it. You may think of the *retail price* or *book value* as a standard for pricing, but neither may be accurate when it comes to shopping on eBay. In fact, I say everything has three prices:

✦ The price a retailer *charges* for an item at the store

✦ The price *everyone* says something is worth

✦ The price an item *actually* sells for on eBay

Understanding the Bidding Action

Okay, you've found the perfect item to track (say, a really classy Hello Kitty wristwatch), and it's in your price range. You're more than interested — you're ready to bid. If this were a live auction, some stodgy-looking guy in a gray suit would see you nod your head and start the bidding at, say, $2. Then some woman with a severe hairdo would yank on her ear, and the price of the watch would jump to $3.

eBay reality is more like this: You're sitting at home in your fuzzy slippers, sipping coffee in front of the computer. All the other bidders are cruising cyberspace in their pajamas, too, but you can't see 'em. (Be real thankful for little favors.)

When you're ready to jump into the bidding fray, find the bidding form (the example shown in Figure 6-1 is a replica necklace) with the Place Bid button at the top of the auction page. If the item includes a Buy It Now option, you see that next to the bid form.

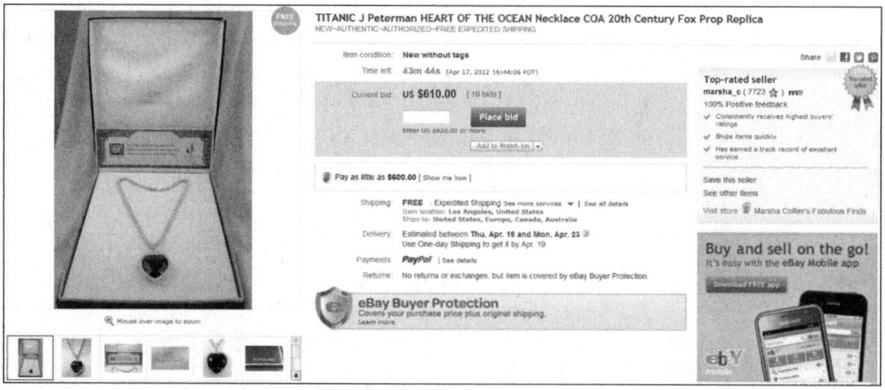

Figure 6-1: You can find the bidding form at the top of every auction page.

Placing your auction bid

To fill out the bidding form and place a bid, first make sure that you're registered. (For help in registering, see Chapter 3.) After you make your first bid on an item, you can instantly get to auctions you're bidding on from your My eBay page. Follow these steps to place a bid:

1. **Sign in to your eBay account, and find an item that you'd like to buy.**

2. **Enter your maximum bid in the appropriate box on your selected item's page.**

   Your bid must be higher than the current minimum bid.

   You don't need to put in the dollar sign, but you do need to use a decimal point — unless you really *want* to pay $1,049.00 instead of $10.49. If you make a mistake with an incorrect decimal point, you can retract your bid (see "Retracting Your Bid in an Emergency," at the end of this chapter).

3. **Click Place Bid (or Buy It Now if you're making a direct purchase).**

   The Review and Confirm Your Bid page, as shown in Figure 6-2, appears on your screen, filling it with all the costs involved in purchasing the item. This is your last chance to change your mind: Do you really want the item, and can you really buy it? The bottom line is this: If you bid on it and you win, you buy it.

4. **If you are sure you want to bid on the item and agree to the terms, click Confirm Bid.**

   After you agree, the Bid Confirmation screen appears.

5. **After you place your bid, you will either be the high bidder . . . or not.**

   You'll know where you stand because a window pops up like the ones shown in Figures 6-3 and 6-4.

Figure 6-2:
The serious part — where you confirm your bid.

Figure 6-3:
Here I'm currently the High Bidder. I'll keep an eye on the action.

Figure 6-4:
My bid was not high enough to beat another user's proxy bid.

eBay considers a bid on an item to be a binding contract. You can save yourself a lot of heartache if you promise *never to bid on an item you don't intend to buy*. Don't make spurious bids on the silly assumption that because you're new to eBay, you can't win; if you do that, you'll probably win simply because you've left yourself open to Murphy's Law. Therefore, before you go to the bidding form, be sure that you're in this auction for the long haul — and make yourself another promise *to figure out the maximum you're willing to spend* — and stick to it.

If you want to practice bidding, go to eBay's Test Bid page at

```
http://pages.ebay.com/education/tutorial/course1/
bidding/
```

Bidding to the max with automatic (proxy) bidding

When you make a maximum bid on the bidding form, you actually make several small bids — again and again — until the bidding reaches where you told it to stop. For example, if the current bid is up to $19.99 and you put in a maximum of $45.02, your bid automatically increases incrementally so you're ahead of the competition — at least until someone else's maximum bid exceeds yours. Basically, you bid by *proxy,* which means the automatic-bid feature stands in for you so your bid rises incrementally in response to other bidders' bids.

No one else knows whether you're bidding automatically, and no one knows how high your maximum bid is. And the best part is that you can be out enjoying your life while the proxy bidding happens automatically.

The *bid increment* is the amount of money by which a bid is raised, and eBay's system can work in mysterious ways. Buyers and sellers have no control over the bid increments that eBay sets. The current maximum bid can jump up a nickel or a quarter or even an Andrew Jackson, but there is a method to the madness (even though you may not think so). To determine how much to increase the bid increment, eBay uses a *bid-increment formula* that's based on the current high bid. Here are examples:

✦ A 5-quart bottle of cold cream has a current high bid of $14.95. The bid increment is $0.50 — meaning that if you bid by proxy, your automatic bid will be $15.45.

✦ A 5-ounce can of top-notch caviar has a high bid of $200. The bid increment is $2.50. If you choose to bid by proxy, your bid will be $202.50.

Table 6-1 shows you what kind of magic happens when you put the proxy system and a bid-increment formula together in the same cyber-room.

Table 6-1			eBay Auction Bid Increments	
Current	*Bid Increment ($)*	*Minimum Bid ($)*	*eBay Auctioneer*	*Bidders*
2.50	0.25	2.75	"Do I hear $2.75?"	Joe Bidder tells his proxy that his maximum bid is $8.00. He's the current high bidder at $2.75.

(continued)

Table 6-1 *(continued)*

Current	Bid Increment ($)	Minimum Bid ($)	eBay Auctioneer	Bidders
2.75	0.25	3.00	"Do I hear $3.00?"	You tell your proxy that your maximum bid is $25.00 and take a nice, relaxing bath while your proxy calls out your $3.00 bid, making you the current high bidder.
3.00	0.25	3.25	"I hear $3.00 from proxy. Do I hear $3.25?"	Joe Bidder's proxy bids $3.25, and while Joe Bidder is out walking his dog, he becomes the high bidder.

A heated bidding war ensues between Joe Bidder's proxy and your proxy while the two of you go on with your lives. The bid increment inches from $0.25 to $0.50 as the current high bid increases.

Current	Bid Increment ($)	Minimum Bid ($)	eBay Auctioneer	Bidders
7.50	0.50	8.00	"Do I hear $8.00?"	Joe Bidder's proxy calls out $8.00, his final offer.
8.00	0.50	8.50	"The bid is at $8.00. Do I hear $8.50?"	Your proxy calls out $8.50 on your behalf, and having outbid your opponent, you win the auction.

The Secret's in the Timing

Brick-and-mortar auctions, such as those held by Sotheby's or Christie's, end when the bidding ends. No auctioneer is going to cut off the feverish bidding for that one-of-a-kind Van Gogh, right? As long as someone is bidding, all systems are go. The last bidder standing wins. Auctions on eBay, however, close at a prescribed time. Because of this fundamental difference in the way eBay runs its auctions, you need to do some special work to make sure that you time your bid as strategically as possible.

You can find out what time an auction ends by simply looking at the auction page. Note that eBay runs on Pacific Time and uses a 24-hour clock (00:00 to 24:00 versus the more familiar 1:00 to 12:00).

To get the serious deals, you may want to synchronize your computer's clock with eBay's. To find out what eBay's official time is, go to

```
http://viv.ebay.com/ws/eBayISAPI.dll?EbayTime
```

Then compare eBay's time with your computer's clock. On most Windows-based computers, the time is in the lower-right corner of the screen on the taskbar.

To change the time on your computer's clock, follow these steps:

1. **Open your Internet browser and visit the following site:**

    ```
    http://viv.ebay.com/ws/eBayISAPI.dll?EbayTime
    ```

    The official clock at the eBay mothership appears, in the form of the Official Time page. Keep the browser open.

2. **Right-click your computer's taskbar where the Date and Time appear.**

    A pop-up menu appears.

3. **Click Adjust Date/Time, and a new window opens, showing your computer's version of "official" time.**

4. **If your clock does not match the official eBay time, click Change Date and Time.**

5. **In the resulting dialog box, type in eBay's "official" time (or adjust the time with the spinners shown in Figure 6-5) and click OK.**

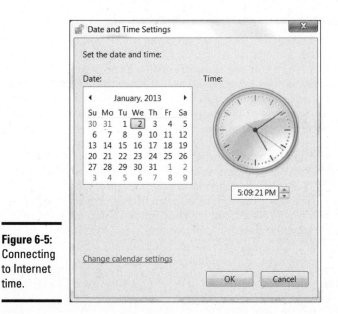

Figure 6-5:
Connecting to Internet time.

Going, going, gone

Although many people list their auctions to end at all hours of the day and night, the amount of bidders in cyberspace is higher during certain hours. Between the hours of 23:00 (that's 11:00 p.m. Pacific Standard Time) and 03:00 (that's 3:00 a.m. Pacific Standard Time), things run a bit slowly on eBay. If you're online at that time, you may be able to take advantage of some very serious bargains. So swallow a shot of espresso and have fun if you're a night owl.

Going, going, gone is the name of the game my daughter and I used to play when we wanted to go sport-shopping on eBay. Visit your favorite eBay category and have fun.

You can choose to view the auctions that are going to end in the next few hours by using the Sort By options from the drop-down menu.

Here you can cruise the auction closing while the world is asleep, and bid to your heart's content to get some great bargains.

Using the lounging-around strategy

Sometimes the best strategy at the beginning of an auction is to do nothing at all. That's right; relax, take off your shoes, and loaf. You may want to make a *token bid* (the very lowest you are allowed) or mark the page to Watch on your My eBay page. I generally take this attitude through the first six days of a week-long auction I want to bid on, and it works pretty well. I do, however, check in every day to keep tabs on important items I'm watching on the My eBay page, and I revise my strategy as time goes by.

If an auction has received no bids 12 hours before the auction ends, the seller has the right to change the minimum bid. Also, if there is a Buy It Now option on an auction, someone can swoop in and purchase the item for the stated price. If you place the minimum as a token bid when you first see the auction, you can foil a Buy It Now from another bidder. (Buy It Now is disabled after a bid is in place.)

If you see an item that you absolutely must have, mark it to watch on your My eBay page (or make a token bid) and revise your maximum bid as the auction goes on. I can't stress enough how important this is.

As you check back each day, take a look at the other bids and the high bidder. Is someone starting a bidding war? Look at the time when the competition is bidding and note any patterns, such as lunchtime bidding. If you know what time your major competition is bidding, you can bid after he or she does (preferably when your foe is stuck in rush-hour traffic).

Using the beat-the-clock strategy

You should rev up your bidding strategy during the final 24 hours of an auction and decide, once and for all, whether you really *have* to have the item you've been eyeing. Maybe you put in a maximum bid of $45.02 earlier in the week. Now's the time to decide whether you're willing to go as high as $50.02. Maybe $56.03?

No one wants to spend the day in front of the computer (ask almost anyone who does), but if you have a smartphone, you might want to use the eBay mobile app while running errands. Just place a sticky note where you're likely to see it, reminding you of the exact time the auction ends. If you're not going to be near a computer when the auction closes, you can also use an automatic bidding software program to bid for you; see "Succeeding by Sniping," later in this chapter, for details.

In the last few minutes

With half an hour left before the auction becomes ancient history, head for the computer and dig in for the last battle of the bidding war. I recommend that you sign on to eBay about 10 to 15 minutes before the auction ends. The last thing you want is to get caught in Internet gridlock and not get access to the eBay website. Go to the items you're watching and click the auction title.

With 10 minutes to go, if there's a lot of action on your auction, click reload or refresh every 30 seconds to get the most current info on how many people are bidding.

Shopping the Machiavellian Way

When you've shopped eBay in a specific category for a while, you may recognize many of the people who win against you in auctions. Don't be surprised that other people in the eBay universe have the same quirky interests as you. Of course, even if that gives you something in common, you may come to dislike their behavior if they outbid you often enough. It's a wretched feeling, being outbid, especially when it happens at the last few seconds.

Take a look, by clicking the Bids, and see if the name of a particular bidder shows up repeatedly. If the high bidder has lots of feedback, he or she may know the ropes — and be back to fight if you up the ante.

eBay has made this tactic difficult by changing the Bidder's ID to a symbol (see Figure 6-6).

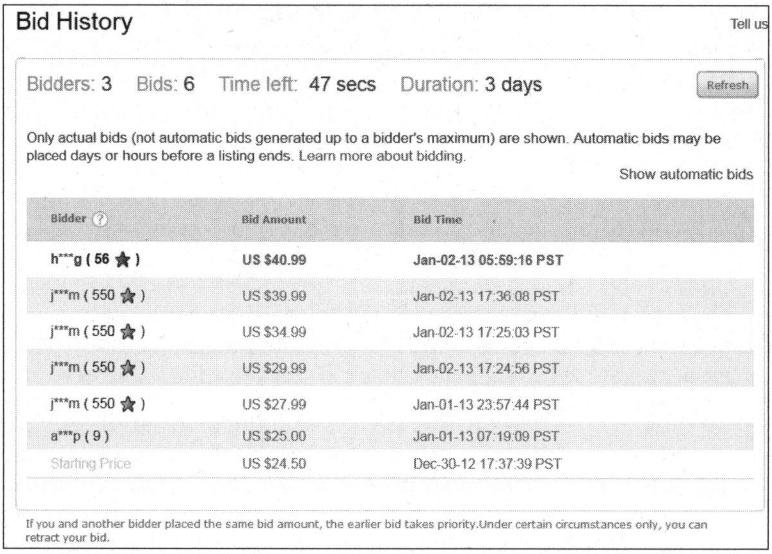

Figure 6-6: eBay's concatenated User IDs showing the bidding history.

Bid History				
Bidders: 3 Bids: 6 Time left: **47 secs** Duration: **3 days**				Refresh

Only actual bids (not automatic bids generated up to a bidder's maximum) are shown. Automatic bids may be placed days or hours before a listing ends. Learn more about bidding.

Show automatic bids

Bidder ⑦	Bid Amount	Bid Time
h***g (56 ⭐)	US $40.99	Jan-02-13 05:59:16 PST
j***m (550 ⭐)	US $39.99	Jan-02-13 17:36:08 PST
j***m (550 ⭐)	US $34.99	Jan-02-13 17:25:03 PST
j***m (550 ⭐)	US $29.99	Jan-02-13 17:24:56 PST
j***m (550 ⭐)	US $27.99	Jan-01-13 23:57:44 PST
a***p (9)	US $25.00	Jan-01-13 07:19:09 PST
Starting Price	US $24.50	Dec-30-12 17:37:39 PST

If you and another bidder placed the same bid amount, the earlier bid takes priority. Under certain circumstances only, you can retract your bid.

You can, however, still find out information on those who are bidding against you in an auction. Click eBay's ersatz User ID for the bidder, and you will see a page like the one shown in Figure 6-7. In this example, I can see that the winner of this auction makes a habit of making a last bid within the last hour.

You can find out the following information from the Bid History Details page:

✦ **The categories the bidder tends to be interested in:** Might as well let your competition do the legwork of finding good auctions for the items you like.

✦ **What time of day the bidder likes to make bids:** You can get a sense of whether the bidder makes a habit of bidding in the last hour (or, as in

Figure 6-6, they bid towards the end of the day) and use this information to your advantage.

✦ **Other bidding habits:** Some bidders like to place an initial bid at the beginning of the auction and then swoop in at the end and snipe. Or they never bid until the end of the auction. Or they never snipe. No matter what strategy your competition chooses, you can come up with a counter-strategy to improve your likelihood of winning.

Figure 6-7:
Bidding
History of
a specific
bidder.

Bid History: Details

Bidding Details

Bidder Information

		30-Day Summary	
Bidder:	c***c (454 ⭐)	Total bids:	9
Feedback:	100% Positive	Items bid on:	9
Item description:	NEW MATTEL 2005 HARD ROCK CAFE BARBIE COLLECTOR EDITION with PIN -NRFB -MINT	Bid activity (%) with this seller:	11%
Bids on this item:	1	Bid retractions:	0
		Bid retractions (6 months):	0

30-Day Bid History

Category	No. of Bids	Seller ?	Last Bid ?
Dolls & Bears > Barbie Contemporary (1973-Now)	1	Seller 1	<1h
Spielzeug > Autos	1	Seller 2	<1h
Computer, Tablets & Netzwerk > Drucker	1	Seller 3	<1h
Spielzeug > Puppen	1	Seller 4	<1h
Toys & Games > Maisto	1	Seller 5	<1h
Modellbau > Busch	1	Seller 6	<1h
Modellbau > Herpa	1	Seller 7	<1h
TV, Video & Audio > HiFi-Systeme/-Kombinationen	1	Seller 8	3d
Spielzeug > Puppen	1	Seller 9	7h

Bidding in odd increments is just one of the many strategies to get you ahead of the rest of the bidding pack without paying more than you should. Many of the strategies in this chapter are for bidders who are tracking an item over the course of a week or more, so be sure you have time to track the item and plan your next move. Also, get a few auctions under your belt before you throw yourself into the middle of a bidding war.

Put in your two cents

Your two cents does matter — at least on eBay. Here's why: Many eBay members round off their bids to the nearest dollar figure or choose familiar coin increments such as 25, 50, or 75 cents. But the most successful eBay bidders have found that adding 2 or 3 cents to a routine bid can mean the difference between winning and losing. So I recommend that you make your proxy bids in odd amounts, like $15.02 or $45.57, as an inexpensive way to edge out your competition. For the first time ever, your two cents may actually pay off!

If you suspect you know who is bidding against you, you can run a bidder search. In Figure 6-8, I ran a bidder search on myself to see who won an auction that I had bid on. I know the User IDs of my bidding rivals. To see a rival's bidding history, do the following:

1. **Click the Advanced Search link, which appears next to the Search box you find on almost every eBay page.**

2. **In the Search links area on the left, click the By Bidder link.**

3. **Enter the User ID of the bidder you want to check out.**

4. **To check the bidder's previous purchases, click to add a check mark in the Include Completed Listings (Last 30 Days) check box.**

   By studying the bidding history, you can see how high the bidder is willing to bid on certain items. This is invaluable information if you want to get a drift of how high *you* have to bid to win the next auction.

5. **Tell eBay whether you also want to see the person's bid even if he or she is not the high bidder.**

   By not selecting the As High Bidder Only option, you get to see the bidder's activity in every transaction, even if the person is not the *current* high bidder. I think you should check all the bidder's auctions to see how aggressively he or she bids on items. You can also see how badly a bidder wants specific items.

   If the bidder was bidding on an item in the past that you're both interested in now, you can get a fairly good idea of how high that person is willing to go for the item this time. Figure 6-8 shows you how this looks.

6. **Choose the number of items you want to see per page.**

7. **Click the Search button.**

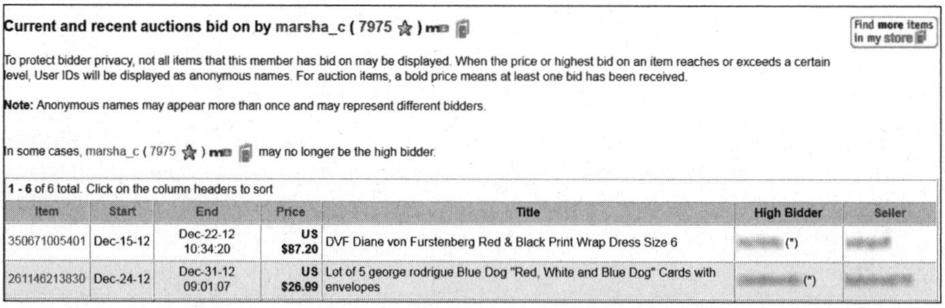

Figure 6-8:
Bidder
Search
results for
me — now
I know who
my nemeses
are!

Current and recent auctions bid on by marsha_c (7975 ☆) ✉ 🖼

Find more items in my store 🖼

To protect bidder privacy, not all items that this member has bid on may be displayed. When the price or highest bid on an item reaches or exceeds a certain level, User IDs will be displayed as anonymous names. For auction items, a bold price means at least one bid has been received.

Note: Anonymous names may appear more than once and may represent different bidders.

In some cases, marsha_c (7975 ☆) ✉ 🖼 may no longer be the high bidder.

1 - 6 of 6 total. Click on the column headers to sort

Item	Start	End	Price	Title	High Bidder	Seller
350671005401	Dec-15-12	Dec-22-12 10:34:20	US $87.20	DVF Diane von Furstenberg Red & Black Print Wrap Dress Size 6	(*)	
261146213830	Dec-24-12	Dec-31-12 09:01:07	US $26.99	Lot of 5 george rodrigue Blue Dog "Red, White and Blue Dog" Cards with envelopes	(*)	

I keep links in my browser to bidder searches on some of my favorite bidders. When I'm in the mood to shop, I just look at what they're bidding on.

My Favorite Bidding Strategies

There used to be a time when I would tell beginning eBay members my favorite methods of bidding and winning, and if there was an eBay employee in earshot, you could see him or her wince. Things are considerably different these days. For example, eBay used to officially oppose the use of third-party payment options — until they purchased PayPal. And when sniping swept the online auction community and became *de riguer,* the eBay Powers That Be didn't endorse the practice. Finally, after some agonizing, the eBay insiders admitted that sniping *does* work in winning auctions.

As a matter of fact, eBay's instructors are now pitching many of the strategies that I've been talking about for years — because they work! While editing this book, my editor even reminisced about just how much the eBay "party line" has changed since I wrote my first book on eBay in 1999.

Hunting for errors

Some of my best buys on eBay were the result of searching for misspellings. Many sellers are in a hurry when they set up their auction listings, and to err is human (and to win, divine). I am more than willing to forgive sellers for their mistakes because the payoff for bargain hunters is, well, a bargain.

Think of alternative spellings when you search for an item. A favorite of mine is *Von Furstenburg* for *Von Furstenberg.* Usually, I search for the correct spelling and find a bunch of items where the bidding can get steep. But when I search for the misspelled version, I may find identical items that have no bids, because I'm the only one who has found the listing. Figure 6-9 shows that eBay is often aware of misspellings when it comes to name brands.

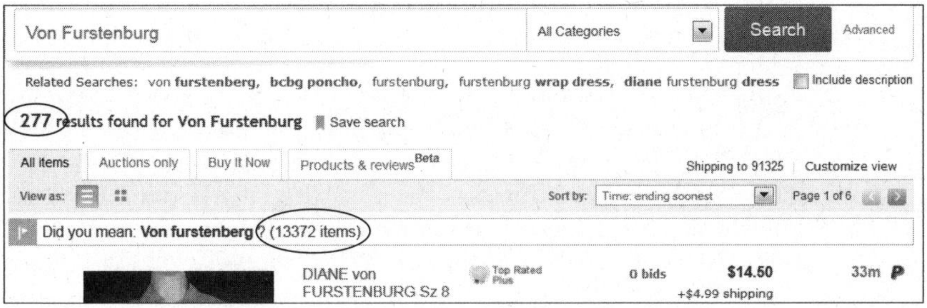

Figure 6-9:
277 misspelled results (versus 13,372 spelled correctly).

| Von Furstenburg | | All Categories | ▼ | Search | Advanced |

Related Searches: von **furstenberg**, **bcbg poncho**, furstenburg, furstenburg **wrap dress**, **diane** furstenburg **dress**   ☐ Include description

277 results found for Von Furstenburg   ☐ Save search

| All items | Auctions only | Buy It Now | Products & reviews ^Beta | | Shipping to 91325 | Customize view |

View as: ▤ ⊞   Sort by: Time: ending soonest ▼   Page 1 of 6 ◁ ▷

▶ Did you mean: **Von furstenberg**? (13372 items)

DIANE von FURSTENBURG Sz 8   Top Rated Plus   0 bids $14.50
+$4.99 shipping   33m ℙ

You can search for both the correct and incorrect spellings by using a search such as *(furstenberg,furstenburg)*. Book II gives you lots more search tricks.

I was also successful during one holiday season, when computer-animated cats were popular (and going for extremely high prices on eBay, because they were sold out everywhere across the country). The brand name was FurReal. I searched for spellings like *fur real* and *furreal* and found many bargains.

eBay smartened up and now sometimes shows alternative spellings — but not always (what is the right way to spell L'Occitane?).

A couple of our favorite misspellings are *neckless* (instead of *necklace*) — currently 1,372 items up for sale — and *vidio* (instead of *video*), for which 242 are currently on the site. I accidentally ran a misspelled search for a popular electronics game and noticed that there were 146 items spelled *Nitendo*. Note that eBay did suggest the proper spelling of *Nintendo*, with 303,218 items.

Researching your item

Sometimes we (that includes me *and* you) find what we think is an incredible deal on eBay. It may well be, especially if we know that the retail price is, say, $80 and we're seeing a Buy It Now or an auction closing at $40. If a low, low price works for you, just go ahead and buy the item if you want it right away. To find the best price for any item on eBay, do your homework to find out what similar items on eBay (or Amazon) tend to sell for.

When you conduct your eBay research, the best strategy is to look at the prices achieved in previous sales. Do a search for completed auctions. Then check an auction's bid history by clicking the number of bids placed on the auction item page (the link appears next to the Winning Bid price). You'll be presented with the screen like the one in Figure 6-10. This will at least give you an idea of how many people are duking it out for the item, if not their actual IDs. You should also click the Show Automatic Bids link on the right, so you can see how many bids were placed by proxy.

Pay attention to the times when bidders are placing their bids, and you may find that the people bidding in the auction are creatures of habit — making their bids about once a day and at a particular time of day. They may be logging on before work, during lunch, or after work. Whatever their schedules, you have great info at your disposal in the event that a bidding war breaks out: Just bid after your competition traditionally logs out, and you increase your odds of winning the auction.

Bidders: 12	Bids: 31	Time Ended: **Jan-04-13 00:42:27 PST**	Duration: **5 days**

(i) This item has ended.

Only actual bids (not automatic bids generated up to a bidder's maximum) are shown. Automatic bids may be placed days or hours before a listing ends. Learn more about bidding.

Show automatic bids

Bidder ⑦	Bid Amount	Bid Time
j***d (3)	**US $255.00**	**Jan-04-13 00:40:54 PST**
a***c (19 ☆)	US $250.00	Jan-03-13 22:19:16 PST
j***d (3)	US $250.00	Jan-04-13 00:40:47 PST
o***s (1)	US $232.50	Jan-03-13 15:51:00 PST
o***s (13 ☆)	US $230.00	Jan-03-13 15:49:57 PST
o***s (1)	US $227.50	Jan-03-13 15:50:57 PST
o***s (1)	US $222.50	Jan-03-13 15:50:54 PST
o***s (1)	US $217.50	Jan-03-13 15:50:52 PST
o***s (1)	US $212.50	Jan-03-13 15:50:49 PST
o***s (1)	US $207.50	Jan-03-13 15:50:46 PST
o***s (1)	US $202.50	Jan-02-13 15:57:22 PST
s***l (28 ☆)	US $200.00	Dec-30-12 21:54:45 PST
o***s (1)	US $200.00	Jan-02-13 15:57:18 PST
o***s (1)	US $195.00	Jan-02-13 15:57:15 PST
o***s (1)	US $190.00	Jan-02-13 15:57:12 PST
o***s (1)	US $185.00	Jan-02-13 15:57:10 PST
o***s (1)	US $180.00	Jan-02-13 15:57:07 PST
o***s (1)	US $175.00	Jan-02-13 15:57:04 PST
o***s (1)	US $170.00	Jan-02-13 15:57:00 PST
o***s (1)	US $165.00	Jan-02-13 15:56:57 PST
o***s (1)	US $160.00	Jan-02-13 15:38:34 PST
y***i (1)	US $150.00	Jan-02-13 08:33:59 PST

Figure 6-10: I don't know who they are, but their bids sure seem persistent.

Early in an auction, there may not be much of a bidding history for an item, but that doesn't mean you can't still check out the dates and times a bidder places bids. You can also tell whether a bidder practices *sniping* (discussed later in this chapter) if his or her bid is in the last few seconds of the auction. You may have a fight on your hands if the bidder uses sniping.

Quick Bidding Tips

When you get a tip, double-check to see who it's coming from. Visit eBay's community boards and chats, and listen to what the others have to say. Before taking anything to heart and changing the way you do things, check the tip-givers' experiences. Are they really experienced on eBay? Or are they selling seminars or passing on the latest misinformation? I love buying from eBay sellers who are also buyers, because they respect and understand what it's like to be a buyer on eBay!

Here are a few short tips that I know really work:

- ✦ **Shop eBay.ca, eh!** That's right. If you're in the U.S.A., why not bid on auctions on the eBay Canada website? In fact, if you're an international bidder and are willing to pay shipping from the United States, you'll have no problem handling Canadian shipping charges.

- ✦ **Place your bids in odd figures.** Many eBay bidders place their bids in the round numbers that match eBay's proxy system. You can win by a few cents if you place your bids in odd numbers like $10.97 or $103.01.

- ✦ **Don't get carried away in a bidding war.** Unless the item is rare, odds are that a similar item will show up on eBay again someday soon. Don't let your ego get in the way of smart bidding. Let your opposition pay too much!

- ✦ **Don't freak out if you find yourself in a bidding war.** Don't keel over if, at the split-second you're convinced that you're the high bidder with your $45.02, someone beats you out at $45.50.

- ✦ **Watch for item relistings.** If you see an item that you want but it has too high an opening bid (or too high a reserve), there's a good chance that no one else will bid on the item, either. Put that auction into your Watch area of My eBay. Then, after the auction ends, double-check the seller's auctions every so often to see whether the item has been relisted with a lower starting bid and a lower (or no) reserve.

- ✦ **Combine shipping when possible.** When you purchase an item, check the seller's other auctions and see whether you're interested in making a second purchase. If you see something else that appeals to you, e-mail the seller to see whether he or she will combine the items in shipping. That way, you can make two purchases for a smaller single shipping bill.

- ✦ **Never bid early, but if you do, bid high.** The only time this "bidding early" business works is if no one else is interested in the auction. Usually, though, the tactic will gear up another eBay user to outbid you because suddenly the item is valuable to at least one person. If you *must* bid before the auction's close, bid high. As a matter of fact, bid a couple of dollars more than you might want to pay. (I mean literally a couple, not a couple hundred.)

- ✦ **Try for a Second Chance offer:** If you get outbid and miss the chance to increase your bid on an auction item, you'd be smart to e-mail the seller and ask whether he or she has any more of the item. You may get lucky, and the seller can send you a Second Chance offer for your high bid.

A seller may send a Second Chance offer to up to four underbidders in the auction under three circumstances: when the winner doesn't pay, when the reserve price wasn't met, or when the seller has more than one of the items that were sold. Any purchase you make in this manner will be covered under eBay Buyer Protection, and you will have the opportunity to leave feedback.

Succeeding by Sniping

Sniping is the fine art of outbidding your competition in the very last seconds of the auction — without leaving them enough time to place a defensive bid. Sniping is my number-one favorite way to win an auction on eBay. When I first touted this method in 1999, it was a fairly new idea. Now everyone knows about sniping, and it's pretty much an accepted bidding method.

Bidders (that is, losing bidders) whine and moan when they lose to a sniper, but they should remember one thing: The high bidder always wins, whether you're sniping or using the automatic bid system. If you're going to snipe, assume that the current bidder has a *very* high-dollar proxy bid in the works.

Some eBay members consider the practice of sniping unseemly and uncivilized — like when dozens of parents used to mob the department-store clerks to get to the handful of Cabbage Patch dolls that were just delivered. (Come to think of it, whatever happened to *those* collectibles?) Of course, sometimes a little uncivilized behavior can be a hoot.

Sniping is an addictive, fun part of life on eBay. I recommend that you try it. You're likely to benefit from the results and enjoy your eBay experience even more — especially if you're an adrenaline junkie.

Sniping techniques for the beginner

Here's a list of things to keep in mind when you get ready to place your snipe bid:

✦ **Know how high you're willing to go.** If you know you're facing a lot of competition, figure out your highest bid to the penny. You should have already researched the item and figured out its value. Raise your bid only to the level where you're sure you're getting a good return on your investment; don't go overboard. Certainly, if the item has some emotional value and you just have to have it, bid as high as you want. But remember, you'll have to pay the piper later. You win it, you own it!

✦ **Know how fast (or slow) your Internet connection is.** Before you start sniping, figure out how long it takes to get your bid confirmed on eBay.

Test it a few times until you know how many seconds you have to spare when placing a bid.

✦ **Don't lose heart if you lose the auction.** Remember, this is a game.

Although sellers love sniping because it drives up prices and bidders love it because it's fun, a sniper can ruin a week's careful work on an auction strategy. The most skillful snipers sneak in a bid so close to the end of the auction that you have no chance to counter-bid. Losing too often, especially to the same sniper, can be a drag.

If your Internet connection is slow and you want to do some sniping, make your final bid two minutes before the auction ends and adjust the amount of the bid as high as you feel comfortable so you can beat out the competition. If you *can* make the highest bid with just 10 seconds left, you most likely will win. With so many bids coming in the final seconds, your bid might be the last one eBay records.

This stuff is supposed to be fun, so don't lose perspective. If you can't afford an item, don't get caught up in a bidding war. Otherwise, the only person who wins is the seller. If you're losing sleep, barking at your cat, or biting your nails over an item, it's time to rethink what you're doing. If it's taking up too much of your life or an item costs too much, be willing to walk away — or log off — and live to bid another day.

To snipe a bid manually (without a sniping service), first make sure you're signed in. Then follow these steps to snipe at the end of the auction:

1. **In the last few minutes of the auction, locate the item you want to win and press Ctrl+N to open a second window on your Internet browser.**

   Keep one window open for bidding, as shown in Figure 6-11.

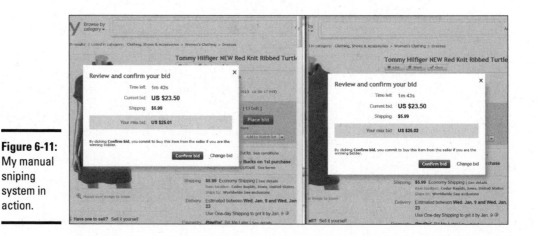

Figure 6-11: My manual sniping system in action.

2. **Continuously click the Reload or Refresh button that appears in the last few minutes of an auction, just above the Place Bid button.**

    By reloading the item continually, you'll be aware when you're in the last 60 seconds of bidding. You also can see instantly whether anyone else is doing any last-minute bidding.

3. **In the bid box of the second browser, type your maximum bid and then click the Place Bid button.**

    You then face a page that, when you press the button, finalizes and confirms your bid on the item. Do not click the Confirm Bid button yet.

4. **As the auction nears its end, confirm your final bid by clicking the Confirm Bid button.**

    You know when the auction is almost over because you're reloading your first browser continually. The longer you can hold off bidding before the auction ends, the better.

If you really want an item bad enough, you may want to set up a backup for your snipe. Try my three-screen system, in which you can place a backup high bid in case you catch another sniper swooping in on your item immediately after your first snipe.

Obviously, if you win with the first snipe, the second window is unnecessary. But if you lose the first one, that second window feels like a real lifesaver! If you're outbid after two snipes, don't cry. The winner paid way more than you were willing to pay. It's not *much* consolation, but rarely is an item so rare that you only see it come on the auction block once in a lifetime.

Auto-sniping your auctions

My daughter says that I can make almost anything high-maintenance, and she may very well be right. When it comes to eBay bidding and winning, a bunch of software programs and websites can help automate your shopping and feedback process. I like that they will bid for me whether I'm near a computer or sleeping peacefully.

Here is one bidding service that I have used successfully: BidRobot. Shown in Figure 6-12, BidRobot deftly places sniping bids for you from its servers. It's won many an auction for me while I've been on the road or busy writing. The service is one of the least expensive out there, charging a low flat rate. Get a three-week free trial (all you can snipe for three weeks!) at

    www.bidrobot.com/cool

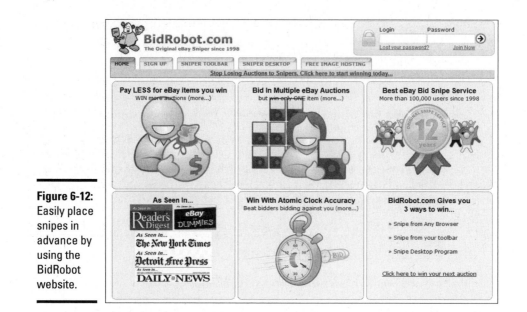

Figure 6-12: Easily place snipes in advance by using the BidRobot website.

BidRobot also has a BidGroup feature to use if you're bound and determined to get the lowest price for an item. This is accomplished by planning a bidding schedule at a set price. The bidding continues until you win your item (or not). Here's how it works.

1. **Search for your item.** Search for your specific item on eBay. You may find a large number of eBay auctions that offer your item.

2. **Select the auctions you'd like to bid on.** Review the listings (checking the seller's feedback, description and eBay Buyer Protection availability) and select six different listings.

3. **Create your first snipe.** Type your first snipe bid in the pale-yellow Bid section (at the very top of the BidRobot bid screen) and select the option to indicate that you want to create a group of bids with the other five auctions.

4. **Group the other auctions.** To bid on other sellers' auctions, scroll down until you find the Pending Bid Group that contains your first item bid. Then use the form in that BidGroup area to add more snipe bids for other auctions in that specific BidGroup. You may add bids for as many additional auctions as you like to this group.

5. **Winning.** If you win any one of the auctions in your BidGroup, the remaining bids in that specific group will not be placed. This is automatic.

Knowing what you're buying

Before you place a bid, be sure that you know the item's *street price,* which is the price that people actually pay — not the MSRP (manufacturer's suggested retail price). You can use the Internet to check prices for many items. In fact, several consumer websites are dedicated to serving savvy consumers by offering this information. You can find prices at www. pricewatch.com or www.shopping. com, and even get price predictions at www.decide.com. Almost everything is also sold on Amazon these days. Why not give its pricing a try at www.amazon.com. You may be comfortable paying slightly more than the street price because the sellers on eBay are small businesses, with many run by people like your neighbor. I'm a big believer in supporting small business. Plus: You have eBay's Buyer Protection behind your purchase.

Retracting Your Bid in an Emergency

We're all human, and we all make mistakes. Luckily for everyone, eBay members are allowed to retract bids under certain circumstances. You may retract your bid if you meet one of the following criteria:

✦ **You accidentally typed the wrong bid amount:** Say you typed $900 but you meant $9.00. Oops. In a case like this, you can retract the bid, but you'd better rebid the proper amount (that original $9.00) immediately, or you may be in violation of eBay's policies.

✦ **The seller has added information to the item description that changes the value of the item considerably:** The bull that was let loose in the seller's shop has changed the mint condition of the Ming vase you just bid on? No problem.

✦ **You can't reach the seller through eBay's e-mail or through the telephone number you got from eBay's find members area:** Seller has gone AWOL, and you have a question about an item you've bid on? You can use eBay's e-mail system by clicking the Contact Member link near the bottom of the listing page. Or to get the seller's telephone number, click the Advanced link (at the top-right corner of most eBay pages) and then click the Find a Member link (on the left side of the page). Next, input your transaction number and the seller's User ID. After checking to make sure that you've begun a transaction with this person, the good people at eBay will send the seller's telephone number in an e-mail message to your registered e-mail address. Your phone number will also be e-mailed to the seller.

Every time you retract a bid, it appears in the feedback area of your eBay feedback page.

Here are a couple of additional restrictions to retracting bids:

✦ **You can retract a bid if it was placed during the last 12 hours of an auction.** If you bid more than once in the last 12 hours of the same auction, you can retract a bid within one hour of placing it. In this case, only that bid will be retracted; any other bid placed before the last 12 hours of the listing remains valid.

✦ **When you retract a bid and the listing has more than 12 hours to go, you wipe out any of your previous bids in the auction.** To reinstate yourself as a bidder, you must bid again.

If you want to retract your bid within the last 12 hours of the auction and you placed the bid before the last 12 hours, you must send an e-mail to the seller asking him or her to cancel your bid. It is up to the seller whether to cancel your bid. A bid retraction isn't a guarantee that you will get out of purchasing the item. Sometimes sellers simply don't have the opportunity or time to cancel a bid. That means you have to buy the item.

You'll probably never need this link, but to retract your bid (or find more information), go to

```
http://offer.ebay.com/ws/eBayISAPI.dll?RetractBidShow
```

eBay vigorously investigates members who abuse bid retractions. Too many bid retractions and you may find yourself suspended from the system.

Chapter 7: Completing the Transaction

In This Chapter

✔ **Buying an item and paying immediately**

✔ **Using plastic**

✔ **Paying through PayPal**

✔ **Contacting the seller**

✔ **Leaving feedback**

The thrill of the chase is over, and you've won (or bought) your eBay item. Congratulations — now what do you do? You have to follow up on your victory and keep a sharp eye on what you're doing. The post-sale process is smooth as silk if you follow the proper procedure.

In this chapter, you get a handle on what's in store for you after you win an auction or buy an item. I clue you in on what the seller is supposed to do to make the transaction go smoothly and show you how to grab hold of your responsibilities as a buyer. You find out about proper post-sale etiquette, including the best ways to get organized, communicate with the seller professionally, and send your payment without hazards. I also brief you on how to handle an imperfect transaction.

Monitoring the Auction Action

Throughout the bidding process, the dollar amounts of items you're winning appear in green on your My eBay⇨Buy⇨Active page shown in Figure 7-1. If you've been outbid, as I have in the figure, they appear in red.

After the auction ends, there's no marching band, no visit from a camera crew, no armful of roses, and no oversized check to duck behind. In fact, you're more likely to find out that you've won the auction from eBay or the Buy⇨Purchase History section of your My eBay page. That's because eBay gets its end-of-auction and transaction confirmation e-mails out pronto. After you win, you can go back to the item and see a checkout link on the item page or click Pay Now on the e-mail you get from eBay. For a look at all the transaction information in the end-of-auction e-mail, see Figure 7-2.

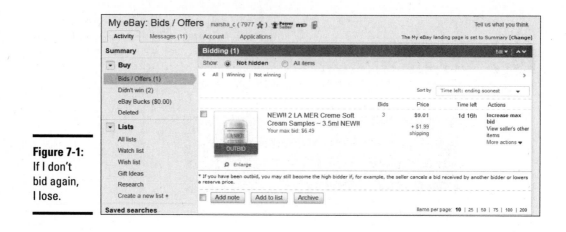

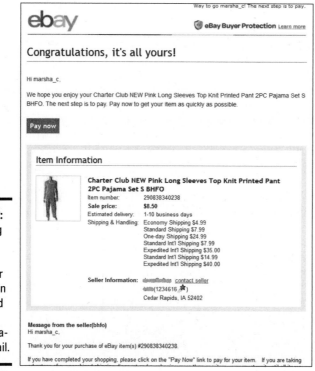

Figure 7-2:
Everything
you need
to know
about your
transaction
is included
in eBay's
Congratula-
tions e-mail.

If you have a smartphone, I recommend that you get eBay's Mobile app (more about the app in Book II, Chapter 2). With this handy tool — shown in Figure 7-3 — you can bid or buy an item wherever you are. When you have bid on an auction with a proxy bid and you win, your phone will ring and let you know that you have won. Isn't the world of mobile apps fabulous?

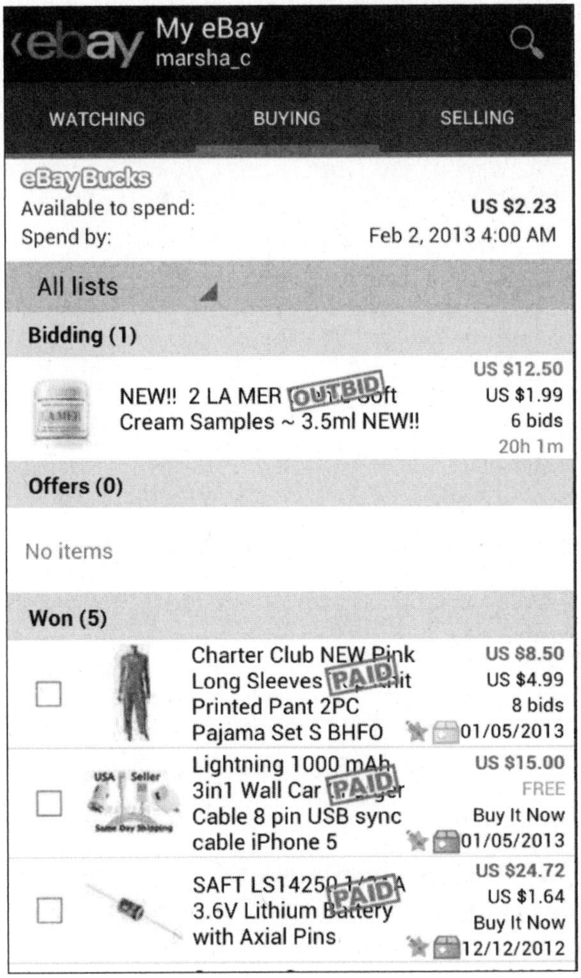

Figure 7-3:
My Buying page on eBay's mobile app, showing purchases and auction bids.

Checking Out

When you buy something in a store, you have to check out as a part of paying. eBay isn't much different. eBay's checkout is a convenient way to pay for your completed auction or purchase with a credit card or eCheck through PayPal. You may also use checkout to pay for your item using another payment service that the seller accepts.

Checkout is integrated directly onto the item page so that you can win and pay for an item in less than a minute, as shown in Figure 7-4.

Figure 7-4:
You've won
the item;
you can
click Pay
Now to pay
immediately.

When you click the Pay Now button, you're taken to the checkout page, where you can make an immediate payment through PayPal. To check out and pay, first take care of some important details on the Confirm Order page (see Figure 7-5):

✦ **Ship To address**. This will be your registered eBay address. If you want the item to be shipped elsewhere, click the Change Shipping Address link.

✦ **Add Message to Seller**. If you want to send the seller a message regarding your purchase, click here; a text box appears, and that's where you type in your message.

✦ **Item title**. Be sure what you're paying for is what you purchased!

✦ **Shipping options**. If the seller offers several shipping options, be sure you select the one that will get the item to you when you need it. eBay lists estimated delivery dates under each option; these are based on the seller's shipping policies.

✦ **PayPal payment method**. You can choose any of the payment methods you have registered with PayPal. Before you click the Confirm and Pay button, be sure to select the appropriate credit card or bank account from the drop-down list that appears when you click the Change link.

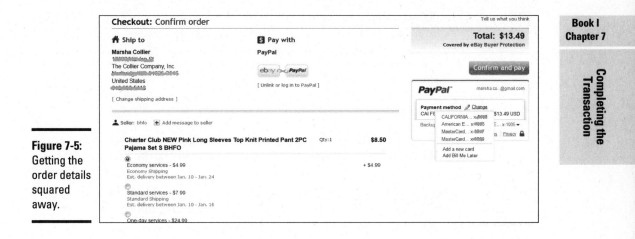

Figure 7-5:
Getting the
order details
squared
away.

When I talk to people about why they don't buy on eBay, the most frequent
answer is that they're afraid of giving out their credit card information.
The second most common reason is that they don't want to send money to
strangers. In addition to all the eBay safeguards that I mention in previous
chapters, the next section gives you further info on how to stay safe when
sending your payment to the sellers. You may be surprised to know that
there are distinct levels of safety in how you can send a payment to a seller.

Using Your Credit Card Safely

The safest way to shop on eBay is to use a credit card whether through
PayPal or direct through the seller's merchant account. eBay Buyer
Protection covers your entire purchase. In the rare instance that your purchase is not covered, most credit card companies will stand behind you if
you encounter problems using your card online.

Knowing your credit card company's policy

Before you start bidding, find out how your credit card company handles
fraud claims. The major credit-card companies — American Express, Discover,
MasterCard, and Visa — have different policies regarding how they stand
behind your online purchases:

✦ **American Express:** American Express offers a "Fraud Protection Guarantee"
for online shoppers. The company claims that there's "no fine print and
no deductible" if you need to rely on American Express to help you fight
a fraudulent transaction.

   `https://www.americanexpress.com/us/content/fraud-`
   `protection-center.html`

✦ **Discover:** Discover offers 100 percent fraud protection. The company offers a secure online account number, which generates a single-use card number each time you shop online so your account number is never transferred over the Internet.

```
https://www.discover.com/credit-cards/help-center/faqs/
soan.html
```

✦ **MasterCard:** The MasterCard Zero Liability program is offered if MasterCard is satisfied that your account is in good standing, you haven't broadcast personal account information online frivolously, and you haven't reported more than two "unauthorized events" in the past 12 months.

It appears that MasterCard's policy is conditional and that they (not you) are the final judge when it comes to determining fraud, so be careful.

```
http://www.mastercard.us/zero-liability.html
```

✦ **Visa:** Visa likes the phrase *zero liability,* as well. Your liability for unauthorized transactions is $0. A new program, called Verified by Visa, lets you set up your own private password that you use with your Visa card any time you use it online at participating merchants.

```
http://usa.visa.com/personal/security/visa_security_
program/zero_liability.html
```

Every once in a while, check your statement, visit your credit card company's website, or call the credit-card company's customer service department to verify its current fraud-protection policy for online purchases.

Never — really, I mean *never ever* — send your credit card information to anyone through e-mail. E-mail is the most insecure way to send information. As your e-mail makes its way from your computer to the recipient's desktop, it makes a whole lot of micro-stops along the way. These stops may take just nanoseconds, but your information is open for reading or storing by outside parties (at least those who have the right expertise) at any stop along the journey.

Adding a layer of protection with an online checkout service

Many eBay sellers use an independent online checkout service that allows them to process shipping information, combine purchases, give an exact shipping total, and receive credit card payments. If the seller uses such a service, you probably see a clickable link in the e-mail that's sent to you to complete the transaction. The link leads you to an online checkout page.

When you come to the point in the checkout process where you must input your credit-card information (see Figure 7-6), look for the following:

✦ **Check the URL for an *s*:** The URL (website address) may change from a prefix of `http://` to `https://` (the s stands for secure).

✦ **Look for a Security Certificate or *SSL*:** You may also see the initials `SSL` in the website's address or somewhere on the page. SSL stands for Secure Socket Layer.

The preceding items indicate that the website uses *security encryption* methods. Translation? No one but you and the merchant can read or view your payment information.

Figure 7-6:
A secure
credit card
checkout.

https://usa.loccitane.com/ecomBag.aspx?c=82&l=1&step=4		Google

L'OCCITANE EN PROVENCE

Welcome Marsha Collier | Logout | Sign In | My Account | Go to Checkout (1)

Boutique Locator | Discover Provence | About Us Search

SALE   SKINCARE   BATH & BODY   FRAGRANCE   HAIRCARE   MEN   INGREDIENTS   BESTSELLERS   WHAT'S NEW

Just for **YOU!** An extra **10% OFF** Sale items* Enter code **VIPSALE**

Call 1-888-623-2880

| SHOPPING BAG | GIFT & SAMPLE OPTIONS | BILLING & SHIPPING | PAYMENT |

Review your Order

SOLD TO	SHIP TO
Marsha Collier	Marsha Collier
CA 91325 United States	CA 91325- United States

EDIT

Product Details	Unit Price	Quantity	Total
Divine Cream Reference: 248782 Size: 1.7 oz	$96.00	1	$96.00
FreeShipPromo: FREE Standard Shipping on orders $60 or more!			

SUB TOTAL	$96.00
SHIPPING	$0.00
Total Taxes	$8.82
TOTAL	$106.82

Gift Wrapping Options   **Payment Method**

Gift invoicing ?

☐ Please hide prices on the recipient's invoice.

Add a Gift Message

EDIT   SUBMIT PAYMENT

Paying with PayPal

PayPal is my preferred method of payment on eBay. I've been happily using PayPal since the company was introduced to eBay, and I've always had positive results. Well, okay, not always. No service can make a slow or lazy seller into the picture of efficiency. The advantage of PayPal, though, is that you don't have to get your hands dirty.

Your credit card company and PayPal

To be a good consumer, you need to take responsibility for your transactions. Be sure you understand your credit card terms and conditions when it comes to third-party payment services. Each credit card company has its own agreement with PayPal — and each company has a different view of how to handle PayPal transactions. For example, Visa and MasterCard treat PayPal as the *merchant of record* in your transactions, meaning that PayPal ends up as the responsible party if you don't receive the merchandise or if you dispute the transaction. If you register a complaint about a charge made on your Visa or MasterCard, the credit card company just yanks the money from PayPal, and it's up to PayPal to settle things with the seller.

At the time of this writing, Discover and American Express treat PayPal transactions somewhat like a cash advance — a money transfer of sorts. I just checked a couple of my past Discover and American Express bills, and the PayPal charges look like any other charges. The only difference is how these credit card companies handle their level of liability in third-party payment services. This is why any complaints about a transaction should go to eBay (or PayPal) first as you are generally covered by Buyer Protection.

The folks at eBay know a good thing when they see it, so they acquired PayPal late in 2002. Now PayPal payments are integrated into eBay's checkout process.

Registering at PayPal

When you register to use PayPal, you have to give your name, address, phone number, and e-mail address. You also have to make up a password.

Make your password more than six characters, and use numbers *and* letters — revisit Chapter 3 in this minibook for more information on registration security.

You have to select a security question. The safest is your first pet's name (many people on Facebook probably know your current pet's name), your city of birth, or the last four digits of your Social Security number. You have to click to put a check mark next to the paragraph that says you have read and agree to PayPal's User Agreement and Privacy policy. (There are links so you can read them.) When you're convinced that you understand what PayPal's all about and what it expects of you, click Sign Up.

PayPal sends you an e-mail confirming your registration. The e-mail arrives, almost instantaneously, at the e-mail address you used at registration, and the message contains a link. When you receive the e-mail, click the link to visit the PayPal site. Enter the password that was used to create your account. Bingo — you're in.

Giving PayPal credit card or checking account information

Of course, you also have to add a credit card number to your PayPal account if you want to pay for anything with a credit card (or plan to sell on eBay). If you don't have a credit card — or would like to occasionally pay for things directly from your bank account — you have to register your checking account.

I can see you beginning to squirm; you're not comfortable giving that type of information to anyone, much less putting it out on the Internet. Relax. PayPal uses military-strength encryption technology to keep your account information safe, so don't be afraid to give up your data.

To register your credit card, you'll have to input the name on the card (the last name is already filled in with the name you registered on the account), the expiration date, and the *card verification number* — the three-digit number on the back of the card, imprinted next to the last few digits of the card number in the area where you sign. (American Express verification numbers are on the front of the card.) PayPal also asks you to supply a billing address.

On an American Express card, the card verification number is the four-digit number on the right side of the face of the card.

When you enter all the information PayPal needs, click the Add button. PayPal submits your information to your credit card company for confirmation. This process may take a minute or so, but eventually your credit card company says you are who you say you are, and the card is added to your PayPal account. You can register four active credit cards.

Registering your checking account is just as easy. You supply the information from the bottom of one of your checks, as shown in Figure 7-7.

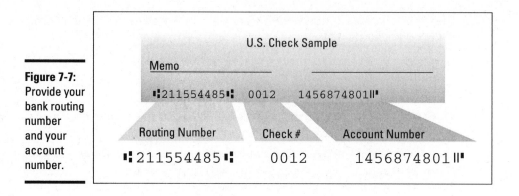

Figure 7-7:
Provide your
bank routing
number
and your
account
number.

U.S. Check Sample

Memo

᛫᛫211554485᛫᛫ 0012 1456874801ꞮꞮ᛫

Routing Number   Check #   Account Number

᛫᛫211554485 ᛫᛫   0012   1456874801 ꞮꞮ᛫

Getting PayPal-verified

For your account to get verified, PayPal must be able to confirm that your
bank account is really yours. If you bank online, you can usually confirm
your account in a few minutes. When PayPal has the information it needs,
it makes two small deposits into that account. (When I say *small*, I mean
small!) After a week or so, call your bank or check your account online and
find out the amount of these two deposits. When you have the amounts, sign
on to the PayPal website with your password, and type the amounts in the
appropriate place. Voilà! Your account is registered — and, not coinciden-
tally, you're verified! PayPal has confirmed that you hold an active account
with your bank. All banks are required to screen their account holders,
and verification authenticates your identity to anyone who does business
with you.

Here are some benefits of being PayPal verified:

✦ You can spend up to $10,000 through PayPal in a single transaction.

✦ You gain a higher level of account security.

✦ You present a confident image as a buyer or seller. Verified status shows
    other PayPal members that you have passed PayPal's security checks.

If you don't want to give up your bank account number, you can become
verified by applying for and being accepted for a PayPal Plus credit card or
PayPal Buyer Credit.

When you first sign up, there are limits on the amount of money you can
withdraw from PayPal, you may only be able to withdraw $500.00 per month.

Luckily, you can remedy this feature by confirming your bank account and
linking your credit cards. After you complete the steps shown here, you're in

the clear. The only limit is that any one withdrawal transfer to a bank can't exceed $100,000.00 USD.

Here's how you can view and lift your withdrawal limit:

1. **Go to PayPal.com and sign in to your account.**

2. **In your Account Overview, click the link near your name that reads** *View Limits*.

3. **On the resulting page, find the link that reads** *Lift Limit* **and click it.**

   You are now ready to roll with the "big guys."

Ways to pay through PayPal

The easiest and most efficient way to pay for eBay purchases is by credit card. If you are not a PayPal-verified buyer, you still have your credit card's fraud-protection guarantee behind you.

eBay sees to it that PayPal is incredibly easy to use because PayPal is the official payment service at eBay. After the auction is over, a link to pay appears. If you prefer, wait until you hear from the seller.

You may also send money directly from your bank account (either savings or checking) through instant transfer or eCheck.

✦ **Instant transfer:** An instant transfer is *immediately* debited from your bank account and deposited into the seller's account — so you'd best be sure you have the funds in your account to back up the purchase *now* (not tomorrow, not next week). PayPal requires you to back up an instant transfer with a credit card, just in case you've miscalculated your account balance.

✦ **eCheck:** You may also write an eCheck, which is just like writing a check, only you don't write it with a pen. Like regular, plain-vanilla paper checks, eChecks take three to four days to clear, and do not post to the seller's account as paid until then.

   The seller will not ship your item until PayPal tells the seller that the eCheck has cleared your bank — so if you're in a hurry, don't use this option.

✦ **Credit card:** You can use your American Express, Discover, Visa, or MasterCard to make your payment through PayPal. The cost of the item is charged to your card, and your statement reflects a PayPal payment with the seller's ID.

Getting the seller's phone number

If you don't receive your item (or something else is amiss) and you've already tried sending an e-mail through eBay Messages, you need to get more contact information. Remember back when you registered and eBay asked for a phone number? eBay keeps this information for times like this.

Know that the eBay Messaging system is monitored by eBay, and the information that it tracks becomes part of the transaction record. If anything weird is going on, it's better to use eBay's system instead of sending an e-mail independently.

To get an eBay member's phone number on a transaction that you're participating in, go back to the Advanced Search: Members: Find Contact Information link. Fill out the Contact Info form by entering the seller's user ID and the number of the item that you're buying, and then click the Search button. If all the information is correct, you automatically see a request-confirmation page; then eBay generates an e-mail message to both you and the other user.

eBay's e-mail message includes the seller's user ID, name, company, city, state, and country of residence, as well as the seller's phone number and date of initial registration. eBay sends this same information about you to the user you want to get in touch with. Most sellers jump to attention when they receive this e-mail from eBay and promptly get the ball rolling to complete the transaction.

If you have a balance in your PayPal account, you must use that money to make your payment; so withdraw your PayPal balance first if you want to pay with a credit card. Payment will then default to using your bank account, so be sure to select a credit card (if that's the way you want to pay) when you're finalizing an eBay transaction.

Sending Payment Promptly and Securely

How many times have you heard the saying "The check is in the mail"? Yeah, I've heard it about a thousand times, too. If you're on the selling end of a transaction, hearing this line from the buyer but not getting the money is frustrating. If you're on the buying end, it's bad form — and may also lead to bad feedback for you.

Being the good buyer that you are, you'll get your payment out pronto. If you've purchased an item and intend to pay by using PayPal, do it immediately — why wait? (The sooner you pay, the sooner you get your item.)

On October 20th, 2008, eBay changed its policies so that paper checks or money orders will no longer be allowed as payment on eBay.

Most sellers expect to get paid immediately after the close of the auction or sale. If, for some reason, you cannot send a PayPal payment right away, be sure to use eBay Messages to let the seller know when you will be paying.

If you have to delay payment for any reason (you have to go out of town, you broke your leg), let the seller know as soon as possible. Most sellers understand if you send them a kind and honest e-mail. Let the seller know what's up; give him or her a date by which the money can be expected, and then meet that deadline. If the wait is unreasonably long, the seller may cancel the transaction

Contacting the Seller

Generally there's no need to contact the seller in a normal transaction. You pay via PayPal and your item should arrive within the timespan estimated by eBay on the item page when you made your purchase.

If you've won an item, it's *de rigueur* for you to use the Pay Now link on the item page as soon as possible after you've won.

If you need to contact the seller before sending payment, you have several ways to find contact information:

✦ **Click the Ask a Question link** on the very bottom of the listing page, which takes you to common questions and answers written out by the seller. If your answer isn't there, you will see a text box where you can send a message through eBay Messages.

✦ **Click the Site Map link,** located way at the bottom of almost every eBay page, and then click the Find a Member link under the Connect heading. On the resulting page, click the link to find Contact Information.

✦ **Click the Advanced Search link** (at the top-right corner of all eBay pages), and then click the Find Contact Information link (on the left side of the page).

eBay doesn't tolerate abuses of its contact system. Make sure that you use this resource to communicate with another user *only* about a specific transaction in which you are participating. To use contact information to complete a deal outside eBay is an infringement of the rules. If you abuse the contact system, eBay can investigate you and you may lose your site privileges.

Leaving Responsible Feedback

Almost any eBay seller will tell you that one of his or her pet peeves about the eBay feedback system is that new community members tend to leave neutral or (even worse) *negative* feedback the moment a shipment arrives and something is wrong. In this section, I tell you what you need to know to avoid getting a bad reputation for being too hard on sellers.

Chapter 5 gives you the long version of leaving feedback on eBay; please read it for detailed information on the new seller ratings. These DSRs (Detailed Star Ratings) allow buyers to get more specific with their transaction feedback.

The DSR part of the feedback system asks you to rate sellers by filling in one to five stars. Why be judgmental? If the transaction went through as promised, why not give the seller five stars? A five-star rating doesn't cost you anything as the buyer, and if the seller is a Top Rated Seller, it can affect a discount they receive on their eBay fees.

Late Delivery

A late delivery is not always the seller's fault. Before dinging a seller's reputation for slow delivery, check the postmark on the package's label. You'll often find that the seller followed through with his or her shipping promise, but the package was held up in transit. The shipping services may deserve a one-star rating, but if the seller shipped right away, why not give that person five stars for a good-faith effort?

Missing or damaged shipment

When a package leaves the seller's hands, it is *literally* (and completely) out of his or her hands. If UPS, Federal Express Ground, or Federal Express Air ships your package, the tracking number can track the item. Here are a few things to remember:

✦ Be sure you know when the seller plans to ship the merchandise, so there's less question about when it will probably arrive. In the top of each listing (under the shipping costs), you will see a delivery time estimate based on the seller's shipping policies. A Top Rated Plus Seller sends items out within 24 hours.

✦ Open your packages immediately upon receipt. A seller can't make a claim on an item that you report damaged in shipping a month after it arrives, so leaving negative feedback for the seller at that point is unfair. Most shippers insist that any and all damage be reported within five days of receipt. Also, if damage has occurred, keep all packing materials for inspection by the carrier.

✦ A seller can't do much about a missing package. Sellers can't even make a claim on a postal shipment until 30 days have passed since mailing. If, however, the tracking information says the package was delivered to your door (and it went missing from there), you have no recourse.

✦ If the item never arrives, only the sender can file a claim with the shipping company and must produce all shipping receipts. Notify the seller immediately by e-mail or telephone upon receiving a damaged shipment. Leaving negative feedback before contacting the seller is just plain unjust.

Item doesn't meet your expectations

If the item arrives and isn't as described in the item description, e-mail the seller. Communication is a good thing — and most sellers want to preserve their reputations. Give the seller the opportunity to work things out with you. Keep in mind these facts:

✦ If a new item in a manufacturer's sealed box arrives damaged, the damage could have happened at the manufacturer and the seller wouldn't even know about it.

✦ A seller may not be as experienced in a particular collectible as you are. If you didn't ask all the necessary questions before bidding, you may have received what the seller *assumed* was a collectible. It's up to the buyer to ask questions before placing a bid.

✦ If you receive the wrong item, the seller might have simply mixed up labels. Don't jump to leave negative feedback. Just notify the seller, who will no doubt work out the mistake with you.

Most important, sellers should be given the chance to prove they care and make good. Most items are always covered by eBay Buyer Protection.

Choosing your words carefully

Good sellers should be rewarded, and potential buyers should be informed. That's why no eBay transaction is complete until the buyer fills out the feedback form. Before leaving any feedback, remember that sometimes no one's at fault when transactions get fouled up. Here are some handy hints on what kind of feedback to leave for a seller:

✦ **Give the seller the benefit of the doubt.** Selling on eBay is a source of income, and most sellers are honest, hardworking people. If the transaction could have been a nightmare, but the seller tried to make it right and meet you halfway, that's an easy call — leave positive feedback.

✦ **Whenever possible, reward someone who seems honest or tried to correct a bad situation.** For example, if the seller worked at a snail's pace but you eventually got your item and you're thrilled with it, you may want to leave positive feedback with a caveat. Something like "Item as described, good seller, but very slow to deliver" sends the right feedback message.

✦ **If the seller worked at a snail's pace but packaged the item adequately and the item was kinda-sorta what you expected, you may want to leave neutral feedback.** That is, the experience wasn't bad enough for negative feedback but didn't deserve praise. Here's an example: "Really slow to deliver, didn't say item condition was good not excellent, but did deliver." Wishy-washy is okay as a response to so-so performance; at least the next buyer will know to ask specific questions.

✦ **If the seller doesn't ship your item or the item doesn't match the description and the seller won't make things right, then you need to leave negative feedback.** But never write negative feedback in the heat of the moment — and *never* make it personal. Life's interesting enough without taking on extra hassles.

Remember that you cannot retract feedback. You are responsible for your words, which will remain on the eBay site forever (with your user ID next to them for all to see). Be sure to leave a simple, factual, and *unemotional* statement. Important things to mention in your feedback are

✦ How satisfied you are with your purchase

✦ The quality of the packaging

✦ The promptness of shipping

✦ The seller's professionalism

✦ The level of communication

If you must leave a negative feedback comment, know that there is karma in this life. If you couldn't resolve things without a problem, chances are the seller wasn't happy with the trading experience, either. Try to work things out first!

Chapter 8: Participating in the Community

In This Chapter

✔ Setting up your About Me and My World page

✔ Having fun in boards, chats, and discussions

✔ Joining an eBay group

eBay is more than just an Internet location for buying and selling great stuff. Most of all, eBay is about people. Today, "social media" is the buzzword — and eBay wants the world to know that it has created (and works hard to maintain) a community. And prime real estate in *this* community costs nothing! As in real-life communities, you participate as much as works for you. You can get involved in all sorts of neighborhood activities, or you can just sit back, mind your own business, and watch the world go by.

As you've probably heard by now, one of the main ways to participate in the eBay community is through feedback (which I explain in detail in Chapters 5 and 7). In this chapter, I show you some other ways to become part of the community. Social media has opened up many new groups — and new ways to share ideas with other sellers who may not want to hang around eBay all day. On the eBay site, you can socialize, get information from other members, leave messages, or just read what everybody's talking about on eBay's message boards, category boards, and corporate announcement board. I include tips on how to use all these places to your best advantage. The tools in this chapter help you solidify your place in the community that is eBay.

Your Home on eBay: About Me

Want to know more about the people behind those user IDs? Thousands of eBay members have created personal web pages on eBay called About Me pages. eBay users with active About Me pages have a Me icon (with a blue lowercase *m* and a red lowercase *e*) next to their user IDs.

If you're on eBay, you *need* an About Me page. Checking out the About Me page for each person you conduct business with gives you an opportunity to get to know those folks. Because eBay is a cyberspace market, you have no other way to let prospective bidders know that you're a real person. (Don't you shop at some stores because you like the owners or people who work there?) The About Me page takes a first step toward establishing a professional and trusted identity at eBay.

The About Me page enables you to personalize yourself as a bidder to sellers and as a business to prospective bidders. (See Figure 8-1 for an example.) Your About Me page also becomes your About the Seller page if you have an eBay store.

An About Me page benefits you also when you buy. Sellers usually like to know about their bidders to build confidence in their trading partners. You can see an example of a personal My eBay page in Figure 8-2.

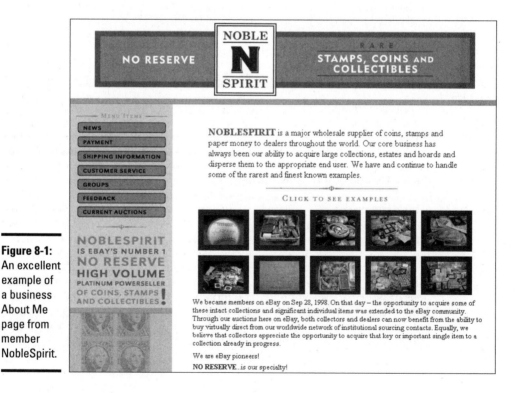

Figure 8-1: An excellent example of a business About Me page from member NobleSpirit.

← Back to previous page

Figure 8-2:
Aunt Patti
tells us
about her
hobbies and
interests.

If you don't have an About Me page, put this book down for a minute and set one up immediately. It doesn't have to be a work of art; just get something up there to tell the rest of the community who you are. You can always go back later and add to (or redesign) it.

The About Me page can also be a deal-maker or a deal-breaker. Once I was looking around eBay for some extra-long cables, and I found several sellers selling just what I wanted. One of the lower-priced sellers had a low feedback rating because he was new on eBay. But he had an About Me page, so I clicked. I found out that the seller was a computer technician by trade and that he and his son made these computer cables together as a family business at home in the evenings. The money they made went to pay for their father-son trips to see their favorite baseball team play. What a great family enterprise! Better yet, he guaranteed the cables. As you might have guessed, I bought the cables, and we both got positive feedback.

Planning and Building an About Me Page

When you plan your About Me page, consider adding the following:

✦ Who you are and in which city you live.

✦ Your hobbies. If you collect things, here's where to let the world know.

✦ Whether you run your eBay business full-time or part-time, and whether you have another career. This is more integral information about you; let the world know.

✦ The type of merchandise that your business revolves around. Promote it here; tell the reader why your merchandise and service are the best!

✦ Your most recent feedback and a list of your current auctions.

To create your page, click the Me icon next to any user's name, scroll to the bottom of the About Me page that appears, find the line that reads "Create or edit my About Me page," and click. You can also click the About Me link on the My eBay Account tab⇨Personal (or Business, depending on your account) Information. Or go to

```
pages.ebay.com/community/aboutme.html
```

Then follow the simple formatted template for your first page and work from there.

When you begin to sell on eBay, your About Me page is an important sales tool — so take your time when you create your page. A well-thought-out About Me page improves your sales because people who come across your items and check out your About Me page can get a sense of who you are and how serious you are about your eBay activities. They see instantly that you're no fly-by-night seller.

Before you create your About Me page, I suggest that you look at what other users have done. eBay members often include pictures, links to other websites (including their personal or business home pages), and links to just about any web location that reflects their personalities. If your purpose is to generate more business, however, I recommend that you keep your About Me page focused on your listings, with a link to your website.

The page can be as simple or as complex as you want. You may use one of eBay's templates as presented, or gussy up the page with lots of pictures and varied text by using HTML.

Sellers with many items on the site often add a message to their About Me pages indicating that they're willing to reduce shipping charges if bidders bid on their other auctions as well. This direct tactic may lack nuance, but it increases the number of people who look at (and bid on) your auctions or fixed-price sales.

Gathering your thoughts

There are several things you must think about prior to setting up your page. Decide beforehand what you want to put into the sections you find on the Enter Page Content form (see Figure 8-3) so you'll be all ready to type when you reach that page:

+ **Page Title:** Come up with a title for your page. It should be as simple as a welcome greeting.

+ **Paragraph 1:** This paragraph can tell a little about you and your hobbies or interests. You can also talk about the items you sell on eBay — but most of all, it should reflect your personality.

In the paragraphs of the About Me page, you can use HTML (see the HTML tab in Figure 8-3) to further customize. The titles, however, are standard and won't permit HTML coding.

+ **Paragraph 2:** Here you can elaborate on your interests and business on eBay. Add more information.

+ **Add pictures**: Pictures are good, too! Let people see who you are, the people you work with, or items from your collections. This is where you "get real" in a visual way.

+ **eBay activity:** Decide what you'd like to show on the page — how many of your most recent feedback comments and whether you'd like to show your current listings on the page.

Don't get carried away with showing your last 100 feedback messages; doing so takes up too much space. Display either 10 or 25 and leave it at that. If visitors want to know more about your feedback rating, they can click your feedback number. (After all, they clicked your Me icon to get here, and that's next to your feedback number.)

+ **Links:** There are strict policies governing the use of links on eBay these days. You can link to your own website, but only from your About Me page. Visit Book III, Chapter 2 for all these details.

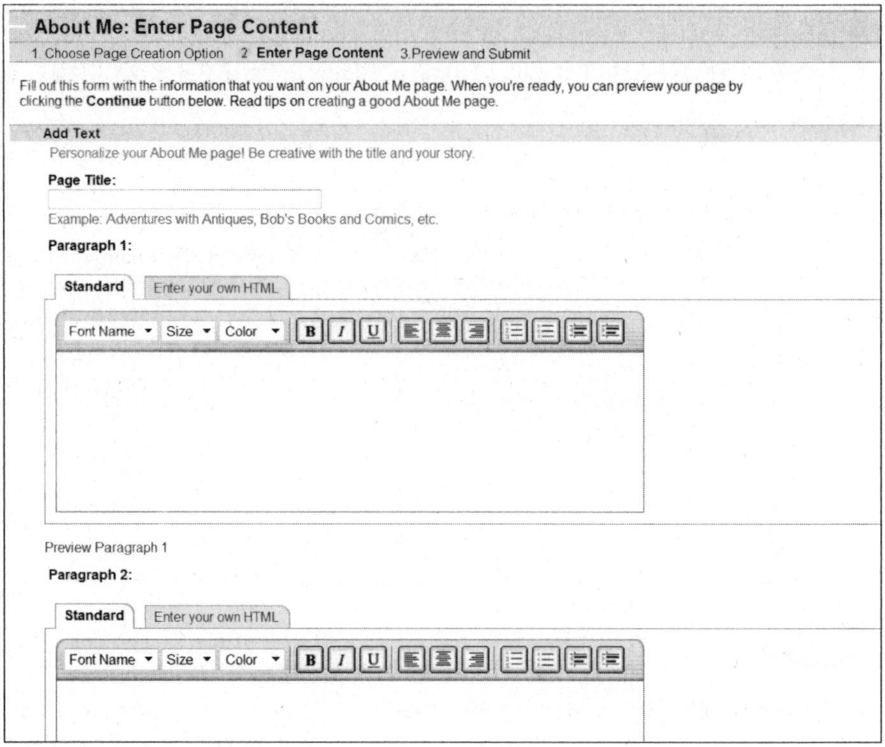

About Me: Enter Page Content

1. Choose Page Creation Option   2. **Enter Page Content**   3. Preview and Submit

Fill out this form with the information that you want on your About Me page. When you're ready, you can preview your page by clicking the **Continue** button below. Read tips on creating a good About Me page.

Add Text

Personalize your About Me page! Be creative with the title and your story.

Page Title:

Example: Adventures with Antiques, Bob's Books and Comics, etc.

Paragraph 1:

Standard   Enter your own HTML

Font Name ▼ Size ▼ Color ▼ **B** *I* U

Preview Paragraph 1

Paragraph 2:

Standard   Enter your own HTML

Font Name ▼ Size ▼ Color ▼ **B** *I* U

Figure 8-3:
eBay's
step-by-step
method
makes
building
your page
easy.

If you've been an advanced user on eBay for a while, consider adding the following to your existing My eBay page:

✦ **Your logo:** If you've designed a logo for your eBay business, be sure to put it on the page.

✦ **Returns policy:** Outline your standard returns policy for your customers.

✦ **Shipping policy:** Explain how you ship and when you ship. Offer discounts on shipping for multiple purchases through your eBay store.

✦ **Searchable index to your eBay store:** Let your customers search your store by apparel size, brand name, or item. You can accomplish this with HTML coding.

✦ **Payment methods:** Let your customers know what payment methods you accept.

Using little-known, eBay-unique HTML tags

It's not highly publicized, but you can use some unique-to-eBay HTML codes to give your My eBay page a custom look. Some of these codes can be combined with others (such as those for bold and color). Play around with them and see what you come up with! The following list gives you the secret codes (sorry, no decoder ring) that you can type into the HTML portion of your text entry:

`<eBayUserID>`: Displays your user ID and real-time feedback rating

`<eBayUserID BOLD>`: Displays your user ID and feedback rating in boldface

`<eBayUserID NOLINK>`: Displays your user ID with no clickable link (useful if you plan to change your ID soon)

`<eBayUserID NOFEEDBACK>`: Displays your user ID with no feedback number after it

`<eBayUserID BOLD NOFEEDBACK>`: Combines two of the previous tags into one

`<eBayFeedback>`: Shows your up-to-the-minute feedback comments in real time

`<eBayFeedback COLOR="red">`: Changes the color of the second line on your feedback comment table to red

`<eBayFeedback TABLEWIDTH="75%">`: Changes the width of your feedback comment table as a percentage of the allowed space (the default value is 90%)

`<eBayItemList>`: Inserts a list of the items you currently have up for sale

`<eBayItemList BIDS>`: Displays everything you're currently bidding on

`<eBayTime>`: Inserts the official eBay time into your text

`<eBayMemberSince>`: Inputs the date and time of your initial eBay registration

Setting up the page

To create your About Me page, do the following:

1. **Click the Site Map link at the bottom of the eBay home page (under Tools).**

   The Site Map page appears.

2. **In the Connect area, click the About Me link.**

3. **If you haven't signed in, type your user ID and password in the appropriate boxes.**

   You're taken to the About Me page, as shown in Figure 8-4.

Figure 8-4:
The About
Me home
page.

4. **Click the Click Here button.**

5. **Decide whether you want to use eBay's easy step-by-step process or enter your own HTML code, and then click Continue.**

   Because entering HTML code assumes you really know what you're doing, I suggest that you choose the step-by-step process.

6. **Enter the following information:**

   • **Page title:** Type the title of your About Me page (for example, *Welcome to Larry Lunch's Lunchbox Place*).

   • **Welcome paragraph:** Type a personal, attention-grabbing bit of text that greets your visitors (something like *Hey, I like lunchboxes a lot — only more exciting*). You have the option of typing in your own HTML coding or using the buttons at the top of the box to change the font, color, size, and attributes (see Figure 8-5). The HTML generator is similar to the Sell Your Item page — and similar to most word-processing programs.

   You can preview your paragraph at any time by clicking Preview Paragraph at the bottom of the text-entry area. If you don't like what you see, close the Preview window and continue to edit your masterpiece.

   • **Another paragraph:** Type text for the second paragraph of the page, such as *Vintage, Modern, Ancient*, or *I Collect All Kinds of Lunchboxes*. Then maybe talk about yourself or your collection (such as, *I used to stare at lunchboxes in the school cafeteria . . . only more, you know, normal*).

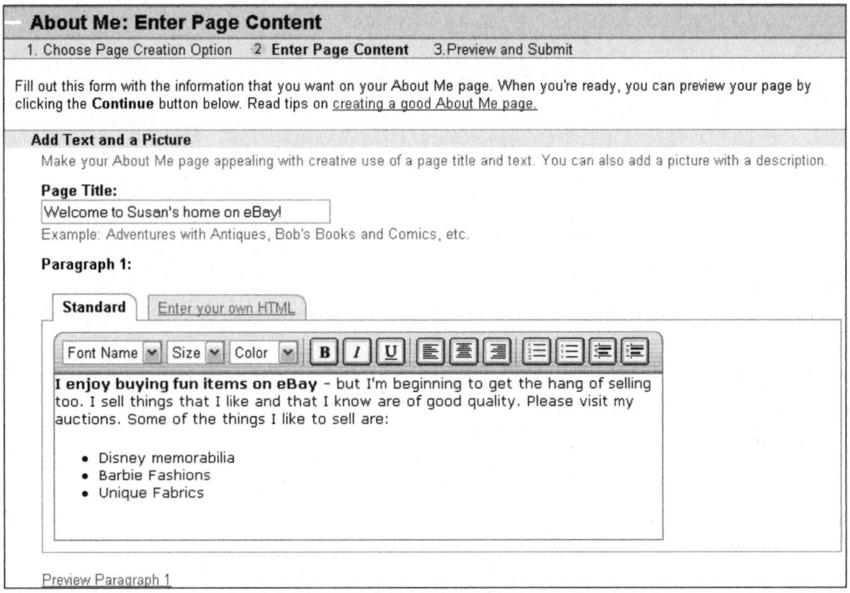

About Me: Enter Page Content

1. Choose Page Creation Option   **2 Enter Page Content**   3.Preview and Submit

Fill out this form with the information that you want on your About Me page. When you're ready, you can preview your page by clicking the **Continue** button below. Read tips on creating a good About Me page.

Add Text and a Picture

Make your About Me page appealing with creative use of a page title and text. You can also add a picture with a description.

Page Title:

Welcome to Susan's home on eBay!

Example: Adventures with Antiques, Bob's Books and Comics, etc.

Paragraph 1:

| Standard | Enter your own HTML |

Font Name ▼ | Size ▼ | Color ▼ | **B** | *I* | U | ≡ ≡ ≡ | ≡ ≡ ≡ ≡

I enjoy buying fun items on eBay - but I'm beginning to get the hang of selling too. I sell things that I like and that I know are of good quality. Please visit my auctions. Some of the things I like to sell are:

- Disney memorabilia
- Barbie Fashions
- Unique Fabrics

Preview Paragraph 1

Figure 8-5:
Entering preliminary text and changing attributes.

- **Picture:** If you're adding a picture, type a sentence describing it, for example: *This is my wife Loretta with our lunchbox collection.*

- **Picture URL:** Type the website address (URL) where people can find your picture. See Book V, Chapter 5 to find out how to upload digital images to your own (probably free) image area.

- **Feedback:** Select how many of your feedback postings you want to appear on your About Me page. (You can opt not to show any feedback, but I think you should put in a few comments, especially if they're complimentary, as in, "Larry sent my lunchbox promptly, and it makes lunchtime a blast! Everybody stares at it. . . .")

- **Items for Sale:** Select how many of your current listings you want to appear on your About Me page. If you don't have any auctions or Buy It Now items at the moment, you can select the Show No Items option.

- **Favorite Links:** Type the names and URLs of any web links you want visitors to see, for example, a website that appraises lunchboxes. ("It's in excellent condition except for that petrified ham sandwich. . . .")

7. **After you've finished entering this information (and are happy with how it looks), click Continue at the bottom of the page.**

Don't worry if you're not absolutely wild about your page on the first pass. The important part is to get it published. You can go back and make changes as often as you want.

8. **On the About Me Preview and Submit page, click the button that corresponds to the layout option you want.**

   You're presented with three layout options, as shown in Figure 8-6.

9. **Scroll down the page and check out what your About Me page will look like.**

   If you don't like your current layout, go back up the page and change the layout.

10. **If you don't like what you see, click the Back button and do some more editing.**

11. **When you're happy with your masterpiece, click the Submit button.**

   You did it. Now anyone in the world with access to the Internet can find your personal About Me page on eBay.

Don't forget to update your About Me page often. A good About Me page makes bidders eager to know more about your auctions. An out-of-date About Me page turns off potential bidders. If you choose to update your page, you need to edit it using HTML. If you don't use HTML, you have to create an entire new page.

You can link to your About Me page from your website or from your e-mail because all About Me pages have their own personal URLs. You can find your About Me page by typing `members.ebay.com/aboutme/` followed by your user ID. Here's the URL for my page (shown in Figure 8-7):

```
members.eBay.com/aboutme/marsha_c
```

Figure 8-6:
Selecting your page layout style — purely a personal decision.

About Me: Preview and Submit

1. Choose Page Creation Option   2. Enter Page Content   3. Preview and Submit

Select a page layout from the three shown here (Layout A is shown below).

⊙ Layout "A"   ○ Layout "B"   ○ Layout "C"

Once you've chosen a layout that you like, click the **Submit** button below.

Note: If you don't have JavaScript enabled on your computer, you'll still be able to choose any of these layouts. However, you won't be able to preview your selection below.

[< Back] [Submit >]

Figure 8-7:
My About
Me page on
eBay.

Reaching the World through Your Profile Page

If blogging is the key to the new web, then your My World profile page is the hub of your eBay user interaction. Your About Me page is there for customers, and the My World page is mostly used by the eBay community. People like to know about other people, and the My World page shows your world, your way.

Just click your user ID on your My eBay page (or any page for that matter) and you'll arrive at your own (ready-to-fill-out) My World page. To visit the hub (okay, here's the URL), just go to

```
http://myworld.ebay.com/
```

and you'll arrive at the My World hub.

If you go to the hub, click the *View My World* button. After you click through, you see a page ready to edit. The page is pre-populated with the items you are selling — but wait — you can add a whole lot more!

To beef up your page, start here.

1. **At the top of your profile page, next to your user ID will be a tiny pencil icon and the word *Edit*. Click Edit.**

Several options open up.

2. **To add your photo and/or a video, click Add Photo/Video.**

The Profile Photo/Video window pops up.

1. *To put a photo on your page, click the Chose File button under the words Select Photo.* A window to your hard drive appears and prompts you to search your computer for a photo. Select your photo from the folder, click Save, and the photo appears on your page.

2. *To add a video in the Profile Photo/Video window that opens, type the YouTube URL for the video you want to share in the Add Video box.* A preview will appear on the right, as shown in Figure 8-8.

3. *When everything looks right, click the Close button.*

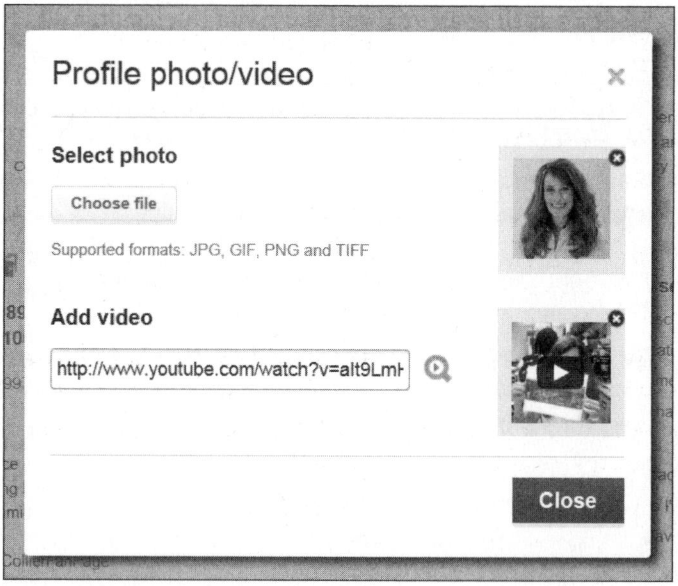

Figure 8-8:
Adding a
photo and a
video.

3. **Under the cartoon word-balloon icon are the words *Write a greeting*. Click this link to add a short introduction for your page.**

4. **Under Connect Social Profile, click the Share icon to connect your account to Facebook.**

This way, folks visiting your profile will be able to join you on the social media network.

5. **Click under the pen icon and a world opens up with places to fill in your Personal and Business Information.**

You don't need to fill in every field. The ones you don't fill in won't appear on the final page. Here are your options:

- **Things I Sell.** The terms you use here to describe your wares are most important; these *keywords* help future bidders find you through eBay's search engine optimization (SEO). Use keywords that will show up in an online search; don't just describe.

- **Things I Buy.** I keep this description very general; I don't believe in tipping my hand to competitors when it comes to bidding.

- **Things I collect.** If you have a particular passion, list it here. You may meet others who have similar interests.

- **Favorites.** Books, movies, music/bands, and TV shows are all options you can add. By including this information, you let other eBay members know more about you.

- **Payment methods.** List the payment methods you accept for payment on eBay here.

- **Shipping information.** List the different vendors and classes of service that you use to send your eBay items.

- **Return policy.** Type in your return policy in the box provided. You may have different return policies for different items, if that's the case, suggest people check your listings.

6. **When you've finished filling in the information that you care to share publicly, go back to the top of the page and click Close Edit.**

Your new profile will appear much the same as mine does in Figure 8-9. You can Visit my profile page at

```
http://myworld.ebay.com/marsha_c
```

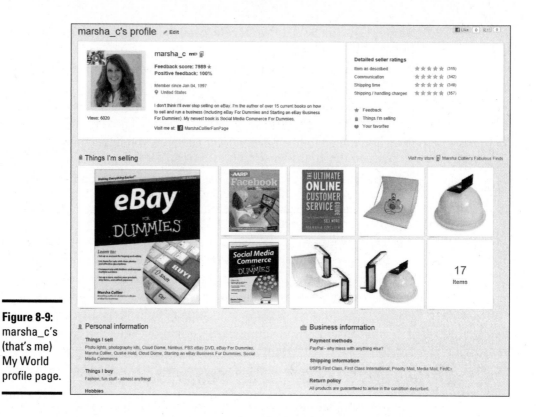

Figure 8-9:
marsha_c's
(that's me)
My World
profile page.

Playing Nice with Other eBay Members

The navigation bar has a handy Community link that connects you to the people and happenings on eBay. eBay has more than 112 million members — a bigger population than some countries — but it can still have that small-town feel through groups and discussion boards. Start on the main page by clicking Community on the navigation bar. Now you can access dozens of category-specific chat and discussion boards, participate in a bunch of general discussion boards, and find help on still other discussion boards.

But there's a whole lot more to the eBay community, as you find out in this section. Take a little time to explore it for yourself.

News and chat, this and that

The Community Overview page is not quite like *The New York Times* ("All the News That's Fit to Print"), but it is the place to go to find all the news, Neighborhoods, chat rooms, and message board links. Figure 8-10 shows you what the page looks like.

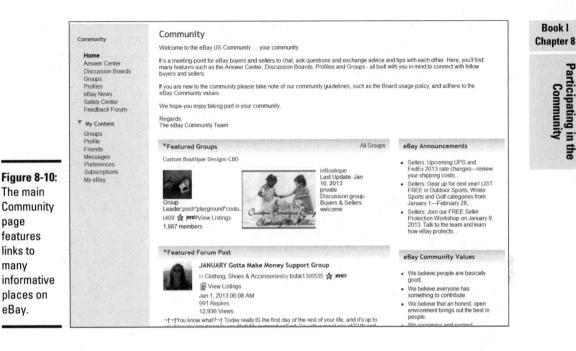

Figure 8-10:
The main Community page features links to many informative places on eBay.

Hear ye, hear ye! eBay's announcements

If you were living in the 1700s, you'd see a strangely dressed guy in a funny hat ringing a bell and yelling, "Hear ye, hear ye!" every time you opened eBay's announcements. (Then again, if you were living in the 1700s, you'd have no electricity, no computer, no fast food, or anything else you probably consider fun — like eBay!) In any case, eBay's announcements are the most important place to find out what's going on (directly from headquarters) on the website. And no one even needs to ring a bell.

The announcements page is where eBay lists new features and policy changes. Visiting this page is like reading your morning eBay newspaper, because eBay adds comments to this page almost every day. You find out about upcoming changes in categories, new promotions, and eBay goings-on. Reach this page by clicking the Announcements link under Community on the eBay top-of-page navigation bar or by going to the following page

```
http://announcements.ebay.com/
```

Figure 8-11 shows you eBay's Announcements, complete with information that could affect your listings.

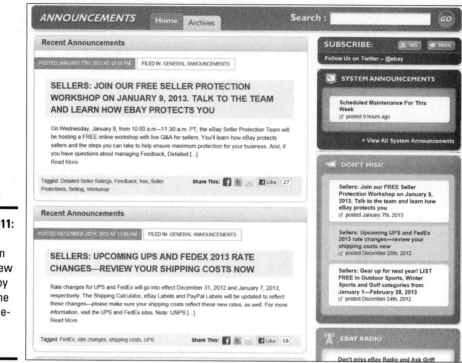

Figure 8-11:
Keep up to date on what's new at eBay by visiting the Announcements board.

When you look at some of eBay's older URL addresses, you may notice a subfolder named /*aw*/. The *aw* harkens back to the day when eBay wasn't eBay — but was AuctionWeb instead (way back when I joined up).

eBay reports outages and system glitches on the system announcement board, at the following address:

```
www2.ebay.com/aw/announce.shtml
```

eBay uses this board also to update users on glitches in the system and when those may be rectified (should you wonder whether the problem is lurking on your computer or on the eBay system).

Whenever eBay introduces new features, explanations, or links, they appear on the Announcements page. Get there by clicking Announcements on the Community drop-down menu in eBay's top navigation bar.

Help! I need somebody

If you ever have specific eBay questions, several eBay discussion forums on the Community page can help you. You can also go directly to the Discussion Boards to pose your question to the eBay members currently in residence.

To get an answer on a discussion board, you need to start a thread by asking a question. Title your thread with your question, and you'll no doubt get an answer to your query posted swiftly. Take a look at the variety of topics in Figure 8-12.

After you've finished reading (or just checking out the index) in this book, you'll have answers to the questions most commonly asked on the site. Use this book as your fun way to participate.

Figure 8-12:
The Discussion Board hub on eBay.

Community
Home
Answer Center
Discussion Boards
Groups
Profiles
eBay News
Safety Center
Feedback Forum

My Content
Groups
Profile
Tags
Friends
Messages
Preferences
Subscriptions
My eBay

Discussion Boards

eBay's discussion boards are a great place to meet other members, get advice, and share and find information on everything from art to travel. Browse the discussion boards below to find an area that interests you.

Subscribe to RSS | Mark All as Read

▼ **Community Center platform General Maintenance Update**

  Learn more about the Community Center Maintenance Updates scheduled to be launched on Wednesday, January 16, 2013.

▼ **Categories**

▼ **Community Help Boards**
About Me page
Auction Listings
Bidding
Buyer Central
Checkout
eBay Mobile
eBay Picture Hosting
eBay Sidebar & Toolbar
eBay Stores
Escrow & Insurance
Feedback
Half.com
International Trading
Miscellaneous
My eBay
Packaging & Shipping
PayPal
Photos & HTML
Policies-User Agreement
Registration
Returns
Reviews & Guides
Search
Seller Central
Technical Issues
Trading Assistant
Trust & Safety (Safe Harbor)
Workshops

▼ **General Discussion Boards**
Building An eBay Business
eBay Cafe
eBay Chat
eBay Friends From All Over
New to eBay Board
Night Owl's Nest
Part-time eBay Sellers
The eBay Town Square
The Front Porch

▼ **Category-Specific Boards**
Animals
Antiques
Art & Artist
Barbie Collectors
Bears and Plush
Book Readers
Booksellers
Business & Industrial
Cell Phones
Childrens Clothing Boutique
Clothing, Shoes & Accessories
Coins & Paper Money
Collectibles
Comics
Computers, Networking & I.T.
Cook's Nook
Country/Rural Style
Custom Made Items and Services
Decorative & Holiday
Disneyana
Dollhouses and Miniatures
Dolls
Dolls Artists and Limited Edition
eBay Motors
Fine Jewelry, Gems & Precious Metals
Handmade/Custom Clothing for Kids
Health & Beauty
Historical Memorabilia
Hobbies & Crafts
Home & Garden
Jewelry & Gemstones
Mid-Century/Modern
Motorcycle Boulevard
Movies & Memorabilia
Music & Musicians
Needle Arts & Vintage Textiles
Outdoor Sports
Photos

Top-rated community help boards

You know you need help, but you don't know which area is best for you. Here's my take on which boards are most helpful:

✓ **Auction Listings Help Board:** This discussion board is a catch-all for many subjects. If you don't see a board specific to your question (or if you post to another board and get no reply), try this one — it's always hopping with lots of peeps (people).

✓ **Photos & HTML Help Board:** Good help from other eBay members for those with specific questions about using HTML and posting pictures in your auctions.

✓ **Technical Issues:** If something isn't working right and you want an answer now (because you're in the middle of putting up a listing), check the Technical Issues Help Board to see whether other members are experiencing the same issue. Many answers to tech issues can be found here.

You can get most eBay-related questions answered by going to eBay's Answer Center, which you get to by clicking the Answer Center link in the Connect area. You then see questions covering almost any topic you can think of regarding listings on eBay. Just post your question and some kindly eBay member will probably suggest an answer.

eBay news and information boards

When eBay rolls out new features or makes a policy change, people want to chat and discuss how these changes will affect their business online. eBay opens a new Board to coincide with each new announcement.

Members who post on these boards often share helpful tips. Newbies may find that *lurking* (reading without posting) on some of these boards helps them find out more about how eBay works. Occasionally, an eBay staffer shows up, which is kinda like inviting Bill Gates to a meeting of new Windows users. eBay staff members are usually hounded with questions.

When a new policy or some sort of big change occurs, these boards are most likely going to fill pretty quickly with discussion about it. On slow days, however, you may need to wade through personal messages and chatting with no connection to eBay. Many of the people who post on these boards are longtime members with histories (as well as feuds) that can rival any soap opera. On rare occasions, the postings can get abusive. Getting involved in personality clashes or verbal warfare gains you nothing. Duck the crossfire and look for the useful stuff.

No matter how peeved the users of a message board may get — and no matter how foul or raunchy the language — no one on eBay ever sees it. eBay uses a built-in vulgarity checker that deletes any (well, okay, *as many as possible*) words or phrases that eBay considers offensive or obscene.

The one cardinal rule for eBay chat boards and message boards is: *No doing business on the board.* No advertising items for sale! Not now. Not ever. eBay bans any repeat offenders who break this rule from participating on these boards.

User-to-user (general) discussion boards

In addition to chat boards, eBay also has *discussion* boards, in which the topics are deliberately open-ended — just as the topics of discussion in coffeehouses tend to vary depending on who happens to be in them at any given time. Check out these areas and read ongoing discussions about eBay's latest buzz. It's a lot of fun and good reading. Post your opinions to the category that suits you. Here are few of my favorites:

+ **The eBay Town Square:** A potpourri of various subjects and topics.

+ **The Soapbox:** The place to voice your views and suggestions to help build a better eBay.

+ **Night Owls Nest:** A fun locale for creatures of the night and their unique postings. (As I'm writing this, for example, there's a thread with spirited advice to a community member who needs help with his "gassy" cat.)

+ **The Park:** An interesting place where community members join in for fun ideas.

Checking Out Other Boards

About a dozen chat rooms on eBay specialize in everything from pure chat to charity work. In this section, I describe a few of these boards.

Café society

The eBay Café message board (eBay's first message board from back when eBay was mostly selling Pez candy dispensers) attracts mostly regulars chatting about eBay gossip. Frequent postings include the sharing of personal milestones and whatever else is on people's minds. You can also find useful information about eBay and warnings about potential scams.

Emoticons: Communicating graphically

When you visit the eBay boards, you may notice that many experienced posters to the board have cute little smiley icons, called emoticons, next to their posts to show emotion. The following table shows how you too can doll up your posts with a little emotion.

You can type the keyboard shortcuts or use the HTML image links to display your chosen icon. Be sure not to put spaces between the characters in the key combinations. Using HTML is pretty easy; for example, `<img src="http://groups.ebay.com/images/emoticons/blush.gif">` gets you the blushing smiley.

Emoticon	Key Combinations	HTML
	X-(	http://groups.ebay.com/images/emoticons/angry.gif
	B-)	http://groups.ebay.com/images/emoticons/cool.gif
	]:)	http://groups.ebay.com/images/emoticons/devil.gif
	:D	http://groups.ebay.com/images/emoticons/grin.gif
	:)	http://groups.ebay.com/images/emoticons/happy.gif
	:x	http://groups.ebay.com/images/emoticons/love.gif
	:|	http://groups.ebay.com/images/emoticons/plain.gif
	:(	http://groups.ebay.com/images/emoticons/sad.gif
	:0	http://groups.ebay.com/images/emoticons/shocked.gif
	:p	http://groups.ebay.com/images/emoticons/silly.gif
	;)	http://groups.ebay.com/images/emoticons/wink.gif

Emoticon	Key Combinations	HTML
	?:|	http://groups.ebay.com/images/emoticons/confused.gif
	:8}	http://groups.ebay.com/images/emoticons/blush.gif
	:_|	http://groups.ebay.com/images/emoticons/cry.gif
	:^0	http://groups.ebay.com/images/emoticons/laugh.gif
	;\	http://groups.ebay.com/images/emoticons/mischief.gif

Giving board

eBay isn't only about making money. On the Giving board, it's also about making a difference. Members in need post their stories and requests for assistance. Other members with items to donate post offers for everything from school supplies to clothing.

If you feel like doing a good deed, conduct a member-benefit auction or donate directly to those in need. For information on how to participate, visit the eBay's GivingWorks at

        http://givingworks.ebay.com/

Sharing Knowledge in Category-Specific Boards

Want to talk about Elvis, Louis XV, Sammy Sosa, or Howard the Duck? More than 30 category-specific chat boards enable you to tell eBay members what's on your mind about merchandise and sales. You reach these boards by clicking their links on the main Community page.

Discussions mainly focus on merchandise and the nuts and bolts of transactions. Category-specific boards are great for posting questions on items that you don't know much about.

You'll get all kinds of responses from all kinds of people. Take some of the help you get with a grain of salt, because some of the folks who help you may be buyers or competitors.

These boards are also great for finding out where to go for more information and to conduct research on specific items. You can also find helpful sources for shipping information about items in that category (such as large furniture in the Antiques section or breakable items on the Glass chat board).

Don't be shy. As your second-grade teacher said, "No questions are dumb." Most eBay members love to share their knowledge.

Joining eBay Groups

If you're the friendly type and would like an instant group of new friends, I suggest you click the Groups link in the Content area. Here you can find thousands of user groups hosted on eBay but run by eBay community members. They may be groups consisting of people from the same geographic area, folks with similar hobbies, or those interested in buying or selling in particular categories.

eBay groups may be public clubs (open to all) or private clubs (invited memberships only) with their own private boards, accessible only by members of the group.

Joining a group is easy: Just click any of the links on the main Groups page, and you're presented with a dizzying array of groups to join. Your best bet is to participate in chats or discussions and find other members that you'd like to join up with.

Book II

Essential Tools

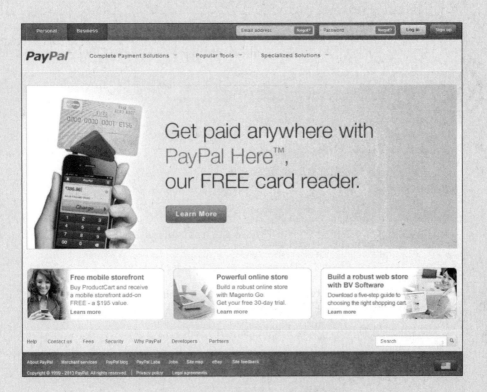

Contents at a Glance

Chapter 1: Researching on eBay

In This Chapter

✔ **Using eBay search**

✔ **Figuring out what's your "Best Match"**

✔ **Working with search results**

✔ **Finding eBay members**

✔ **Figuring out the category structure**

Think of walking into a store and seeing thousands of aisles of shelves containing millions of items. Browsing the categories of items up for sale on eBay can be just as pleasantly boggling, without the prospect of sore feet. One of the best parts about shopping on eBay is that you can find just about everything, from that esoteric lithium battery to new designer dresses (with matching shoes) to pneumatic jackhammers. New or used, it's all here — lurking in the millions of daily listings.

Start surfing around the site, and you instantly understand the size and scope of what you can find for sale. You may feel overwhelmed at first, but the folks at eBay have come up with lots of ways to help you find exactly what you're looking for. But finding the nuggets (deals) can be like searching for the proverbial needle in the haystack. The search tips in this chapter will put you ahead of your competition for finding deals, and instruct the pricing and timing of your own listings.

Looking for Items with eBay's Search Engine

Anyone can find items to purchase on eBay. Finding bargains or researching selling prices accurately, on the other hand, requires a bit more finesse. The key is to understand how to search the site for hidden treasures. Just as knowing how to browse the categories is important, knowing how to work the search engine expertly will steer you in the right direction to find your item for the lowest price.

Prior to 2012, eBay's search engine worked in a different way. The search engine was based on traditional Boolean search operators that let you refine searches in depth. Some of these operators (such as searching for two instances at once) still work (see Table 1-1 later in this chapter). But IMHO (in my humble opinion) some of the most helpful search techniques have been retired in (eBay's) hopes of providing a better user experience.

Going where the Search button takes you

The single most important button on any eBay page is the Search button. When you type some keywords in the search text box and click this button, you'll be presented with a list of items that match your keywords on eBay.

Should you want a more advanced type of search, click the Advanced link next to the Search button. You're sent to the Advanced Search: Find Items page, which will have your search options in a box on the left side of the page, as shown in Figure 1-1. Three sections of advanced searches — Items, Stores, and Members — are available; each enables you to search for information in a different way.

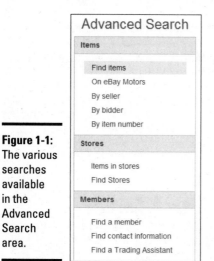

Figure 1-1:
The various searches available in the Advanced Search area.

To enhance your search, ask eBay search to check both item titles and item descriptions. Select the check box next to Search Title and Description to open up your search. You'll get more hits if you select the Search Title and Description check box, but you may also get too many items that are out of your search range.

Under the Items section, you can choose the following types of searches:

✦ **Find Items:** Search by keywords or item number. Type the keywords that describe an item (for example, *Superman lunchbox* or *antique pocket watch*) and click Search, and you can see how many matching items are available on eBay.

✦ **On eBay Motors:** Looking for something related to wheels or an engine? Click here to see the form specifically designed for eBay Motors searches.

✦ **By Seller:** Every person on eBay has a personal user ID (it's the name you use to conduct transactions). Use the Items by Seller search if you liked the merchandise from a seller's auction and want to see what else the seller has for sale. Type the seller's user ID, and you get a list of every item that person is selling.

✦ **By Bidder:** User IDs help eBay keep track of every move a user makes at eBay. If you want to see what a particular user (say, a fellow *Star Trek* fan) is bidding on, use the Items by Bidder search. Type a user ID in the By Bidder search box, and you get a list of everything the user has won.

✦ **By Item Number:** Every item that's up for auction on eBay is assigned an item number, which is displayed next to the item name on its page. To find an item by number, just type the number and click Search.

The second search section is Stores. When you click the link to search in Stores, you can search by two options:

✦ **Items in Stores:** eBay stores have an additional search engine. Listings of items in eBay stores appear on a regular search for items.

✦ **Find Stores:** If you know an eBay store name or description, you can type a store name — or portion of a store name — and find the store you're looking for.

The final search section is Members:

✦ **Find a Member:** Here you can type the user ID of any eBay member to view his or her feedback profile, About Me page, or user ID history.

✦ **Find Contact Information:** When you are in a transaction with someone, you can type the person's user ID and the number of the transaction to receive an e-mail containing the phone number of your trading partner. This works only if you have a current bid or have bought an item.

✦ **Find a Trading Assistant:** Clicking this option enables you to search for someone in your area who will sell your goods on eBay for you. Visit Book IV, Chapter 3 to see how you can become a trading assistant (because certainly this book will help you turn into a Top Rated seller).

**Book II
Chapter 1**

**Researching
on eBay**

The first nine of your favorite searches appear in a drop-down list on every page in the search-hub area.

Performing a basic search in Advanced

It's your choice — you can make your search as complex (or confusing) as you want by using the gazillions of options on the Advanced Search page. You can also choose to keep it somewhat basic. I know, it sounds a tad bizarre, but the basic Find Items search is a bit more advanced than typing a few keywords into a box. You do have more options.

On this search form, you'll see innumerable boxes. You can fill out some or all of them. The more information you type into this form, the more precise your search can be.

To illustrate this, try a basic search as you might do from the regular text Search box. It's a lot easier to find your items in that simple method. Stumped on what words to use in your search? Consider the item you're trying to find. Look at it and determine which words best describe it. Suppose that your favorite china pattern has been discontinued and you want to search eBay for some missing pieces. To find the pieces quickly, follow this process:

1. **Determine the manufacturer's name.**

   Since I'm looking for a plate, I turn over the plate I have to look on the back for the manufacturer's name — it's Dansk!

   If you don't have all the information you need, check out the manufacturer's website or a website that specializes in the item you're looking for.

2. **Determine the name for the series, collection, pattern, or design.**

   Sometimes an item has more than one name. For example, I'm searching for Bistro (the name of the collection) and Maribo (the pattern name).

3. **Narrow your search even further, if possible or necessary.**

   For example, I need to replace a salad plate.

4. **Enter the words for your search.**

   I typed *Dansk Bistro Maribo salad* into the keyword box. If someone has listed an item with all those words in the title, I'll be lucky and pull up some winners. However, it's more likely that the words in your initial search have been buried in the description.

5. After you get your search results, you can narrow your search by searching in a category.

Use the drop-down list at the top of the results to limit your search to a particular main (or *top-level*) category, for example, instead of searching all eBay categories. This might be a good idea if you know for sure where the item is listed.

I often leave the category selection alone so that my search encompasses all categories. Sometimes sellers (when listing many items at once) make mistakes and list in the wrong category. That's when you can find a real deal.

But items often cross over categories. When they do, eBay lists (on the left side of the page) the actual categories where the search items were found. From my search results (pictured in Figure 1-2), I can see that my salad plates are listed in the sub-category of Pottery & China. In this instance, I'm lucky that they're listed in only one area, so it's clear that I've found exactly what I'm searching for.

eBay displays — below the core Buy-It-Nows and Auction listings — the items that both match my search and can be found in eBay Stores.

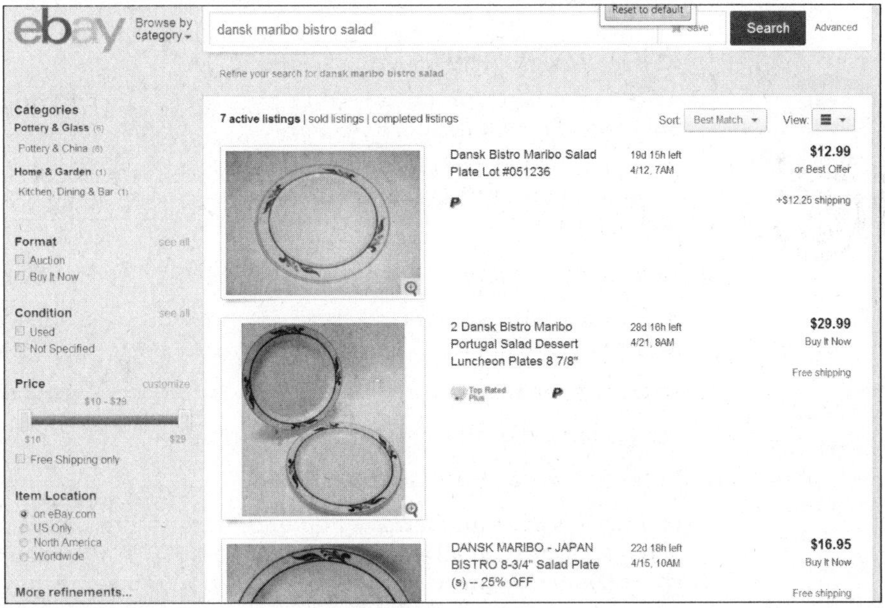

Figure 1-2:
Search
results for
my salad
plates.

6. **Tell eBay how you want the results arranged by using the Sort drop-down list shown in Figure 1-3.**

For example, if you want to check out auctions in order of how soon they're closing, choose Time: Ending Soonest. (This is my favorite option — you might miss the deal of the century while you're sifting through hundreds of listings in another order.) From the Sort drop-down list, choose one of the following options:

- *Best Match:* This is eBay's default when you search for an item. Searches are based on the eBay search engine's algorithms, and this search is (loosely) tied to item availability, seller reputation, and adherence to eBay policies. The precise definition of Best Match isn't public, but eBay described it this way:

  Along with the listing keywords and other information, one of the most important elements in this calculation is the historical buyer behavior on the site for similar searches.

  I generally prefer my searches as *Time: Ending Soonest*, but *Best Match* in my searches finds items in eBay's featured order.

  I can tell you that sellers, according to their information on the Seller Dashboard, rise and fall in search results according to buyer satisfaction and detailed seller ratings (DSRs). Also, offering *free shipping* (as long as you're in good standing as a seller) will bring your items higher up in Best Match searches.

Here's another reason, that, as a buyer, you might not want to penalize a seller just because *"I* don't *give anyone five stars."* Those Star ratings mean a whole lot to sellers; please be generous when you've had a good transaction. (Rant over.)

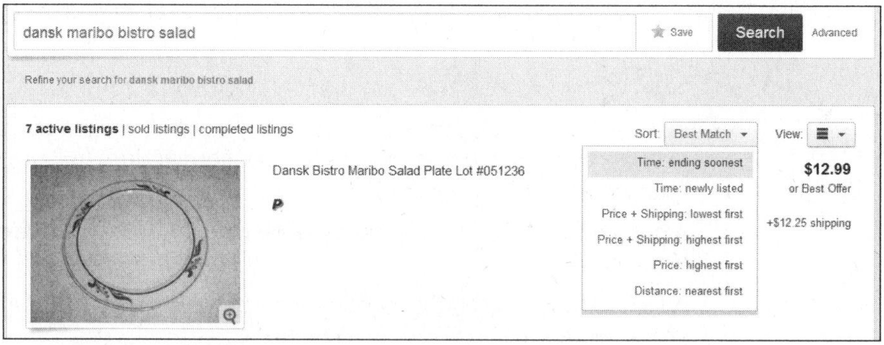

| dansk maribo bistro salad | ☆ Save | **Search** | Advanced |

Refine your search for dansk maribo bistro salad

7 active listings | sold listings | completed listings   Sort: Best Match ▾   View: ☰ ▾

Figure 1-3:
Select how
you want to
search for
your item.

Dansk Bistro Maribo Salad Plate Lot #051236

Time: ending soonest
Time: newly listed
Price + Shipping: lowest first
Price + Shipping: highest first
Price: highest first
Distance: nearest first

$12.99
or Best Offer

+$12.25 shipping

- *Time: ending soonest:* Listings closing first appear at the top of the results.

- *Time: newly listed:* The most recently posted items are listed first.

- *Price + Shipping: lowest first:* Search results are presented based on the combined cost of shipping to your ZIP code and the price of the item. They're listed in order from lowest-priced to highest-priced.

- *Price + Shipping: highest first:* This search, too, is based on the combined cost of shipping and the current cost (or high bid) on the item. Items are listed from highest- to lowest-priced.

- *Price: highest first:* This sort of ignores the shipping costs and goes right to the heart of the search; the price of the item. This is useful when you're searching for, say, a 1967 Corvette and you want to buy a car, not a Hot Wheels toy.

- *Distance: nearest first:* If you're looking for a bunny-style, wrought-iron boot scraper or something as huge as a stove, you might want to buy from a seller who is close by to save shipping costs (you may even be able to pick up the item).

Book II
Chapter 1

Researching on eBay

7. **Use the View drop-down list to select how you want to view the results.**

   You've got three choices:

   - *List View:* This is the standard eBay format of the item picture on the left and the listing information to the right.

   - *Gallery View:* This view shows you the search results in boxes. By mousing (hovering) over a box, the item will pop out so you can view it in more detail (as shown in Figure 1-4).

   - *Customize:* Choosing the Customize view option opens a small window like the one in Figure 1-5, where you can preset your preferences for future searches.

8. **Select how many items you want to see on a page.**

   eBay searches default to 50 items per page. You may want to see more or less depending on the speed of your connection. In List view, the options are 25, 50, 100, and 200.

9. **After you've filled in all your search preferences, click the Search button.**

   A list of items matching your search appears, in the order and format you selected in the Sort and View areas.

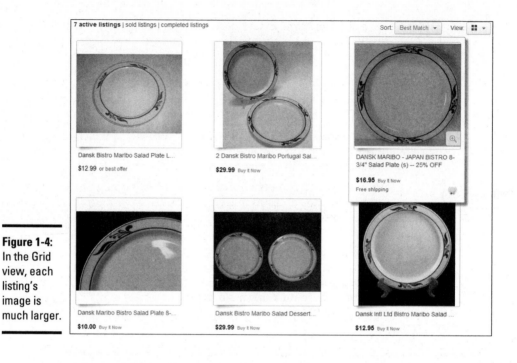

Figure 1-4: In the Grid view, each listing's image is much larger.

Figure 1-5: Customize your search preferences in this box.

If you want to search completed items to get an idea of what the salad plate has sold for before, click the Sold Listings link (next to the Active Listings link at the top of your search results). This search returns results of items that have already ended. This is my favorite search option on eBay; I use it as a strategic bidding and pricing tool. How? If you're bidding on an item and want to know whether the prices are likely to go too high for your pocketbook, you can use this search option to compare the current price of the item to the selling price of similar items from auctions that have already ended. You can see Sold Listings items that have completed within the last 90 days. (If an item hasn't sold, it will be viewable for last 30 days.)

Refining even the most basic search

You can refine an advanced search even further by using more of the options offered in the Advanced Search area. Don't be intimidated; you need to understand just a few more bells and whistles.

Here are some of the additional options you'll find in the Advanced Search: Find Items area:

✦ **Words:** You can choose to search

  • *All words, any order*

  • *Any words, any order*

  • *Exact words, exact order*

  • *Exact words, any order*

  To save yourself time, scan Table 1-1. It features shortcuts you can use in the basic Search box to get the same results as the preceding options — and more.

✦ **Exclude words from your search:** If you're looking for some silver flatware, for instance, and you want it to be solid, not plated, you could type *plated*. That search would exclude any item listings that contain the word *plated*.

✦ **Price:** Here's where you can narrow your search to a specific price range. I don't recommend using this option because you never know what you might miss.

✦ **Buying formats**: Since eBay has three main buying formats, you can search them individually:

  • *Auctions:* If you love the thrill of bidding, you can limit your search to auctions only. (But why? There may be a better deal in Buy It Now.)

  • *Buy It Now:* This option comes in handy when you simply must purchase something immediately. This would work well for the pair of tickets you've found to *The Producers* or when you're about to run out of your favorite moisturizer and don't have time to make it to the store within the next week to pick some up.

- *Classified Ads:* In some categories, such as Real Estate, sellers put up classified ads that prompt you to contact the seller to find out more or complete the transaction.

✦ **Location:** You can elect to see your results from all items on eBay or you can search by country.

- *On eBay.com:* Search eBay, no matter which country. Other options are US Only, Worldwide, or North America.

- *Available To:* Select a country from the drop-down list, and the search engine looks for items from sellers willing to ship to that country.

- *Located In:* Use the drop-down box to find items from the country you specified.

✦ **Currency:** If you have (so to speak) a yen to pay for your item with a foreign currency, you can search for sellers who accept the following:

- *Any currency*
- *U. S. dollar*
- *Australian dollar*
- *Canadian dollar*
- *Euro*
- *Indian rupee*
- *New Taiwan dollar*
- *Pounds sterling*
- *Swiss franc*

✦ **Only Show Items from Specific Sellers:** If you want to locate an item being sold by up to ten sellers, you can type their user IDs here, separating each user ID from the others by a comma or a space. If you want to find items excluding certain sellers, click the drop-down list and list the offending sellers in the text box.

Also, under Show Results, you can select options to display only particular items:

✦ **Items near you:** If you're selling or buying something big that you can't (or don't want to) ship or pick up, this option allows you to specify local pickup or select a mileage range of 10 to 2,000 miles of a ZIP code or popular city.

✦ **Items being sold for charitable organizations through eBay Giving Works:** If you're looking for items being sold only to benefit nonprofits, you may indicate that preference here.

Should you not want to go through this tedious, step-by-step check-mark thing every time you want to make a thorough search, you might want to memorize the shortcuts in Table 1-1. You can type these shortcuts in any simple search box on any eBay page to get a specialized search.

Table 1-1   Shortcut Symbols for Conducting Speedy Searches

Symbol	*Effect on Search*	*Example*
No symbol, multiple words	Returns auctions with all included words in the title.	*olympus mount* might return an item for an Olympus camera or an item from Greece. ***Remember:*** You can filter by category after you run a search.
"Term in quotes"	Searches items with the exact phrase within the quotes.	*"stuart little"* is more likely than *stuart little* to return items about the mouse because the search returns the words in the exact order you request.
Words enclosed in parentheses, separated by a comma and with no space	Finds items related to either item before or after the comma.	*(kennedy,nixon)* returns items with either of these diverse President's names in the title.
Minus sign	Excludes results with the word after the minus sign.	*signed –numbered* finds limited edition items that are signed but not numbered.
Minus symbol and parentheses	Finds items with words before the parentheses but excludes those within the parentheses.	*Packard –(hewlett,bell)* finds those rare Packard auto collectibles.
Parentheses	Searches the main word plus both versions of the word in parentheses.	*political (pin,pins)* searches for *political pin* or *political pins*. Be sure not to put a space in this search.

Searching for Items by Seller

The next search option in the Items search area helps you find items by seller. After spending time on eBay, you'll find that you have favorite sellers. You can always access a seller's other items for sale by clicking the View Seller's Other Items link on a listing page.

If you intend to follow the items for sale from certain sellers, it's a good idea to save them in your My eBay page lists. (For more on that, see Chapter 5 of this minibook.)

Here's a way to see whether one of your competing sellers has an item like yours up for sale:

1. **Click the By Seller link under Items in the Advanced Search box.**

2. **On the resulting page, type the eBay user ID of the seller you want to find.**

3. **Select options to filter the listings that the search will return:**

- *Show Completed Listings Only:* Select this check box if you want to see listings that this specific seller has completed in the past. You can choose to see all current and previous auctions, as well as auctions that have ended in the last day, last week, or past 15 days, as shown in Figure 1-6.

- *Show Close and Exact User ID Matches:* Sometimes you may not remember the exact User ID of someone. For example, I am marsha_c. You might not remember the underscore between the *a* and the *c.* When you click this option, you see all IDs that are similar to mine (although without the underscore, my ID doesn't show up at all).

Figure 1-6:
You can search for all open or completed listings by an individual seller.

Items by seller

Enter seller's user ID

marsha_c

Find items offered by a particular seller.

☑ Show completed listings only | Last 15 days ▼

Last 15 days

☐ Show close and exact user ID | Last 7 days

Last day

Sort by:

Best Match ▼

Results per page

50 ▼

[Search]

4. **Choose the order in which you want to see search results from the Sort By drop-down list.**

   If you want to see the auctions that are closing right away, choose Time Ending Soonest.

5. **Choose how many items you want to see on a page from the Results per Page drop-down list.**

6. **Click the Search button.**

**Book II
Chapter 1**

**Researching
on eBay**

Understanding the icons

When you see your search results, you may notice tiny icons next to some of the items. Here's a key to what those little pictures mean.

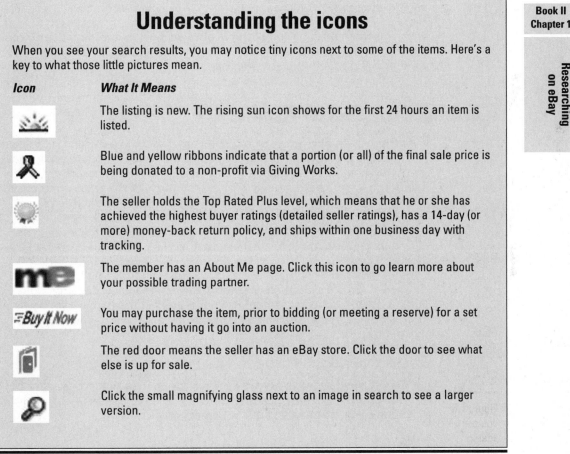

Icon	What It Means
	The listing is new. The rising sun icon shows for the first 24 hours an item is listed.
	Blue and yellow ribbons indicate that a portion (or all) of the final sale price is being donated to a non-profit via Giving Works.
	The seller holds the Top Rated Plus level, which means that he or she has achieved the highest buyer ratings (detailed seller ratings), has a 14-day (or more) money-back return policy, and ships within one business day with tracking.
me	The member has an About Me page. Click this icon to go learn more about your possible trading partner.
Buy It Now	You may purchase the item, prior to bidding (or meeting a reserve) for a set price without having it go into an auction.
	The red door means the seller has an eBay store. Click the door to see what else is up for sale.
	Click the small magnifying glass next to an image in search to see a larger version.

Searching for Items by Bidder

Also on the Advanced Search page is the Items by Bidder option. Sellers and buyers alike use it when an auction is going on to figure out their strategies. A bidder search is similar to a seller search, except you can add a few bidding filters. You can see every item the bidder has won.

You may be wondering why you'd ever want to run a bidder search. Well, when you've been outbid by the same person several times, you might not need to ask that question. If you want an item badly enough, you'll become interested in the bidding patterns of others. (See Book I, Chapter 6 for more bargain-shopping secrets.)

When researching your competition, always check out other bidders' completed auctions as well as the times they've been outbid. This will give you a good grasp of their bidding *modus operandi.*

Working with Search Results

With the growth of eBay, search results have become more and more complex. But the results page gives you lots of extra clues for narrowing your quest and homing in on exactly what you want. These clues are especially handy when you've performed your search through the text search boxes on most eBay pages, rather than initiating your search from the "official" Advanced Search page hub. Take a look at Figure 1-7 — the results of my search for *x-10 home unit* (a home automation device) — and notice that eBay came up with quite a few items that weren't even close to what I was looking for.

On the left side of search results, scroll down and look for an area called Format. From here you can narrow your results in a way that may better suit your shopping plans. You can use the Format area to sort your results in these ways:

✦ **Auctions:** Click this tab if you want to see only items up for auction.

✦ **Buy It Now:** If you've placed a search for an item that you want to buy now, this is for you. Click this tab and you'll see the items that match your query that can be bought immediately.

Figure 1-7:
Posters?
Football
jerseys?
I'll have to
refine my
search.

By clicking the See All link next to the Format selection, you see a dialog box
where you can narrow your search further. Figure 1-8 shows the filtering
options possible when you click Show Only.

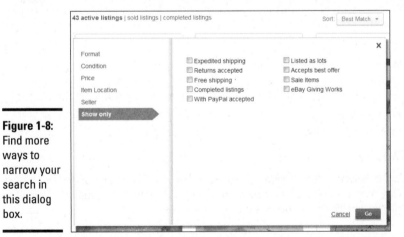

Figure 1-8:
Find more
ways to
narrow your
search in
this dialog
box.

You can also sort your results by listings ending soonest, newly listed items,
the lowest or highest price plus shipping, the nearest location, and PayPal

items first, Best Match or Category. All these options are available on the main search page, but you can sort on the results page as well.

Matching categories

On the left side of the page, the top links are matching categories, which can be very helpful. In the search in Figure 1-9, I'm still looking for my *x-10 home unit*. Reviewing all results might be time-consuming. So rather than going through pages of results, I look at the category list on the left and see a category that looks promising: Computer/Tablets and Networking.

Figure 1-9:
Select a
category
that
matches
your search
to home
in on your
item.

Refining a search with other options

On the search results page are a few more options that allow you to further refine your search. Here are some you might like to use:

✦ **Sold Listings and Completed Listings:** At the top of the results, you'll find the perfect way to refine your search when you're doing research on how an item will sell for — or how much you should expect to pay.

✦ **Free Shipping:** In the left column, you can select a box to isolate your search to only those sellers who offer free shipping.

✦ **Price:** Narrow your search to a specific price range.

✦ **Item Location:** When you're signed in, your ZIP code is filled in by default, but you can type in any ZIP code. You also select the mileage from a drop-down list.

In the quest for even more minutiae, a link at the bottom of this box allows you to customize the search queries even further. You can definitely take a good thing too far, and this is getting pretty close.

Finding eBay Members

With millions of eBay users on the loose, you may think it's hard to track folks down. Nope. eBay's powerful Advanced Search page kicks into high gear to help you find other eBay members in seconds.

In the Advanced Search, Members area, you can

✦ **Find a member:** If you know a friend's e-mail address, you can input it on this page to find out whether he or she is registered on eBay (after you type in a supplied verification code).

✦ **Find contact information:** If you're involved in a transaction with someone, you can click this link to have the person's phone number e-mailed to you. Because this information is confidential, you must be involved in a transaction with the person. You'll be asked to type the other member's user ID and the transaction number you're dealing with before this information is sent out.

To protect privacy and prevent possible harassment, you'll have to be in a transaction with your friend before you get any information.

Book II
Chapter 1

Researching on eBay

Understanding eBay's Category Hierarchy

Understanding eBay's categories was a lot easier when there were just a few. I remember thinking that the quantity of categories was daunting when the site boosted the number up to the unthinkable 4,000.

Now that the total number of categories is around 20,000 — including child (or sub-) categories — the time has come to either abandon all hope of understanding them or to take things in hand and appreciate the elegance and organization of a system that's just beyond the realm of comprehension. You may never totally understand the category structure, but that's okay — what's important is knowing which categories the sellers use most frequently.

eBay is constantly revisiting the way people search for items on the site. Understanding the tips in this chapter will give you a distinct advantage when you're shopping.

How the structure works

Go ahead, ask me what I'm interested in. Let's see; I like art, golf, photography, fashion — I won't bore you with the rest, but it sounds like a fairly benign list, doesn't it? I'm sure your list of interests is straightforward too. Right?

Well, not quite. Say you like golf as much as I do. You might just click Sporting Goods then find Golf and click.

Surprise! The Sporting Goods category is made up of hundreds of child categories of everything from golf balls to Pittsburgh Penguins jerseys. eBay's Golf landing page goes a long way to help you find what you're looking for.

This hasn't been done to confuse you, but as of this moment, there are 558,377 active listings in Golf. eBay's refinements allow you to visit areas where your sports interest might take you. To accommodate the countless items for sale that sports aficionados, collectors, and participants list, eBay had to create a lot of small areas.

Drilling down to your item

Depending on what you're looking for, things can get downright confusing. For example, suppose I want to find items relating to my dog, a somewhat obscure breed called Schipperke. You might think I have it made. I mean, how could a category for such an esoteric breed of dog be anything but very simple? A search for Schipperke will net me over 3,000 listings!

Schipperkes have their own category in the main category of Collectibles➪ Animals➪Dogs on eBay (not real dogs, just the collectible type). eBay has categories in Collectibles for almost every breed of dogs. Know anybody who collects dog-related items? See what I mean about mystifying? Currently, 450 Schipperke items are listed in the category.

But there are more auctions. When I ran a top of page text search on *Schipperke,* I came up with 3,162 active listings, as shown in Figure 1-10.

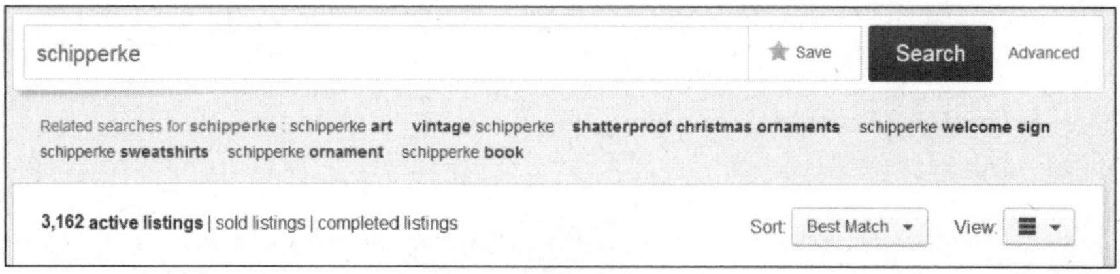

Figure 1-10: Looking for *Schipperke* in any category.

Items for *Schipperke* (and its misspellings) were listed in these second-level categories (each of which branch into many more):

   Clothing, Shoes & Accessories: In 6 child categories

   Collectibles: In 11 categories

Jewelry & Watches: In 5 child categories

Home & Garden: In 8 child categories

Pet Supplies

eBay Motors

Crafts: In six 6 categories

Art: In 2 child categories

Stamps

Books: In 5 child categories

Cameras & Photo

Toys & Hobbies

Business & Industrial

Pottery & Glass

Coins & Paper Money

I hope you realize where I'm going with all this. Even though I chose an arcane item, searching only through the specific category designated for it would have affected my search significantly. I would have missed some of the more interesting items.

Chapter 2: Researching Collectible Prices

In This Chapter

✔ Pricing new products via mobile

✔ Researching collectible items and values

✔ Common-sense buying guidelines

✔ Using online information in your research

A s one who wants to sell products, you need to know how to price what you're selling. If you don't know what your item is worth, then your sale might not net the highest profit. If you don't know the facts or what to say, your well-written title and detailed description (combined with a fabulous picture) may still not be enough to get the highest price for your item. If you don't know how to make your item easy to find, it may not be noticed by even the hardiest of collectors.

Knowing your item is a crucial part of successful selling on eBay. New item pricing can be all over the board, and knowing how much an item will sell for — before you purchase it — will help you make educated stocking decisions. Collectible items may be appraised or listed in a book for a high value, but what you care about is the price at which the item will actually sell. Imagine someone uncovering a hoard of the same type of item you're selling and, not knowing the value of it, dumping it on eBay with low Buy It Now prices. This scenario would drive down the value of the item within a couple of weeks. Great for buyers — but not so great for sellers.

The best advice you can follow as you explore any free-market system is *caveat emptor* — let the buyer beware. Although you can't guarantee that every one of your transactions will be perfect, if you research items thoroughly before you bid, you won't lose too much of your hard-earned money — or too much sleep.

Pricing New Products for eBay via Mobile

So let's say you're out at a store that's slashing prices to liquidate stock. Lots of merchandise seems very resellable to you, but which will net the most profit?

My personal arsenal of tools for determining the sales potential of merchandise lies in my smartphone. All products have a scannable, numeric-based, Universal Product Code (UPC or barcode). Every product has a unique barcode, all of which follow an identical format (as shown in Figure 2-1).

Figure 2-1:
A sample layout for the UPC found on all products for sale.

This barcode carries information about a product and pricing for retailers and is scanned when you purchase a product. The barcode covers two steps in managing a retail business: monitoring the purchase and tracking inventory.

That all said, scanning a product prior to buying it and putting it up for sale will help you make smarter business decisions. Of course, your go-to app would be the eBay app, which at printing time is available for iPhone, iPad, Android, Blackberry, and Windows devices. You can use mobile apps on your smartphone, tablet, or *phablet* (a popular term for larger smartphones that double as small tablets). Figure 2-2 shows the eBay app on my Android tablet.

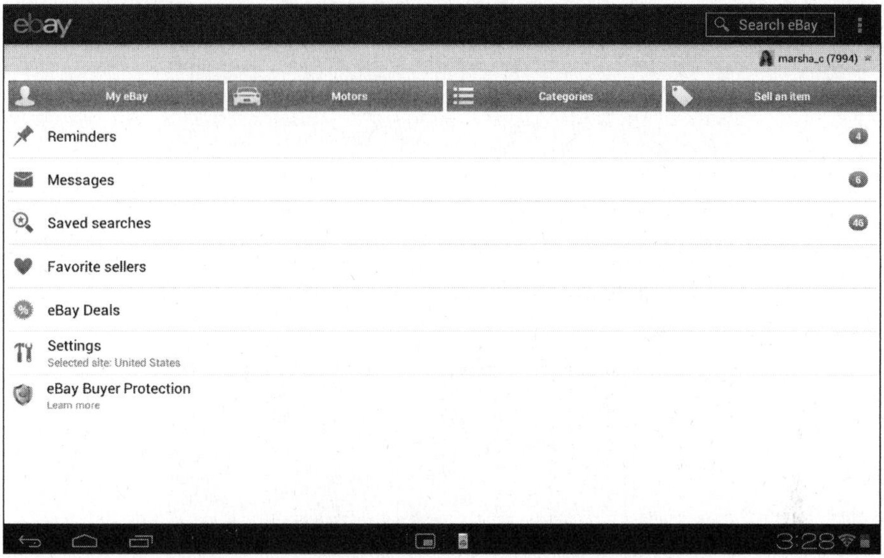

Figure 2-2:
The app appears the same on most tablets and smart-phones.

Book II Chapter 2

Researching Collectible Prices

When you click the Search icon in the upper-right corner, a drop-down menu appears, prompting you to type in your search query or to scan a barcode, as shown in Figure 2-3.

To scan a barcode, the app will fire up the scanning module. Scanning uses your camera to catch the barcode, so line up your camera and center the barcode within the scanning boundaries shown in Figure 2-4.

Android phones also give you the option to tap the microphone icon on the app and "say" the product name. Miraculously, the name will appear in the search box and give you results for your search, as in Figure 2-5.

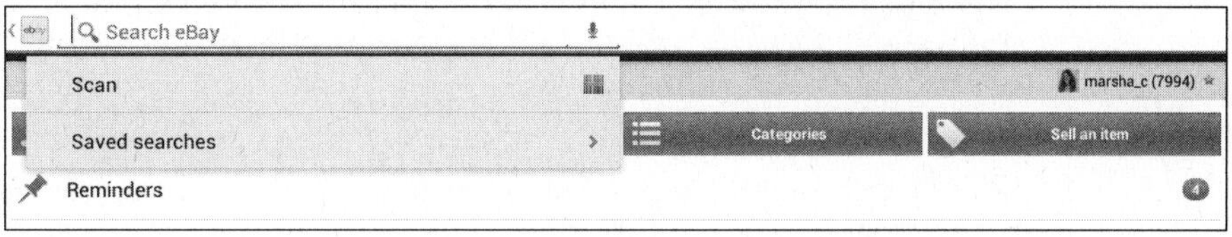

Figure 2-3:
Click here to activate the barcode scanner.

Figure 2-4:
Scanning
a barcode
with the Red
Laser app.

The results of your search will show items matching your search that are
currently being sold on eBay. By clicking the Refine button, you can narrow
your search to Sold items and get an idea of whether the item is actually selling on eBay — and for how much.

Figure 2-5:
An eBay
app search
using Voice
command.

On the off chance that the item is not being sold on eBay, you can use some super shopping apps to compare prices for your item, whether on the web or close to your home. Here are a few I really like:

✦ **RedLaser:** This app (owned by eBay) is a useful shopping scanner and it also stores loyalty cards and clip coupons. When you're looking for bargains, you can use RedLaser to check out library books and even to flag allergens in foods.

✦ **Prime shopping and Price Check:** The Amazon shopping app has a scanner built in (or you can type or speak a search) to find the price of an item if it is selling on Amazon. Amazon Price Check finds the item on Amazon, as well as items for sale from other vendors online. Figure 2-6 shows screens from both apps.

✦ **ShopSavvy:** Shown in Figure 2-7, this is a popular app for both Android and iOS. Scan the barcode or type in the name of an item. If an item is available locally, the app can display its location on a map with a blue dot next to it (if it's in stock). And you get online prices (also shown in Figure 2-7) as well.

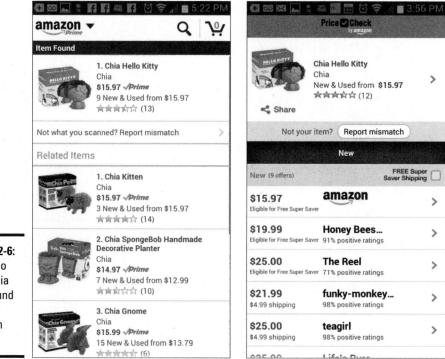

Figure 2-6: My Hello Kitty Chia was found on both Amazon apps.

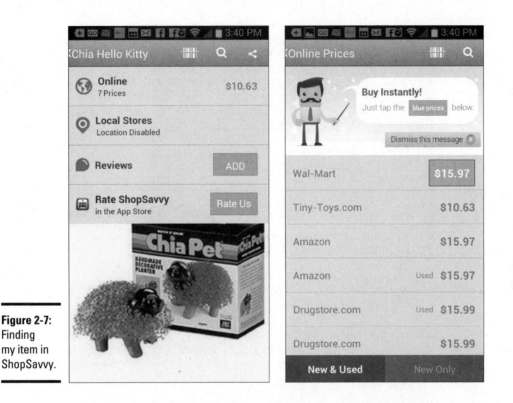

Book II
Chapter 2

Researching
Collectible Prices

Figure 2-7:
Finding
my item in
ShopSavvy.

✦ **Milo:** This app (also owned by eBay and shown in Figure 2-8), is a local shopping app. Scan in the barcode, enter your ZIP code, and Milo will find which stores near you carry the item, and at what price.

Figure 2-8:
Milo
handles
local
search from
barcode
scanning.

Finding Pricing Trends on eBay

If you're just starting out on eBay, chances are you like to shop and you also collect items that interest you. You'll find out early in your eBay adventures that a lot of people online know as much about collecting as they do about bidding — and some are serious contenders.

Understanding grading terms

One of the keys to establishing value is knowing an item's condition, typically referred to as an item's *grade*. The following table lists the most common grading categories that collectors use. The information in this table is used with permission from (and appreciation to) Lee Bernstein.

Category (Also Known As)	What It Means	Example
Mint (M, Fine, Mint-In-Box [MIB], 10)	A never-used collectible in perfect condition with complete packaging (including instructions, original attachments, tags, and so on) identical to how it appeared on the shelf in the original box.	Grandma got a soup tureen as a wedding present, never opened it, and stuck it in her closet for the next 50 years.
Near Mint (NM, Near Fine, Like-New, 9)	The collectible is perfect but no longer has the original packaging or the original packaging is less than perfect. Possibly used but must appear to be new.	Grandma used the soup tureen on her 25th anniversary, washed it gently, and then put it back in the closet.
Excellent (EX, 8)	Used, but barely. Excellent is just a small step under Near Mint, and many sellers mistakenly interchange the two, but Excellent can have very minor signs of wear. The wear must be a normal, desirable part of aging or so minor that it's barely noticeable and visible only upon close inspection. Damage of any sort is not "very minor." Wear or minor, normal factory flaws should be noted. (Factory flaws are small blemishes common at the time of manufacture — a tiny air bubble under paint, for example.)	Grandma liked to ring in the New Year with a cup of soup for everyone.
Very Good (VG, 7)	Looks very good but has defects, such as a minor chip or light color fading.	If you weren't looking for it, you might miss that Grandma's tureen survived the '64 earthquake, as well as Uncle Bob's infamous ladle episode.
Good (G, 6)	Used with defects. More than a small amount of color loss, chips, cracks, tears, dents, abrasions, missing parts, and so on.	Grandma had the ladies in the neighborhood over for soup and bingo every month.
Poor (P or G-, 5)	Barely collectible, if at all. Severe damage or heavy use. Beyond repair.	Grandma ran a soup kitchen.

Grading is subjective. Mint to one person may be Very Good to another. Always ask a seller to define the meaning of the terms used. Also, be aware that many amateur sellers may not really know the different definitions of grading and may arbitrarily add Mint or Excellent to their item descriptions.

**Book II
Chapter 2**

**Researching
Collectible Prices**

How can you compete? Well, in addition to having a well-planned bidding strategy (covered in Book I, Chapter 6), knowing your stuff gives you a winning edge. I've gathered the opinions of two collecting experts to get the info you need about online collecting basics. I also show you how one of those experts puts the information into practice, and I give you a crash course on how items for sale are (or should be) graded.

The values of collectibles go up and down. *Star Wars* items are a perfect example. Values skyrocket during the release of the latest movie, but then settle to a considerably lower level. Any published book of value listings is valid only for the *moment* the book is written. If you stay on top of your market in a few specialties, you'll be aware of these market fluctuations. If you're looking for the highest price for *Star Wars* items, for example, instead of looking to liquidate excess inventory, I'd hold those items until they hit the pop culture charts again.

Determining the "going price" of a particular item on eBay is as simple as performing a Completed Items search. I acquired a few vintage (mint) ashtrays from the iconic Playboy Club, so join me as I check out the value.

1. **Type in the keywords in the search text box at the top of every page and click the Search button.**

   The resulting page shows you how many items that match your keywords are being sold on eBay at that moment. If you get too many results, add an extra keyword that better describes your item and repeat the search. I found 51 active listings (as shown in Figure 2-9).

2. **Scroll down the page and look at the images of items for sale, making note of which ones actually match your item.**

   From here, you get an idea of the prices that sellers are asking.

3. **Choose an option from the top of the search results. They are**

   - *Active listings:* Shows the exact number of items currently up for sale on eBay that match your selected keywords.

   - *Sold Listings:* Shows you only the items that actually sold. In my search, 135 items had sold. To get an idea of the highest price I can get for the item, I used the sort option, shown in Figure 2-10, by selecting Price: Highest First from the Sort drop-down menu. What an eye-opener! These results showed me exactly which variations of my item were the most valuable — and which keywords work the best to attract customer's eyes.

**Book II
Chapter 2**

**Researching
Collectible Prices**

Figure 2-9:
Fifty-one
listings
matching
"Playboy
Club
Ashtray"
are up for
sale right
now.

- *Completed Listings:* Clicking this option shows you how many listings have run their course and are over. If the item sold, the final price is indicated in green text. If the item hasn't sold, you see the final price in red. In my search, I found 191 completed listings. By studying this data, you can get an idea of a good starting price to set for your item to encourage sales and higher bids.

4. **For the deepest research, click the individual items that garnered the highest prices and see how the seller described the item.**

   Smart sellers tell the stories behind collectibles and add appropriate keywords to their titles!

In my search, I see listings for the same item that sold from $5.99 up to $22! Why? From just the data shown here, the sellers who received the lowest final sale prices put their items up for sale when several others were selling the same item. eBay is a supply-and-demand venue. Even if an item is rare, the final sale price will go down if there are too many up for sale.

Figure 2-10: Sort search results for Sold listings with highest prices first.

Following Collectible-Buying Guidelines

Buying collectibles on eBay can be a unique market unto itself. But certain rules still apply. Here are a few things to keep in mind when buying collectibles on eBay:

+ **Get all the facts before placing a bid or clicking Buy.** Study the description carefully and make your decisions accordingly. Find out whether all original parts are included and whether the item has any flaws. If the description says that the Fred Flintstone figurine has a cracked back, e-mail the seller for more information.

+ **Don't get caught up in the emotional thrill of bidding.** First-time buyers (known as *Under-10s* or newbies because they have fewer than ten transactions under their belts) tend to bid wildly, driven by emotions. If you're new to eBay, you can get burned if you just bid for the thrill of victory without first thinking about what you're doing.

I can't stress how important it is to determine an item's value *before* you bid. But because value is such a flighty thing (depending on supply and demand, market trends, and all sorts of other cool stuff), I recommend that you get a general idea of the item's current value and use this ballpark figure to set a maximum amount of money you're willing to bid for that item. Then *stick* to your maximum and don't even think about bidding past it. If the bidding gets too hot, there's always another auction.

To find out more about bidding strategies, Book I, Chapter 6 is just the ticket.

✦ **Know what the item should cost.** Buyers used to depend on *price guides* — books on collectibles and their values — to help them bid. But price guides are becoming a thing of the past. Sure, you can find a guide that says a *Lion King* Broadway poster in excellent condition has a book price of $75, but if you do a search on eBay, you'll see that they're actually selling for under $20. (Hint: When *was* that guide published, anyway?)

When your search on eBay turns up what you're looking for, average the completed prices that you find. Doing so gives you a much better idea of what you need to spend than any price guide can.

Book II
Chapter 2

Researching
Collectible Prices

✦ **Timing is everything, and being first costs.** In the movie-poster business, if you can wait three to six months after a movie is released, you get the poster for 40 to 50 percent less. The same goes for many new releases of collectibles. Sometimes you're wiser to wait and save money.

✦ **Be careful of presale items.** You may run across vendors selling items that they don't have in stock at the moment but that they'll ship to you later. For example, before the second *Harry Potter* film came out, some vendors ran auctions on movie posters they didn't have yet. If you had bid and won, and for some reason the vendor had a problem getting the poster, you'd have been out of luck. Don't bid on anything that can't be delivered as soon as your payment clears.

✦ **Being too late can also cost.** Many collectibles become more difficult to find as time goes by. Generally, as scarcity increases, so does desirability and value. Common sense tells you that if two original and identical collectibles are offered side by side, with one in like-new condition and the other in used condition, the like-new item will have the higher value.

✦ **Check out the seller.** Check the seller's feedback rating (the number in parentheses next to the person's user ID) before you buy. If the seller has many comments with very few negative ones, chances are good that this is a reputable seller. Better yet? If you find a Top Rated Seller badge next to the seller's name, you can pretty much count on a positive experience.

If you miss winning an auction and are offered a side deal, beware! Side deals off the eBay site are strictly prohibited. If you conduct a side deal and are reported to eBay, you can be suspended. Not only that, but buyers who are ripped off by sellers in away-from-eBay transactions shouldn't look to eBay to bail them out. They're on their own. Second-chance offers, on the other hand, are eBay-legal — and safer.

Quizzing the seller

You should ask the seller certain questions when making a collectible purchase. Assume that the object of your desire is a collectible GI Joe action figure from 1964 to 1969 (by the way, these items are selling for top dollar as I write this book!). In this section, I list some questions you should ask. The information here can give you an idea of what to ask when determining your maximum bid on other collectibles as well (or whether an item is even *worth* bidding on). As you imagine, the more you know before you place a bid, the happier you're likely to be when you win.

This checklist can save you considerable hassle:

+ **Find out the item's overall condition.** For GI Joe, look at the painted hair and eyebrows. Expect some wear, but overall, a collectible worth bidding on should look good.

+ **Be sure the item's working parts are indeed working.** Most GI Joe action figures from this period have cracks on the legs and arms, but the joints should move and any cracks should not be so deep that the legs and arms fall apart easily.

+ **Ask whether the item has its original parts.** Because you can't really examine actual items in detail before buying, e-mail the seller with specific questions relating to original or replacement parts. Many GI Joe action figures are rebuilt from parts that are not from 1964 to 1969. Sometimes the figures even have two left or right hands or feet! If you make it clear to the seller before you buy that you want a toy with only original parts, you'll be able to make a good case for a refund if the item arrives as rebuilt as the Six Million Dollar Man.

+ **Ask whether the item has original accessories.** A GI Joe from 1964 to 1969 should have his original dog tags, boots, and uniform. If any of these items are missing, you will have to pay around $25 to replace each missing item. If you're looking to bid on any other collectible, know what accessories came as standard equipment with the item.

+ **Know an item's value before you bid.** A 1964 to 1969 vintage GI Joe in decent shape, with all its parts, sells for around $500 without its original box. In a recent auction, a "Vintage 1967 GI Joe Green Airborne MP Set RARE Excellent" — without box — sold for $895. If you are bidding on a GI Joe action figure and are in this price range, you're okay. If you get the item for less than $400, congratulations — you've nabbed a bargain.

+ **If you have any questions, ask them *before* you bid.** Check collectors' guides, research similar auctions on eBay, and Google the web for unbiased third-party advice.

Hey, experts have been buying, selling, and trading collectible items for years. But just because you're new to eBay doesn't mean you have to be a newbie for decades before you can start bartering with the collecting gods. I wouldn't leave you in the cold like that — and neither would eBay. You can get information on items you're interested in, as well as good collecting tips, right on the eBay website. Visit the category-specific discussion boards in the Community area. You can also search the rest of the web or go the old-fashioned route and check the library.

Keep in mind that there truly are several prices for an item. The retail (or manufacturer's suggested retail price — MSRP) price, the book value, the secondary market price (the price charged by resellers when an item is unavailable on the primary retail market), and the eBay selling price. The only way to ascertain the price an item will go for on eBay is to research completed auctions.

Useful publications

I used to recommend that buyers and sellers research items by going out to the local newsstand and buying a special-interest magazine based on the type of merchandise they sell. With the advent of digital publishing, finding current printed magazines is like hunting up a tool from the past. On the other hand, you may be able to find vintage copies of magazines for sale on the web, eBay, or Amazon. These magazines contain a wealth of knowledge — but remember that those articles were written at an earlier stage of the items' rarity and salability; be sure to check current market conditions. You can also find websites that specialize in selling back issues of magazines. Figure 2-11 shows a search of www.biblio.com for *Barbie Bazaar* magazine, netting seven back issues for sale.

Following are a few publications (some have current websites) that can offer strategic information on collectibles:

✦ *Action Figure Digest*: Find out who's hot in the action-figure biz in this monthly magazine that ceased publication around 2007.

✦ *Antique Trader*: This magazine has been the bible of the antiques collecting industry for more than 40 years. Visit its online home at www.antiquetrader.com for more articles and subscription information.

✦ *Autograph Magazine*: This online magazine gives the lowdown on the autograph business, as well as samples of many autographs for identification. Its site, www.autographmagazine.com, features many current articles.

Figure 2-11:
Searching
biblio.com
for vintage
collectible
magazines.

+ ***Barbie Bazaar:*** Once this was the official Mattel magazine, packed with everything Barbie! You'll not find a website, but back issues of these magazines have valuable information on Barbie collecting.

+ ***Dolls Magazine:*** Still alive and with an active website, *Dolls Magazine* is filled with good info. Check the site at www.dollsmagazine.com.

+ ***Coin World:*** This respected magazine has many online services available for a free registration on their website, at www.coinworld.com (featured in Figure 2-12).

+ ***Goldmine:*** At www.goldminemag.com, this place is the hub for CD and vinyl collectors. The website has many current articles and information on rare issues.

Book II
Chapter 2

Researching
Collectible Prices

Figure 2-12:
The Coin
World
website.

+ **Numismatic News:** Another standard, *Numismatic News* is still publishing a print edition after more than 50 years. The website at `www.numismaticnews.net` has valuable current information for coin collectors and offers downloads with current coin values and identification information.

+ **Sports Collectors Digest:** Takes sports collectibles to the highest level. Visit the website at `www.sportscollectorsdigest.com`, read the stories, and sign up for a free e-mail newsletter.

+ **Linn's Stamp News:** Still alive and kicking on the web at `www.linns.com` is the venerable *Linn's Stamp News*. First published in 1931, the magazine carries on a tradition for stamp collectors on its website.

+ **Teddy Bear & Friends:** If you're looking for information on collecting teddy bears, `www.teddybearandfriends.com` is the place.

It seems that every leading magazine has its own website. In the next section, I mention some useful sites for pricing references.

Online Sources of Information

Because you're all so Internet-savvy (what's better than getting the information you want at a millisecond's notice?), I assume you plan to visit the magazine websites that I mention in the preceding section. In this section, I give you a few more fun online sources where you can pick up some more insight about your items.

Other websites

Many websites devoted to different collectible areas list prices at recently completed auctions. These auctions are the best evaluation of an item's value because they're usually directed toward specialists in the collectible category. Most of the participants in these auctions *really* know their stuff.

You may have to poke around the following websites to find the prices realized at auction, but once you do, you'll have the Holy Grail of estimated values. Look for links that point to auction archives. Many of these sites will consign an item from you as well, and sell it to their audiences:

✦ **Artprice:** This art auction site, at www.artprice.com, charges for its searches by artist but has an immense database.

✦ **Autographs and More — now part of Heritage Auctions:** According to the site, Heritage Autographs Library has the greatest free collection of authentic autographs on the planet at www.autographs.com.

✦ **Collectors Universe:** This is a major destination for coins, cards, stamps, and more at www.collectors.com.

✦ **Promotional Glass Collector's Association:** For collectible advertising glasses, check out this at www.pgcaglassclub.com (you've got to see this stuff!). And there's an online database of items at www.glass411.info.

✦ **Professional Coin Grading Service:** Find a U.S. coin-collecting price guide at www.pcgs.com/prices.

✦ **Lyn Knight Auctions:** Find currency auctions at www.lynknight.com.

If you're researching prices to buy a car on eBay, look in your local newspaper to get a good idea of prices in your community. You should also check out sites on the Internet. I've had many of my friends (and editors) visit the various sites, and we've settled on www.nadaguides.com because it seems to give the most accurate and unbiased information.

Online search engines

If you don't find the information you need on eBay, don't go ballistic — just go elsewhere. Even a site as vast as eBay doesn't have a monopoly on information. The Internet is filled with websites and Internet auction sites that can give you price comparisons.

Your tablet, phone, or computer can connect to powerful outside servers (really big computers on the Internet) that have their own fast-searching systems called *search engines.* Remember, if something is out there and you need it, you can find it in just a matter of seconds. Here are the addresses of some of the web's most highly regarded search engines or multi-search-engine sites:

✦ **Google** (www.google.com)

✦ **Bing** (www.bing.com)

✦ **Yahoo!** (www.yahoo.com)

The basic process of getting information from an Internet search engine is pretty simple:

1. **Type the address of the search-engine site in the Address box of your web browser.**

   You're taken to the website's home page.

2. **Find the text box next to the button labeled Search or something similar.**

3. **In the text box, type a few words indicating what interests you.**

   Be specific when typing search text. The more precise your entry, the better your chances of finding what you want. Look for tips, an advanced search option, or help pages on your search engine of choice for more information about how to narrow your search.

4. **Click the Search (or similar) button or press Enter on your keyboard.**

   The search engine presents you with a list Internet pages that have the requested information. The list includes brief descriptions and links to the first group of pages. You'll find links to additional listings at the bottom if your search finds more listings than can fit on one page (and if you ask for something popular, like *Twilight,* don't be surprised if you get millions of hits).

There will also be a link to click that will show you images that match your search — if you're not quite sure in identifying your item. Find the picture that matches the item to find out more.

Always approach information on the web with caution. Not everyone is the expert he or she would like to be. Your best bet is to get lots of different opinions and then boil 'em down to what makes sense to you. And remember — *caveat emptor*. (Is there an echo in here?)

Authentication services

Some companies provide the service of *authenticating* (verifying that it's the real deal) or authenticating and *grading* (determining a value based on the item's condition and legitimacy). To have these services performed on your items, you'll have to send them to the service and pay a fee.

Following are a few excellent sites for grading coins:

✦ **Professional Coin Grading Service (PCGS):** This service, at `www.pcgs.com`, is considered to be the top of the line in coin grading. This company's standards are strict, but coins graded by PCGS usually sell for higher prices.

To catch up on the latest pricing on American coins, go to PCGS (see Figure 2-13). This site has an elaborate online price guide for all coin grades.

✦ **American Numismatic Association Certification Service (AMNACS):** This service was sold to Amos Press in 1990, and you can find out more at `www.anacs.com`.

✦ **Numismatic Guaranty Corporation of America (NGCA):** The site, `www.ngccoin.com`, offers information as well as a mail-in grading and certification service for your coins.

✦ **PCI Coin Grading Service (PCI):** PCI, the longstanding coin-grading service at `http://pcicoins.com`, is under new management.

Stamp collectors (or those who have just inherited a collection from Uncle Steve) can get their stamps authenticated by the American Philatelic Society. Visit this site for more information: `http://stamps.org/Stamp-Authentication`.

For comic books, Comics Guaranty, LLC (CGC) at `www.cgccomics.com/grading` will seal (enclose in plastic to preserve the quality) and grade at a discount for eBay users.

Figure 2-13:
The PCGS
website
has many
links and
an up-to-
date price
guide at no
charge.

Sports cards and sports memorabilia have a bunch of authentication services. If you acquired your autograph or item of memorabilia directly from the player or team, you can ensure its authenticity. Having the item authenticated may or may not get you a higher price at eBay. Try these sites:

✦ **Professional Sports Authenticator (PSA):** Go to www.psacard.com for more info.

✦ **Online Authentics:** This service, at www.onlineauthentics.com, reviews autographs by scans online or by physical review.

The best way to find a good authenticator in your field is to search the items on eBay and see who is the most prominent authenticator listed in the descriptions. For example, in the coins area, coins from certain grading services get higher bids than those from other services. You can also go to an Internet search engine (such as Google or Yahoo!) and type the keywords *coin grading* (for coins). You'll come up with a host of choices; use your good sense to see which one suits your needs.

Not all items need to be officially authenticated. Official authentication does add value to the item, but if you're an expert, you can comfortably rate an item on your own in your auctions. People will know from your description whether you're a specialist. Your feedback will also work for you by letting the prospective bidder or buyer know that your merchandise from past sales has been top-drawer.

Chapter 3: Five-Star Customer Service via Eloquent Communications

In This Chapter

✔ **Brushing up on your writing skills**

✔ **Creating Auto Answers**

✔ **Customizing eBay's transaction messages**

*B*usiness is business and, if you're in business, you must remember that your customers are number one, and they deserve your very best "five-star service." Businesses become successful by inspiring a "wow" when it comes to servicing customers and selling quality merchandise. The image that you project through your e-mails and listings identifies you to prospective shoppers as a professional — or not. Your e-mails should be polite and professional. Your listings shouldn't make prospective buyers feel like you're hustling them, sneaking in hidden fees, or being pushy with severe rules when they're trying to make a purchase.

You don't have to have the most beautiful listings on eBay to succeed. Instead, you need products that sell — and willingness to take the time to build good customer relations! This is what gives the small-time entrepreneur a distinct advantage over the mega-company that branches its sales onto eBay. In this chapter, I cover some ways — from writing effective descriptions to sending cordial communications — to let your customers know that they're number one in your book.

Communicating in Writing Takes a Little Effort

Perhaps English class wasn't your favorite, but good grammar and proper spelling and punctuation in your communications portray you as a pro. As a writer, I constantly troll the grammar and punctuation websites to brush up on my writing skills. (Okay, I also have brilliant editors covering up my transgressions. . . .)

Throughout the rest of this section, I provide some examples of effective e-mail messages. Study these and also check out a few online business letter examples. And don't forget good manners. You don't want to be too formal, but you do want to be personable and polite.

At least 20 percent of the time that I send an inquiry to a seller, I don't get a response — guaranteeing that I won't be buying that product from that source. I refuse to buy from someone who doesn't care enough to respond to a question. When I do get responses, many are terse, brusquely written notes. Sellers who take the time to write a short, considerate reply that includes a greeting and a thank-you get my business.

Always respond to messages sent through eBay Messages quickly, clearly, and politely — and with a teeny sales pitch when possible. And by all means, use this opportunity to point out other listings you have that may also interest the writer. (Now *that's* customer service.)

Anticipating Initial Buyer Inquiries

A relevant item description is the key to initial customer satisfaction. If you answer all possible questions within a well-written description, there will be less need for the customer to wonder about your item. (In Book III, Chapter 3, you find a full breakout of the information that your item description should include.)

Why would you want to make your item description try to pre-answer initial inquiries from buyers? Here are a couple of reasons:

✦ **You may lose a sale if you don't.** Other sellers may have the same item with a more complete description, and it's just as easy for customers to buy from a seller they know is selling just what they want.

✦ **Your Detailed Seller Ratings may be affected if the description is missing.** eBay feels that most transactions need not include communication past the buyer reading your description. For that reason, your feedback will receive an automatic five-star rating if you satisfy these three criteria:

  • *You specify one-day handling time and upload tracking information within one business day.*

  • *There are no buyer- or seller-initiated communications in eBay Messages.*

  • *There are no requests for contact information between you and the buyer.*

This is not to say that cordial communication with a prospective buyer is undesirable. The opposite is true. If you do get an inquiry, be sure to answer as quickly as humanly possible, and give the customers all the information they need.

Use eBay's options to manage Questions & Answers for your buyers. This way, if your customers scroll to the bottom of your description and click *Ask a Question*, they're taken to your Auto Answers.

Follow these steps to set up your Auto Answers:

1. **Go to your My eBay page by clicking the link in the upper-right of most eBay pages.**

2. **Mouse over the Account tab, and click the Manage Communications with Buyers option, as shown in Figure 3-1.**

   You arrive at an area where you can customize your questions and e-mail messages. (I discuss e-mail best practices in the later sections of this chapter.)

Figure 3-1:
Accessing your buyer communications options.

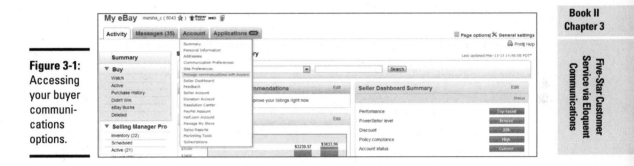

3. **Scroll down the page to the Manage questions and answers section and click Edit.**

4. **On the resulting page, select the check boxes to indicate which communications you want to provide for your buyers.**

   As shown in Figure 3-2, your options are

   • *Allow buyers to provide special instructions on their order during check-out.* This option is most important because buyers may have special instructions for delivery or may just want to reach out and say Hi. (Both are part of making your customer happy.)

   • *Allow buyers to contact you from your active listings.* If you don't indicate (in the Show Q&A box shown here) that you want to have Auto Answers for your listing, you must select the check box here. But I highly recommend using eBay's Auto Answers system.

   • *Show Q&A.* When a buyer clicks Ask a Question, your Auto Answers will appear on the listing page.

5. **Scroll down the page and click a topic shown to see what eBay supplies as an Auto Answer.**

   These Auto Answers are automatically generated from the details you input (or have on file with eBay) when you list your item.

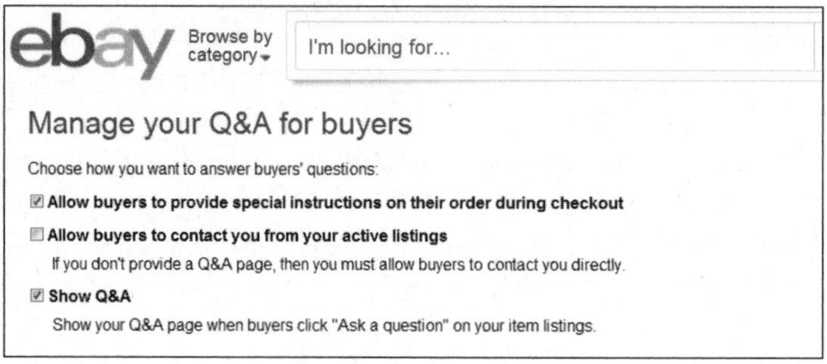

Figure 3-2:
Click the
check box
to indicate
your
preferences
for
communi-
cation.

ebay   Browse by category ▾   I'm looking for...

Manage your Q&A for buyers

Choose how you want to answer buyers' questions:

☑ **Allow buyers to provide special instructions on their order during checkout**

☐ **Allow buyers to contact you from your active listings**
   If you don't provide a Q&A page, then you must allow buyers to contact you directly.

☑ **Show Q&A**
   Show your Q&A page when buyers click "Ask a question" on your item listings.

6. **(Optional) Create your own questions and answers if you have other specifications you want the customer to know about.**

   To do so, here's the drill:

   a. *From the list, select the topic to which your answer applies.*

   b. *Click the Add a Question link.*

   c. *In the Add Your Own Q&A dialog box that appears, type your question and answer, as I show in Figure 3-3.*

7. **Type in as many custom Q&As as you wish, changing topics in the Topic list as needed. When you're finished, click the Submit button at the bottom.**

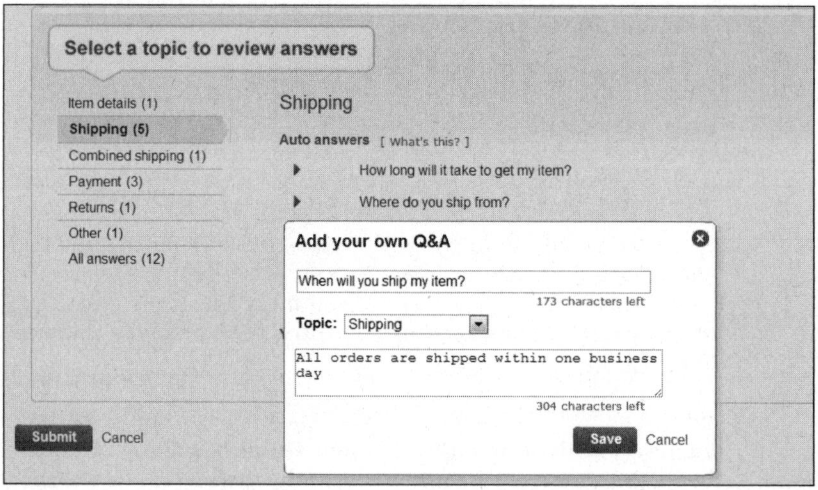

Figure 3-3:
Create
your own
questions
to appear in
your Auto
Answers.

Select a topic to review answers

Item details (1)
Shipping (5)
Combined shipping (1)
Payment (3)
Returns (1)
Other (1)
All answers (12)

Shipping

Auto answers [What's this?]

▸   How long will it take to get my item?

▸   Where do you ship from?

Add your own Q&A   ⊗

When will you ship my item?
                              173 characters left

Topic: Shipping ▾

All orders are shipped within one business
day
                              304 characters left

                              Save Cancel

Submit Cancel

Communicating through eBay Messages

When a prospective buyer has a question or wants to send you an offer on an item, and you permit such communications, you will know about it in two ways: through e-mail or your eBay mobile app. You'll get a notification from eBay alerting you that a question has been asked. A best offer e-mail will arrive in your e-mail inbox and look something like the message in Figure 3-4.

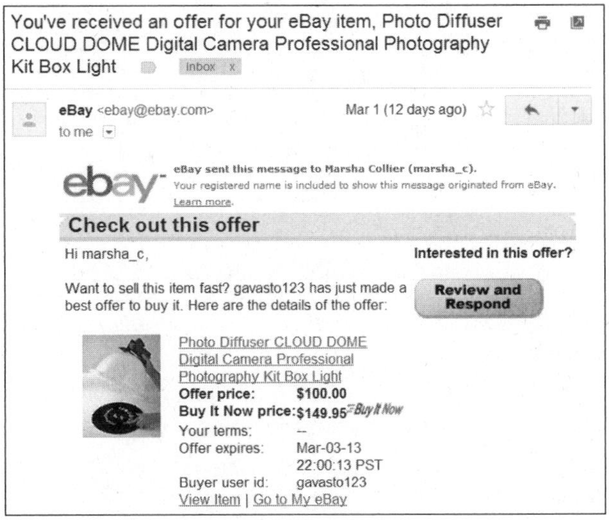

Figure 3-4: E-mail notification of a best offer on one of my listings.

Responding to an eBay message

When you receive an e-mail message from a buyer, you *can* click the Review and Respond button in the e-mail and go directly to the online question to post your response, or for safety's sake, go directly to your My eBay page and click the Messages tab. You can also respond from the eBay mobile app: Just open the app and select Messages from the opening screen shown in Figure 3-5.

When you visit your eBay message box, you can find, read, and respond to your customer's message.

You can also go directly to the item page, where you'll see the notice that you have a question to answer. Click the link and you're taken to the message page where you can respond to the question. (This is the same page that the e-mail links to.)

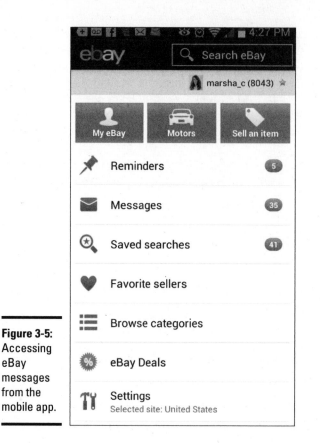

Figure 3-5:
Accessing
eBay
messages
from the
mobile app.

Making your response friendly, helpful, and productive

When answering a question, a brief and straightforward response is good. For example, I wrote the following note in response to a question regarding the condition of the Christmas tree in one of my auctions:

Hello,

Yes, the aluminum Christmas tree in my auction is in excellent condition. The 58 branches are full and lush and will look great for the holidays. Please write again if you have any more questions or concerns.

Don't forget to check my other listings for a color wheel and a revolving tree turner. They would look great with this tree, and I can combine them for shipping.

Thank you for writing,

Marsha
`http://stores.ebay.com/Marsha-Colliers-Fabulous-Finds`

Isn't that pleasant? The note addresses the question in a respectful and personable manner. Writing a note like this doesn't take long. You should be doing it.

Putting your eBay store URL in your signature is a great way to get new customers to view your other merchandise.

Personalizing Your Buyer's Communication

Your eBay business can easily run on auto-pilot because eBay will automatically send e-mail messages to buyers at various points in the transaction:

✦ The moment a buyer purchases an item

✦ Once a buyer completes checkout and has paid

✦ When the buyer hasn't paid after a few days

✦ When an order is updated with tracking and shipping information

✦ To remind the buyer to leave Feedback (about a month after the transaction)

Have you ever received a bulk-generated, boilerplate e-mail? The other party hasn't bothered to fill in half the blanks, and you're almost insulted just by having to read it? Receiving a note like this after you've requested that the seller combine purchases (and the letter pays no attention to your request) is especially annoying. E-mails can cross, but a personal approach goes a long way with customers.

Customizing an automatic message

Although eBay's e-mails (without alteration) are pretty good (a *buyer-success* purchase e-mail is shown in Figure 3-6), any eBay seller can customize that first e-mail. And why shouldn't you?

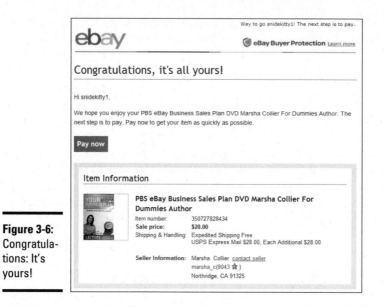

eBay Buyer Protection Learn more

Congratulations, it's all yours!

Hi snidekitty1,

We hope you enjoy your PBS eBay Business Sales Plan DVD Marsha Collier For Dummies Author. The next step is to pay. Pay now to get your item as quickly as possible.

Pay now

Item Information

PBS eBay Business Sales Plan DVD Marsha Collier For Dummies Author

Item number:	350727828434
Sale price:	**$20.00**
Shipping & Handling:	Expedited Shipping Free
	USPS Express Mail $28.00, Each Additional $28.00

Seller Information: Marsha Collier contact seller
marsha_c(8043 ☆)
Northridge, CA 91325

Figure 3-6:
Congratula-
tions: It's
yours!

To customize an e-mail message, follow these steps:

1. **Go to your My eBay page, mouse over Account tab, and click the link to go to the Manage Communication with Buyers area.**

   On the resulting page are samples of the eBay-generated e-mails.

2. **Click the button to show the Buyer Wins e-mail. Find the link in the lower-right corner that prompts you to Add a Message.**

3. **Click Add a Message to go to the form page shown in Figure 3-7.**

   If you have a business logo, you can insert it in the e-mail. Or if you have an eBay store, you can insert your store header at the top of the e-mail.

4. **Type your message to the buyer (up to 2,000 characters) in the text box.**

   eBay can auto-insert data from your transaction when you select an item from the Add to Message list at the right of the text box; Figure 3-7 shows a selected item in curly brackets. The contents for these items — shown in Tables 3-1 and 3-2 — are generated from eBay's records on the transaction and will appear in your e-mail.

5. **After you've finished your message, click Save, and this customized message will go out to all your buyers.**

**Book II
Chapter 3**

Figure 3-7:
Using
eBay's
data in
your e-mail
message.

**Five-Star Customer
Service via Eloquent
Communications**

Table 3-1   Auto-Text Options for Buyer and Seller Information

Buyer information	*AutoText Option*	*Seller information*	*AutoText Option*
Buyer User ID	{BUYERUSERNAME}	Seller User ID	{SELLERUSERNAME}
Buyer name	{B_FULLNAME}	Seller name	{S_FULLNAME}
Buyer first name	{B_FIRSTNAME}	Seller first name	{B_FIRSTNAME}
Buyer last name	{B_LASTNAME}	Seller last name	{B_LASTNAME}
Buyer street 1	{B_STREET1}	Seller email address	{S_EMAIL}
Buyer street 2	{B_STREET2}	Seller phone number	{S_PHONE}
Buyer city	{B_CITY}	Seller street 1	{S_STREET1}
Buyer state	{B_STATE}	Seller street 2	{S_STREET2}
Buyer zip code	{B_ZIPCODE}	Seller city	{S_CITY}
Buyer country	{B_COUNTRY}	Seller state	{S_STATE}
		Seller zip code	{S_ZIPCODE}
		Seller country	{S_COUNTRY}

Table 3-2   **Auto-Text Options for Transaction Information**

Transaction information	*AutoText Option*	*Additional Info*
Sales record number	{SALESRECORDNUMBER}	
Item number	{ITEM#}	
Item title	{TITLE}	
Link to listing	{ITEMLINK}	
Shipping Options	{SHIPPING_OPTIONS}	
Track shipment link	{TRACKSHIPMENTLINK}	
Notes to buyer	{BUYER_NOTE}	
Discounts or Charges	{OTHER_FEES}	
Closing price	{OTHER_FEES}{CLOSING$}	This field is the price per item. Use the {QUANTITY} variable to reflect multiple purchases when your buyer buys more than one item in a single transaction.
Total price	{TOTAL$}	
Quantity	{QUANTITY}	
Feedback link	{FEEDBACKLINK}	Adds a link to the Feedback page.
Refund Amount	{REFUND_AMOUNT}	
Variation details	{VARIATION}	
Favorites list	{FAVORITESLIST}	Includes a link to a page where buyer can add you to their favorite sellers and stores list.
S&H fee {S&H}	{S&H}	
Tax	{TAX}	US site only.
Tax State	{TAX_STATE}	
Payment accepted	{S_PAYMENT}	Lists which payment methods are accepted.
Payment instructions	{PAYMENTINSTRUCTIONS}	Lists accepted payment methods and other relevant information.

Transaction information	AutoText Option	Additional Info
Shipping calculator	{SHIPPINGCALCULATOR}	
Transaction table	{TXTABLE}	Includes table with item, quantity and price.
Checkout link	{PAYNOWLINK}	US, CA, and UK sites only.
Shipped date	{SHIPPEDDATE}	

If you're a Selling Manager Pro (explained on Book VIII) subscriber, you have the option of adding your own message to most of eBay's automatic messages. Figure 3-8 shows an e-mail sent to a customer, and it contains the package tracking information. In the next section, I offer you some suggested text.

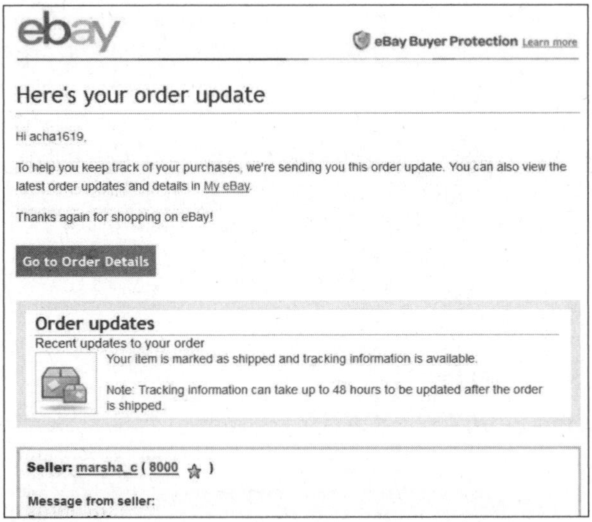

Figure 3-8: Order updates e-mail.

The order confirmation e-mail

I know that you probably aren't going to send out a payment received letter for every transaction, especially when they're paid through PayPal. But it would surely be nice if you did. Staying in constant communication with your buyers will make them feel more secure with you — and with buying on eBay. You want them to come back, don't you?

When you receive payment and are ready to ship, sending a short note like the following (again — eBay makes this easy with Selling Manager Pro) helps to instill loyalty in your customer:

Hi, {BUYERUSERNAME},

Your payment was received for {ITEMTITLE} *and your item will ship tomorrow. Please e-mail me when it arrives so that I can hear how pleased you are with your purchase.*

When the transaction is over, I hope you will leave five-star, positive feedback for me because building a good reputation on eBay is very important. I'd really appreciate it, and I'll be glad to do the same for you.

Thank you for purchasing my item,

{S_FULLNAME}
{SELLERUSERNAME}

Say thank you — I mean it! What do all the successful big-name department stores have in common? Yes, great prices, good merchandise, and nice displays. But with all things being equal, customer service always wins, hands down.

Updating shipping information

The automatic order update e-mail goes out from eBay or PayPal once you input your tracking number and mark the item as shipped. By inserting the tracking number into the PayPal payment record, you cover two bases: Your buyer is notified of shipping, and PayPal has the record that you've shipped an item.

Subject: Your item is on the way!

Hi, {BUYERUSERNAME}

Thank you for buying my {ITEMTITLE}. *Please know that my goal is to give you the "five-star service" that you deserve as my customer. Your item will always reach you within a few days of your purchase, since I ship as soon as possible.*

Your package's tracking number appears on this e-mail and on your My eBay Order Details page.

If there is any question when the package arrives, PLEASE e-mail me imme-diately. Your satisfaction is my goal, and I'm sure any problem can be easily taken care of.

Sincerely,

{S_FULLNAME}

{SELLERUSERNAME}
http://stores.ebay.com/yourstorenamehere

When the e-mail is sent to your customer, your message will be inserted under eBay's shipping notification and graphics. Your message portion will look like the e-mail in Figure 3-9.

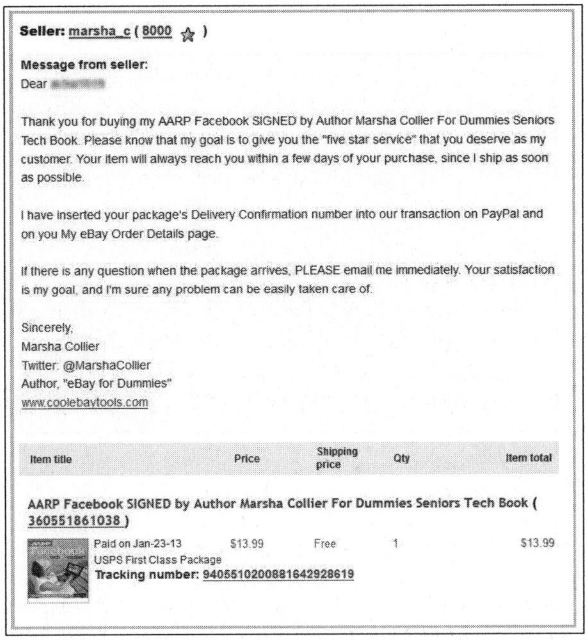

Seller: marsha_c (8000 ☆)

Message from seller:
Dear ████████

Thank you for buying my AARP Facebook SIGNED by Author Marsha Collier For Dummies Seniors Tech Book. Please know that my goal is to give you the "five star service" that you deserve as my customer. Your item will always reach you within a few days of your purchase, since I ship as soon as possible.

I have inserted your package's Delivery Confirmation number into our transaction on PayPal and on you My eBay Order Details page.

If there is any question when the package arrives, PLEASE email me immediately. Your satisfaction is my goal, and I'm sure any problem can be easily taken care of.

Sincerely,
Marsha Collier
Twitter: @MarshaCollier
Author, "eBay for Dummies"
www.coolebaytools.com

Item title	Price	Shipping price	Qty	Item total
AARP Facebook SIGNED by Author Marsha Collier For Dummies Seniors Tech Book (360551861038)				
Paid on Jan-23-13 USPS First Class Package **Tracking number:** 9405510200881642928619	$13.99	Free	1	$13.99

Figure 3-9:
The personalized text as it appears to your customer.

Chapter 4: Letting PayPal Help You Manage the Money

In This Chapter

↙ **Understanding the PayPal system**

↙ **Deciding which account is best for you**

↙ **Seeing how PayPal protects you**

↙ **Uncovering your payment history**

In the early days of online auctions, eBay transactions were an iffy proposition. You would send a check to your trading partner, wait for the check to clear, and then wait for the item to arrive, all of which seemed interminable. There was little feedback in the beginning, so it was difficult to separate the good sellers from the bad. The most widely accepted form of payment was the money order, but that wasn't as reliable as a check since you had no way to know when the money order cleared. Yet, in our small (but growing) community, we weren't afraid to send money orders to strangers. Heck, some sellers even shipped merchandise *before* they received payment! Things were a lot simpler, if riskier, in the old days.

Now that eBay is a huge, global marketplace, having a secure and reliable method for accepting (and making) payments for your eBay transactions is crucial. PayPal fits the bill, and it has a great track record. See the nearby sidebar, "From x.com to PayPal . . . what a story!" for a brief look at PayPal's origin and the foundation of its position as a trusted method of exchanging money.

If you've read any of my other books, you know that I've been a huge fan of PayPal from the beginning. PayPal is one of the safest and least-expensive ways for an online seller to accept payments. For a small retailer, PayPal fees can be much more cost-effective than those associated with a credit card merchant account. In this chapter, I tell you about the types of PayPal accounts, how you use PayPal to accept payments, and also, how PayPal can help you pay for your own purchases or personal money transfers. You also find out how PayPal supports your efforts to keep accurate records of all your transactions, which is a big help at tax time!

From x.com to PayPal...what a story!

To solve the problem of *no-good-way-to-pay-for-online-auctions*, a bright man, Elon Musk (yes the same person who founded Tesla Motors and Space Exploration Technologies: SpaceX), came up with the concept of e-mailing money; you could even beam cash to someone's Palm Pilot! There was no charge for using this service, which was even more amazing! Signing up for the program gave you a $10 credit for becoming a member. You also received a $10 bonus for each friend you convinced to join. (The maximum amount that any user could get in bonuses was $1,000, but that's no small change!)

With numbers like that, the early eBay (née AuctionWeb) crowd signed up quickly, and x.com became the most widely used service on the Internet, the first mover and shaker in online person-to-person payments.

eBay countered, acquiring Billpoint in the spring of 1999 with hopes of launching its own payment service in a partnership with Wells Fargo. In a disaster of bad timing, the service was not available to eBay members until the second quarter of 2000. Meanwhile, x.com — now reborn as PayPal — was growing by leaps and bounds and quietly taking over the market.

PayPal went public in February of 2002 to an encouraging Wall Street. The feud between PayPal and Billpoint heated up. The number of customers who signed up with Billpoint couldn't keep pace with the number joining PayPal. PayPal posted a profit, while Billpoint was losing millions per year. In October 2002, eBay bit the bullet and acquired PayPal in a deal valued at $1.5 billion. Billpoint was then simply phased out of the site.

Understanding How PayPal Works

Joining PayPal is just the beginning, and the benefits far outweigh any fees charged to sellers. There's no charge to the buyer to pay for an online purchase — or to send money to anyone.

Payment methods supported by PayPal

You have several ways to fund the money you send to another party through PayPal:

✦ **Instant transfer:** Sending money this way means the money is immediately credited to the recipient's account. That person can then transfer the money to his or her personal bank account without delay. If you want to send a transfer, you must have a credit or debit card registered with PayPal as a backup for your funds — just in case your bank denies the transfer. It's just like writing a secure check — without exposing any of your personal information (such as your checking account number) to another party.

✦ **eCheck:** Sending an eCheck isn't as "instant" as an instant transfer. It's just like writing a check from your checking account; it can take from three to five days for an eCheck to clear. You don't need a backup source of funds when you use eCheck.

✦ **PayPal balance:** If someone sent you money through PayPal or you've sold something on eBay, you have a balance in your PayPal account. This balance is first applied to any purchases you've made. Then, when your account has no balance, you can choose to pay by credit card. It's simplest to keep your books balanced if you withdraw any PayPal balance to your business checking account before you make a purchase.

✦ **Credit card:** Charge it! Putting your PayPal purchases on a credit card is a good idea. Not only are you protected by PayPal, but your credit card company also backs you up in case of fraud.

You can register multiple credit cards on your PayPal account and select a different one for different types of purchases. That way, you can place personal purchases on one account and business purchases on another. It makes end-of-year bookkeeping a lot easier!

Sending money

PayPal breaks types of payments into categories based on what you're paying for. You can pay for *almost* anything in the world on the PayPal system (as long as the recipient has an e-mail address). A few things that you *can't* pay for with PayPal include most items related to gambling, adult content or services, and buying or selling prescription drugs from noncertified sellers. If you're planning to send payments for something that may be a tad questionable, I recommend a visit to the PayPal help area to be sure your item is currently in the clear. You can find the Acceptable Use Policy for the United States here:

```
https://cms.paypal.com/us/cgi-bin/?cmd=_render-content&
     content_ID=ua/AcceptableUse_full&locale.x=en_US
```

After you sign into your PayPal account and click the Send Money tab, you can send money from PayPal in the following ways:

✦ **Paying for eBay items:** When you buy an eBay item on eBay, you need to pay through the eBay Checkout system.

✦ **Goods (other):** By clicking this radio button, you can send money to anyone in the world for goods purchased anywhere other than eBay.

✦ **Services:** You can send payment for a service performed (see Figure 4-1) for you or your business, such as web design, bookkeeping, psychic readings — your imagination can get carried away here.

✦ **Personal:** Use this when you need to send money to your kid in college or pay back your roommate for saving you from great embarrassment when you left your wallet at home on a double date.

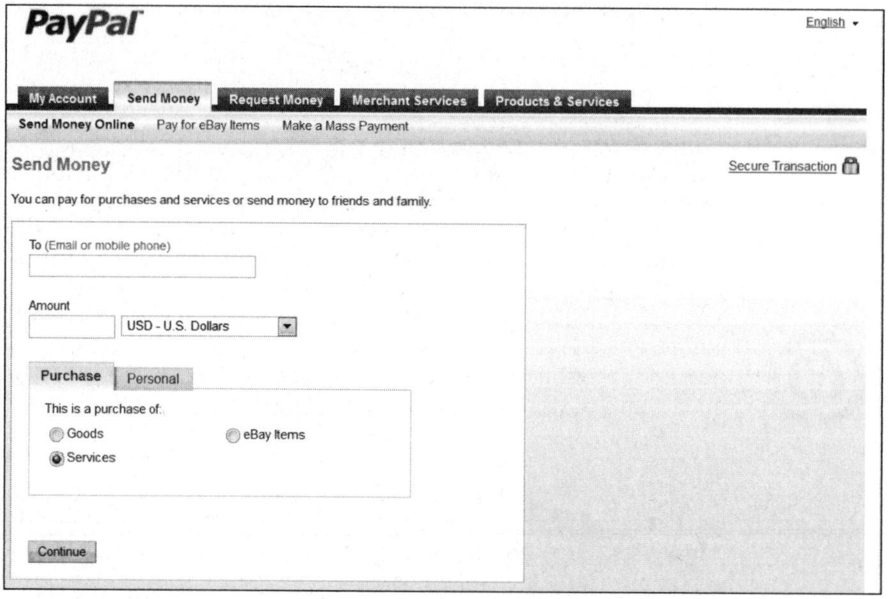

Figure 4-1:
Sending
money
through
PayPal.

PayPal screenshot showing the Send Money page with To, Amount fields, Purchase/Personal tabs, and a Continue button.

When you're using the cash-advance feature for the Send Money⇨Personal payment type, consider using a payment method other than credit card to avoid possible credit card fees for a cash advance.

Sorting Out PayPal's Different Accounts

PayPal has three types of accounts to accommodate everyone from the casual seller to the professional business: Personal, Business, and Premier accounts.

PayPal Personal account

When you begin your career with PayPal, you may want to sign up for a Personal account. With this basic account from PayPal, you can send and receive money (non-credit-card payments) for free. PayPal Personal accounts are for only one person and not for a business. (You can't have a joint Personal account, either.)

Business and Premier accounts

The PayPal accounts for the professional seller (Business and Premier) allow you to accept credit card payments, get a debit card, and participate in PayPal's high-yield money market fund. A Premier account is held in an individual's name (although it may still be for a business); a business account can be held in a business name and allows multiple login names. At these account levels, you have access to a customer service phone number.

A fee is levied on all money you receive through PayPal at this level. PayPal has a standard rate and a merchant rate, as shown in Table 4-1. The merchant rate has three tiers, based on your monthly sales volume. When you open your account, you're charged the standard rate. After your sales grow and you've been receiving more than $3000 per month through PayPal for three consecutive months, you can apply for a merchant account.

Table 4-1	PayPal Seller Transaction Fees in U.S. Dollars	
Rate	*Monthly Sales Level*	*Fee*
Standard	Up to $3,000.00	2.9% + 30¢ U.S.
Merchant	From $3,000.01 to $10,000.00	2.5% + 30¢ U.S.
Merchant	From $10,000.01 to $100,000.00	2.2% + 30¢ U.S.
Merchant	Greater than $100,000.00	Call PayPal at 1-888-818-3928.

Note: If you receive payment from a buyer in another country, you are charged a 3.9 percent transaction fee, plus a fixed fee based on the currency received.

The fees (for any type of account) when accepting payments via the PayPal Here card reader and smartphone app (shown in Figure 4-2) are as follows:

✦ 2.7 percent when you swipe a credit card in the reader

✦ 3.5 percent plus 15¢ per transaction when you type a card number into the app

Figure 4-2:
The PayPal Here card reader allows you to swipe credit cards for payments.

PayPal's Protection Plans

Safety: Isn't that what paying for things online is all about? Safety for the buyer *and* safety for the seller are primary concerns in the minds of those doing business online. PayPal has created protection policies for both parties.

PayPal purchase protection

As a buyer who pays for eBay items through PayPal, you are protected under these circumstances:

✦ **You didn't receive the item you paid for with PayPal.** PayPal refers to this as an *item not received dispute.* When you pay for an item through PayPal, the seller must produce a tracking number that you can use to chart the transit of your package. If the item is valued over a certain amount, you may be required to sign a delivery confirmation when it gets to your door.

✦ **You received an item you paid for with PayPal but it is "significantly not as described."** This can mean many things, such as you received a completely different item, the condition was misrepresented, parts were missing, the item was damaged in transport, or you received a counterfeit version of the item.

This kind of protection doesn't cover you when you're merely disappointed with an item when you open the box. It also won't cover downloadable software or digital items — even if you buy them on eBay.

✦ **You were charged for something you didn't purchase, and you report it within 60 days**. With PayPal, you're covered by the $0 Liability for Eligible Unauthorized Transactions program.

When your purchase is made on eBay, it's covered by eBay Buyer Protection. PayPal is used by many online merchants for payment processing.

Following are a few rules for using the purchase-protection system and making claims:

✦ **Number of claims:** You may make only one claim per PayPal payment.

✦ **Timing:** Your claim must be made within 45 days of your PayPal payment.

✦ **Participation:** You must be ready and willing to provide information and documentation to PayPal's buyer protection team during the claims process.

PayPal seller protection

Don't think that sellers get left out of the protection scenario. You do have some protection against unwarranted claims made on your online and eBay sales; it's called (logically enough) *seller protection.*

To see whether your transaction is covered under seller protection, follow these steps:

1. **In your payment received e-mail from PayPal, click the View the Details of the Transaction link.**

2. **Sign into your PayPal account.**

3. **Scroll down the Transaction Details page to the buyer's shipping address.**

You'll see whether the shipping address is confirmed. (PayPal confirms the address by making sure that the credit card billing address matches the shipping address.) If it is confirmed, you must ship to that address to be protected.

When your transaction is protected, should any fraud be involved (a stolen credit card or identity hoax), you will not lose the money. PayPal guarantees the transaction.

If you receive a PayPal payment and the buyer requests you ship to an address other than the address on the transaction details page, drop the buyer a note and ask about the address. At this point, depending on the reply you receive, decide for yourself whether you're willing to take the risk. Remember that you will not be covered under seller protection if you ship to an unconfirmed address.

What's this "PayPal-verified" business all about?

Being *PayPal-verified* is an important rating for both seller and buyer. It means that someone has checked and you really are who you say you are. Becoming verified isn't a big deal. All you have to do is register your checking account with PayPal. (Remember when you opened an account at the bank? They got information about you to be sure you were *you*, didn't they?)

PayPal will make two teeny (less than $1) deposits into your checking account. After these have been transferred to your account, you can log back in to your PayPal account and confirm the two amounts. That's it — and you get free pennies, too!

If you live outside the United States, you become verified by adding a credit card to your account and enrolling in the Expanded Use program, which is a similar confirmation scheme.

Surprise! There are a few other rules and restrictions. For sellers to be protected, they must

+ **Ship to a confirmed address.** You must ship to the buyer's address exactly as displayed on the transaction details page.

+ **Ship within seven days.** The item must leave your place of business within seven days of receiving payment. In the case of a pre-sale or customized item, you must post the delivery time in your listing.

+ **Accept single payment from a single account.** You must have accepted one payment from one PayPal account to pay for the purchase. (No multiple-account payments for an item.)

+ **Ship tangible goods.** Seller protection is not available for services, digital goods, and other electronically delivered items.

+ **Provide proof of shipping.** You need to provide a tracking number so the shipment can be tracked online. The transaction details page must show that you shipped to the buyer's address. For items valued $250 and over, you must be able to produce a signed signature delivery confirmation.

If you use an automated shipping solution such as Endicia (at www.endicia.com), you also just copy and paste the delivery confirmation numbers onto the PayPal page. PayPal will send an e-mail to the buyer with the information for the buyer's records.

If PayPal is required by the buyer's issuing credit card company to respond immediately to resolve a chargeback situation, you must provide all information within three days.

At this writing, seller protection is available for many of the eBay International sites. Check with the PayPal site by clicking the Worldwide link at the bottom of PayPal's pages for any changes in this policy.

Downloading Your Transaction History from PayPal

I've been running a home-based business since the mid-1980s. Because I came from a corporate background working in the newspaper business, I've always known that keeping my books clean is of utmost importance. Recordkeeping has always been the bane of my existence. When I began my home-based business, the first thing I did was to hire a lawyer and a CPA to teach me what I had to do.

Recordkeeping means keeping track of everything: Every penny, sou, farthing, or ruble that you spend or take in. In the United States (and in most other countries), we have a pesky thing called taxes. We all have to turn in tax returns of several types when we run a business — and they'd better be correct. There may come a day when you receive a letter from a State or Federal tax agency asking to take a look at your books. This is simply a nice way of saying the dreaded word, *audit.*

The best defense against an audit is to have backup records. The more records you have proving your business income and expenses, the less painful your audit will be. One excellent piece of data to have at your fingertips is your PayPal transaction history.

Besides meeting tax-reporting requirements, keeping accurate records keeps you on top of your business dealings. (See Book IX for more about how good recordkeeping helps your business succeed.) PayPal helps you with this all-important recordkeeping by providing reports on your buying and selling activity with these features:

✦ **24/7 availability:** PayPal allows you to customize and download your transaction reports at any time. You might want to consider downloading your reports on a monthly or quarterly basis — as well as generating one big report at the end of the year.

Or you may want to download the reports to coincide with your state sales-tax payments (for backup documentation) or to keep a record of your monthly totals.

✦ **Various formats:** You can download reports in several formats. The most flexible is a comma-delimited file that you can open and edit in a spreadsheet program, such as Excel or Microsoft Works.

Preparing to download your PayPal data

PayPal is great when it comes to giving you control over your reports. You can narrow your downloads to incoming transactions for a one-day period or see all transactions for the year or more.

You may need all the information that PayPal gives you, but PayPal can give you information overkill. Here I go over some of the options PayPal provides so you can decide which types of information are important for you to keep in your permanent record.

All your downloadable PayPal reports can contain the following information by default:

✦ **Date:** The date each PayPal transaction occurred.

✦ **Time:** The time the payment was made.

✦ **Time zone:** The time zone used for recording transactions in your PayPal account.

✦ **Name:** The name of the person to whom you sent money or from whom you received money.

✦ **Type:** The type of transaction that occurred: deposit, withdrawal, ATM withdrawal, payment sent, payment received, and so on.

✦ **Status:** The status of the transaction (cleared, completed, denied, and so on) at the time you download the file.

✦ **Gross:** The gross amount involved in the transaction (before any fees are deducted).

✦ **Fee:** Any PayPal fees charged to the transaction.

✦ **Net:** The net dollar amount of the transaction. This is the total received, less any PayPal fees.

✦ **From e-mail:** The e-mail address of the sender.

✦ **To e-mail:** The e-mail address of the recipient.

If you use different e-mail addresses to classify different types of sales, this can be a good sorting point for your reports. For example, I receive payments for my personal auctions to one e-mail address, and payments for my business to another.

When you want to customize the download, you can pick and choose what data you really need to have on hand:

+ **Item ID:** That strange combination of letters and numbers that PayPal assigns to each transaction. Decide whether this is important for your records. (I don't use it.)

+ **Item title:** The title of the listing related to the transaction.

+ **Shipping amount:** The amount the buyer paid for shipping. It's a good idea to use this field because it helps you separate merchandise revenue from shipping revenue.

+ **Auction site:** If you're collecting money from other sites through PayPal, you might want to include this link so that you can sort your sales by auction site.

+ **Buyer ID:** You may want to keep a record of your customer's eBay IDs.

+ **Item URL:** The Internet address of the auction or transaction. (For eBay, the URLs are on the site for up to 90 days — here you can go back a year.)

+ **Closing date:** The date the transaction closed. The record will always contain the date the payment posted to your PayPal account, whether you indicate a closing date here or not.

+ **Shipping address:** The address to which the item was shipped.

+ **Counter party status (verified versus unverified):** A record of whether your buyer was PayPal-verified.

+ **Address status (confirmed versus unconfirmed):** Shows whether the address you shipped to was confirmed.

+ **Sales tax:** Information about sales tax you collected.

Book II
Chapter 4

Letting PayPal
Help You Manage
the Money

Downloading and customizing your reports

To get your reports from PayPal, follow these steps:

1. **Go to** www.paypal.com **and log in to your account with your e-mail address and password.**

   After you're logged in, the top of your page displays various tabs.

2. **Click the My Account tab.**

3. **Mouse over the History item on the navigation bar and click Download History on the resulting drop-down menu, as shown in Figure 4-3.**

   You land on the Download History page. Before you start clicking anything, consider customizing your reports by choosing only the data you want from all the available data described in the previous section.

4. **Scroll down the page to indicate your level of customization.**

   You can customize the fields you require in your download through the links at the right, shown in Figure 4-4.

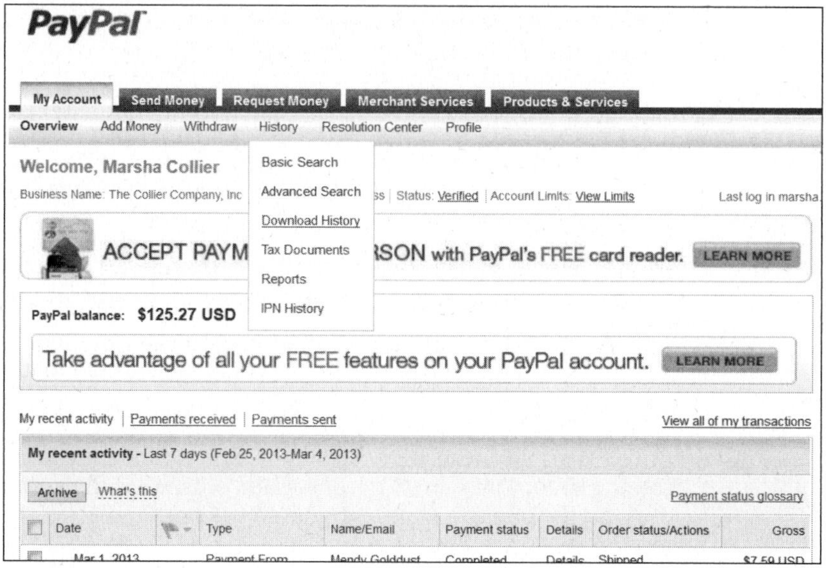

Figure 4-3:
Accessing
downloads
from the
PayPal
navigation
bar.

Figure 4-4:
Requesting
a download.

5. **Click the Customize Download Fields link.**

   You're taken to a page where you can further refine the data you need.

6. **Select the fields you want to include by putting a check mark in the box next to the desired data.**

   For details on the different options, see the previous section.

7. **Click Save.**

   You're returned to the Download History page (refer to Figure 4-4). Your customization is saved for future report downloads.

8. **Specify the dates that you want to span in the downloaded report.**

   You can do either of the following:

   • *Click the Custom Date Range option and type dates in the From and To fields.*

   • *Click the Last Download to Present option.*

   If you're a seller in the U.K., your page will look slightly different from the one pictured here. Your dates will be in DD/MM/YY format.

9. **Select a format for your download from the File Types for Download drop-down list.**

   Your choices include

   • *Comma-delimited file:* This type of file downloads with the `.csv` extension. After you've downloaded a comma-delimited file, you can open it easily in Microsoft Excel by double-clicking, as shown in Figure 4-5.

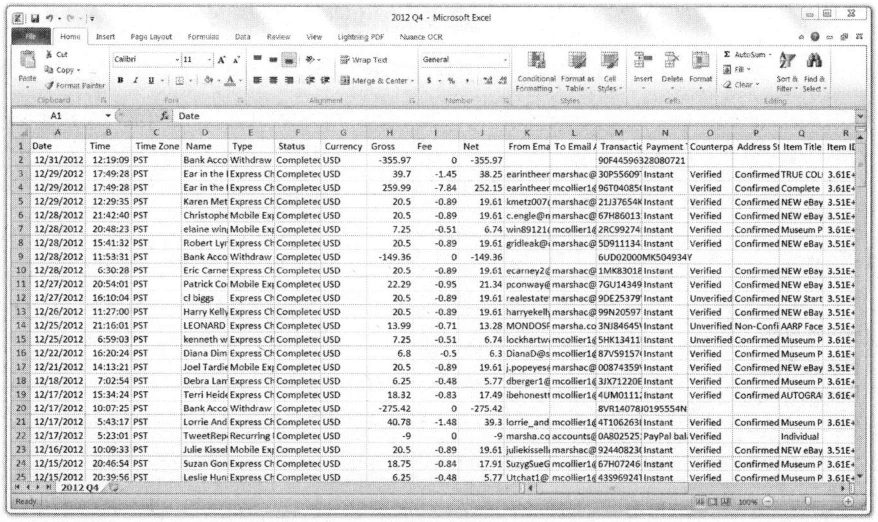

Book II
Chapter 4

Letting PayPal
Help You Manage
the Money

Figure 4-5: Opening a comma-delimited file in Excel.

- *Tab-delimited file:* This file downloads with the `.txt` extension. It can be opened not only in a spreadsheet program but also as a text file in Windows Notepad or a word processing program such as Microsoft Word for Windows.

- *Quicken or QuickBooks file:* These files download in the native format, ready to import into these Intuit bookkeeping programs. Just remember: After these files are imported, they're in there for good.

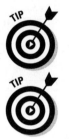

Saving these files for spreadsheet use does not limit you as to what version of which program will open what file in the future. The `.txt` and `.csv` files are universal files that can be opened on any PC with basic spreadsheet capabilities.

By opting for a spreadsheet file as your record of customers, you're not bogging down a bookkeeping program with hundreds and eventually thousands of records of one-time buyers. Even a robust program like QuickBooks will max out at around 14,000 customers!

10. **Click the Download History button.**

If you've asked for a long timeframe (such as a year), go make yourself a cup of joe. When you come back, your file will be ready to download.

Saving and Editing Your Reports

If your report isn't ready immediately, PayPal will send you an e-mail to let you know when your download is ready. You will be prompted to go to your Download Recent History Logs page, shown in Figure 4-6.

Figure 4-6:
Downloading
my fourth-
quarter 2012
transactions
for my state
sales-tax
filing.

Click the Download Log button to save the file to a folder on your computer. A pop-up window prompts you to select the folder in which you want to save the file.

I recommend setting up a folder that contains only Internet and eBay sales files.

After the file is saved, you can open it. Figure 4-7 shows a downloaded history file ready to open in Microsoft Excel. In this format, you can re-sort the columns, total the sales, and delete unnecessary columns. This file is now part of your eBay business archive, should the day come that you need to produce it. Be sure to back it up, just in case.

**Book II
Chapter 4**

Letting PayPal
Help You Manage
the Money

Figure 4-7:
The downloaded CSV file, ready to be opened.

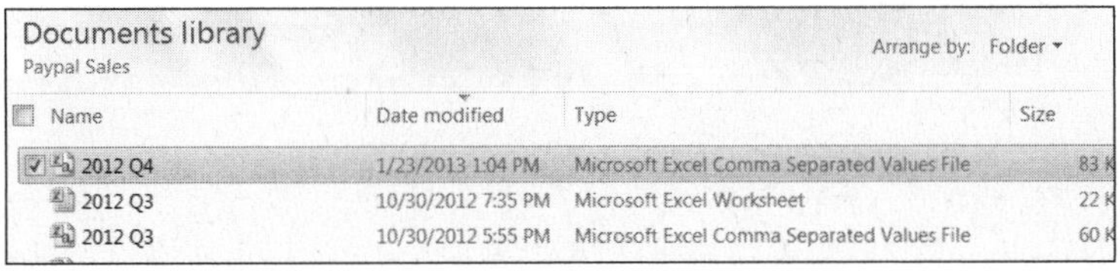

Documents library Paypal Sales				Arrange by: Folder ▾
Name	Date modified	Type	Size	
☑ 2012 Q4	1/23/2013 1:04 PM	Microsoft Excel Comma Separated Values File	83 K	
2012 Q3	10/30/2012 7:35 PM	Microsoft Excel Worksheet	22 K	
2012 Q3	10/30/2012 5:55 PM	Microsoft Excel Comma Separated Values File	60 K	

Some CPAs recommend that you keep these files for up to seven years. To be safe, check with your own tax professional, who understands the needs of your particular tax situation.

Chapter 5: Using eBay's Management Tools

In This Chapter

✔ **Signing in**

✔ **Understanding the parts of the My eBay hub**

✔ **Checking out the Summary area**

✔ **Organizing purchases on the Buy page**

✔ **Setting your preferences on the Account page**

✔ **Getting on board with Selling Manager**

*e*Bay offers you an amazing variety of tools. Because the site is constantly changing, few of us know where all these Easter eggs are or even how to use them. It's always an eye-opener when I poke around the site and find a new tool or useful shortcut.

Although I love (and use) eBay's management tools, many solid third-party services and tools are available. Book VIII lets you in on some of my favorites.

Aside from the tools I tell you about in this chapter, the most important shortcut I can give you is to remind you to sign in and select the box that says "Stay signed in" before you attempt to do anything on eBay. This way, you can do the vast majority of your eBay business without being bugged for your password.

Signing In to Get Going

Before you do almost anything on eBay, it's best to sign in. What would be more of a waste of time than to find an item you want, at the price you'd love to pay, with only two minutes to go — and not be signed in? (See the sidebar "The lowdown on sign-ins" for more information.) You must be signed in to bid, sell, or buy, so just do it!

1. **Click the Sign In link at the top of any eBay page.**

(If you're already signed in, the link will read Sign Out.) You're sent to the Sign In page.

2. **Type your user ID and password, as shown in Figure 5-1.**

Type your registered eBay user ID (not your e-mail address). Your user ID and e-mail address aren't interchangeable on the site.

ebay Welcome to eBay

Sign in

User ID

marsha_c

Password

••••••••••••

Forgot your user ID or password?

☑ Stay signed in (Uncheck if you're on a shared computer)

[Sign in]

New to eBay?

Get started now. It's fast and easy!

[Register]

eBay Buyer Protection covers your **purchase price + original shipping.**
It's FREE and automatically included. Learn more ▸

Figure 5-1:
Click Sign In
and you are
ready
to deal!

If you ever forget your eBay password, you can click the Forgot your User ID or Password links or go directly to the following:

```
https://scgi.ebay.com/ws/eBayISAPI.dll?FYPShow
```

If you remember the answer to the question you were asked during the eBay registration process, you can create a new password immediately.

3. Click the Sign In button.

You're now signed in and ready to do almost anything on eBay! You're brought to your My eBay Summary page.

The lowdown on sign-ins

Your computer holds your sign-in information for an entire day (unless you sign out). If you have more than one user ID or share a computer with other people, be sure to sign out when you're finished. For your protection, you still have to type your password for actions involving financial or personal information such as these:

✔ Changing your user information such as e-mail address, user ID, payment methods, or credit card information

✔ Going from a buyer account to a seller account

✔ Selling an item in a different browser session

✔ Choosing to clear your browser cookies

✔ Posting in the Community Discussion Boards, Chat, Answer Center, or Groups

Occasionally, eBay may ask you to enter a verification code when you sign in. This is simply an additional security feature that prevents people from using the site inappropriately through automated registrations.

Taking Charge on Your My eBay Page

The number-one tool available at no cost to every eBay user is the My eBay page. This area of the site is unmatched for its organizational boost to your buying and selling activities. After you've registered on the site, you have a My eBay page automatically, so let's delve into exactly what it can do for you.

I call My eBay a page, but it's really an *area* — a group of several pages held together with links. The My eBay area gives you control of everything you are doing (or would like to do) on eBay.

REMEMBER

You have to sign in to the site before you can use the My eBay area. To get to your My eBay page, click the My eBay link on the eBay navigation bar, which is at the top of every eBay page.

My eBay is divided into seven areas: Summary, Buy, Lists, Saved Searches, Saved Sellers, Purchase History, and Sell. Additionally, there are tabs for Activity (which encompasses the sections just listed; shown in Figure 5-2), Messages, and Account. Most are described in Table 5-1.

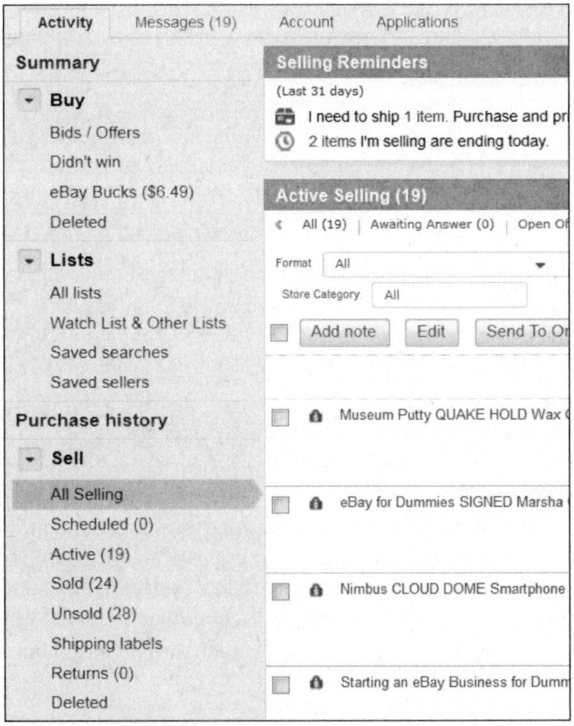

Book II
Chapter 5

Using eBay's
Management Tools

Figure 5-2:
Navigation
links on the
My eBay
page.

Activity	Messages (19)	Account	Applications

Summary

- **Buy**
  - Bids / Offers
  - Didn't win
  - eBay Bucks ($6.49)
  - Deleted
- **Lists**
  - All lists
  - Watch List & Other Lists
  - Saved searches
  - Saved sellers

Purchase history

- **Sell**
  - All Selling
  - Scheduled (0)
  - Active (19)
  - Sold (24)
  - Unsold (28)
  - Shipping labels
  - Returns (0)
  - Deleted

Selling Reminders

(Last 31 days)

🗄 I need to ship 1 item. Purchase and pr
🕐 2 items I'm selling are ending today.

Active Selling (19)

‹ All (19) | Awaiting Answer (0) | Open Of

Format   All ▾

Store Category   All

☐ Add note   Edit   Send To Or

☐ 🔒 Museum Putty QUAKE HOLD Wax (

☐ 🔒 eBay for Dummies SIGNED Marsha (

☐ 🔒 Nimbus CLOUD DOME Smartphone

☐ 🔒 Starting an eBay Business for Dumm

You can visit each Activity by clicking links in the left column on the side of the page. The top-level links of each My eBay area presents you with a summary of the activity in that area. The links below the top link take you to specific data, without making you scroll through a long page.

Table 5-1	In a Snapshot: Views of the My eBay Area
Click Here	*To See This on Your My eBay Page*
Summary	A page summarizing your My eBay area, with notifications of actions that need follow-up on the balance of the My eBay pages.
Buy	Every item for sale that you're watching, bidding on, or have made offers on, as well as any auctions you've lost.
Lists	A collection of links to the items on your wish list, Watch list, and any custom list you chose to make: favorite categories, searches, sellers, and stores.
Saved Searches	When you perform a search on eBay, you are prompted to save the search. When you save, that search will appear in this area.
Saved Sellers	When you come across a seller who sells the types of items that interest you, click to save, and that seller will appear here. (**Hint:** My user ID is marsha_c.)
Purchase History	When you make a purchase on eBay, the transaction information lands here. When your seller ships the item, the tracking number will be posted so you can check on the status of the shipment.
Sell: All Selling	All the information about any items you're selling on eBay.
Tab: Messages	A separate tab to a direct and secure place to view the latest information about eBay. You no longer have to worry about phishing spam that pretends to be from eBay. When eBay has something to tell you, it appears here.
Tab: Applications	Clicking here will take you to eBay's App store and show you the ones that you are subscribed to.
Tab: Account	This contains links to several important areas: your eBay account information, such as seller's fees and invoices; the most recent feedback comments about you, links that send you to all the feedback you've left and received, an area where you can respond to feedback; and finally, preferences you can specify so that eBay performs just as you want it to.

Below the My eBay Summary (under the Activity tab) are convenient short-cuts to services and answers you may need while doing business on eBay (see the left of Figure 5-3). You can choose to specify which links appear here by clicking the *Edit Shortcuts* link. Clicking this link presents you with a box of options. You may then select topic links for display on your page, as shown on the right in Figure 5-3.

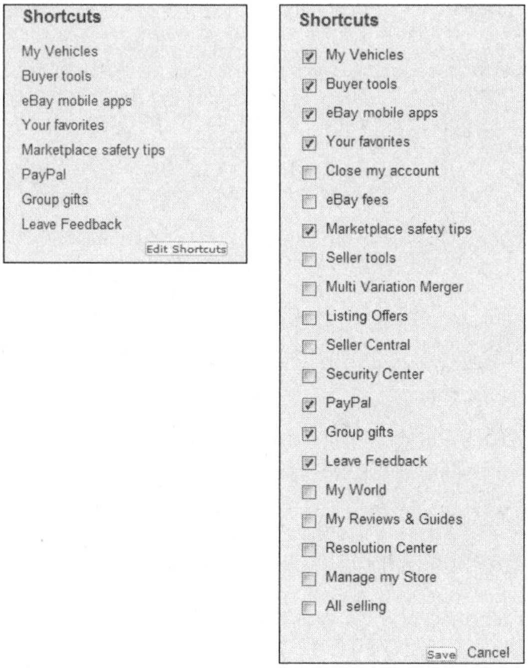

Book II
Chapter 5

Using eBay's
Management Tools

Shortcuts

My Vehicles
Buyer tools
eBay mobile apps
Your favorites
Marketplace safety tips
PayPal
Group gifts
Leave Feedback

Edit Shortcuts

Shortcuts

☑ My Vehicles
☑ Buyer tools
☑ eBay mobile apps
☑ Your favorites
☐ Close my account
☐ eBay fees
☑ Marketplace safety tips
☐ Seller tools
☐ Multi Variation Merger
☐ Listing Offers
☐ Seller Central
☐ Security Center
☑ PayPal
☑ Group gifts
☑ Leave Feedback
☐ My World
☐ My Reviews & Guides
☐ Resolution Center
☐ Manage my Store
☐ All selling

Save Cancel

Figure 5-3:
Your
Shortcuts
links (left)
and all
those
available
(right).

The links you see may repeat on the different pages of your My eBay area.

Before you freak out because you have a question about something on eBay that you can't remember the answer to, double-check the eBay Customer Support pages. You can always find help when you click the Customer Support link on the navigation bar.

Looking at the My eBay Summary Page

Until you set your preferences (as to which page you want to automatically open your My eBay area to — see the "Site Preferences link" section further on), you land on the Summary page. A friend's is shown in Figure 5-4. *Note:* When you subscribe to Selling Manager (which I do and you should), it will replace the All Selling box.

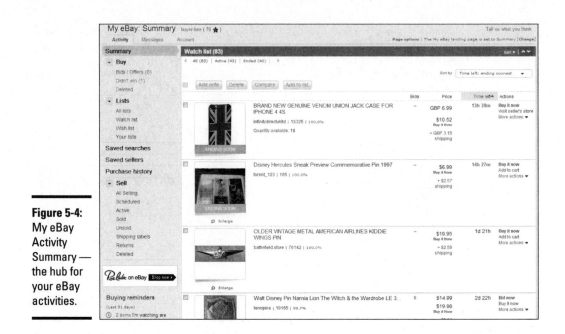

Figure 5-4:
My eBay
Activity
Summary —
the hub for
your eBay
activities.

The Summary page gives you a snapshot of your current eBay business. It provides data about your buying and selling business, and supplies links to the items.

When you are a buyer, this area tells you about

✦ Items you're watching

✦ Items you're bidding on

✦ Items you've been outbid on (for which you may need to up your bid)

✦ Feedback that you need to leave for items you've purchased

If you have a Watch list (more on that further on), it will appear front and center on this page, as well as in the Lists category.

When you sell on eBay, the Sell: All Selling area will provide info on

✦ Questions about items pending from prospective customers

✦ Items you have sold

✦ Any items that are in the Returns process

✦ Items you're selling

✦ How many items you haven't sold

You can customize what you'd like to appear on most of the My eBay pages when you click the My eBay link in the navigation bar. Then click the Change link in the right corner next to these words: *The My eBay landing page is set to Summary* (refer to Figure 5-4). Figure 5-5 shows you how to select the landing page option from a drop-down list.

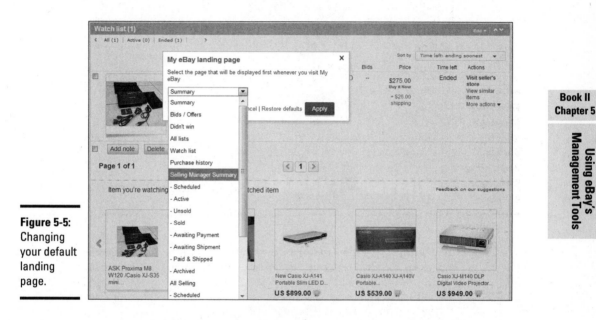

Figure 5-5: Changing your default landing page.

Should you subscribe to any of eBay's paid services such as eBay Stores, there will also be a link to your subscription area. In addition, a link is provided to any important notices from eBay regarding changes in its policies or services.

Tracking Your Buying Activity on My eBay

The Buy page is the hub for keeping track of your bids, your wins, items you're watching, and any items you didn't win. This area of My eBay helps you control everything you're currently shopping for on the site. I check this page several times a day to see the progress of items I'm interested in.

Bids/Offers

When you place a bid, eBay registers it in the Bids/Offers area, as shown in Figure 5-6, and displays a clickable link to the item.

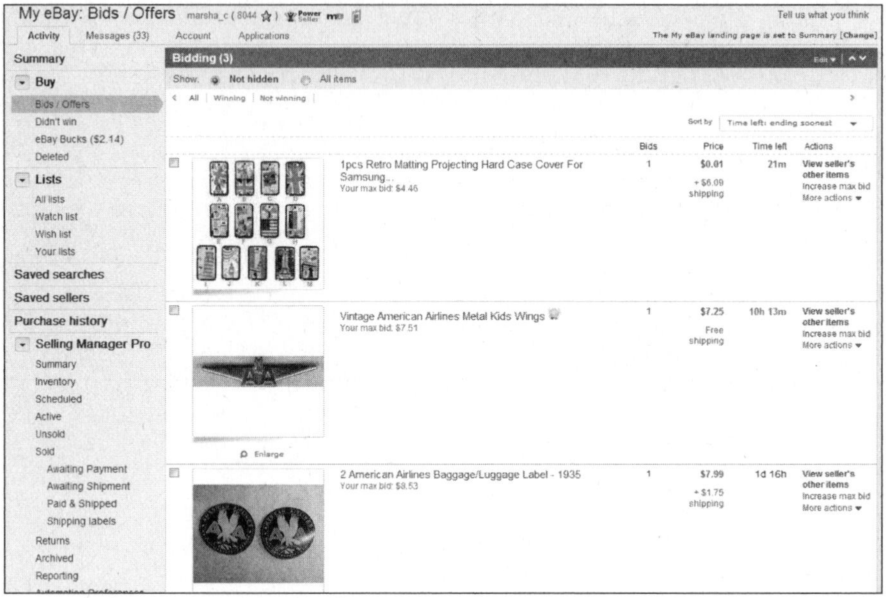

Figure 5-6:
Keeping
track of
your bidding
and buying
activity.

When shopping, if you don't check on your mobile device, make the bidding page a daily stop on eBay, so you can see the status of your bids:

✦ Bid amounts in green indicate that you're the high bidder in the auction.

✦ Bid amounts in red indicate that your bid is losing. If you want to increase your bid, simply click the auction title to go to the auction.

✦ The Your Max Bid area reminds you of the amount of your highest bid; if you see a bid that surpasses your own, you'll know it's time to throw in another bid to stay in the game.

✦ As auctions on which you've bid end, they are transferred to the Didn't Win section or the purchase page, based on your success or failure in the bidding process.

You can make notations on your bidding or item-watching. Just click the drop-down menu to the right of the item you want to annotate, click the Add Note button (as I've done in Figure 5-7), and then add the information.

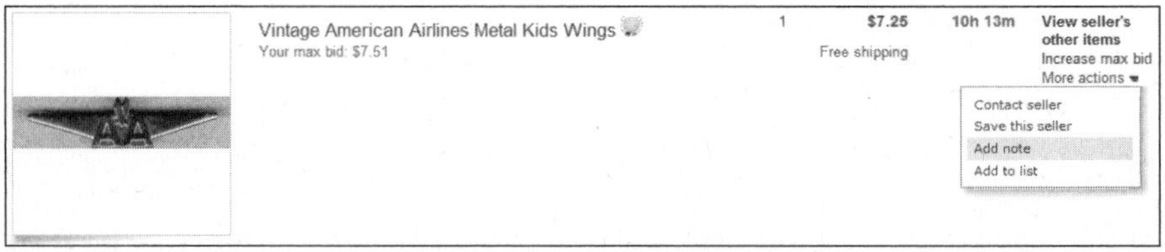

Figure 5-7:
Write a note
to remind
yourself
about the
item.

Didn't win

Sniff . . . the Didn't Win page is a very sad place. Clicking this link in the Buy section brings you to a page that lets you know when you've been outbid and lost the opportunity to purchase an item. This option isn't there to rub your nose in all the auctions you've lost — it's a handy tool that lets you search the seller's *other* items for something similar, or search the category for a similar item.

eBay Bucks

Loyalty programs keep you coming back for more, and eBay Bucks (shown in Figure 5-8) gives you rewards for the money you spend on eBay. Every calendar quarter, eBay totals up the amount you've spent on the site in qualifying categories and issues (currently) an eBay Bucks certificate worth two percent of your total. This certificate can be used toward the purchase of any item on the site for the following quarter after it's issued.

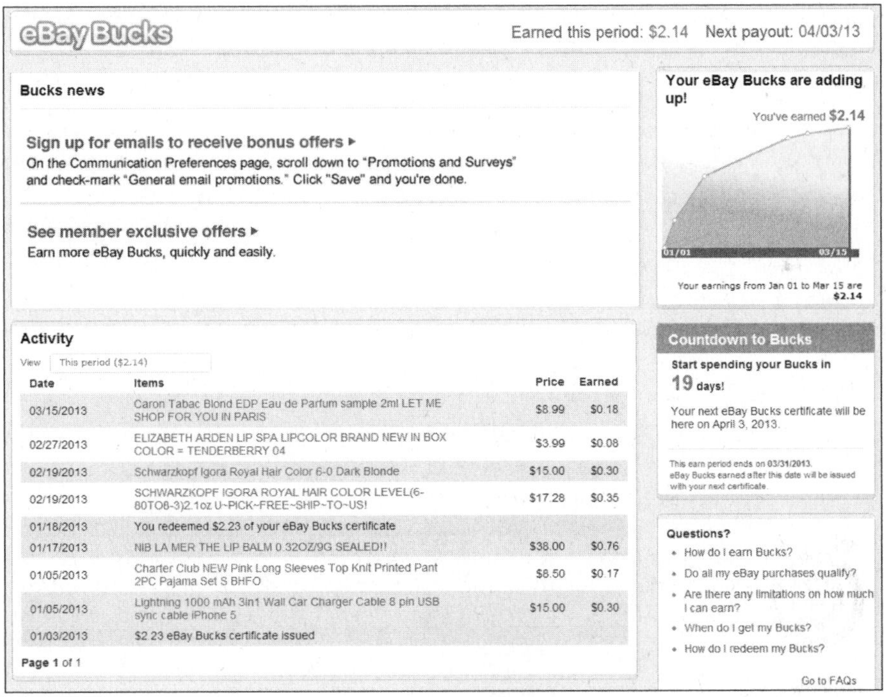

Figure 5-8:
Keep track
of your
eBay Bucks
earnings on
this page.

Organizing My eBay Lists, Searches, and Purchases

If you sell and have an interest in a few categories, eBay lists can make your search for new items easier. Saved sellers bring you back to product specialists you like, and saved searches help you track trends and find some bargains to resell on eBay.

Lists: Watch list

I'll bet you've seen an item that made you think . . .

> *I don't want to bid (or buy) this just now, but I'd like to buy it if it's a bargain!*

And you've probably seen the *Watch this item* link at the top of each listing page. Click it to add that item to your Watch list, which is available from your My eBay page.

Clicking the Watch list link from My eBay brings you to the Watch list (see Figure 5-9), one of the most powerful features of the My eBay Lists area. If you're watching items, you'll see a notation on the page, indicating how many auctions you're currently watching. This page lists each watched item with a countdown (time left) timer, so you know exactly when the auction will close. When a listing on your watch list gets close to ending, you can swoop down and make the kill — if the price is right.

Figure 5-9:
Sit back and observe with the My eBay Watch List.

Here are two great ways to use the Watch list:

✦ **As a buyer:** Are you interested in an item? You can observe the bidding action — the number of bids and how fast the price is rising (or not) — without showing your hand to the competition.

The watch-list function helps me keep my bargain-hunting quiet. Everybody knows when you're bidding on an item; nobody knows when you're watching the deals like a hawk. When you're looking for bargains to buy and resell, you may not want to tip off the competition by letting them know you're bidding.

✦ **As a seller:** Also a handy marketing tool, the Watch list allows you to store listings from competitive sellers. That way, you can monitor the status of items similar to ones you plan to sell later — and see whether the items are selling high or low, which helps you to decide whether it's a good time to sell.

Saved Searches link

A tool that comes in handy for sellers as well as buyers is the Saved Searches area of My eBay where you can accumulate a bucket load of your favorite searches. When you want to see whether any of your searched-for items are available for sale, simply click the search name. If there are no items matching your search, you see the words *Your search returned 0 items* below the search words in the list (see Figure 5-10).

Book II
Chapter 5

Using eBay's
Management Tools

☐	diane von dion *Your search returned 0 items*	Dresses	View items Edit search More actions ▾
☐	diane von domina (6.8)		View items Edit search More actions ▾
☐	diane von domino	Keywords:diane von domino	View items Edit search More actions ▾
☐	diane von heronette 6		View items Edit search More actions ▾
☐	diane von jiwon	Women's Clothing	View items Edit search More actions ▾
☐	Diane von white dress		View items Edit search More actions ▾
☐	ebay varsity jacket *Your search returned 0 items*		View items Edit search More actions ▾
☐	express ce* jeans *Your search returned 0 items*		View items Edit search More actions ▾

Figure 5-10: Items showing no results in my saved searches.

Are you always looking for certain things on eBay? For example, maybe you plan to search frequently for a Callaway Seven Heaven Wood — whatever. Add it to your list of saved searches and you won't have to type *Callaway*

Seven Heaven Wood more than once. By organizing your saved searches, you can search for your favorite items with a click of your mouse on the title links.

You can view saved searches, change them, delete them, or indicate that you'd like to receive e-mail notification when a new matching item is listed. To add an item search to the list, run a search from the search box on any eBay page and click the Save button with a star icon that appears next to your search text. The next time you reload your My eBay Saved Searches page, your new favorite search will be listed.

When you click the Save button, a window pops up, asking you to name the search and giving you the option to receive e-mails when new items match your search. Click the check box next to this option, and you won't have to go to your Saved Searches area; you'll be notified by e-mail instead (refer to Figure 5-11). eBay sends its robot to check listings each night, so you'll get a notification of new listings the next morning.

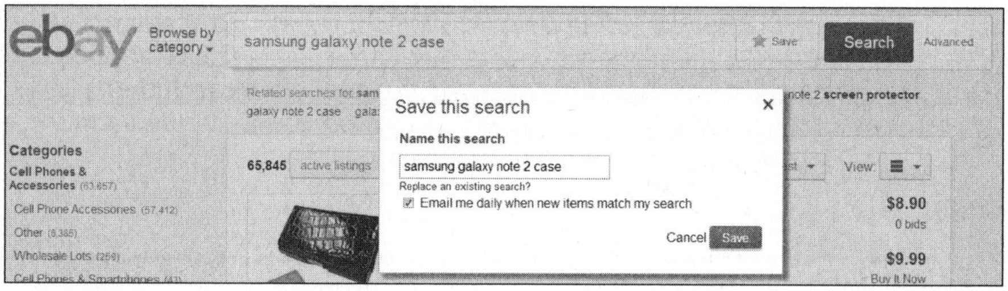

Figure 5-11: Save in your Saved searches and/or opt to receive daily e-mails notifying you.

Be sure to use all the search tricks and shortcuts I show you in the table in Chapter 1 of this minibook. These are single-line searches that you normally would perform from the search boxes on the eBay pages.

Keeping track of favorite searches is a valuable tool when you're looking for particular items to resell and want to find them at bargain prices. Also, when you have a unique collectible for sale, you can monitor the current selling prices.

Saved Sellers link

When you've been on eBay for awhile, you will find that certain sellers carry a specific type of merchandise that interests you. By saving their user IDs in the Saved Sellers area, you'll be able to revisit their current items for sale without having to run a seller search. Remember that the purpose of the My eBay page is to have all your controls in one area.

From a seller's point of view, Saved Sellers is where you can keep a list of people who sell items similar to what you sell. You can check up on them and see what they're selling, when they're selling it, and for how much. It's a helpful timing tool that can prevent you from listing a similar item at the same time of their auctions.

Saved Sellers is handy also when your competition is selling an item that you plan to sell, but at a deeply discounted price. When that happens, don't offer yours until they sell out of the item, at which time the price will most likely go back up — supply and demand, remember? I have a few quality wholesalers and liquidators under Saved Sellers, too, and search for lots that I can resell at a profit.

To add a seller to your Saved Sellers list, just go to one of their items for sale. If you are actively searching items, and find a seller with goods you like, just click the Save this Seller link in the Seller Information box on the item page.

**Book II
Chapter 5**

**Using eBay's
Management Tools**

Purchase History link

Clicking the Purchase History link in the My eBay navigation area displays all the items you've won as far back as the last 60 days, as shown in Figure 5-12. The Purchase History page is the go-to place to check on any items that you're waiting to receive. It's also a convenient way to keep track of your expenditures, especially if you are buying for resale.

If you do not see pictures next to your items, just click Edit, then Customize at the upper-right and make them appear.

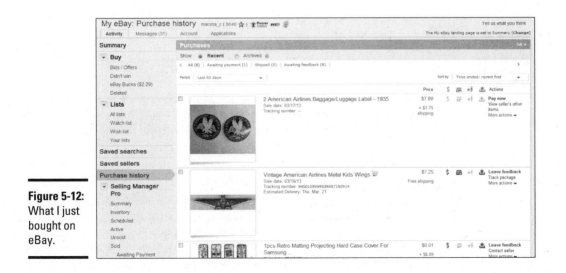

Figure 5-12:
What I just
bought on
eBay.

Helpful features on the Purchase History page include the following:

✦ **Listing title:** A link to the listing. I always use this when an item arrives so I can be sure that the item I received is exactly as advertised.

✦ **Item sale date and price paid:** Helps you remember when you purchased the item.

✦ **Estimated delivery date:** Based on the seller's mode of transit, eBay estimates how long the item should take to get to your door. If it hasn't arrived within a day or so (barring snowstorms and natural disasters), it doesn't hurt to contact the seller to check on the shipping status.

✦ **Tracking number:** When the seller has shipped, and the seller inputs the tracking number to the transaction record, the number will appear in this area. You can click the tracking number to see the progress (or delivery confirmation) of your item, as I did in Figure 5-13.

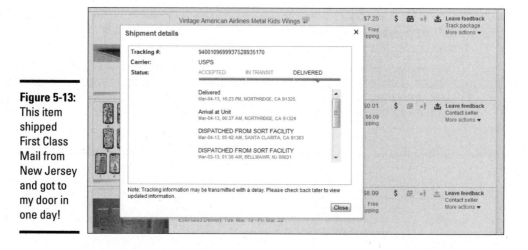

Figure 5-13: This item shipped First Class Mail from New Jersey and got to my door in one day!

✦ **Drop-down menu:** Click the More Actions drop-down menu to the far right of any item you've purchased, and you'll be able to perform actions related to your transaction. Here are some important ones:

• *Contact Seller:* This link sends you to the seller's smart answers page. If you don't see the answer to your question, you can send a message to the seller through eBay messaging.

• *Resolve a Problem:* Say the item arrives and it's not what you expected. Personally, at that point I consider it my first choice (as buyer) to contact the seller through the contact link and try to work out an issue, but if you want to use this link, the seller will receive a message subject lined with your "issue."

- *Return This Item:* If the seller has a return policy, you can use this link to initiate a return and resulting refund.

- *Sell This Item:* If you purchased the item to resell, or just figured out you really don't want it, click here and you go to a Sell an Item page.

✦ **Icons:** Each item's listing has four icons that appear dimmed until the selected action is taken. A *dollar sign* indicates whether you've paid for the item, a *star next to a pen* indicates that you've left feedback, a *small package* lets you know that the seller has notified eBay that the item has been shipped, and *an envelope with a star on top* indicates whether feedback has been left for you.

Using My eBay to manage your sales

For the new seller, the tools on the Selling pages are great. They're simple and get right to the point. To run an eBay business, small sellers can use the All Selling page with the Sell an Item form for individual listings, and these tools should be sufficient.

On the Selling page, you can view details like these for your active listings:

- **Links to listings:** Each listing title is a clickable link you can use to go instantly to an item's page.

- **Current price:** This is the starting price of your item (if you have no bids) or the current price based on bids received.

- **Reserve price:** This handy feature reminds you of the reserve price that you've set on an item. There's nowhere else to check this.

- **Quantity available:** Here's where you can see how many of the item are still available for purchase on the site. When an eBay store item is listed, this feature shows you how many are left, as well as the original quantity you listed.

- **# of bids:** When you see that the price is rising on an item, check out this column to see how many bids have been placed to date.

- **Views/Watchers:** This is the number of views your item page received, and the number of people who have selected the item for their Watch list.

- **Time left:** In this column, you can see how much time is left (to the minute) in your listing.

- **Actions:** This is the handiest column of all. Here you have a link that lets you list a similar item. This is particularly handy if you want to use a template again for another item. It also allows you to revise a listing, add to the description, end a listing, or edit promotions if you have a store.

Visit Book III, Chapter 5 for an in-depth look at how the My eBay: All Selling area can help you manage your eBay business. After you have a larger number of items for sale, I recommend you upgrade your page to eBay's free Selling Manager tool. (Find out more in the "Ramping Up with Selling Manager" section later in this chapter.)

eBay saves your transaction information for up to three years. Transactions made prior to 60 days can be viewed in your Archived purchase history. To view transactions from prior years, select the Archived radio button at the top of the list. Then, from the drop-down menu (shown in Figure 5-14), select the year you want to view.

Figure 5-14: In this view, I can view all my purchases back to 2011.

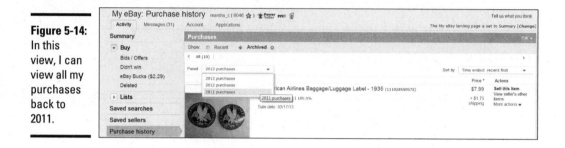

My eBay: Account Tab

The Account tab (which links to the My Account page) lets you know how much you owe eBay and how much they'll charge your credit card that month. This is a quick and easy way to check your most recent invoice, payments and credits, and your account; all these links are located in one area. You can also access your PayPal account to see, for example, when deposits were sent to your checking account.

The Account tab is also a place where you can find a drop-down menu that links to the many areas that affect your selling procedures and account data (you can see mine in Figure 5-15). This section tells you about some of the important links you'll find on this menu.

Personal Information link

Click the Personal Information link to get to the Personal Information page, which holds all the links to your personal information on eBay. This is where you can change your e-mail address, user ID (without losing your feedback), password, and credit card information — and also edit or create your About Me page. You can also change or access any registration or credit card information that you have on file at eBay. There's even a link you can use to change your home address on record.

Figure 5-15:
Links
available
from the
Account tab.

Keeping all your contact information up to date on eBay is important. If the eBay folks should ever find that any of the contact information is wrong, they may suspend your membership.

Another link, Communication Preferences, takes you to where you can specify how you want to receive information from eBay and handle your member-to-member communications.

By using the eBay mobile app, you can get instantaneous notifications on your smartphone. My personal favorite is the cash register sound I hear when someone pays for one of my items on PayPal.

Site Preferences link

A handy feature of the Site Preferences area (see Figure 5-16) is the opportunity to customize the settings you see here by clicking the Show link and then the Edit link for that preference. For example, under General Preferences, you can save extra clicks by changing preferences to keep yourself "Signed in on this computer."

You may as well click through every option every once in a while. That way, you'll be sure you have things set up just the way you want them for conducting business on eBay.

Site Preferences	Show all
Use Preferences to change your eBay settings for payment, selling, etc. With Buyer Requirements, you can block certain buyers from bidding on or purchasing your items.	
Selling Preferences	
Sell Your Item form and listings Edit your Sell Your Item form preferences and other listing preferences.	Show
Selling Manager Pro	Show
Payment from buyers Edit Checkout, PayPal, and other payment options you offer buyers.	Show
Shipping preferences Offer shipping discounts for combined purchases and create shipping calculator rate options.	Show
Promoting Similar Items on eBay Pages and Emails These preferences have been moved to Marketing Tools	Hide
Share your content Consider photos I upload in the listing process for inclusion in the eBay product catalog and other product offerings.	Show
Share your eBay items with friends You can share your items with other social networking websites.	Show
Logos and branding Display your logo and send customized emails to buyers.	Moved to Manage communications with buyers
Buyer requirements Block certain eBay buyers from bidding on or purchasing your items.	Show
Manage communications with buyers Manage your questions and answers (Q&A) Page.	Moved to Manage communications with buyers
Unpaid Item Assistant Let eBay open and close unpaid item cases for you automatically.	Show
eBay Giving Works Edit your nonprofit communication preferences.	Show
Return preferences	Show
General Preferences	
Reviews & Guides Display Reviews & Guides icon.	Show
Advertising Preferences	Hide

Figure 5-16:
My eBay Site Preferences page.

Seller Dashboard

Customer service is what it's all about when you're building and maintaining a business on eBay, so this space should be a regular stop for you. It'll keep you apprised of how you're doing with your customer service. Your average DSR (Detailed Seller Ratings) will appear in a box at the top of the page.

Each title on this page links to deeper information on your personal seller performance. There's a lot of revealing data here, so be sure to click these links regularly to see where you can improve your customer relations (and status with eBay).

If you're a Top Rated Seller, the Seller Dashboard is a very important place — because this is where you can keep track of your Final Value fee discount (which is based on your ratings). Take a look at my page (in Figure 5-17) for an example. Click the See Your Reports link near the top-right to generate reports on how your feedback has fared.

Seller dashboard				
Summary	ⓘ	**Seller performance numbers**		Updated daily ⓘ

Performance	Top-rated
PowerSeller level	Bronze
Discount	20%
Policy compliance	High
Account status	Current
FAST 'N FREE eligibility	14%

Transactions: **468**
See your reports

Average detailed seller ratings	Your average	Low ratings (1s and 2s)
Item as described	5.00	0.00% (0)
Communication	4.99	0.00% (0)
Shipping time	4.98	0.00% (0)
Shipping and handling charges	5.00	0.00% (0)

Buyer Protection cases	Your percentage (count)
Opened cases	0.00% (0)
Closed cases without seller resolution	0.00% (0)

Performance numbers are from transactions with buyers in the United States.

Seller standing ⓘ

eBay   Your performance standards on the last evaluation are Top-rated

Status: On track for 03/20/13

You met the requirements to be a Bronze PowerSeller

BRONZE

You earned 20% off final value fees on your eligible listings.
Invoice: 02/28/13 See invoice

20%

See how eBay calculates your discount.

Figure 5-17:
My Seller
Dashboard
page.

Feedback link

In Book I, I talk all about the importance of feedback to the eBay community. In the Feedback area of the Account page, you can keep track of all your feedback duties. Feedback is a most important function of your eBay transactions; don't forget to leave some for your trading partners!

When you click the Feedback link, you can see your listings from the last 90 days. You see a star to the far right of a transaction if you've left feedback. (The star will be grayed out if you haven't.) If your trading partner has left feedback for you, you see a sign in a comment-cloud icon — a plus sign means positive feedback and a minus sign means negative.

At the very bottom of the page, eBay shows you recent feedback that has been left for you. But it's much easier to click the feedback number next to your user ID to see your most recent feedback.

There's also a link on the top that takes you to the Feedback Forum, where you can perform many feedback-related functions, including these crucial two:

✦ **Reply and Follow Up:** Responding to feedback left for you is especially important, especially if the feedback is less than stellar. Every story has two sides. Make sure yours is prompt and professional.

✦ **Request Feedback Revision:** If you've solved a problem and turned an unhappy customer into a happy one, you can request that the person re-examine the feedback left earlier.

Should you want to check feedback for a specific eBay member, there's a Find a Member search box where you can type in his or her user ID and go to the Find a Member page.

Subscriptions link

Click the Subscriptions link, and you'll be able to see just which additional selling tools you're paying for. From here, you can upgrade, downgrade, or unsubscribe.

Ramping Up with Selling Manager

When you've been bitten by the selling bug, it's a natural transition to go from a monthly listing of a few items to dozens or more. When you've reached that point, you are officially running an eBay business. Congratulations!

This new level of eBay participation has a good and a bad side. The good is that you're making considerably more cash than you did before starting to sell on eBay. The bad? You have to keep closer track of the details. So it's time to start investing in tools to keep your business professional.

The first tool that can help smooth your transition makes the process of running eBay auctions and sales consistent — Selling Manager. This section tells you what Selling Manager does, but Book VIII goes into more of the app's intricacies.

Book III, Chapter 4 gets into eBay's free Turbo Lister program (it gets your items on the site without putting you through the slow, sometimes torturous Sell an Item form). As with Turbo Lister, Selling Manager is a suite of tools for managing your selling business from any computer (as long as it has an Internet connection). eBay gives these apps to sellers for free; you just have to sign up for them.

First glimpse of Selling Manager

To subscribe to your free Selling Manager app, follow these steps:

1. **On your My eBay page, click the Account tab.**

2. **Click Subscriptions in the menu that appears.**

The resulting page shows you which subscriptions are available to your account.

3. **Click the eBay Selling Manager (or Selling Manager Pro) Learn More link.**

4. **Read the information on the resulting Selling Manager page, and then click the Sign Up Now link.**

eBay's Selling Manager

Selling Manager Pro works much like Selling Manager: It replaces the Selling area of your My eBay page with its own summary of your current transactions (see the figure). Many sellers (even PowerSellers) rely on Selling Manager to handle their eBay management chores. I subscribe to Selling Manager Pro, so you'll see some additional options in the figure. Visit Book VIII, Chapter 1 to decide which version is right for you.

From Selling Manager, you can

✔ **View listing status.** You can see which sales activities you've completed and what you still have to do.

✔ **Send custom e-mail and post feedback.** Customize your e-mail templates and set up stored feedback comments to help you run through the post-sales process quickly.

✔ **Relist in bulk.** Relist multiple sold and unsold listings at once.

✔ **Maintain sales records.** See individual sales records for every transaction, including a history of the transaction status.

✔ **Print invoices and shipping labels.** Print labels and invoices directly from sales records.

✔ **Download sales history.** Export your sales records to keep files on your computer.

✔ **Keep track of items that qualify for relisting.** Relisting an item that hasn't sold may qualify for a listing fee refund when the item sells upon the second listing. There's a link in Selling Manager that will show you what qualifies.

Selling Manager Pro Summary			Last updated:Mar-17-13 16:40:47 PDT

Select a view ▾ | | | Search

Listing Improvement recommendations — Edit

We have no recommendations to improve your listings right now.

At a glance — Edit

GMS (USD)	24 hrs	7	30	90	120
$4710					
$3200					$3917.81
$2400				$3082.76	
$1600					
$800			$1035.43		
	$23.99	$140.20			

Time in days

Listing Activity — Edit

	Sales	# of Listings
Active Listings	$0.00	20
Listing with offers		0
Ending within the next hour		0
Ending today		0
Listings with questions		0
Listings with bids		0
Ended Listings (Last 90 days)		63
Duplicate listings not visible to buyers		0
Sold		6
Unsold		57
Eligible for Relist Fee credit		0
Scheduled Listings		1

Seller Dashboard Summary — Edit

Status

Performance	Top-rated
PowerSeller level	Bronze
Discount	20%
Policy compliance	High
Account status	Current

Go to your dashboard

Sold (last 90 days) — Edit

	Sales	# of Listings
All	$3,028.41	104
Awaiting Payment	$0.00	0
Buyers eligible for combined purchases		0
Awaiting Shipment	$52.48	3
Paid and waiting to give Feedback		0
Paid and Shipped	$2,975.93	101
Shipped and waiting to give Feedback		0
Resolution Center	$0.00	0
Returns	$152.00	1
Eligible for unpaid item case		0
Unpaid item cases require your response		0
Eligible for final value fee credit		0
Items not received or not as described		0

You're now subscribed to Selling Manager. eBay automatically populates Selling Manager with your information from the My eBay: Sell page. The Sell link will change to Selling Manager when it's all set up.

If you can't find the links to Selling Manager and other tools, try typing this into your browser:

```
http://pages.ebay.com/sellerinformation/sellingresources/
    sellingtools.html
```

With Selling Manager, you can click the link on your My eBay page to view a summary of all your selling activities.

The Summary page lists at-a-glance statistics so you can quickly see what's going on with your sales, at any time — from any computer. Links to other pages in the Selling Manager tool also appear on the Summary page.

If you plan to exceed 100 transactions a month, consider using Selling Manager Pro, which costs $15.99 per month. The Pro version has bulk feedback and bulk invoice-printing features and incorporates inventory management.

Scheduled link

The Scheduled link on the Summary page takes you to any auction, fixed-price listing, or store listing you've sent to eBay through Turbo Lister (or listed on the Sell an Item page) and scheduled as pending for a later starting date or time. In addition, you can view, edit, or reschedule these pending listings through a link on the Summary page.

When you enter the Scheduled Listings area by clicking the Scheduled link on the Summary page, you can go directly to the listing. If you want to promote your listing-to-be in social media (or create a link to it from elsewhere on the Internet), you can do so using the URL of the pending listing.

From this page, you can confirm all information about pending sales, as well as make any changes to the listing or to the scheduling time.

Active link

Click the Active link under Sell on the Summary page, and you can observe the bidding action just as you can from the Sell page. The color coding that indicates bidding activity works the same way as on the Sell page, and links to your listings are accessible with a click of your mouse.

For more about active listings, visit the Summary page, which includes links to items ending within the hour and those ending within the next 24 hours.

Sold in Selling Manager

The Sold feature (which you get to by clicking the link on the Summary page), is where Selling Manager really shines. You'll find quite a few handy links here, including these:

✦ **Awaiting payment:** This is where items that have been won or bought are listed before a payment is made.

✦ **Awaiting payment, buyers eligible for combined purchases:** When a customer buys more than one item from you, the transactions will show up here. By clicking this area, you can easily combine the transactions for several items into a single invoice, to give the buyer the benefit of a reduced shipping cost. (Also, by combining purchases, the buyer will pay only once through PayPal, and you'll be charged only one transaction fee, versus multiple).

✦ **Awaiting shipment:** If you input the fact that a buyer has sent payment, or if the buyer pays using PayPal, the transaction automatically moves to this category.

✦ **Paid and waiting to give feedback:** Once an item is paid for, a reference to it appears here so you can keep track of the feedback you need to leave.

✦ **Paid and shipped:** These are (you guessed it) items that the buyer has paid for and that you've indicated as shipped on the transaction record.

Book II
Chapter 5

Using eBay's
Management Tools

Archived link

From the Archived link, you can access completed transactions that you have set to archive in the Sold area. You can also download this information to your computer. These are good records, so download them and keep them.

To indicate that you've shipped an item, click the record number next to the item and scroll down to the Sales Status & Memo area. Click Save, and the record moves from the Paid and Ready to Ship page (under Sold Listings) to the Paid and Shipped page.

Tracking payments from eBay's Selling Manager

Selling Manager makes many selling processes considerably easier. The number to the right of the Paid and Ready to Ship link on the Summary page indicates that you have items ready to ship. To see the details on these items, just click this link. You see each transaction; a bold dollar-sign icon to the right of a listing confirms that a payment has been made.

Book III

Selling Like a Pro

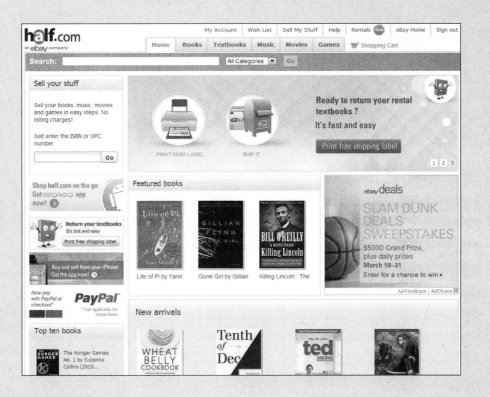

Contents at a Glance

Chapter 1: Be Sure Your Listings Make Cents

In This Chapter

✔ **Knowing the costs of selling an item**

✔ **Getting more punch with options**

✔ **Figuring Final Value Fees**

✔ **Understanding the different types of auctions**

✔ **Including PayPal costs**

✔ **Knowing hidden shipping and handling expenses**

Selling on eBay is a good idea for anyone. You clean out your garage, sell things you might have thrown away anyway, and make a profit. What a wonderful marketplace! You can make money in your spare time and enhance your lifestyle with just a few clicks on your keyboard and mouse.

When you decide to sell on eBay in earnest, however, you can run into problems. Few eBay sellers have a background in retailing or marketing, and eBay is all about retailing and marketing. In this chapter, I give you tips on pricing strategies. The first item on the agenda is to understand all the fees involved with running an e-business on eBay.

Keeping an Eye on Where the Pennies Go

It doesn't seem so much to list an item, plus pay a small Final Value Fee. Of course, a few cents (maybe dollars) go to PayPal. One by one, these minute amounts tend to breeze by even the most experienced seller. You don't really see your eBay fees, because they're not directly deducted from your sales. eBay bills you at the end of the month. It's easy to lose track of your costs unless you are keeping *very* good books (more about tracking costs in Book IX, Chapter 3).

Be sure you're making a profit

I recently purchased a selection of women's apparel to sell. My cost per item was $9.99. To remain competitive, I offered free shipping, which probably will cost me another $4 (including the cost of the mailer). Other eBay sellers smartly zeroed in on the same items of apparel — and I don't mind the competition — as long as my items sell. But some of the other sellers didn't continue to be so smart and may be cheating themselves out of money. They priced their listings at $14.99 and offered free shipping. At this point, I have to say: Do the math. Is it worth the time to source an item and then sell it for just a few pennies profit? Not in my book. When you price your items, price them within the going market. Selling an item cheaply will not give you an ROI (return on investment) that will make you happy in the long run. Truth.

All those nickels, dimes, and quarters add up. The hundreds (thousands?) of people who are selling items on the site for $1 can't be making much of a profit — not even enough for a pack of gum! To avoid this low-profit trap, you must be keenly aware of every penny you spend on listing fees, Final Value Fees, listing options, and PayPal fees.

Becoming complacent and blithely ignoring your eBay costs as you list items for sale can be easy to do. As a person in business for yourself, you must take into account outgoing expenses as well as incoming revenues. The cost of your initial listing (does your time to write and photograph not have a cost?) is just the beginning of your advertising budget for that item. You have to factor in the cost of all the listing options and features you use as well. After all that, you also pay a Final Value Fee to eBay after the item sells. (For fees regarding your eBay Store, check out Book VIII, Chapter 4.)

In this section, I review the costs for listing an item to sell on eBay. But if you use a credit card payment service, those folks also charge a fee. Later in this chapter, I examine the costs of some popular credit card payment services.

Insertion (listing) fees

If you don't have an eBay store, you are entitled to 50 free listings per calendar month (beginning at 12:00:00am Pacific Time on the first day of each month and ending at 11:59:59 pm Pacific Time on the last day of the month). That means the listings are free of *insertion fees*. After that, the fee is a straightforward $.30 per listing, whether it's a fixed-price listing or an auction. Adding extra listing features adds more to the listing fee. For example, when you place a reserve on an auction, you're charged an insertion listing upgrade fee based on the *amount* of the reserve price.

Free listings are not available in the Real Estate, Motors: Boats, Cars & Trucks, Motorcycles, Other Vehicles & Trailers, and Powersports, and some Business & Industrial categories.

What listings count toward your free limit? See the following:

✦ New listings (whether auction or fixed price)

✦ Relisted items when eligible (that is, when you relist an item that didn't sell the first time)

✦ Listings ended early, or those that eBay ends early due to an eBay policy violation

✦ Duplicate identical auction listings (even if one or more of those listings are removed for policy violation by eBay)

If your item doesn't sell, you do have the option of relisting your unsuccessful item. Your relisted item will count as an additional listing for the month. Writing a better title, starting with a lower opening bid, or adding a snappier description and better pictures may help in selling the item.

Reserve-price auction fees

In a *reserve-price auction,* you're able to set an undisclosed minimum price for which your item will sell, thereby giving yourself a safety net. Figure 1-1 shows an auction in which the reserve has not yet been met. Using a reserve-price auction protects the investment you have in an item. If, at the end of the auction, no bidder has met your undisclosed reserve price, you aren't obligated to sell the item and the high bidder isn't required to purchase the item.

Figure 1-1:
Never mind the reserve — I can't afford the starting bid.

2010 Lamborghini Gallardo 2dr LP560-4
Lamborghini Gallardo Twin Turbo 1250 Horsepower Silver Convertible Low Mileage

Item Location:	Henderson, Nevada, United States
Time left:	4d 00h (Mar 31, 2013 14:53:20 PDT)
Bid history:	0 bids

Starting bid: **US $269,999.00**
Reserve not met

Your maximum bid: US $ [   ] Place bid

(Enter US $269,999.00 or more)

Add to Watch list

Enlarge   Get low monthly payments

Second chance to sell!

If your auction goes above the target sales price and you have more of the item in stock, you can offer items in stock to your underbidders. The figure shows you where you can click from your My eBay Sold Items area to make a Second Chance Offer. Click to offer the item to under-bidders for their most recent high bids. You will

also find a link to make a Second Chance offer on the Closed Item page.

You will be charged only Final Value Fees — not a second relisting (insertion) fee — if the person purchases the item. The second chance offer will also not count toward your free listings per month.

TITANIC J Peterman HEART OF THE OCEAN Necklace COA 20th Century Fox Prop Replica

Winning bid: **US $660.00**

Bidders: 8   Bids: 20   Time Ended: Apr-17-12 16:44:06 PDT   Duration: 5 days

Your item sold for US $660.00

Only actual bids (not automatic bids generated up to a bidder's maximum) are shown. Automatic bids may be placed days or hours before a listing ends. Learn more about bidding.

Show automatic bids

Bidder (show email addresses)	Bid Amount	Bid Time	Location*	Shipment Status	Action
(275)	US $660.00	Apr-17-12 16:44:00 PDT	United Kingdom	--	**Send invoice** **More actions ▾**
(13)	US $650.00	Apr-17-12 11:11:01 PDT	Belgium	--	Send second chance offer
(57)	US $600.00	Apr-16-12 13:32:19 PDT	United Kingdom	--	Send second chance offer
(26)	US $580.00	Apr-16-12 07:09:59 PDT	Canada	--	Send second chance offer
(57)	US $555.00	Apr-16-12 13:14:27 PDT	United Kingdom	--	Send second chance offer
(25)	US $550.00	Apr-15-12 15:16:42 PDT	Canada	--	Send second chance offer
(13)	US $520.00	Apr-15-12 07:14:10 PDT	Belgium	--	Send second chance offer
(57)	US $502.00	Apr-15-12 14:04:07 PDT	United Kingdom	--	Send second chance offer
(13)	US $500.00	Apr-15-12 07:07:05 PDT	Belgium	--	Send second chance offer
(57)	US $480.00	Apr-15-12 07:31:49 PDT	United Kingdom	--	Send second chance offer
(57)	US $465.00	Apr-15-12 07:31:31 PDT	United Kingdom	--	Send second chance offer
(774)	US $411.00	Apr-14-12 13:04:31 PDT	92647-6991	--	Send second chance offer
(168)	US $410.00	Apr-14-12 20:12:28 PDT	91733-2733	--	Send second chance offer

For example, if you have a rare coin to sell, you can start the bidding at a low price to attract bidders to click your auction and read your description. If you start your bidding at too high a price, you might dissuade prospective bidders from even looking at your auction, and you won't tempt them even to bid. They may feel that the final selling price will be too high for their budgets. You want to get the auction fever going with lots of bidders!

Everyone on eBay is looking for a deal or a truly rare item. If you can combine the mystical force of both of these needs in one auction, you have something special. The reserve-price auction enables you to attempt — and perhaps achieve — this feat.

The reserve-price auction is a safety net for the seller but often an uncomfortable guessing game for the prospective bidder. To alleviate buyer anxiety, many sellers put reserve prices in the item description, allowing bidders to decide whether the item will fit into their bidding budgets.

Should you have a change of heart, you can lower or even remove your reserve price after you receive a bid on the item.

Placing a reserve price on one of your auctions means that the item will not sell until the bidding reaches the reserve price. When your reserve-price item does sell, you've sold your item at a profit (let's hear it for optimism!). The reserve fee is based on the reserve price you set, as outlined in Table 1-1, so be sure to set the reserve high enough to cover the fee and *still* give you a profit.

Why not spell out the amount of your reserve price within your listing description? That way, there's a good chance the buyers will know what they're in for. Why not also offer free shipping in a reserve auction to take the edge off.

Book III
Chapter 1

Table 1-1	eBay Reserve Auction Fees*
Starting Price ($)	*Fee*
0.01–199.99	$2.00
200.00 and up	1% of reserve price (maximum of $50.00)

Reserve fee for eBay Motors is a flat $15.00.

If your item doesn't sell the first time with a low starting price and a reserve, you can always relist it at a slightly higher starting price without a reserve.

eBay's Optional Listing Features

eBay listings have many options and upgrades. Figure 1-2 shows how even a random search on eBay listings can yield examples of some very popular listing options.

Figure 1-2:
A search
showing
eBay option
upgrades.

When you come to the point in listing your item that brings you to eBay's optional listing features, you see the headline, "Get more bids with these optional features! Make your item stand out from the crowd!" Sounds pretty good, doesn't it? But getting carried away by these options is easy — and can lead to spending all your expected profits before you earn them.

When I was teaching eBay University's Advanced Selling class, I quoted statistical success rates for the different features, but in the real life of *your* business, success varies from item to item and category to category.

If you take the boldface option and then your listing appears in a category full of boldface titles, the bold just doesn't have the potential to boost your return on investment. In fact, your listing might stand out more *without* the bold option.

I recap the cost of the various eBay listing options in Table 1-2. Weigh the pros and cons in terms of how these options affect your eBay business. Will spending a little extra money enhance your item enough to justify the extra cost? Will you be able to make the money back in profits? You must have a good understanding of what the options are — and when and how you can use them to fullest advantage.

Table 1-2	eBay Listing Upgrade Fees		
Option	*Auction All Durations*	*Fixed Price 3, 5, 7, and 10 day*	*Fixed Price 30 day and "Good Til Cancelled"*
Subtitle	$0.50	$0.50	$1.50
Bold	$2.00	$2.00	$4.00
Listing Designer (FREE to Selling Manager Pro Subscribers)	$0.10	$0.10	$0.30
Gallery Plus	$0.35	$0.35	$1.00
Buy It Now (Auction Only - FREE to non-Store Subscribers)	$0.01–$9.99: $0.05; $10–$24.99: $0.10; $25–$49.99: $0.20; $50. and up: $0.25		
International Site Visibility	$0.01–$9.99: $0.10; $10.–$49.99: $0.20; $50. and up: $0.40	$0.50	$0.50
List in two categories	Double insertion and Listing Upgrade fees		
Value Pack (Gallery Plus, Listing Designer & Subtitle)	$0.65	$0.65	$2.00
Ten-day duration	$0.40	$0.40	

When doing business on eBay, you may have to pay a store fee, an insertion fee, and a Final Value Fee. If you accept credit card payments, you must pay an additional fee to the payment service. Estimate your expenses from these basics before you consider spending money for advertising.

**Book III
Chapter 1**

**Be Sure Your
Listings Make Cents**

Subtitle

You may use a maximum of 80 characters for your item's title. Title search is the de facto search standard on eBay. From the statistics I've seen during years on the site, more than 98 percent of searches were made for title only, versus title and description. So how can you make your item stand out when it shows up with hundreds of other items that look the same? Use the subtitle option!

Notice the subtitle under one of the listings in Figure 1-3. This is your opportunity to add just enough tantalizing text to your listing — text that is readable by prospective buyers as they quickly scan search results or browse category offerings. Subtitles work very well if you are one of several sellers selling the same item at a similar price — it sets your listing apart from the others. A caveat: This additional text will be picked up in a search only if the person chooses to search both titles *and* descriptions, but will be visible on any page where your item shows up. The fee for this option is $.50 to $1.50.

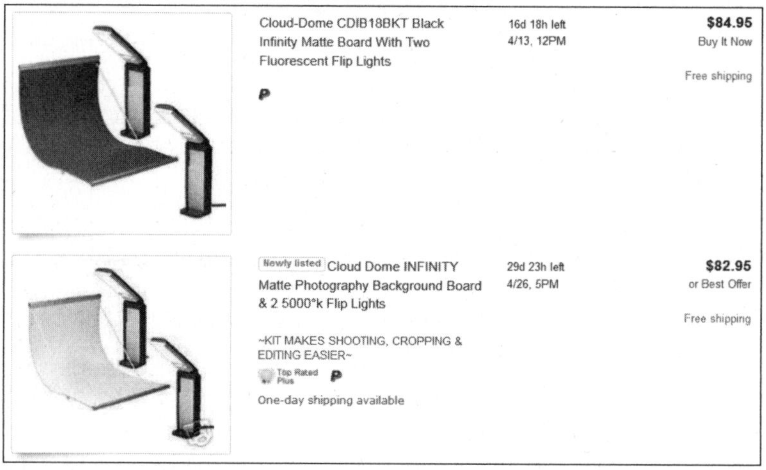

Figure 1-3:
I set my items apart from the competition by using subtitles.

Cloud-Dome CDIB18BKT Black
Infinity Matte Board With Two
Fluorescent Flip Lights

16d 18h left
4/13, 12PM

$84.95
Buy It Now

Free shipping

Newly listed Cloud Dome INFINITY
Matte Photography Background Board
& 2 5000°k Flip Lights

29d 23h left
4/26, 5PM

$82.95
or Best Offer

Free shipping

~KIT MAKES SHOOTING, CROPPING &
EDITING EASIER~

Top Rated
Plus

One-day shipping available

When your item has something special about it or could use some extra description, the subtitle option allows you more space to give the browsing shopper vital information.

Listing Designer

eBay comes up with options to fill the needs (or wants, in this case) of users. Some sellers enjoy putting colorful graphics around their descriptions. Listing Designer will include pretty graphics and help you design your description, placing pictures in different places on the page. But if you have a good description (creatively done with HTML color and emphasis) plus a good picture (inserted creatively with the HTML code I give you in Book V), your item will draw bids just the same as if you spent $.10extra (per listing) for the Listing Designer option.

I offer a "Cool *Free* Ad Tool" in the Tools area of my `coolebaytools.com` website that allows you to give your description some structure (and will insert a web-hosted photo where you might want to add some text). Thousands of my readers are using it every day; please do, with my compliments!

If you want your descriptions surrounded by graphics, just make sure that the graphics within your description aren't too large. Otherwise the pages load too slowly over some connections.

Using a graphics template to brand your listings on eBay, giving them a uniform look is a great idea. If you want to use a template, decide on one and make it your trademark.

Boldface

The Boldface option is a favorite and probably the most-used option in the eBay stable. A listing title in **boldface type** stands out in a crowd, unless . . . you got it, unless it's in a category loaded with boldface titles. If the $2 to $4 that eBay charges for this benefit is in your budget, odds are it will get you a good deal more views than if you didn't use it.

Applying boldface to your item title spices it up and pulls it off the page right into the reader's eye. Unfortunately, bold type tacks an additional $2 to $4 onto your listing cost — so you'd better be in a position to make a good profit from the item. Also make sure your research shows that the item can sell for your target price.

View counter

Counters have become a popular free option in the online world. Placed on your page when you list your item, the counter ticks up each time someone loads your page from eBay. A counter can impress bidders and convince them they're viewing a hot deal. It can also impress other sellers to run out and sell the identical item.

A counter is a terrific tool for marketing your auctions — sometimes. If you have an auction with no bids and a counter that reads a high number, newbie bidders may be dissuaded from taking a flyer and bidding on your auction. Their thinking goes something like this: If that many people looked at this auction and didn't bid, something must be wrong with the item. They'll tend to doubt their own instincts as to what is and isn't a good deal.

In a situation such as this, however, what might be going on is that savvy bidders are just watching your auction, waiting to bid at the last minute.

A *hidden counter* shields the numbers from the eyes of casual lookie-loos. The figures are available only to you in the Active listings area of your My eBay page.

Buy It Now

The Buy It Now feature for auctions, shown in Figure 1-4, has a few significant benefits. If you have a target price for the item you're listing, make that your Buy It Now price. You can also use this option during frenzied holiday shopping times or with hot items. Be sure to stay within the rules and post a Buy It Now price of at least 30 percent above your opening bid and perhaps you'll get a bite, er, sale.

Figure 1-4: See the Buy It Now button just below the Place Bid button?

The Buy It Now feature disappears when someone bids on the item or, if you've placed a reserve on the auction, when a bidder meets your reserve price. To use this feature, you must have a feedback rating of at least 10 and have a PayPal account in good standing.

Adding the Final Value Fees

eBay's version of the Hollywood back-end deal is the Final Value Fee. Big stars get a bonus when their movies do well at the box office; eBay gets a cut when your item sells. When the revenue is posted, eBay charges the Final

Value Fee to your account in a matter of seconds. Then, if you don't have an eBay Store, you pay a flat 10 percent of your final selling price including any shipping you charge the buyer.

If you have an eBay Store, the fee varies by category. You can find the Final Value Fee structure for eBay Stores in Book VIII, Chapter 5.

A classified ad in the Real Estate category is *not* charged a Final Value Fee, and eBay doesn't charge a percentage Final Value Fee on an auction in the Real Estate category as in other categories. You pay a flat FVF of $35 for Timeshares and Land and no FVF for Commercial or Residential. But in the Automotive category, you pay a flat Successful Transaction Services Fee of $125 for vehicles if your auction ends with a winning bidder (and the reserve has been met).

When you're selling a vehicle (car, truck, or RV) through eBay Motors, you're getting a great deal as a seller: You pay $0 to list your item, and the successful listing fee is only $125 when the item sells.

Know Your Options in Auctions

An auction is an auction is an auction, right? Wrong! eBay has four types of auctions for your selling pleasure. Most of the time you'll run traditional auctions, but other auctions have their special uses, too. After you've been selling on eBay for a while, you may find that one of the other types of auctions better suits your needs. In this section, I review these auctions so you fully understand what they are and when to use them.

Traditional auctions

Traditional auctions are what made eBay famous. You can run a traditional auction for 1, 3, 5, 7, or 10 days, and when the auction closes, the highest bidder wins. I'm sure you've bid on several and won at least a few. I bet you've also made money running some of your own.

You begin the auction with an opening bid, and bidders will bid up your opening price into a healthy profit for you (I hope).

Best Offer

If you've got a fixed-price listing, you can opt to insert a button under your sales price that encourages buyers to make you an offer on your item. This is probably one of the oldest sales methods around. (In some countries, it's an insult to buy something at the posted price; haggling is part of their retail culture.)

So, if you love the thrill of haggling (I don't, really), you can insert the Make Offer button in your listings at no extra charge. See Figure 1-5 for an example. When someone makes an offer on one of your items, eBay sends you an e-mail asking that you reply regarding whether the proposed price is acceptable to you.

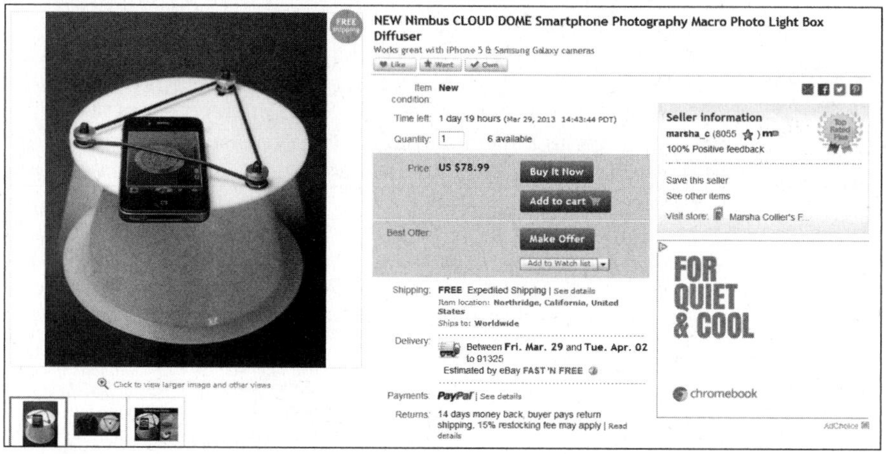

Figure 1-5:
Maybe I'll make a deal on this.

[Screen capture of eBay listing: NEW Nimbus CLOUD DOME Smartphone Photography Macro Photo Light Box Diffuser. Works great with iPhone 5 & Samsung Galaxy cameras. Item condition: New. Time left: 1 day 19 hours (Mar 29, 2013 14:43:44 PDT). Quantity: 1, 6 available. Price: US $78.99. Buy It Now. Add to cart. Best Offer: Make Offer. Add to Watch list. Shipping: FREE Expedited Shipping. Item location: Northridge, California, United States. Ships to: Worldwide. Delivery: Between Fri. Mar. 29 and Tue. Apr. 02 to 91325. Estimated by eBay FAST 'N FREE. Payments: PayPal. Returns: 14 days money back, buyer pays return shipping, 15% restocking fee may apply. Seller information: marsha_c (8055) 100% Positive feedback. Save this seller. See other items. Visit store: Marsha Collier's F. FOR QUIET & COOL chromebook.]

Restricted access auctions

eBay won't allow certain items to be sold in nonrestricted categories, so you must list them in the Adult Only category of eBay. eBay makes it easy for the user to find or avoid these types of items by making this area accessible only after the user agrees to the terms and conditions of the area, as shown in Figure 1-6.

Items in the Adult Only category are not openly accessible through the regular eBay title search, nor are they listed in Newly Listed Items. Anyone who participates in auctions for items in the Adult Only category on eBay, whether as a bidder or a seller, must have a credit card on file on eBay for verification.

Do not attempt to slip an adults-only auction into a nonrestricted category. eBay doesn't have a sense of humor when it comes to this violation of policy, and may relocate or end your auction. eBay might even suspend you from its site.

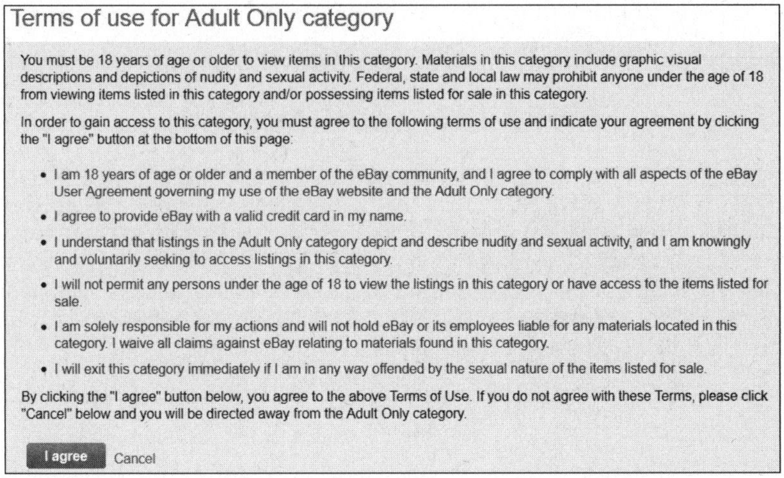

Terms of use for Adult Only category

You must be 18 years of age or older to view items in this category. Materials in this category include graphic visual descriptions and depictions of nudity and sexual activity. Federal, state and local law may prohibit anyone under the age of 18 from viewing items listed in this category and/or possessing items listed for sale in this category.

In order to gain access to this category, you must agree to the following terms of use and indicate your agreement by clicking the "I agree" button at the bottom of this page:

- I am 18 years of age or older and a member of the eBay community, and I agree to comply with all aspects of the eBay User Agreement governing my use of the eBay website and the Adult Only category.

- I agree to provide eBay with a valid credit card in my name.

- I understand that listings in the Adult Only category depict and describe nudity and sexual activity, and I am knowingly and voluntarily seeking to access listings in this category.

- I will not permit any persons under the age of 18 to view the listings in this category or have access to the items listed for sale.

- I am solely responsible for my actions and will not hold eBay or its employees liable for any materials located in this category. I waive all claims against eBay relating to materials found in this category.

- I will exit this category immediately if I am in any way offended by the sexual nature of the items listed for sale.

By clicking the "I agree" button below, you agree to the above Terms of Use. If you do not agree with these Terms, please click "Cancel" below and you will be directed away from the Adult Only category.

I agree   Cancel

Figure 1-6:
You must agree to the legalities to enter the Adult Only category.

Private listings

The eBay Advanced Search page features an area where you can conduct a bidder search. You can find a list of the items that you've bid on in the past 30 days. Anyone not signing in on your eBay account sees a list of only the items you've won — but that's no real help. One December, my daughter told me that she didn't want a particular item — something that I had just bid on — for Christmas. My creative daughter had been regularly perusing my bidding action on eBay to see what I was buying for the holidays! A private listing would have kept my shopping secret.

Private sales also work well for the buyers who avail themselves of the services of the psychics, card readers, and fortune tellers on eBay and don't want their friends to think they are . . . well, you know. Sometimes it's just best to keep things quiet. No one needs to know just how much you choose to pay for something. As a seller, you have the option (at no extra charge) of listing your item as private.

The private auction is a useful tool for sellers who are selling bulk lots to other sellers. It maintains the privacy of the bidders, and customers can't do a bidder search to find out what sellers are paying for the loot they plan to resell on eBay.

AUCTION ANECDOTE

Not quite adult enough . . .

I was surprised to see a private auction listed on one of my favorite eBay seller's list. She usually doesn't sell items like "Fringe Black BRA 36B SEXY SEXY SEXY," so I looked through this seller's past auctions. I saw that she didn't get any bids when she listed the bra in the restricted (adults-only) area of eBay in the category Everything Else: Mature Audiences: Clothing, Accessory. When she put the bra up for private auction in the category Clothing & Accessories: Women's Clothing: Lingerie: Bras: General, she got five bidders and sold the item. I guess it wasn't sexy enough for the "adult" crowd!

The private auction can save you the potential embarrassment associated with buying a girdle or the tie that flips over to reveal a racy half-nude on the back.

Although the private auction is a useful tool, it may intimidate a novice user. If your customer base comes from experienced eBay users and you're selling an item that may benefit by being auctioned in secret, you might want to try this option.

PayPal Gets Its Cut

When you've sold your item, do you think that's the end of the fees? Nope! If your customer pays using PayPal, you're faced with additional fees. However, having a PayPal Premier or Business account is important for building your commerce for these reasons:

+ eBay buyers look for the PayPal option because it offers them a high level of protection against fraud.

+ Most customers prefer to pay with a credit card, either to delay the expense or to have complete records of their purchases.

+ From a seller's point of view, using PayPal can be cheaper than having a direct-merchant credit card account.

+ PayPal helps with your paperwork by offering downloadable logs of your sales that include all PayPal fees. eBay fees are not included; you're on your own for the recordkeeping on those.

A PayPal Business account requires the account to be registered in a business name. A Premier account allows you to do business under your own name.

Check out Book II, Chapter 4, which covers the PayPal services and fees in depth.

Setting Sensible Shipping Costs

Buyers who visit the eBay site are bargain shoppers. They want to get their items at the lowest possible prices. They're also more cognizant about the "hidden" expense buried in the item's shipping and handling fees. When you set these fees, you must take into account every expense involved in your packing and shipping. You can't make your shipping area a losing proposition.

However, many eBay sellers have increased their shipping prices to outrageous amounts. But when the shipping fee equals a third of the item's cost, a prospective bidder may think twice about placing a bid. Of course, if the item is big or the buyer wants it fast, he or she may feel better about paying higher shipping costs.

eBay penalizes sellers who charge high shipping fees and rewards sellers who offer Free Shipping by giving the free shippers better visibility in the Best Match search results. Try listing your item by including the shipping amount in your selling price and offer Free Shipping. Then offer buyers a second shipping option for Priority Mail (faster shipping) at a charge. Your item will still get the benefit of eBay's Free Shipping search preference.

Business is business, and when you're on eBay to make a profit, every penny counts. In this section, I tell you how to evaluate all the costs involved with packing and shipping the items you sell. I also show you how to use the tools at your disposal — such as eBay's shipping calculator — to make the best decisions about how much to charge your buyers for shipping costs.

Forewarned is smart

After you know all the eBay fees involved in selling your item, you can play around with the pricing and figure out how much your Buy It Now (or target selling) price should be. Remember to include the following costs when pricing your items:

- ✔ How much you paid for the item you want to resell

- ✔ The "Freight In" amount (the cost of shipping the item to you)

- ✔ The cost of shipping the item to your buyer

For information on organizing your shipping area, be sure to read Book VII.

When calculating shipping costs, don't assume that all you have to worry about is just the cost of your postage. You also have per-item costs for boxes, padded mailers, shipping tape, labels, and pickup or service fees from your carriers. Now and again, you may even pay the college kid across the street five bucks to schlep your boxes for you. Expenses show up in the strangest places.

In addition to adding up the packing and shipping supplies, you need to amortize the monthly fees from any online postage shipping services. Should you occasionally pay for a pickup from the carrier, you need to add that expense to the shipping charges, too. The following list runs down some of the expenses involved:

+ **Padded bubble mailers:** Select an average-size padded mailer that works for several types of items you sell. Selecting a few average sizes for all your products works well because it's cheaper to buy in quantity. Even if a few of your items could fit in the next-size-down mailers, buying the bigger size by the case gives you a considerable discount. Why keep five sizes of mailers in stock in quantities of 100 if you don't have to? If you don't use all the bigger ones, you can always sell them. And besides, padded envelopes don't go bad.

  Don't be misled by packaging suppliers' claims of low-cost mailers. They *usually* don't include the shipping costs in these price estimates.

  When you price your cost-per-piece, be sure to include (as part of your cost) what you have to pay to get the item shipped to you. For example, if you purchase your mailers — say #4s (9½ x 14½) — by the hundred, they may cost you $.39 each. If you buy a case of 500, they may cost only $.29 each. By buying in quantity, you save $.10 per mailing envelope! The more business you do, the more significant the savings.

+ **Packing peanuts:** I must admit that storing all those packing peanuts is a real drag. But here's where buying in bulk equates to huge cost savings. I just checked one of my favorite vendors, www.bubblefast.com, and found a *free-shipping* offer. From Bubblefast, you can purchase antistatic packing peanuts in lots of various sizes:

  3.5 cubic feet for $11.25 = $3.21 per cubic foot

  7 cubic feet for $21.90 = $3.13 per cubic foot

  14 cubic feet for $42.00 = $3.00 per cubic foot

  It's no surprise that the 14-cubic-foot deal turns out to be the most economical. eBay sellers such as Bubblefast sell packing peanuts for almost *half* what they cost when purchased from a brick-and-mortar retailer.

(That's because a store you can walk into has to use up square footage to store these babies, which means a higher cost.)

Here, in a nutshell (sorry, I couldn't resist), is my solution to peanut storage: Fill a drawstring-type trash bag with packing peanuts, and then tie the drawstring. Screw some cup hooks into the rafters of your garage and hang the bags from the rafters. You can store a bunch of peanuts there! *Be sure to recycle!*

✦ **Packing tape:** You need a stock of clear packing tape. The common size for a roll is 2 inches wide by 110 feet long. Shipping tape comes in two thicknesses, 1.6 mil and 2 mil; the heavier tape makes a better seal in larger packages and costs pennies more. I searched eBay and found these deals on 2 mil tape, the following prices *include* shipping:

> 6 rolls = $14.98 = $ 2.50 per roll
>
> 12 rolls = $21.45 = $ 1.79 per roll
>
> 18 rolls = $26.45 = $1.47 per roll

Again, compare prices before buying.

✦ **Boxes:** I won't take you through the various costs of boxes because *hundreds* of sizes are available. Shop eBay (but often the shipping prices are too high), and also check out www.uline.com for boxes at reasonable prices. For the example, let's just say a typical box will cost $.55 each.

✦ **G&A (general and administrative) costs:** For the uninitiated (translation: you never had to do budgets at a large corporation), G&A represents the costs incurred in running a company. But the principle is familiar: Time is money. For example, the time it takes you to research the costs of mailers, tapes, and boxes on eBay is costing you money. The time it takes you to drive to the post office costs you money. You won't actually put a figure on this just now, but it's something you need to think about — especially if you spend half an hour at the post office every other day. In effect, that's time wasted. You could be finding new sources of merchandise instead.

✦ **Online postage service:** If you're paying around $10 a month for the convenience of buying and printing online postage, that's an expense too. If you ship 100 packages a month, that amortizes to $.10 per package.

If you're questioning whether you need an online postage service, here's my two cents: Being able to hand your packages to the postal carrier beats standing in line at the post office, and having records of all your shipments on your own computer is worth the monthly fee.

Table 1-4 shows you the cost for mailing a tiny padded envelope cushioned with packing peanuts. Before you even put postage on the package, you could possibly be spending $.52 — not including your time.

Table 1-4	**Sample Shipping Costs**
Item	*Estimated Cost per Shipment ($)*
Padded mailer	0.29
Peanuts	0.07
Tape	0.02
Mailing label	0.04
Postage service	0.10
Total	0.52

If you're shipping many packages a month, read Book IX, which tells you how to use QuickBooks to easily and simply track your shipping costs.

Chapter 2: Understanding the Finer Points of Selling

In This Chapter

✔ **Discovering successful selling strategies**

✔ **Selling in other areas of eBay**

✔ **Following the rules**

E-commerce has made a turnaround. When eBay CEO, John Donahoe, joined the company eight years ago, auctions were in a rut. And as the brick-and-mortar businesses opened online web stores, shoppers looked for more traditional transactions. Customers wanted to just "buy" products.

On today's eBay, 70 percent of all items are sold at fixed prices (this includes Buy It Now listings), and 30 percent of its sales are auctions. This is not to say that auctions (for the time being) are not popular; many high-dollar profits are made from auctioning unique, rare, and high-demand items. Understanding how eBay sales work is important to anyone who wants to sell on the site.

You can buy the "inside secrets" of eBay from lots of places; e-books and webinars abound these days. Some of these authors and instructors try to convince you that only *they* have the surreptitious bits of knowledge — gleaned from years (months?) of experience on the site — that reveal what's Really Going On. Truth be told, the online e-commerce market changes so quickly that eBay can barely keep up with it — the profile of the online shopper changes constantly. How likely is it that anybody has the ultimate answer?

Sure, you hear mysterious rumors of the way to sure-fire profits (cue up *The X-Files* theme in the background). Start an auction at a certain day and time, run a fixed-price listing a certain amount of days, and you'll automatically make more money? Puh-leez! The only one who rakes in profits with that information is the guy who's selling it to you! In addition to reflecting market deviations, eBay changes its search metrics continually — so there is no hard-and-fast answer for securing high profits.

Before deciding to hire an eBay mentor or pay for a program; ask for the mentor's or instructor's eBay User ID. By taking a look at the type(s) of items the person sells (are they varied?), the frequency of sales, feedback, and where that seller's items show up in Best Match search, you'll get a good idea of how successful the seller really is.

I've interviewed many eBay high-volume sellers (*PowerSellers*) including the most elite, those who have attained Top Seller status. Almost all agree that eBay theories are bunk; you've got to watch the site and follow its change announcements. However, the sellers do have some practical preferences for when and how they conduct their eBay business. This chapter gets to the gist of these preferences — and the corresponding best practices.

Auction Selling Strategies

The basic plan for running an auction is the same for everyone, except for decisions regarding the timing of the auction and the starting price. If you speak to 20 eBay sellers, you'll probably get 20 different answers about effective starting bids and when to end your auction. The big answer is "it depends" — it depends on your category, your seller status, how you describe your item, and even your photos. Until you develop your own philosophy based on a success ratio, I'd like to give you the tools to make a sound decision. What works for one seller may not work as well (or at all) for another.

You can also successfully promote your eBay sales online and offline, and you can legally offer your item to the next highest bidder if an auction winner doesn't come through with payment — or even if you have more than one of the item in stock. I discuss a few of these practices in this section.

The ideas in this chapter come from my own experience and discussions with current eBay PowerSellers. These ideas are merely suggestions of methods and starting points that work for others. You definitely need to test them out to find out which practices work — for you and for the types of items you sell.

Starting the auction bidding

The most generally accepted theory about starting bids is that setting the bidding too high scares away new bids. But again, the variable is based on how much the item is worth or even how much it costs.

Some sellers begin the bidding at the price they paid for the item, including known eBay and PayPal fees, thereby protecting their investment. This is a good tactic, especially if you bought the item at a price far below the current going rate on eBay.

To determine the current going value for your item, I recommend searching for the item through the sold listings, which I explain in Book II, Chapter 1. If you know that the item is selling on eBay for a certain price and that there is a demand for it, starting the bidding at a reasonably low level can be a great way to increase bidding and attract prospective bidders to view your auction.

Years of advertising experience can't be wrong. If your item is in demand and people are actively buying, start the bidding low. Retail stores have done this for years with ads that feature prices starting at $9.99 or $14.98. Note that Wal-Mart ends prices in $.97 or $.54 when they're on sale in a store, but on its website, the items' prices end evenly at $.00. Even television commercials advertising automobiles quote a low starting price. (To get the car as shown in the ad, of course, you may end up paying twice the quoted price.)

When sellers know that they have an item that will sell, they often begin their bidding as low as 99 cents. Because of the eBay *proxy bidding system* (which maintains your highest bid as a secret, increasing it incrementally when you're bid against), it takes *more* bids (due to the smaller bidding increments) to bring the item up to the final selling price.

The downside is that new bidders who aren't familiar with the system may bid only the minimum required increment each time they bid. This can be frustrating, and they may quit bidding because it might take them several bids to top the current bid placed by someone who is familiar with the proxy bid system. eBay offers up a tip when the bidder places a bid that doesn't meet the current bid in the system, as shown in Figure 2-1.

Figure 2-1:
The initial
page
suggested
placing a
bid of $53.00
or more.

Very few of us remember the proxy increments by heart, so as a refresher, I give you the goods in Table 2-1.

Table 2-1	Auction Proxy Bidding Increments
Current High Bid ($)	*Bid Increment ($)*
0.01–0.99	0.05
1.00–4.99	0.25
5.00–24.99	0.50
25.00–99.99	1.00
100.00–249.99	2.50
250.00–499.99	5.00
500.00–999.99	10.00
1000.00–2499.99	25.00
2500.00–4999.99	50.00
5000.00 and up	100.00

Auction length

Another debatable philosophy is auction timing. People are always asking me how long to run auctions and what's the best day to end an auction. You have to evaluate your item and decide which of the following is the best plan:

✦ **One-day auction:** Did you just get a load of an item that sells as fast as you post it on the site? A Buy It Now feature on any auction can bring great results, but that will work only if the item is super-hot!

If people are aggressively bidding up an item — and they really gotta have it — you may do best by starting the bidding low and listing the item with a one-day format.

The best way to use a one-day listing is if your item is time-sensitive, for example, event tickets, airline tickets, vacation packages, or tee times. A one-day listing gives you the immediacy — and the time to ship a physical ticket — if necessary.

To list an item for one day, you must have a feedback score of at least 10. If you don't, the option to list for one day won't show up on the item listing form.

When you list in a one-day format, your listing goes right to the top of the *Time: Ending Soonest* sort. Many savvy shoppers view their searches by Listings Ending First (rather than the eBay default of Best Match). With a one-day format, you can pretty much choose the time of day your item will be at the top.

This format can also be successful if you have an item that's the current hot ticket in pop culture. I used this format when I sold some *Friends* TV-show memorabilia a while back. The 24-hour auction opened at midday before the final episode of the show — and ended the next day — at a healthy profit!

If your competitors start their auctions at $.99 with a reasonable Buy It Now price, you'll find that bidders negate Buy It Now offers pretty quickly by placing a bid — which makes it no longer a Buy It Now item — and the item goes to auction. Retaliate by listing your item with a starting bid at just a dollar or so below your Buy It Now price (and make that price at least $.50 below the competition's), and your items may be snapped up more quickly. Keep in mind that for this strategy, your item needs to be in demand!

Buy It Now pricing must be at least 30 percent over your listing's starting price.

✦ **Three-day auction:** If, the item's price will shoot up right after you post it, a three-day auction works just fine. And it's great for those last-minute holiday shoppers looking for hard-to-find items.

A three-day auction is good, for the same reasons that a one-day auction is good — only it's better for the faint of heart and nervous Nellies (like me) because it gives your item more time on the site — more of a chance to sell.

With the Buy It Now feature, you can pretty much accomplish the same thing as you would with a short-term auction. When you list your item for sale, set a price at which you're willing to sell the item immediately; this is your Buy It Now price.

✦ **Five-day auction:** A five-day auction gives you two days more than a three-day auction and two days less than a seven-day auction. That's about the size of it. If you just want an extended weekend auction or your item is a hot one, use it. Five-day auctions are useful during holiday rushes, when gift-buying is the main reason for bidding.

✦ **Seven-day auction:** Tried-and-true advertising theory says that the longer you advertise your item, the more people will see it. On eBay, this means that you have more opportunities for people to bid on it. The seven-day auction is a staple for the bulk of eBay vendors. Seven days is long enough to cover weekend browsers and short enough to keep the auction interesting.

✦ **Ten-day auction:** Many veteran eBay sellers swear by the ten-day auction. Sure, eBay charges you an extra $.40 for the privilege, but the extra three days of exposure (it can encompass two weekends) can easily net you more than your extra cost in profits.

A ten-day auction is good for special collectibles or an expensive item that isn't normally on the site. Putting up a ten-day auction (start Friday night so you get exposure over two weekends) is a near-perfect way to attract bidders.

Your auction closes exactly one, three, five, seven, or ten days — *to the minute* — after you start the auction. Try not to begin your auctions when you're up late at night and can't sleep: You don't want your auction to end at two in the morning when no one else is awake to bid on it. If you can't sleep, schedule your auctions on the site or prepare your listings ahead of time with the Turbo Lister program (which I discuss in Chapter 3) and upload them for future launching when your part of the world is ready to shop.

The specific day you close your auction can also be important. eBay is full of weekend browsers, so including a weekend of browsing in your auction time is a definite plus. Often auctions that end late Sunday evening through Monday close with high bids.

You'll need to do some research to determine the best times to run your auctions and for how long. The best person to figure out the closing information for your auctions is you. Use the tools and, over time, you'll work out a pattern that works best for you.

Figuring out What Day to End an Auction

Back when eBay counted its listings by the hundreds (and then low thousands), it clearly made a difference what day of the week you chose to end an auction. That is, when the number of buyers and sellers on eBay was relatively small, matching your auction time with the bidders' online habits was important. Now that eBay spawns as many as 112 million listings a day — with countless buyers and lookie-loos visiting the site — you find the eBay shoppers looking for bargains at virtually all hours of the day and night. So for a traditional auction, you can choose almost any ending time and know that you'll still have some healthy bidding action.

The wildcards in the mix are the Buy It Now and fixed-price transactions, which have become wildly popular — and successful. Although they don't always follow a daily pattern of sales, they can still follow the preferred auction-ending days you find in this section.

To figure out when to end an auction, you need to know when to start it. Figures 2-2, 2-3, and 2-4 are the top preferred timelines for running a sale on eBay.

You may notice that all these preferred datelines end on a Sunday. Sunday is the top-ranked ending day for auctions by eBay sellers.

Figure 2-2: A timeline for a three-day auction.

Sunday	Monday	Tuesday	Wednesday	Thursday	Friday	Saturday
1	2	3	4	5 8:00 PM PST	6	7
8 8:00 PM PST	9	10	11	12	13	14
15	16	17	18	19	20	21

Figure 2-3: This is seven days of auction action.

Sunday	Monday	Tuesday	Wednesday	Thursday	Friday	Saturday
				1	2	3
4 8:00 PM PST	5	6	7	8	9	10
11 8:00 PM PST	12	13	14	15	16	17
18	19	20	21	22	23	24

Figure 2-4: A full ten days of bidding frenzy (if you're lucky).

Sunday	Monday	Tuesday	Wednesday	Thursday	Friday	Saturday
	1	2	3	4 8:00 PM PST	5	6
7	8	9	10	11	12	13
14 8:00 PM PST	15	16	17	18	19	20
21	22	23	24	25	26	27

I can't list everyone's opinions on the subject — that would probably confuse you anyway — so here are the item-ending days ranked in order from most to least popular:

1. Sunday

2. Monday

3. Thursday

4. Tuesday

5. Wednesday

6. Saturday

7. Friday

 Test out auction-ending days to coordinate these dates with the specific type of items you sell. Some buyers (say, men who buy golf goods during lunch hour and women who buy collectibles while their husbands are out golfing on weekends) can throw these days a curve.

Knowing What Time to Start Your Auction

The only way to figure out when to end your auction is by planning when to start it. An auction beginning at 12:00 will end at that same time on the ending day.

eBay time is military time in the Pacific time zone. Table 2-2 converts the eBay clock to real time for your time zone. Make a photocopy of this table and keep it by your computer. (Even after all these years, it still takes too much time to decipher eBay time without a printed chart.)

If you ever need to check your time zone or want to know exactly what time it is in eBay-land, point your browser to

```
http://viv.ebay.com/ws/eBayISAPI.dll?EbayTime
```

and you'll see the map pictured in Figure 2-5.

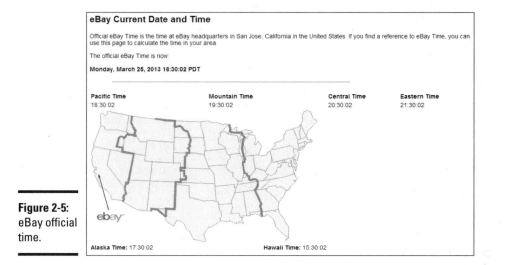

eBay Current Date and Time

Official eBay Time is the time at eBay headquarters in San Jose, California in the United States. If you find a reference to eBay Time, you can use this page to calculate the time in your area.

The official eBay Time is now:

Monday, March 25, 2013 18:30:02 PDT

| Pacific Time | Mountain Time | Central Time | Eastern Time |
| 18:30:02 | 19:30:02 | 20:30:02 | 21:30:02 |

Alaska Time: 17:30:02   Hawaii Time: 15:30:02

Figure 2-5:
eBay official
time.

Table 2-2	eBay Time versus Continental U.S. Time			
eBay Time	**Pacific**	**Mountain**	**Central**	**Eastern**
0:00	12:00 a.m.	1:00 a.m.	2:00 a.m.	3:00 a.m.
1:00	1:00 a.m.	2:00 a.m.	3:00 a.m.	4:00 a.m.
2:00	2:00 a.m.	3:00 a.m.	4:00 a.m.	5:00 a.m.
3:00	3:00 a.m.	4:00 a.m.	5:00 a.m.	6:00 a.m.
4:00	4:00 a.m.	5:00 a.m.	6:00 a.m.	7:00 a.m.
5:00	5:00 a.m.	6:00 a.m.	7:00 a.m.	8:00 a.m.
6:00	6:00 a.m.	7:00 a.m.	8:00 a.m.	9:00 a.m.
7:00	7:00 a.m.	8:00 a.m.	9:00 a.m.	10:00 a.m.
8:00	8:00 a.m.	9:00 a.m.	10:00 a.m.	11:00 a.m.
9:00	9:00 a.m.	10:00 a.m.	11:00 a.m.	12:00 p.m.
10:00	10:00 a.m.	11:00 a.m.	12:00 p.m.	1:00 p.m.
11:00	11:00 a.m.	12:00 p.m.	1:00 p.m.	2:00 p.m.
12:00	12:00 p.m.	1:00 p.m.	2:00 p.m.	3:00 p.m.
13:00	1:00 p.m.	2:00 p.m.	3:00 p.m.	4:00 p.m.
14:00	2:00 p.m.	3:00 p.m.	4:00 p.m.	5:00 p.m.

(continued)

**Book III
Chapter 2**

**Understanding
the Finer Points
of Selling**

Table 2-2 *(continued)*

eBay Time	Pacific	Mountain	Central	Eastern
15:00	3:00 p.m.	4:00 p.m.	5:00 p.m.	6:00 p.m.
16:00	4:00 p.m.	5:00 p.m.	6:00 p.m.	7:00 p.m.
17:00	5:00 p.m.	6:00 p.m.	7:00 p.m.	8:00 p.m.
18:00	6:00 p.m.	7:00 p.m.	8:00 p.m.	9:00 p.m.
19:00	7:00 p.m.	8:00 p.m.	9:00 p.m.	10:00 p.m.
20:00	8:00 p.m.	9:00 p.m.	10:00 p.m.	11:00 p.m.
21:00	9:00 p.m.	10:00 p.m.	11:00 p.m.	12:00 a.m.
22:00	10:00 p.m.	11:00 p.m.	12:00 a.m.	1:00 a.m.
23:00	11:00 p.m.	12:00 a.m.	1:00 a.m.	2:00 a.m.

Here's the consensus of some experts in order of ending-time preference (in eBay time; check the table for a translation):

1. 18:00 to 22:00

2. 21:00 to 0:00

3. 15:00 to 18:00

4. 13:00 to 16:00

Here are the worst eBay times to end an auction:

1. 2:00 to 6:00

2. 0:00 to 3:00

This information should give you some good ideas for your own auction sales.

Selling Items through Fixed Price Sales

Because e-commerce has morphed and consumer preferences have changed, you need to consider a more balanced approach to your sales. Only after trial and error will you know how your specific products sell best — and what combination of listings will help you hit that sweet spot. In the recent era of e-commerce, folks like to come to a site to buy items outright at a given price as well as participate in auctions.

eBay Stores are a great way to offer fixed-price items, but even without a store, you can list fixed-price items on the regular eBay site. (Find out more about the costs of running an eBay Store in Book VIII.)

Fixed-price listings have a slightly different pricing structure on the site. You are given a certain amount of free listings on the site each month.

✦ **No eBay Store:** Sellers without an eBay Store get up to 50 free auction or fixed-price listings.

✦ **Basic Store sellers:** Up to 150 free listings a month.

✦ **Premium Store sellers:** Up to 500 free listings a month.

✦ **Anchor Store sellers:** Up to 2,500 free listings a month.

After you've used your initial free listings, any fixed-price listing — regardless of starting price or number of items for sale — costs 30 cents. This is for a 3-, 5-, 7-, 10-, or 30-day listing, or a Good Till Cancelled listing. Great news, eh? If you're selling media, the cost is even lower. Items listed in the categories of Books, Music, DVDs & Movies, and Video Games are charged only 5 cents per listing for the same durations!

Sounds great, huh? Well, there's a catch. (You knew there'd be a catch, didn't you?) You've got Final Value Fees to consider. Chapter 1 (in this minibook) charts them all; Book VIII, Chapter 4 provides further insights.

Making Money in Other eBay Zones

There's more to eBay than just the auction site. Don't lose a selling opportunity by not checking into the other viable areas described in this section.

eBay's half-brother: Half.com

Half.com, founded in July 1999, was the brainchild of Joshua Kopelman. He observed the insufficiencies of retailing in the area of used mass-market merchandise and went to work on developing a new outlet for secondhand merchandise. Kopelman's site was so successful that eBay bought out Half.com after its first year of business in 2000 for roughly $350 million. Half.com ranks as one of the Internet's most visited sites; currently Alexa, the web-info resource(http://www.alexa.com/), estimates that the site has around 7.8 million daily visits.

The Half.com home page (at http://www.half.ebay.com/) is shown in Figure 2-6. Half.com currently lists millions of items, including books, CDs,

DVDs, video games, and game systems. In a smart turn, Half.com recently added the capability for shoppers to rent textbooks.

Because Half.com is part of eBay, your feedback follows you to the site.

Selling at Half.com is different from selling at your eBay (or other online) store only because you're selling in a head-to-head, fixed-price marketplace. Your item is listed against more of the same item from other sellers (shown in Figure 2-7). Half.com isn't a home for your store; you might say that each item has its own store, complete with competing sellers.

From a seller's point of view, the best features of Half.com are these:

✦ The item listing is free.

✦ The item stays on the site until the item is sold or until you take it down.

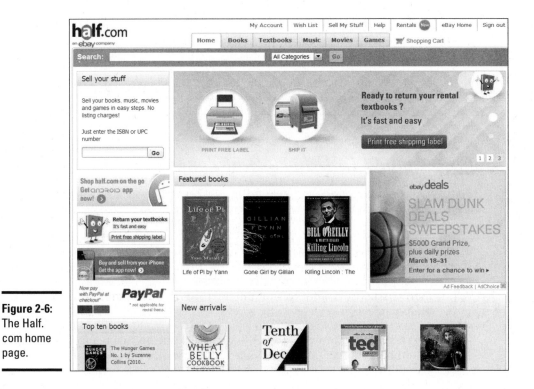

Figure 2-6: The Half. com home page.

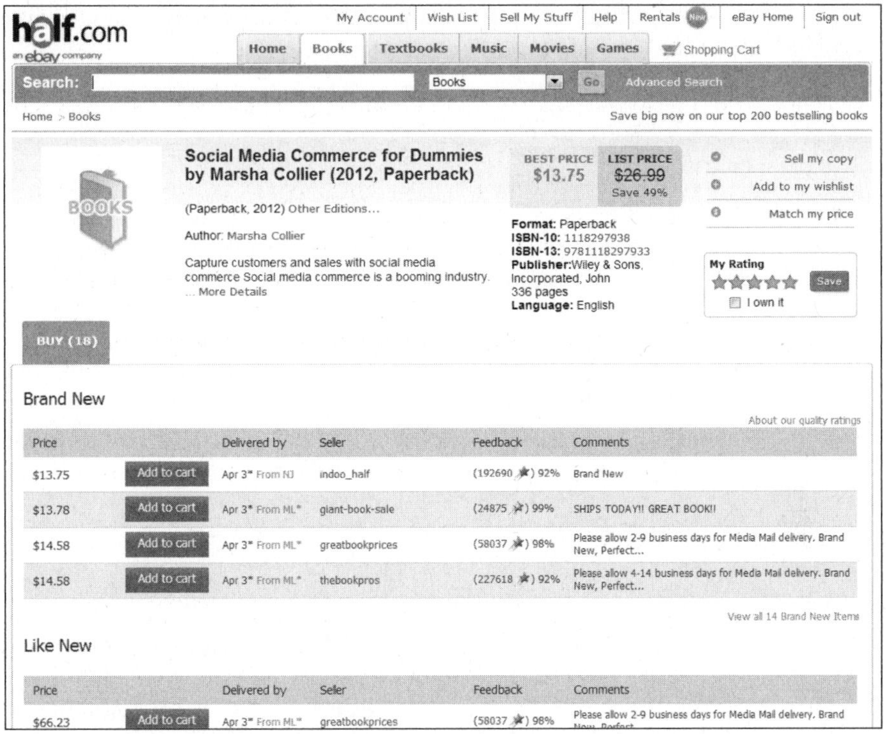

Figure 2-7:
An item
page on
Half.com.

Just like your My eBay page, Half.com has a very user-friendly area where you can control your selling. You'll find it under My Account: Inventory. You can change the prices for your books right there — no need to access individual listings!

To list an item for sale at Half.com, you first need to locate the item's Universal Product Code (UPC) or, if you're selling a book, the International Standard Book Number (ISBN).

Here are some pointers about finding the right codes and listing items on Half.com:

✦ In case you're wondering what an ISBN is, turn this book over and find the bar code on the back. The number written above it is this book's ISBN.

✦ If you don't want to bring all your books, CDs, movies, or games to your computer so you have the UPC or ISBN handy, scan your items using an inexpensive handheld scanner (make sure it's a model that holds the scans in memory).

✦ If you don't have an item's outer box with the UPC, search Half.com from any of its pages for your particular item (including its brand name). When your search comes up with the exact item, copy down the code number and use it with your listing, or click the Sell Your Stuff link on the item page.

✦ You'll find that when you apply the UPC or ISBN in your listing, Half.com comes up with an image of your item, so you don't even have to take a picture for your sale. When an item is out of print, Half.com may not have an image to upload with the listing. In this case, the text *Image not available* appears in the area where the picture would appear. (Half.com allows you to upload your own picture.)

✦ Half.com has an amazing database of items in the books, music, movie, and video-game categories to help you find the specs of whatever item you want to list. But if your item doesn't have a code, you can upload your own photo and even add a 1,000-word description.

When someone searches on Half.com for an item, such as a book, a listing of all sellers who are selling that book appears. The listings are classified by the book's condition — categorized as Like New or Very Good — depending on what the seller entered. The list price of the book is included, as well as a comparison of selling prices on the eBay site. Also, when a prospective buyer searches and finds a book or coded item, a box appears in the corner of the listing with a price comparison of the item from various other online sales sites.

Half.com charges a commission after your item sells, as shown in Table 2-3. Commissions for items sold in the Books, Music, Movies, Games, and Game System categories are a percentage of the selling price of the item. The shipping cost is not added to the selling price.

Table 2-3	Half.com Sales Commissions
Selling Price Plus Shipping ($)	*Half.com Commission (%)*
0–50.00	15.0
50.01–100.00	12.5
100.01–250.00	10.0
250.01–500.00	7.5
500.01 and up	5.0

For example, if you're selling a paperback book for $37.00, here's what happens:

1. Buyer buys your paperback, which is priced at $37.00.

2. Half.com charges the buyer $3.99 for Media Mail shipping and handling costs.

3. You pay Half.com a 15 percent commission, which is $5.55 on a $37.00 item.

4. You get a shipping reimbursement of $2.64.

   See Table 2-4 for Half.com shipping reimbursements.

5. Half.com sends you a net payment of $34.09.

Table 2-4	Half.com Shipping Reimbursements	
Item	*Media Mail*	*Expedited (Usually Priority Mail)*
Hardcover book	$3.07 for the first item	$5.24 for the first item
	$1.40 for each additional item	$3.49 for each additional item
Paperback book	$2.64 for the first item	$5.20 for the first item
	$1.19 for each additional item	$2.24 for each additional item
Music and DVDs	$2.39 for the first item	$5.20 for the first item
	$1.03 for each additional item	$1.99 for each additional item
VHS movies	$2.14 for the first item	$5.20 for the first item
	$1.19 for each additional item	$1.99 for each additional item
Audio books	$2.64 for the first item	$5.20 for the first item
	$1.15 for each additional item	$1.94 for each additional item
Games	$2.89 for the first item	$5.20 for the first item
	$1.15 for each additional item	$1.99 for each additional item

Automotive? Go eBay Motors

Anything and everything automotive can go in the eBay Motors category (see Figure 2-8), and it will sell like giant tires at a monster truck rally. Following are just a few of the car-related items that fit in this category.

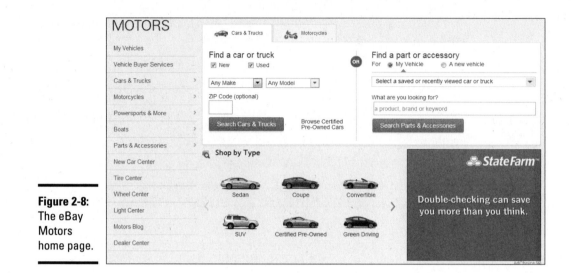

Figure 2-8:
The eBay
Motors
home page.

Car parts

Got used car parts? eBay has an enormous market in used car parts. One seller I know goes to police impound sales and buys wrecks — just to get some valuable parts that he can resell on eBay.

New car parts are in demand, too. If your local auto-parts store is blasting out door handles for a 1967 Corvette (a vehicle for which it's hard to find parts), it wouldn't hurt to pick up a few to resell on Motors. Sooner or later, someone's bound to search eBay looking for them. If you're lucky enough to catch the trend, you'll make a healthy profit.

Cars

Yes, you can sell cars on eBay. In fact, used-car sales have skyrocketed online thanks to all the people who find eBay to be a trusted place to buy and sell used vehicles. The most expensive vehicle ever sold on eBay was a 1959 Ferrari 250 GT California; it sold for $3,260,100. Sold via the mobile app was a Mercedes SLR McLaren for $240,001. (I told you those odd amount bids, can make a difference.)

Selling vehicles on eBay is a natural business for you if you have access to good used cars, work as a mechanic, or have a contact at a dealership that lets you sell cars on eBay for a commission or on a consignment basis. (For the ins and outs of consignment selling, check out Book IV, Chapter 3.)

To complete your sale, eBay Motors features Vehicle Purchase Protection that covers up to $50,000, vehicle history reports, vehicle inspection and escrow services, and one-click access to vehicle shipping quotes from GigMoves. Access eBay Motors and its services from the eBay home page or by going directly to www.ebaymotors.com.

If you want to sell lower-priced vehicles (those that have a lot of miles and might not be worth shipping cross-country) locally, you may avail yourself of the Local Classified ad feature. The ad appears for seven days in eBay Motors to buyers that are within 200 miles of your ZIP code. For a low-volume seller, it is free to list and sell. After you've posted more than seven listings in a calendar year, the fee is $15.

Different fees apply when you sell a vehicle on eBay Motors nationally. To encourage sellers to list and sell vehicles on the site, eBay has set up a tiered system of fees. The first four vehicles you list in a 12-month period are charged no listing fees, but have a higher transaction fee when the sale is successful. The fees are based on the final selling price. Take a look at Tables 2-5 and 2-6 for significant differences.

Table 2-5   National Listing Fees for Low-Volume Sellers

Category	Insertion Fee	Sale of up to $2,000	Sale over $2,000
Cars & Trucks, RVs & Campers, and Commercial Trucks	Free	$60	$125
Motorcycles, Powersports, Trailers, and Boats	Free	$60	$125
Powersports under 50cc	Free	$10	$10
All other vehicles	Free	$60	$125

Table 2-6   National Listing Fees for High-Volume Sellers

Category	Insertion Fee	Sale of up to $2,000	Sale over $2,000
Cars & Trucks, RVs & Campers, and Commercial Trucks	$50	Free	Free
Motorcycles, Powersports, Trailers, and Boats	$20	$30	$60
Powersports under 50cc	$10	$10	$10
All other vehicles	$20	$30	$60

Although many people who have found the vehicle of their dreams on eBay are more than happy to take a one-way flight to the vehicle location and drive it home, shipping a vehicle is a reasonably-priced alternative. On your listing, eBay can supply a link to give you a quick estimate of shipping fees to the buyer's ZIP code. Figure 2-9 shows the estimates I got to ship a car from Pensacola, Florida to Northridge, California.

Figure 2-9: Quick shipping estimates in eBay Motors.

> **Shipping Quotes**   PROVIDED BY GigaMoves
>
> Hire an auto transport company to ship this vehicle to your door. Four companies have provided estimated costs for shipping this 2008 Cadillac CTS from Pensacola, Florida 32514 to Northridge, California 91325-3816 on 04/13/2013.
>
> | Company | | Cost Estimate | Quote Number | Contact Information |
> |---------|--|---------------|--------------|---------------------|
> | uShip | Best price, best service...guaranteed! Feedback-rated transporters you can trust. | $805 | 11916321 | 800-264-7447 M-W 8-7,Th-Sa 8-6,Su 12-5 CST |
> | ALPINE AUTO | The most efficient auto shipper with the most competitive prices. | $926 | 9957605 | 888-444-0079 M-F 7-6pm MST, Sat 0-Noon MST |
> | DAS | With over 55 years in business and 1,000,000 deliveries, we know shipping! | $1059 | 68235287 | 800-827-6998 M-F 7AM-9PM, Sat 8AM-6PM CST |
> | UNITEDROAD | More than 2 million cars shipped annually, A + BBB Rating, 98% On Time, Door to Door Service | $1408 | 43250984 | 866-608-6277 M-F 9am-8pm; Sat 9am-1pm EST |
>
> Click "Get custom quotes" to get a personalized quote from one or more of these companies.
>
> `Get custom quotes`

Here are just a few things to keep in mind if you plan to sell cars on eBay:

✦ To sell a vehicle on eBay Motors, you must enter the Vehicle Identification Number (VIN) on the Sell an Item page. This way, prospective buyers can access a vehicle history report to get an idea of the condition of the car.

✦ An item that you've listed on eBay Motors will appear in any search, whether a potential buyer conducts a regular eBay search or a search in eBay Motors.

✦ If your reserve isn't met in an eBay Motors auction, you may still offer the vehicle to the high bidder through the Second Chance option. You may also reduce your reserve during the auction if you feel you've set your target price too high.

Real estate: Not always an auction

eBay Real Estate at `www.ebay.com/chp/real-estate` isn't always an auction. Because of the wide variety of laws governing the sale of real estate, eBay auctions of real property are *not* legally binding offers to buy and sell. However, putting your real estate on eBay (see Figure 2-10) is an excellent way to advertise and attract potential buyers. When the auction ends, neither party is obligated (as they are in other eBay auctions) to complete the real estate transaction. The buyer and seller must get together to consummate the deal.

Figure 2-10:
Look!
Gold mines!

Nonetheless, eBay real estate sales are popular and the sales are growing by leaps and bounds. You don't have to be a professional real estate agent to use this category, although it may help when it comes to closing the deal. If you know land and your local real estate laws, eBay gives you the perfect venue for subdividing those 160 acres in Wyoming that Uncle Regis left you in his will.

For less than the cost of a newspaper ad, you can sell your home, condo, land, or even timeshare on eBay Real Estate in the auction format. You can also choose to list your property in an ad format, accepting not bids but *inquiries* from prospective buyers from around the world. On the Sell an Item form, you must specify special information about your piece of real estate.

In Tables 2-7 and 2-8, I provide a listing of fees that you can expect to encounter on eBay Real Estate. *Note:* When your listing sells in the Land, manufactured Home, and Timeshares for Sale categories, you're charged a Notice Fee of $35.00.

Table 2-7   Timeshare, Land, and Manufactured Homes

Type of Fee	Fee Amount
Auction/Fixed Price listing for 1-, 3-, 5-, 7-day (Add 40 cents for a 10-day auction.)	$35.00
Auction/Fixed Price 30-day	$50.00

(continued)

Book III
Chapter 2

Understanding
the Finer Points
of Selling

Table 2-7 *(continued)*

Type of Fee	Fee Amount
Classified Ad 30 days	$150.00
Classified Ad 90 days	$300.00
Final value (Notice) fee	$35.00
Reserve fee (refunded when property sells)	$0.01 to $199.99: $2.00; $200.00 and up: 1% of reserve price (up to $50)

Table 2-8 Residential, Commercial, and Other Real Estate

Type of Fee	Fee Amount ($)
Auction/Fixed Price listing for 1-, 3-, 5-, 7-day (Add 40 cents for a 10-day auction.)	$100.00
Auction/Fixed Price 30-day	$150.00
Classified Ad 30 days	$150.00
Classified Ad 90 days	$300.00
Final Value Fee	0

Selling by the Rules

There are a lot of *shoulds* in this world. You *should* do this and you *should* do that. I don't know who is in charge of the *shoulds,* but certain things just make life work better. If you follow the advice on these pages, your eBay business will thrive with a minimum of anguish. If you've ever had a listing pulled by eBay, you know that anguish firsthand and don't want to have it again.

In the real world, we have to take responsibility for our own actions. If we buy a flat-screen TV set (in the box) for $25 from some guy selling them out of the back of a truck, who do we have to blame when we take it home and the box is full of cardboard? You get what you pay for, and you have no consumer protection from a seller of possibly "hot" (or nonexistent) TVs. Responsible consumerism is every buyer's job. Lawsuit upon lawsuit gets filed — and some are won — when buyers feel they've been ripped off, but my best advice is that if you stay clean in your online business, you'll keep clean.

eBay is a community, and the community thrives on the five basic values listed here:

✦ We believe people are basically good.

✦ We believe everyone has something to contribute.

✦ We believe that an honest, open environment can bring out the best in people.

✦ We recognize and respect everyone as a unique individual.

✦ We encourage you to treat others the way that you want to be treated.

eBay is committed to these values, and it says so right on its website. eBay believes that community members should "honor these values — whether buying, selling, or chatting." So *should* we all.

Is what you want to sell legal?

Although eBay is based in California and therefore must abide by California law, sellers do business all over the United States. Therefore, items sold at eBay must be governed by the laws of every other state as well. As a seller, you're ultimately responsible for both the legality of the items you sell *and* the way that you transact business on eBay. Yes, you can sell thousands of different items on eBay. But do you know what you *aren't* allowed to sell?

The eBay User Agreement outlines the rules and regulations regarding what you can and can't sell, as well as all aspects of doing business on eBay. If you haven't read it in a while, do so. You can find it at the following address:

```
http://pages.ebay.com/help/policies/user-agreement.html
```

eBay's policies can change from time to time. As an active seller, you should make sure that you're notified of any changes. You'll be notified when eBay makes changes to the User Agreement, through your eBay Message Center.

By now, you should have a firm grasp of the rules and regulations for listing auctions. But in addition to knowing the rules for listing items, you must consider the items themselves. In this section, I detail the three categories of items to be wary of: prohibited, questionable, and potentially infringing. Some are banned, period. Others fall in a gray area. You're responsible for what you sell, so you'd better know what's legal and what's not.

If you're found in violation of eBay's listing restrictions, you may be penalized in a variety of ways, including

✦ Listing cancellation

✦ Limits on account privileges

✦ Account suspension

✦ Forfeit of eBay fees on cancelled listings

✦ Loss of PowerSeller status

You may think it's okay to give away a regulated or banned item as a bonus item with your auction. Think again. Even giving away such items for free doesn't save you from potential legal responsibility.

Prohibited and restricted items

A prohibited item is banned from sale at eBay. You can't sell a prohibited item under any circumstances. Take a look at the upcoming list. A little common sense tells you there's good reason for not selling these items, including liability issues for the seller. (For example, what if you sold alcohol to a minor? That's against the law!)

Restricted items involve more shades of gray. They may involve the sale of dangerous or sensitive items that may not be prohibited by law. eBay sets these limitations as a result of input by members of the eBay Community and others. eBay has a strong Offensive Material Policy which covers items of merchandise that "promote or glorify hatred, violence, racial or religious intolerance, or items that promote organizations with such views." As you can imagine, this is a slippery slope for some sellers.

The following is just a partial list; the current complete list can be found at `http://pages.ebay.com/help/policies/items-ov.html`

Adult Material

Alcohol*

Animals and wildlife products

Art

Artifacts, grave-related items, and Native American arts and crafts

Counterfeit currency or stamps

Counterfeit items

Credit cards

Drugs and drug paraphernalia

Embargoed goods from prohibited countries

Firearms, ammunition, replicas, and militaria

Government IDs and licenses

Human remains and body parts

Lockpicking devices

Lottery tickets

Mailing lists and personal information

Medical devices

Multilevel marketing

Postage meters

Prescription drugs

Recalled items

Satellite and cable TV descramblers

Stocks and other securities**

Stolen property

Surveillance equipment

Tobacco

Travel***

USDA-prohibited plants and seeds

*No alcoholic beverages can be sold on the eBay U.S. website, except for pre-approved sales of wine.

**Old or collectible stock certificates may be sold, provided that they're canceled or are from a company that no longer exists.

***All sellers wanting to rent out their own lodging must first register with eBay Travel verification.

Check the following address for updates:

```
http://pages.ebay.com/help/sell/questions/prohibited-
items.html
```

Questionable items

Determining whether you can sell a *questionable item* is tricky. Under certain circumstances, you may be able to list the item for sale at eBay. To fully understand when and if you can list a questionable item, visit the links that I highlight in Table 2-10.

Table 2-10	Partial List of Questionable Items and Where to Find the Rules Regulating Them
Can I Sell This?	*Go Here to Find Out**
Alcohol	/alcohol.html
Art	selling-art.html
Artifacts	/artifacts.html
Autographed Items	/autographs.html
Batteries	/hazardous-materials.html
Contracts and tickets	/contracts.html
Electronics equipment	/electronics.html
Event tickets	/event-tickets.html
Food	/food.html
Freon and other refrigerants	/hazardous-materials.html
Hazardous materials	/hazardous-materials.html
Human parts and remains	/remains.html
International trading — sellers	/international-trading.html
Mature audiences	/mature-audiences.html
Offensive material	/offensive.html
Pesticides	/pesticides.html
Police-related items	/police.html
Presale listings	/pre-sale.html
Recalled Items	/recalled.html
Stamps	/selling-stamps.html
Stocks and other securities	/stocks.html
Slot machines	/slot-machines.html
Used clothing	/used-clothing.html
Used medical devices	/medical-devices.html
Weapons and knives	/firearms-weapons-knives.html

* All URLs begin with http://pages.ebay.com/help/policies.

The Chanel-style purse

In the early days on the site, I listed a quilted leather women's purse that had a gold chain strap, which I described as a Chanel-style purse. Within two hours, I received an informational alert from the eBay listing police. I described the item to the best of my ability, but found that it became a potentially infringing item. My use of the brand name *Chanel* caused my auction to come under the violation of keyword spamming.

In its informational alert, eBay described my violation:

"Keyword spamming is the practice of adding words, including brand names, which do not directly describe the item you are selling. The addition of these words may not have been intentional, but including them in this manner diverts members to your listing inappropriately."

Ooops! You can see how my ingenuous listing was actually a violation of policy. Think twice before you add brand names to your auction description. Thankfully, the eBay police judge each violation on a case-by-case basis. Because my record is clear, I merely got a reprimand. Had my violation been more deliberate, I might have been suspended.

Potentially infringing items

Potentially infringing items follow a slippery slope. If you list a *potentially infringing item,* you may infringe on existing copyrights, trademarks, registrations, or the like. Get the idea? These items are prohibited for your own protection.

Items falling under the "potentially infringing" category are generally copyrighted or trademarked items, such as software, promotional items, and games. Even using a brand name in your auction as part of a description (known as *keyword spamming*) may get you into trouble.

Repeating various un-trademarked keywords can get you in trouble as well. eBay permits the use of as many as five synonyms when listing an item for sale. A permissible example of this might be: purse, handbag, pocketbook, satchel, and bag. Adding many un-trademarked keywords would cause the auction to come up in more searches.

Knowing eBay's Listing Policies

eBay itself does not sell merchandise. eBay is merely a venue that provides the location where *others* can put on a giant e-commerce party (in other words, *sell stuff*). To provide a safe and profitable venue for its sellers, eBay must govern auctions that take place on its site. eBay makes the rules; you and I follow the rules. I like to think of eBay as the place that lets you hold your senior prom in its gym. When I was in school, my classmates and I had to follow the rules or see our prom cancelled. If we don't agree to follow eBay's rules, a safe and trusted eBay community can't exist.

eBay has some hard-and-fast rules about listing your items. One rule is that you must list your item in the appropriate category (that only makes sense). In this section, I highlight a few other rules that you should keep in mind when listing. What I discuss isn't a definitive list of eBay listing policies and rules. Take time to familiarize yourself with the User Agreement (which details all eBay policies and rules) at the following address:

```
http://pages.ebay.com/help/policies/user-agreement.html
```

I recommend that you check the eBay User Agreement regularly for any policy changes.

Duplicate listings

Remember the old supply-and-demand theory from your economics class? When people list the same items repeatedly, they drive down the item's going price while ruining all the other sellers' opportunities to sell the item during that time frame.

eBay allows you to list as many identical auctions as you want, but only one without bids will show on eBay at a time. And you may not have more than one listing of a fixed-price item. Sellers who want to "game" the system in this way, by listing a huge number of the same item, need to think twice.

When alcohol was a collectible

Many people collect rare and antique bottles of liquor or wine. I even sold a bottle of Korbel champagne (whose bottle artwork was designed by Frank Sinatra) on eBay in 1998. Korbel bottles have featured artwork by designer Nicole Miller and comedienne Whoopi Goldberg, as well as designs by Tony Bennett, Frank Sinatra, and Jane Seymour.

People also collect Jim Beam bottles, Dug decanters, and miniatures that are even more valuable when they're full. You *can* sell these on eBay as long as they are empty.

Pre-selling: Not worth the hassle

A seller I once knew presold Beanie Babies on eBay. She had a regular source that supplied her when the new toys came out, so she fell into a complacent attitude about listing presales. Then her supplier didn't get the shipment. Motivated by the need to protect her feedback rating (and by the fear that she'd be accused of fraud), she ran all over town desperately trying to get the Beanies she needed to fill her orders. The Beanies were so rare that she ended up spending several hundred dollars more than what she had originally sold the toys for, just to keep her customers happy.

eBay policy states that the display of multiple identical items from the same seller will be *limited to only one at a time without bids* in search results. So what's the point? If you're going to list an item that many times, at the very least be sure to list it in different categories. That's a rule, but it also makes sense. Nothing drives down the price of an item faster than closing identical auctions, one after another, in the same category. eBay also requires that you list your item in a category that's relevant to it.

State it up front: Drop-shipping and product-sourcing listings

In many situations, being the first seller to put a popular item up for sale can get you some high bids. And if you can guarantee in your auction description that the item will be available to ship within 30 days of the purchase or the auction closing, you can sell items from a product sourcer or drop-shipper. However, if you're not completely sure that you'll have the item in time, I don't recommend that you even attempt such a listing.

Before you set up such listings (for presale or drop-shipping), check out the Federal Trade Commission 30-day rule covering these matters, which you can find at the following address:

```
http://business.ftc.gov/documents/alt051-selling-internet-
prompt-delivery-rules
```

Ix-nay on the bonuses, giveaways, raffles, or prizes

Because eBay sells to every state in the United States, it must follow explicit laws governing giveaways and prizes. Each state has its own set of rules and

Book III
Chapter 2

Understanding
the Finer Points
of Selling

regulations, so eBay doesn't allow individual sellers to come up with their own promotions.

If your auction violates this rule, eBay might end your listing.

Search and browse manipulation by keyword spamming

Keyword spamming happens when you add words, usually brand names, to your auction description that don't describe what you're selling (for example, describing that little black dress as Givenchy-style when Givenchy has nothing to do with it). Keyword spamming manipulates the eBay search engine by including an unrelated item in the listing for a copyrighted or trademarked item, and then diverting bidders to an auction of other merchandise. Sellers use keyword spamming to pull viewers to their auctions after viewers have searched for the brand name. To attract attention to their listings, some sellers use *not* or *like* along with the brand name, such as *like Givenchy.*

Here are the problems with keyword spamming:

✦ It's a listing violation and causes your auction to fall under potentially infringing items for sale on eBay. The wording you choose when you run this kind of auction manipulates the eBay search engine and prospective bidders.

✦ It's frustrating to the potential buyers trying to use the search engine to find a particular item, and it's unfair to other eBay sellers who've properly listed their items.

Keyword spamming can take many forms. Some merely mislead the prospective bidder; others are infringements on legal rights. A few of the most common are

✦ Superfluous brand names in the title or item description

✦ Using something like "not brand X" in the title or item description

✦ Improper trademark usage

✦ Lists of keywords

✦ Hidden text

This violation is often white text on a white background or hidden text in HTML code. The white text resides in the auction HTML, so it shows up in the search but is not visible to the naked eye. Sneaky, eh? And prohibited.

✦ Drop-down lists

TIP

The eBay Verified Rights Owner program

eBay can't possibly check every auction for authenticity. But to help protect trademarked items, it formed the Verified Rights Owner (VeRO) program.

Trademark and copyright owners expend large amounts of energy to develop and maintain control over the quality of their products. If you buy a "designer" purse from a guy on the street for $20, it's probably counterfeit, so don't go selling it on eBay.

eBay works with VeRO program participants to educate the community about such items. They work also with verified owners of trademarks and copyrights to remove auctions that infringe on their products. If eBay doesn't close a suspicious or blatantly infringing auction, then both you and eBay are liable for the violation.

To participate in the VeRO program, the owners of copyrights and trademarks must supply eBay with proof of ownership. To view the VeRO program information, go to

```
http://pages.ebay.com/help/
tp/vero-rights-owner.html
```

To report a violation of something you have legal rights to, download this form on eBay:

```
http://pics.ebay.com/aw/
pics/pdf/us/help/community/
NOCI1.pdf
```

Note: eBay cooperates with law enforcement and may give your name and street address to a VeRO program member.

To view a list of other VeRO members' About Me pages, go to

```
http://pages.ebay.com/help/
community/vero-aboutme.html
```

To get the latest on eBay's keyword spamming policy, go to

```
http://pages.ebay.com/help/policies/search-manipulation.
html
```

Limited linking from your listings

Few issues set sellers to arguing more than eBay's rules on linking. In your auction item description, you *can* use the following links:

✦ One link to an additional page that gives further information about the item you're selling.

✦ A link that sends a member to eBay messages so that the buyer can send you an e-mail.

✦ Links to more photo images of the item you're selling.

✦ Links to your other auctions on eBay and your eBay store listings.

✦ One link to your About Me page, besides the link next to your user ID that eBay provides.

`http://pages.ebay.com/help/policies/listing-links.html`

Chapter 3: Listing Items for Sale

In This Chapter

↙ **Organizing your sales**

↙ **Prepping for the listing**

↙ **Setting up a solid description**

↙ **Making changes after the sale is posted**

Are you ready to make some money? Yes? (Call it an inspired guess.) Are you on the threshold of adding your items to the hundreds of thousands that go up for auction (or fixed-price sale) on eBay every day? Some items are so hot that the sellers quadruple their investments. Other items, unfortunately, are so stone-cold that they may not even register a single bid.

In this chapter, I explain all the facets of the Sell an Item page — the page you fill out to get your merchandise up for sale. You get some advice that can increase your odds of making money, and you find out the best way to position your item so buyers can see it, bid on it, or buy it outright. I also show you how to modify, relist, and end your listing.

Getting Ready to List Your Item

After you decide what you want to sell, find out as much as you can about it and conduct a little market research. Then you should have a good idea of the item's popularity and value.

Before you list, make sure that you have the following bases covered:

✦ **The specific category under which you want the item listed:** Ask your friends or family where they'd look for such an item — and remember the categories that were most successful when you conducted your market research with the eBay search function. Using a product UPC (or ISBN) number when you search may also give you a clue to a proper item category.

To find out which category will pay off best for your item, run a search and then select the Sold Listings option. See how many fixed-price listings and auctions of that item are running (and whether people are bidding on them). Then click the Sold Listings link at the top of your search results. Sort your results by Price and Shipping: Highest First, and then look over the most successful transactions to see which categories they're listed in. For more information on eBay's search, visit Book II, Chapter 1.

✦ **What you want to say in your item description:** Jot down your ideas. Take a good look at your item and make a list of keywords that describe your item. *Keywords* are single descriptive words that can include

- Brand names

- Size of the item (citing measurements if appropriate)

- Age or date of manufacture

- Condition

- Rarity

- Color

- Size

- Material (fabric)

- . . . and more

✦ **An idea of what picture (or pictures) of your item you want to post at the top and/or put inside your description:** Pictures help sell items, but you don't have to use them if you're selling media items (eBay will supply them for you). Pictures in the description are important if you include descriptive text on your images. eBay no longer allows images with text to appear in the top level photos in search. (If you want to know more about using pictures in your auctions, see Book V.)

✦ **The price at which you think you can sell the item:** Be as realistic as you can. (That's where the market research comes in.)

The Sell an Item form is where your listing is born. Filling out your paperwork requires a few minutes of clicking, typing, and answering all kinds of questions. The good news is that when you're finished, your sale is up for all to see.

Before you begin, you have to be registered with eBay as a seller. If you still need to do so, go to Book I, Chapter 3 and see how to fill out the preliminary cyber-paperwork. If you've registered but haven't provided eBay with your financial information (credit card or checking account), you'll be asked for this information before you proceed to sell. Fill in the data on the secure form. Then you're ready to set up your listing.

Deciding on a Sales Format

Selling an item can be like the dizzying menu in a Chinese restaurant: You have three ways to sell an item on eBay. Three ways may not seem to be very dizzying, unless you're trying to decide just which format is the best for you.

Here's what you need to know about each type:

✦ **Online auction:** This is the tried-and-true traditional sale format on eBay. You can combine this auction with the Buy It Now feature, for those who want the item immediately. Often, if you're selling a collectible item, letting it go to auction may net you a much higher profit — remember to do your research before listing.

✦ **Fixed-price listing:** A fixed-price sale is easy for the buyer to complete; it's just like shopping at the corner store. The only problem is that many potential buyers may lean toward an auction because of the perception that they *may* get a better deal.

✦ **Classified Ad:** If you don't want to put real estate up for auction and you'd like to correspond with the prospective buyers of a property, this is the option for you.

Say, for example, that you want to list a traditional eBay auction. Or perhaps you want to sell your item for a fixed price. In any case, to find eBay's Sell an Item page from the eBay home page, just click Sell in the upper-right navigation bar and select Sell an Item.

Getting Your Sales Specifics in Order

Yes, the Sell an Item form looks daunting, but filling out its many sections doesn't take as long as you may think. Some of the questions you're asked aren't things you even have to think about; just click an answer and off you go. Other questions ask you to type information. Don't sweat a thing; all the answers you need are right here.

When listing your item, here's the info you're asked to fill out (each of these items is discussed in detail later in this chapter):

✦ **User ID and password:** If you're not signed in, you need to do so before you list an item for sale.

✦ **Category:** The category where you've decided to list your item (required).

✦ **Title:** The name of your item (required).

✦ **Description:** What you want to tell eBay buyers about your item (required). After you've written a brilliant title for your listing, prospective buyers click and scroll down to your description. Do they have to dodge through pointless verbiage, losing interest along the way? Or do you get right down to business and state the facts about your item?

✦ **Adding Pictures:** Decide which images of your item you want to upload to show off your listing. Book V has more information on using images in sales.

✦ **Quantity:** The number of items you're offering in an auction is always one, but you can run a fixed-price listing with multiple items.

✦ **Starting Price:** This would be the Minimum bid for an auction or the sale price for a fixed-price listing.

✦ **Duration:** The number of days you want the listing to run (required).

✦ **Reserve price:** The hidden target price you set for an auction. This is the price that bidders must meet before you'll sell this item (optional). eBay charges you a fee for this feature.

✦ **Private listing:** You can keep the identity of all bidders secret with this option (optional). This option is used only in rare circumstances (such as when you're selling psychic readings and your customers might not want their proclivities made public).

✦ **Buy It Now:** You can sell your auction item directly to the first buyer who meets this price (optional).

✦ **List item in two categories:** If you want to double your exposure, you can list your item in two categories. Note that double exposure equals double your listing fees (optional). For some items, eBay does not permit a two-category listing.

✦ **Boldface title:** A selling option to make your item listing stand out. eBay charges $2 to $4 for this feature (optional).

✦ **Ship-to locations:** Here's where you can indicate where you're willing to ship an item. If you don't want to ship out of the United States, check only that option. You can select individual countries as well (optional).

You may want to consider whether you want to be in the international shipping business. If you don't ship internationally, you're blocking a bunch of possible high bidders. Give it a try and see how it works for you.

✦ **How you will ship:** Select the options that apply as to how you plan to ship the item.

Meeting your customers

eBay is a person-to-person marketplace. Although many sellers are businesses (like you), the perception is that sellers on eBay are individuals (versus businesses) earning a living. The homespun personal approach goes a long way to being successful when you're selling on eBay. One of the reasons many buyers come to eBay is that they want to support the individuals who have the gumption to start their own small enterprises on the site.

+ **Shipping charges:** Your listing will get preference in search if you offer free shipping. Consider building that expense into your price.

+ **Immediate payment:** Fill out this area if you want to require the buyer to pay immediately through PayPal (optional).

Since I'm talking here about listing an item for sale, I briefly go over some high points on strategies — but be sure you also check out Chapter 1 to get some serious insight on listing strategies.

Selecting a Category: The How and Why

Book III
Chapter 3

Many eBay sellers will tell you that selecting the exact category isn't crucial to achieving the highest price for your item — and they're right. The bulk of buyers (who know what they're looking for) just input search keywords into eBay's search box and look for their items. Potential buyers also may select a category and — just as if they were window-shopping in the mall — peruse the items and see whether one strikes their fancy.

Listing Items for Sale

For best positioning in search results, be sure to select the appropriate category for your item. If you pick an unrelated category, you run the risk of your listing being removed from the site as a listing violation.

On the first page of the Sell an Item form, you will select the main category for your item. After you select your main category, you land on the official working portion of the Sell an Item page.

With tens of thousands of categories, finding the right place for your item can be daunting. You need to apply some marketing techniques when deciding where to place your auctions. You can list an item in two categories, but you have to pay double for that. Does your budget allow for it?

Consider these ideas and techniques for finding the right category for your item:

✦ **Check out other sellers' successes:** To find where other sellers have successfully sold items that are similar to yours and see the prices the items sold for, you can search Sold items. You may find that your item is listed successfully in more than one category.

✦ **Find out who's currently selling your item (and where):** Check the active listings; are lots of people selling your item? If you see that you're one of 40 or 50 people selling the item, you need to get exacting about where to list yours. Evaluate the item and its potential buyers. In what categories would someone shopping for your item search?

✦ **Use appropriate subcategories to catch in-the-know buyers:** Most bidders scan for specific items in subcategories. For example, if you're selling a Bakelite fruit pin, don't just list it under Jewelry; keep narrowing your choices. In this case, you can put it in a costume jewelry category that's especially for Bakelite. I guarantee that the real Bakelite jewelry collectors out there know where to look to find the jewelry they love.

As you start the listing process, eBay gives you a tool to find where the bulk of sellers are selling your item. Simply type three or four keywords (or a UPC or ISBN number in case of media) in the first step's search box and click Search to answer the question: "What do you want to sell today?" If eBay has your item in its catalog, the item's category will be automatically selected. Figure 3-1 shows you how easy it is to find where your item is being sold.

The next page, Find a Matching Category, shows you a list of scrollable categories that may match the item you searched for. This list is based on existing listings of items that match your keywords, as shown in Figure 3-2.

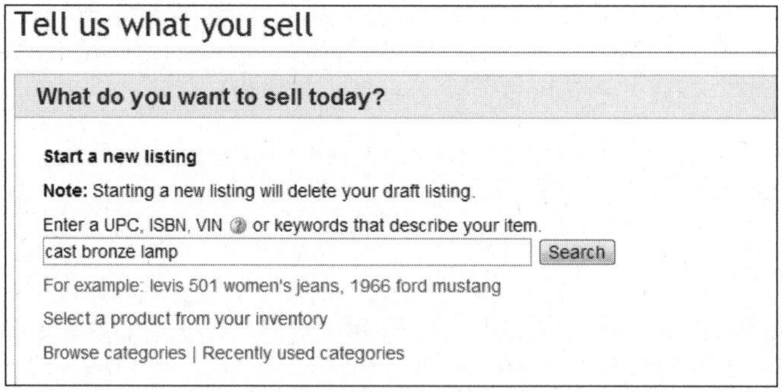

Figure 3-1:
Let eBay help you select the proper category for your item.

Tell us what you sell

What do you want to sell today?

Start a new listing

Note: Starting a new listing will delete your draft listing.

Enter a UPC, ISBN, VIN ⓘ or keywords that describe your item.

| cast bronze lamp | Search |

For example: levis 501 women's jeans, 1966 ford mustang

Select a product from your inventory

Browse categories | Recently used categories

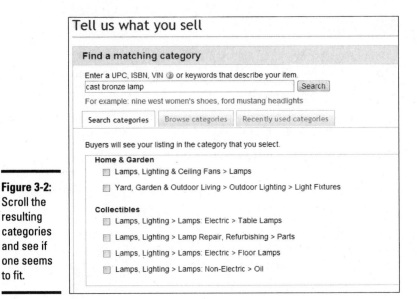

Figure 3-2: Scroll the resulting categories and see if one seems to fit.

You can select your item's category from this Search Categories tab, or click the Browse Categories tab for a deeper look. eBay offers you a wealth of choices in a handy point-and-click way. If you're unfamiliar with the types of items you can actually find in those categories, you may want to check out a category before you choose it to describe your item. Figure 3-3 shows you how to use the Browse Categories tool to narrow down subcategory selection.

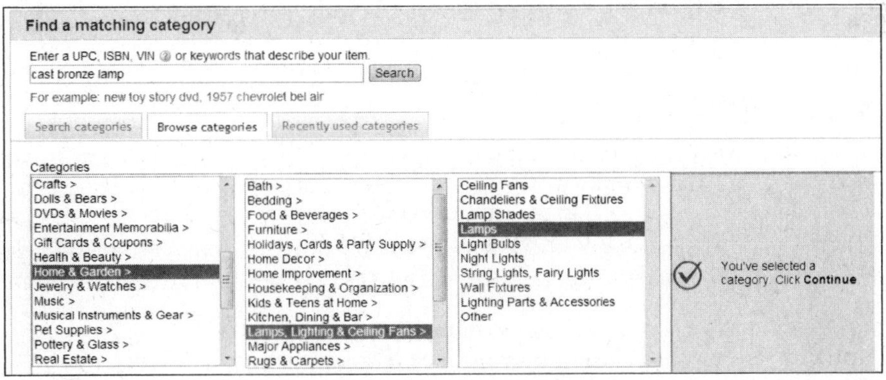

Figure 3-3: Narrowing to subcategories.

To select a category, here's the drill:

1. **Click one of the main categories in the pane on the left.**

   On the next pane to the right, you see a list of subcategories.

2. **Select the most appropriate subcategory in the pane to the right.**

   eBay makes it easy to narrow the category of your item: Just keep clicking until you hit the end of the line.

3. **Move to the next pane and** continue selecting subcategories until you've narrowed your listing category as much as possible.

   You know you've come to the last subcategory when eBay announces, `You've selected a category. Click Continue.`

If you've chosen to list an item, bid on an item, or even just browse in the Everything Else: Adult Only category, you need to follow separate, specific guidelines because that category contains graphic nudity or sexual content that may offend some community members. You must

✦ Be at least 18 years of age (but you already know that all eBay customers must be 18 or older)

✦ Have a valid credit card

✦ Complete a waiver stating that you're voluntarily choosing to access adults-only materials

If you have erotic items that are not quite that racy, you might like to sell them in a private auction, see the "I Want to Be Alone: The Private Auction" section, later in this chapter.

Creating the Perfect Item Title

After you figure out what category you want to list in, eBay wants to get down to business.

The most valuable onscreen real estate on eBay is the 80-character title of your item. The majority of buyers do title searches (in my research, around 98 percent of searches are performed by *title* only), and that's where your item must come up to be seen! So the onus is on you to give the most essential information right away to grab the eye of the reader who's just browsing. Be clear and informative enough to get noticed by eBay's search engine. Figure 3-4 shows examples of good titles. Note how some sellers beefed up the titles by using the Subtitle option.

TOM FORD silk POLKA DOTS narrow FORMAL eyelash Fringe scarf NWT Authentic!

8' wide Black & White Checkered Checker Flooring Floor Trailer Continuous Vinyl
Priced per linear Ft. Customize your exact size needed!

LOUIS VUITTON Multicolor Belt Black Gold Buckle LV Paris Black 70 28

Starting an eBay Business for Dummies SIGNED Marsha Collier How to Sell NEW Book
FREE SHIPPING~Priority Mail $2.99~SOLD BY AUTHOR

Skechers Women's Size 9.5 Shape Ups XF - Accelerators Walking Toning Shoes 12320

Dexter: The Complete Season 1-6 (DVD, 2012, 24-Disc Set) BRAND NEW Fast Shipping

AAA 8" Sparkling Golden & White CALCITE Terminated CLUSTER Cave from Morocco

Figure 3-4: These item titles are effective because they're clear, concise, and easy on the eyes.

Here are some ideas to help you write your item title:

✦ Use the most common name for the item.

✦ If the item is rare or hard to find, mention that.

✦ Mention the item's condition and if it's new.

✦ Mention the item's special qualities, such as its style, model, or edition.

✦ Avoid jargon or unusual characters, such as $, hyphens, and L@@K (or WOW), because they just clutter up the title — buyers rarely search for them.

Ordinarily, I don't throw out French phrases just for the fun of it. But when making a profit is an issue, I definitely have to agree with the French that choosing or not choosing *le mot juste* can mean the difference between having potential buyers passing by your item and having an all-out bidding war on your hands. Read on for tips about picking *the best words* to let your auction item shine.

Look for a phrase that pays

Here's a crash course in eBay lingo that can help bring you up to speed on attracting buyers to your auction. The following words are used frequently in eBay auctions and can do wonders to jump-start your title:

✦ Mint

✦ One of a kind (OOAK)

✦ Vintage

✦ Collectible

✦ Rare

✦ Unique

✦ Primitive

✦ Well-loved

There's a science to figuring out the value of a collectible (called *grading*). Do your homework before you assign a grade to your item. If you need more information on what these grades actually mean, Book II, Chapter 2 provides a translation.

Getting eyes on your listing with eBay Labs

Keywords! Keywords! Keywords! I can't stress enough that keywords are essential in your title. *Keywords* are single words that people would naturally use to search for an item. For example, if you're selling a shirt, common keywords for your title might include words that tell

✦ Color

✦ Size

✦ Fabric

✦ Manufacturer's name

✦ Whether it's a men's, women's, or children's garment

✦ Whether it's new or used, such as NWT (New With Tags)

A secret place to find accurate keywords that users search for on eBay is in eBay's fairly hidden eBay Labs tool, an example of which is shown in Figure 3-5. You can find this page at

```
http://labs.ebay.com/erl/demoto/to?
```

Type in some basic keywords for your item and the eBay Labs tool will let you know what keywords are the most popular for your item.

eBay acronyms and initialisms at a glance

The initialisms and the phrases in a prior section "Look for a phrase that pays" aren't the only marketing standards you have at your eBay disposal. As eBay has grown, so has the lingo that members use as shortcuts to describe their merchandise. Table 3-1 gives you a handy list of common abbreviations and phrases used to describe items. (**Hint:** "Mint" means "may as well be brand new," not "cool chocolate treat attached.")

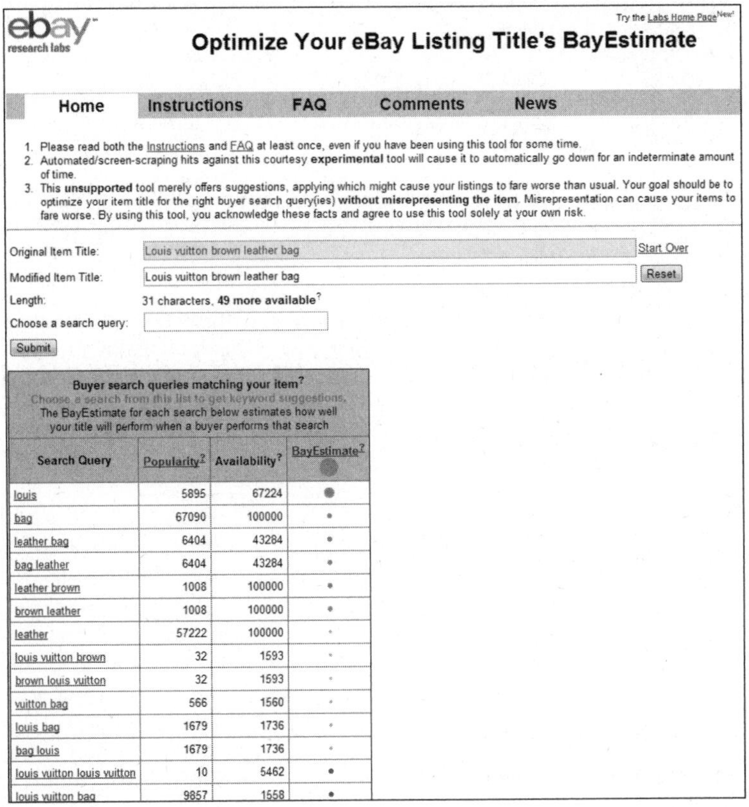

Book III
Chapter 3

Listing Items
for Sale

Figure 3-5:
Get eBay's help with finding accurate keywords.

Table 3-1	A Quick List of eBay Abbreviations	
eBay	*What It Abbreviates*	*What It Means*
MIB	Mint in Box	The item is in the original box, in great shape, and just the way you'd expect to find it in a store.
MIMB	Mint in Mint Box	The box has never been opened and looks like it just left the factory.
MOC	Mint on Card	The item is mounted on its original display card, attached with the original fastenings, in store-new condition.
NRFB	Never Removed from Box	The item has never been opened.

(continued)

Table 3-1 *(continued)*

eBay	*What It Abbreviates*	*What It Means*
COA	Certificate of Authenticity	Documentation that vouches for the genuineness of an item, such as an autograph or painting.
NOS	New Old Stock	Merchandise is new and unopened, but may have been stocked (or on the shelf) for a while.
OEM	Original Equipment Manufacture	You're selling the item and all the equipment that originally came with it, but you don't have the original box, owner's manual, or instructions.
OOAK	One of a Kind	You are selling the only one in existence!
NR	No Reserve Price	A reserve price is the price you can set when you begin your auction. If bids don't meet the reserve, you don't have to sell. Many buyers don't like reserve prices because they don't think that they can get a bargain. (For tips on how to allay these fears and get bids in reserve price auctions, see the "Using your secret safety net — reserve price" section.) If you're *not* listing a reserve for your item, be sure to let bidders know.
NWT	New with Tags	An item, possibly apparel, is in new condition with the tags from the manufacturer still affixed.
NWOT	New, but Without Store Tags	Generally a new article of apparel that is missing the store tags, but is unused.
HTF, OOP	Hard to Find, Out of Print	Out of print, only a few ever made, or people grabbed up all there were. (HTF *doesn't* mean you spent a week looking for it in the attic.)

Normally, you can rely on eBay abbreviations to get your point across, but make sure that you mean it and that you're using it accurately. Don't label something MIB (Mint in Box) when it looks like it's been Mashed in Box.

You'll find more eBay (and social media) abbreviations on my website, `www.coolebaytools.com/tools/online-acronyms-and-ebay-abbreviations`. (Or click the Tools tab at `www.coolebaytools.com`, and then click the FAQ on Online Acronyms and eBay Abbreviations.)

Don't let your title ruin your listing

Imagine going to a supermarket and asking where you can find the *stringy stuff that you boil* instead of asking where the spaghetti is. You might end up with mung bean sprouts — delicious to some, but hardly what you had in mind. That's why you should check and recheck your spelling. Savvy buyers use the eBay search engine to find merchandise; if the name of your item is spelled wrong, the search engine may not find it. Poor spelling and incomprehensible grammar in descriptions also reflect badly on you. If you're in competition with another seller, the buyer is likelier to trust the seller *hoo nose gud speling.*

In my travels, I meet so many interesting people with lots of great stories about their forays on eBay. One of my favorites is the story told to me by a lovely lady in Salt Lake City. She brought to my class her biggest eBay bargain. She won a Shaquille O'Neill signed basketball on eBay for 1 cent! Yep, one red cent (plus shipping). I'll bet that seller had a rude surprise when his listing closed! Oh, you want to know why such a valuable collectible sold for so little? The seller couldn't spell Shaquille and listed the all-important name in the item's title as *Schackeel.*

If you've finished writing your item title and you have spaces left over, *please* fight the urge to dress the title up with lots of exclamation points and asterisks. No matter how gung-ho you are about your item, the eBay search engine may overlook your item if the title is encrusted with meaningless **** and !!!! symbols. If bidders do see your title, they may become annoyed by the virtual shrillness and ignore it anyway!!!!!!!!! (See what I mean?)

Another distracting habit is overdoing capital letters. To buyers, seeing everything in caps is LIKE SEEING A HYSTERICAL SALESPERSON SCREAMING AT THEM TO BUY NOW! All that is considered *shouting,* which is rude and tough on the eyes. Use capitalization SPARINGLY, and ONLY to finesse a particular point or feature.

Giving the title punch with a subtitle

A useful feature on eBay is the availability of subtitles. eBay allows you to buy an additional 55 characters as a subtitle, which will appear under your item title in a list formatted search. The fee for this extra promotion is $0.50 ($1.50 for 30 days), and in a few circumstances, it is definitely worth your while. Any text that you input will really make your item stand out in the crowd — but (you knew there would be a *but,* didn't you?) these additional 55 characters won't come up in a title search. So if you have all those words in your description, the words will be found either way with a title-and-description search.

Creating Your Item Description

After you hook potential bidders with your title, reel 'em in with a fabulous description. Don't think Hemingway here; think infomercial (the classier the better). Figure 3-6 shows a concise description of the item for sale. You can write a magnificent description, as well — all you have to do is click the box and start typing.

Figure 3-6:
Writing
a good
description
can
mean the
difference
between
success and
failure.

Karen Neuburger Size M Night Shirt - Brand New w tags

I just love this nightshirt with the Cappuccino, latte, coffee espresso print! Dream the softest, coziest dreams in Karen Neuburger sleepwear. Always in the softest knits. Always relaxed in silhouette. And so comfortable, you'll never want to take them off.

Chosen as one of Oprah's favorite things:
"These are my favorite pajamas! Made with the finest brushed cotton, they come in a variety of colors."—Oprah

- Soft and cozy interlock knit fabric
- Pullover nightshirt falls above the knee
- Three button Henley placket
- Machine wash cold, tumble dry low
- 60% cotton 40% polyester

Sizing: S (6-8) M (10-12) L (14-16) XL (18-20)

Composing the description

Here's a list of suggestions for writing an item description:

✦ **Write a factual description.** Do you carefully describe the item, stating every fact you know about it? Do you avoid the use of jargon? Does the description answer almost any question a potential buyer might ask? If not, do some revising.

✦ **Accentuate the positive.** Be enthusiastic when you list all the reasons everyone should buy the item. Unlike the title, the description can take up as much space as you want. Even if you use a photo, be precise in your description — tell the reader, for example, the item's size, color, and fabric. Refer to "Creating the perfect item title," earlier in this chapter, for ideas on what to emphasize.

✦ **Include the negative.** Don't hide the truth of your item's condition. Trying to conceal flaws costs you in the long run: You'll not only get tagged with bad feedback, but the buyer can get his or her money back from PayPal if it arrives "not as described." If your vintage item has a scratch, a nick, a dent, a crack, a ding, a tear, a rip, missing pieces, replacement parts, faded color, dirty smudges, or a bad smell (especially if cleaning might damage the item), mention it in the description. If your item has been overhauled, rebuilt, repainted, or hot-rodded, say so. You don't want the buyer to send back your merchandise because you weren't truthful about imperfections or modifications. This type of omission can lead to losing the item and having the money taken out of your PayPal account.

✦ **Include short, friendly banter.** You want to make the customer feel comfortable shopping with you. Don't be afraid to let your personality show!

✦ **Update your My eBay page.** Let people know a little about you and who they're dealing with. When customers have to decide between two people selling the same item and all else is equal, they'll place their bids with the seller who makes them feel secure.

✦ **Limit the number of auction rules (or terms of sale).** Some sellers include a list of rules that's longer than the item's description. Nothing turns off a prospective buyer like paragraph after paragraph of rules and regulations. If you really *must* put in a litany of rules, use the following bit of HTML to make the size of the text smaller: `<font size=-1>`.

✦ **Choose a reasonable typeface size.** Many users are now looking at eBay on mobile devices. If you design your listings for a large computer display, your typefaces may be way too large for the average user. Forcing a user to scroll leads to frustrated customers. I recommend something in the range of 10 to 14 points, depending on the typeface you choose.

✦ **Be concise and to the point — don't ramble!** As my sixth-grade English teacher user to say, "Make it like a woman's skirt: long enough to cover the subject, yet short enough to keep it interesting." Too many sellers these days drone on and on, causing bidders to have to scroll down the page several times. You can quickly lose your audience this way. They'll look for a listing with a less complicated look.

Jazzing it up with HTML

When you type in your description, you have the option of jazzing things up with a bit of HTML coding, or you can use eBay's HTML text editor, described in Book V, Chapter 3. If you know how to use a word processor, you'll have no trouble dressing up your text with this tool. Table 3-2 shows you a few HTML codes that you can insert into your text to help you pretty things up.

**Book III
Chapter 3**

*Listing Items
for Sale*

Table 3-2	A Short List of HTML Codes	
HTML Code	*How to Use It*	*What It Does*
`<b></b>`	`<b>cool collectible</b>`	**cool collectible** (bold type)
`<i></i>`	`<i>cool collectible</i>`	*cool collectible* (italic type)
`<b><i></b></i>`	`<b><i>cool collectible </i></b>`	***cool collectible*** (bold and italic type)
`<font color=red> </font>`	`<font color=red>cool collectible</font>`	Selected text appears in red
`<font size=+1> </font>`	`<font size=+3>cool </font> collectible`	cool collectible (font size normal+1 through 4, increases size *x* times)
` `	`cool collectible`	cool collectible (inserts line break)
`<p>`	`cool<p>collectible`	cool collectible (inserts paragraph space)
`<hr>`	`cool collectible <hr>cheap`	cool collectible ——— cheap (inserts horizontal rule)
`<h1></h1>`	`<h1>cool collectible </h1>`	**cool collectible** (converts text to headline size)

You can go back and forth from the HTML text editor to regular input and add additional codes here and there by selecting the View/Edit HTML check box (when you're in the HTML text editor). You can prepare your listings ahead of time in an HTML composer in the Mozilla SeaMonkey suite (see Book V, Chapter 3 for more details) and save them to your computer as plain TXT files (I do). That way, pre-designed listings are always retrievable for use (just copy and paste) no matter what program or form you're using to list them.

Listing Multiples of an Item for Sale with Variations

Whether you have 20 of one item, or the same item in different variations (size or color), eBay has a handy way to list multiple items in one listing. For a fixed-price sale for multiple items that are all the same, just indicate the number you have in the appropriate box on the Sell an Item page.

When you have different sizes or colors for an item, you'll want to list with variations. A listing with variations will look similar to the listing shown in Figure 3-7, where the buyer can choose size, type, color, and so forth from drop-down lists.

Figure 3-7: How the customer views a variations listing.

The option to include variations in a listing may not show up on the Sell an Item page, but after you select one of the categories where variations are permitted, a window like the one shown in Figure 3-8 pops up. You can then select the Yes option to answer the question "Do you want to include variations in this listing?" and click Continue.

Currently, you can create listings with variations in the following categories:

✦ Baby

✦ Clothing, Shoes & Accessories

✦ Crafts

✦ Health & Beauty

+ Home & Garden (most sub-categories)
+ Jewelry & Watches
+ Pet Supplies
+ Sporting Goods
+ eBay Motors Apparel & Merchandise

eBay provides you with a list of common variation details when you click the Add Variation Detail link. If you have custom variations, click Add Your Own Detail. You can select up to five variation details — such as Color, Size, Width, Material, and Style — with up to 30 values for each detail.

A multi-variation listing may appear higher in search results. Putting up multiple listings for the same item is fruitless; eBay won't show more than one identical auction listing from a single seller at one time in search results and may remove identical listings from the site.

A matching set of cuff links is considered one item, as is the complete 37-volume set of *The Smith Family Ancestry and Genealogical History since 1270.* If you have more than one of the same item, I suggest that you sell the items one at a time, because you will more than likely get higher final bids for your items when you sell them individually.

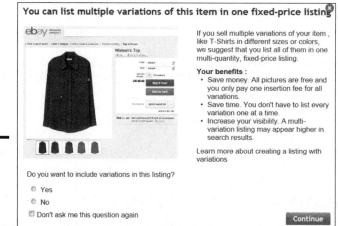

Figure 3-8:
Selecting
the option
to include
variations.

Setting Bids, Prices, and Reserves

What do a baseball autographed by JFK, a used walkie-talkie, and a Jaguar sports car have in common? They all started with a $.99 minimum bid. eBay requires you to set a *minimum bid,* the lowest bid allowed in an auction. You may be surprised to see stuff worth tens of thousands of dollars offered for auction starting just a under a buck. These sellers haven't lost their minds. Neither are they worried someone could end up tooling down the highway in their $100,000 sports car for the price of a burger. They protect their final sale price with a reserve. (Keep reading; I explain in the later section "Using your secret safety net — reserve price.")

Before you set a minimum bid, do your homework and make some savvy marketing decisions. If your auction isn't going as you hoped, you *could* end up selling Grandma Ethel's Ming vase for a dollar. See "Making Midcourse Auction Corrections," later in this chapter, to see how you can make changes in your listing if you've made some egregious error.

Setting a minimum bid — how low can you go?

Setting an incredibly low minimum is a subtle strategy that gives you more bang for your buck. You can use a low minimum bid to attract more bidders who will, in turn, drive up the price to the item's real value — especially if, after doing your research, you know that the item is particularly hot.

The more bids you get, the more people will want to bid on your item because they perceive it as hot.

If you're worried about the outcome of the final bid, you can protect your item by using a *reserve price* (the price the bidding needs to reach before the item can be sold). This ensures that you won't have to sell your item for a bargain-basement price because your reserve price protects your investment. The best advice is to set a reserve price that is the lowest amount you'll take for your item, and then set a minimum bid that is ridiculously low. However, use a reserve only when absolutely necessary because some bidders pass up reserve auctions.

Going with a Buy It Now price

eBay's Buy It Now (*BIN* in eBay-speak) is available for single-item auctions. This feature allows buyers to purchase an item *now.* Have you ever wanted an item really badly and you didn't want to wait until the end of an auction? If the seller offers Buy It Now, you can purchase that item immediately.

When listing an item this way, just specify the amount the item can sell for in the Buy It Now price area — the amount can be whatever you want. If you choose to sell a hot item during the holiday rush, for example, you can make the BIN price as high as you think it can go. If you just want the item to move, make your BIN price the average price you see the item go for on eBay.

After your item receives a bid, the BIN option disappears and the item goes through the normal auction process. If you have a reserve price (as well as a BIN price) on your item, the BIN feature doesn't disappear until a bidder meets your reserve price through the normal bidding process. To list an auction with Buy It Now, the price needs to be at least 30 percent higher than the starting price.

The Buy It Now price will remain, if there is a bid that doesn't reach 50 percent of your BIN price in certain categories:

1 Motors, Parts & Accessories (eBay Motors)

2 Tickets

3 Clothing, Shoes & Accessories

4 Cell Phones & Accessories

Using your secret safety net — reserve price

Here's a little secret: The reason sellers list big-ticket items such as Ferraris, grand pianos, and high-tech computer equipment with a starting bid of $.99 is because they're protected from losing money with a reserve price. The *reserve price* is the lowest price that must be met before the item can be sold. It is not required by eBay but can protect you. For this feature, eBay charges an additional fee that varies depending on how high your reserve is.

For example, say you list a first-edition book — John Steinbeck's *The Grapes of Wrath*. You set the starting price at $.99 and the reserve price at $80. That means people can start bidding at $.99, and if at the end of the auction the book hasn't reached the $80 reserve, you don't have to sell the book.

As with everything in life, using a reserve price for your auctions has an upside and a downside. Many choosy bidders and bargain hunters blast past reserve-price auctions because they see a reserve price as a sign that proclaims "No bargains here!" Many bidders figure they can get a better deal on the same item with an auction that proudly declares *NR* (for *no reserve*) in its description. As an enticement to those bidders, you see lots of NR listings in auction titles.

If you need to set a reserve on your item, help the bidder out. Many bidders shy away from an auction that has a reserve, but if they're really interested, they will read the item description. To dispel their fears that the item is way too expensive or out of their price range, add a line in your description that states the amount of your reserve price. "I have put a reserve of $75 on this item to protect my investment; the highest bid over $75 will win the item." A phrase such as this takes away the vagueness of the reserve auction and allows you to place a reserve with a low opening bid. (You want to reel 'em in, remember?)

On lower-priced items, I suggest that you set a higher minimum bid and set no reserve.

If bids don't reach a set reserve price, some sellers offer an underbidder a second chance offer or relist the item for another whack at the buying public.

Timing Your Auction: Is It Everything?

Although I discuss auction length in depth in Chapter 2 of this minibook, it's important to mention a bit more here. eBay gives you a choice of auction length: 1, 3, 5, 7, or 10 days. Just click the number you want in the box. If you choose a 10-day auction, you add $.40 to your listing fee.

My auction-length strategy depends on the time of year and the item I'm selling, and I generally have great success. If you have an item that you think will sell pretty well, run a 7-day auction (be sure to cover a full weekend) so bidders have time to check it out before they decide to bid. However, if you know that you have a red-hot item that's going to fly off the shelves — such as a rare toy or a hard-to-get video game — choose a 3-day auction. Eager bidders tend to bid higher and more often to beat out their competition if the item's hot and going fast. A 3-day auction is long enough to give trendy items exposure and ring up bids.

No matter how many days you choose to run your auction, it ends at exactly the same time of day as it starts. A 7-day auction that starts on Thursday at 9:03:02 a.m. ends the following Thursday at 9:03:02 a.m.

Although I know the folks at eBay are pretty laid back, they do run on military time. That means they use a 24-hour clock set to Pacific time. So 3:30 in the afternoon is 15:30, and one minute after midnight is 00:01. Questions about time conversions? Check out www.timezoneconverter.com or look at the table in Chapter 2. And so you don't have to keep flipping back to that page, I also include a printable conversion chart of eBay times in the Tools area of my website (www.coolebaytools.com).

With listings running 24 hours a day, 7 days a week, you should know when the most bidders are around to take a gander at your wares. Here are some times to think about:

✦ **Saturday and Sunday:** Always run listings over a weekend. People log on and off eBay all day to look for desired items.

✦ **Holiday weekends:** If a holiday weekend's coming up around the time you're setting up your auction, run your auction through the weekend and end it a day after the "holiday" Monday. This gives prospective bidders a chance to catch up with the items they perused over the weekend and plan their bidding strategies.

✦ **Time of day:** The best times of day to start and end your auction are during eBay's peak hours of operation, which are 5:00 p.m. to 9:00 p.m. Pacific Time, right after work on the West Coast. Perform your completed auction research, however, to be sure that this strategy applies to your item, because this timing depends on the item you're auctioning.

Unless you're an insomniac or a vampire who wants to sell to werewolves, don't let your auctions close in the middle of the night. Not enough bidders are around to cause last-minute bidding that would bump up the price.

I Want to Be Alone: The Private Auction

In a *private* auction, bidders' User IDs are kept under wraps. Sellers typically use this option to protect the identities of bidders during auctions for high-priced big-ticket items (say, that restored World War II fighter). Wealthy eBay members may not want the world to know that they have the resources to buy expensive items. Private auctions are also held for items from the Adult Only category. (Gee, there's a shocker.)

The famous sign pictured in almost every piece of Disney promotion (for the first 40 or so years of Disneyland's existence) was put up for sale on eBay in 2000. The sign was purchased by actor John Stamos for a high bid of $30,700. Unfortunately for John, the Disney auctions did not use the Private Auction feature. After news of the winner's name hit the tabloids, the entire world knew John's eBay user ID! He had to change his ID in a hurry to end the throngs of lovey-dovey e-mail messages headed to his computer!

Adding Visuals to Highlight Your Item

With so many listings posted daily on eBay, you need some way to get your listing noticed. Adding visual interest to catch a potential buyer's eye is one way. As you fill out the Sell an Item page, take advantage of the visual elements that eBay offers.

A picture is worth a thousand words

Clichés again? Perhaps. eBay requires that you have at least one image to illustrate what you are selling. You can add up to 12 pictures on your listing for free, as shown in Figure 3-9. You can find the images (after the listing is over) in My eBay⇨Completed Listings for 90 days.

If you want to host your pictures on a website or other server, you can use the *copy web files* uploader. Your pictures will then be optimized automatically for use on eBay. You may also add web-hosted images to your description. See Book V, Chapter 5 for the necessary coding and instructions.

For the best quality, eBay recommends that you upload images that are more than 1600 pixels in height or width.

Listing Designer

How many times have you seen an item on eBay laid out on the page all pretty-like with a fancy colorful border around the description? If that sort of thing appeals to you, eBay's Listing Designer can supply you with borders for almost any type of item for $0.10. Will the pretty borders increase the amount of bids your auction will get? It's extremely doubtful. A clean item description with a couple of good, clear pictures of your item is all you need.

**Book III
Chapter 3**

**Listing Items
for Sale**

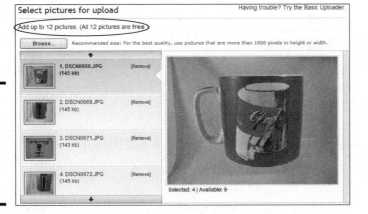

Figure 3-9:
Upload images to eBay with a couple of mouse clicks!

Listing the Payment Methods You'll Accept

Yeah, sure, eBay is loads of fun, but the bottom line to selling is the phrase "Show me the money!" You make the call on what you're willing to take as money from your auction's high bidder. eBay offers the following payment options — just select the ones that you like:

✦ **Personal check, cashier's check, bank transfers, or money orders.** These are only permissible as payment for capital equipment, Real Estate, Adult Only, and some Motors categories, or when a customer picks up an item in person. As a seller, you want to get paid with as little risk as possible. The only drawback? You have to wait for the buyer to mail the money.

✦ **Credit cards:** If you accept credit cards, using PayPal is the cheapest and most convenient way to go. If you have a merchant account through a retail store, be sure to select the little check boxes next to the credit cards you accept. eBay also allows sellers to accept credit card payments from ProPay, Skrill, or the merchant credit card account you've set up for your business.

✦ **Online escrow:** An option for selling vehicles in eBay motors, an escrow service, `escrow.com`, acts as a referee, a neutral third party. This service charges you a percent of the sale price.

Where You Are and Where You'll Ship To

When listing an item for sale on eBay, you come to the area where you need to input your payment and shipping information. You have the option of offering free shipping, a flat rate, or offer calculated shipping. The charges appear in a box at the top and the bottom of your item description.

But how you handle shipping — and its associated cost for your buyers — depends on what you're shipping (how big it is), where you're shipping it, and the carrier you decide to use. So take a bit of time to consider your location and your shipping options before you fill out this section.

Offering free shipping helps sell items. Studies have proven that customers prefer to buy items online that offer free shipping.

eBay has some rules about shipping

eBay has rules about how much you can charge for shipping in certain categories. Some greedy sellers would charge egregious amounts for shipping their items, so eBay cracked down and made maximum shipping limits. Table 3-3 gives you the current shipping charge limits as of April 12, 2013.

Table 3-3	Shipping Charge Limits by Category	
Category: Books		
Subcategory	*Type of Merchandise*	*Maximum Shipping Charge*
Accessories	Address Books	$4.00
	Blank Diaries & Journals	$5.00
	Book Covers	$5.00
	Book Plates	$3.00
	Bookmarks	$3.00
	Other	$3.00
Antiquarian & Collectible	Antiquarian & Collectible	$4.00
Audiobooks	Audiobooks	$4.00
Catalogs	Catalogs	$4.00
Children's Books	Children's Books	$4.00
Cookbooks	Cookbooks	$4.00
Fiction Books	Fiction Books	$4.00
Magazine Back Issues	Magazine Back Issues	$5.00
Nonfiction Books	Nonfiction Books	$4.00
Other	Other	$4.00
Textbooks, Education	Textbooks, Education	$4.00
Wholesale & Bulk Lots	Audiobooks	$10.00
	Books > 101-500	$20.00
	Books > 11-50 Items	$8.00
	Books > 51-100 Items	$15.00
	Books > 6-10 Items	$6.00
	Books > More than 500	$30.00
	Books > Up to 5 Items	$6.00
	Magazines	$8.00
	Other	$6.00

Book III
Chapter 3

Listing Items
for Sale

(continued)

Table 3-3 *(continued)*

Category: DVDs & Movies

Subcategory	Type of Merchandise	Maximum Shipping Charge
DVD, HD DVD & Blu-ray	DVD, HD DVD & Blu-ray	$3.00
Film	Film	$6.00
Laserdisc	Laserdisc	$6.00
Other Formats	Other Formats	$3.00
UMD	UMD	$5.00
VHS	VHS	$3.00
VHS Non-US (PAL)	VHS Non-US (PAL)	$5.00
Wholesale Lots	DVDs > 101-250 Items	$30.00
	DVDs > 11-50 Items	$15.00
	DVDs > 251-500 Items	$60.00
	DVDs > 501-1000 Items	$120.00
	DVDs > 51-100 Items	$25.00
	DVDs > Up to 10 Items	$10.00
	Mixed Lots	$10.00
	Movies Accessories	$17.00
	Other	$10.00
	VHS > 101-500 Items	$30.00
	VHS > 11-50 Items	$15.00
	VHS > 51-100 Items	$25.00
	VHS > More than 500 Items	$120.00
	VHS > Up to 10 Items	$10.00

Category: Music

Subcategory	Type of Merchandise	Maximum Shipping Charge
Accessories	Accessories	$5.00
Cassettes	Cassettes	$3.00

Category: Music

Subcategory	Type of Merchandise	Maximum Shipping Charge
CDs	CDs	$3.00
DVD Audio	DVD Audio	$3.00
Other Formats	Other Formats	$3.00
Records	Records	$4.00
Super Audio CDs	Super Audio CDs	$3.00
Wholesale Lots	Cassettes	$10.00
	CDs > 101-500 Items	$30.00
	CDs > 11-100 Items	$20.00
	CDs > More than 500 Items	$60.00
	CDs > Up to 10 Items	$10.00
	Other Formats	$10.00
	Records > 11-50 Items	$15.00
	Records > More than 50 Items	$25.00
	Records > Up to 10 Items	$10.00

Category: Video Games

Subcategory	Type of Merchandise	Maximum Shipping Charge
Accessories	Accessories	$6.00
Games	Games	$4.00
Internet Games	Games > Guild Wars	$6.00
	Games > World of Warcraft	$3.00
	Software & PC Versions	$6.00
Other	Other	$4.00
Systems	Systems	$15.00
Vintage Games	Vintage Games	$6.00
Wholesale Lots	Accessories	$10.00
	Console Systems	$50.00
	Games	$9.00
	Other	$9.00

**Book III
Chapter 3**

**Listing Items
for Sale**

Setting shipping and handling terms

Before you list your item, think about the details related to shipping your merchandise. Here are some of your choices for where you'll ship:

✦ **Ship to the United States only:** This option is selected by default; it means you ship only domestically.

✦ **Will ship worldwide:** The world is your oyster. But make sure that you can afford it.

✦ **Will ship to United States and the following countries:** If you're comfortable shipping to certain countries but not to others, make your selections here. Your choices appear on the item page.

When you indicate that you will ship internationally, your listing can show up on the international eBay sites (for a small fee), which is a fantastic way to attract new buyers! eBay has lots of international users, so you may want to consider selling your items around the world. If you do, be sure to clearly state in the description all extra shipping costs and customs charges.

You also get to set the method and fees related to shipping. eBay buyers love seeing a flat shipping fee. If you can convince yourself to find a reasonable midway point, a fixed shipping price may just beat your competition. Figure 3-10 shows you the Sell an Item form's area to fill in for a flat shipping rate.

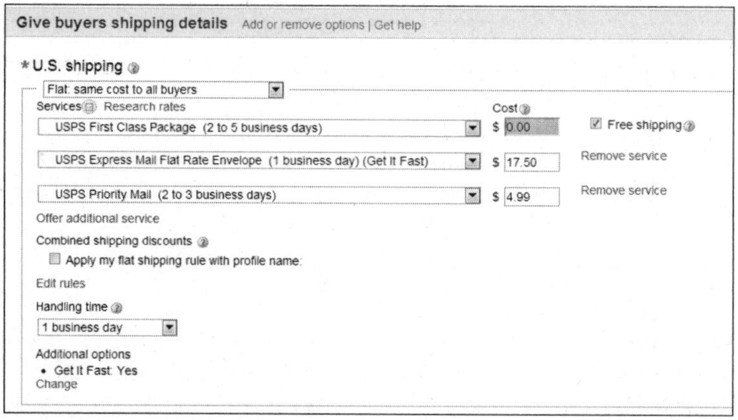

Figure 3-10:
The form you use for flat shipping rates.

Give buyers shipping details   Add or remove options | Get help

＊U.S. shipping ⓘ

[Flat: same cost to all buyers ▼]

Services ⓘ Research rates   Cost ⓘ

[USPS First Class Package (2 to 5 business days) ▼] $ [0.00]   ☑ Free shipping ⓘ

[USPS Express Mail Flat Rate Envelope (1 business day) (Get It Fast) ▼] $ [17.50]   Remove service

[USPS Priority Mail (2 to 3 business days) ▼] $ [4.99]   Remove service

Offer additional service

Combined shipping discounts ⓘ

☐ Apply my flat shipping rule with profile name:

Edit rules

Handling time ⓘ

[1 business day ▼]

Additional options
• Get It Fast: Yes
Change

Also in the form's shipping details, you can set a handling time, which is more attractive when you say you will ship within a (business) day of receiving the customer's money. eBay puts the phrase "Get it fast" on these listings when you also offer overnight shipping.

Combining free shipping with 1-day handling earns your listing the designation *Fast 'n Free,* as shown in Figure 3-11. This delivery-truck icon attracts a lot of eyes when customers are searching. Plus, eBay gives a boost to items having this designation in Best Match search results.

Figure 3-11:
Get your
item
shipped
Fast 'n Free!

> On or before **Thu. Apr. 11** to 91325
> Estimated by eBay FAST 'N FREE ⓘ

Using eBay's shipping calculator

When your item weighs two pounds or more, you may want to use eBay's versatile shipping calculator to determine your flat shipping-and-handling cost or to quote a calculated shipping cost. Using the shipping calculator has these advantages:

✦ **It accounts for variable rates:** Because UPS and the U.S. Postal Service now charge variable rates for packages of the same weight, based on distance, using the calculator simplifies things for your customers (and for you). *Note:* Be sure you've weighed the item.

✦ **It includes your handling amount:** The calculator allows you to input a handling amount and adds it to the overall shipping total — but does not break out these amounts separately for the customer.

Figure 3-12 shows how simple the calculator is. You may select up to three levels of shipping per item.

You can check out the associated costs by clicking the Show Rates button, which shows you all shipping costs, so you can decide to ship with either the U.S. Postal Service or UPS. I always test my packages from a California ZIP code (because that's where I live) to a New York ZIP code. Doing this gives me an estimate for Zone 8, which is the most expensive option (coast-to-coast by distance) when shipping in the U.S.

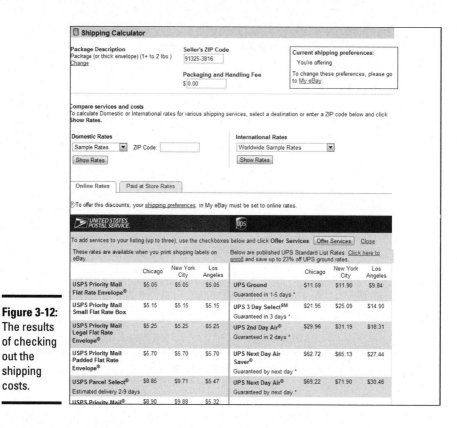

Figure 3-12:
The results
of checking
out the
shipping
costs.

eBay's shipping calculator does not include Domestic First class (can be used for up to a 1-pound package) or First Class International (can be used for up to a 4-pound package). It also does not offer the options for domestic Regional Flat Rate Priority boxes (see Book VII for more details).

You can check out the fees for different shipping services also (after signing in) by using the full eBay shipping calculator located at

```
http://cgi3.ebay.com/aw-cgi/eBayISAPI.dll?emitseller
shippingcalculator
```

The proper shipping price appears on the item page based on the shopper's registered ZIP code, so they will know immediately how much shipping will be to their location. Follow these steps in the Sell an Item process to have eBay calculate the charges for you:

1. **In the Shipping area, choose Calculated: Cost Varies by Buyer Location from the drop-down menu, as shown in Figure 3-13.**

2. **Select your package's type and weight from the drop-down lists, and fill in package dimensions as needed.**

3. **Select a carrier from the drop-down lists (as shown in Figure 3-14).**

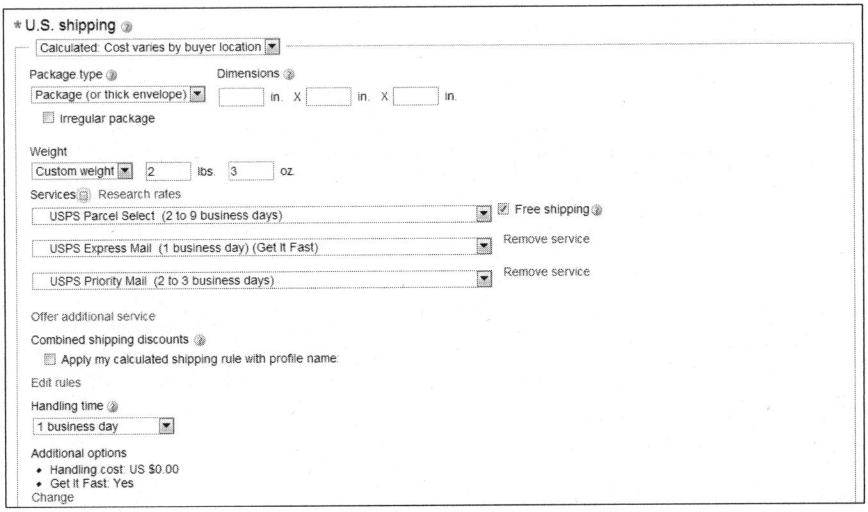

Figure 3-13: The Calculated shipping-rates form.

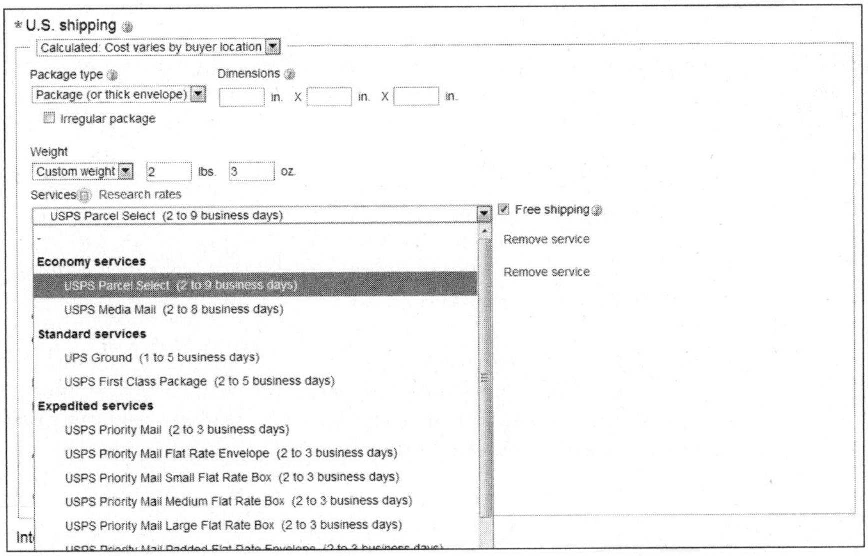

Figure 3-14: Selecting a shipping service from the drop-down list.

4. **In the additional options, click to add a Handling Cost to cover your shipping expenses.**

   When adding your packaging and handling charges, don't worry that the buyers will see these individual fees. eBay combines this amount with the shipping cost and shows the total as one shipping price.

   After you've input all your information, you can forget about shipping charges, because eBay takes over. Check out Book VII for more information on shipping options — and on how to mechanize the process.

Checking Your Work and Starting the Sale

After you've filled in all the blanks on the Sell an Item page and you feel ready to join the world of e-commerce, follow these steps:

1. **Click the Review button at the bottom of the Sell an Item page.**

   You go to the Verification page, the place where you can catch mistakes before your item is listed. The Verification page shows you a condensed version of all your information and tallies how much eBay is charging you in fees and options to run this auction. You can also click to see a preview of how your auction description and pictures will look on the site.

   You also may find the Verification page helpful as a last-minute chance to get your bearings. If you've chosen a general category, eBay asks you whether you're certain there isn't a more appropriate category. You can go back to any of the pages that need correcting by clicking the appropriate tab at the top of the Verification page. Make category changes or any other changes and additions, and then head for the Verification page again.

2. **Check for mistakes.**

   Nitpick for common, careless errors; you won't be sorry. I've seen eBay members make goofs such as the wrong category listing, spelling and grammatical errors, and missing information about shipping, handling and payment methods.

3. **When you're sure everything is accurate and you're happy with your item listing, click the Submit My Listing button.**

   A Listing Confirmation page pops up. At that precise moment, your sale begins, even though it *may* be as much as an hour before it appears in eBay's search and listings updates. If you want to see your listing right away and check for bids, your Confirmation page provides a link for that purpose. Click the link, and you're there.

All listing pages come with this friendly warning: *Seller assumes all responsibility for listing this item.* Some eBay veterans just gloss over this warning after they've been wheeling and dealing for a while, but it's an important rule to remember. Whether you're buying or selling, you're always responsible for your actions.

For the first 24 hours after your sale is underway, eBay stamps the Item page with a funky sunrise icon next to the listing in the category listing page or search results page. This is just a little reminder for buyers to come take a look at the latest items up for sale.

Making Midcourse Auction Corrections

If you made a mistake filling out the Sell an Item page but didn't notice it until after the listing is up and running, don't worry. Pencils have erasers, and eBay allows revisions. You can make changes at two stages of the game: before the first bid is placed and after the bidding war is underway. This section explains what you can (and can't) correct — and when you have to accept the little imperfections of your Sell an Item page.

Making changes before bidding begins

Here's what you can change about your auction before bids have been placed, as long as your auction does not end within 12 hours:

+ The title, subtitle, or description
+ The item category
+ The item's Minimum Bid price
+ The item's Buy It Now price (you can add or change it)
+ The reserve price (you can add, change, or remove it)
+ The URL of the picture you're including with your auction
+ A private-auction designation (you can add or remove it)

When you revise a listing, eBay puts a little notation on your page that reads: Description (revised).

To revise a listing (or auction before bids have been received), follow these steps:

1. **Go to the item page and click the Revise Your Item link.**

This link appears only if you've signed in on eBay. If the item hasn't received any bids, a message appears on your screen to indicate that you may update the item.

You're taken to the Revise Your Item page, which outlines the rules for revising your item. At the bottom, the item number is filled in.

2. **Click Revise Item.**

You arrive at the Revise Your Item page which looks uncannily like the Sell an Item form.

3. **Scroll down to the area you'd like to change.**

4. **Make changes to the item information.**

5. **When you've finished making changes, click the Continue button at the bottom of the page.**

A summary of how your newly revised listing appears in search is on your screen. If you've incurred any additional fees, the amount is listed at the bottom of the page. If you want to make more changes, click the Back button of your browser or the Edit Listing link.

6. **When you're happy with your revisions, click Submit Revisions.**

Making changes in the last 12 hours

If your auction is up and running and already receiving bids, you can still make some slight modifications to it. Newly added information is clearly separated from the original text and pictures. In addition, eBay puts a time-stamp on the additional info in case questions from early bidders crop up later.

After your item receives bids, eBay allows you to add to your item's description. If you feel you were at a loss for words in writing your item's description — or if a lot of potential bidders are asking the same questions — go ahead and make all the additions you want. But whatever you put there the first time around stays in the description as well.

Follow the same procedure for making changes before bidding begins. When you arrive at the Revise Your Item page, you can *only* add to your description, add features, or add further payment information.

Don't let an oversight grow into a failure to communicate — and don't ignore iffy communication until the listing is over. Correct any inaccuracies in your listing information *now* to avoid problems later on.

Always check your e-mail (or your My eBay messages) to see whether bidders have questions about your item. If a bidder wants to know about flaws, be truthful and courteous when returning e-mails. As you get more familiar with eBay (and with writing descriptions), the number of e-mail questions will decrease. If you enjoy good customer service in your day-to-day shopping, here's your chance to give some back.

Book III
Chapter 3

Listing Items
for Sale

Chapter 4: Listing via eBay's Turbo Lister

In This Chapter

✔ **Knowing the requirements**

✔ **Downloading the software**

✔ **Preparing your listing**

Not much in this world is free, but eBay offers you a free, convenient tool you can use to list your items for sale: Turbo Lister. This powerful application helps you organize your items for sale, design your descriptions, and then upload them to the site. It organizes (and saves) your pre-designed descriptions for future use, and your items disappear from the program only if you delete them.

I like Turbo Lister because it's simple and easy to use, with a built-in WYSIWYG (What You See Is What You Get) HTML editor that makes preparing your eBay listings offline a breeze. You can also copy and paste in your pre-made templates made in SeaMonkey (see Book V Chapter 3). After you've input your items and are ready to list, you can just click a button and they're all listed at once. You can also stagger listings and schedule them for a later date (for a fee). In this chapter, you get an inside look at how Turbo Lister works.

I have been using Turbo Lister since the dark ages of eBay and have managed to archive over 150 listings. The great news: I can reuse the templates I've designed in the past and can also update old listings to sell items with them again.

 Turbo Lister is an excellent way to archive your eBay item descriptions. Just keep an accompanying folder with the pictures and you can relist an item years later!

Features and Minimum Requirements

Turbo Lister is robust software with the following features:

✦ **Self-updates:** Turbo Lister automatically updates itself regularly from the eBay site and includes any new eBay enhancements so your listings always take advantage of eBay's latest features. Whenever you fire up the program, it loads and then immediately checks with the eBay server for updates. This can take a few minutes, so if you plan on listing items ASAP, be sure to open Turbo Lister ahead of time and give it a few minutes to work its update magic.

✦ **Templates:** Predesigned templates are built into the program's Listing Designer. If you use one of eBay's themes or layouts, you will be charged an additional $.10 on top of your listing fees (unless you subscribe to Selling Manager Pro, in which case they are free). If you'd prefer, use a template of your own design to jump-start your description without incurring extra charges, by pasting your template into the HTML view. You can even use templates from other sources (such as those in Book V, Chapter 3), as long as they are in HTML format.

✦ **WYSIWYG interface:** If you choose to design your own ads from scratch, you can do it with Turbo Lister's easy-to-use WYSIWYG layout tool.

✦ **Bulk listing tool:** Prepare your listings whenever you have the time. When you're ready to launch a group of them, just transfer them to the upload area, and, well, upload them.

✦ **Item preview:** You can preview your listings to be sure they look just as you want them to.

✦ **All item listing capabilities are available offline:** By using Turbo Lister (and its constant auto-upgrading), you don't sacrifice any of the features available to you when you list on the site using the Sell an Item form.

Although this software is definitely useful, you have to decide whether it's really for you. The first thing to check is whether your computer meets Turbo Lister's minimum requirements:

✦ Your computer must be a PC, not a Mac (sorry, Mac users). You have to have the Windows 2000, XP, Vista, or Windows 7 operating system.

✦ The processor must be at least a Pentium II (the faster your processor, the better).

✦ You must have at least 128 MB of RAM. 256 MB is recommended. Easy. . . . The more RAM you have, the better things work.

✦ You should have at least 250 MB of free space on your hard drive to run the installation.

✦ Microsoft Internet Explorer version 5.5 or later. (I have no idea why having any version of Internet Explorer is a requirement; Turbo Lister runs on its own.)

To check your version of Internet Explorer with the browser open, click the Help menu and then choose About Internet Explorer. The top line of the resulting dialog box displays your Internet Explorer version number.

Downloading and Starting Turbo Lister

To use Turbo Lister, you must first download it at

```
http://pages.ebay.com/sellerinformation/selling
resources/turbolister.html
```

After you install Turbo Lister on your computer, you can list your sales on the easy-to-use form. What could be more convenient?

After you get to the Selling Tools page, download Turbo Lister. Follow these steps:

1. **Click the Download Now button.**

The requirements for using Turbo Lister appear at the bottom of the page.

2. **Click the Save File link.**

Clicking Save file downloads Turbo Lister.

3. **Double-click to open the file once it downloads.**

The Windows Security warning appears, cautioning that you're about to download something foreign to your computer. Click Yes; clicking No doesn't open the file. Just trust me (and eBay) and click Yes.

From this point on, installation is automatic. Voilà! Turbo Lister is on your computer.

Note that this procedure first downloads a small setup version of the program that checks your computer for preinstalled files. When that task is finished, Turbo Lister checks back with mothership eBay and automatically downloads any files it needs.

After you've installed the program, you'll see a new icon on your desktop; a little green man juggling magic pixie dust over his head. This is the icon for Turbo Lister. Double-click it and you'll see the Turbo Lister splash screen with eBay's tips of the day. This screen pops up every time you open the program. You may find it annoying and that it wastes precious seconds of your time. To avoid seeing the tips, select the check box labeled *Do not show me this screen again*, and then click Start Here. The splash screen will be forever banished.

When the program is open, the first thing you do is to set up a new Turbo Lister file:

1. **Select the Start option from the opening screen, and click Next.**

2. **Fill in your eBay user ID and password, and then click Next.**

Turbo Lister now wants to connect back to eBay to retrieve your eBay account information.

3. **Make sure your Internet connection is live and then click the Connect Now button.**

In a minute or so, a small window opens, asking you to give eBay permission to access your eBay data, as shown in Figure 4-1.

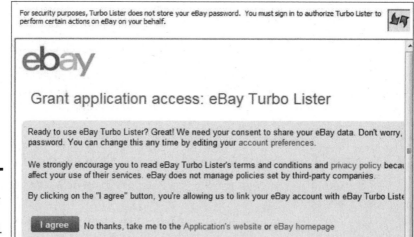

Figure 4-1:
Linking your
account to
Turbo Lister.

4. **Click I Agree, if you do. Otherwise click a link next to No Thanks, Take Me to the . . . .**

   You can choose either of these destinations:

   - Application's website
   - eBay Homepage

5. **Click Finish.**

   The program fires up and is ready to list.

Preparing an eBay Listing

Now that you have Turbo Lister at hand, you can prepare hundreds of eBay listings in advance — and launch them with a single mouse click. Or, if you want to start your auctions at a particular date and time, you can select a scheduled item launching format. (Find more on that in the later section "Uploading Listings to eBay.")

Follow these steps to list an item for sale:

1. **Click the New button (the one with the sunburst symbol) in the upper-left corner.**

2. **Select Create New Item from the drop-down menu.**

   A page appears, as shown in Figure 4-2, ready for you to enter your title, subtitle, and lots of other information.

   You can save bunches of time if you write your titles and descriptions in Notepad or Word, at your leisure, before you go into Turbo Lister. You can use your own templates or use the Design View to doll up your text.

3. **In the Title box, enter the title.**

   If you want to use a subtitle, type that as well. Subtitles are handy for adding selling points that accompany your title in search results.

4. **Select your category from the Category drop-down list and then click Select.**

   You are presented with a screen that lists all eBay categories in a hierarchal format. The main categories are listed with a plus sign next to them. When you find your main category, click the plus sign to see the subcategories

**Book III
Chapter 4**

**Listing via eBay's
Turbo Lister**

displayed, as shown in Figure 4-3. To drop even lower into the world of nether-categories, keep clicking plus signs next to subcategories. You know you've hit the bottom rung of the category ladder when you see only a minus sign.

5. **If you have an eBay Store, select a category for the item in your store from the Store Category drop-down list.**

   This area is automatically populated from your eBay Store when eBay updates your Turbo Lister installation.

6. **Continue filling in the blanks, uploading pictures, and choosing from lists. When you're finished, click Save.**

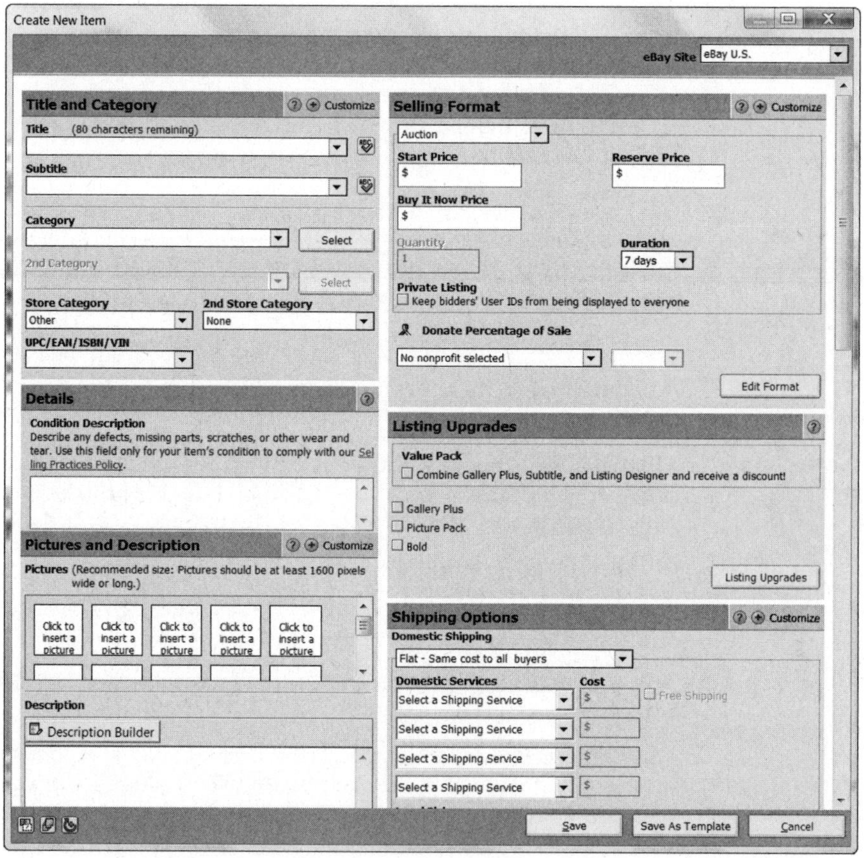

Figure 4-2: All of eBay's Sell an Item information is on one page (with links).

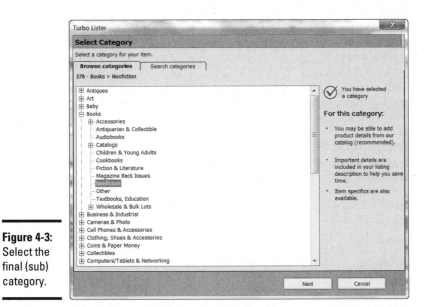

Figure 4-3:
Select the final (sub) category.

Importing your existing eBay listings

If you have items listed on eBay (that you've listed through the Sell an Item page or with eBay's relisting feature), you can import those listings into Turbo Lister for future use and relisting. Just click the File➪Import Items to add your current eBay listings to your Turbo Lister archive. If you want to sync your listings, use the Synchronize button on the toolbar.

In a moment or two, you're presented with a complete tally of everything you have listed for sale on the site. You'll also see (if you've indicated you want this information) sold and unsold items. All these listings automatically import into Turbo Lister, and you can then save your listings as templates or for uploading at a later date.

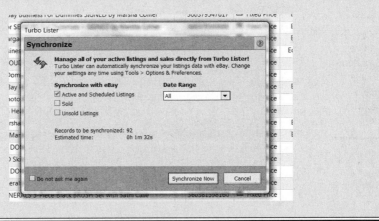

Designing Your Listing

When it comes to designing your listing, you have several options. If you pre-design your description in an HTML tool, you merely need to copy and paste the coding into the description box. Also, Turbo Lister makes designing your item listing a snap — with a few easy-to-use features in its Listing Designer tool, found in the Description Builder.

✦ **WYSIWYG HTML design form:** In the Create New Item form, this feature is somewhat hidden. But if you click the Description Builder button, a new window pops up to reveal the HTML design form. You can base your item description on this very easy-to-use design tool. In the Design View tab, the tool gives you a toolbar similar to the text formatting toolbar in Microsoft Word (see Figure 4-4), so the buttons are most likely familiar.

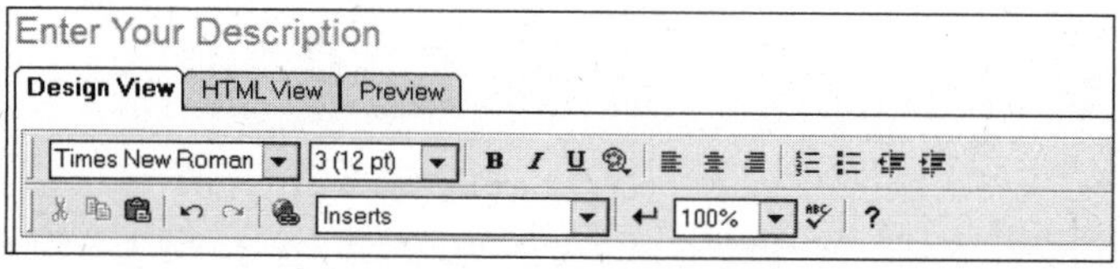

Figure 4-4:
The Design
View
toolbar.

Enter Your Description

| Design View | HTML View | Preview |

Times New Roman | 3 (12 pt) | **B** *I* U 🔍 | ≡ ≡ ≡ | ≣ ≣ 律 律

✂ 📋 📋 | ↩ ↪ | Inserts | ↵ | 100% | ✓ | ?

✦ **Templates and themes:** I'm sure you've seen eBay listings with nice graphics in the borders. These come from eBay's easy-to-use theme templates, which are listed on the left side of the Design View tab. You may select any of these colorful templates to enhance your listing. Themes make the listing look pretty, but they may draw attention away from the selling strength of your pictures. Remember that your good description and a quality photo will sell your item. Also keep in mind that eBay charges an additional $.10 to use these themes in your listing. You don't have to use any of the themes; just be sure *not* to select the box next to Use Designer.

✦ **Layout:** These options are available only if you are going to pay for using Listing Designer. You may select from Standard, Photos Left, Photos Right, One Photo Top, Photos Bottom, or Slide Show.

When you use eBay Picture Services, the first 12 pictures are free. If you have photos where you have embedded descriptive text, they must be in the item description — and be hosted online.

eBay has included a photo-icon tool that allows you to include your own images hosted on the web. Click the link on the left to Change Photo hosting and select web. A photo icon will appear, and you can type in the URL of your picture (shown in Figure 4-5). There's also a command in the edit bar to insert a hyperlink into your description (see Figure 4-6) so you can have the prospective buyer e-mail you with a click of the mouse.

✦ **HTML view:** If you have a smattering of HTML knowledge, you may want to edit your listing design in HTML view. You can also insert your hosted images by entering supplementary coding into the HTML view. (See Book V, Chapter 3 for additional information about coding and inserting your pictures in the description area.) Also, if you have your own predesigned template, you can copy and paste the HTML for the template into the HTML view box.

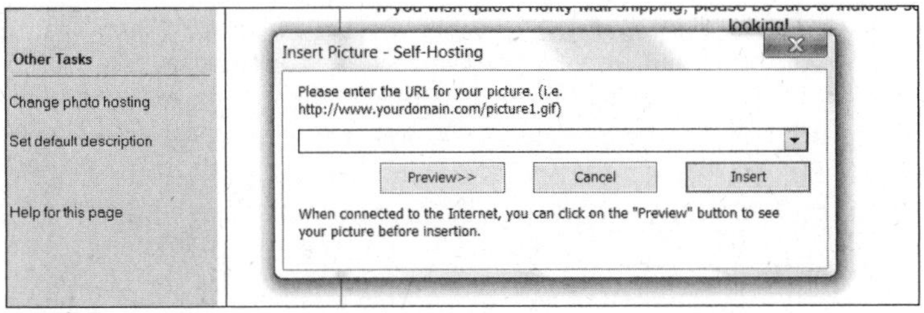

Figure 4-5: Inserting photo URL insert in the description area.

> Other Tasks
>
> Change photo hosting
>
> Set default description
>
> Help for this page
>
> **Insert Picture - Self-Hosting** ✕
>
> Please enter the URL for your picture. (i.e. http://www.yourdomain.com/picture1.gif)
>
> [Preview>>]   [Cancel]   [Insert]
>
> When connected to the Internet, you can click on the "Preview" button to see your picture before insertion.

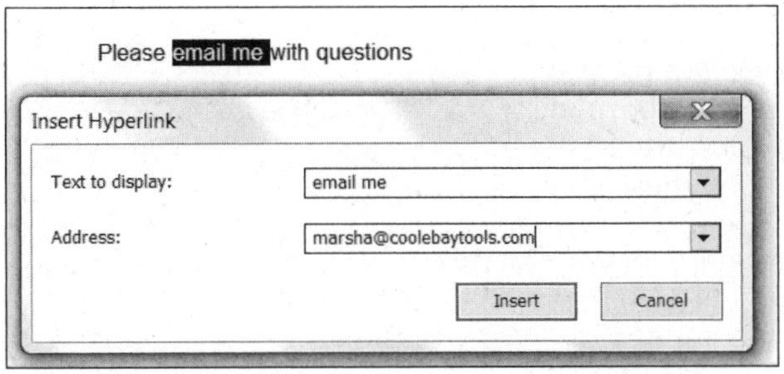

Figure 4-6: Inserting an e-mail link in the description area.

> Please **email me** with questions
>
> **Insert Hyperlink** ✕
>
> Text to display: email me
>
> Address: marsha@coolebaytools.com
>
> [Insert]   [Cancel]

Book III Chapter 4

Listing via eBay's Turbo Lister

At any time during the design process, click the Preview tab to see what your listing looks like in an Internet browser.

At the end of the Create New Item form is a Save as Template button. Suppose you've finally designed a simple template that you'd like to use over and over for your auctions. (I have two pet templates — one with a vertical picture and one with a horizontal picture. They may be simple, but I use them again and again.) You can save any listing you've created as a template — and then merely substitute the new text the next time you want to use that template format.

Filling In Item Specifics

Now it's time to get all the little details into your listing, such as the number of days to run the listing and your shipping and payment information. You do all this in the sections on the right side of the page, as shown in Figure 4-7.

eBay fills in much of this information for you. To edit the information pertaining to an option, such as pricing information in the Selling Format section, click the Edit button for the appropriate section (in this case, Edit Format). Clicking the Change button displays a small menu for adding text or changing defaults. After you've made your changes, click OK.

Save time by saving repetitive text as the default. For example, when you want all your listings to have the same information in Payment Instructions or Payment Methods, select the Save for Future Listings check box in the detail section that appears when you click that section's Edit button. This saves the information as the default. You can always change the information on a case-by-case basis when listing another item.

After you've filled out all the information in the Turbo Lister form, click Save.

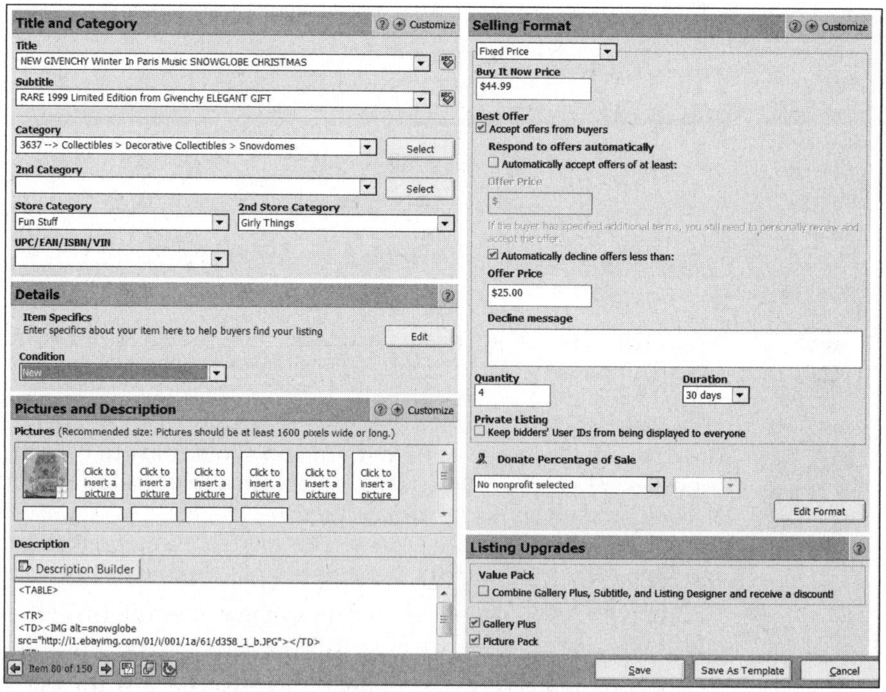

Figure 4-7:
Finishing up
your listing
with the
final details.

Organizing Your Listings

After you've put together a few listings, your Turbo Lister item Inventory will look something like Figure 4-8. Just click the link on the left to get to the Inventory tab, which shows your listing activity in the middle grid and your folder structure on the left. You can look at all your items, including those in folders, by clicking the Inventory link. To see the contents of a particular folder, just click the folder name.

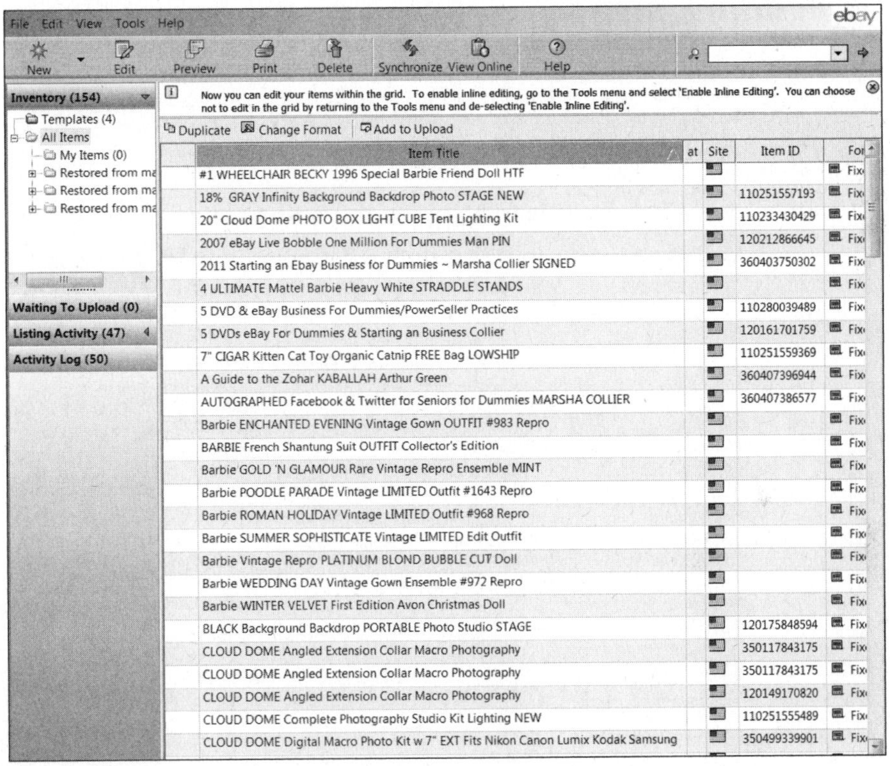

Figure 4-8: My Turbo Lister item Inventory view.

Note that you can add folders to the tab's folder list to hold inventories for different categories of items. To create a folder and move items into it, follow these steps:

1. **Open the Turbo Lister program.**

   By default, you see your inventory view after the tip of the day.

2. **Near the top of the screen, click the arrow just to the right of the New button and select the command to create a new folder.**

3. **Give your new folder a name, and then click OK.**

   The folder appears in the folder list on the left side of the screen.

4. **To move a listing to a different folder, highlight the listing and drag it to the folder.**

   To move multiple listings at once, press the Control key or the Shift key and then click the listings.

Uploading Listings to eBay

After you've input a few listings, you may want to upload them so they will become active on eBay. Turbo Lister makes it easy to upload items from your items Inventory on your computer to eBay. Start in the default view in Turbo Lister and follow these steps:

1. **Click the title to highlight the listing you want to upload.**

2. **If you want to schedule the listing to upload at a later date or time, select the Schedule option (at the top of the screen) and choose a date and time.**

3. **Drag the item to the Add to Upload button, at the top of the item list.**

   Your listing is copied to the listings Waiting to Upload tab, as shown in Figure 4-9.

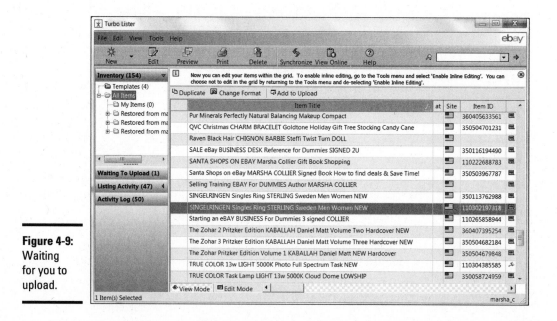

Figure 4-9:
Waiting
for you to
upload.

4. **Repeat Steps 1 through 3 to upload additional listings.**

   You can define the order in which your listings upload to eBay by high-lighting the item you want to move on the listings' Waiting to Upload page and then clicking the up or down arrow at the top of the list.

5. **To send items to eBay to be listed immediately, click the Waiting to Upload bar and then Upload All.**

   eBay calculates your fees before posting the listings; you can approve or cancel the upload before the listings go live on the site.

6. **Approve the upload, and your items will be live on the site.**

Chapter 5: Running Your Business on My eBay

In This Chapter

✔ Understanding the All Selling area

✔ Sending out notices and invoices

✔ Relisting items

✔ Working with bidding-management tools

For the beginning or small seller, the My eBay page will simply help you manage your sales by giving you a complete view of what's going on in your eBay business. When you start running more listings than you can handle comfortably with My eBay, you may want to consider upgrading your My eBay page to Selling Manager or Selling Manager Pro. (See Book VIII, Chapter 1 for more information.)

This chapter explains how you can get the most out of the My eBay: All Selling page, and how it can benefit your business.

Managing Your All Selling Area

eBay provides some smooth management tools on your My eBay, All Selling summary page. You can track items you currently have up for sale and items you've sold. The All Selling page is a quick way to get a snapshot of the dollar value of your auctions and fixed-price listings.

The My eBay: All Selling home page, which is shown in Figure 5-1, is a long page if you have many items for sale. The left-hand navigation links on the Activity tab let you quickly hop to the area you want to examine. This page has several areas:

Links to selling areas

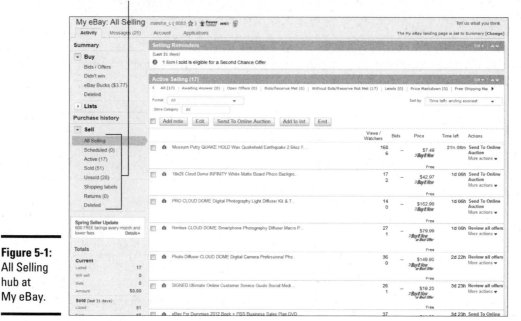

Figure 5-1:
All Selling
hub at
My eBay.

✦ **Scheduled:** If you've scheduled listings to begin at a later time, you can link to them here.

✦ **Active:** The listings shown in the middle of the page give you a clear idea of what's going on with your eBay sales.

✦ **Sold:** Click this link and find the list of items you've (thankfully) sold.

✦ **Unsold:** Follow this link to the netherworld of unsold items. It's time to relist, Sell Similar, or put these items in your store. (Find out how in the section "Relisting Items without Extra Work," later in this chapter.)

✦ **Shipping Labels:** Clicking this link takes you to a searchable archive of the shipping labels you've printed. You can also check tracking information in this area.

✦ **Returns:** If a customer initiates a return through eBay, the progress of the return appears in this area.

✦ **Deleted:** After you process a return, the transaction goes into the Deleted folder where you can view it for up to 120 days.

eBay's handy icons

On the My eBay page, eBay uses a very colorful and handy group of icons to signify tasks to be accomplished or to indicate certain actions. Take a look at the figure to see the icons and what they stand for.

Icon Legend

⚒	Auction Format
🔒	Fixed Price Format
📋	Classified ad Format
✷	Second chance offer
🖩	Checkout complete
$	Item Paid
💳	Item Shipped
★📄	Left Feedback
★	Feedback Received
$◄	Payment was refunded
$	Item Partially Paid
🔵	Request Total
📘	Relisted

 If you manually scroll waaaay down the page, you'll see far too much information. To avoid all that scrolling, click the links on the left side of the page to go to each individual area on its own page.

eBay's All Selling area allows you to customize various pages. Also, hidden features help you perform "paperwork" tasks. These features are available in different areas, so before I tell you what each page can do, you should be familiar with the pages.

Organizing with My eBay: Active Selling

With Active Selling page, shown in Figure 5-2, you can keep an eye on any questions you receive from buyers, open offers, bids/reserves met, your fixed-price sales, and the progress of your auctions.

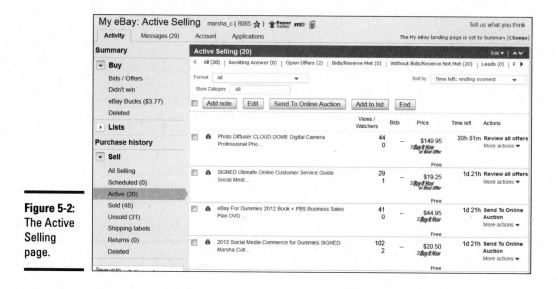

Figure 5-2:
The Active
Selling
page.

The general layout

At the bottom of the left-hand column of links, you'll see your Totals, which give you an idea of your sales during the past 31 days. eBay also shows the total items currently up for sale. The total dollar amount of the items that have been bid on appears with these totals.

Depending on how you customize the view (which I describe in the next section), you can see how many bids your auctions have, whether your reserves have been met, and how much time remains before the auction closes. By clicking an auction title, you can visit the auction to make sure your pictures are appearing or to check your bid counter.

Don't be frustrated if you don't have a ton of bids. Many, many people watch auctions and don't bid until the last minute, so you may not see a lot of bidding activity on your page when you drop in to look. Be sure to customize your page and select the # of Watchers option so you can get a grip on how many people are interested in your item.

Customizing your display

To customize what you see when you go to your My eBay page, just click the Change link that appears to the right of the words *The My eBay landing page is set to XXXXX*. Some of us prefer the Summary page to show up first, and others prefer to see the All Selling page. It's up to you. Click the Change link at the upper right to set your options. After you click it, you see the pop-up window with a drop-down list shown in Figure 5-3.

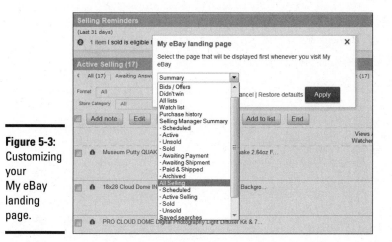

Figure 5-3:
Customizing your My eBay landing page.

Filtering your view

By clicking the Edit drop-down menu at the upper right of any Selling view, you can preset what you'd like to see in the display, using the Customize options shown in Figure 5-4.

In addition to selecting presets for the listings you'd like to see, you can perform several actions via the links and drop-down menus at the top of the Active Selling page. Here's the rundown:

✦ **View:** Beneath the Active Selling title bar, a group of links enable you to filter important listings. You can select for viewing

All to see all your active listings.

Awaiting Answer to view eBay Messages that are unanswered in your mailbox.

Open Offers to find out when eBay members have made offers on fixed-price listings (those for which you say that you would entertain offers).

> *Bids/Reserve Met* to look at auctions where you've had some bidding activity.
>
> *Without Bids/Reserve Not Met* to see those auctions without bids or with bids that are too low.

✦ **Sort:** Next to Sort By, click the down-facing arrow to order your listings by

> *Time Left*: Ending Soonest or Newly Listed
>
> *Price:* Lowest First or Highest First
>
> *Format*: Auctions First
>
> *High Bidder ID*
>
> *Watchers:* Highest or Lowest Number
>
> *Views*: Highest or Lowest Number

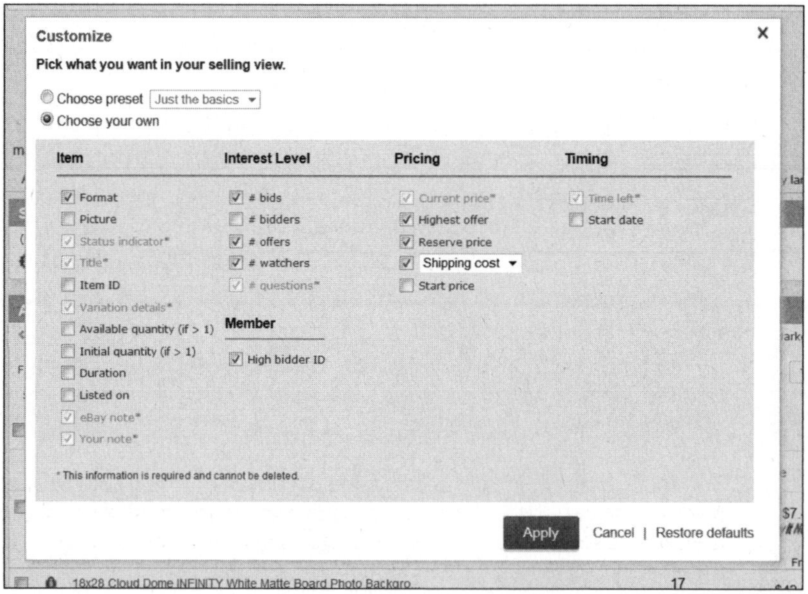

Figure 5-4: Selecting the format of items shown on the Active Selling page.

Taking action when necessary

Make sure you pay attention to the More actions drop-down menu that appears at the end of each listing line (see Figure 5-5). This menu has powerful options that allow you to do the following:

✦ **Sell Similar:** List an item similar to the one on your page (more on making Sell Similar work for you in later sections of this chapter).

✦ **Revise:** Change a listing that has no bids.

✦ **Add to Description:** Add text to your listing's description *after* the listing has bids.

✦ **End Item:** When the dog plays tug-of-war with your item, you can end the listing. (Find more about ending a listing in the "Ending your listing early" section near the end of the chapter.)

✦ **Add Note:** If you want to add a notation (which only you can see and only on this page), select the check box to the left of the item title and then click the Add Note button at the top of the listings. Just type your comment on the page that appears and click Save.

✦ **Add to List:** If you want to make a list that contains some of your items, you can, and add them here.

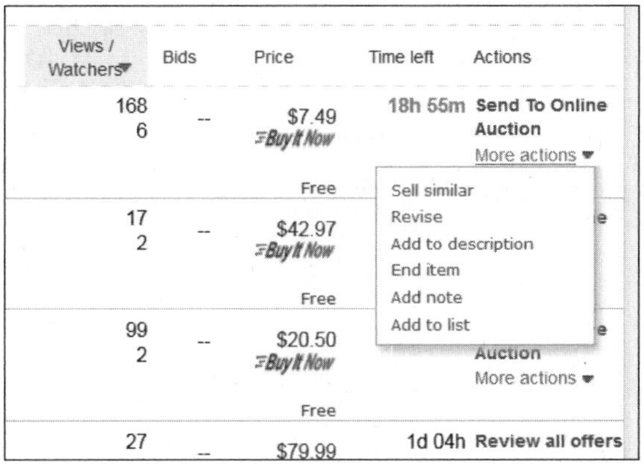

Figure 5-5:
Action options for active listings.

Views / Watchers	Bids	Price	Time left	Actions
168 6	--	$7.49 *Buy It Now*	18h 55m	Send To Online Auction More actions ▼
		Free		Sell similar
17 2	--	$42.97 *Buy It Now*		Revise Add to description End item
		Free		Add note
99 2	--	$20.50 *Buy It Now*		Add to list Auction More actions ▼
		Free		
27	--	$79.99	1d 04h	Review all offers

**Book III
Chapter 5**

Running Your
Business on
My eBay

Auction prices that appear in green have received one or more bids (and met any reserves you've set). Auctions in red haven't received any bids or the reserve price hasn't been met.

Using the Tools on the My eBay: Sold Page

Clicking the Sold link (on the Activity tab at the left side of the page under the Sell header) takes you to a list of all the items you've sold.

The Sold page keeps a concise view of your sales in one place, as shown in Figure 5-6. You can use this page in lieu of fancy management software; it actually offers you some very accessible actions. If you're selling hundreds of items, your list will probably be too long to monitor individual items — but you can view the total current price of the items that sold on the left.

The Sold items page has the following features and information, which I'm sure you'll find helpful in completing your transactions:

✦ **Check box:** Select the check box next to an item listing to perform a task on one or more of them. Options you see at the top of the list of items include Add to List, Add Note, Add Tracking Number, and Print Shipping Labels.

✦ **Buyer's user ID and feedback rating:** The eBay User ID of the winner of the sale.

✦ **Total Items:** If the transaction was for multiple items, the number of items is displayed here.

✦ **Item title:** A direct link to the auction. You can click this link to check on your auction and see the other bidders, should you want to make a Second Chance Offer.

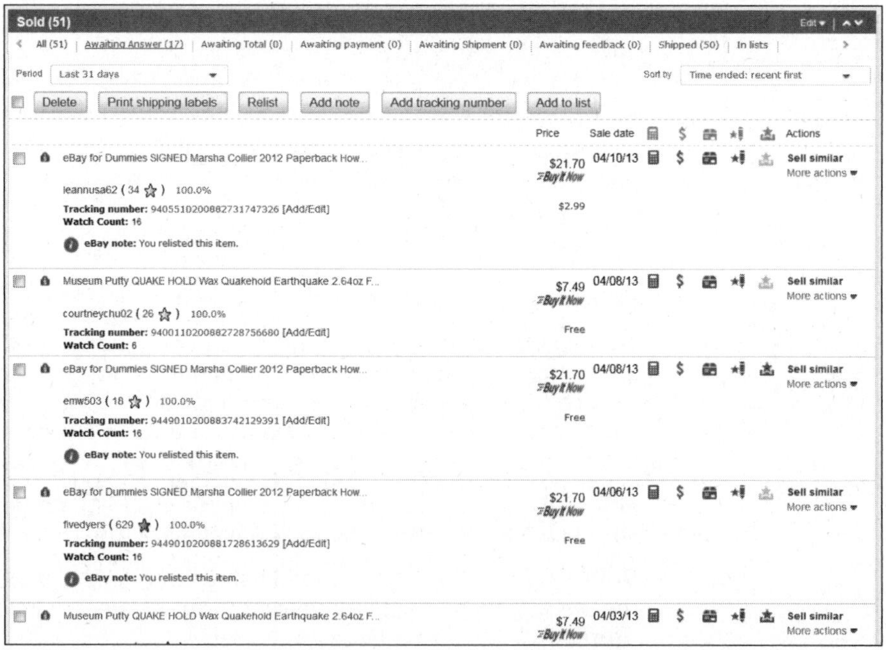

Figure 5-6: The Sold items page in My eBay.

✦ **Tracking number:** You can add or edit a shipment tracking number here — as well as click the number to view the shipment's progress and when it was delivered.

✦ **Sale price:** The final selling price for your item.

✦ **Shipping price:** If the buyer paid extra for shipping, the amount will appear under the sale price, or you will see the word *Free*.

✦ **Sale date:** Keep an eye on the end date so you can be sure you get your payment as agreed.

✦ **Actions:** Under this heading, you find a hidden drop-down list (More Actions) that works with the transaction, offering options for various actions you can take. Here are a few of the more important ones:

   • *Contact Buyer:* When you choose this option, a window appears where you can send a buyer a note regarding his or her order.

   • *View PayPal Transaction:* This option takes you to the transaction's page on PayPal. (You'll have to sign in to your PayPal account.)

   • *Print Shipping Label:* You can print a shipping label from here. See Book VII, Chapter 2 for other professional-shipping label options.

   • *Leave Feedback:* Leave feedback with a single click once you've heard that the item arrived safely and your customer is happy.

   • *Second Chance Offer:* This option appears only in the case of an auction where there were underbidders (losers). Click here to make a Second Chance offer to one of your underbidders if you have multiple items for sale.

   • *Sell Similar:* When you want to list a similar item (or relist a sold one) you can do it quickly here.

   • *Report This Buyer:* If you have a problem with your transaction because a buyer violates any rules, click here to let eBay know.

   • *Relist:* Use this option to relist your item on the site.

✦ **Icons:** My eBay has several icons that appear dimmed until you perform an action from the Actions drop-down menu. You may also click the icons at the top of the list to sort your listings by auctions completed, although most sellers prefer to keep the listings in the default chronological order (with newest sale date on top). Here's what the icons mean:

   • **Mini Calculator:** The buyer has completed checkout (supplying a shipping address and a planned payment method).

   • **Dollar sign:** The buyer has paid using PayPal, or you've noted that the buyer has paid with a different form of payment available on the drop-down list within the sale record.

Book III
Chapter 5

**Running Your
Business on
My eBay**

- **Shipping box:** You've indicated that the item has shipped.
- **Star with Pen:** You've left feedback for the buyer.
- **Star on an envelope:** The buyer has left you feedback.

Connecting with your Customers and Checking the Money

Thank goodness — somebody submitted a winning bid on one of your items in an auction. It's a good feeling. When I get those end-of-transaction e-mails from eBay, I whisper a silent *yeah!* Then I hold my breath to see whether the buyer will go directly to PayPal and make the payment. Usually that's what happens. More and more buyers are getting savvy and understand about paying immediately after winning an item.

New buyers and those who buy or win multiple items from you (my favorite kind of buyer!) may wait to hear from you regarding payment and shipping. Many newbies feel more comfortable hearing from you and knowing who they're doing business with. Also, in the case of multiple purchases, you may have to recalculate the postage. The sooner you contact the buyer, the sooner you'll get your payment.

Notifying winners

eBay sends out an end-of-transaction e-mail to both the buyer and the seller. The e-mail is informative to the seller and a welcome e-mail for the buyer.

Figure 5-7 shows you a typical "yippee, you won" e-mail. It's brightly colored and joyful, probably designed to evoke some strong level of excitement in the buyer.

The e-mail to the buyer has a Pay Now button, but includes more concrete information about the transaction:

- ✦ Item title and number.
- ✦ The final bid or sale price.
- ✦ Quantity (if the purchase was for more than one).
- ✦ Seller and buyer's User ID.

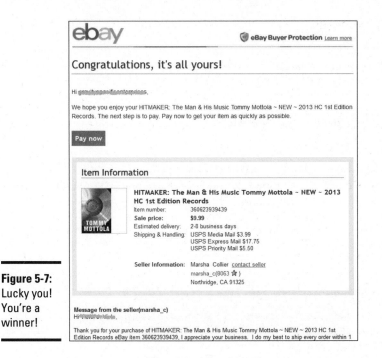

Book III
Chapter 5

Running Your
Business on
My eBay

Figure 5-7:
Lucky you!
You're a
winner!

+ A link for viewing the item. This link is good for up to 90 days. Note that this is the only place you get this link, and unless you subscribe to eBay's Selling Manager, you'd better keep hold of it. Sold items remain on your My eBay page for 60 days, but the items disappear from the eBay search engine within two weeks.

+ A link so that the buyer can contact the seller.

+ A buyer's link to complete checkout and pay.

+ If the seller has set up custom e-mails to go along with these notices, that message will appear at the bottom of the confirmation.

That's a lot of information, and I'll bet the average user just glances over it and either deletes it (bad idea) or files it in a special folder in his or her e-mail program.

If you think eBay's notification is good enough, it's time to rethink your customer service policy. An e-mail to the buyer at this point is important. Customer contact is the key to a good transaction. If the buyer sprints directly to PayPal and sends you some money to pay for a purchase, a special e-mail from you would be nice. Thank the buyer for the payment and mention when the item will ship, as detailed in the next section, "Sending invoices."

Sending invoices

Sometimes buyers don't pay immediately, so when the sale is final, the items go into the Sold area. Here's where you can keep track of the sale. You can check whether the buyer has paid with PayPal as well as the transaction status. If the buyer has completed checkout, you can get his or her information by clicking the Next Steps/Status link. If the buyer hasn't completed checkout, you can click the Send Invoice button to send the buyer an invoice. Very handy.

If you haven't heard from the buyer after three days (the prescribed eBay deadline for contact), you may need to resend your invoice or send an e-mail message.

After the transaction is complete (which means the item has arrived and the buyer is happy with his or her purchase), you can click the handy Leave Feedback link to leave feedback about the buyer.

Tracking payments in My eBay: Sold

You've created a winning ad, run a successful auction or sale, notified the winner, and sent off an invoice. Now it's time for the big payoff: getting the money in hand for your item. eBay and PayPal work in concert to offer several tools to notify you when a payment is made.

Once again, the Sold items area of My eBay comes to the rescue. As if by magic, every time one of your buyers makes a payment through the PayPal service, your My eBay page indicates that the item has been paid by changing the dollar-sign icon from dimmed to solid. Take a look back at Figure 5-6, and note that items have been paid using PayPal.

Stimulating Sales from the My eBay: Unsold Page

The Unsold page, shown in Figure 5-8 indicates the items that didn't sell. To get to that area, scroll way down the page or click the Unsold link under the Sell header (on the Activity tab at the left side of the page).

You may customize this page in the same way that I illustrated for the Active Selling page in the earlier section, "Filtering your view."

You can take several actions on this page to get your items back up for sale. You can bulk-relist by placing check marks in the boxes to the left of the listings and then clicking the Relist button at the top.

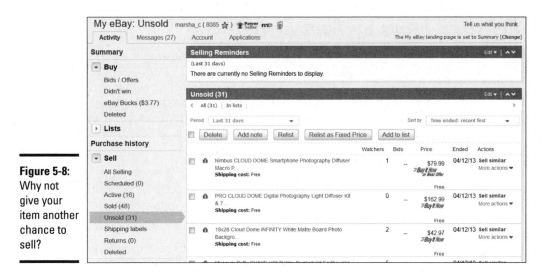

Figure 5-8:
Why not give your item another chance to sell?

But wait! Before you automatically relist, find out whether there's a reason your item didn't sell. Run a search on the item to see whether someone else is selling the same thing at a bargain-basement price. If so, perhaps you could lower your price, or better yet, rethink your title and description. You can also opt to wait a few weeks to see if the competition runs out of stock.

Some of the actions you can easily perform on this page:

+ **Relist:** Use this option so that you can get a free relist credit for the first run of an auction if your item sells the second time. You may relist in bulk or one item at a time, hopefully giving your listing a thorough once over (and tweaking the title or description) to better improve the listing's appearance in search results.

+ **Sell Similar:** Try this if the item hasn't sold after a second auction relisting (or if the item is a similar fixed-price item). This option starts the cycle in eBay's computer fresh as new.

+ **Relist as Fixed Price:** If an auction didn't succeed, perhaps the item would be best as a Fixed Price listing (consider adding the Make Offer option as well). I tell you more about changing up your listings in the next section.

+ **Add to List:** Use this option for items that you would like to add to a list. You can start a new list or use eBay's suggestions for Watch List, Wish List, Research, or Gift Ideas.

Relisting Items without Extra Work

One of the most efficient ways to run an eBay business is to stock the same item in quantity. After getting some eBay experience under your belt, you're bound to find several items that you're comfortable selling. And if you follow my suggestions in Book IV, you'll buy multiples (dozens? cases? pallets?) of the items at a seriously discounted price. When you have all these items lying around the garage, your goal is to get them into buyers' hands at a profit.

In Book VIII, I talk about opening an eBay store. But in addition to your own store, you should be running auctions or seven day listings on the eBay site. Why? They are the key to drawing buyers into your store to purchase (or notice) your other items.

I know several sellers who bought items in such bulk that they're stocked with the item to sell once a week for the next few years! That's a good thing only if the product is a staple item that will always have a market on eBay.

Relisting after a sale

Yeah! Your space-age can opener with a built-in DVD player sold at auction! Since you have three dozen more to sell, the quicker you can get that item back up on the site, the sooner you'll connect with the next customer.

When bidders lose an auction on eBay, one of the first things they do is search for somebody offering the same item. The sooner you get an item relisted (or similarly listed in a fixed-price sale), the sooner a disappointed underbidder will find your item. Of course, relisting the item also makes it available to other interested bidders who may not have seen the item before.

If at first you don't succeed

Boo! Your Dansk Maribo dinner plate didn't sell. Don't take it personally. It's not that someone out there doesn't love you. It doesn't mean your merchandise is trash. It's just that this particular week, no one was looking for Maribo plates (go figure).

Often eBay shoppers shop with no discernable pattern. No one may want your item at a certain price one week, and then you may sell five or six the next week. It happens to me all the time.

When relisting, you often need to make adjustments. Perhaps the keywords in your title aren't drawing people to your listing. To help you figure out whether the problem is you or the market, search for other, similar items to see whether anyone is buying. If there's just no bidding activity (you're selling bikinis in January?), perhaps that item needs to be retired from eBay for a while.

Consider some other variables. Are other items selling on the site with a lower starting price? If you can comfortably lower your price, do so. If not, wait until other sellers run out of the item. Then put yours up for auction — you may just get more bidding action if you're one of the few sellers offering the same item.

I have quite a few items that I purchased by the case — right along with a bunch of other eBay sellers. They desperately dumped theirs on the site, without paying any attention to the competition. I waited and got my target price for the item the following season.

eBay is a supply and demand marketplace. If the supply exceeds the demand, prices go down. If you have an item that sells as fast as you can list it, prices go up.

Okay, time to relist (or Sell Similar)

eBay gives you many ways to relist an item. Because this chapter features My eBay, I cover that method here. Figure 5-9 shows the seller's version of a sold item (only the seller sees this when he or she is signed in), which includes the Sell a Similar Item link. If you happen to be at the item page, this link will work. The most convenient place to handle relisting will be from your My eBay page.

Figure 5-9:
Yeah! My
item sold!

To sell a similar item, from the My eBay: Sold page, click the More Actions drop-down list next to the listing and choose the Sell Similar option. Now the review step of the Sell an Item form appears. You can make any changes you want — or not!

You can go to the My eBay: Unsold page to relist unsold items for a possible listing-fee credit (in the case of auctions) in the same fashion.

eBay Bidding Management Tools

Most eBay users don't know the extent of eBay's seller-specific services. And sometimes sellers are so involved with selling that they don't take the time to find out about new helper tools. So I've gone deep into the eBay pond to dig up a few excellent tools to help you with your online business. Even if you've used some of these before, it might be time to revisit them because eBay has implemented quite a few changes during the past year.

Canceling bids

Did you know that you don't have to accept bids from just anyone? Part of the business is watching your bidders. With bidding-management tools, you can save yourself a good deal of grief.

You could have any number of reasons for wanting to cancel someone's bid. Here are a few more legitimate reasons for canceling a bid:

✦ The bidder contacts you to back out of the bid; choosing to be a nice guy, you let him or her out of the deal.

✦ You're unable to verify the bidder's identity through e-mail or the phone.

✦ You need to end the listing early.

You can get to the cancellation form directly by typing the following in your browser:

```
http://offer.ebay.com/ws/eBayISAPI.dll?CancelBidShow
```

Setting eBay buyer requirements

If you don't want certain buyers bidding on your auctions, you can remove their capability to do so. Setting up a list of bidders that you don't want to do business with is legal on eBay. If someone that you've blocked tries to bid on your auction, the bid won't go through. A message will be displayed notifying the bidder that he or she can't bid on the listing and should contact the seller for more information.

Many eBay sellers bemoan the fact that international buyers bid on their items, when the items clearly state that they do not ship internationally. Also, they get upset when a bidder with minus-level feedback wins an item.

Quit whining and do something about it! On your My eBay⇨Account⇨ Site Preferences page, you can set defaults that will affect your bidders. On this page, scroll to Site Preferences: Buyer Requirements.

Click the Show, then Edit link to change your preferences. On the Select Requirements page (see Figure 5-10), click the check boxes for those buyers you don't want to be permitted to bid on your items. Some of the requirements you can set block buyers who

✦ Don't have a PayPal account

✦ Have unpaid items recorded on their account

✦ Are registered in countries to which you don't ship

✦ Have reportedly violated eBay policies

✦ Have a negative feedback score

✦ Have bought a specified number of your items in the last 10 days

If any of your bidders meet the requirements for blocking and attempt to bid, they will see a notice saying they are unable to bid.

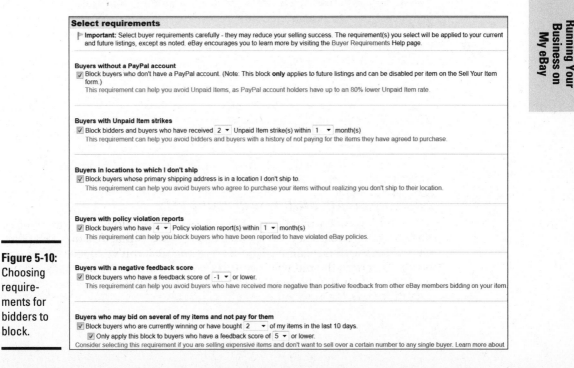

Figure 5-10: Choosing requirements for bidders to block.

You can block as many as 5,000 users from buying your items. However, I recommend that you use this option only when absolutely necessary. Situations — and people — change, and it's best to try to clear up problems with particular bidders.

In the case of some international buyers, I found that they send me a message to ask me to ship to them. I check their feedback, and if it's clear to me that they know the ropes, I can put their User IDs on my Buyer Requirements Exception list and they're free to win my item.

You can block buyers from the Buyer/Bidders Management page. You may find a link at the bottom of your Selling Manager Pro page or go directly to

```
http://pages.ebay.com/services/buyandsell/bidder
management.html
```

or

```
http://cgi1.ebay.com/ws/eBayISAPI.dll?bidderblocklogin
```

You can reinstate a bidder at any time by going to the Blocked Bidder/Buyer List and deleting the bidder's User ID from the list.

Ending your listing early

You may decide to end a listing early for any number of reasons. If any bids are on your auction before ending it, you are duty-bound to sell to the highest bidder. So before ending an auction early, it's polite to e-mail everyone in your bidder list, explaining why you're canceling bids and closing the auction. If an egregious error in the item's description is forcing you to take this action, let your bidders know whether you're planning to relist the item with the correct information.

After you've e-mailed all the bidders, you must then cancel their bids by using the bid cancelation form; for the link to this form, see an earlier section "Canceling bids."

When ending a listing that has bids, the seller has the option of canceling all bids or leaving the bids, thus making the high bidder the winner of the closed listing.

To end a listing, use the drop-down list next to the listing on the Active Selling page. Click the More Actions drop-down menu next to the item and choose End Item to end your listing (shown in Figure 5-11). You can also go directly to

```
http://offer.ebay.com/ws/eBayISAPI.dll?EndingMyAuction
```

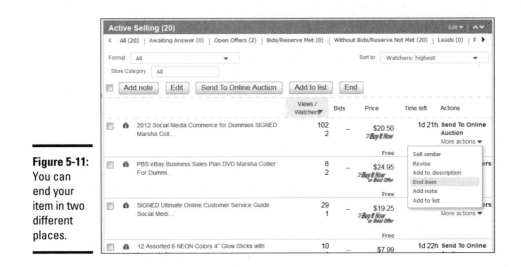

Following are some legitimate reasons for ending your sale:

+ **An error occurred in the minimum bid or reserve amount.** Perhaps your spouse really loves that lamp and said you'd better get some good money for it, but you started the auction at $1.00 with no reserve. In this case, it is better to go to the listing and make revisions.

+ **The listing has a major error in it.** Maybe you misspelled a critical keyword in the title.

+ **The item was somehow lost or broken.** Your dog ate it?

I don't recommend canceling an auction unless you absolutely have to because it's just bad business. People rely on your auctions being up for the stated amount of time. They may be planning to bid at the last minute, or they may just want to watch the action for a while. Also, if you have bids on the item, you may be in violation of one of eBay's policies.

Book IV

Sourcing Merchandise

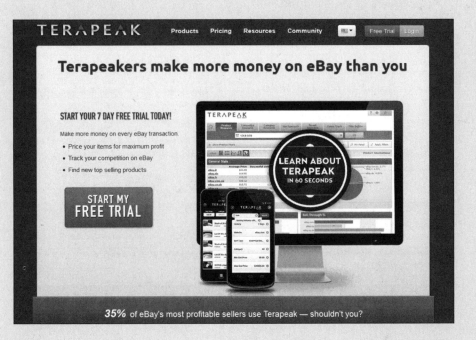

Contents at a Glance

Chapter 1: Understanding Online Retailing

In This Chapter

- ✔ Evaluating your six-month merchandise plan
- ✔ Using demographics to market your business
- ✔ Knowing your market — right now
- ✔ Catching trends
- ✔ Knowing what's hot on eBay
- ✔ Discovering what's hot online

I'll bet it's no surprise to you that most eBay sellers lack a solid retail background or education. Most of us come from different walks of life, and just about all most of us know about retailing is shopping — that's probably how we first found eBay. Now, that game is about to change. The more we choose to sell, the more our businesses grow, and the more we need to know about the business of retail.

eBay sellers use many types of business models. Some sellers are constantly on the prowl for new products and stock their merchandise as soon as they find a deal. Others follow the trends and try to get stock of the latest and greatest gizmo that they hope will sweep the country (and eBay). And sellers who run their businesses by selling for others are constantly beating the pavement for new customers to serve. Then there's the new eBay entrepreneur. Just like a brick-and-mortar retailer, today's online sellers have to keep up on the trends so they can stock up on the most popular items for the coming seasons.

Be sure you understand how you want to run your own business. Ask yourself the following questions and give some thought to your answers:

1. **Who is your customer?** Know their demographics and where you can find them. (Book VI gives you solid insights on how to use social media to your best advantage.)

2. **Does your business or eBay Store have an image to maintain?** Are there some products you just wouldn't carry — no matter how profitable they might be?

3. **What is your price point policy?** Do you have a specified profit margin in mind?

4. **How important is customer service to your business?** How far will you go to reach out to buyers?

After you've faced these issues and given your business an identity, you're ready for the next steps. In this chapter, I help you see how to organize and run your business like a pro.

Taking Aim with a Six-Month Merchandise Plan

The eBay seller buys merchandise to sell on eBay and perhaps also on other marketplaces. These online sellers are always looking for new sources and wholesalers. But many of the folks who sell on eBay specialize in a particular type of item, such as dolls, sports cards, lighting fixtures, or apparel. Their eBay business is organized; they sell their merchandise and then buy more to replenish their stock. Is this the best way to handle things? It definitely works for most, but those who study retailing know that there's a far more organized way.

One of the first things you learn when studying retail buying is the use of a six-month merchandise plan. It's the ultimate tool in the arsenal of a successful retail buyer. Although it was originally designed for brick-and-mortar retailers, I've adapted it here for online sellers.

Here's what establishing a six-month merchandising plan gives you:

✦ **A clear, concise look at your business activity:** After you fill out the plan, you'll be able to combine it with the reports generated by your bookkeeping program to get a clear, concise picture of your online business. (I explain bookkeeping best practices in Book IX.) This is a business and not a guessing game, and handling your business in a professional manner will save you a great deal of time and money.

I admit that running by the seat of your pants is fun and exciting, but it's not a solid business practice. One of the reasons I started my own business is that an unorganized business format appealed to me. To my dismay, I soon learned that organization and planning really *did* make a difference in my bottom line.

✦ **A basis for growth plans:** Anyone who has participated in management in a corporation knows about the annual plan. Every year in many organizations, management gets together (with Ouija and dart boards) to projects sales, expenses, and profits for the coming year. From this annual exercise, the budget for the coming year arises. These are the magic numbers that form everyone's annual raises — along with the company's plans for growth.

✦ **A set of attainable and repeatable goals:** So, assuming that eBay sellers are online retailers, retail evaluation could help eBay sellers make sound business decisions. Making a merchandise plan is a good step in that direction. A merchandise plan covers six months at a time and sets sales goals. It also helps estimate how much money must be spent on merchandise (and when) so that a particular season's success can be replicated and magnified.

Pulling Together Your Inventory Data

You need a few numbers to get your merchandising plan on paper. If you aren't using bookkeeping software yet, you must put together a report that reflects the dollar value of your existing inventory. (Book IX, Chapters 2 and 3 will give you more insights.) If you are using bookkeeping software, you can get these numbers easily from the program's Inventory Valuation report:

✦ **BOM:** The value, in dollars, of your beginning-of-month inventory

✦ **EOM:** The value, in dollars, of your end-of-month inventory

The EOM figure for a specific month is the same as the BOM figure for the following month. For example, the end-of-month figure for April is the same as the beginning-of-month figure for May.

✦ **Gross sales:** Total revenue from sales (not including shipping and handling)

✦ **Markdowns:** Total revenue of merchandise you have sold on eBay below your target price

To put together your six-month plan, you need to have sales history for a six-month period. To get a good historical picture of your sales, however, it's preferable to have at least an entire year's worth of figures.

Your six-month plan can be based on your total online sales or only one segment of your business. For example, if you sell musical instruments along with many other sundry items, but you want to evaluate your musical-instrument sales, you can use just those figures for a six-month plan for your music department.

What you're going to establish is your *inventory turnover* — that is, measure how much inventory sells out in a specified period of time. The faster you turn over merchandise, the sooner you can bring in new merchandise and increase your bottom line. You can also evaluate whether you need to lower your starting price to move out stale inventory to get cash to buy new inventory.

When you prepare your six-month plan, set out the months not by the regular calendar but by a *retail calendar,* which divides the year into the seasons of fall/winter (August 1 through January 31) and spring/summer (February 1 through July 31). This way, if you want to refer to top national performance figures in trade publications or on the Internet, you can base your figures on the same standardized retail seasons.

Using the Formulas That Calculate Your Data

Okay, I can admit that bigger minds than mine came up with standard formulas for calculating business success. These formulas are used by retailers around the world. If you're not pulling the figures from a bookkeeping program, you can make the calculations as follows:

✦ EOM stock = BOM stock + Purchases – Sales

✦ BOM stock = EOM stock from the previous month

✦ Sales + EOM – BOM = monthly planned purchases

You can make your calculations in dollar amounts or number of units of the item. To figure out how much of an item to buy, you must know how much you have left in stock.

Prepare a chart for your own business, similar to the one shown in Table 1-1. Study your results and find out which months are your strongest. Let the table tell you when you might have to boost your merchandise selection in lagging months. It will help bring your planning from Ouija board to reality.

Table 1-1   **Sample Six-Month eBay Merchandise Plan**

Fall/Winter	*Aug*	*Sept*	*Oct*	*Nov*	*Dec*	*Jan*	*Total*
Total sales	$2875.00	$3320.00	$3775.00	$4150.00	$3950.00	$4350.00	$22,420.00
+ Retail EOM	$1750.00	$3870.00	$4250.00	$3985.00	$4795.00	$4240.00	$22,890.00
+ Reductions	$575.00	$275.00	$250.00	$175.00	$425.00	$275.00	$1975.00
− Retail BOM	$3150.00	$1750.00	$3870.00	$4250.00	$3985.00	$4795.00	$21,800.00
= Retail purchases	$2050.00	$5715.00	$4405.00	$4060.00	$5185.00	$4070.00	$25,485.00
Cost purchases	$3310.00	$3540.00	$4725.00	$5150.00	$2775.00	$3450.00	$22,950.00
% of season's sales	12.82%	14.81%	16.84%	18.51%	17.62%	19.40%	
% of season's reductions	29.11%	13.92%	12.66%	8.86%	21.52%	13.92%	
Average stock	$3815.00						
Average sales	$3735.00						
Basic stock	$1000.00						

**Book IV
Chapter 1**

**Understanding
Online Retailing**

Marketing to Your Customers

When you're in business, you can't just consider yourself a retailer; you have to be a marketer too. The Internet enables sellers in the United States to market across a massive geographic area. I'm sure you know how large the area is, but what about the *people* you sell to? You've heard of advertising being targeted to the lucrative 18-to-49 age demographic, but what about all the other age groups? Who are *they?* If you learn about your customers, you'll know how to sell to them. It's all about targeting.

Decide who buys what you want to sell — or, better yet, decide with whom you want to deal. If you don't want to deal with e-mails from teenage gamers, for example, perhaps you shouldn't be selling items that Gen N (defined in a moment) is gonna want.

Marketers often provide blanket definitions about the population based on their stages in life, what they're expected to buy, and in which activities they participate. Generational cohorts are formed less by biological dates than by life experiences and influences. We all know that outside influences make a big difference in how we look at things; they also affect how and why we buy things.

Table 1-2 gives you the population figures of the United States. With the knowledge from this table, you can better decide just how many people are potential shoppers for your products in the future. The 2010 census pegged the country at a total population of 308,745,538, and a median age of 37.2 years old.

Table 1-2	U.S. Census 2010*	
Age Range	*Population*	*Change from 2000 to 2010*
20–24	21,585,999	13.8%
25–34	41,063,948	2.9%
35–44	41,070,606	–9%
45–54	45,006,716	19.5%
55–59	19,664,805	46%
60–64	16,817,924	55.6%
65–74	21,713,429	18.1%
75–84	13,061,122	5.7%
85-100	5,440,069	28.3%

* The United States Census is taken every ten years. The next census will occur in 2020.

Monetizing your talent

If you're talented in any way, you can sell your services on eBay. Home artisans, chefs, and even stay-at-home psychics are transacting business daily on the site. What a great way to make money on eBay — make your own product!

Many custom items do well on eBay. People go to trendy places (when they have the time) such as Soho, the Grove, or the Village to find unique custom jewelry. They also go to eBay. There's a demand for personalized invitations, cards, and announcements — and even return address labels. Calligraphic work or computer-designed items are in big demand today, but no one seems to have the time to make them. Savvy sellers with talent can fill this market niche.

Knowing the Current Market

Just as successful stockbrokers know about individual companies, they also need to know about the marketplace as a whole. Sure, I know about the newly reissued Furbies out there, and so does nearly everyone else. To get a leg up on your competition, you need to know the big picture as well. Here are some questions you should ask yourself as you contemplate making buckets of money by selling items at eBay:

✦ **What items have the buzz?** If you see everyone around you rushing to the store to buy a particular item, chances are good that the item will become more valuable as stocks of it diminish. The simple rule of supply and demand says that whoever has something everyone else wants stands to gain major profits.

✦ **Do I see a growing interest in a specific item that might make it a big seller?** If you're starting to hear talk about a particular item, or even an era ('70s nostalgia? '60s aluminum Christmas trees? Who knew?), listen carefully and think of what you own — or can get your hands on — that can help you catch a piece of the trend's action.

✦ **Should I hold on to this item and wait for its value to increase, or should I sell now?** Knowing when to sell an item that you think people may want is a tricky business. Sometimes you catch the trend too early — and find out that you could have commanded a better price if you'd waited.

Other times you may catch a fad that's already passé. It's best to test the market with a small quantity of your hoard, dribbling items individually into the market until you've made back the money you spent to acquire them. When you have your cash back, the rest will be gravy.

✦ **Is a company discontinuing an item I should stockpile now and sell later?** Pay attention to discontinued items, especially toys and collectibles. If you find an item that a manufacturer has a limited supply of, you could make a tidy profit. If the manufacturer ends up reissuing the item, don't forget that the original run is still the most coveted and valuable.

✦ **Was there a recall (due to non-safety issues), an error, or a legal proceeding associated with my item?** If so, how will it affect the value of the item? For example, a toy recalled for reasons other than safety may no longer be appropriate, but it could be rare and collectible if sealed and intact.

Some people like to go with their gut feeling about when and what to buy for resale at eBay. By all means, if instinct has worked for you in the past, factor instinct in here, too. If your research looks optimistic but your gut says, "I'm not sure," listen to it; don't assume you're just hearing that lunchtime taco talking. Test the waters by purchasing a couple of the prospective items for resale. If that sale doesn't work out, you won't have a lot of money invested, and you can credit your gut with saving you some bucks.

Catching Trends in the Media

Catching trends is all about listening and looking. You can find all kinds of inside information from newspapers, magazines, television, and of course, the Internet. Believe it or not, you can even find out what people are interested in these days by bribing a kid. Keep your eyes and ears open.

In the news

The media (online or on paper) is bombarded with press releases and inside information from companies the world over. Look for stories about celebrities and upcoming movies and see whether any old fads are experiencing a resurgence. (You can sell such items as *retro chic*.)

Read the accounts from trade conventions, such as the New York Toy Fair or the Consumer Electronics show. New products are introduced and given the thumbs-up or thumbs-down by journalists. Use that information to help determine the direction for your area of expertise.

On television

No matter what you think of television, it has an enormous effect on which trends come and go and which ones stick. Why else would advertisers sink billions of dollars into TV commercials? For example, at the zenith of its popularity, the *Oprah Winfrey Show*, could turn a book into an overnight bestseller with one appearance by its author. Tune in to morning news shows and afternoon talk shows. The producers of these shows are on top of pop culture and move fast to be the first to bring you the next big thing. Take what they feature and think of a marketing angle. If you don't, you can be sure somebody else will.

Catch up with youth culture . . .

. . . or at least keep good tabs on it. If you remember cranking up The Beatles, The Partridge Family, or KISS (say what?) until your parents screamed, "Shut off that awful noise," you may be at that awkward time of life when you hardly see the appeal of what young people are doing or listening to. But if you want tips for hot items, tolerate the awful noise and listen to the kids around you. Children, especially preteens and teens, may be the best trend-spotters on the planet.

Check out other media

Websites and blogs geared to the 18-to-34 age group (and sometimes to younger teens) can help you stay on top of what's hot. See what the big companies are pitching to this target audience (and whether they're succeeding). If a celebrity is suddenly visible in every other headline, be on the lookout for merchandise relating to that person. (Are we talking hysteria-plus-cash-flow here, or just hysteria?)

Join social networks

So, you say you haven't been to Facebook, haven't started to use Twitter, and don't have a blog or boards on Pinterest? Wow, you're living in the days of low-res TV! This online social scene is the place to be. The *social web* (as it's called) is branded with the top of the top; the most happening things and products. Join the fun on some social networks, and you'll soon have a clue to what the "hip kids" are doing now. Book VI gives you insight on the where, how, and when to jump in.

Finding eBay's Soon-to-Be-Hot Sellers

Everyone wants to know what the hot ticket is on the eBay site. They want to know what's selling best so that they can run out, buy it, and *make big money* on eBay. Whoa, there, big fella.

As you may know, I'm not a believer in the notion that eBay is a get-rich-quick program. Nobody has or can give you secret information that magically transforms you from a garage seller to a warehouse tycoon overnight. You get there by studying the market and finding out what works and what doesn't. There are no shortcuts. That said, here's where you can find information on what's hot or what's going to be hot on the site.

**Book IV
Chapter 1**

**Understanding
Online Retailing**

Hot on the home page

New shoppers to the site generally enter from the home page. In case you haven't noticed, eBay suggests categories on a flyout menu on the home page. By clicking the top-level categories on those menus, you can see the hottest categories within each area. In Figure 1-1, for example, I've highlighted Crafts because it's listed as the top category in Home, Outdoors and & Décor.

Arriving in the Crafts category, I see (in Figure 1-2) some top-selling items. Now wouldn't I be the smart one if I were to list items that coincided with the top-selling items on the site? You bet!

Figure 1-1: Select a category within your business interests.

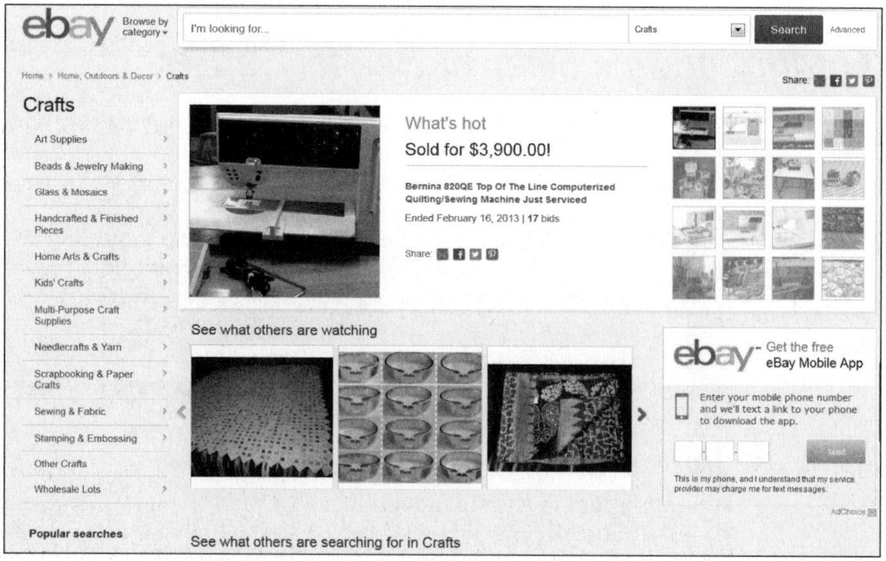

Figure 1-2: Selling for top dollar in the Crafts category.

Marketplace Research by Terapeak

Terapeak is an application that evaluates eBay item sales on an ongoing basis. Visit the eBay Marketplace Research page at

```
http://pages.ebay.com/marketplace_research
```

Or visit the page directly by going to Terapeak's website (shown in Figure 1-3) at

```
http://www.terapeak.com/
```

On the Terapeak website, eBay sellers (and buyers, if they so wish) can access up to 365 days of eBay data on completed listings. By doing so, you can get a firm grip on the demand for items you're planning to sell — with charts trending the average bids per item, number of completed items, and more. You also have access to the top searches within a category — or the entire site — to see what buyers are searching for.

There's much more data available these days since eBay partnered with Terapeak, a service I have used for ages. This company developed an eBay toolset that can really dig deep and do research for you. You'll be amazed at the data you see — especially when you've narrowed down the items you're interested in selling to just a few. Too much research can cause your eyes to glaze over and make you see funny spots in front of your face. (That doesn't happen to you? Okay, perhaps it's just me.)

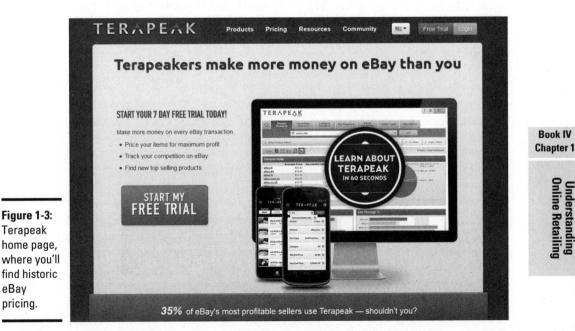

Figure 1-3:
Terapeak home page, where you'll find historic eBay pricing.

Book IV Chapter 1

Understanding Online Retailing

All this excellent data isn't free — but you can get a seven-day free trial.

For $49.95 a month or a discounted annual subscription at $239.40 ($19.95 a month), you can really go to town and access huge amounts of historic data for all eBay sites. Why not at least give it a try for a month? Research a bunch of items, and think about what you will sell next. You can always sign up again later to check out how things are trending in the future. By consulting Terapeak's data, you can dip your toe in first and save some of your hard-to-come-by cash for actually *buying* the merchandise you're going to sell.

Checking Out the Buzz Online

The eBay website is the world's host for popular culture. If it's hot, people come to eBay to look for it. You should also look on the Internet to find the buzz. By *buzz* I mean the latest gossip, rumor, or thing that's talked about at the water cooler at work. Something that's the buzz can become a trend — and *trends* are those periodic waves of people buying the latest gotta-have items.

You can find the beginnings of buzz in any news report or on your Internet provider or web portal's home page. Although Google publishes their most popular searches in their annual Zeitgeist, Yahoo! for example, has Yahoo!'s Trending Now stories at `buzz.yahoo.com`. It's a compilation of items that have received the largest number of searches on their system. You can see what's new on the list, what's going up in popularity, and what's going down.

Chapter 2: Sourcing Merchandise Like the Pros

In This Chapter

✓ Taking the mystery out of finding merchandise

✓ Getting the best wholesale deals

✓ Finding unusual (and cheap) deals

I'm often asked, "Where do I find merchandise to sell?" This, of course, is followed by "What can I sell to make the highest profit?" Good questions. But what successful seller has an answer they want to give to the competition? Did Macy's tell Gimbel's?

When eBay PowerSellers have a good, solid source of merchandise, they're not likely to share the name of that source with anyone — nor would any offline retailer. (Think about it a minute.) When I was teaching a class for advanced sellers at eBay Live (eBay's user convention), I was asked *the* question in an auditorium-size room filled with PowerSellers. I answered a question with a question: Were there any PowerSellers in the audience who would like to share their sources with the rest of the group? You could have heard a pin drop. So I upped the ante — "I'll pay anyone $10 for one solid source" — still silence. Business is business.

When someone is willing to sell you attendance to a webinar or a list of merchandise sources, you can bet the list contains old, fairly public vendors. Also, these folks are in the business of selling lists. If they were so successful, why aren't they filling their coffers with eBay profits?

The bottom line is that all successful sellers seek out their own sources. What works for one may not work for another. Methods for finding goods that I include in this chapter are gleaned from my own research, as well as from interviews with successful online retailers.

Tips for the Modest Investor

If you're interested in making money in your new eBay venture but you're starting with limited cash, follow this list of inventory dos and don'ts:

✦ **Do** start small. Think about the many collectibles that are sitting around your home. Earn your eBay stripes by selling things where it's safe to make a mistake or two. Consider finding collectibles at garage sales and resale stores as well.

✦ **Don't** spend more than you can afford to lose. If you shop at boutiques and expensive department stores, buy things that you like to wear yourself (or give as gifts) in case they don't sell.

✦ **Do** try to find something local that's unavailable nationally. For example, if you live in an out-of-the-way place that has a local specialty, try selling that on eBay.

✦ **Don't** go overboard and buy something really cheap just because it's cheap. Figure out who would want the item first.

✦ **Do** consider buying in bulk, especially if you know the item sells well or is inexpensive. Chances are good that if you buy a couple and they sell well on eBay, the item will be sold out by the time you try to buy more. If an item is inexpensive (say $.99), I always buy at least five. If no one bids on the item when you hold your auction, you're only out $5. (Why not check the store's return policy?)

As a denizen of the Internet, no doubt you'll receive tons of unsolicited e-mails guaranteeing that the sender has the hottest-selling items for you to sell on eBay. Think about this for a second. If you had the hot ticket, wouldn't you be selling it on eBay and making the fortune yourself? These people make money by preying on those who think there's a magic way to make money on eBay. There isn't. It takes old-fashioned elbow grease and research.

Buying for Retail: The Basic Course

If you're not sure what you want to sell for profit — but you're a shop-till-you-drop person by nature — incorporate your advanced shopping techniques into your daily routine. If you find a bargain that interests you, chances are you have a knack for spotting stuff that other shoppers would love to get their hands on.

Figuring out who's who in the industry

Industrial-strength sourcing is not for the faint-hearted, nor for those who lack the needed licenses and sales permits. (Book IX fills you in on how to get those; to play with the big boys, you'll have to produce these documents just to get in the door.)

It would be so very simple if you could just buy merchandise from a manufacturer. But that's rarely the case. The wholesale game requires a full team of players to participate, and each player performs a different task, as follows:

✔ **Manufacturers:** Buying directly from a manufacturer may get you great prices, but that may not be the place for a beginner to start. Manufacturers usually require large minimum orders from retailers. Unless you have a group of other sellers (perhaps a friend who owns a retail store?) to split your order with, you may have to make your purchase from a middleman.

An exception to the large-quantity requirement may be in the apparel industry. Because apparel has distinct, rapidly changing fashion seasons, a quick turnover in merchandise is a must. Apparel manufacturers may allow you to make small purchases toward the end of the season to outfit your eBay Store. It never hurts to ask.

✔ **Wholesalers:** Here's your first step to finding your middleman. Wholesalers purchase direct from the manufacturer in large quantities. They sell the merchandise to smaller retailers who can't take advantage of the discounts offered by manufacturers for large orders.

Find a wholesaler who is familiar with (or better yet, specializes in) the type of merchandise you want to sell. Obviously, someone who specializes in prerecorded DVDs and videos will not have a clue about the fashion market — and vice versa.

Don't forget to check local wholesalers, as described in the "Finding merchandise locally" section later in this chapter.

✔ **Manufacturer's reps:** These are generally the type of people you'll meet at trade shows or marts. They represent one or many noncompeting manufacturers and sell their merchandise to retailers for a commission.

✔ **Jobbers or brokers:** These independent businesspeople buy merchandise anywhere they can at distressed prices. They deal mostly in liquidation or salvage merchandise. To find out more about this source, see Chapter 4 in this minibook.

Don't forget to negotiate. Almost everything in the wholesale merchandise world is negotiable. Although merchandise may have a set price, you may be able to get a discount if you offer to pay on delivery or within ten days. Ask whether you can get help with shipping costs and perhaps promotions. Or you may earn a discount if you promote wholesalers' products through banner ads. Ask, ask, ask. The worst you can hear is no.

When you're new at eBay selling, you probably want to get your feet wet first before shelling out large sums for wholesale merchandise. Some great deals are available in the open market for resale!

Joining the hunt for e-Bay inventory

Check your favorite eBay category and see what the hot-selling item is. Better yet, go to your favorite store and make friends with the manager. Store managers will often tell you what's going to be the new hot item next month. After you're armed with the information you need, search out that item for the lowest price you can, and then give it a shot on eBay.

Keep these shopping locales in mind when you go on the eBay hunt:

✦ **Upscale department stores, trendy boutiques, outlet stores, or flagship designer stores** are good places to do some market research. Check out the newest items and then head to the clearance area or outlet store and scrutinize the bargain racks for brand-name items.

✦ **Discount club stores** such as Sam's Club and Costco made their mark by selling items in bulk to large families, clubs, and small businesses. In case you haven't noticed, these stores have upscaled and sell just about anything you could want. And both Sam's Club and Costco have websites: http://auctions.samsclub.com and www.costco.com.

Just now I visited the Sam's Club auction site. I found this Dr. Seuss *The Lorax* gift set going (in minutes) for perhaps the minimum bid of $14. (See Figure 2-1.)

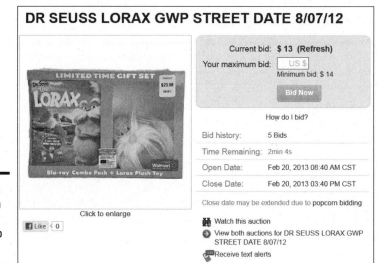

Figure 2-1: An auction on the Sam's Club website.

I made a quick jump to eBay and searched for this gift set in sold items. I found that four sets had been sold recently at the price of $39.95 plus shipping, as shown in Figure 2-2. This example represents a pretty sweet profit potential. Note in Figure 2-1 that Sam's Club links to another auction for the same item — it's another one in five hours where the high bid is only $6.

Figure 2-2:
The same item selling for a lot more on eBay.

4 sold listings | active listings | completed listings   Sort: End Date: recent first ▾   View: ☰ ▾

Dr. Seuss' THE LORAX GIFT SET - includes DVD + BLU-RAY plus Lorax Plush Toy NEW   Feb-11 06:58   **$39.95** Buy It Now +$2.99 shipping

Top Rated Plus

View similar active items | Sell one like this

In another book, I talked about a special on the Costco website, www.costco.com, for a new *Snow White & the Seven Dwarfs* DVD. For $18.49, you could pre-order the *Snow White* DVD and get a second Disney DVD for *free*. When there's an offer like this, you can sell two items on eBay for the price of one. If I had followed my own advice — bought a case of this deal and held some for future sales — I'd be in the money today. It seems that Disney movies are released for a limited time only.

Now, when checking the Costco site, I find these women's summer skorts on sale for $9.99 (shipping and handling included). On eBay they were selling in multiple listings for $26.99. Figures 2-3 and 2-4 show you how profit can be made. By looking at the completed listings, I could even see which colors and sizes netted the highest profit, so I bought $200-worth for my spring/summer eBay sales.

Stores like Costco have a 90-day return policy. Keep track of your merchandise cycle and return when you need to.

✦ **Dollar stores** in your area. Many of the items these places carry are *overruns* (too many of something that didn't sell), *small runs* (too little of something that the big guys weren't interested in stocking), or out-of-date fad items that need a good home on eBay. I've found profitable books, Olympics memorabilia, and pop-culture items at this type of store.

Figure 2-3: Women's skorts at Costco.

Figure 2-4: More than double the money on eBay.

It's not unusual for dollar-store warehouses to sell direct to a retailer (that's you). Find out where the distribution warehouse is for your local dollar store chain and make contact. The 99¢ Only stores, for example, have a wholesale unit called Bargain Wholesale that runs out of their City of Commerce, California offices. Bargain Wholesale also has a website (see Figure 2-5) which is open to anyone with legitimate resale credentials.

Figure 2-5:
Download
Bargain
Wholesale's
catalog
on the
company
site.

✦ **Thrift stores** are packed with used — but often good-quality — items. And you can feel good knowing that the money you spend in a nonprofit thrift shop is going to a good cause. Some branches of Goodwill and the Salvation Army receive merchandise from a central warehouse. Ask the manager (whom you've befriended) when the truck regularly comes in.

Goodwill Industries is definitely geared up for the 21st century. You can shop at its online auctions (see Figure 2-6) and get super values on the best of their merchandise. Don't forget to check the going prices on eBay before you buy. Have fun at www.shopgoodwill.com.

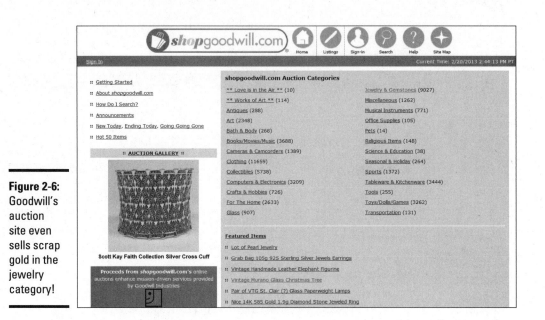

Figure 2-6:
Goodwill's auction site even sells scrap gold in the jewelry category!

✦ **Garage, tag, moving, and estate sales** offer some of the biggest bargains you'll ever come across. The stuff you find at estate sales is often of a higher quality. Keep an eye out for "moving to a smaller house" sales. These are usually people who have raised children, accumulated a houseful of stuff (collectibles? old toys? designer vintage clothes?), and want to shed it all so that they can move to a condo in Palm Springs.

When an item is new but has some collectible potential, I suggest you buy in bulk, sell some of the item to repay your investment, and save the balance for later. This strategy has paid off for me a good many times with Disney films, Barbies, and Andy Warhol dinnerware.

✦ **Liquidation and estate auctions** are two types of auctions where you can pick up bargains. Before you go to any auction, double-check payment terms and find out whether you must bring cash or can pay by credit card. Also, before you bid on anything, find out the *hammer fee,* or *buyer's premium.* These fees are a percentage that auction houses add to the winner's bid; the buyer has the responsibility for paying these fees.

When a company gets into serious financial trouble, its debtors (the people to whom the company owes money) obtain a court order to liquidate the company to pay the bills. The liquidated company then sells its stock, fixtures, and even real estate in a liquidation auction. Items sell for just cents on the dollar, and you can easily resell many of these items on eBay. Use Google or Bing and search *auctioneers: liquidators.* You can also contact local offices to get on mailing lists.

Estate auctions are the higher level of estate garage sales. Here you can find fine art, antiques, paper ephemera, rare books, and collectibles of all kinds. These auctions are attended mostly by dealers, who know the local going prices for the items they bid on. But because they're buying to sell in a retail environment, their high bids will generally be the wholesale price for your area. And local dealers are buying what's hot to resell in your city — not what's going to sell across the country. That entire market will probably be yours.

✦ **Newspaper auction listings** are an excellent source of merchandise for resale, particularly the listings of liquidations and estate auctions (usually appear on Saturday) and the daily classified section, which often has ads that announce local business liquidations. Do not confuse any of these with garage sales or flea-market sales (run by individuals and a great source for one-of-a kind items). Liquidation and estate sales are professionally run, usually by licensed liquidators or auctioneers, and involve merchandise that may be new but is always sold in *lots* (in a quantity) rather than one item at a time.

If your local newspaper has a website, use its online search to view the classifieds for major liquidations, estate auctions, or other similar deals. Right there online, you can often find just what you're looking for locally. To find the paper's website, run a search on Google like the one shown in Figure 2-7.

Figure 2-7:
A Google search for *newspaper classified los angeles* brings up plenty of hits to peruse online.

Google | newspaper classified los angeles

Web   Images   Maps   Shopping   More ▾   Search tools

About 119,000,000 results (0.67 seconds)

Ad related to **newspaper classified los angeles** ⓘ

Los Angeles Classifieds - ClassifiedAds.com
www.classifiedads.com/
Search For **Classifieds Los Angeles**! Thousands of Ads in **Los Angeles**

Classifieds   Jobs
Vehicles   Rentals

Classifieds - Los Angeles Times
classifieds.latimes.com/
Search **Classifieds** for. In Category. All Categories, Antiques, Arts & Crafts ... 50 miles, 100 miles, 250 miles, Entire US. Place an Ad with the **Los Angeles** Times!

Los Angeles Times -- Los Angeles Jobs & Employment - latimes.com
www.latimes.com/**classified**/jobs/
Help wanted ads for jobs in **Los Angeles** and the rest of the U.S. from the LA Times. ... Management, Manufacturing, Marketing, Media - Journalism - **Newspaper**, Nonprofit - Social Services ... Job **classifieds** from Times partner CareerBuilder ...

Los Angeles Daily News Classifieds
daily**news**.kaango.com/
Post **classifieds** ads and search **classifieds** ads in Woodland Hills, California for **Los Angeles** Daily **News** in Autos: For Sale or Lease, Autos: Services & Parts, ...

Los Angeles Classifieds | Local Classified Ads | Oodle
www.oodle.com/regions/la/
From jobs to pets, apartments to cars, find **Los Angeles classified** ads on Oodle. ... **newspapers** and disorganized **classified** sites, Oodle has all local **classifieds** ...

✦ **Going-out-of-business sales,** some of which run week by week, with bigger discounts as time goes by. Don't be shy about making an offer on a quantity of items.

Going-out-of-business sales can be a bonanza, but be careful and don't be misled. Many states require businesses that are putting on a going-out-of business sale to purchase a special license that identifies the business as *really* going out of business. Some store ads may read "Going Out for Business" or some similar play on words, so you need to be sure that you're going to the real thing.

✦ **Flea markets or swap meets** in your area may have some bargains you can take advantage of.

✦ **Gift shops at museums, monuments, national parks, and theme parks** can provide eBay inventory — but think about where to sell the items. Part of your selling success on eBay is *access*. People who can't get to Graceland may pay handsomely for an Elvis mini-guitar with the official logo on the box.

✦ **Freebies** are usually samples or promotion pieces that companies give away to introduce a new product, service, or, best of all, a media event. Hang on to these! If you receive handouts (lapel pins, pencils, pamphlets, books, interesting napkins, flashlights, towels, stuffed toys) from a sporting event, premiere, or historic event — or even a collectible freebie from a fast-food restaurant — they could be your ticket to some eBay sales. For example, when *Return of the Jedi* was re-released in 1997, the first 100 people to enter each theater got a Special Edition Luke Skywalker figure. These figures are still highly prized by collectors and when the next part of the *Star Wars* saga was released, the prices on this figure went up yet again.

When you go to the cosmetic counter and buy a way-too-expensive item, ask for tester-sized samples. Name-brand cosmetic and perfume samples of high-priced items sell well on eBay. Also, look for *gift with purchase* deals. If it's a specialty item, you can usually sell it on its own to someone who'd like to try a sample, rather than plunge headlong into a large purchase. Less-special items can be grouped together as lots. Be sure to put the brand names in the title.

One of my mottoes is "Buy off-season, sell on-season." You can get great bargains on winter merchandise in the heat of summer. January's a great time to stock up on Christmas decorations, and the value of those trendy vintage aluminum trees doubles in November and December. Cashmere sweaters, too! In the winter, you can get great deals on closeout summer sports merchandise. It's all in the timing.

Looking for resale items on eBay

Another place to find items to sell is on eBay itself. Look only for good-quality merchandise to resell. Remember that the only way to make a living on eBay is to sell quality items to happy customers so that they'll come back and buy from you again.

Be sure to search eBay auction titles for the following:

✦ **Keywords:** wholesale, resale, resell, closeout, surplus

✦ **Key phrases:** "case of" (see Figure 2-8), "wholesale lots," "case quantity," "lot of," "pallet of"

Use the quotation marks (but not the commas) in the key phrases because this forces the search engine to find the words in the exact order.

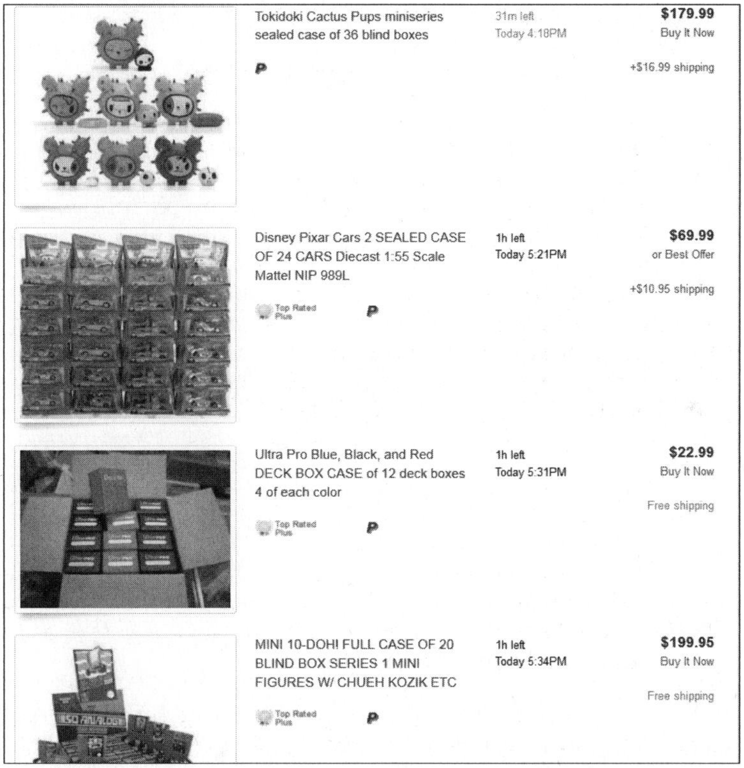

Figure 2-8: A "case of" search in the Toy category finds a sweet deal on Disney Pixar Cars.

Also be sure you check out the wholesale categories on eBay. After noticing how many sellers were buying from other sellers, eBay set up wholesale sub-categories for almost every type of item. You can find the wholesale items in most categories. Go to the eBay home page and click Shop by Category. Then click See All Categories in the pop-up window that appears. Scroll down the list of categories, and select the favorite category in which you sell, click the More link, and find the Wholesale Lots subcategory. Just click that link to get to the deals, as shown in Figure 2-9.

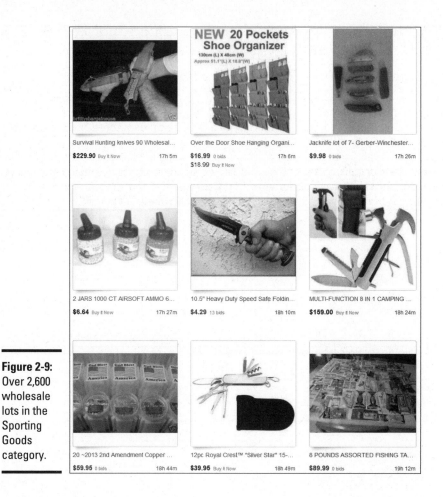

Figure 2-9:
Over 2,600 wholesale lots in the Sporting Goods category.

Buying Wholesale

After you get the hang of finding items in stores to resell on eBay, it's time to move to the wholesale source. As a side note, I want you to know that although my eBay business is based on wholesale merchandise, I still love going to the sources mentioned in the last section and finding great deals to resell. It's become a fun hobby! Don't we all love to find a piece of merchandise that we *know* we can sell for a profit?

Okay, you want to set up shop on eBay. You kind of know what type of merchandise you want to sell, but you don't know where to turn. Anyone in the brick-and-mortar world who plans to open a new store faces the same quandary: finding merchandise that will sell quickly at a profit.

Tuesday Morning

One of my editors is going to kill me for mentioning one of her favorite eBay merchandise sources, but here it is: Tuesday Morning, which has more than 500 stores scattered over the United States. They sell first-quality designer and brand-name closeout merchandise at deep, deep discounts — 50 to 80 percent below retail. The key here is that the store sells recognizable brand names, the kind of items that eBay shoppers look for. I've seen items at their store from Samsonite, Gucci, Limoges, Wedgwood, Royal Doulton, Madame Alexander, and even Barbie! Find your local store or shop at their website, `www.tuesday morning.com`. The following is a great example of the bargains you can find. On the left, see the item on the Tuesday Morning site at $49.99; on the right, it's close to $117 in an eBay listing. Nice profit margin!

Limoges CLEARANCE Hinged
Birdcage w/ 2 Doves
$49.99 $162.50

NEW! Limoges Porcelain BIRDCAGE
Trinket Box Doves Birds Kissing
Wedding CHAMART

$117.00 Buy It Now   8d 21h 9m

Merchandise that sits around doesn't give you cash flow, which is the name of the game in *any* business. (*Cash flow* = profit = money to buy better, or more, merchandise.) I spoke to several successful retailers and they all gave me the same answers about where they began their quest. The upcoming sections give you a look at the answers these retailers shared.

Setting up to buy

Purchasing wholesale merchandise may require that you have your state's *resale license,* which identifies you as being in the business. Be sure that you have one before you try to purchase merchandise directly from another business. Also, when you have a resale number and purchase merchandise from another business — known as a *business-to-business* (B2B) transaction — you probably won't be charged sales tax when you purchase your stock because you'll be *paying* sales tax when you sell the items. Go to Book IX, Chapter 1 to find out how to get that magic resale number.

When you have your resale number, you can go anywhere you want to buy merchandise. If you want to buy direct from a manufacturer, you can. Unfortunately, many manufacturers have a minimum order amount, which may be more than you want to spend (and you'd get more of a particular item than you'd ever want at once). To remedy that, see whether you can find independent retailers who buy in quantity — and who will (perhaps) let you in on some quantity buys with manufacturers. I often buy in with a couple of local shops when they purchase their orders.

To gain access to legitimate wholesale sources, you must be a licensed business in your city or county. You also usually have to have a resale permit and tax ID number from your state. (See Book IX, Chapter 1 for details.)

Finding merchandise locally

Always remember that the cost of shipping the merchandise to you adds a great deal of expense. The higher your expense, the lower your return may be. The more you buy locally to resell, the more profit you can make.

The first place most potential retailers go is to the local wholesale district. These are immediate merchandise sources, within driving distance of your home.

Regional merchandise marts

Your next stop — should you be lucky enough to live in a major metropolitan area — is to find out whether there's a merchandise or fashion mart near you. These are giant complexes that hold as many as several thousand lines of merchandise in one area.

Merchandise marts are hubs for wholesale buyers, distributors, manufacturers, and independent sales representatives. They have showrooms within the property for manufacturers or their representatives to display their current merchandise. Under one roof, you may find both fashion and gift merchandise for your eBay business.

See Table 2-1 for a representative sprinkling of the many marts across the country. This is not a comprehensive list, just one to get your mind moving; I have a much more thorough list in the Tools area of my website www. coolebaytools.com. You can contact the individual marts for tenant lists and more information. If you're a legitimate business, the marts will be more than happy to teach you the ropes and get you started.

Table 2-1   Wholesale Merchandise Marts

Name	Location	Website Address	Trade Shows
Americas Mart	Atlanta, Georgia	www.americasmart.com	Apparel, jewelry, shoes, fashion accessories, gifts, home furnishings
California Market Center	Los Angeles, CA	www.californiamarket center.com	Apparel, accessories, textiles, toys, gifts, furniture & décor, garden accessories, stationery, personal-care products
The Merchandise Mart	Chicago, Ill	www.mmart.com	Apparel, office, home, decorative accessories, textiles, gifts
The Chicago Market	Chicago, IL	www.shopchicago market.com	Apparel, home furnishings, antiques, gifts, bridal
Columbus Marketplace	Columbus, OH	www.thecolumbus marketplace.com	Gifts, garden, home furnishings, décor
Dallas Market Center	Dallas, TX	www.dallasmarket center.com	Apparel, gift products, decorative accessories, home furnishings, lighting, garden accessories, floral, and gourmet
Denver Merchandise Mart	Denver, CO	www.denvermart.com	Apparel, gifts, souvenirs, gourmet, collectibles, home décor
The L.A. Mart	Los Angeles, CA	www.lamart.com	Gifts, home décor, furnishings
Miami Merchandise Mart	Miami, FL	www.miamimart.net	Apparel, gifts, accessories, home décor
Minneapolis Gift Mart	Minneapolis, MN	www.mplsmart.com	Gifts, home décor, accessories
New York Merchandise Mart	New York, NY	www.41madison.com	Gifts, home décor, accessories
San Francisco Gift Center & Jewelry Mart	San Francisco, CA	www.sfgcjm.com	Apparel, jewelry, home furnishings, gifts, jewelry, stationery
The New Mart	Los Angeles, CA	www.newmart.net	Contemporary clothing and accessories

When you go to each mart's website, you'll find hundreds of links to whole-sale sources. Many marts also send you a directory of the manufacturers represented in the mart.

Wholesale trade shows

By checking out the links to the marts listed in Table 2-1, you'll also end up with links to the thousands of wholesale trade shows that go on across the country each year. Trade shows are commonly held in convention centers, hotels, and local merchandise marts.

A super source for finding gift shows is the `greatrep.com` website, shown in Figure 2-10. Here you find a list of all the major gift shows — with click-able links to contact information for the show coordinators. For more on GreatRep.com, see the "Buying Online for Resale" section later in this chapter.

When visiting a show or a mart, view all merchandise before you place an order. Bring a notebook with you to make copious notes of items you find interesting and where you find them.

Figure 2-10: Check the GreatRep.com website for an updated trade show schedule.

Necessary ID for trade shows and marts

Professional trade shows and marts are not open to the general public, and they want to keep it that way. When you attend these venues, they want to be sure that you represent a business. Following is a list of items that you may be asked to provide, as proof that you are a retailer:

✔ Business cards

✔ A copy of your current resale-tax certificate or state tax permit

✔ Current occupational or business tax license

✔ Proof of a business checking account or a letter of credit from your bank (if you're applying for credit)

✔ Financial statement

✔ Cash and checks

Be sure to check with the organization sponsoring the trade show or mart before attending so that you'll have everything you need. Don't let this list scare you — wholesale marts are fun, and the organizers and vendors will do everything they can to help you make your retailing venture a success!

These trade shows are gargantuan bourses of hundreds of wholesale vendors all lined up and ready to take your orders. The vendors have samples of the merchandise in the lines they carry and are delighted to answer all your questions about their products, credit applications, and minimum orders. These shows are designed to move products to retailers like you!

Few trade shows are more exciting than the Consumer Electronics Show (CES), sponsored by the Consumer Electronics Association. If you buy breakthrough technologies to sell online, this show is a must! You'll find the latest in everything high-tech, including digital imaging, electronic gaming, home electronics, car audio, home theater, and satellite systems. You'll see what's new — but more importantly, you'll see what will be passé in a hurry — great merchandise to sell (in a timely way, of course) on eBay.

CES draws more than 100,000 buyers each year, and the vendors are there to sell their goods to *you*. Visit the CES website at www.cesweb.org to get an idea of the excitement that the show generates.

See whether the item is selling on eBay before you make your purchase. Bring your tablet or laptop and conduct research either on the spot or later in the day for next-day purchases. *Getting* a good deal is one thing — selling it on eBay is another.

Buying Online for Resale

I've come across many legitimate sources of goods on the Internet. But the Internet is loaded with scam artists; it's up to you to check vendors out for yourself before spending your hard-earned money. Even if I mention sellers here, I want you to check them out as if you know nothing about them. I can't guarantee a thing; all I know is that at the time of this writing, they were reliable sources for eBay merchandise.

Craigslist

If you haven't visited Craigslist in a while, you're missing quite a bit. You'll find anything and everything listed in the free local classifieds, and you never know when there will be something worthwhile to resell. This site is always worth at least a once-a-week visit. Much of the stuff on the site is listed by people who are too afraid (or maybe just technophobic) to sell on eBay. Focus on your category of interest and go to town. I did exactly that and found the item shown in Figure 2-11, a Cartier Love bracelet selling for $150. This item sells on eBay for up to $3,000!

Before buying an item like the one pictured in Figure 2-11, definitely check the authenticity. Buyer beware — it's most likely a fake.

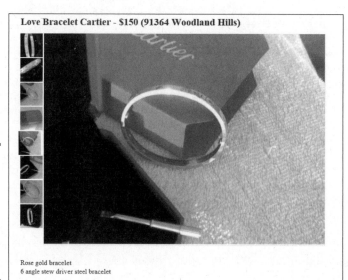

Love Bracelet Cartier - $150 (91364 Woodland Hills)

Rose gold bracelet
6 angle stew driver steel bracelet

Figure 2-11: Craigslist is a super source for purchasing used items from technophobes.

Tips for buying wholesale online

Because the online world can be fraught with problems, keep in mind the following:

- ✔ **Protect your e-mail address.** Check every site you sign up with for a privacy policy. Watch out for wording like this in the Privacy Policy: "Our Privacy Policy does not extend to our affiliated sellers or advertisers. They are free to maintain their own privacy policy independent of us." Again, get an anonymous e-mail address to spare yourself spam.

- ✔ **Look for an *About Us* page.** Be sure the site has an address and a phone number. Call the number to see whether it is a "real" business, not a fly by night. While you're at it, see how you're treated on the phone.

- ✔ **Look for safety seals.** Seeing the Better Business Bureau Online, TrustE, or SquareTrade logo on the website can bolster trust in the company.

- ✔ **Check out the shipping costs.** Sometimes the shipping can cost more than the item. Before placing your order, make sure you know all the shipping costs and terms.

You must have a Federal tax ID number (that's your identification to do business) to even register on most legitimate wholesale sites. Finding wholesale websites with this restriction is a *good* thing. It's another way to verify that you're dealing with a true wholesale supplier.

B2B wholesale clearinghouses

Legitimate online sites for retailers are rare. Many of the business to business (B2B) merchants and wholesale directories reflect nothing but flea-market goods and highly marked-up drop-shipping items. Don't be disappointed. That doesn't mean you can't find a deal on some great merchandise. The benefit of the Internet is that you have access to many sources. The challenge is to find the good, solid, reliable sources of information, like the following:

- ✦ **MadeInUSA.com:** One of the best ways to find an item to sell is to find that item in your everyday life. If you have the manufacturer's name but no contact information, go to the company website at www.madeinusa. com (see Figure 2-12), which has a huge database of manufacturer contact info.

- ✦ **GreatRep.com:** At www.greatrep.com, you find a website directory (refer to Figure 2-10) where buyers (that's you) can hook up with manufacturer's representatives that carry lines of merchandise in the wholesale giftware, home furnishings, and furniture industries. It's fantastic! After you register (and provide your state resale license), you have access to listings of thousands of manufacturers. In the listings you may find out how much they require for a minimum order and you can request a catalog.

Figure 2-12:
Search more than 300,000 manufacturers at this website.

Buying directly from online wholesalers

Following are a few sources that have some unusual merchandise. I've bought from almost all of them:

✦ **Liquidation.com:** If you like auctions (and I *know* you do), check out www.liquidation.com. This is a massive all-auction website that has incredible deals on all types of merchandise, as shown in Figure 2-13. One of the things that I love about this site is that most individual auctions provide a link to the *manifest* — a list of every piece of merchandise in the lot. If you click the View Manifest link at the top of the auction page, you see a piece-by-piece list of the items included in the lot you're bidding on.

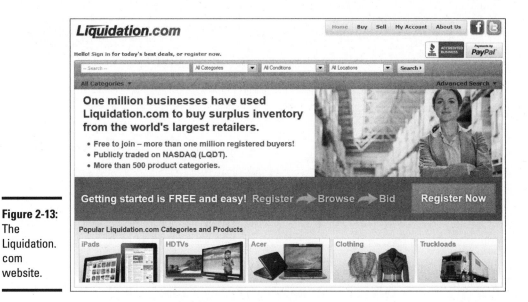

Figure 2-13:
The
Liquidation.
com
website.

It's best to buy from vendors closer to your geographic area because after you add the shipping fee, you might be paying too much for your lot. Liquidation.com can refine your searches to your location in the country, and it has a shipping calculator to help you know ahead of time how much your shipping may be.

✦ **Oriental Trading Company:** The Oriental Trading Company has been in business for a long time. I used to buy from their catalog for school and charity affairs. This site offers everything from crafts to costumes to party goods — and all priced perfectly for resale on eBay. Use your practiced eye (and completed search) to ferret out the unique items that will sell. Visit them at www.orientaltrading.com.

✦ **Big Lots Wholesale:** If you're familiar with the Big Lots stores scattered around the country, you have an idea of what you can buy at biglots wholesale.com. A quick click to their website showed me that they were loaded with great deals on everything from health and beauty items to toys to lawn and garden tools. A seller's tax ID number is required to get pricing on this site.

Chapter 3: Selling Other People's Stuff Online

In This Chapter

↙ **Organizing your consignment business**

↙ **Competing with consignment store chains**

↙ **Becoming a Trading Assistant on eBay**

↙ **Promoting your consignment business**

↙ **Writing an effective consignment contract**

Consignment sales are a popular way for you to help non-techie types by selling their items on eBay. Lots of sellers do it, and several retail locations base their business on it. This chapter gives you a close-up look at consignment selling. Essentially you take possession of the item from the owner and sell it on eBay. You're responsible for taking photos and marketing the auction on eBay — for a fee. In addition to the money you earn selling on consignment, you also get excellent experience for future auctions of your own merchandise

Getting Organized to Sell for Others

To set up your business for consignment sales, you should follow a few guidelines:

1. Design a consignment agreement (a binding contract), and send it to the owners of the merchandise before they send you their items. Doing so ensures that all policies are set up in advance and that no questions will arise after the transaction has begun.

2. Have the owners sign and give the agreement to you (the consignor) along with the item.

3. Research the item based on past sales so you can give the owners an estimated range of what the item might sell for on eBay.

4. Photograph the item carefully (see Book V for some hints) and write a thoughtful, thorough description.

5. Handle all e-mail inquiries as though the item were your own; after all, your fee is generally based on a percentage of the final sale.

Traditional auction houses handle consignment sales in a similar fashion.

Competing with the Drop Off Stores

Several chains have opened up across the country with brick-and-mortar locations accepting merchandise from the general public to sell on eBay. By becoming an official Trading Assistant, you can compete with the big boys in your own area.

The best part is that if you're running your eBay business out of your home, from a garage, or from a low-rent industrial office, you're a step ahead of the big guys who have to pay high rents in fancy neighborhoods to get their drop-in business. They also have to hire people who are familiar with running auctions on eBay — and aren't you *already* set up for that?

Don't worry about the competition! You may hear about the many eBay consignment stores that are opening up. (As a matter of fact, some are selling franchises for this business for up to $15,000!) You already know how to sell on eBay. (Franchise? You don't need a stinkin' franchise!) Use your good sense (and positive feedback) to build your own eBay consignment store.

Following are some of the chains that sell goods on eBay for consumers:

✦ AuctionItToday, www.auctionittoday.com

✦ iSold It, www.i-soldit.com

✦ Instant Auctions, www.instantauctions.net

Retail locations have a much higher cost of business than you do. They need to be open for set hours a day and have several employees on duty at all times. Many of these stores won't accept an item worth less than $75. There's still a lot of profit left for you in the realm of under-$75 items.

Table 3-1 shows the fees charged by consignment chain stores, as of this writing.

Table 3-1	Consignment Chain Fees	
Chain	*Sold Price*	*Fee Percentage*
Instant Auctions	Up to $499.99	28%
	$500 - $999.99	23%
AuctionItToday	Up to $500	30%
	$500 and up	38%
iSold It	up to $500	35%
	over $500	20%

In addition to the fees shown in Table 3-1, these chains (of course) also charge for all eBay and PayPal fees. Some also charge a minimum commission per item. Keep an eye out in your own area should a store open so you can keep up with the competition.

What do you charge for all your work? I can't give you a stock answer for that one. Many sellers charge a flat fee for photographing, listing, and shipping that ranges from $5 to $10 per item, plus as much as a 40 percent commission on the final auction total (to absorb eBay fees). Other sellers base their fees solely on the final sale amount and charge on a sliding scale, beginning at 50 percent of the total sale, less eBay and payment service fees. You must decide how much you think you can make on an item.

Table 3-2 gives you some ideas based on the input I've received from some successful eBay consignment sellers. (These percentages may be in addition to the listing fee and gallery charges.)

Table 3-2	Sample Progressive Commission Schedule
Final Value ($)	*Your Commission*
Under 50	40%
50.01–150.00	35% of the amount over $50
150.01–250.00	30% of the amount over $150
251.00–500.00	25% of the amount over $500
501.00–1000.00	20% of the amount over $500
Over 1000	15%

Remember that you can always choose to charge a flat commission, if that works best in your area. Check out the eBay Trading Assistants in your area to see what they charge.

Becoming Listed in the eBay Trading Assistant Directory

What is an eBay Trading Assistant? Simply put, an eBay Trading Assistant sells merchandise for people on eBay. A more complex definition is that a Trading Assistant (TA) sells items on consignment for those who are not familiar with the eBay site or simply don't want to bother to learn the ropes.

The first thing to take into consideration before becoming a Trading Assistant is to be sure you are familiar with the eBay site and its rules and regulations and — most of all — are experienced in selling items at a profit. To be a successful Trading Assistant, you need to know how to research items on eBay and how to parlay keywords into winning auction titles.

The Trading Assistants Program home page (see Figure 3-1) appears on the eBay site at

```
http://pages.ebay.com/tahub/
```

To find a Trading Assistant in your area, click the link to find a Trading Assistant and you'll be taken to a search page. Potential customers can search for a Trading Assistant in their area to sell their items by typing in a ZIP code.

This page is promoted on the eBay site to new users and in eBay promotions. Being listed on this page will help your customers find you.

eBay makes it very clear that whether you fulfill the requirements for listing in the Trading Assistant Directory or not, being a Trading Assistant is a privilege. If eBay receives complaints about your services, they have the right to remove you from the Trading Assistant Directory. Following are eBay's requirements:

✦ **Listings:** You must have sold at least ten items in the previous three months.

✦ **Feedback rating:** You must maintain a minimum rating of 100 or higher, with a minimum of 98 percent positive comments.

✦ **Activity:** You must have continued to sell at least ten items in the previous three months and maintain ten sales per each three-month period.

✦ **Follow Terms.** eBay offers a style guide that outlines the use of the eBay brand. eBay takes the use of its name and graphics seriously, so if you intend to become a Trading Assistant, you must respect the privilege. You can see the details at

```
ebaytradingassistant.com/index.php?page=userAgreements&
type=taSG
```

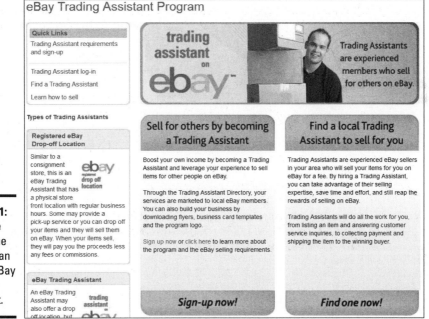

Figure 3-1: Visit here to become listed as an official eBay Trading Assistant.

You may notice on the directory-search screen that there's an option to search for buySAFE-bonded sellers. This is a real selling point when it comes to doing business with strangers. A seller who's *bonded* is basically backed by insurance. (See Book VIII, Chapter 2 for more on joining buySAFE, whose website is at www.buysafe.com.) Note that in Figure 3-2, several buySAFE-bonded sellers show up in a search of Los Angeles, California.

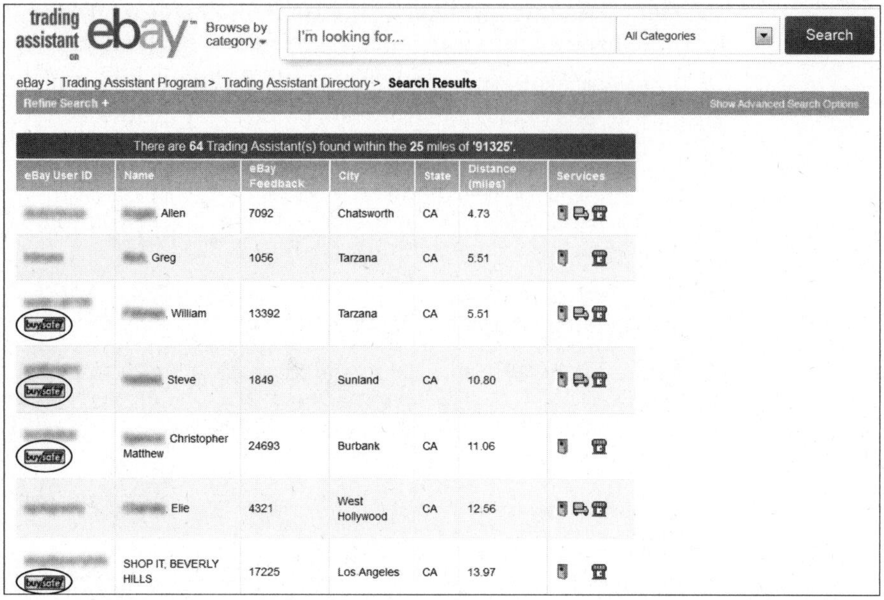

trading assistant on ebay
Browse by category
I'm looking for...
All Categories
Search
eBay > Trading Assistant Program > Trading Assistant Directory > Search Results
Refine Search +
Show Advanced Search Options
There are 64 Trading Assistant(s) found within the 25 miles of '91325'.
eBay User ID | Name | eBay Feedback | City | State | Distance (miles) | Services
Allen | 7092 | Chatsworth | CA | 4.73
Greg | 1056 | Tarzana | CA | 5.51
William | 13392 | Tarzana | CA | 5.51
Steve | 1849 | Sunland | CA | 10.80
Christopher Matthew | 24693 | Burbank | CA | 11.06
Elie | 4321 | West Hollywood | CA | 12.56
SHOP IT, BEVERLY HILLS | 17225 | Los Angeles | CA | 13.97
buySAFE

Figure 3-2: buySAFE-bonded sellers receive choice positions in search results.

As a Trading Assistant, you acquire merchandise and sell it on eBay on consignment. You are also responsible for the following:

- **Consulting with consignors about their items.** Know the details that might affect how you sell what you're selling. Get the goods on the goods before you post.
- **Researching the value of the item.** Many non-eBay users may have unreasonable expectations of the price their items will sell for. It's your duty to check this out beforehand and explain the realities to them.
- **Coordinating the listing.** Take digital photos and write a complete and accurate description of the item.
- **Keeping a close accounting of fees and money collection.** Whether you use hard copy or software, be diligent and consistent.

That's not much in the way of requirements, so get ready to become a TA.

REMEMBER

Becoming a Trading Assistant does *not* make you an employee, agent, or independent contractor of eBay. Make sure you refer to yourself as an independent business.

When you sign up as a Trading Assistant, you have to fill out a form describing your business to prospective customers. Think through the things you want to say before posting them. Your information here works like an ad for you. Following are the items to put on your Trading Assistant Profile page:

✦ **Personal information:** This includes your eBay user ID, your real name and address, and the languages spoken. Your personal information appears in the listing, such as the one from a professional Trading Assistant, *borntodeal*, shown in Figure 3-3.

✦ **Category specialty:** If you specialize in a particular category, be sure to mention it. You may indicate eBay home page categories.

✦ **Service description:** In this area you can say as little or as much as you like about your eBay experience and the services you provide. Remember that the more you communicate in advance, the more successful you'll be.

Here is a sample service description (also look at the Specialties and Services in Figure 3-4):

> I've been active on the site since 1996 and am an eBay PowerSeller. I specialize in selling all types of eBay items and am particularly familiar with the fashion category. I can handle large numbers of listings. Please contact me so that we can discuss your particular needs and time availability.

> I can visit your home within 15 miles from my place of business to inventory the items. I will list, ship, and provide you with an itemized list of all items sold with the sale price and my fees.

Figure 3-3: Trading Assistant Directory Contact Information box.

borntodeal (24693 ⭐) buysafe

Contact this Assistant

Member Profile   Items for Sale

eBay Seller Information

Feedback Score: 24693
Positive Feedback: 100%
eBay member since 1999 in US

Specialties

Contact Information

Name:
Christopher Matthew Spencer

BusinessName:
"BORNTODEAL" on eBay

Web Site:
http://www.borntodeal.com

Address:
1130 North Lima Street
Burbank, CA 91505
US
Map

Contact:
☎ 818.567.4000 (Primary)
☎ 800.252.5352 (Secondary)
✉ borntodeal@gmail.com

Drop-off Location:
🕐 Hours:
Monday: 9:00 AM - 5:00 PM
Tuesday: 9:00 AM - 5:00 PM
Wednesday: 9:00 AM - 5:00 PM
Thursday: 9:00 AM - 5:00 PM
Friday: 9:00 AM - 5:00 PM
Saturday: Closed - Closed
Sunday: Closed - Closed

🛒 I am a Registered eBay Drop Off Location.

🏪 I offer drop off service.

Pickup:
Not Available.

- Advertising
- Comics
- Sewing
- Paper
- Disneyana
- Science Fiction
- Clocks
- Science, Medical
- Transportation
- Breweriana, Beer
- Tobacciana
- Vanity, Perfume & Shaving
- Trading Cards
- Casino
- Holiday, Seasonal
- Postcards
- Linens, Fabric & Textiles
- Pens & Writing Instruments
- Animals
- Knives, Swords & Blades
- Lamps, Lighting
- Metalware
- Religions, Spirituality
- Rocks, Fossils, Minerals

Services

Service Description:
"borntodeal" is a Burbank, California company with experts who make it a breeze for anyone to sell their high-value items on eBay. Once your item sells, we give you a check!
We specialize in top-brands, non-profit fundraising and handling high-value estates.
We proudly have over 26,000 positive feedbacks on eBay and we can help you get the best price for what you want to sell!
With a strong commitment to environmental protection, The Chase Group Auction Management ensures our customers we are providing the very best in recycling stewardship and employee care and in addition to helping you sell unwanted items, we also help protect our environment by taking usable, valuable items and finding them a new owner thereby avoiding landfills and waste that might otherwise hurt the environment. All operations are carried out with a constant awareness of our clients need for security and minimal environmental impact.
We handle everything from the time you drop of your merchandise until we cut your check, you can just sit back and watch the action online.

- Research and value your items to get you top dollar
- Professionally photograph your items and post high quality photos of them
- Store your items in our warehouse
- Manage the entire selling process - do the auction posting, handle all calls and emails, track the auction, collect the payment and ship the item(s)
- Pay all of the eBay listing and final value fees, as well as PayPal fees
- Send you a check

Figure 3-4:
The Specialties and Services area.

✦ **Policy description:** Ensure that consignees understand your policies. A sample description follows:

> I will list your items for two listing cycles, spread up to 30 days. If items do not sell, they will be returned to you. Items must be in my possession to be submitted to eBay unless contractual arrangements are made in advance. I handle all correspondence and shipping. A consignment contract is required. I also do independent consulting specializing in Internet auctions and their application to your business.

✦ **Fee description:** This is where you need to do some research. Search your ZIP code on the Trading Assistants Directory page and see what other fees are being charged in your area. After you have an idea of what you want to charge, you can put that information here.

Take a look at the descriptions for the Trading Assistant shown in Figure 3-5. There's no question about how this seller handles his business after you read this text. See if you can come up with text that will sell your services without being overbearing.

You can provide incentives for higher-value items by charging lower commissions (such as "40 percent if the item sells for less than $50, but 30 percent if the item sells for more"). Also, charging a higher percentage and including fees allows an easier fee discussion with the client (for example, "40 percent and all fees included versus 30 percent and you pay all the fees, which include . . .").

Figure 3-5:
Company
description
portion of
a Trading
Assistant
listing.

> **Fees:**
> Depending upon the volume and value of the items you have to sell, we offer fee structures to fit the situation. Since every circumstance is unique, let's discuss yours and work out the best fee arrangement possible. Typically we share 50/50 revenue on sales.
>
> **Terms And Conditions:**
> We are seeking items that have a value of $100 or more per individual item.
>
> We have handled charity fundraising opportunities for celebrities and well-known corporations as well. If you are looking to develop a cause-marketing project for your charity and have a desire to set it up without making mistakes along the way, we offer consulting in that area too.

Many Trading Assistants also quote transaction fees for listing with a reserve price (knowing it probably won't sell because the consignor doesn't have a fair guess at the market valuation).

When you've decided everything you need to list, click the Trading Assistant Requirements and Sign-up link on the Trading Assistant home page (mentioned at the beginning of this chapter). Fill out the forms and, just like magic, you've become a Trading Assistant.

Promoting Your Business

When I was working in the newspaper advertising business, we had a saying about someone who opened a new store: If all the advertising they do is their Grand Opening ad and nothing after, it won't be long before you'll be seeing the Going Out of Business sale ad. The same is true with your Trading Assistant business.

Adding the Trading Assistant logo to your listings

Your best customers may come from people who see your existing items when browsing eBay. Why not show all viewers that you're a Trading Assistant by including the Trading Assistant logo in your listings. When prospective customers click the link, as shown in Figure 3-6, they'll be sent to your Trading Assistant Information page (just as if they searched for you in the directory).

Quite rightfully, eBay has very strict rules about the usage of the Trading Assistants logo. It may be used

✦ On each page of your website.

✦ In your print advertising or marketing materials for Trading Assistant on eBay services.

Figure 3-6:
The eBay
Trading
Assistant
Program
logo with a
link to the
Directory
listing.

I am a Trading Assistant
I can sell your stuff on eBay!

✦ On your eBay listings.

✦ Your About Me page on eBay.

✦ On tradeshow booths (only one TA Logo allowed; with sizing restrictions).

✦ On business cards, you may use the TA Logo to indicate that you are a Trading Assistant. The TA Logo must be no larger than one-half inch wide, and must appear below your name and / or logo. The following disclaimer must also appear on the front or back of the card, in type no smaller than 8 points: "I am not an employee or agent of eBay, Inc."

The Trading Assistant Logo may NOT be used

✦ On your résumé.

✦ In business proposals.

✦ On vehicles.

✦ On your event banners.

✦ On clothing, including company uniforms.

✦ On merchandise (such as duffel bags, baseball caps, coffee mugs, and so forth).

Add the Trading Assistant logo when your regular eBay business is slow, and take it out when you're overly busy. That way, you can control the amount of work you have.

To add the link to your listings, you have to use a little HTML. Don't panic. It's easy. You can easily download the code from the Trading Assistant's secure area, or just use the following code. Add this HTML code at the end of your listing description, replacing *marsha_c* with your eBay User ID:

```
<p align="center"><img src="http://pics.ebaystatic.com/aw/pics/logos/logoUS_R_
   TA_RGB_141x106.jpg" alt="I am a Trading Assistant on eBay" width="141"
   height="106" border="0" longdesc="TA Logo" /></a></p>
<p align="center" class="style3"><a href="http://ebaytradingassistant.com/
   directory/index.php?page=profile&ebayID=
   marsha_c" target="_blank">I am a Trading Assistant<br>I can sell your stuff
   on eBay!</a></p>
```

That's all. Now the link and button shown in Figure 3-6 appear in your eBay listings.

Posting flyers

Why not design a flyer that you print on your own printer. Put it up at the supermarket, the car wash, the cleaner — anywhere and everywhere flyers are allowed.

Even if you don't see flyers in a retail location, ask the owner of the business if you can put one up — maybe even offer a discount to the business owner for selling their items on eBay in exchange.

To get to the eBay Trading Assistant logos and Toolkit, sign into your eBay Trading Assistant account and go to

```
http://ebaytradingassistant.com/index.php?page=home
```

Then scroll down and click the Trading Assistant Style Guide link to can find the current graphical offerings from eBay.

You might want to make a flyer like the one shown in Figure 3-7, which includes small tear-off strips where you can place your contact information. When people see your promotion, they can just snip off your phone number (or e-mail address) and contact you when they get home.

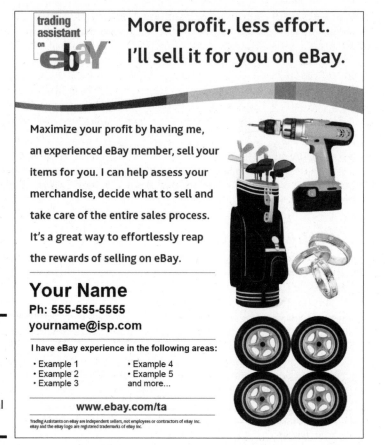

Figure 3-7:
Excellent
eBay
Trading
Assistant
promotional
flyer.

Handling Your Business Professionally

How you conduct your business can demonstrate to your customers that you're a responsible person. You need to present a professional appearance when you meet your client, and you should have a professional attitude in your dealings.

Being professional also means anticipating possible problems. In addition to being very clear about financial issues with your clients (especially fees and the realistic selling value of your clients' merchandise), you may want to consider getting additional insurance to cover the merchandise you're holding in your home.

You may also want to consider designing a few forms to reinforce your clients' awareness that this is your business and that you know it well. For example:

✦ **Inventory form:** This form lists the entire inventory you receive from the client and should include as detailed a description of the item as your client can supply. Also, include the minimum amount (if any) the client will accept for the item — this will be your reserve price if necessary.

✦ **Sales agreement:** Professional Trading Assistants have their clients sign a sales contract. Read on for some good suggestions about what to put in your contract. You may want to have a lawyer look at your contract before you use it.

The following information was graciously supplied by eBay's successful Trading Assistants, Kate and Phil Bowyer. It includes quotes from their own Trading Assistant contract that cover many things you might overlook when you put together your own contract. This, of course, is not a full agreement, but it provides some of the salient points.

Be sure to include an explanation of the consignment process:

✦ The Consignor will bring item(s) to the Seller, who, upon both parties signing this contract, will take possession of the items for the duration of the auction.

✦ Acceptance of any item consigned will be at the Seller's sole discretion.

✦ The Seller will inspect the item(s) for quality and clean if necessary (a fee may apply).

✦ The Seller will take quality photographs and write an accurate description of item(s).

✦ The Seller will research eBay for similar items to assure proper pricing.

✦ The Seller will start the auction(s) and handle all aspects of the sale including correspondence with bidders.

✦ The Seller will collect payment from the winning bidder ("Buyer") at the end of the auction and will ship the item(s) in a timely manner, once funds have cleared.

✦ The Seller will follow up the sale by contacting the Buyer to make sure the Buyer is satisfied with the transaction.

✦ Once the Seller and Buyer are satisfied with the transaction, payment will be made to the Consignor.

✦ The Seller will keep the Consignor aware of the auction progress by telephone or e-mail and by supplying the Consignor the auction number(s) to track the item(s) themselves.

✦ The Seller will return unsold item(s) to the Consignor upon payment of outstanding fees.

It's also a good idea to provide the consignor with a statement of items sold, summarizing the total purchase price, all fees, and the amount the consignor receives.

✦ **Outline your fees:** "The Consignor will be billed the actual rates and fees as incurred for all services, to include the Seller's *00%* Commission. Any services or upgrades requested by the Consignor will carry the exact fee and will be deducted from payment, or after three (3) failed auction listings, will be due to the Seller payable in cash. If the auction sells, these fees will be subtracted from the winning bid before the Consignor receives payment."

Be sure to include a copy of current eBay fees: listing, options, reserves, PayPal, and final value fees.

✦ **Outline the terms of your commission:** "The Seller's commission for this service is a percentage based on the auction's winning bid. If the auction does not sell, the Consignor is only responsible to pay the applicable insertion and reserve price auction fees. An Unsold Reserve fee of *$0.00 [fill in your amount]* will be due to The Seller for a reserve price auction that does not sell."

✦ **Be sure you don't guarantee the item will sell.** "If an item does not sell, the Seller will re-list it two additional times. The Seller may contact the Consignor to discuss combining individual items into lots to attract buyers. The Consignor's verbal consent, or e-mail consent, will be documented in the Consignor's file and will serve as a revision to this contract. After a third unsuccessful listing, the Consignor will be billed for the fees associated with all three auctions, plus a $5.00 surcharge. Items will be returned to the Consignor upon payment of those fees. Items not claimed within 14 days from the end of the final listing will become the property of the Seller."

✦ **Protect yourself and your eBay reputation:** "The Consignor of said item(s) consents to the sale of said item(s) based on the terms described in this agreement. The Consignor also attests that said item(s) are fully owned by the Consignor and are not stolen, borrowed, misrepresented, bogus, etc."

You might also mention that you will only sell the item if eBay policies allow the item to be sold.

"The Seller will do everything possible to secure the safety of the Consignor's item(s), however, the Seller is not responsible for any damage to the item, including fire, theft, flood, accidental damage or breakage, and acts of God. The Consignor releases the Seller of any such responsibility for any unforeseen or accidental damage."

I choose to protect myself additionally, because reputation on eBay is paramount. I have a small business rider on my homeowner's insurance that covers merchandise in my home up to $5,000. It's an inexpensive addition to your policy — *definitely* worth looking into.

✦ **Ending a sale prematurely:** "If such an instance arises that the Consignor demands the item(s) to be pulled, the Consignor will pay a cancellation fee of $75. Items will not be surrendered to the Consignor until this fee is paid in cash."

✦ **Protect yourself from possible shill bidding:** An important line you should add protects you from possible shill bidding. How about: The Consignor also agrees not to place a bid on an auction that the Seller has listed for the Consignor (hereafter "Shill Bid") on eBay, nor to arrange for a Shill Bid to be made on the behalf of the Consignor by a third party. If the Consignor or an agent of the Consignor submits a Shill Bid on an auction listed by the Seller, the Consignor agrees to pay all fees, commissions, and penalties associated with that auction, plus a $75.00 fine, and the Seller may refuse to grant auction services to the Consignor in the future.

Again, I strongly suggest that you get professional advice before putting together your own contract or agreement.

**Book IV
Chapter 3**

**Selling Other
People's Stuff
Online**

Chapter 4: Sourcing Liquidation and Drop-Shipping

In This Chapter

✔ **Speaking like a merchandiser**

✔ **Understanding the different types of salvage**

✔ **Practicing safe shopping**

✔ **Drop-shipping without drop-kicking your customers**

You're likely to find various levels of quality when you look for merchandise to resell on eBay. Receiving a box of ripped or stained goods when you expected first-quality merchandise can be disheartening. If you take the time to evaluate the condition of the merchandise you're interested in buying, you save time (and money) in the long run. But to make that evaluation, you need to know what the industry language tells you about the quality of the merchandise.

In addition to qualifying the goods you buy, take the time to qualify the processes and partners you use. For example, *drop-shipping* (shipping goods straight from the stockpile to the consumer) has become a popular method for moving merchandise sold on eBay, but it comes with many caveats. For example, eBay has a policy about preselling items, so be sure to check it out — and make sure your drop-shipper has the merchandise ready to go when you place your order. Use this chapter to become a savvy buyer of goods to resell *and* an effective mover of those same goods.

Know the Lingo of Merchandisers

To help ensure that industry jargon won't trip you up, this section describes the lingo you need to know and offers pointers on making the right decisions about your merchandise and methods. Here are some terms you're likely to come across:

✦ **Job lots:** A *job lot* simply refers to a bunch of merchandise sold at once. The goods may consist of unusual sizes, odd colors, or even some hideous stuff that wouldn't blow out of your online store if a hurricane blew through. Some of the merchandise (usually no more than 15 percent) may be damaged. Super discounts can be had on job lots — and if the lot contains brand names from major stores, you may be able to make an excellent profit.

A good way to find a *jobber* (someone who wants to sell you job lots) on the Internet is to run a Google search on *wholesale jobber*. Another great place to find a jobber is in the phone book or industry newsletter classifieds.

✦ **Off-price lots:** If you can get hold of top-quality, brand-name items in off-price lots, you can do very well on eBay. These items are end-of-season *overruns* (more items were made than could be sold through normal retailers). You can generally find this merchandise toward the end of the buying season.

Many eBay sellers, without having the thousands of dollars to buy merchandise, make friends with the salespeople at manufacturers' outlet stores (where the merchandise may land first). Others haunt places like TJ Maxx, Marshall's, and Burlington Coat Factory for first-rate deals.

Search the classified ads of genuine trade publications for items to buy in bulk. Publications such as *California Apparel News* have classifieds that are accessible online. Visit their website at `www.apparelnews.net` and click Classifieds (see Figure 4-1). Subscribing to their online publication will no doubt get you quicker access to the choice sample and merchandise sales.

✦ **Liquidations:** All eBay sellers think of liquidations as the motherlode of deals. And yes, they may *be* the motherlode of deals — if you can afford to buy and store an entire 18-wheeler truckload of merchandise. That takes a great deal of money and a great deal of square footage, plus the staff to go through each and every item.

The merchandise can be an assortment of liquidations, store returns, salvage, closeouts, shelf pulls, overstocks, and surplus goods. Some items may be damaged but repairable; others may be perfectly salable. As much as 30 percent or more of a truckload may be useless. Buying liquidation merchandise is a gamble but can have advantages. By buying a full truckload, you have a wide breadth of merchandise, you pay the lowest amount for it, and some of it may be good for spare parts. Just make sure beforehand that you have a place to put it all.

Save yourself some money. Don't go on eBay and buy some wholesale list for $5. You can get the same names by running a Google search on the term *wholesale*. Every true wholesaler's website has a place where authorized dealers (that could be you) can log in. Try searching for *dealer login* along with a category name, such as *dealer login golf* (as I've done in Figure 4-2).

Figure 4-1:
Access industry classifieds on the California Apparel News website.

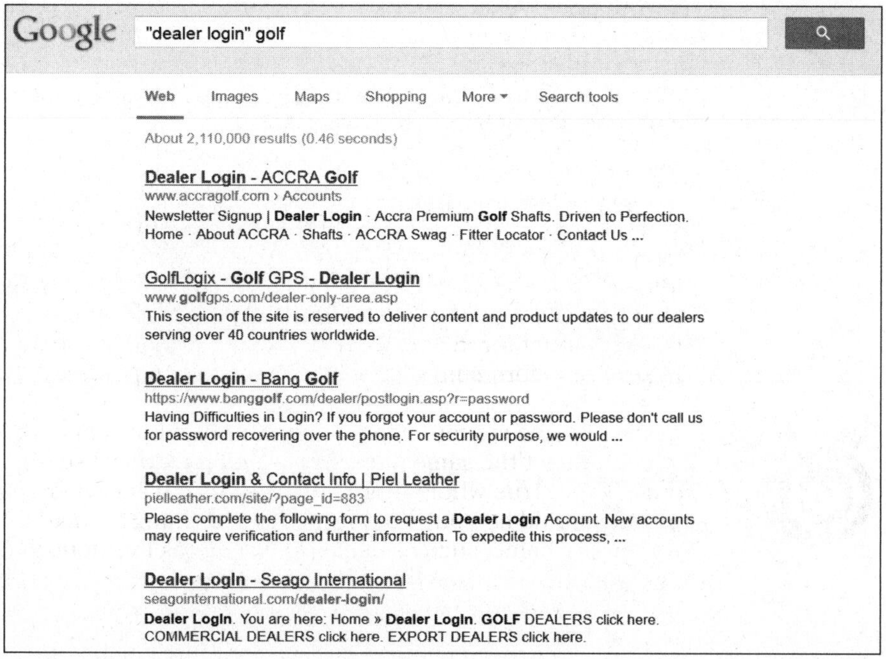

Figure 4-2:
I've found over 2 million legitimate wholesale resources for golf items.

Getting the 411 on refurbished goods

You can find great deals on refurbished electronic merchandise on eBay. Unfortunately, refurbished merchandise gets an unnecessarily bad rap. Very smart people may tell you to be wary of refurbished merchandise. Great advice . . . I guess. I tell people to be wary of *all* merchandise.

The way I figure it, refurbished merchandise has been gone over by the manufacturer twice — new merchandise has been gone over only once. I buy refurbished merchandise all the time. Let me explain what refurbished merchandise is and why it can be such a bargain. Refurbished merchandise can fall into one of these categories:

- **Canceled orders:** This is merchandise in perfectly good shape. Say a customer makes a special order and then changes his or her mind, or the order is somehow mucked up ("I ordered a PC. You sent me a Mac!"). Something has to be done with the merchandise. Enter you, the savvy shopper.

- **Evaluation units:** An evaluation unit is a piece of equipment that is sent to a member of the media or to a corporation for testing or review. Evaluation units must be returned to the manufacturer, and the manufacturer may decide to unload them.

- **Store returns:** This is probably pretty obvious to you, right? Joe Customer buys something in a store, takes it home, and opens it, only to decide that he doesn't really want

it. By law, as soon as the box is opened, a piece of merchandise can never be sold as new again, even if the merchandise was never used.

- **Defective units:** This is a piece of merchandise deemed defective by either the store or by the user and returned to the manufacturer.

- **Overstocks:** When a manufacturer comes out with a new model, the company may take back the older models from retailers in an effort to encourage them to stock more of the newer, faster, cooler model.

Whenever an item is returned to the manufacturer for any reason and the original box has been opened, the item (whether it's a television, a computer, a camera, or some other technical device), must be reconditioned to the manufacturer's original quality standards. Any non-functioning parts are replaced with functioning components and the item is repackaged. The manufacturer usually gives refurbished items a 90-day warranty.

When buying refurbished goods, be sure the original manufacturer was the one doing the reconditioning. I'm sure that some technical geeks can fix things just fine in their garages, but you don't have the same level of protection (as in, you don't have a warranty from a reliable source) if you buy a piece of equipment that wasn't fixed by the manufacturer.

Salvage: Liquidation Items, Unclaimed Freight, and Returns

The easiest to buy for resale, *salvage merchandise* is retail merchandise that has been returned, exchanged, or shelf-pulled for some reason. Salvage can also encompass liquidation merchandise and unclaimed freight. Generally, this merchandise is sold as-is and where-is — and may be in new condition. To buy this merchandise directly from the liquidator in large lots, you must have your resale (sales tax number) permit and be prepared to pay the shipping to your location.

Several types of salvage merchandise are available:

✦ **Unclaimed freight:** When a trucking company delivers merchandise, a manifest accompanies the freight. If, for some reason, a portion of the shipment arrives incomplete, contains the wrong items, or is damaged, the entire shipment may be refused by the merchant. The trucking company is now stuck with as much as a truckload of freight. The original seller may not want to pay the freight charges to return the merchandise to his or her warehouse (or want to accept blame for an incorrect shipment), so the freight becomes the trucker's problem. The trucking companies arrive at agreements with liquidators to buy this freight in the various areas that the liquidators serve. This way, truckers are never far from a location where they can dump, er, drop off such merchandise.

✦ **Returns:** Did you know that when you return something to a store or mail-order house, it can never be sold as new again (in most states anyway)? The merchandise is generally sent to a liquidator who agrees in advance to pay a flat percentage for goods. The liquidator must move the merchandise to someone else. All major retailers liquidate returns, and much of this merchandise ends up on eBay or in closeout stores.

If you're handy at repairing electronics or computers, you'd probably do very well with a specialized lot. You may easily be able to revitalize damaged merchandise, often using parts from two unsalable items to come up with one that you can sell in like-new working condition.

✦ **Liquidations:** Liquidators buy liquidation merchandise by truckloads and sell it in smaller lots. The merchandise comes from financially stressed or bankrupt companies that need to raise cash quickly.

The liquidation business has been thriving as a well-kept secret for years. As long as you have space to store salvage merchandise and a way to sell it, you can acquire it for as low as ten cents on the dollar. When I say you need storage space, I mean lots of space. To buy this type of merchandise at bottom-of-the-barrel prices, you must be willing to accept truckloads — full 18-wheelers, loaded with more than 20 pallets (4 feet x 4 feet x 6 or 7 feet) — of merchandise at a time. Often these truckloads have *manifests* (a document detailing the contents of the shipment) listing the retail and wholesale price of each item on the truck. If you have access to the more-than-10,000-square-feet of warehouse that you'll need to unpack and process this amount of merchandise, you're in business.

I'm a fan of Liquidatation.com and often find myself scrolling their home page to see the current offerings (see Figure 4-3). Buying from them at a good price can mean healthy profits.

✦ **Seasonal overstocks:** My motto is "Buy off-season, sell on-season." At the end of the season, a store may find its shelves overloaded with seasonal merchandise (such as swimsuits in August) that it must get rid of to make room for the next season's stock. These brand-new items become salvage merchandise because they're seasonal overstocks.

✦ **Shelf-pulls:** Have you ever passed up one item in the store for the one behind it in the display because its box was in better condition? Sometimes the plastic bubble or the package is dented, and you'd rather have a pristine one. That box you just passed up may be destined to become a *shelf-pull*. The item inside may be in perfect condition, but it's cosmetically unsalable in the retail-store environment.

Some liquidation items, unclaimed freight, and returns may be unsalable. Although you'll acquire many gems that stand to bring you profit, you'll also be left with a varying percentage of useless items.

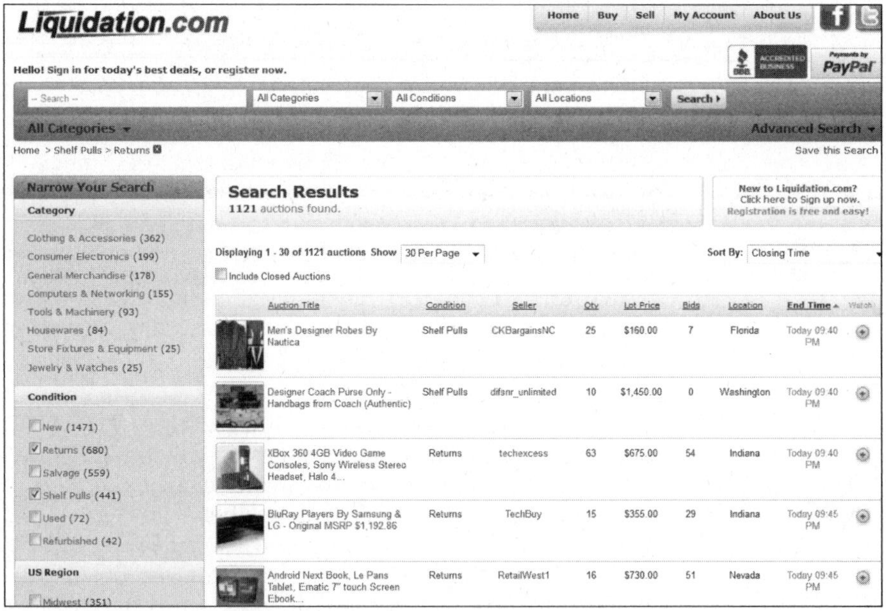

Figure 4-3:
Liquidation. com's currently closing returns auctions.

Buying liquidation merchandise on eBay

Liquidation merchandise can be new, used, or trashed. Searching through a liquidator's eBay auctions is like digging through the "Final Sale" bin at a store, where prices are marked down to absurd levels.

Liquidators buy merchandise from companies that are in financial distress and need to raise cash quickly. The kinds of issues companies face can vary — the why isn't important. All you need to know is that you can get access to some astonishing deals because some of it is sold in lots on eBay.

Merchandise arrives by the truckload. From there the merchandise is unloaded, inspected, and sorted — and then the fun begins. Some of the merchandise can be put together in wholesale *lots* (the goods are grouped by the pallet or by the case and sold to wholesalers or retail-

ers), and some of the merchandise may be put aside to be sold to sellers for resale on eBay.

Buying items from liquidators can be a risky enterprise. There's no warranty, and no one you can complain to if something is wrong with the item. All items are always sold *as is* and *where is*. Essentially, what you see is what you get; if it works, it's a bonus.

Here are some tips for buying this type of item:

- ✔ **Look for "sealed in the box":** Look at the picture and read the description carefully. If the description states that the item is sealed in the manufacturer's packaging, you have a pretty good chance that the item is in new condition.

- ✔ **Don't spend a bundle:** This kind of goes without saying, right? It's supposed to be a bargain.

Some liquidation sellers sell their merchandise in the same condition that it ships in to their location, so what you get is a crapshoot. You may lose money on some items while making back your money on others. Other sellers who charge a bit more will remove less-desirable merchandise from the pallets. Some may even make up deluxe pallets with better-quality merchandise. These loads cost more, but if they're filled with the type of merchandise that you're interested in selling, you'll probably write better descriptions and subsequently do a better job selling them.

Before you glaze over and get dazzled by a low, low price on a lot, check the shipping cost to you *before* you buy. Many so-called wholesalers will lure you in with bargain-basement prices, only to charge you three times the normal shipping costs. Do your homework before you buy!

Book IV
Chapter 4

Sourcing
Liquidation and
Drop-Shipping

Staying Safe When Buying Online

Nobody offers a quality or fitness guarantee when you buy liquidation merchandise. You could end up with pallets of unsalable merchandise, and you must steer quickly away from anyone who guarantees that you'll make money. Remember that liquidation merchandise is always sold as-is.

Unfortunately, this market can be rife with unscrupulous sellers who are middlemen. They buy the truckloads, go through everything with a fine-tooth comb, and pull out all the saleable merchandise. Then they repack the pallets with what's left, and sell those to unsuspecting newbies who think that they *may* get a good deal.

When buying online, it's hard to know about the company you're dealing with because you've probably just found them after performing a web search. When you find a source from which you want to buy merchandise by the pallet, check out a few things before spending your hard-earned cash:

✦ **Get an anonymous free e-mail address from Gmail before signing up for any mailing lists or newsletters.** Some websites that offer these publications make most of their money by selling your e-mail address to spammers. If you give them an anonymous e-mail address, the buckets of spam will never end up in your *real* mailbox. (I learned about that the hard way.)

✦ **Raise your shields if the wholesalers also link their websites to miscellaneous make-big-profits-on-eBay websites.** They may be making most of their money from commissions when the e-book of "road-to-riches secret tips" is sold to you.

✦ **Be sure the site has a phone number.** Give them a call and see how you're treated. It's no guarantee of how they'll treat you if you're unhappy with a purchase, but you may get a human being on the phone (rare and precious these days).

✦ **Look for a physical address.** Do they have a place of business or is the company running out of some guy's pocket cellphone? (Often it's not a good sign if there's no place to *hang* a sign.)

✦ **Ask for references.** Seeing the Better Business Bureau Online, TrustE, or SquareTrade logo on the website can bolster trust in the company. (They have to qualify for those seals.)

✦ **Before you purchase anything, go to eBay and see whether that item will sell — and for how much.** Often you find hundreds of listings for an item with no bids. Check completed auctions and be sure that the item is selling for a solid profit over what you expect to pay for it (including shipping).

✦ **Never buy anything just because it's cheap.** That was true in Thomas Jefferson's day and is still true today. Be sure you can actually *sell* the merchandise. (I also learned *this* the hard way.)

✦ **Guarantee:** Does the source guarantee that you *will* make money or that you *can* make money by buying the right merchandise? Remember that no one can guarantee that you'll make money.

✦ **References:** Does the supplier offer on its website references that you can contact to find out some usable information on this seller's items and the percentage of unsalable goods in a box or pallet?

✦ **Look for *FOB*.** That means *freight on board.* You will be charged freight from the location of the merchandise to your door. The shorter the distance, the cheaper your freight costs.

Before doing business on any website, be sure its owners have a privacy policy that protects your personal information. Also check for an About Us page and make sure the page talks about the business and the people behind it. I hate to be repetitive, but be sure you can reach a human being on a phone or in person (with a street address) if need be.

Dealing with Drop-Shippers

A *drop-shipper* is a business that stocks merchandise, sells the merchandise to you (the reseller), but ships it directly to your customer. By using a drop-shipper, you transfer the risks of buying, storing, and shipping merchandise to another party. You become a *stockless* retailer with no inventory hanging around — often an economical, cost-effective way to do business.

The following steps outline the standard way to work with most drop-shippers on eBay:

1. Sign up on the drop-shipper's website to sell their merchandise on eBay or in your web store. Check out their terms before you sign up; make sure there's no minimum purchase.

2. Select the items from their inventory that you want to sell. The supplier gives you descriptive copy and photographs to help make your sales job easier.

3. Post the item online and wait (fidgeting with anticipation) for someone to buy it.

**Book IV
Chapter 4**

**Sourcing
Liquidation and
Drop-Shipping**

4. As soon as your buyer pays you for the item, e-mail the drop-shipper (or fill out a special secure form on their website) and pay for the item with your credit card or PayPal.

5. Relax while the drop-shipper ships the item to your customer for you.

6. If all goes well, the item arrives quickly and safely.

You make a profit and get some positive feedback.

The drop-shipper's website provides you with descriptions and images. Fine. But you and everybody else who sells that item on eBay will have the same photos and descriptive copy. Do yourself a favor and get a sample of your item, take your own pictures, and write your own description. Then at least you have a chance at beating the competitive sameness on eBay.

Drop-shipping works especially well for web-based retail operations. Web stores can link directly to the drop-shipper to transmit shipping and payment information. When you're selling on eBay, it's another thing. There's more competition and you can't list hundreds of items at no additional cost.

Listing items on eBay costs money and may build up your expenses before you make a profit. You can't just select an item from a drop-shipper and throw hundreds of auctions on eBay without losing money. That is, unless your item is selling like gangbusters at an enormous profit. If that were the case, believe me, there would be another eBay seller buying directly from the manufacturer and undercutting your price.

I must interject that I bought (for research) several drop-shipper lists from eBay sellers. I am saddened to report that I couldn't find *any* that fulfilled my security requirements for doing business with an unknown business online. The drop-shippers whose merchandise I could track had a penchant for flooding the eBay market by selling the same item to way too many sellers — thereby driving down the price. I also found little brand-name merchandise available. If any of my readers find a reputable drop-shipper who allows room for profit on eBay, please e-mail me through my website. I think this is a business that *could* work, but only if the right businesses (and business practices) were involved.

It's one thing to sign up for a free newsletter — or even to register with a particular site — but it's something else to have to pay to see what the drop-shipper intends to offer you. *You should not pay anything in advance for the opportunity to check out a drop-shipper's merchandise.*

Drop-shipping to your customers

Some middlemen, wholesalers, and liquidators specialize in selling to online auctioneers through a drop-ship service. Some crafty eBay sellers make lots of money selling lists of drop-shipping sources to eBay sellers — I hope not to you. Dealing with a drop-shipper means that you don't ever have to take possession of (or pay for) the merchandise. You're given a photo and, after you sell the item, you give the vendor the address of the buyer. They charge your credit card for the item plus shipping, and then ship the item to your customer for you.

This way of doing business costs *you* more and lowers your profits. Your goal as a business owner is to make as much money as you can. Because the drop-shipper is in business too,

they'll mark up the merchandise (and the shipping cost) so they can make their profit.

Be careful when using a drop-shipper. Ask for references. See whether a zillion sellers are selling the same merchandise on eBay — and not getting any bites. Also, what happens if a drop-shipper runs out of an item that you've just sold? You can't just say "oops" to your buyer without getting some nasty feedback. It's your online reputation at stake. If you find a solid source and believe in the product, order a quantity and have it shipped to your door. Don't pay for someone else's mark-up just for the convenience of having them ship to your customers.

Finding a good drop-shipper

Thousands of web companies are aching to help you set up your online business. Some of them are good solid companies with legitimate backgrounds, but others are just trying to get your money. These guys hope you don't know what you're doing; they're betting you'll be desperate enough to send them some cash to help you get your share of the (har, har) "millions to be made online."

Consider the following when you're choosing drop-shippers to work with:

✦ **Skepticism is healthy.** When you come across websites that proclaim that they can drop-ship thousands of different products for you, think twice. *Thousands?* I don't know many stores that *carry* thousands of items — if they do, they have vast square footage for storage and hundreds of thousands of dollars to invest in merchandise. Most drop-shipping services don't. A much smaller offering of merchandise may indicate that the drop-shipper has the merchandise ready to ship and isn't relying on ordering it from someone for you.

Book IV
Chapter 4

**Sourcing
Liquidation and
Drop-Shipping**

✦ **Look out for long lines of distribution.** Drop-shippers are often middle-men who broker merchandise from several sources — for example, from other middlemen who buy from brokers (who in turn buy from manufac-turers). The line of distribution can get even longer — which means that a slew of people are making a profit from your item before you even buy it "wholesale." If even one other reseller gets the product directly from the distributor or (heaven forbid) the manufacturer, that competitor can easily beat your target selling price. If you're considering doing business with drop-shippers, verify that they actually stock the merchandise they sell.

Coping with the inevitable out-of-stock

What happens when you sell an item and you go to the distributor's site and find that it's sold out? Before your heart stops, call the drop-shipper. Perhaps those folks still have one or two of your items around their warehouse and took the item off the website because they're running too low to guarantee delivery.

If that isn't the case, you're going to have to contact your buyer and 'fess up that the item is currently out of stock at your supplier. I suggest calling your customers directly in this situation; they may not be *as* angry as they might be if you just e-mailed them. Offer to refund the money immediately. Somebody else's foul-up may net you bad feedback, but that risk goes along with using drop-shipping as a business practice.

Book V

Presenting Your Items

Contents at a Glance

Chapter 1: Your eBay Photo Studio

In This Chapter

✔ Setting up a photo studio

✔ Looking into digital camera features

✔ Scanning your items

✔ Buying other tools for your photo studio

Welcome to the world of *imaging*, where pictures aren't called pictures but *images*. Pictures taken with a digital camera or scanned on a scanner can be cropped, color-corrected, and made near-perfect with simple software. Crisp images draw attention to your listings and grab viewers by the lapels.

Sellers, take heed and read why you should use well-made digital images in your listing pages:

✦ If you don't have a crystal-clear picture, potential customers may wonder whether you're deliberately hiding the item from view because you know something is wrong with it. Paranoid? Maybe. Practical? You bet.

✦ Fickle shoppers don't even bother reading an item description if they can't take a good look the item.

✦ Aside from using eBay's catalog photos (when available) taking your own pictures shows that you have the item in your possession. It is also required by eBay in most categories. Lazy sellers take images from a manufacturer's website to illustrate their possibly bogus sales on eBay. Why risk being suspect? Snap a quick picture!

✦ Everyone's doing it. I hate to pressure you, but depending on the category, several images are the custom on eBay. So if you're not using more than one, you're not reaching the widest possible number of people who would consider your item. From that point of view, you're not doing the most you can to serve your potential customers' needs.

So which is better for capturing images — a digital camera or a digital scanner? As with all gadgets, here's the classic answer: It depends. For my money, it's hard to beat a digital camera. But before you go snag one, decide what kind of investment (and how big) you plan to make in your eBay business. If you're already comfortable taking photos with your smartphone and it does a good job for now, keep on using it. Using an all-in-one printer with a scanner can balance out your photo needs. The scoop on both alternatives is coming right up.

Setting Up Your Studio

Taking pictures for eBay? No problem! You have a digital camera and you know how to use it. Just snap away and upload that picture, right? Sorry, but no. There's a good way and a bad way to take photos for eBay — and believe it or not, the professional way taught by many instructors isn't necessarily the best way.

I recommend that you set up a mini photo studio for your eBay pictures. That way, you won't have to clean off your kitchen counter every time you want to take pictures.

If you must use the kitchen counter, a desktop, or even a chair (as in Figure 1-1), be sure to use an inexpensive infinity photo background, which you can find on — where else? — eBay.

You need several basic things in your photo studio; the extras you need are based on the type of merchandise you're selling. An eBay *generalist,* someone who sells almost anything online — like me! — should have quite a few extras for taking quality photos.

I often use a photo cube combined with small clamp lights (shown in Figure 1-2), true color lamps, or tall floodlights. A photo cube works well for larger detailed and collectible objects — as well as any object that will fit in it. By using a translucent fabric cube, you can fully illuminate your item and have no resulting glare, harsh shadows, or detail burnout.

Hands down, the equipment for photographing jewelry and teeny, tiny items is the Cloud Dome (see "Other Studio Equipment" further on). It not only helps with lighting, but also holds your camera or smartphone steady for difficult to light or super-magnified (*macro*) shots.

What you find in this section might be more than you thought you'd need to produce good pictures. But your photographs will help sell your merchandise, so you need to consider this part of your business seriously. Of course, if you sell only one type of item, you won't need such a varied selection of stuff, but you should have the basic photo setup.

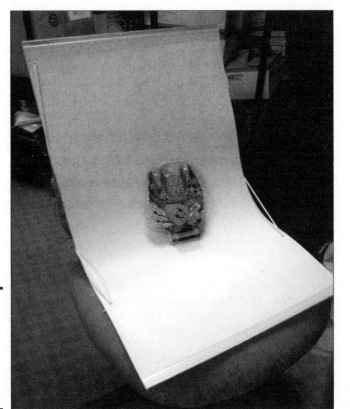

Figure 1-1:
Sometimes
a chair
works
well — add
some light
and voila!

Figure 1-2:
Using a
photo cube
in the dining
room to
photograph
antiques.

Your #1 Tool: A Digital Camera

Digital cameras are mysterious things. You may read about *megapixels* (a million pixels) and think that more is supposed to be better, but that doesn't apply to eBay or to web images. Megapixels measure the image resolution that the camera is capable of recording. For eBay use, the most you need from a camera is a miniscule 2 megapixels, or 1600 x 1200 in size, which allows for cropping. Images uploaded to eBay's picture hosting are optimal when they're at least 500 pixels wide. The eBay servers will perform magic on your pictures and reduce them down sharply.

If you're going to self-host because you want to show multiple images of your items within a listing description, beware! With so many online shoppers using mobile devices, your images may not show up clearly on smaller screens. If you use a high-resolution camera, you'll have a pixel-bloated picture that takes a looooong time to load online.

The camera you use for eBay is a personal choice. Would-be big-time sellers starting out in an eBay business (with no experience on the Internet) usually go out and buy the most expensive digital camera they can find. Maybe having lots of megapixels is a macho thing, but a camera with a bunch of megapixels is the last thing you need for eBay images.

You don't need a million pixels, but you do need the following:

✦ **Quality lens:** I'm sure anyone who has worn glasses can tell the difference between a good lens and a cheap one. Really cheap cameras have plastic lenses, and the quality of the resulting pictures is accordingly lousy. Your camera will be your workhorse, so be sure to buy one from a company known for making quality products.

✦ **Removable media:** Most cameras can connect to your PC with a USB cable, and many sellers are happy with that type of connection. Others find that taking their camera to the computer and using cables and extra software to download pictures to the hard drive is annoying. Removable media eliminate this annoyance. Here's a starter list of removable storage media:

• **Secure digital card (SD, SDHC or SDXC):** This amazing little piece of technology (the size of a postage stamp) is one of the most durable of the small media. It's encased in plastic, as is the CompactFlash card and the Memory Stick. It also uses metal connector contacts (rather than pins and plugs like other cards), making it less prone to damage. These cards can be found to hold up to 2 TB (a single terabyte = 1024 gigabytes).

• **Mini and Micro Secure Digital cards:** If the matchbook-size SD card wasn't small enough, manufacturers decided to miniaturize them further — and increase the amount of data they can carry. The mini version is about the size of a postage stamp and the micro? When I first saw this card, I was afraid to touch it. It's about the size of my pinky nail and can hold up to an astounding 64 GB (check out Figure 1-3). The micro card can often be purchased with an adapter that will allow it to be inserted into a carrier so it can be used in any standard SD card slot.

- **Memory Stick:** A tiny media card (about the size of a piece of chewing gum and as long as a AA battery), the Memory Stick is a Sony device used in most Sony products. Memory Sticks now hold as much as 256 GB. One of the great things about a Memory Stick is that it can be used in numerous devices besides cameras, including PCs and digital video recorders.

Figure 1-3:
You'll find many sizes and adapters for SD cards.

You may find that you use more than one type of medium with your digital camera. And because you can record any type of digital data on these types of removable media, you may find other uses for them. For example, sometimes when I want to back up files (or move larger files) and don't have access to my flash drive, I copy them onto one of my camera memory cards in the reader on my desktop computer, and then transfer the files by plugging the card into the adapter on my laptop.

✦ **Optical zoom versus digital zoom:** Two characteristics to keep in mind when looking for a camera are convenience and *optical* zoom. Choose a camera that is easy to use and has the accessories you want. Also, make sure that the optical-zoom capabilities will help you capture the level of detail that your merchandise requires.

When shopping for your camera, find one with the highest-power optical zoom that you can afford. *Optical zoom* is magnified by the camera's lens (using the camera's internal optics), producing a vivid picture.

Digital zoom is valuable with a camcorder when you're shooting moving pictures, because the eye can't focus as easily as the camera on moving results. When your camera uses digital zoom, it does the same thing as enlarging a picture in photo-editing software. The camera centers the focus over half the focal plane, and uses software interpolation to enlarge the picture. This makes your image slightly fuzzy.

✦ **Tripod mount:** Have you ever had a camera hanging around your neck while you're trying to repackage some eBay merchandise that you've just photographed? Or perhaps you've set down the camera for a minute and then can't find it? Avoid this hassle by using a tripod to hold your camera. Tripods also help you avoid blurring your pictures if your hands are a bit shaky. To use a tripod, you need a *tripod mount*, the little screw-hole that you see at the bottom of some cameras. Later in this chapter, I give you some tips on finding the right tripod.

✦ **Macro setting capability or threading for a lens adapter:** These features will come in handy if you plan to photograph coins, jewelry, or small detailed items. A camera's macro setting enables you to get in really close to items while keeping them in focus. Usually the macro mode can focus as close as 1 inch and as far away as 10 inches. A small flower icon in the camera's menu normally signifies the macro setting. A threaded lens mount is an alternative that enables you to add different types of lenses to the camera for macro focus or other uses.

The average camera's *focal length* (focus range) is from three3 feet to infinity. If you have a camera that says the macro focus range is set at 5.1 inches, it means you can't focus it clearly on an object any closer than 5.1 inches. Macro pictures require a steady hand (or you can affix your camera to a Cloud Dome or — at the very least — to a tripod); any vibration can blur your image.

✦ **Battery life:** When you're choosing your camera, be sure to check into the length of time the camera's battery will hold a charge. The last thing you want to do is run out of juice at the wrong moment. Consider the following:

- Keep a spare battery on hand. I keep a battery (which replaces two AA batteries) in my bag so I'll be prepared if my camera battery runs low while I'm on the road.

- Invest in a charger and rechargeable batteries. I have a rechargeable backup battery for my camera in the office. These batteries last a long time and are worth the investment.

Cameras have presets for different focal ranges, and they're usually set in meters. (There's an *m* following the focus range number.) Just so you won't forget, a meter is approximately three feet in distance.

✦ **White-balance setting:** This is a tricky feature. Most eBay digital photographers set the camera to Auto (if there is a setting) and hope for the best. If you can adjust the white balance, do so. Manufacturers use different presets. The list of options can include settings for incandescent lights, twilight, fluorescent lights, outdoor, indoor, or shade. All these lighting situations have different color temperatures, as I discuss in the "Lighting" section later in this chapter.

REMEMBER It's worthwhile to take the time to play with the various white-balance settings of your camera in the different places where you normally photograph eBay merchandise. Make notes on settings that give you the truest colors in your digital images.

✦ **Autofocus and zoom:** These options just make life easier when you want to take pictures, and should be standard features.

Taking pictures with your smartphone

Whether you use an Android, iPhone, or Windows phone, smartphone cameras are packing in many of the features previously only found in expensive cameras.

My Samsung Galaxy Note II sports an 8-megapixel camera with options for image stabilization, manual focus, ISO and WB controls, metering options, guidelines, and more. It also has voice activation so I don't have to fumble to tap the touchscreen; I just have to say, "Capture" and the camera takes the shot.

Fair warning, for any product pictures you take with any smartphone: Never use the flash.

Using the standard lights as I recommend in this chapter will give you a better outcome.

I don't recommend that you rely on your smartphone for taking all your eBay product pictures. Although smartphones have great cameras, they don't offer optical zoom — and cameras generally have much larger image sensors. Cloud Dome (manufacturer of the light diffusing domes) now makes a teeny version for smartphone photography. Named Nimbus, this diffuser has a 4.5-inch focal length. In most cases, only use a smartphone when you can see good results.

The bottom line is that you should buy a brand-name camera. I often still use an antique Nikon CoolPix for shooting; and more often use a Canon PowerShot. The CoolPix is way outdated, but it's also loaded with all the bells and whistles I need for eBay photos and for some reason, I can always find it. My smartphone camera comes in handy when I want to get a picture taken quickly because it is always at hand.

I bet you could find a camera that fits your needs right now on eBay. Keep in mind that, in our tech-savvy society, many digital camera users buy the newest camera available and sell their older, low-megapixel cameras on eBay for a pittance. Many professional camera stores also sell used equipment.

Scanning Your Wares

Scanners have come a long way in the past few years. A once-expensive item can now be purchased new for a little more than a $100. If you sell books, autographs, stamps, or documents, a scanner may be all you need to shoot your images for eBay.

When shopping for a scanner, don't pay too much attention to the resolution. Some scanners can provide resolutions as high as 12,800 dpi, which is more data then you need when you print the image. But to dress up your eBay auctions, all you need is (are you ready?) 96 to 150 dpi! That's it. Your images will look great, won't take up much storage space on your computer's hard drive, and won't take forever to load when a buyer looks at them. Basic scanners can scan images up to 1200 dpi, so even they are more powerful than you need for your eBay images. As with digital cameras, I recommend you stick with a brand-name scanner.

You should use a *flatbed* scanner, on which you lay out your items and scan away. I replaced my old scanner with a Wi-Fi-enabled HP Color LaserJet Multifunction printer, which is not only a scanner but also a printer, a fax, and a color copier (see Figure 1-4). It's available on the web for as low as $250 and fulfills all my office needs as well. These nifty flatbed units are available new on eBay. I've seen HP inkjet models, new in box, sell for as low as $100.

A few tips on scanning images for eBay:

✦ If you're taking traditionally processed photographs and scanning them, print them on glossy paper because they'll scan much better than those with a matte finish.

✦ You can scan 3-D items, such as a doll, on your flatbed scanner and get some respectable-looking images. To eliminate harsh shadows, lay a black or white T-shirt over the doll or her box so that it completely covers the glass. This way, you will have a clean background and get good light reflection from the scanner's light.

✦ If you want to scan an item that's too big for your scanner's glass, simply scan the item in pieces, and then reassemble it to a single image in your photo-editing program. The instructions that come with your software should explain how to do this.

✦ Boxed items are a natural for a flatbed scanner. Just set them on top of the glass, and scan away. You can crop the shadowed background with your photo-editing software.

Figure 1-4:
A tap on the touch screen and I can scan wirelessly from my desk.

Other Studio Equipment

What you find in this section might be more than you thought you'd need for photographing your items. But photographs can help sell your merchandise, so you need to take this part of your business seriously. Of course, if you sell only one type of item, you won't need such a varied selection of stuff, but you should have the basic photo setup.

Tripod

A *tripod* is an extendable, three-legged aluminum stand that holds your camera. You should look for one that has a quick release so if you want to take the camera off the tripod for a close-up, you don't have to unscrew it from the base and then screw it back on for the next picture.

The legs should extend to your desired height, lock in place with clamp-type locks, and have a crank-style, geared center column so you can move your camera smoothly up and down for different shots. Most tripods also have a *panning head* for shooting from different angles. You can purchase a tripod from a camera store or on eBay for as low as $25.

Power supplies

If you've ever used digital cameras, you know that they can blast through batteries faster than sugar through a 5-year-old. A reliable power supply is a must. You can accomplish this in a couple of ways:

✦ **Rechargeable batteries:** Many specialists on eBay sell rechargeable batteries and chargers. Choose quality Ni-MH (nickel-metal hydride) batteries because this kind, unlike Ni-Cad (nickel-cadmium) batteries, has no "memory effect." That means you don't have to totally discharge them before recharging.

✦ **Lithium-ion batteries:** These batteries (available in many sizes) are the longest lasting and lightest batteries available, but they're also expensive. Then some smart guy figured out a way to put two batteries into one unit; considerably cutting the price. These batteries can average 650 photos before you have to change them.

Lighting

Trying to take good pictures of your merchandise can be frustrating. If you don't have enough light and use the camera's flash, the image might be washed out. If you take the item outside, the sun might cast a shadow.

The autofocus feature on many digital cameras doesn't work well in low light. I've seen some eBay sellers use a flash and instruct their children to shine a flashlight on the item as they photograph it from different angles — all the while hoping that the color isn't wiped out.

After consulting specialists in the photo business to solve the problem of proper lighting for digital cameras, I put together an inexpensive studio lighting set for online product photography. Please check my website (www. coolebaytools.com) for information on how to obtain this package. It's the same one that I successfully use in my home photo studio (refer to Figures 1-1 and 1-2).

Professional studio lights can be expensive, but you might be able to find a set for around $150. (You need at least two lights, one for either side of the item, to eliminate shadows.) Search eBay for used studio lighting; I'm sure you'll find a good deal.

If you're photographing small items, you can successfully use an Ott-Lite or a less expensive, generic true-color version, as shown in Figure 1-5. The lamp's bulb is a full-spectrum, daylight 5000K florescent tube, good enough for jewelry photography. This same light is used for grading diamonds.

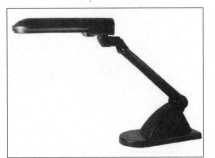

Figure 1-5:
True-color and folding diamond-grading flip lights.

The *color temperature* of a light, which ranges from 2500°K to 7800°K, is a number given to a lighting condition. The K after the number signifies the Kelvin temperature range. Actual daylight color temperature is about 5500°K, and it's best to get your lighting as close to that as you can. Using a bulb with a daylight number is important because it's a *pure neutral*, which means that it throws no blue or yellow cast on your images.

Photo cube

How much do I love my photo cube? I could write a poem! It allows me to take the most detailed photos of antiques and specialty items at night in my home. It works incredibly well wherever I use it because my kit includes two true-color lights. The nylon cube diffuses the light so that there are no harsh shadows and I don't burn out minute details with too much light. Take a look at the details in Figure 1-6.

Figure 1-6:
The fine details in this antique ivory carving really show up due to the spectacular lighting diffused by the photo cube.

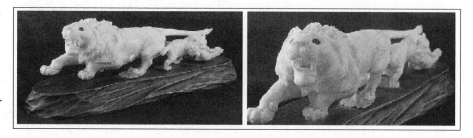

Photo background and stage

Backgrounds come in many shapes and sizes. You can get paper, fabric, or use one of the portable photo stages for smallish items:

✦ **Seamless:** In professional photo-talk, *seamless* is a large roll of 3-foot (and wider) paper that comes in various colors and is suspended and draped behind the model and over the floor. (Ever wonder why you never see the floor and wall come together in professional photos?) Photographers also drape the seamless over tabletop shots. Some people use fabrics such as muslin instead of seamless.

✦ **Fabrics:** I recommend using neutral fabrics (such as white, light gray, natural, and black) for photographing your merchandise so the color of the fabric doesn't clash with or distract from your items. Some of the photo cubes on eBay come with great low-wrinkle fabric backgrounds as well.

✦ **Portable Photo background:** A portable photo stage is another valuable tool for taking pictures indoors or out. Textured ABS plastic is manufactured so you can set it in a curve shape (see Figure 1-7); the stage can be set on any surface — and will permit you to take a clean picture without extraneous backgrounds. You can store it flat on a bookshelf till you need it next.

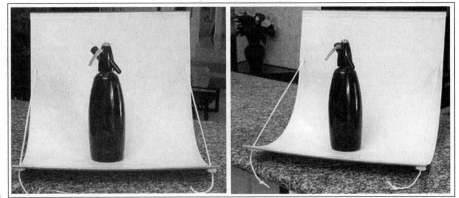

Figure 1-7:
Easy
kitchen-
counter
eBay
photography
(just crop
out the
back-
ground).

Cloud Dome

If you're going to photograph a lot of jewelry, collectible coins, or other metallic items, you'll probably become frustrated at the quality of your pictures. Metallic objects seem to pick up random color from any kind of light you shine on them for picture-taking. Bad results: Gold jewelry will photograph with a silver tone, and silver will look gold-ish!

After conferring with lots of eBay photo gurus, I was told the secret of getting crisp, clear, close-up pictures: Use a Cloud Dome. It stabilizes your camera (just as if you were using a tripod) and filters all unwanted color tones, resulting in image colors that look like your item.

The Cloud Dome is a large plastic bowl on which you mount your camera. You take your pictures through the dome. The translucent white plastic diffuses the light so your item is lit evenly from all sides, eliminating glare and bad shadows. Check out the manufacturer's website at `www.clouddome.com` to see some amazing before-and-after pictures.

Cloud Dome also makes a smaller version for smartphone photography, called the Nimbus. The Cloud Dome also manages to get the best images from gems. You can actually capture the light in the facets! Pearls, too, will show their luster. Several eBay members (including yours truly) sell the Cloud Dome; I highly recommend it! In Chapter 2 of this minibook, I show you how to use it.

Props

To take good photos, you need some props. Although you may think it strange that a line item in your accounting program will read *props,* they do qualify as a business expense. (Okay, you can put it under "photography expenses" — *props* just sounds so Hollywood!)

How often have you seen some clothing on eBay from a quality manufacturer, but you just couldn't bring yourself to bid more than $10 because it looked like it had been dragged behind a car and then hung on a hanger before it was photographed? Could you see how the fabric would hang on a body? Of course not.

Mannequin

If you're selling clothing, you'd better photograph it on a mannequin. If you don't want to dive right in and buy a mannequin, at least get a body form to wear the outfit. Just search eBay for *mannequin* to find hundreds of hollow forms selling for less than $20. If you sell children's clothing, get a child's mannequin form as well. The same goes for men's clothes. If worse comes to worst, find a friend to model the clothes. There's just no excuse for hanger-displayed merchandise in your auctions.

I got my mannequin (Midge) at a department store's liquidation sale here in Los Angeles. I paid $25 for her. Her face is a little creepy, so I often crop her head out of the photos. She has a great body and everything she wears sells at a profit. Many stores upgrade their mannequins every few years or so. If you know people who work at a retail store, ask when they plan to sell their old mannequins; you may be able to pick one up at a reasonable price.

Display stands, risers, and more

Jewelry doesn't photograph well on a person's hand and looks a lot better when you display it on a stand (see Figure 1-8) or a velvet pad. If you're selling a necklace, why not display it on a necklace stand, not on a person. You can find these on eBay by searching *jewelry display stand* and can be bought for under $10.

Risers can be almost anything that you use to prop up your item to make it more attractive in a picture. Put riser pieces that aren't attractive under the cloth that you use as a background. Keep a collection of risers and propping materials in your photo area so they're always close at hand.

Figure 1-8:
eBay listing
featuring a
professional
jewelry
display.

You wouldn't believe what the back of some professional photo setups look like. Photographers and photo stylists think resourcefully when it comes to making the merchandise look good — from the front of the picture, anyway! Throughout my years of working with professional photographers, I've seen the most creative things used to prop up items for photography:

✦ **Bottles of heavy stuff:** A photographer I once worked with used little bottles of mercury to prop up small boxes and other items in a picture. Mercury is a heavy liquid metal — but also a poison, so I suggest you try the same technique with small bottles (prescription bottles work well) filled with other weighty stuff (how about sand?).

✦ **Beeswax and clay:** To set up photos for catalogs, I've seen photographers prop up fine jewelry and collectible porcelain with beeswax (the kind you can get from the orthodontist works great) or clay. Beeswax is a neutral color and doesn't usually show up in the photo. However, you must dispose of beeswax afterward, often because it picks up dirt from your hands and fuzz from fabric.

✦ **Museum Gel or Quake Hold:** These two products are invaluable when you want to hold a small object at an unnatural angle for a photograph. (They're like beeswax and clay, but cleaner.) Museums use this putty-like product to securely keep breakables in one place — even during an earthquake! Museum Gel can sometimes be difficult to remove from items (and can leave a residue), so that's why I use Quake Hold putty for my eBay items.

✦ **Metal clamps and duct tape:** These multipurpose items are used in many photo shoots in some of the strangest places. For example, if your mannequin is a few sizes too small for the dress you want to photograph, how do you fix that? Don't pad the mannequin; simply fold over the dress in the back and clamp the excess material with a metal clamp, or use a clothespin or a small piece of duct tape to hold the fabric taut.

Chapter 2: Mastering eBay Photography

*P*hotography has always been a passion for me. The hobby led me (at the age of 10) from developing film in a tiny storage-closet darkroom through my first side-advertising job for a camera store (yes, I was always a moonlighter) to a great professional gig taking photographs of NASCAR auto racing for magazines and newspapers. When designing catalogs, I worked with professional catalog photographers and picked up pro tricks for setting up pictures, buffing up the merchandise, and making everything look picture-perfect. In this chapter, I pass on the tips and shortcuts to you. Use these ideas to take great pictures that flatter your merchandise and help you sell!

Photo Guidelines

The idea behind using images in your auctions is to attract tons of potential buyers. With that goal in mind, you should try to create the best-looking images possible, no matter what kind of technology you're using to capture them.

Point-and-shoot may be okay for a group shot at a historical monument, but illustrating your item for sale is a whole different idea. Whether you're using a traditional digital camera or a mobile device to capture your item, some basic photographic guidelines can give you better results:

✦ **Do** take the picture of your item outside, in filtered daylight, whenever possible. That way the camera can catch all possible details and color. If you can't take your images during the day, use a Cloud Dome and a good set of true-color lights, either on clamps or stands.

✦ **Do** forget about fancy backgrounds; they distract viewers from your item. Put small items on a neutral-colored, nonreflective towel or cloth; put larger items in front of a neutral-colored wall or curtain. You'll crop out almost all the background when you prepare the picture on your computer before uploading the image.

✦ **Do** avoid getting yourself in the photo by shooting your pictures from an angle. If you see your reflection in the item, move and try again.

One of my favorite eBay pictures featured a piece of fine silver taken by the husband of the lady selling the piece on eBay. Silver and reflective items are hard to photograph because they pick up everything in the room in their reflection. In her description, the lady explained that the man reflected in the silver coffeepot was her husband and not part of the final deal. She handled that very well! To solve this reflective problem, take pictures of silvery objects in a photo cube or dome.

✦ **Do** use extra lighting. These days, a digital camera's flash mode will wash out most colors. Turn off the flash and add extra photo lighting. Use extra lighting, even when you're taking the picture outside. The extra lighting acts as *fill light* — it adds more light to the item, filling in some of the shadowed spots.

✦ **Do** try to get as close to the item as you can. This will permit you to upload your images immediately — without the need for photo editing in a software program.

✦ **Do** take two or three acceptable versions of your image. You can choose the best one later before you upload.

✦ **Do** take extra close-ups of detailed areas that you want buyers to see (in addition to a wide shot of the entire item), if your item relies on detail.

✦ **Do** make sure that the items are clean. Cellophane on boxes can get nasty-looking, clothing can get linty, and all merchandise can get dirt smudges. Not only will your items photograph better if they're clean, they'll sell better, too. Farther along in this chapter, I give you some tips on cleaning specific items.

If you're selling coins, don't clean them! If your coin is of any value at all, the price will plummet (and your selling reputation be ruined) once the savvy coin collector discovers your efforts.

✦ **Do** make sure that you focus the camera; nothing is worse than a blurry picture. If your camera is a fixed-focus model (it can't be adjusted), get only as close as the manufacturer recommends. Automatic-focus cameras measure the distance and change the lens setting as needed. But just because a camera has an autofocus feature doesn't mean that pictures automatically come out crisp and clear. Low light, high moisture, and other things can contribute to a blurred image. Double-check the picture before you use it.

When you list a used item other than in the books, movies, music, and video games categories, you cannot use the eBay catalog stock photo in the primary photo position. You *must* upload your own photo. Also, lifting another seller's photos is against eBay's rules, so be sure to report any photo-thieving sellers you find to eBay's Security Center at

```
http://pages.ebay.com/securitycenter/
```

Avoid using incandescent or fluorescent lighting to illuminate the photos you take. Incandescent lighting tends to make items look yellowish, and fluorescent lights lend a bluish tone to your photos. An exception is *GE Reveal* incandescent bulbs, which throw a good natural light. LED lights give a nice bright white light.

Photographing the Tuff Stuff: Coins and Jewelry

I've been selling on eBay since 1997 and thought I was pretty good at showing off and selling my wares. But then I purchased a small lot of Morgan silver dollars to resell. I figured, no problem, I'd take my standard digital picture and sell away. Oops, my mistake. The digital pictures made my beautiful silver coins look gold!

Then came my next challenge: photographing some silvertone and goldtone costume jewelry. My setup — with its perfect positioning, beautiful lighting, and black velvet jewelry pads — looked stunning. The pictures should have been perfect. But the silvertone looked gold, and the goldtone looked silver. What's the deal?

The deal is lighting — specifically, the need for ambient lighting. *Ambient* light (light that occurs naturally) is the best light for photographing many types of items, especially shiny items. I thought back to when I worked with catalog photographers who took pictures of jewelry — and I remembered the elaborate setup they used to produce the sparkling images you see in the ads. And although I can closely re-create the experts' silk tents with photo cubes, the minimalist lighting and multiple light flashes per exposure that are part of the professional photographer's setup can't be duplicated easily at home.

Enter the Cloud Dome, a giant bowl that you place upside-down over the object you want to photograph. This bowl evenly diffuses ambient room light over the surface area of the object. This way, you can produce quality digital images in average room lighting. The Cloud Dome also helps with the following:

✦ **Eliminating camera shake:** When taking close-focus, highly zoomed-in pictures, holding your camera steady is of utmost importance. Using a tripod is difficult with close-up pictures, so using a Cloud Dome is the best option because your camera mounts directly to the Dome and is held as still as if you were using a tripod.

✦ **Consistent lighting:** When you use flash or flood lighting alone (without a Cloud Dome) for pictures of metallic objects, your photographs can include shiny hotspots from reflections (off walls and ceilings), washed-out areas from the glare of the lights, shadows, and loss of proper color.

Shooting with the Cloud Dome

The Cloud Dome looks like a giant Tupperware bowl with a camera mount attached. Figure 2-1 shows a Cloud Dome being set up to photograph jewelry (on the right). The image next to it shows the new Cloud Dome for smart-phone cameras, the Nimbus.

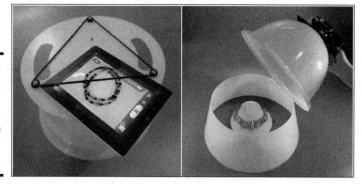

Figure 2-1: Taking pictures with the Cloud Dome and the Nimbus.

Follow these steps to take a picture with the Cloud Dome:

1. **Attach your camera to the Cloud Dome's mount with the lens positioned so that it peers into the hole at the top of the dome.**

2. **Place your item on top of a contrasting background.**

   See the following section, "Tips for taking Cloud Dome pictures," for ideas on choosing a background.

3. **Place the dome with camera attached over your item.**

4. **Check the item's position through your camera's viewfinder or LCD screen.**

   If the item is not in the center, center it. If you feel you need additional lighting to bring out a highlight, use a lamp outside the dome.

5. **Focus your camera and shoot the picture.**

Many items benefit from being photographed through a Cloud Dome, especially the following:

✦ **Jewelry:** I've found that taking pictures with the Dome keeps the gold color gold and the silver color silver. Also, using the Cloud Dome helps your camera pick up details such as engraving and the metal surrounding cloisonné work. It also gives pearls and gold their unique luster and soft reflection, as shown in Figure 2-2.

Figure 2-2:
A quartz stone with gold inclusions and diamonds, photographed with the Cloud Dome.

✦ **Gems and stones:** I've seen some beautiful pictures taken of gems and stones with the Cloud Dome. To achieve a special look, you can use a Cloud Dome accessory, a reversible gold-and-silver reflector. Especially when you use the silver side, facets of diamonds glisten as if they were in the pinpoint lights at the jeweler's. You may also want to focus a floodlight or lamp on the outside of the dome for extra sparkle.

✦ **Coins and stamps:** The Cloud Dome allows you to hold the camera steady for extreme close-ups. It also allows you to photograph coins without getting any coloration that is not on the coin. For both coins and stamps, the Cloud Dome helps you achieve sharp focus and true color.

✦ **Holographic or metallic accented items:** If you've ever tried to photograph collector cards, you know that the metal accents glare and holograms are impossible to capture. Also, the glossy coatings confuse the camera's light sensors, causing overexposed highlights.

✦ **Reflective objects:** Items such as silverware or even computer chips reflect a lot of light when lit properly for photos. The Cloud Dome diffuses the light so that the pictures become clear. Check out the before-and-after photos in Figure 2-3.

Figure 2-3: Computer chips, before and after shooting with the Cloud Dome.

Tips for taking Cloud Dome pictures

Surprisingly, there's little learning curve to using a Cloud Dome. The simple steps in the preceding section attest to this fact. What may take you more time is discovering the tips and tricks that help you achieve professional-looking results. This section should kick-start your discovery process:

✦ **Focus, focus:** Due to the focus limitations of many of today's digital cameras, I found it best to use the Cloud Dome with the extension collar (often sold along with the dome), which allows you to have your camera 17 inches away from the item if you're photographing on a flat surface.

✦ **Get in close to your item:** When attempting *macro* (extreme close-up) photography, the Cloud Dome holds your camera still while you shoot the picture. If you prefer, after you've centered your item, stand away and take the picture using your camera's self-timer.

✦ **Find upstanding items:** If your item is vertical and doesn't lend itself to being photographed flat, use the Cloud Dome's angled collar, which allows you to shoot the item from an angle instead of from the top.

✦ **Keep background where it belongs:** When selecting a background for your item, choose a contrasting background that reflects the light properly for your item. Make it a solid color; white is always safe, and black can add dramatic highlights.

Prepping and Photographing Clothing

When photographing apparel for eBay, the one rule is: Take the *best picture* you can and move on to the next item so that you can hurry up and list all the items for sale. Period.

And even though I've just said there's only one rule, I also know that taking the *best picture* involves a bit of preparation on your part. Figure 2-4 shows the results of an eBay search for the keyword *dress*. Which of these items looks better — the ones laid out on the floor or those on a mannequin or model? A designer dress in this search probably would have sold for twice the amount if it had been displayed on a mannequin!

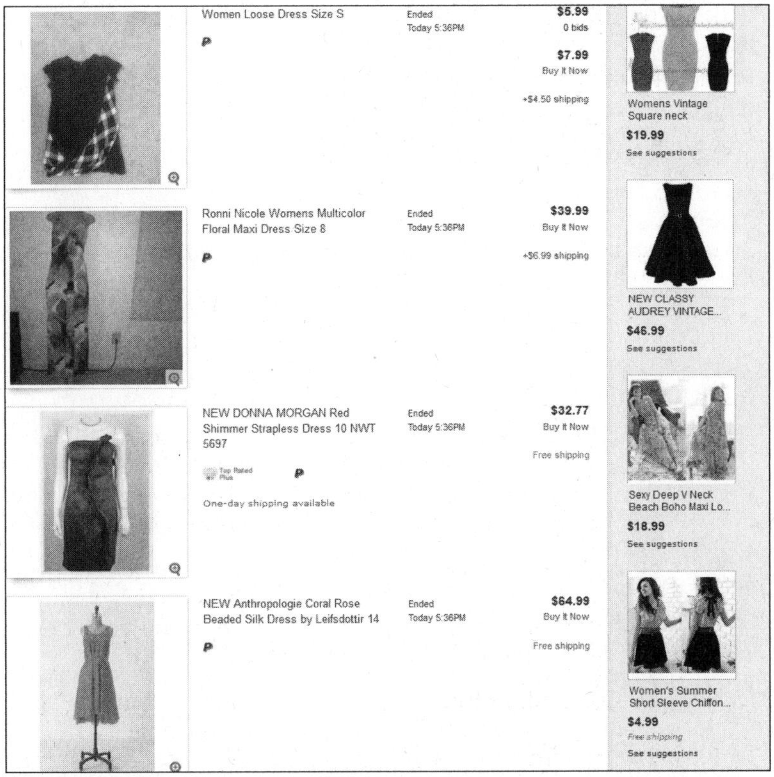

Figure 2-4: Random search for *Dress* in the Women's Apparel category on eBay.

One of the worst ways to photograph clothing is on a tabletop or folded on the floor. The camera misses essential details in the folded items, and you miss the opportunity to show off the clothing in all its glory — as worn on a body. To get the highest final price, give your clothing an authentic, lifelike appearance.

Scanning photographs from a catalog is just as much of a copyright violation as stealing a picture from the manufacturer's website. eBay may end your listing if such a violation is reported.

Apparel photography can be tricky by all measures, especially when you don't have a model. Using a model is a great idea if you have plenty of time to spare. When you work with a model (even if it's a son or daughter or a friend), you'll have to take many shots of the person wearing the same item, because you want the model to look as good as the clothing, and vice versa. Not a timesaver.

What's the best way to shoot fashion for eBay? Assembly-line style. Henry Ford had it right. Have everything assembled in one area and the process can go smoothly and quickly. In this section, I tell you about how to prepare your studio, your props, and your clothing to get the best picture for the least effort. And best of all, the time you spend preparing the clothes to photograph also makes them customer-ready. Now, *there's* a timesaver!

Cleaning and pressing essentials

Before you photograph your clothing, make sure the clothing itself imparts the image you want your buyers to see. For example, remove any loose threads and lint that has accumulated on the fabric.

Have the following items handy to help you with the cleaning and pressing chores:

+ **Garment rack:** When you unpack your merchandise from the carton it was shipped to you in, it can look pretty ragged. And if you've purchased some hanging merchandise and it's in tip-top shape, you'll want to keep it that way. Hanging the merchandise on a garment rack (as shown on the left in Figure 2-5) keeps it fresh-looking so it looks great when you get ready to ship.

+ **Steamer:** Retail stores, clothing manufacturers, and drycleaners all use steamers. Why? Because steaming the garment with a steam wand is kinder to the fabric and takes wrinkles out in a hurry. Steam penetrates the fabric (not crushing it, as does ironing) and seems to make the fabric look better than before.

Steaming is also five times *faster* than ironing (and not as backbreaking), so that's why it's truly the professional's choice. Steaming garments is a breeze; see for yourself on the right in Figure 2-5.

Figure 2-5:
Making
clothes look
their best
for listing
on eBay.

A handheld travel steamer will work for beginners who sell one or two apparel items a month. Although you can steam a garment with a professional-style steamer in a minute or two, you might have to work on a garment with a travel steamer for 15 minutes. If you're thinking about selling a quantity of clothes on eBay, a professional-style, roll-base steamer is what you should look for.

I use a Jiffy Steamer that I've had for quite a while. (I bought it on eBay and got a great deal.) It's the same kind they use in retail stores, only slightly smaller.

✦ **Dryel:** A popular, reasonably priced, home dry-cleaning product you use in your dryer, Dryel can be used with almost any type of garment (be sure to double-check the packaging before you use it). After going through a Dryel treatment, clothes come out of the dryer sweet and clean. The starter kit even comes with a spot remover. You can buy Dryel at your local supermarket.

According to eBay rules, all used clothing must be cleaned before it is sold on the site. Even if the vintage garment you have up for sale is clean, it can always benefit by a roll in the dryer with Dryel. New garments, too, benefit; Dryel removes any smells that have clung to the garment during its travels.

✦ **Spot cleaners:** I recommend that you use spot cleaners only if you know what you're doing. Some really great ones out there will remove a small spot, but you'd best practice first on items that you're *not* selling.

Steaming hot tips

Keep these tips in mind when steaming the clothes you sell on eBay:

✔ Always keep the steam head in an upright position so that the condensation inside the hose drains back into the steamer.

✔ Run the steam head lightly down the fabric.

✔ Hang pants by the cuff when steaming.

✔ Don't let the steam head come directly in contact with velvet or silk; otherwise you may spot the fabric.

✔ Steam velvet (or any fabric with a pile) from the reverse side.

✔ Heavy fabrics may do better by steaming from the underside of the fabric.

✔ When you're through steaming your clothes for eBay, try steaming your mattresses and furniture. Steaming has been proven to kill a majority of dust mites and their accompanying nastiness.

Assembling your fashion photo studio

Photographing fashion right takes a little time, but the right tools make the project easier. Here's a list of some of the items you'll need when photographing clothing:

✦ **Mannequin body double:** You don't want to deal with supermodels and their requirements for nonfat vanilla lattes, so you have to find someone who will model the garments and not give you any grief. Figure 2-6 pictures my mannequin, Midge, who has sold lots of dresses on eBay for me.

Figure 2-6: Midge modeling a vintage fur (photo was cropped before listing).

Full-body mannequins can be purchased on eBay for about $100. (Dress forms for as little as $25). I bought Midge from a local store that was updating their mannequins. Major department stores often liquidate their display merchandise through online sales, so keep your eyes peeled for auctions of store fixtures.

Keep in mind that you needn't spend a mint on a brand-new model. If your mannequin is used and has a few paint chips — so what?

Following are some less expensive alternatives to a mannequin:

- **Molded body form:** Before you decide to jump in with both feet, you might want to try using a hanging *body form* — a molded torso that has a hanger at the top. You can find molded styrene forms on eBay for as little as $20. If you decide to stay in the apparel-vending business, you can always upgrade to a full-size mannequin.

- **Dressmaker's adjustable form:** You can also use a dressmaker's form to model your eBay clothing. The best part about using these is that you can adjust the size of the body to fit your clothing. You can often find new or good-condition used ones on eBay for under $40.

✦ **Vertical photo lights on stands:** To light your merchandise, you'll do best to invest in some floodlights. You don't have to spend a mint, but as you'll see when you start taking pictures, the little flash on your camera can't accentuate the good parts of your apparel. You may want to stop the flash on your camera from going off altogether when you take pictures of clothes, because too much light coming from the front will wash out the detail in the fabric.

Place the mannequin in the middle of your studio area. Situate a floodlight on either side, closer to the camera than to the mannequin. Your setup will be a V-shape, with your mannequin at the point, your floodlights at the top of each V-side, and you (or a tripod) holding the camera in the middle at the top of the V. Adjust the distance that you place your lights as needed. Be sure to tilt the light heads to pick up extra detail in the clothing.

✦ **Clothespins:** To fit your clothing on the mannequin, use clothespins to take up any slack in the garment (be sure to place the clothespins where the camera won't see them). Before you think I'm crazy, I'll have you know that clothespins were used in almost every apparel photo shoot that I've participated in. Think about it: The clothing you're selling will come in different sizes and may not always hang right on your mannequin.

eBay Gallery of Horrors

This section shows you a bunch of big-time don'ts. We've seen images like these all over eBay at one time or another.

Mistake #1

Figure 2-7 shows a nice item, but the picture suffers from two major flaws:

Figure 2-7:
Glaring
errors here!

✦ **A glare from the camera's flash shows in the cellophane on the item.** This can be avoided by turning the item slightly at an angle so that the flash doesn't give off such a bright glare.

✦ **The price sticker is smack on the front of the item.** Often you'll buy things for resale that have stickers. Be a pro — use a commercial product (see Chapter 1) to remove stickers.

Mistake #2

Don't dress your picture with props to decorate the scene. Your photo should be a crisp, clean image of the product you're selling, and only that. Figure 2-8 shows a common eBay seller mistake. What a cute teddy — but what are you selling here?

Mistake #3

I never knew how much colorful upholstery people had in their homes. I've seen items photographed on plaid, floral, and striped fabrics (see Figure 2-9). It distracts from your item. Don't do it.

Figure 2-8:
You're
selling
what?

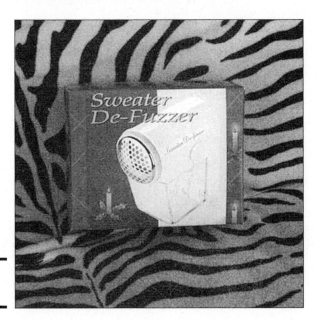

Figure 2-9:
Nice sofa!

Mistake #4

I'm sure the item in the box shown in Figure 2-10 is desirable, but who can make that judgment without seeing the item? Take the item out of the box. If the box is a crucial part of the deal (as in collectibles), be sure to mention that the box is included in the sale.

Figure 2-10:
Peek-a-boo.

If you can't open the box without ruining the value of the item, pull in for a macro close-up. When you have a quantity of the item, bite the bullet and open one up. A good picture gets you higher bids, and perhaps that loss of one item will be made up by the higher bids on the sales with good pictures.

Mistake #5

Can you say *close-up?* Use the zoom on your camera to fill the frame with a full picture of your item. Draw your camera close to the item so the prospective customer can see some detail. Don't take a wide picture of the area around the item, like the shot shown in Figure 2-11. Don't just rely on cropping the picture in an image-editing program; that only makes the image smaller.

Figure 2-11:
Pay no
attention to
the object
on the
carpet.

Chapter 3: Designing Your Website, Listings, and Blogs with HTML

In This Chapter

✔ Writing descriptions that sell

✔ Using eBay's HTML tool

✔ Buffing up your auctions with basic HTML

✔ Making friends with tables

✔ Generating auction descriptions and Templates with SeaMonkey

✔ Creating an ad — fast

I must admit, the very thought of coding used to terrify me. HTML sounds terribly geeky. Yet HTML isn't all that scary after you realize that it's just a fancy name for HyperText Markup Language, an easy-to-use language for creating online content. All you need to know is the markup part.

HTML uses tags to mark pages to include elements such as text and graphics in a way that web browsers understand. A web browser sees the tags, and knows how to display the document (that is, the web page). HTML also makes possible the whole work of links. When you click a link, you jump to another place: another web page, document, or file, for example.

HTML can save you money when it comes to your own website. A little knowledge of HTML will allow you to build your own online store quite simply and insert PayPal Buy Now (or Add to Cart) buttons. By learning a few HTML tricks, you won't have to pay extra for an e-commerce-enabled store from your domain host.

Do you look good on mobile?

A lot of business is transacted via mobile apps. And you can be sure that some buyers will view any website you are selling from on a mobile device. And so, looking attractive on a mobile device is job one.

In 2012, eBay mobile sales totaled $13 billion. This amount more than doubles the mobile sales in 2011. PayPal mobile handled almost $14 billion in payment volume; that's more than triple the prior year. Mobile purchases are expected to climb, and eBay estimates up to $20 billion in 2013.

Applying this chapter's information on using HTML in the Sell an Item form will boost your sales merely by making your listings appear more attractive. In the meanwhile? To see what your visitors will see, check your website on Google's test site at

```
http://www.google.com/think/
collections/make-website-work-
across-multiple-devices.html
```

Luckily, you don't have to be a coder to produce enticing web pages or eBay listings. My personal knowledge of HTML gets me only so far, so I often use tools like Mozilla's SeaMonkey to create designs for my e-mails, blog, website, or eBay listings. I've developed several templates so that all I have to do is replace the text each time I want to repeat a layout. Imparting a specific "look" to all your online business makes your outreach appear far more professional. This chapter shows you how to do that, too.

In addition, the eBay listing creation form has an area where you can input your own HTML, as well as a designer that you use like a word processor to format text. I show you how to make this convenient tool do magic with your listings.

Before You Format: Writing Descriptions that Sell

Many eBay sellers somehow think that putting colorful graphics and lots of logos in their listings will entice more customers to buy. Unfortunately, that's pretty far from the truth. People go to your listings to find information and a great deal on something they want, not to be entertained. They need to see the facts, placed cleanly and neatly on the page.

The addition of many unrelated images to your description may cause another problem: A slower-than-normal page-load time for visitors with slower connections. If loading your page takes too long, most people will go to another listing.

So what should you do to attract buyers? I spent most of my career in the advertising business, and the byword of good advertising is, "Keep it simple!" An organized and well-written selling description will outsell dancing bears and pictures of your children every time.

When you write the descriptions for your items, be sure that you describe your items clearly and completely. Mention everything about the item; be honest and even mention flaws or damage. When you're honest up front, you'll have a happy buyer.

After you list all the facts, get excited and add some energetic text in your description. Think infomercial! Think Shopping Channel! They make things sound so good that you feel that you *must* have whatever item they're selling. You can do the same, if you just take the time. In Book III, Chapter 3, I give you basic pointers on writing the best auction descriptions possible.

HTML the Easy eBay Way

Luckily, you don't have to know a lot of code to produce fancy eBay descriptions. The Create your listing form has an excellent (but basic) HTML generator that has features similar to a word processor, as shown at the top of Figure 3-1 (where you see 'em just below the Standard and HTML tabs).

To apply any of these features (such as bold or italic) to your text, you simply highlight the text and click one of the buttons.

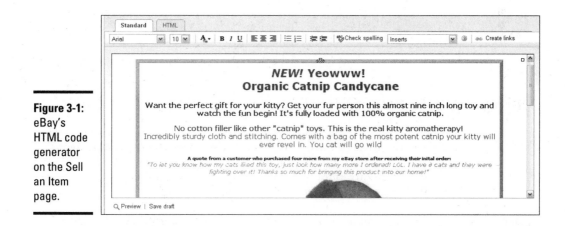

Figure 3-1: eBay's HTML code generator on the Sell an Item page.

When inputting text, you may notice that eBay's tool inserts a line space after text when you start a new paragraph. If you want the text to wrap (as in the headline of Figure 3-1) and not have a blank space between text lines, hold down the Shift key while you press the Enter (or Return) key. That forces an HTML line break instead of a paragraph break.

Starting at the top left in Figure 3-1, you see three drop-down lists. Click to the right of each box and the following options appear:

✦ **Font name:** Apply different fonts to your text. Play around with the different fonts to see which ones you prefer. Figure 3-2 shows you the fonts from which you can choose.

Figure 3-2:
The different fonts that eBay currently offers.

Arial	**Arial Black**	Comic Sans	Courier	Georgia
Impact	Times	Trebuchet	Verdana	

✦ **Size:** You can increase or decrease the size of the type. It reads in numbers, or point size. The smallest is 8-point and the largest is 36-point.

✦ **Color:** Want to add some color to your text? Just highlight the text and select black, blue, red, green, yellow, or brown from the plethora of colors available.

After these three drop-down lists, you see a row of buttons:

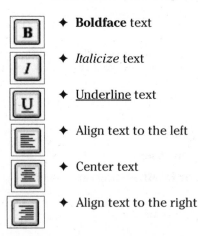

✦ **Boldface** text

✦ *Italicize* text

✦ <u>Underline</u> text

✦ Align text to the left

✦ Center text

✦ Align text to the right

 ✦ Create a numbered list

✦ Create a bulleted list

✦ "Outdent," or move indented text back to the left

✦ Indent text to the right

✦ Check the spelling in your description

Next you'll come to an amazing and powerful tool. Do you have text (or HTML) that you'd like to have in all your listings? Most of your listings? Click the Inserts box, shown in Figure 3-3, and you'll see some basic inserts for your text that eBay created based on your seller's profile. To add an insert to your description, simply place your cursor where you'd like the insert to appear, and click that selection from the menu.

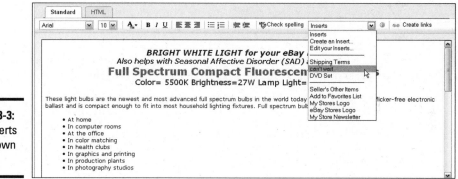

Figure 3-3:
The Inserts
drop-down
list.

You can even create custom inserts of up to 4,000 characters! Create inserts for frequently used text, such as promotional messages, custom policies, or warranty information. Just follow these steps:

1. **Choose Insert⇨Create an Insert.**

The screen shown in Figure 3-4 appears.

2. **In the first box, type a name for your insert.**

3. **In the second box, type your text or HTML coding (up to 4,000 characters).**

4. **When you're through, click the Save button.**

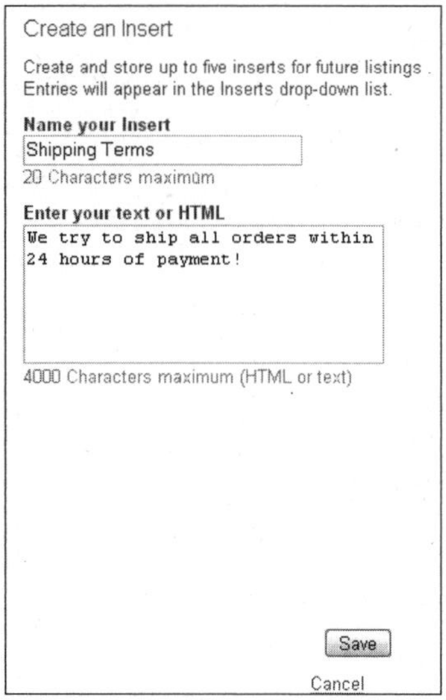

Create an Insert

Create and store up to five inserts for future listings .
Entries will appear in the Inserts drop-down list.

Name your Insert

Shipping Terms

20 Characters maximum

Enter your text or HTML

We try to ship all orders within
24 hours of payment!

4000 Characters maximum (HTML or text)

Save

Cancel

Figure 3-4:
Creating
a custom
insert.

After you create your custom insert, you can add it to any of your descriptions with a click of your mouse. How convenient!

Getting Friendly with HTML

When you want to fancy up any page that appears on the web, knowing a bit of HTML will be a valuable tool in your arsenal. When it comes to sales on eBay, you *could* use one of eBay's stock graphic themes. Or you could insert your own graphics into your listing; it wouldn't cost you any extra fees and would brand your listing as yours. Even if you do use one of eBay's lovely graphic designs, you might still want to format your text. The tricky stuff is where HTML coding comes in.

You can also use HTML to insert multiple pictures into your descriptions to better promote your item. This won't cost you extra, and you can still use up to 12 free photos from eBay for your top-of-listing images. According to eBay policy, any images with descriptive text on them must appear in your description. For information on how to upload your images to a server for inclusion into your description, see Chapter 5 in this minibook.

What HTML can do

Take a look at Figure 3-5. It contains an auction description I typed in the Notepad program (which you can find under Windows Accessories).

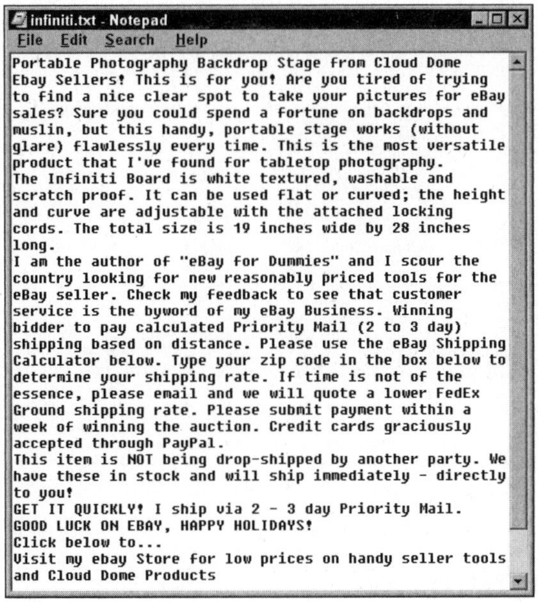

Figure 3-5:
Raw
description
text in
Notepad.

If I add some appropriate HTML coding to the file, the auction page looks a whole lot different, as you can see in Figure 3-6. Pretty cool, eh?

How HTML works

HTML uses a series of codes to give the browser information (commands) about how to display items, such as when text should be bold or italic, or when text is actually a link. And HTML uses angle brackets (< >) to mark those command codes. What's within the brackets is an instruction rather than actual text; only the text of your description will appear on your page.

Figure 3-6:
Listing
description
dolled up
with HTML.

In the example that follows, the *b* and *i* in brackets indicate that text between them should be formatted bold and italic, respectively. Notice that there is both a start formatting and end formatting indication (<b> starts bold formatting and </b> ends it.) Here's one example:

HTML start and end tags: `<b><i></i></b>`

Tags with text between them: `<b><i>eBay tools</i></b>`

The resulting text on your page: ***eBay tools***

Table 3-1 lists many common HTML tags to get you started. If you want to stay compatible with XHTML (Extensible HyperText Markup Language) and the latest HTML5, start getting in the habit of using lowercase for your tags.

Table 3-1	Basic HTML Codes	
Text Codes	*How to Use Them*	*What They Do*
`<b></b>`	`<b>eBay tools</b>`	**eBay tools** (bold type)
`<i></i>`	`<i>eBay tools</i>`	*eBay tools* (italic type)
`<b><i></i></b>`	`<b><i>eBay tools</b></i>`	***eBay tools*** (bold and italic type)
`<font color=red></font>`	`<font color=red>eBay tools </font>`	Selected text appears in red. (This book is in black and white so you can't see it.)
`<font size=+1></font>`	`<font size=+3>eBay tools</font>`	eBay tools (font size normal +1 through 4, increases size *x* times)
` `	`eBay tools`	eBay tools (inserts line break)
`<p>`	`eBay<p>tools`	eBay tools (inserts paragraph space)
`<hr>`	`cool eBay<hr>tools`	cool eBay ─────── tools (inserts horizontal rule)
`<h1></h1>`	`<h1>eBay tools</h1>`	**eBay tools** (converts text to headline size)
List Codes	*How to Use Them*	*What They Do*
`<ul><li></ul>`	`<ul><li>I accept <li>PayPal <li>Money Orders <li>Checks</ul>`	I accept • PayPal • Money Orders • Checks
`<ol><li></ol>`	`<ol><li>I accept <li>PayPal <li>Money Orders <li>Checks</ol>`	I accept 1. PayPal 2. Money Orders 3. Checks

(continued)

Table 3-1 *(continued)*

Linking (Hyperlink) Codes	How to Use Them	What They Do
`<img src>`	`<img src="http://www.yourwebsite.com/imagename.jpg">`	Inserts an image from your server into the description text
`<a href= >`	`<a href= http://www.yourwebsite.com/shippinginfo.htm>Click here for shipping info</A>`	When selected text is clicked (in this instance, *Click here for shipping info*), the user's browser goes to the page you indicate in the URL
`target=_blank`	`<a href= http://www.yourwebsite.com/shippinginfo.htm target=_blank>`	When inserted at the end of a hyperlink, it opens the page in a separate browser window

Table Codes	How to Use Them	What They Do
`<table border>`	`<table border=4>`	Puts a border around your table at a width of 4 pixels
`<table></table>`	`<table> sample text sample text</table>`	The table command must surround *every* table
`<tr><td></td></tr>`	`<tr><td>text</td><td>text</td></tr><tr><td>text</td><td>text</td></tr>`	Table row `<tr>` must be used with `<td>`. Table data to end and open new boxes text text text text

A few things to keep in mind about HTML:

✦ Don't worry about affecting your design by pressing Enter at the end of a line. You must use a command to go to the next line on the final product, so pressing Enter on your keyboard has no effect on what the page looks like.

✦ Most HTML coding has a beginning and an ending. The beginning code is in angle brackets <>. To end the formatting, you repeat the code in brackets, only this time with a slash to end the command </>.

✦ It's not necessary to put the paragraph command at the beginning and at the end of the paragraph. This is one command that doesn't need a close. Just put the command <p> where you want the breaking space to occur. This applies also for a horizontal rule, <hr>. Just place the command where you want the line, and it will appear.

✦ People have different fonts set up on their computers, so they may not have the special unique style font you want to display. Be sure to list alternative fonts for your text. If you don't, different browsers may substitute other fonts that might look *really* funky on some readers' pages.

Following is a listing description showing the HTML code in bold so it's easier to spot:

```
<center><font face='verdana,helvetica,arial' color='crimson'
    size=5>
<b>Portable Photography Backdrop Stage<br>from Cloud Dome</b>
</font></center>
<center><font face='verdana,arial,helvetica,sans serif'
    color='black' size=4>
Ebay Sellers! This is for you! Are you tired of trying to
    find a nice clear spot to take your pictures for eBay
    sales? Sure you could spend a fortune on backdrops and
    muslin, but this handy, portable stage works (without
    glare) flawlessly every time. This is the most versatile
    product that I've found for tabletop photography. </font>

<br><center><font face='verdana,arial,helvetica,sans serif'
    color='black' size=2>
The Infiniti Board is white-textured, washable, and
    scratchproof. It can be used flat or curved; the height
    and curve are adjustable with the attached locking cords.
    The total size is 19 inches wide by 28 inches long. <p>
<img src="http://www.collierad.com/whiteboard.jpg">
<font face='verdana,arial,helvetica,sans serif' color='black'
    size=2><center>
I scour the country looking for new reasonably priced tools
    for the eBay seller. Check my feedback to see that
    customer service is the byword of my eBay Business.
    Winning bidder to pay calculated Priority Mail (2- to
    3-day) shipping based on distance. Please use the eBay
    Shipping Calculator below. Type your zip code in the box
    below to determine your shipping rate. If time is not of
    the essence, please e-mail and we will quote a lower FedEx
    Ground shipping rate. Please submit payment within a week
    of winning the auction. Credit cards graciously accepted
    through PayPal.<br>
<b>This item is NOT being drop-shipped by another party. We
    have these in stock and will ship immediately - directly
    to you!<br></font>
```

```
<font face="verdana,arial,helvetica,sans serif"
   color="crimson" size=2><i>
GET IT QUICKLY! I ship via 2 - 3 day Priority Mail.</b> </
   i></font><p>
<i><font face="verdana,arial,helvetica,sans serif"
   color='black' size=3><p>
Click below to... <br>
<a href= http://cgi6.ebay.com/ws/eBayISAPI.dll?ViewSellersOt
   herItems&include=0&userid=marsha_c&sort=3&rows=50&since=-
   1&rd=1 target=_blank>
Visit my eBay Store <b><i>for low prices </i></b>on handy
   seller tools and Cloud Dome Products</a></b></font></
   center>
```

Add Pictures to Your Description

"How do I put pictures in my listing's description area?" Here's the answer to the question I'm asked most when I teach a class on eBay. Many sellers have more than one picture within the auction description area. By putting extra images in the description, they can show more of the item details that may coincide with the verbiage in the description. This isn't magic; you can do it too. Just add a tiny bit of HTML code. Don't freak out on me, now; you can do this. Here is the HTML code to insert one picture in your auction:

<img src=http://www.*yourserver*.com/*imagename*.jpg**>**

Be sure to use the angle brackets (they're located above the comma and the period on your keyboard) to open and close your code.

When you want to insert two pictures, just insert code for each picture, one after the other. If you want one picture to appear below the other, use the HTML code for line break, <br>. Here's how to write that:

<img src=http://www.*yourserver*.com/*imagename1*.jpg**>
**
<img src=http://www.*yourserver*.com/*imagename2*.jpg**>**

Note that the HTML code shown here is boldfaced to help you spot it, but it's not necessary to bold your HTML code when you *use* it.

Using HTML Table Codes to Make Templates

Have you ever noticed how some people manage to have a photo on both the right or the left sides of their descriptions? It's not that difficult to do. You add a little HTML code to the listing using a feature called *tables*.

For example, Figure 3-7 shows a picture contained in a table on the left side of the description. (By the way, when the full version of this auction ran on eBay, with the kind cooperation of the people on *The View,* we raised more than $1,000 for UNICEF!)

Figure 3-7:
A listing
using tables
with the
picture on
the left.

The HTML code for this description goes like this. (The `<tr>` and `<td>` codes create the table format.)

```
<table align=center cellpadding=8 width='80%' border=7
    cellspacing=0 bgcolor='white'>
<tr><td>
<center><font face='verdana,helvetica,arial' color='crimson'
    size=5>
<b>"The View"<br>Cast Autographed<br>Coffee Mug</b></font><p>
<img width=250 src='http://images.auctionworks.com/viewmug.
    jpg'>
</td>
<td>
<center><font face='verdana,helvetica,arial' color='crimson'
    size=3>
<b><i>Signed by</i><br><b>Joy Behar<br>Star Jones<br>Barbara
    Walters<br>Meredith Vieira</b>
</font><p>
<font face='verdana,arial,helvetica,sans serif' color='black'
    size=2>
```

```
<b>All you fans of <i>The View </i>, this is your chance to
    own a coffee cup autographed by all four stars of the
    show. The proceeds from this auction will be donated
    to UNICEF. The winner will be announced on ABC's <i>The
    View</i> TV show on Monday. We'll be checking this auction
    live on the show on Wednesday, April 23rd, 2003 with
    Marsha Collier, the author of <i>"eBay for Dummies"</i></
    b>.</font><p>
<font face='verdana,arial,helvetica,sans serif' color='black'
    size=1>
Shipping will be via Priority Mail. Credit cards are accepted
    through PayPal. </font>
</center></td></tr></table>
```

After you get the hang of it, tables aren't scary at all. As a matter of fact, if you want to use my templates for your listings, be my guest!

Think twice before loading up your description with buckets of pictures. List the item and take a look at it in the eBay Mobile app to be sure it looks OK. Remember that visitors who are using mobile devices can "spread" (by placing their fingers on the screen) to enlarge text. You can always go back and revise the item until you think it looks just right.

Creating Your Own HTML Designs and Templates

When you're ready to take on design in earnest, it really helps to have a few item-description templates all set up and ready to go. This is what the big brands do (granted, some do a better job than others). Although it's fun to play around with using different graphics as you sell on eBay — and I must admit, I've seen some cute ones — having a standardized look establishes you as a branded, professional seller. After all, how often does eBay change its look? The answer is, not too often. The colors and the basics of design remain the same because such is eBay's (very valuable) brand.

What might go into a template? You can insert your logo within your description, or put links to your About Me page or your store, for example. Think of your template becoming your brand. Many auction-management services offer predesigned templates for descriptions, but their services can often cost big bucks. Save yourself the money, put together your own template, and update it as design trends change.

Keeping things simple and showing off your product will result in more sales. Getting carried away with graphics that have nothing to do with your item is distracting.

In this section, I show you how to design simple templates using SeaMonkey. It's an all-in-one (like this book), free Internet application suite that grows with you. I use it for the Composer module (a WYSIWYG — What You See Is What You Get — HTML editor). The more HTML you understand, the more you can do with Composer. To make life even easier, in the next section, you use an HTML generator on my website to create a template that you can customize with a little extra knowledge of HTML.

Downloading SeaMonkey

Few things in this life are absolute necessities, but photos and good design definitely are. It's a good idea to start developing templates by building a simple one that includes a space for a photo. Because I like to use much of what the Internet offers for free . . . I use a Mozilla program called SeaMonkey Composer to do just that.

SeaMonkey is a free, fully functional Windows or Mac Internet suite from Mozilla (the same folks who brought to you Firefox). It consists of a web browser, an e-mail and news-client program, and an HTML editor. In other words, you can get all these programs in one. Many people enjoy occasionally switching from Internet Explorer or Firefox to the feature-rich, faster, less-memory-hogging SeaMonkey. I use it because I like the HTML editor Composer.

You can download the free suite at `www.seamonkey-project.org`.

Because SeaMonkey is a *suite* (meaning it has several programs all in one), you decide which program you want to run when you click the SeaMonkey icon. If you just want to use the HTML editor Composer (as I do), take the following steps:

1. **After downloading the software, install it by double-clicking the SeaMonkey icon.**

   You might just want to play with its superfast web browser and maybe get a feel for its other features . . . but right now? I'm using the Composer.

2. **Click the Window link in the toolbar.**

3. **Select Composer from the drop-down menu.**

   A blank new window will open with the Composer ready to go.

Adding text and graphics

After you open SeaMonkey Composer, you'll see that it looks like an eBay or Word page layout, but it has far more features. The most important for you to see are the four tabs at the bottom of the screen. These tabs enable you to view your template in several ways:

✦ **Normal.** This is your standard design mode, where you can highlight text — change it or color it — and add pictures or tables, as shown in Figure 3-8.

✦ **HTML Tags.** This view shows you your template with the symbols of the tags you have created. Check out Figure 3-9.

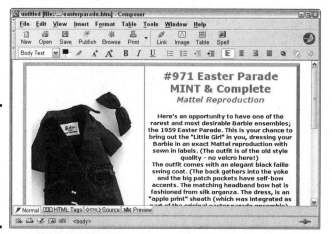

Figure 3-8: It took just a few seconds to put together this simple template.

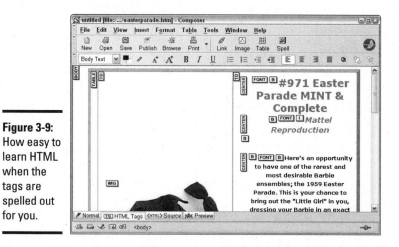

Figure 3-9: How easy to learn HTML when the tags are spelled out for you.

✦ **HTML Source.** Figure 3-10 shows the raw HTML code that you see when you click the Source tab. From this view, you can save the template to your hard drive and change the text at will through the Normal tab.

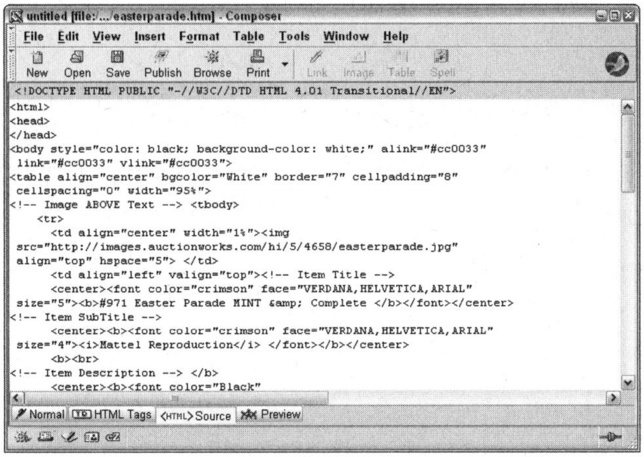

Figure 3-10:
Just copy
and paste
this source
code into
the eBay
Sell an Item
form and
voila!

✦ **Preview.** This tab displays your work in pretty much the same way as the Normal setting, but it's good to double-check that everything is perfect before you save it.

In the following steps, you create a table that contains a photo on the left and text on the right:

1. **Click the Table button on the toolbar or choose Tools⇨Insert Table.**

   An Insert Table screen appears.

2. **If you want a photo next to your text, indicate 1 row with 2 columns, as in Figure 3-11.**

   This creates a table with two cells side by side.

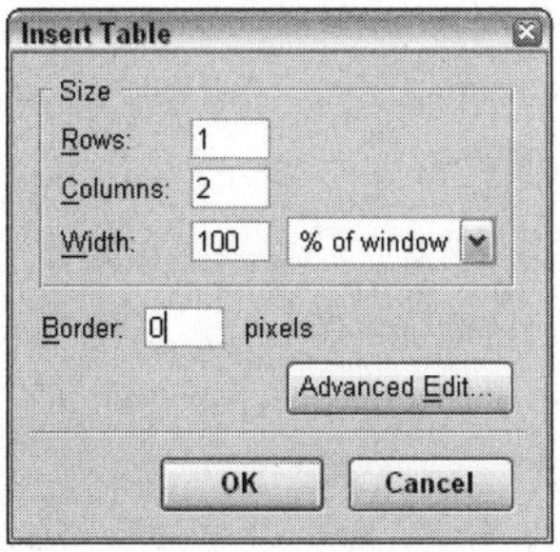

Figure 3-11:
Creating a
table with
two cells.

3. **Click OK.**

The table screen disappears, and you see the table or the HTML coding (as shown in Figure 3-12) for two cells on the screen.

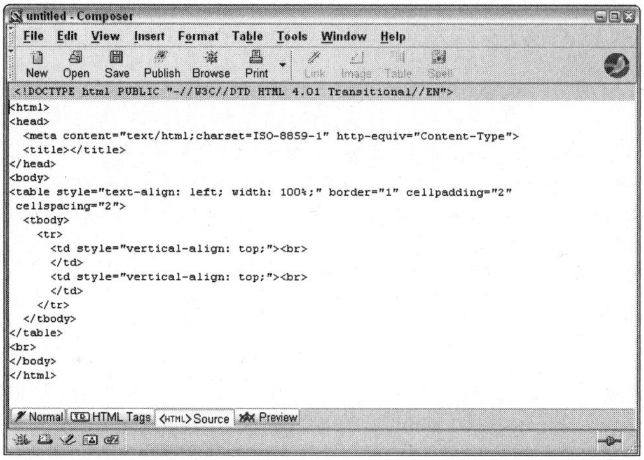

Figure 3-12: Coding for a 2 x 1 table in the SeaMonkey screen.

```
untitled - Composer
File  Edit  View  Insert  Format  Table  Tools  Window  Help

New  Open  Save  Publish Browse  Print      Link  Image  Table  Spell

<!DOCTYPE html PUBLIC "-//W3C//DTD HTML 4.01 Transitional//EN">
<html>
<head>
  <meta content="text/html;charset=ISO-8859-1" http-equiv="Content-Type">
  <title></title>
</head>
<body>
<table style="text-align: left; width: 100%;" border="1" cellpadding="2"
 cellspacing="2">
  <tbody>
    <tr>
      <td style="vertical-align: top;"><br>
      </td>
      <td style="vertical-align: top;"><br>
      </td>
    </tr>
  </tbody>
</table>
<br>
</body>
</html>

Normal  HTML Tags  <HTML> Source  Preview
```

4. **Click the Row 1 Cell 1 on the screen, (in Source mode this would be between the HTML opening and closing codes (<td> and </td>), and then click the Image button (it looks like a little picture) on the toolbar.**

The Image Tag dialog box appears.

5. **In the Image Properties box, type the Internet address (URL) where your image is stored.**

You can get the URL from your image hosting service, from your website, or by locating the image on the Internet and copying the URL from the top of your browser screen. If you want to alter the size of your image, you can also type the width or height (or both), in pixels, in the Dimensions boxes.

6. **Click OK.**

The HTML code for the image appears inside the text area.

7. **Click the Row 1 Cell 2 on your screen, and enter the description text you want to appear next to the picture.**

For convenience, you can also open a listing description you've already written in Windows Notepad, and copy and paste it into the space.

Adding HTML formatting

If you've already written your description text, you can paste it into the open window. But if you do that (as Figure 3-13 shows), all the sentences run together in one mammoth paragraph.

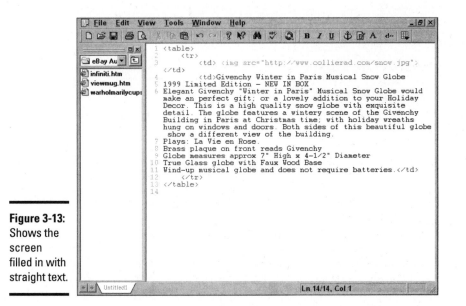

Figure 3-13:
Shows the screen filled in with straight text.

To distinguish and emphasize parts of your description — and to simply make it look better — you can add HTML text attributes as follows:

1. **Highlight the text you want to change.**

2. **Click the button on the toolbar for the text formatting style you want to apply.**

The *B* button is for **bold,** *I* is for *italic,* and *U* is for <u>underline</u>. The formatting is applied automatically.

After some final tweaking, the final description looks like Figure 3-14.

Figure 3-14:
A beautiful, quickly created listing!

Givenchy Winter in Paris Musical Snow Globe
1999 Limited Edition - NEW IN BOX

Elegant Givenchy "Winter in Paris" Musical Snow Globe would make an perfect gift; or a lovely addition to your Holiday Decor. This is a high quality snow globe with exquisite detail. The globe features a wintery scene of the Givenchy Building in Paris at Christmas time; with holiday wreaths hung on windows and doors. Both sides of this beautiful globe show a different view of the building.

- Plays: La Vie en Rose.
- Brass plaque on front reads Givenchy
- Globe measures approx 7" High x 4-1/2" Diameter
- True Glass globe with Faux Wood Base
- Wind-up musical globe and does not require batteries.

Choose File⇨Save to save your HTML when you're happy with the results. When you're ready to use that auction description, just open the file, copy the code, and paste it into the eBay auction description area (be sure you're typing in the area under the HTML tab) for the appropriate item.

When inserting HTML code into your listings, be sure you have the HTML tab selected, or your listing will look like a bunch of code (which isn't very attractive).

SeaMonkey has many other features, including custom colors, anchors, and spell checker. After you've created a template or two, poke around and see how fancy you can get with this small (but powerful) program.

Getting a Quick, Basic Template

Because there are times you're in too much of a hurry to fool with *anything*, I've put a free ad tool on my website:

    www.coolebaytools.com

When you land on my home page, click the link in the navigation bar labeled Tools. On the resulting page, click the Cool Free Ad Tool link and you jump to the instant template page, shown in Figure 3-15.

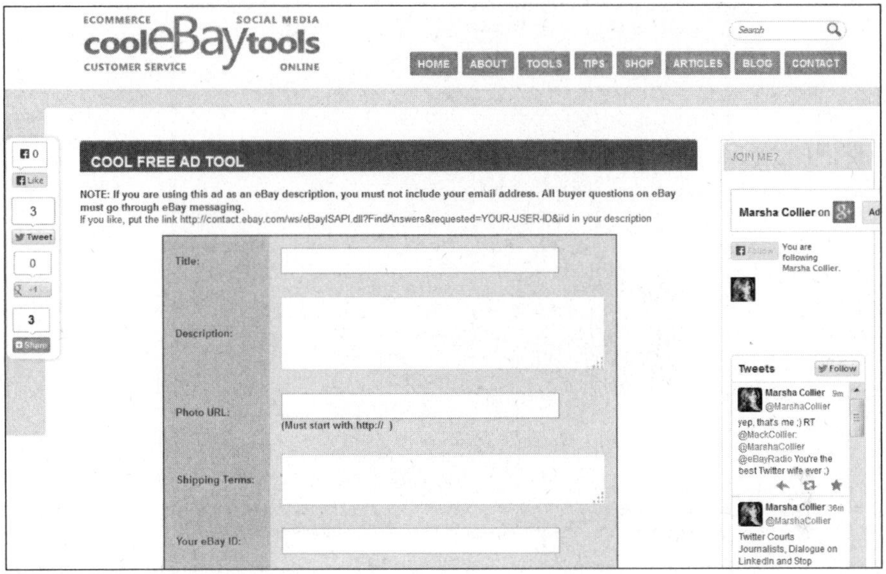

Figure 3-15:
The Cool Free Ad Tool page on my site.

To set up a quick eBay template using this tool, follow these steps:

1. **In the Title box, type the headline for your description.**

2. **In the Description box, enter a description.**

   You can copy and paste prewritten text from Notepad or a word-processing program, or just write your copy text as you go along.

3. **In the Photo URL box, enter the URL of your image.**

4. **In the Shipping Terms box, type the pertinent information (optional).**

5. **Enter your eBay User ID.**

   The address is used to put code in your description that links to your My eBay messages.

6. **Select the border, background, and navigation font colors from the drop-down lists. Type a size for the navigation font as prompted.**

7. **Click the View Ad button.**

   You see how your new listing description looks. Mine is shown in Figure 3-16.

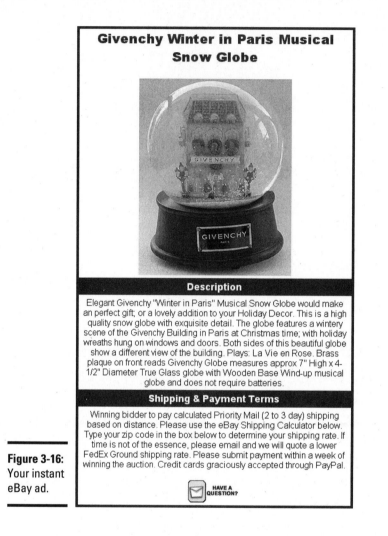

Figure 3-16:
Your instant
eBay ad.

Scroll down until you see a box containing the description's HTML code, as shown in Figure 3-17.

You can copy and paste this code directly into the eBay description area of the Sell Your Item form (or any eBay listing tool). You can also add HTML codes and even another picture to your item description.

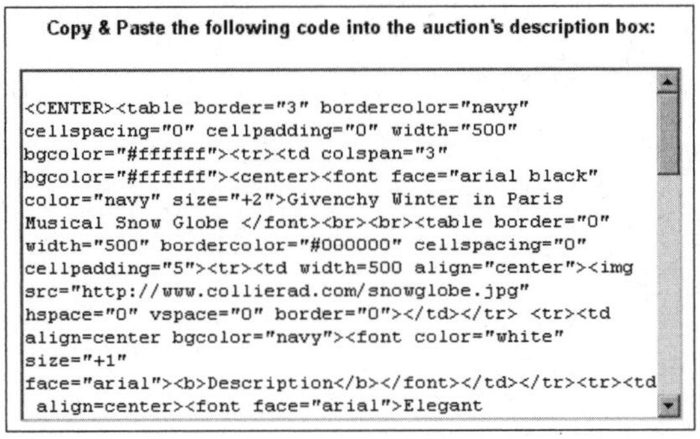

Figure 3-17:
HTML
coding
for your
auction.

Copy & Paste the following code into the auction's description box:

```
<CENTER><table border="3" bordercolor="navy"
cellspacing="0" cellpadding="0" width="500"
bgcolor="#ffffff"><tr><td colspan="3"
bgcolor="#ffffff"><center><font face="arial black"
color="navy" size="+2">Givenchy Winter in Paris
Musical Snow Globe </font><br><br><table border="0"
width="500" bordercolor="#000000" cellspacing="0"
cellpadding="5"><tr><td width=500 align="center"><img
src="http://www.collierad.com/snowglobe.jpg"
hspace="0" vspace="0" border="0"></td></tr> <tr><td
align=center bgcolor="navy"><font color="white"
size="+1"
face="arial"><b>Description</b></font></td></tr><tr><td
align=center><font face="arial">Elegant
```

Chapter 4: Getting Your Photos Ready for eBay

In This Chapter

✔ **Getting the photo's file size right**

✔ **Considering photo-editing software**

✔ **Touching up your photo**

*I*n this chapter, I show you how fast you can get the photos you take — or the scans you make — ready for presentation online. No eBay seller should spend hours playing with and perfecting images for listings (although some do). One pass through a simple image-editing software program gets any reasonable picture Internet-ready. In this chapter, I tell you only what you need to know to appropriately resize and touch up your item photos.

Then, after your pictures are, well, picture-perfect, look to Chapter 5 in this minibook for some easy ways to upload your images to the web.

Size Matters

The prime concern to have about the pictures you put on eBay is size — that's right; in this case, size does matter. If you are using eBay's Picture Hosting services, images need to be at least 500 pixels on the longest side because the service converts them to optimal resolution for the page. When you use your own hosted images in the listing description, you need to optimize the files to a reasonable size yourself. The picture file size needs to be limited so you don't bog down the prospective buyer's viewing of description (especially if you're using multiple images). Why? That's easy. The larger your item's picture files, the longer the browser takes to load the item page. And four out of five eBay users will click back out to avoid a long page load. (I'm guessing that you don't want your listings to elicit that behavior.)

Keep in mind that images placed with eBay's Picture Hosting will expire (disappear) automatically 90 days after the end of the listing. Be sure to save copies of any images you may need in the future on your own computer.

To get a better idea of the size for the images you use online, remember that no matter which camera setting you choose, your image should be designed to be viewed on a monitor. Lower resolution is just fine because the average computer monitor isn't an HDTV.

The average resolution for new monitors increases as technology improves, but it's still surprisingly low when you compare that resolution to available camera settings. (Keep in mind that many eBay shoppers may not be concerned with being on the cutting edge of technology, and so may not have the latest computer equipment.) The most popular settings for laptops and desktops (in pixels) are

✦ 1366 x 768

✦ 1024 x 768

✦ 1280 x 800

These settings determine the number of pixels that can be viewed on the screen. No matter how large your monitor is (whether 15, 17, or even 21 inches), it shows only as many pixels as you determine in its settings. On larger screens, the pixels just get larger — and make your pictures fuzzy. That's why most people with larger screens set their monitors for a higher resolution.

Knowing that your shoppers might have made the move to mobile devices (tablets and smartphones) should affect your image decisions. Typical tablet displays tend not to have a resolution higher than 1024 x 768. Smartphone screen resolutions can vary greatly. The iPhone originally sported a 480 x 320 display, and today's iPhone 5 has an 1136 x 640 display. My phone is an anomaly; the Galaxy Note II has a very large, 5.5-inch display and a resolution of 1280 x 720.

Remember that scanned images are measured in dpi (dots per inch). Do not confuse this with a monitor's pixels per inch (ppi). The average monitor is only 72 to 96 ppi so why scan your images any higher? Consider that a Faceboook cover photo is 851 pixels wide; when displayed full-width at 72 ppi, the image would be over 11 inches wide.

The higher the resolution, the smaller the text and images will appear on any device. To see your images clearly on a mobile device, the viewer may have to zoom to enlarge. They don't want to squint!

If you use eBay for your all eBay items, setting your image size is not a huge issue. eBay picture hosting applies a compression algorithm that forces your pictures into eBay's prescribed size.

The more compression put into computer images, the less sharp they appear. So you might as well use your camera or image-editing program to set your images to a monitor-friendly size before uploading them.

Here's a checklist of tried-and-true techniques for preparing elegantly slender, fast-loading images to display on eBay:

✦ **Set your image resolution at 72 pixels per inch**. You can do this with the settings for your scanner. Although 72 ppi may seem like a super-low resolution, it only nibbles computer space, shows up fast on a buyer's screen, and looks great on eBay.

✦ **When using a digital camera, set the camera to no higher than the 2 MB, 1600 x 1200 format**. That's about perfect for any monitor. You can always crop the picture if it's too large.

✦ **For use in your description, make the finished image no larger than 480 pixels wide.** When you size your picture in your image software, it's best to keep it no larger than 300 x 300 pixels or 4 inches square. These dimensions are big enough for people to see the image without squinting, and the details of your item show up nicely. When using eBay Picture hosting, eBay requires images to be a minimum of 500 pixels on the longest side (1600, they say, is optimal).

✦ **Crop any unnecessary areas of the photo**. You need to show only your item; everything else is a waste.

✦ **If necessary, use your software to darken or change the photo's contrast.** When the image looks good on your computer screen, the image looks good on your eBay page.

✦ **Save your image as a JPG file**. When you finish editing your picture, save it as a JPG file. (To do this, follow the instructions that come with your software.) JPG is the best format for eBay; it compresses information into a small file that builds fast and reproduces crisply on the Internet.

✦ **Check the total size of your image**. After you save the image, check its total size. If the size hovers around 100K or smaller, eBay users won't have a hard time seeing the image in a reasonable amount of time.

Adding the Artist's Touch

Pictures don't always come out of the camera in perfect form. However, you can do a few tweaks to bring them into perfection range:

✦ **Alter the size:** Reduce or increase the size or shape of the image.

✦ **Change the orientation**: Rotate the image left or right; flip it horizontally or vertically.

✦ **Crop the background**: Sometimes there's a little too much background and not enough product. Don't waste precious bandwidth on extraneous pixels. To *crop* your image means to cut away the unnecessary part of the picture.

✦ **Adjust the brightness and contrast**: These two functions usually work together in most photo programs. By giving your picture more brightness, the picture looks brighter (duh). Raising contrast brings out the detail, and lowering it dulls the difference between light and dark.

✦ **Sharpen**: If your camera was not perfectly in focus when you took the picture, applying a photo-editing program's sharpening feature can help. If you sharpen too much, however, you can destroy the smoothness of the image.

If your image needs any more help than these alterations, it's probably easier and faster to just retake the picture.

Image-Editing Software

eBay sellers use a wide array of image-editing software. As a matter of fact, some listing software has built-in mini-editing capabilities. (See Book VIII for more on third-party software for eBay.) Choosing software for your images is like choosing an office chair. What's right for some people is dreadful for others. You might want to ask some of your friends what software they use — and take a look at it.

When you buy a camera, it will no doubt arrive with media that includes some type of image-editing software. Give the software a try. If it works well for you, keep it. If not, check out the two options I mention later.

Every image-editing software program has its own system requirements and capabilities. Study the software that comes with your camera or scanner. If you feel that the program is too complicated (or doesn't give you the editing tools you need), investigate some of the other popular programs. You can get some excellent shareware (software that you can try before you buy) at download.cnet.com.

I used to be happy using Photoshop, but it's a large and expensive program. It's also a bit of overkill for eBay images. Two other new tools have caught my eye: LunaPic and Fast Photos.

Using Microsoft's simple photo editor

Microsoft Office Picture Manager is a software program included with Microsoft Office suite starting with the 2003 version through the 2010 version. (It replaced Microsoft Photo Editor, which had been included with the Microsoft Office suite since Office 97). Picture Manager offers basic picture-editing features, and it may be a good place to start. If you have Microsoft Office (2003, 2007, or 2010), you find Picture Manager on your Start menu under Microsoft Office Tools.

To edit an image in Microsoft Office directly on your computer, follow these steps:

1. **Right-click the image in one of your folders.**

2. **From the menu that appears, select Open With and then Microsoft Office.**

   Although it seems a less-than-intuitive tweak, Microsoft chose to remove the reference to Picture Manager from the menu options. Go figure. Meanwhile, your image opens in the photo editor, as shown in Figure 4-1.

3. **If the toolbars and panes don't appear when the photo editor opens, click View⇨Task Pane.**

4. **In the Task pane, click Edit Pictures and all the necessary commands to complete your masterpiece will appear.**

Figure 4-1:
A hidden feature in Microsoft Office makes quick photo edits easy.

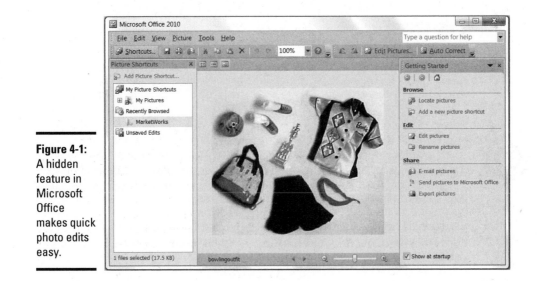

Microsoft Office Picture Manager gives you some useful tools: You can auto-correct, fix "red eye," enhance color, adjust brightness and contrast, compress, resize, crop, and rotate. It's about all you need if you take a good photo to begin with. Clicking the Auto Correct button works well to correct the quality of an image. Click Export Pictures, and in the resulting Export task pane, you can choose the exact size for the final image.

Perfecting your picture online in LunaPic

You need to know that I can be lazy. When it comes to editing my images for eBay, I'm still looking for a magic wand. Sometimes I'm too lazy to open a program. So in my laziness, I browsed the Internet and found a free online photo-editing website, www.lunapic.com.

Although I prefer to use a program on my computer, LunaPic works great for quick, on-the-fly editing that I often need. You can even edit pictures on someone else's computer because there's no need to install software. Take a look at Figure 4-2. Here's LunaPic, a website that makes photo editing as easy as getting a burger at the drive through window.

Register on the site, and you have full photo-editing capabilities. Upload photos from your computer (or webcam) to the site, perform your touch-up, and then save and download! LunaPic has a full-featured toolset on the site; in it, you find tools to adjust brightness, contrast, and color, and to sharpen your images — and many more.

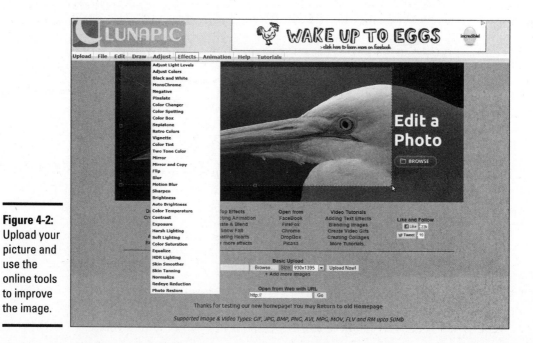

Figure 4-2: Upload your picture and use the online tools to improve the image.

Quick touchup and FTP in Fast Photos

If PhotoShop is too expensive and complex (it really is for eBay purposes), you might be happy giving Fast Photos by Pixby Software a try. It's a simple, all-in-one photo-editing program designed especially for e-commerce and eBay sellers. The developer of the software knew exactly what processes online sellers need for their images and included just those — and nothing else. There are tools for cropping, JPEG compression, sharpening, resizing, enhancing, rotating, and adding watermark text and borders.

The software is a PC application that runs on Windows (versions 7, Vista, and XP). For a 21-day free trial, visit the Fast Photos website at www.pixby.com/.

I said that Fast Photos is all-in-one because it not only allows you to touch up your images quickly, but also has a built-in FTP program so that you can upload your images immediately after editing them.

Editing an image for eBay in Fast Photos is simple:

1. **Open the program.**

2. **Click Browse and find the directory containing your image.**

3. **Find the photo, click it (see Figure 4-3), and then click the Add to Tray button (near the top of the screen).**

Figure 4-3:
Selecting a photo for editing in Fast Photos.

4. Choose Edit.

5. Click to perform any of the following tasks, as shown in Figure 4-4.

- **Rotate**: If you've shot your picture sideways or upside down, you can rotate it here.

- **Crop**: In Crop mode, a gray rectangle appears with corner dots. Click a corner dot, drag the rectangle until it closes in on your item, and then click Apply.

- **Enhance**: Brighten, darken, increase, or decrease the contrast and work with image gamma and color. Don't worry — everything you do is visible onscreen and can be undone if you mess things up.

- **Resize**: You can resize your image to the standard eBay sizes or make the image a custom size.

- **Sharpen**: Is your image a little fuzzy? Click here to bring out the details.

- **Add border**: If you want a border or a drop shadow on your image, you can apply it here (only for use in your descriptions).

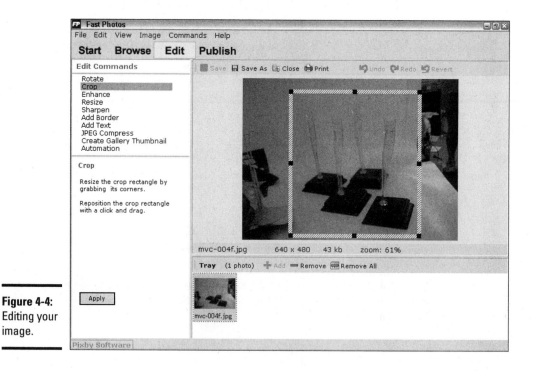

Figure 4-4:
Editing your
image.

- **Add text**: Type your user ID so you can watermark the images within your description (which helps dissuade those who try to use your images as their own).

- **JPEG compress**: By moving a sliding bar, you can compress the image as much as you dare. The more you compress, the less detailed the image will be.

6. **To save the changes you've made to your image, click Save As and give your file a name.**

Now you can upload your newly edited image to the web. Just choose Publish (on the toolbar).

To set up an FTP account for uploading, click the Add button on the Publish screen. The screen shown in Figure 4-5 appears. Input the data required for your FTP server, click OK, and then upload your image with a mouse click.

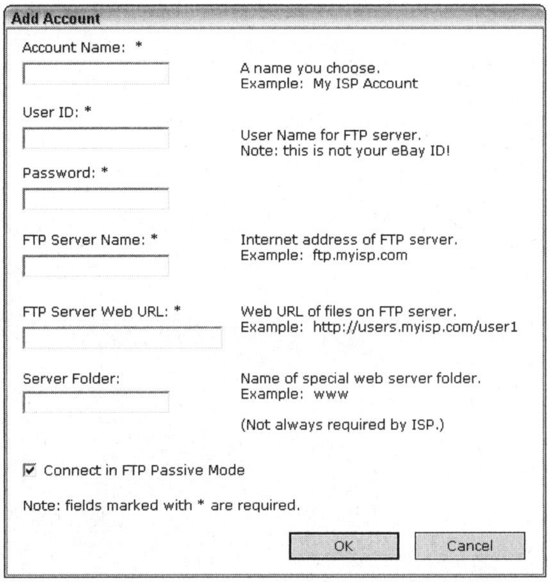

Add Account

Account Name: *

A name you choose.
Example: My ISP Account

User ID: *

User Name for FTP server.
Note: this is not your eBay ID!

Password: *

FTP Server Name: *

Internet address of FTP server.
Example: ftp.myisp.com

FTP Server Web URL: *

Web URL of files on FTP server.
Example: http://users.myisp.com/user1

Server Folder:

Name of special web server folder.
Example: www

(Not always required by ISP.)

☑ Connect in FTP Passive Mode

Note: fields marked with * are required.

[OK] [Cancel]

Figure 4-5:
Fill in the form with your FTP information.

There is also a batch mode so you can edit and upload entire groups of images at once. Check out Chapter 5 in this minibook for more information on uploading your images.

Chapter 5: Getting Your Photos on eBay and the Web

After you get your image perfect (following the suggestions in Chapter 4), it's time to emblazon it on the web for all the world to see. Uploading the images you use for your online networks, website, and blogs are fairly straightforward. But when it comes to photos for eBay sales, you have a few choices. In this chapter, I tell you about storing your photos and images — and also about how to get them to where they need to be to appear in your listings.

Finding a Home for Your Pictures

Because your image needs an address, you have to find it a good home online. You have several options:

✦ **eBay Picture Hosting**: This is eBay's stock and trade for storing your listing images. To place up to 12 images on a listing at no charge, this is what you need to use. Images from eBay Picture Hosting appear at the top-left of your listing. Visitors can click the individual photos to show one in the main photo frame. When a potential buyer views your item on eBay's Android mobile app, the pictures scroll horizontally at the top of the screen when the user swipes. iPhone and iPad users must tap a photo to scroll through.

✦ **An image-hosting website:** Websites that specialize in hosting pictures are popping up all over the Internet. Some charge a small fee; others are free. The upside here is that they're easy to use.

Some users are still convinced that they have to pay for an image-hosting service — but that's rarely the case these days.

✦ **Your website**: If you have your own website, it's easy to make a separate folder there to store your images for eBay listings. You can name your photos and access them with a URL directing eBay to the picture hosted on your site's server.

If you are selling a car, know that eBay Motors does not offer 12 top-of-listing images for free. You get four images at no charge; additional photos cost 15 cents each, up to 24 pictures total. You may also choose to purchase a Picture Pack, which will cover all 24 pictures, for $2. You can opt to host your own images, placing the top four in eBay Picture Hosting and the balance within your description.

Using eBay's Picture Hosting

I highly recommend that your first move be to take advantage of the 12 free pictures per listing from eBay's Picture Hosting. First, it's available at no charge; second, Picture Hosting offers many other benefits, such as ease of uploading.

eBay has two different methods for listing an item. Generally, when you click Sell an Item from the top-of-page navigation bar, you get the Basic Listing tool. For more options and the capability to post a more complete listing, click the Switch to Advanced Tool link at the top of the page (shown in Figure 5-1) to go to the Advanced Listing tool.

At this point, I'll go back to my basic assumptions about you. I assume you know how to list an item on eBay — or, at the very least, you can make your way through the Sell an Item form and get to the Add Pictures step.

When you get to this step, you need to upload a picture to eBay, whether or not you have pictures in your description. Why? Because eBay requires at least one image in the listing (remember, you can upload up to 12 pictures for free) and because your uploaded picture becomes part of the ultra-important top area of the item page, as shown in Figure 5-2. This picture will also be the default for use as your all-important image in search results.

**Book V
Chapter 5**

**Getting Your
Photos on eBay
and the Web**

Click here for the Advanced Listing tool.

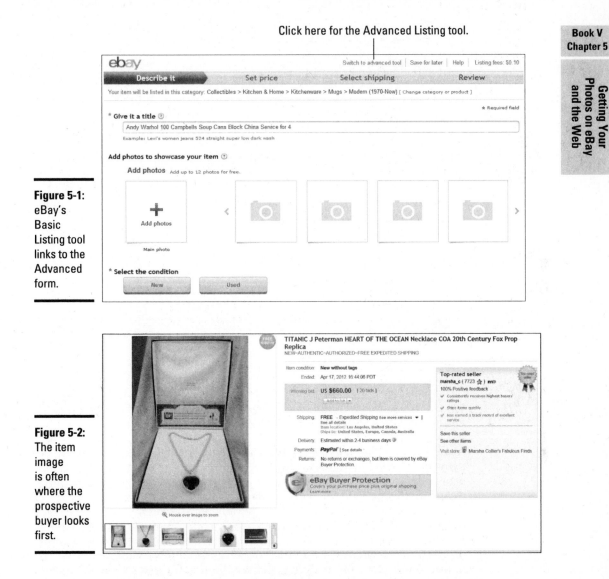

Figure 5-1:
eBay's
Basic
Listing tool
links to the
Advanced
form.

Figure 5-2:
The item
image
is often
where the
prospective
buyer looks
first.

I suggest that you use eBay's Picture Hosting for your primary images. The
12-image limit that eBay offers should suffice for most listings. If you want to
include more photos in the description because the item is rare or detailed,
host the other images elsewhere.

Uploading your picture to eBay

In this section, I assume that you've already taken a picture, uploaded or scanned it, and saved it somewhere on your computer's hard drive.

For organization's sake, you might consider making a subfolder called *eBay Photos* in your Pictures folder. That way you can always find your eBay pictures quickly, without searching through photos of your family reunion.

eBay offers two versions of image uploading. The Basic version, which is shown in Figure 5-3, enables you to upload eBay-ready images as they appear on your computer. If you want to rotate or crop the picture, you need the Standard uploader. You'll be using that more-advanced version in the steps that come later in this section.

Figure 5-3: eBay's Classic picture hosting.

When you reach the part of the listing form that asks you to add pictures, notice the Add or Remove Options link. Clicking this link causes a window to pop up, as in Figure 5-4. Select the check box next to Show the Option for Using Pictures Hosted on Your Web Server (Self Hosting) if you need more than the 12 pictures that eBay will host for you. If you want your uploaded images to be watermarked with your eBay User ID or camera icon, select those options as well. Then click Save.

Clicking the Add Pictures button opens a Select Pictures for Upload window, as shown in Figure 5-5. Click the Browse button to open a window showing your hard drive's folders. Find and select the eBay-ready images you want to upload. After you select the images from your computer, they will appear in the Pictures area of this window. Click the Upload button at the bottom and (surprise) your pictures upload to eBay's servers.

**Book V
Chapter 5**

Getting Your
Photos on eBay
and the Web

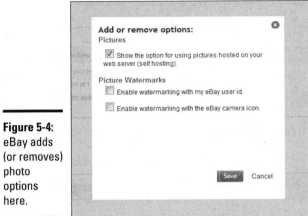

Figure 5-4:
eBay adds
(or removes)
photo
options
here.

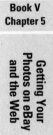

Figure 5-5:
Pictures
uploaded for
your eBay
listing.

To get more options — for example, cropping, rotating, and minor editing functions — click the leftmost tab at the top of the window to go to the
enhanced photo uploader, which is shown in Figure 5-6.

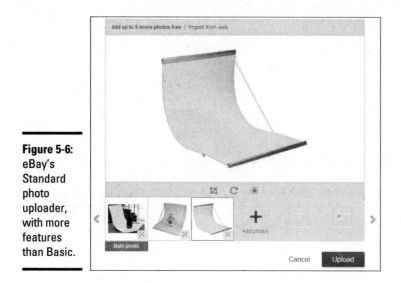

Figure 5-6:
eBay's
Standard
photo
uploader,
with more
features
than Basic.

Then, to upload your picture, follow these steps:

1. In the Standard uploader window (refer to Figure 5-6), click the Upload button.

A window pops up, prompting you to open an image file on your computer.

2. Navigate to the directory that holds your eBay images on your computer.

3. Click the image in the browsing window.

The image name appears in the filename box.

4. Click the Open button.

The selected image appears in the picture frame.

5. To rotate the image, click the circular arrow tool.

6. Crop the image as needed:

a. *Click the crop box in the lower center of the larger image.*

Two squares appear at opposite corners of the image.

b. *Click the frame on the outside of your image, and move the bar until the offensive area is cropped out.*

You can crop from the sides, top, and bottom of the picture.

Book V
Chapter 5

Getting Your
Photos on eBay
and the Web

7. When you're finished, click Continue.

A pop-up window notifies you that your picture is being uploaded to eBay's picture server.

eBay's uploader tools automatically make your pictures the perfect size for eBay. But don't forget that you get the best picture quality when you use images with 1600-pixel height or width (minimum is 500 pixels).

Understanding the costs

You may notice that you have the option to use more pictures in your listings. eBay charges for any additional images over the limits noted in Table 5-1. You can include more images at no extra cost by hosting them on a server (more on that later).

Table 5-1	eBay Picture Hosting Fees		
Feature	*Auction Listing ($)*	*Fixed Price 3-, 5-, 7-, 10-Day Duration*	*Fixed-Price 30-Day, Good Till Cancelled*
Up to 12 pictures	Free	Free	Free
Gallery Plus	0.35	0.35 per 30 days	1.00
eBay Motors (after the 4 free pictures)	0.15	0.15	N/A
eBay Motors Picture Pack (up to 24 pictures)	N/A	N/A	2.00

The Gallery option is no longer an option. The small photo of your item that appears next to your listing *is* the Gallery picture — and it's free.

When most people first get the urge to dazzle prospective buyers with additional pictures, they often insert more images in the description area. Let's talk about where you can host these images.

You will find several third-party sites that will also host your eBay images. There's more on those options in Book VIII, Chapter 2.

Using Your Free Web Space

If you have a website, no doubt you have plenty of storage space. Make a new folder and store your images for your eBay sales there.

In this section, I show you some easy ways to upload your pictures to your website and import them into your eBay listings. Doing so gives you the opportunity to offer the prospective buyer more views of the items you have up for sale.

Internet service providers may supply you with an image upload area, but they may require you to use File Transfer Protocol (FTP) to upload your images. You may be able to find a free or shareware (requiring a small fee) FTP program on sites such as the following:

✦ www.tucows.com

✦ http://download.cnet.com/windows/

If you use the Fast Photos image-editing program (described in Chapter 4 of this minibook), you get an FTP program as part of the software at no extra charge! Also, I've been using the Firefox browser, and I really like it. It has a free FTP program, FireFTP, that's reliable and easy to use. FireFTP has never given me a whit of a problem, and I highly recommend it.

You can add FireFTP to your Firefox browser (Mac or PC) by choosing Tools⇨Add-ons from the Navigation menu. Doing so takes you to a web page where you can search for FireFTP (and lots of other interesting add-ons). You can download the add-on directly by visiting

    http://fireftp.net/

After you install the program, open it and follow these steps to upload a file to your server:

1. **Click Manage Accounts ⇨New.**

The Account Manager appears.

2. **Type in the name of your website in the Account Name box.**

3. **Where prompted, type the FTP address for your account and then click Next.**

Book V
Chapter 5

Getting Your
Photos on eBay
and the Web

4. **Type the user name and password that you use to log in to your web-site account. Then click OK.**

5. **Click the Browse button (shown in Figure 5-7) to locate the directory on your computer where you store your eBay images.**

6. **Click OK and you're good to go.**

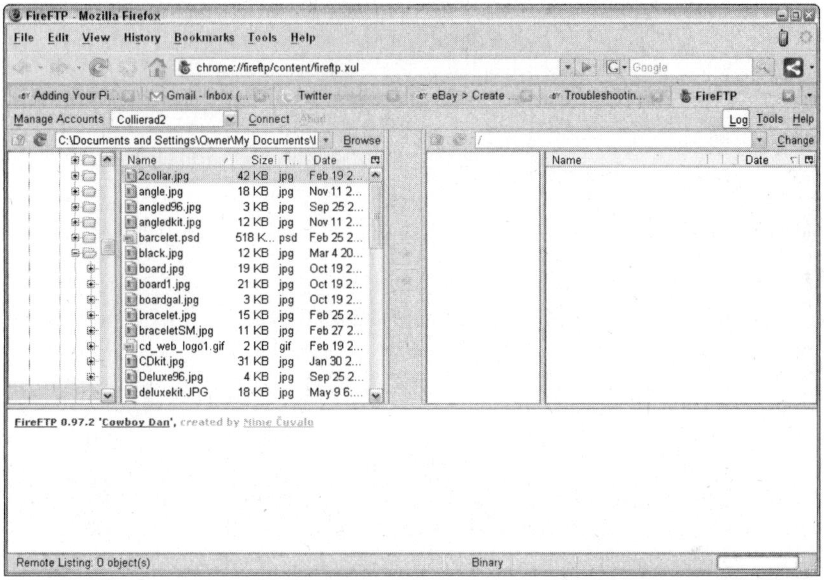

Figure 5-7:
Selecting your default directory.

From this point on, every time you click the Connect button, FireFTP logs on to your web space and displays the screen shown in Figure 5-8. Note that the left side of the program is open to the directory you selected as the default for your eBay images. The right side of the screen shows what is currently on your ISP-provided home page.

To upload an image, highlight it and click the transfer arrow in the center. Faster than I could take a screen shot (okay, I took it anyway, and it's Figure 5-9), the image is uploaded to my web space.

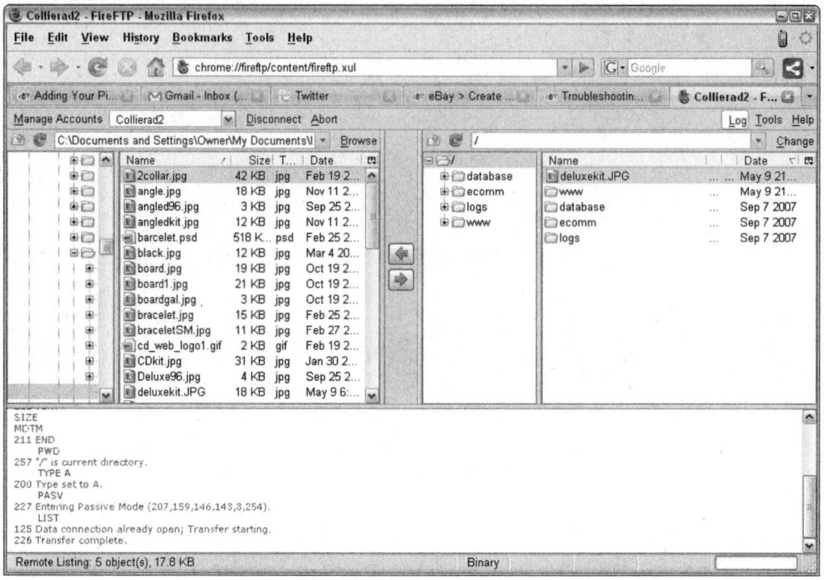

Figure 5-8:
Signing on
to your FTP
space.

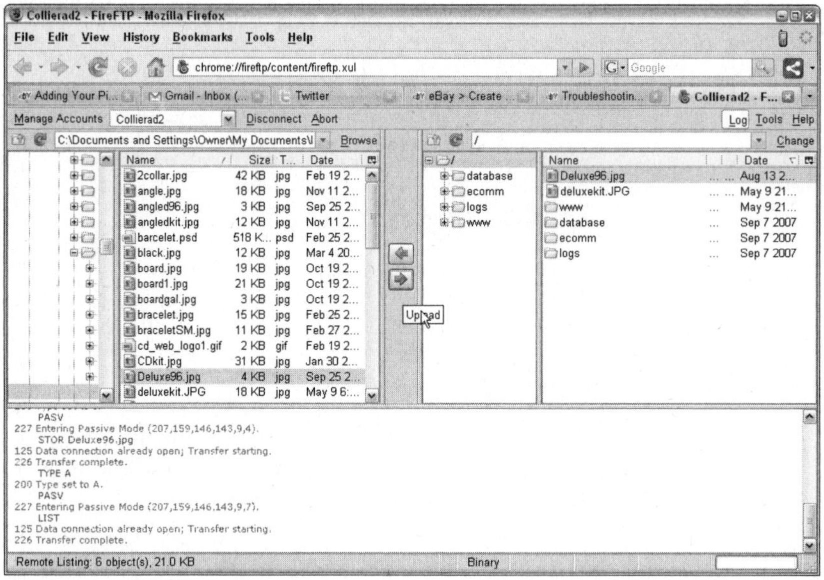

Figure 5-9:
Instant
image
upload!

Book VI

Extending Your Reach

Visit www.dummies.com/extras/ebaybusinessaio for tips on putting your best face forward online.

Contents at a Glance

Chapter 1: Developing Your Web Presence

In This Chapter

✔ Embracing the idea of web presence

✔ Finding and choosing your space online

✔ Deciding on the perfect website name

✔ Registering the perfect name

Your eBay store is important to your business, but it doesn't replace a website (hopefully an e-commerce site). You should establish your own presence on the web, outside of eBay. And although you should link your site to eBay, don't miss out on the rest of the Internet population.

You *don't* have a website yet? Perhaps you're spending all your spare online time on Facebook? (I suspect that may be true.) You might also consider a blog to back up your online selling efforts. Even if you don't sell directly from anywhere other than eBay (although I wish you would), a blog can help build your reputation as an online seller.

You *do* have a website? Have you taken a good look at it lately to see whether it's up to date? (I recently gave my site a facelift and love the new look.) Does your site link to your eBay listings or have its own online store? I hope so.

Whether or not you have a website or blog, give this chapter at least a once over. I provide a lot of detail about websites, from thinking up a name to choosing a host. If you don't have a site, I get you started launching one. If you already have a site, read the pointers about finding the best host. For the serious-minded web-based entrepreneur (that's you), I also include a few important marketing tips.

Knowing Why Web Presence Is Important

Having even a small website (at the very least) gives you experience in setting one up and establishes a web presence. When you're ready to jump in for real, you can always upgrade to a full-on business site and include your old site. I've had a blog on Blogger at `mcollier.blogspot.com` since 2004, and when I upgraded my `coolebaytools.com` site, I integrated the Blogger site within it.

My example brings up a classic question: What is the difference between a blog and a website? The term *blog* is shortened from the term *web-log*, which originally meant that someone published a journal online on a regular basis. The online journal was a web log of that person's life. In today's world, a blog is not just for emotional meandering; most businesses have one to give a personal touch and share news with their readers.

The main difference between a blog and a website is that a blog is meant to be updated regularly with new content, whereas a website's content is more static and changes rarely. Of course, if you have a blog linked to your website, you can update content there while keeping the static, evergreen content intact. Take a look at almost any brand's site; you will probably see a link to an accompanying blog in the navigation bar. A blog is now considered a *type* of website.

A blog is a more touchy-feely communication tool, and a website is a more concrete representation of your business as a whole. Think of a website as a digital storefront for your business. And keep in mind that a website is of utmost importance if you have a retail location. In my book, *Social Media Commerce For Dummies* (also published by Wiley; you can find it at `www.dummies.com`), I give you all the up-to-date information on how to make your website shine — and convert visitors to buyers.

Your customers need to visit your blog and actually read its content for it to be a valuable resource for your business. Countless blogs receive just a few hits a day; if your customers are busy, a marketing-oriented blog may be the last place they want to visit. The goal is to engage reader's interest, so don't just write about business; write about topics that you enjoy and that your readers will find interesting. You might want to direct your blog's focus to a range of broader-interest topics. Bottom line: Have a plan for regular postings and an objective to focus on before you start writing your blog entries.

Free Web Space — a Good Place to Start

Although I love the word *free,* in real life it seems like nothing is *really* free. *Free* generally means something won't cost you too much money — but may cost you a bit more in time. When your site is free, you may give up the opportunity to have your own direct URL (Universal Resource Locator) or domain name. That is available usually for a small extra fee. You may also have to put up with ads appearing on your site, or not; it depends from whom you get the free space.

I much prefer a free web space with no ads, but that seems to be asking a lot. Surprisingly, there are a few very good, reliable places. The most flexible free sites for an eBay seller allow you to upload images that you can share in your eBay descriptions. Take a look at Table 1-1, where I compare some popular options for free web space.

Table 1-1	Free Web Space			
Site	*Blog or Website*	*Total Storage*	*Sharable Images w URL*	*Design Tools*
Webs.com	Website	40 MB	Yes	Yes
Wix.com	Website	500 MB	No	Yes
Google Blogger *	Blog	30 GB*	No	Yes
WordPress.com	Blog	3 GB2	No	Yes

* Storage on all Google Apps is shared from your Google Drive total storage of 30 GB

You might want to consider using a quick and easy HTML generator such as the one in Mozilla's free SeaMonkey. You can use this with the Firefox FireFTP upload extension for a complete web hookup. (See Book V Chapter 3 for more information on the SeaMonkey program.)

Your first web pages may be simple, and that's okay. You have to get used to having a website before you can really use it for commerce. Put up a home page that links to a few product-related pages and your eBay listings, and, voilà, you're in business. If you're feeling more adventurous about your website, check out the next section, where I describe a handful of website hosts.

Paying for Your Web Space

If you've been on the Internet for any length of time, you've been bombarded by hosting offers through your daily spam. A web-hosting company houses your website code and electronically doles out your pages and images to your web page's visitors.

If you take advantage of PayPal's free Pay Now buttons or shopping cart, you can turn a basic-level hosted site into a full-on e-commerce store without paying additional fees to your hosting company. The PayPal tools are easily inserted into your pages with a snippet of code provided by PayPal. (See Chapter 3 in this minibook for more information.)

Before deciding to spend money on a web-hosting company, check it out thoroughly. Go to that company's site to find a list of features offered. If you still have questions after perusing the website, look for a toll-free number to call. You won't find any feedback ratings like you find on eBay, but the following are a few questions to ask (don't hang up until you're satisfied with the answers):

✦ **How long has the company been in business?** You don't want a web host that has been in business only a few months and operates out of the founder's basement. Deal with folks who have been around the Internet for a while (hence know what they are doing). Is the company's website professional-looking? Does the company look like it has enough money to stay in business?

✦ **Who are some of the company's other clients?** Poke around to see whether you can find links to sites of other clients. Take a look at who else is doing business with the hosting company and analyze the sites. Do the pages and links come up quickly? Do all the images appear in a timely manner? Websites that load quickly are a good sign.

✦ **What is the downtime-to-uptime ratio?** Does the web host guarantee *uptime* (the span of time its servers stay operational without going down and denying access to your site)? Expecting a 99-percent-uptime guarantee is not unreasonable; you're open for business — and your web host needs to keep it that way.

✦ **How much web space do I get for my money?** For the most basic website on web.com (not to be confused with webs.com mentioned above) you can get 300GB of storage for $2.99 a month; you'd better be getting a lot if you're paying more for it.

✦ **Does the web host offer toll-free technical support?** When something goes wrong with your website, you need it corrected immediately. You must be able to reach tech support quickly without hanging around on the phone for hours. Does the web host have a technical support area on its website where you can troubleshoot your own problems (in the middle of the night, if needed)?

Whenever you're deciding on any kind of provider for your business, take a moment to call its tech-support team with a question about their services. Take note of how long you had to hold and how courteous the techs were. Before plunking down your hard-earned money, you should be sure that the provider's customer service claims aren't merely that — just claims.

✦ **What's the policy on shopping carts?** In time, you may need to install a shopping cart on your site. Does your provider charge extra for that? If so, how much? In the beginning, a convenient and professional-looking way to sell items on your site is to set up a PayPal shopping cart or PayPal Pay Now buttons. When you're running your business full-time, however, a shopping cart and a way to accept credit cards is a must.

✦ **What kind of statistics will you get?** Visitors who go to your website leave a bread-crumb trail. Your host collects these statistics, so you'll be able to know which are your most and least popular pages. You can know how long people linger on each page, where they come from, and what browsers they're using. How your host supplies these stats to you is important.

✦ **Is there a desktop design tool?** If you're not a web-design expert, having a WYSIWYG (What You See Is What You Get) design tool will make life a lot easier. If your web host has themes or templates, you're good to go. Figure 1-1 shows you the page from Network Solutions that offers design templates. Using a ready-made (but customizable) template can help make the initial site setup somewhat painless for the non-technically inclined.

✦ **Are there any hidden fees?** Does the web host charge exorbitant fees for setup? Charge extra for statistics? Impose high charges if your bandwidth suddenly increases?

✦ **How often will the web host back up your site?** No matter how redundant a host's servers are, a disaster may strike, and you need to know that your website won't vaporize. *Redundancy* (having duplicate copies of your data and site functionality) is the safety net for your site.

Table 1-2 provides a comparison of the costs for the most basic offerings. In the rest of this section, I fill you in on the details about the four web-hosting companies listed in the table. Make sure you check out the company websites for the most current information since the features offered change (almost as often as eBay does).

Keep in mind that **200 MB of disk storage space can host as many as 6000 HTML pages**. My entire website, `coolebaytools.com`, including WordPress plugins, fills only 55 MB!

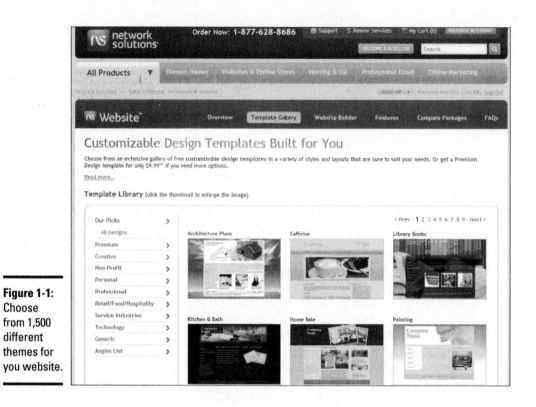

Table 1-2	Comparing Entry-Level Hosting Costs*			
Feature	**AT&T Website Hosting**	**Network Solutions.com**	**Web.com**	**Yahoo! Small Business**
Monthly plan cost	$10	$6.95 with 3 year term	9.96 paid yearly	$4.99
Disk space storage	?	5 GB	300 GB	100 GB
Data transfer/ month	?	50 GB	Unlimited	1000 GB
DIY web-design tools	Yes	Yes	Yes	Yes
24/7 toll-free tech	Yes	Yes	?	?
E-mail	100	1000	10	250

* Does not take into account any promotional first-year discount offers.

$10 private domain registration

In the never-ending battle of the giants, Google is offers free web space through Blogger and $10 domain registration (per year). Private registration is important because it prevents anyone from looking up who owns your website — and then deluging you with spam and other "offers."

New domains are instantly configured with a complete array of Google applications: personalized Gmail, Google Calendar, instant messaging, online document editing, and more. It's also loaded (at no charge) with other features.

✔ Full DNS control and management so you can move your domain settings to another web host

✔ Private registration at no additional cost to protect your personal information

✔ Free domain locking to protect you from unauthorized domain transfers

You can find this Google feature when you register at

```
www.blogger.com/
```

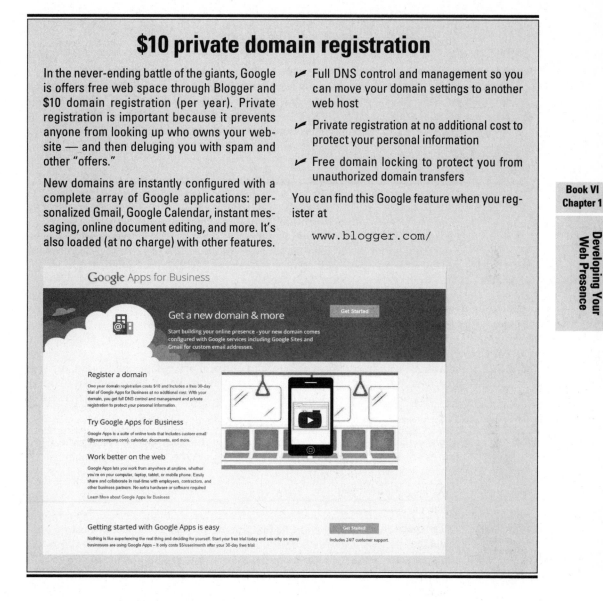

Naming Your Baby

What to name the baby, er, website? It's almost as much of a dilemma as deciding on your eBay user ID or eBay store name. If you don't have an existing company name that you want to use, why not use the same name as your eBay store? Register and lock it up now so that you can keep your brand forever.

Domain parking

Suppose you've come up with a brilliant name for your site and your business gets really big and famous. Then someone else uses your website's name but registers it as a `.net` — while yours is a `.com`. To avoid this situation, make sure you register both domains (`.com` and `.net`) and park them with your registrar.

That way any permutations of your domain will point to your active website. For example, `www.ebay.net` and `www.ebay.org` are registered to (guess who?) `ebay.com`. You can check the owner of any domain name at any of the web-hosting or registrar sites.

Name your site with a word that identifies what you do, what you sell, or who you are. And be sure you like it — because once it's yours and you begin operating under it and establishing a reputation, it'll be with you 20 years from now when you're still selling online. (I know, it should only happen!)

A few websites offer wizards to help you decide your domain name. A particularly intuitive one can be found at the following:

```
http://snapitnow.com/
```

In a small, web-based form, you input your primary business type and keywords that describe your business. The wizard then displays a large number of options and also lets you know whether the options are available. Very convenient.

Before you attempt to register a name, you should check to be sure it isn't anyone else's trademark. To search an updated list of registered United States trademarks, go to the following and use the electronic trademark search system:

```
www.trademarksearchforfree.com
```

After a search, you may want to trademark your site name. Go to `www.legalzoom.com`, an online service that can help you with that. It offers online trademark applications and also refers you to an attorney if you'd like to use one; just go to the site for further information.

Registering Your Domain Name

Talk about your junk e-mail. I get daily e-mails advising me to `Lose 40 pounds in 40 days, accept credit cards now,` and of course `REGISTER MY NAME NOW!` The last scam seems to be geared to obtaining my e-mail address for other junk mail lists rather than trying to help me register my website. Choosing a *registrar* (the company that handles the registering of your site name) is as important as choosing the right web host. You must remember that the Internet is still a little like the Wild West — and that the cyber-equivalent of the James Gang might be waiting to relieve you of your hard-earned cash. One of the ways to protect yourself is to understand how the registry works (knowledge *is* power), so read on.

Before you decide on a registrar for your domain name, take a minute to see whether the registrar is accredited by ICANN (Internet Corporation for Assigned Names and Numbers — the international governing body for domain names) or is reselling for an official ICANN-accredited registrar. (You'll have to ask who they register with.) The Accredited Registrar Directory is updated constantly at the U.S. Department of Commerce's InterNIC site, so check the following for the most recent list:

```
www.internic.com/regist.html
```

For a comparison of registration fees as of this date, see Table 1-3.

Table 1-3	Yearly Domain Name Registration Fees	
Registrar	*Registration Fee ($) per year*	*URL Forwarding ($)*
Google.com	10.00 (private registration)	Free
yahoo.com	9.95 (free with web hosting package)	Included
namesarecheap.com	14.00	Included
networksolutions.com	24.99 (free with hosting package)	12.00

You'll usually get a substantial discount from the more expensive registrars when you register your domain name for multiple years — a good idea if you plan on staying in business. Also, if you register your name through your hosting service, you might be able to cut the prices in Table 1-3 in half! The only drawback is that your prepaid registration might go out the window if you choose to change hosting companies.

Making your personal information private

ICANN requires every registrar to maintain a publicly accessible whois database that displays all contact information for all domain names registered. Interested parties (or, for that matter, fraudsters) can find out the name, street address, e-mail address, and phone number of the owner of the site by running a whois search on the domain name. You can run a whois search by going to `www.whois.net` and typing the domain name in question.

Unfortunately, this information can be useful to spammers who spoof your e-mail address as their fake return address to cloak their identity;

identity thieves, stalkers, and just about anyone up to no good may also take an interest. To see the difference between private and public registrations, run a whois search on my website, `www.coolebaytools.com/` — which is private — and `www.ebay.com`, which is public.

Registrars such as Network Solutions offer private registration for an additional $9 a year (Google for FREE). Check to see whether your registrar offers this service. For updated information on private registration, visit my website.

If you're registering a new domain name but already have a site set up with your ISP, you need a feature called URL forwarding, or web address forwarding. This feature directs any hits to your new domain name from your existing long URL address. Some registrars offer this service, but watch out for hidden surprises — such as a "free" offer of the service, which means they'll probably smack a big fat banner at the bottom of your home page. Your registrar should also have some available tech support. Trying to troubleshoot DNS issues is a job for those who know what they're doing! Remember, sometimes you *do* get what you pay for.

Chapter 2: Marketing Tools for Your Web Presence and Social Media

In This Chapter

- ✔ Advertising on the web
- ✔ Getting listed in a search engine
- ✔ Connecting with customers on social media (Twitter, Facebook, and so on)

After you set up your website (whether blog or business site) and eBay Store, it's time to let the world know about it. Having spent many years in the advertising business, I can spot businesses that *want* to fail. They open their doors and expect the world to beat a path to them and make them rich. This doesn't happen — ever.

You must take a proactive approach to letting the world in on the goodies you have for sale. This means spending a good deal of time promoting your site by buying keywords on Google, getting your URL into a search engine, and taking advantage of social media. There are no shortcuts.

In this chapter, I tell you about ways to exploit the promotional opportunities you find online. For example, you'll be pleasantly surprised to learn that a simple link to your website from your eBay About Me page will draw people to your site initially.

In my book *Social Media Commerce For Dummies*, I go deeply into using social media to reach new customers. (You can find it at www.dummies.com.)

Advertising with Google AdWords

Wouldn't it be cool if you could run ads all over the Internet at a low price? You can!

Google's cost-per-click (CPC) offering, AdWords, is used by nearly every business on the web. If you are a regular user of Google search, you should be noticing small ads on the right side of your search results, often under a headline called Sponsored Links. I used to think these ads were expensive links from high-dollar operations — until I found out the truth. If you take a look at the results of a Google search in Figure 2-1, you'll see the ads that companies bought to show up on searches for my name on the right. (By the way — notice that my eBay Store shows up in page 3 of a Google search on my name. A word to the wise.)

According to numerous sources, 1,722,071,000,000 searches were performed on Google in 2011; that's about 4,718,000,000 per day. Google AdWords allow you to create the profitable little ads that accompany each of these searches. You choose keywords to let Google know where to place your ads. Certainly you can come up with some relevant keywords to promote your website or eBay Store.

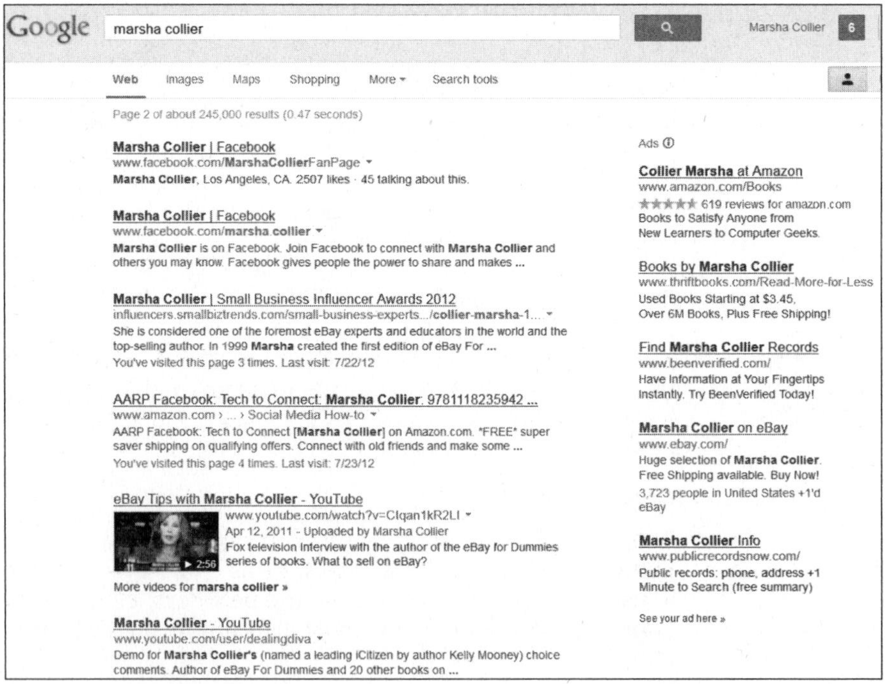

Figure 2-1: Okay, I googled myself.

You pay for such an ad only when someone clicks on it. Want to know more? Go over to `www.google.com/AdWords`. Once you're there, you can go over the details and set up your own campaign.

For your campaign, keep the following in mind:

✦ **Keywords and keyword phrases:** Come up with a list of keywords that would best describe your merchandise. Google allows you to estimate, based on current search data, how often your selected keyword will come up every day. Google will also estimate your daily cost, based on how many people click that word. That can be a shocking number. Don't worry — not everyone who sees your ad will click it — but if they did, eeyow!

✦ **CPC (cost-per-click):** You determine how much you'll pay for each click on your keywords. You can pay as little as $.05 a click. The dollar amount you place on your clicks makes the basis for how often your ad appears.

✦ **CTR (click-through rate):** This statistic reflects how many people click your ad when they see it. If your CTR falls below .5 percent after 1,000 impressions, AdWords may slow or even discontinue your ad views. When one of your keywords isn't passing muster, it will be indicated on your reports.

✦ **Daily budget:** You can set the cap in dollars on how much you'll spend a day. Otherwise, if you had some really hot keywords, you could spend thousands on clicks.

Setting up an AdWords account takes a while and some thinking. So wait until your mind is clear (Saturday morning?) and sit down at the AdWords site with a cup of coffee.

Google gives you excellent step-by-step instructions after you're signed in at `www.google.com/AdWords`. This is the general process:

1. **Decide whether you want to target your ads geographically.**

You can pinpoint your market if you'd like, or you can blast the entire world. Choose from a list of 14 languages, 250 countries, or as far down as 200 United States regions.

2. **Create your ad.**

This is not as easy as I thought. You can create only three lines of ad text with a total of 95 characters. Be as concise as possible. Don't throw in useless adjectives. Figure out the perfect 95 characters that will sell your site to the world. You must also supply the URL for your website or eBay Store.

3. **Select your keywords.**

   Type your keywords and key phrases in the box provided. You can use Google's Keyword Suggestion tool to help you out. Because this is your initial pass and won't be etched in granite, feel free to take some wild stabs and see what happens.

4. **Choose you maximum CPC (cost per click) and then click Calculate Estimates.**

   Here's where the sticker-shock gets you. The displayed data lets you know which keywords you can afford to keep and which ones must be discarded. If you want to change your CPC amount, do so and click Recalculate Estimates. The Traffic Estimator calculates how much, on average, you'll end up spending in a day.

5. **Specify your daily budget.**

   There will be a prefilled amount that would ensure that your ad stays on top and gets full exposure every day. (No, Mr. Google, I do not want to spend $50 a day on my keywords.) Set a cap on your budget and Google will never exceed it. You may make it as low as you want; there's no minimum spending amount.

6. **Enter your e-mail address and agree to the terms.**

7. **Enter your billing information.**

   You're minutes away from your ads going live on the Google index.

Here's an intriguing fact: Your ads may also appear on other places on the Internet where Google feeds ads.

Getting Your Site Visible on a Search Engine

For people to find your site (and what you're selling), they must be able to locate you. A popular way people do this is by searching with a search engine, so you should submit your site to search engines. Go to the search engines that interest you and look for a link or a help area that will enable you to submit your site. Be sure to follow any specific instructions on the site; some may limit the amount of keywords and the characters in your description.

To submit your URL to search engines, you need to do a little work (nothing's easy, is it?). Write down 25 to 50 words or phrases that describe your website; these are your *keywords.* Now, using as many of those keywords as you can, write a description of your site. With the remaining words, create a list of keywords, separating each word or short phrase with a comma. You can use these keywords to add meta tags to the header in your HTML document for your home page. *Meta tags* are identifiers used by search-engine *spiders,* robots that troll the Internet looking for new sites to classify on search engines. Specifying a meta tag in HTML looks like this:

```
<meta name = "insert your keywords here separated by commas"
      content = "short description of your site">
```

Catch attention on Google

Have you ever googled your eBay Store or website? I did, by searching for the name of my eBay Store, which includes my name. Figure 2-2 shows you the results.

You, too, should Google yourself, your website, and eBay Store to see where and if it's listed. If you find nothing, you're missing out on a huge opportunity for free promotion. Google runs spiders (just picture the way a spider runs — swiftly and all over the place) that scour the Internet on a monthly basis, looking for data to add to the Google index.

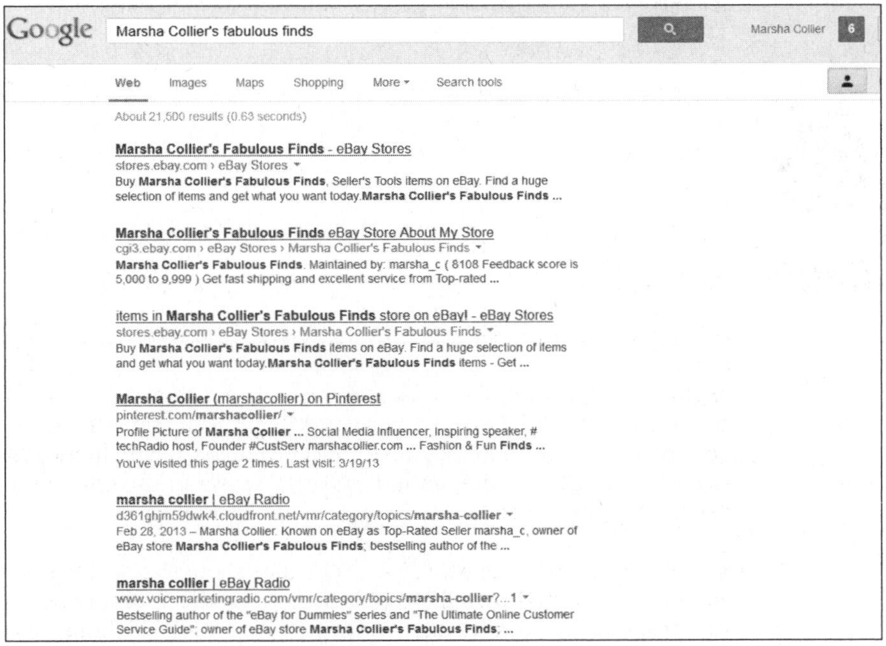

Book VI
Chapter 2

Marketing Tools for Your Web Presence and Social Media

Figure 2-2:
Wow! My eBay Store shows up!

Thousands of sites (and you do know that since your eBay Store has a unique URL, it's considered to be a website) are added to the Google index every time their spiders crawl the web.

If your eBay Store *isn't* listed, go to

```
www.google.com/submityourcontent/#
```

as pictured in Figure 2-3. When you get to this page, follow the instructions to get your eBay Store URL indexed. To find your store's URL, click the red *store* tag next to your eBay user ID to go to your store, and then copy and paste the URL (in the address line of your browser) into the URL line on the form. When I went to my eBay Store, I got this URL:

```
http://stores.ebay.com/Marsha-Colliers-Fabulous-Finds
```

That's the URL I use in my e-mail and printed propaganda to promote my store.

There are no guarantees here, but odds are you'll find your little shop on Google within a few weeks. To get the full benefit of Google's massive power, be sure to register and verify your business website on Google's Webmaster Tools at

```
www.google.com/webmasters/tools/
```

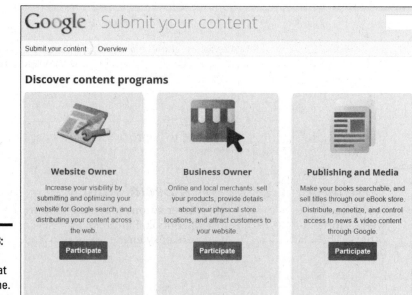

Figure 2-3: Get your free shot at the big time.

Get listed on Bing and Yahoo!

You will find that dealing with certain webmaster tools entails a fairly strong learning curve. So if you just want to get your site in line to appear in Bing's search. Just go to

```
www.bing.com/toolbox/submit-site-url
```

The simplest form on the Internet — show in in Figure 2-4 — appears. Just type in the URL of your homepage, type in the captcha code you see, and you are good to go.

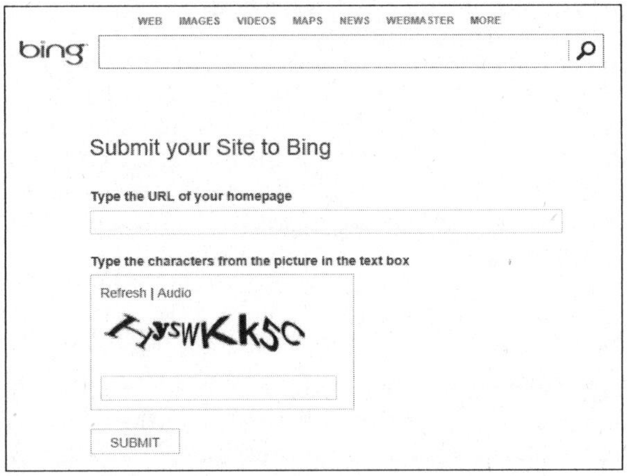

**Book VI
Chapter 2**

**Marketing Tools for
Your Web Presence
and Social Media**

Figure 2-4:
Submitting your site's URL.

To be listed on Yahoo! it takes a bit more effort. Bing has taken over the submission chores for Yahoo!. I'm afraid things will get a bit complex here. You need to sign up for Bing Webmaster Tools at

```
www.bing.com/toolbox/webmaster
```

By signing up here, you will be able to improve your site's performance in both Bing and Yahoo! searches.

Casting for Customers in Social Media

Social media hosts networking conversations on many sites around the web — for example, on Twitter, Facebook, Pinterest, Google+, and a myriad others. These sites are places where easy engagement can lead to customer enticement.

In this conversational atmosphere, you can expect to

+ **Sell:** Promote online and offline sales by posting promotions, discounts, and offers.

+ **Find new customers:** Find people who are interested in a new vendor. Unhappy customers tend to be verbal on social media; maybe you're the new vendor *they* are looking for.

+ **Build community:** Join with others in your industry to share information. Connect with prospective and current customers to ultimately help drive new business.

+ **Observe the competition:** Follow friendly (or unfriendly) competition to see how they handle social media outreach.

+ **Engage in customer service:** Through connecting online, you can successfully engage with customers who are in need of help.

Your investment in social media networking may take a bit of time to pay off, but pay off it will. (Just stick with it.) I fully cover topics related to conversing through social media in my book *Social Media Commerce For Dummies*.

Building a Community on Twitter

Twitter is a convenient format for building an online community. If the thought of marketing through short-and-sweet messages appeals to you, Twitter may be the place for your online customer connections.

Some quick Twitter stats:

+ Twitter has an estimated 500 million registered users and 200 million active users.

+ Estimated total tweets average 400 million per day; that's 750 tweets per second.

+ Thirty percent of Twitter users have an income of more than $100,000.

+ Twitter handles more search queries than Microsoft's Bing and Yahoo! combined.

For Twitter to work for your social commerce, you have to follow people, listen, and take action by engaging in the conversation. Take the time to interact and foster relationships within the Twitter community. (Later on, I show you how to find people to follow who will compliment your brand.)

Participating is not terribly hard because Twitter's tweets are limited to 140 characters. If you send text messages on your phone, you're given room for 160 characters, so moving from text messages to tweeting isn't a big jump. After you get the hang of short messaging, tweeting can become second nature.

When promoting on Twitter

Your plan for Twitter should be to engage a good number of followers, drawing them to your business and brand. Become their virtual friend and turn them into evangelists for your businesses. Twitter is not a numbers game unless you're a multinational company (and have the staff to run the account).

When you Tweet, be discreet: Be sure that your self-promotional tweets stay at a low number. People are not on Twitter to be sold to, they are there to engage. If your account is constantly sending out marketing-style Tweets, you'll find that relatively few people will follow your account back — or you may be overrun by other promotional bots.

Social media scientist and data-cruncher Dan Zarrella from Hubspot studies social media posts to find out which get the greatest attention. In contrast to Twitter — where information is exchanged among personal tweets — Facebook posts with a higher number of self-referential words (such as *I* and *me*) tend to get more Likes. Note that these posts aren't marketing messages; they're posts that involve you and your involvement with your business and customers.

Choosing who to follow

Twitter can work only when you follow other people and they follow you back. How do you get people to follow you? By commenting on another tweet, re-tweeting, tweeting content, or just jumping into a conversation that interests you.

Your first step is to go to the Twitter home page, at `https://twitter.com`, and type your full name, your e-mail address, and a password. Then click Sign Up for Twitter, as shown in Figure 2-5.

Figure 2-5:
Enter a bit of data and you're in! Fill out your bio on the following page.

After you register on Twitter, things may seem a little lonely. I signed up in early 2008 and was befuddled by the blank page that stared back at me. Twitter will post suggestions for people you might want to follow. You can also try the following:

✦ **TweetFind:** The home page (at http://www.tweetfind.com/) says "Twitter Directory with Social Listings — Grow your Social Media Presence Today." Use TweetFind (shown in Figure 2-6) to search keywords in user bios as they have been input on Twitter. You can also search job titles, topics, or any specific keywords that may help you find someone you might be interested in following.

TweetFind presents search results in order of relevance to your keywords, so more valid results appear at the top. Most important, you can click any user's name to see a profile page with more information. Note the Klout and PeerIndex influence scores when these show up on profile pages. They are proprietary rating metrics — and an industry standard: Higher scores indicate a person with greater influential activity (based on that user's influence and engagement on Twitter).

Figure 2-6:
TweetFind connects businesses and consumers.

✦ **Twellow:** Billing itself as the *Twitter Yellow Pages*, this site (at `http://www.twellow.com/`) has been indexing and categorizing Twitter since 2007. Twellow makes following new people a breeze. On the home page, select a category or subcategory from a drop-down menu to see a list of Twitter users whose bios (or personally selected categories on Twellow) match your search. You can also type in the search box the keyword of a topic you want to follow.

If you read the user's details and decide that you want to follow the person, click the Follow button below the user's profile picture, as shown in Figure 2-7.

Figure 2-7:
Click the Follow button below the profile picture to follow the person.

You can narrow your keyword or topic searches to your immediate geographic area, which is particularly valuable if your business does not currently do online sales. On the search results page, click the city at the top-right of the list and Twellow will narrow the search to a reasonable distance. Note that the displayed city is generated from your Internet service provider and may not exactly match your location.

After you set up your Twitter account, select your topics and register them on Twellow so that your account becomes indexed and available for others to find when they search the site.

Making Friends and Fans on Facebook

Making friends with strangers can feel creepy, especially on a personal Facebook page. But your prospective customers are all strangers until you interact with them.

I hope you have a personal Facebook page where you connect with friends and family. I do, and since I had a personal page long before Facebook allowed business pages, I have many business contacts there as well. This is the perfect way to get a feel for how Facebook works. When you post personal items, however, be sure to post them to appear only on the news feeds of close friends and family.

But to build your brand on Facebook, you have to start a business page. The hard part is moving business friends away from your personal page to your fan page. As I've said before, in today's social media, business has become personal. So unless you're new to Facebook, you will have some adapting to do.

Facebook business page benefits

A personal page is fun for connecting and sharing, but Facebook business pages have far more flexibility. The trade-off is that your business page will take a bit more finesse to maintain because it blends personal contact and marketing.

✦ You can have more than 5,000 friends (fans or Likes on your business page). Do you want that many? The answer is yes if you plan on selling anything online.

✦ You can use your business name as the page title, making it easier for the page to be indexed by Google. This helps your business's SEO (search engine optimization) and may add strength to the listing position of your business website.

✦ Those who Like the page are opting in for your updates. Treat this valuable resource with respect and don't barrage them with promotions.

✦ You can customize the page into a mini-site that includes contact forms, sales pages, blog feeds, contests, and even a store.

✦ Statistics are available on each individual post on your page, as shown in Figure 2-8.

✦ Status updates are filtered by Facebook's EdgeRank algorithm, which places what it deems to be the most relevant content in news feeds. Business pages can use a paid ad tool to enhance the number of views a single post garners. (I have seen success with a budget as small as $5 a day.)

✦ You can purchase ads that point to your business page or your website. These ads, which appear in Facebook's right-side border, can be targeted using 15 criteria and even more subcriteria. You can narrow the audience to a city and even to a specific ZIP code.

Figure 2-8:
See how far a post on your business page has spread.

Engaging and building your audience

It's time to be your charming self. As the head of your business, your business page should reflect you. In the beginning, you may feel as though you're talking to yourself and a dozen or so family and friends. But don't give up. Slow and steady wins the race.

Only one in five posts on your Facebook business page should be promotional. The other four posts should be about something your audience will appreciate but not directly about your business.

Find other businesses, perhaps in your field or neighborhood, with which you are friendly and Like their pages from your business page.

Chapter 3: Tapping PayPal Resources to Expand Sales

In This Chapter

✔ Making PayPal's tools work for you

✔ Embedding PayPal payment buttons into your website

✔ Using PayPal on mobile devices

PayPal was founded with a desire to give its customers plenty of extras for their loyalty — and it offers tons of tools to enhance a seller's online selling experience. The tools and fees charged by PayPal are unmatched by any other online payment service.

And if you think that PayPal is just for an eBay business, think again! Before eBay purchased PayPal, approximately 15 percent of PayPal's revenues came from online gaming. When eBay took over in late 2002, PayPal no longer received revenue from this arena. And there's good news for us: Today eBay offers the same tools — and more — to process PayPal payments on your own personal or business websites. In this chapter, you discover how to build revenue by expanding sales to your own site — and even going mobile — with the help of PayPal.

Enabling PayPal Payments on Your Website

After you get a few items in your garage or business location that you stock in quantity, you've got the makings of your own webstore. Don't let the thought of this spook you. You *can* do it! Aside from selling in your eBay Store, you can sell directly from a website or even from a Facebook store. In time, as your eBay business grows into your own website, you'll find that using PayPal as your payment provider is a great deal. And you pay the same transaction fees — to PayPal only — for processing your credit card sales.

Build business by including your website URL in your e-mail signature, letting the world know you're open for business 24/7.

The first step is to create a website (see Chapter 1 in this minibook). When you have the site up and running, here's what you need to know about using PayPal as a payment tool:

✦ **Incorporating payment buttons is easy:** Buy Now or Add to Cart buttons are the most basic way to enable sales through PayPal from your site. These buttons are easy to insert (see the next section)— you don't have to be a computer whiz to create the links because PayPal makes that process almost automatic.

✦ **The fees are what you're used to:** There's no fee to use this service beyond the standard processing fee that PayPal charges when someone buys an item on eBay. All you need is a verified PayPal Premier or Business account. (Check out Book II, Chapter 4 for information on the various types of PayPal accounts.)

✦ **The procedure is familiar, too:** When someone buys something from your website, the procedure is the same as when someone pays for an eBay item. You receive an e-mail from PayPal telling you that a web payment (versus an eBay payment) has been received. The e-mail subject includes the item number or that you've assigned to the product sold.

PayPal also integrates with shopping -cart and e-commerce software for an additional charge. In this chapter, you examine the free options for new or smaller sellers. If you need help integrating PayPal into shopping-cart software, your website provider will have all the information you need.

Incorporating the Payment Buttons

Enabling your website to accept PayPal payments is as simple as placing the PayPal button on your site. To create a payment button on your site, first sign in to your PayPal account. From there, follow these steps:

1. **Click the Merchant Services tab, at the top of the page, as shown in Figure 3-1.**

You arrive at the Merchant Services area shown in Figure 3-2.

2. **Click the Create Payment Buttons for Your Website link.**

3. **On the resulting page, click the Create Buttons button.**

You see the page where you create buttons for the items you're selling on your site, as shown in Figure 3-3.

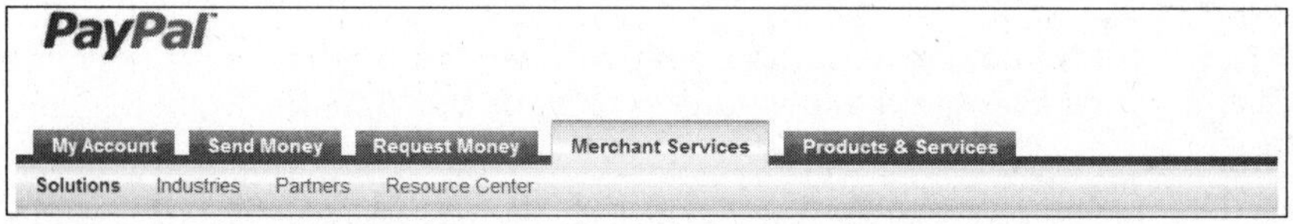

Figure 3-1:
The first step in creating a button.

PayPal

| My Account | Send Money | Request Money | Merchant Services | Products & Services |

Solutions   Industries   Partners   Resource Center

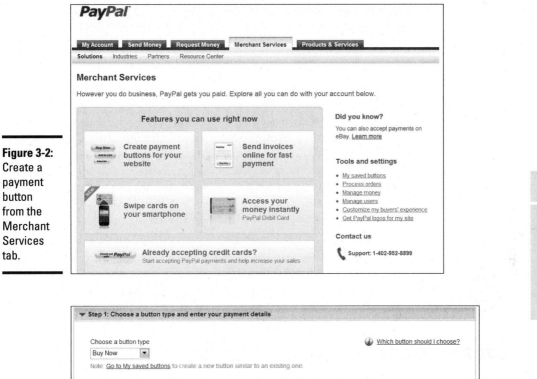

Figure 3-2: Create a payment button from the Merchant Services tab.

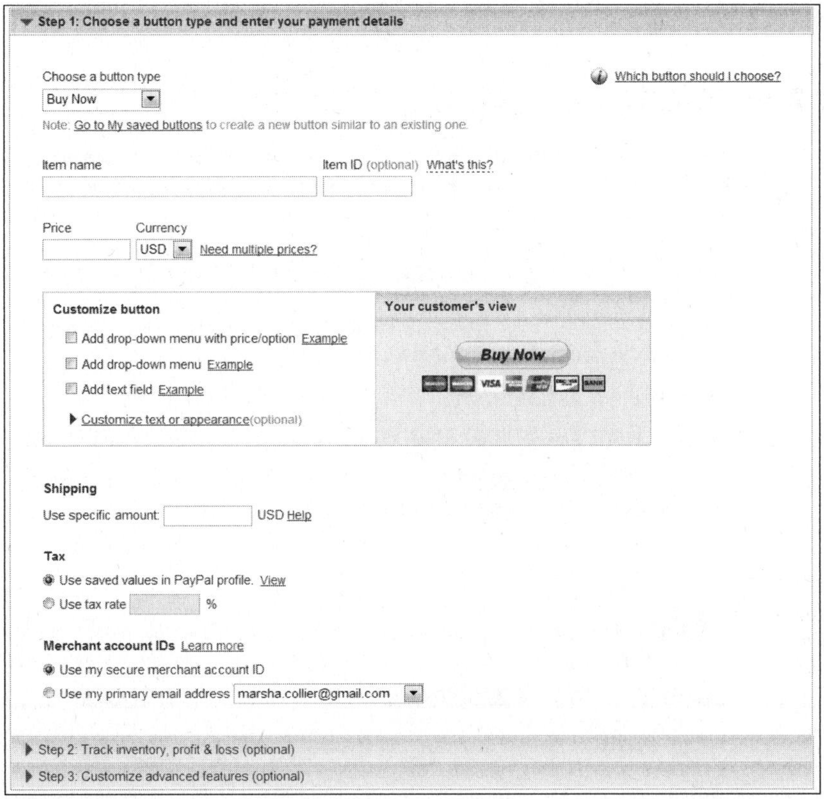

Figure 3-3: Creating a web-payment button.

4. **From the drop-down list, select the type of button you want to use to accept payments.**

   In this example, I chose the Buy Now button, but you can choose any from the following table.

Button	*What It Does*
	With this Buy Now button, customers can click and immediately be brought to PayPal to complete their payment. Use Buy Now for merchandise or if your customer is buying services (for example, a psychic reading, bookkeeping, or consulting).
	Customers can use the Add to Cart button to select one or more items from your website and place them in a shopping cart when you're selling physical merchandise.
	Associate the Subscribe button with your items if you're selling subscriptions to a newsletter or collecting dues for a membership.
	If you have a website where you'd like to get donations — here's the right button. It's an excellent way for nonprofits to get additional funds.
	Choose the Buy Gift Certificate button if you're selling gift certificates to your store.
	The Installment Plan button allows your customers to purchase your item and pay over time with PayPal.

   PayPal enables you to customize the buttons by clicking the Customize Text or Appearance link under Customize Button on the left.

5. **Enter your item information, including the item name, ID, price, currency, shipping amount, and tax.**

   Here's a list of all the items you're asked to enter:

   • **Item name:** Type in the name of the product (or service) you will sell with this button.

   • **Item ID (optional):** Give your item an ID number or use the standard SKU for the product.

   • **Price:** Enter the item price here.

   • **Currency:** Decide what currency you're accepting for your purchases. (If you're in the United States, go for the dollars.)

- **Customize Button options:** If your item has options (if, for example, it comes in different sizes or colors), you can create a custom drop-down list for your payment page so the customer can choose.

- **Shipping**: Enter the amount you charge to ship the item.

- **Tax:** Select your state and enter the appropriate sales tax to be applied to your in-state purchases. If you already have a sales-tax provision in your PayPal profile, you see it listed here. PayPal automatically applies the sales tax for sales shipped within your state.

6. **If you don't like the button you chose as it's pictured, click the Customize Text or Appearance link in the Customize Button section to see more options.**

I like using the buttons that include the different credit card icons so that folks who aren't familiar with PayPal will know that they can use any credit card.

7. **Click the Step 2 tab for the option to track inventory.**

Unless you want to update your button every time you receive new merchandise, I suggest that you leave this option blank.

8. **If you want to add custom features, click the Step 3: Customize Advanced Features (Optional) tab.**

On this tab, you can add extended options for your button. Included (definitely use these!) are the following:

- **Quantity:** If you'd like your customers to be able to purchase more than one of your item at a time, you may indicate that here by giving the buyers a quantity field to fill in.

- **Allow customer to add special instructions:** If you'd like your buyers to be able to write you a note (40 character limit), select the Yes check box.

- **Shipping address:** Select the Yes check box if you'd like the customer's shipping address. I guess it would be kind of useless *not* to ask for a shipping address when you're expected to ship the item somewhere, huh?

- **Insert your logo:** To add a logo to your payment page, type the URL where the file is stored. PayPal will place the logo on your payment page.

The logo you use must be sized at 150 x 50 pixels or PayPal won't accept it.

- **Checkout landing page:** If you want your customers to land on a specific page after they've purchased an item — setting up a thank-you page on your website is a nice idea, for example — enter that URL here.

- **Cancel Transaction page:** If you want to include a page where people are taken if they cancel the transaction before completing it, you can insert that address here. If you don't specify a page, they will land at a PayPal web page that allows cancellation of the transaction.

9. **Click Preview.**

   You see a sample of the page your customer will see after making a web payment to you.

10. **If the page is okay, click the Create Button Now button.**

11. **If you want to go back and edit, click the Edit button.**

That's all there is to creating your first Buy Now button and the payment page that appears when it's clicked. When you get the hang of it for one item, you can reuse many of the settings for other items that you sell.

Repeating the PayPal button process

When you have created a payment button, there's no need to go through the entire process for each item. Just familiarize yourself with the various button options and change those entries as needed for each item.

When shoppers click a payment button on my site, they land on my Cool eBay Tools customized PayPal payment page (shown in Figure 3-4, complete with custom logo). The PayPal payment page is a secure page (as indicated by the lock icon) that users access directly from PayPal. The URL for the page begins with `https`; the `s` at the end indicates that the site is secure.

Figure 3-4:
The customized payment page.

COOL eBay TOOLS

Your order summary

Descriptions	Amount
Quake Hold Putty	$6.99
Item price: $6.99	
Quantity: 1	
Item total	**$6.99**
Shipping and handling:	$2.50
	Total $9.49 USD

Choose a way to pay

PayPal 🔒

▾ Pay with my PayPal account
Log in to your account to complete the purchase

Email

PayPal password

Log In

Forgot your email address or password?

▸ Don't have a PayPal account?
(Optional) Join PayPal for faster future checkout

Going Mobile with PayPal Here™

In today's mobile-enabled world, you may find an opportunity to sell goods or services through means other than your website accessed on a desktop computer. You can now accept credit cards processed though PayPal on your smartphone with the PayPal Here credit card reader, shown in Figure 3-5.

The card reader is available for free to any PayPal account, just go to `www.paypal.com/here`. It plugs into (and works through) the microphone jack of almost any of the current smartphones. The magic happens when the reader is combined with a free app that's downloadable from the iOS (iPhone) or Android Play Stores; it enables you to swipe a credit card to deposit the funds immediately into your PayPal account.

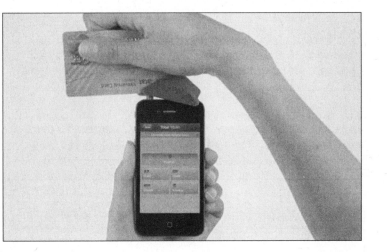

Figure 3-5:
The PayPal Here card reader.

Although other smartphone credit card readers are available, none have PayPal's support behind them. Other benefits come with PayPal Here:

✦ **Low transaction fee.** Although using PayPal Here does incur slightly higher transaction fees than processing a payment online, the current rate (2.7 percent plus $.15 per transaction), it beats the competition.

✦ **You can manually enter credit card numbers.** Entering a credit card number manually is handy for phone transactions, but the fee is considerably higher: 3.50 percent plus $0.15.

✦ **You can accept checks online.** You can accept and process check payments without going to the bank. The app enables you to accept check payments of $1,000 or less by typing in the check amount, then scanning the check with your smartphone camera. At this time, there is no charge for accepting check payments.

✦ **You can send receipts to customers by e-mail or text message.** This feature gives your customer a receipt for the transaction.

Always accept payments via PayPal online whenever possible. A customer may want to pay you with a credit card when picking up (or when you deliver) an item, and that's a convenience for them. But realize that your seller protection through PayPal exists solely on the web. PayPal Here transactions are not eligible for Seller Protection — so, if possible, have your customers pay you on the web before they get their items.

Book VII

Storing and Shipping

Contents at a Glance

Chapter 1: Organizing Your Merchandise and Shipping Area

In This Chapter

✔ **Organizing your stock**

✔ **Keeping inventory**

✔ **Packing up**

✔ **Buying stamps without a trip to the post office**

The more SKUs you sell, the more confusing the storing and packing of all those items can get. As you build your eBay business, the little side table you use for storing eBay merchandise isn't going to work anymore (and I think you'll want your dining room back). You need to begin to think industrial. Even part-time sellers can benefit by adding professional touches to their business organization.

In this chapter, I emphasize the importance of setting up and organizing your back office. I cover everything from stacking your stock to keeping inventory to getting those indispensable packing materials and saving time by buying postage online. Organization will be your byword. Dive right in. The sooner you read this chapter, the sooner you can build your eBay back office and get down to business.

The Warehouse: Organizing Your Space

Whether you plan to sell large items or small items, you need space for storing them. As you make savvy purchases, maintaining an item's mint condition will be one of your greatest challenges. In this section, I cover the details of what you'll need to safeguard your precious stock.

Shelving your profits

Before you stock the shelves, it helps to have some! You also need a place to put the shelves: your garage, a spare room, or somewhere else. For the home-based business, you have a choice between two basic kinds of shelves:

✦ **Plastic:** If you're just starting out, you can always go to the local closet-and-linen-supply store to buy inexpensive plastic shelves. They're light and cheap, but they'll buckle in time.

✦ **Steel:** If you want to do it right the first time, buy steel shelving. The most versatile steel shelving is the wire kind (versus solid steel shelves), which is light and allows air to circulate around your items. Steel wire shelving assembles easily; I put mine together without help. You can combine steel-wire shelving units to create a full wall of shelves. Each shelf safely holds as much as 600 pounds of merchandise.

To save you time, I researched the subject and found some readily available, reasonably priced shelves. Just go to Target or Costco and look for Seville Classics four-shelf commercial shelving, sold in 36- and 48-inch-wide units. Seville Classics also has an eBay store where you can buy from them direct. Look for them at

```
http://stores.ebay.com/Seville-Classics
```

You can easily convert a garage or a spare room to a professional and functional stock room. Figure 1-1 shows a portion of my stock area.

Box 'em or bag 'em?

Packing your items for storage can be a challenge. For smaller items, pick up some plastic bags in sandwich, quart, and gallon sizes. When items are stored in plastic, they can't pick up any smells or become musty before you sell them. The plastic also protects the items from rubbing against each other and causing possible damage. If you package them one item to a bag, you can then just lift one off the shelf and put it directly into a shipping box when a listing sells.

Your bags of items will have to go into boxes for storage on the shelves. Clear plastic storage boxes, the kind you often find at superstores, are great for bulky items. They're usually 26 inches long, so before you buy these big plastic containers, make sure that they'll fit on your shelving comfortably and that you'll have easy access to your items. Smaller see-through plastic boxes with various compartments (such as the type home-improvement stores carry for storing tools) work great for storing very small items.

Using cardboard office-type file storage boxes from an office supply store is another option. These cardboard boxes are 10 x 12 x 16 inches, which is a nice size for storing medium-size products. At around $1 each, they're the most economical choice. The downside is that you can't see through cardboard boxes, so if your label falls off, you have to take the box off the shelf and open it to check its contents. The upside is that they are inexpensive.

TIP

When using these large plastic bins, it's always a good idea to tape a pad of Post-it notes on the end of the box so you can quickly identify the contents. For more advanced users, how about using a Dymo labelmaker and re-create the bar code as well as the product name? That way you can scan the code when you remove an item to keep track of inventory.

Speaking of bins, Figure 1-2 shows you the bins in the small-parts area of the warehouse of eBay seller banderson-at-fuse. His setup isn't exactly what the home seller will need, but it sometimes helps to see how the big guys do it.

Figure 1-1: A portion of my merchandise storage area.

Figure 1-2:
Nice, organized little bins of products at Barry Anderson's eBay business.

Keeping Track of What You Have

Savvy sellers have different methods of handling inventory. They use everything from spiral-bound notebooks to sophisticated software programs. Although computerized inventory tracking can simplify this task, starting with a plain ol' handwritten ledger is fine, too. Choose whichever works best for you, but keep in mind that as your eBay business grows, a software program that tracks inventory for you may become necessary.

Most of these systems wouldn't work for a company with a warehouse full of stock — but will work nicely in an eBay sales environment. Many sellers tape sheets of paper to their boxes to identify them by number, and use that as a reference to a simple Excel spreadsheet for selling purposes. Excel spreadsheets are perfect for keeping track of your listings as well, but if you're using a management service or software, you don't need both for physical inventory.

Planning: The key to good organization

When I had to put my eBay merchandise in order, I was busy with my regular business, so I hired a friend to organize my eBay area. This decision turned out to be one massive mistake. My friend organized everything and put all my items in boxes — but didn't label the boxes to indicate what was stored in each. To this day I still haven't recovered — and don't know where a bunch of my stuff is!

A bit of advice: Think things out and plan where you'll put everything. Organize your items by theme, type, or size. If you organize before planning, you might end up with organized disorganization. The figure shows some merchandise organized, labeled, and stored at an eBay seller's warehouse.

You may also want to use Excel spreadsheets for your downloaded PayPal statements, to hold information waiting to transfer to your bookkeeping program. I post my sales each time I make a PayPal withdrawal (a couple of times a week). I keep the PayPal downloads only for archival purposes.

When you're running a full-time business, however, you have to keep Uncle Sam happy with a dollars and cents accounting of your inventory, so keep your inventory records in a standardized program such as QuickBooks (discussed in Book IX, Chapter 3). I describe a variety of auction-management software and websites, many of which include physical inventory tracking features.

In my eBay business, I keep my inventory record in QuickBooks. Each time I purchase merchandise for my business, I post it in the program. When I post my sales each week, QuickBooks automatically deducts the sold items from my inventory. I then do a physical inventory as product stock runs low.

The Shipping Department: Packin' It Up

In this section, I review some of the things you must have for a complete, smooth-running shipping department, such as cleaning supplies and packing materials. The *handling fee* portion of your shipping charges pays for these kinds of items. Don't run low on them — and pay attention to how you store them. They must be kept in a clean environment.

Pre-packaging clean up

Be sure the items you send out are in tip-top shape. Here are a few everyday chemicals that can gild the lily:

✦ **WD-40:** This decades-old lubricant works very well at getting price stickers off plastic and glass without damaging the product. And if the plastic on a toy box begins to look nasty — even when stored in a clean environment — a quick wipe with a paper towel and a dash of WD-40 will make it shine like new. It also works well for untangling jewelry chains and shining up metallic objects.

✦ **Goo Gone:** Goo Gone works miracles in cleaning up gooey sticker residue from nonporous items.

✦ **Vamoose.** Is there a smoker in your house? Cigar or cigarette smoke can permeate most items. Even if you're an occasional smoker, this product is worth its weight in gold. It's a chemical miracle that totally removes these stale, smoky smells. Read up about it on the web at www.vamooseproducts.com and find it in their eBay store at

```
http://stores.ebay.com/
    cigaretteandtobaccoelimination
```

✦ **un-du Adhesive Remover:** This amazing liquid easily removes stickers off cardboard, plastic, fabrics, and more without causing damage. It comes packaged with a patented miniscraper top that you can use in any of your sticker-cleaning projects.

Removing musty smell from apparel items

Clothing can often pick up odors that you just don't notice. I recently bought a designer dress on eBay from a seller who had the typical disclaimer in her description: "No stains, holes, repairs, or odors. Comes from a smoke-free, pet-free home."

Unfortunately, the minute I opened the box I could smell the musty odor of an item that had been stored for a very long time.

To prevent that stale storage odor, keep a package of Dryel in-dryer dry cleaning sheets around. This is a safe, do-it-yourself product. Just toss your better eBay clothing items in the patented Dryel bag with the special sheet and toss it in the dryer as per the instructions on the box. Your garment will come out smelling clean — and wrinkle free. For more information, visit their website at www.Dryel.com.

Packing materials

The most important area where sellers drop the time-and-money ball is in shipping. I buy hundreds of items from eBay and have seen it all when it comes to packing, padding, and shipping. I've seen money thrown out the window by e-commerce retailers who used incorrect packing materials; too often the wrong stuff is expensive in the first place, and increases the final weight of the package — and shipping cost.

The packing materials that you use for your shipments can either make or break your bottom line in the Shipping Income/Expense column of your business reports.

Prudent packing can be a boon to your business because having lower shipping costs can often make the difference between a profit and none (and offering free shipping affects your position in eBay's search). This is especially true when several people have the same item up for sale, with a minuscule difference in the item's selling price. *Hint:* Free shipping always wins.

Pay attention to packing. It's only expensive if you don't know what you're doing. You can ship your items in quality packing, keep buyers happy, and still make a dollar or so on each item for your handling fees.

Buying your shipping materials online is trés economical. eBay shipping supply e-tailers make their living selling online. Their overhead is much lower than that of any retail outlet. Even after paying shipping to get the bubble wrap to your door, you save money and time. Most of these sellers ship the same day they get your order.

Only use as much packing material as you need to get the item where it's going and ensure it arrives intact. This saves time, money, and space.

Using void fill

Nope! Void fill is not a new drug to prevent hunger pangs when dieting. *Void fill* is the industry term for the stuff you use to fill up space in shipping boxes to keep items from rolling in transit. (It's really the modern term for the old-fashioned word *dunnage*.)

There are many forms of void fill, and the best kind depends on the item you're shipping. Here are the most popular types, and a description of their plusses and minuses.

So that you can always be sure that your items will arrive at their destinations in one piece, you'll want to keep the following on hand at all times:

✦ **Air packing pillows:** I found out about these nifty little pillows because they seem to come in packages from all the major online stores. I store them as they come in — in my packing area — and recycle them in my outgoing packages.

Buying air packing pillows from sellers on eBay is economical, mainly because the manufacturing and shipping costs are low. What these folks are essentially shipping you is 99 percent air (something the post office hasn't yet figured out how to charge for). You can find air pillows in the Business and Industrial category. Some sellers sell the uninflated pillows with a small hand-size air pump to fill the pillows.

Air packing pillows are perfect for filling in the area around smaller boxed items that you want to double box. They are also handy if you have breakables that you've prewrapped in bubble wrap; just use the pillows to fill out the box. They're crushproof and can support about 150 pounds without a blowout.

✦ **Bubble wrap:** Made up of air-filled cushions of polyethylene, bubble wrap is supplied in rolls of different widths and lengths (see Figure 1-3). It shines for those who wrap delicate, breakable items. When wrapping an item with bubble wrap, wrap it one way and then the other, and then affix some packing tape to make your item an impenetrable ball. Depending on your product, you may have to carry two sizes of bubble wrap to properly protect the goods. Bubble wrap is reasonably priced (check out the many vendors on eBay) and adds next to no weight to your packages.

Figure 1-3: Different sizes of bubble wrap.

When you purchase bubble wrap, be sure you buy the perforated, or tear-off, kind. Cutting a giant roll of bubble wrap with a box cutter can be a dangerous proposition.

✦ **Plain old white newsprint:** In the right shipping situation, plain white newsprint is fantastic. eBay sellers dealing in glass, china, and breakable knickknacks often use white newsprint to wrap each piece before placing it in a box full of packing peanuts.

White newsprint is cheap and easy to store. The bad news? It's heavy when you use too many sheets to wrap the product. If you feel you would like to use newsprint, I suggest you buy it by the roll and use a table-mounted roll cutter to cut the exact size you need. (This is the kind of thing you may have seen in old-time butcher shops and delis.) This setup helps you to avoid using too much paper.

✦ **Styrofoam packing peanuts:** Every serious eBay seller has to have a stock of packing peanuts. When properly placed in a box, peanuts fill every nook and cranny and cushion your shipment to make it virtually indestructible. They're handy for padding Tyvek envelopes and filling boxes so that items don't shift around. A bonus: They're cheap and if you recycle them, they don't hurt the environment.

When packing with peanuts, the key is to not go short in the land of plenty. Use enough peanuts to fill the box completely; leaving any airspace defeats the point of using the peanuts in the first place.

Book VII Chapter 1

Organizing Your Merchandise and Shipping Area

Storing pesky packing products

Storing shipping supplies is the tricky part. I store peanuts in the bags they were shipped in (note the ones in the figure) or in 33-gallon plastic trash bags, and then hang the bags on cup hooks around the garage ceiling. (By the way, bags of peanuts make great bumpers in the garage.) To store my bubble wrap from Bubblefast, I hung a broomstick with wire from the rafters. I made the broomstick into a dispenser (of sorts).

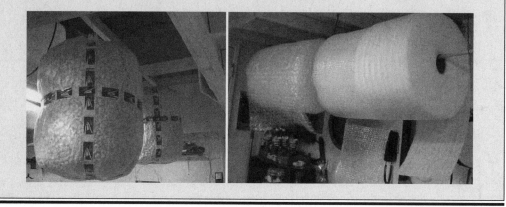

More packing supplies

Your shipping department needs just a few more items. Don't forget to include the following at the outset of your packing career:

✦ **Plastic bags:** Buy plastic bags in bulk to save money. Make sure you buy various sizes and use them for both shipping and storing. Even large kitchen or trash bags are good for wrapping up posters and large items; the plastic protects the item from inclement weather by waterproofing the item.

✦ **Two- or three-inch-wide shipping tape:** You'll need clear tape for securing packages and to place over address labels to protect them from scrapes and rain. I once received a package with an address label soaked with rain and barely legible. Don't risk a lost package for want of a few inches of tape.

✦ **Hand-held tape dispenser:** You need a way to get the tape off the roll and onto the box. Using a tape dispenser can be a bit tricky to the uninitiated, but once you get than hang of it, you'll be sealing up boxes in no time flat!

Shipping in mailing envelopes

You'll be shipping your stuff in an envelope or a box. Don't be quick to discount shipping in envelopes. Any item under 13 ounces can be shipped via First Class mail — and that can represent quite a savings.

Mailing envelopes come in many types of materials. Some are sturdier than others. Here's what many eBay sellers use:

✦ **Polyvinyl envelopes:** If you've ever ordered clothing or bedding from any of the television-shopping clubs, this is what they came in. Polyvinyl envelopes are lightweight and puncture- and tear-resistant. They are the most durable envelopes available. Who says you *have* to ship in boxes?

✦ **Tyvek envelopes:** You know those really cool, indestructible white envelopes you get from the post office or FedEx? They're made of DuPont Tyvek, a spun-bonded olefin fiber. Tyvek has all the benefits of vinyl envelopes, plus it breathes (allows air to reach your product) and has a higher strength-to-weight ratio than other envelope materials. (That "ratio" business means it's very strong, yet feather-light.)

✦ **Bubble-padded mailers:** These envelopes are lined with small bubbles, similar to bubble wrap. They're great for shipping a variety of items and are the most popular with eBay sellers (see Figure 1-4).

Bubble-lined mailers come in different materials:

• Plain-paper bubble mailers are the cheapest way to go, but they can be damaged in the mail if you use them to ship heavy items. The way around that problem is to wrap cheap, clear packing tape once around the envelope in each direction.

• Vinyl bubble mailers aren't expensive and are a super protective way to ship. They're 15 percent lighter than paper bubble mailers and are water-resistant.

If you send items that can fit nicely into bubble-padded envelopes, use them. This type of envelope is perfect for mailing small items or clothing using First Class mail. The envelopes are available in quantity (an economical choice) and don't take up much storage space. Table 1-1 shows you the industry-standard sizes of bubble envelopes and their suggested use.

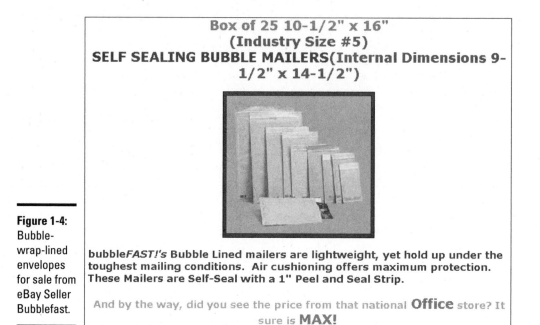

Box of 25 10-1/2" x 16"
(Industry Size #5)
SELF SEALING BUBBLE MAILERS(Internal Dimensions 9-1/2" x 14-1/2")

bubble*FAST!'s* Bubble Lined mailers are lightweight, yet hold up under the toughest mailing conditions. Air cushioning offers maximum protection. These Mailers are Self-Seal with a 1" Peel and Seal Strip.

And by the way, did you see the price from that national **Office** store? It sure is **MAX!**

Figure 1-4:
Bubble-wrap-lined envelopes for sale from eBay Seller Bubblefast.

Table 1-1		Standard Bubble-Padded Mailer Sizes
Size	*Measurements (in Inches)*	*Suggested Items*
#000	4 x 8	Collector trading cards, jewelry, coins
#00	5 x 10	Postcards, paper ephemera
#0	6 x 10	Doll clothes, CDs, DVDs, Xbox or PS2 games
#1	7 1/44 x 12	Cardboard-sleeve VHS tapes, jewel-cased CDs and DVDs
#2	8 1/2 x 12	Clamshell VHS tapes, books
#3	8 1/2 x 141?2	Toys, clothing, stuffed animals
#4	9 1/2 x 141?2	Small books, trade paperbacks
#5	10 1/2 x 16	Hardcover books, dolls
#6	12 1/2 x 19	Clothing, soft boxed items
#7	14 1/2 x 20	Much larger packaged items, framed items, plaques

Mechanizing your labeling

Printing labels on your printer is convenient until you start sending out a dozen packages at a time— then cutting the paper and taping the label gets too time-consuming. Plus, those cut-out labels are not professional. I highly recommend you do yourself a favor and get a label printer. Yes, they can be expensive, but you can find some great deals on eBay. I bought my heavy-duty, professional Eltron Zebra 2844 thermal label printer on eBay for one-fourth the retail price. (Search eBay for *zebra 2844*.) It's saved me countless hours. Another good label printer for beginners is the Dymo LabelWriter 4XL.

Boxing your items

Depending on the size of the items you sell, you can purchase boxes in bulk at reliable sources. Because you have a resale number, look in your local yellow pages for wholesale boxes (you still have to pay tax, but the resale number identifies you as a business and often can result in lower prices). Try to purchase from a manufacturer that specializes in B2B (business-to-business) sales. Some box companies specialize in selling to the occasional box user.

You also need to know a little about what it takes to make a sturdy box. The *de facto* standard for quality in general-use shipping boxes is 200-pound double-wall corrugated.

You can save big money if your items fit into boxes that the post office supplies and you plan on using Priority Mail. The U.S. Postal System (USPS) will give you all the boxes and mailing envelopes you need free, and it offers plenty of sizes. See Table 1-2 for available sizes.

Table 1-2	Free Priority Mail Packaging
Size (in Inches)	*Description*
7 9/16 x 5 7/16 x 5/8	DVD box
9 1/4 x 6 1/4 x 2	Large video box (#1096L)
7 9/16" x "5 /16" x "1-3/8	Electronic media
5 3/8" x 8 5/8" 1 5/8"	Small flat-rate
11 1/2" x 13 1/8" x 2 3/8"	Medium (#1097)

(continued)

Table 1-2 *(continued)*

Size *(in Inches)*	*Description*
11-7/8" x 3-3/8" x 13-5/8"	Flat-rate medium (FBR2)
12 3/8 x 15 1/4 x 3	Large (#1095)
12 1/8" x 13.3/8" x 2 3/4"	Medium (#1092)
10" x 7" x 4 3/4"	Regional Rate A1
10 15/16" x 2 3/8" x 12 13/16"	Regional Rate A2
12" x 10 1/4" x 5"	Regional Rate B1
14 3/8" x 2 7/8" x 15 7/8"	Regional Rate B2
14 3/4" x 11 3/4" x 11 1/2"	Regional Rate C
6 x 38	Large triangle tube
6 x 25	Small triangle tube
7 x 7 x 6	Small square (BOX4)
12 x 12 x 8	Medium square (BOX7)
11 x 8 1/2 x 5 1/2	Medium flat-rate (FBR1)
23 11/16" x 11 3/4" x 3	Large board game flat-rate
12" x 12" x 5-1/2"	Large flat-rate box
7.5 X 5.125 X 14.375	Priority Mail shoebox
11.625" X 15.125	Tyvek envelope
9 1/2" x 12 1/2"	Padded flat-rate envelope
6 x 10	Cardboard envelope
12 1/2 x 9 1/2	Flat-rate cardboard envelope
5 x 10	Cardboard window envelope

To order your boxes, labels, forms, and just about anything else that you'll need to ship Priority Mail, go to the Postal Store (see Figure 1-5) at `http://shop.usps.com/`. Orders can take up to a month to arrive, so be sure to order before you need more boxes.

Figure 1-5:
Order shipping supplies from the USPS.

Buying Postage Online

In 1999, the United States Postal Service announced a new service: *information-based indicia* (IBI) postage that you can print on envelopes and labels right from your PC. In this section, I give you the details on the two main Internet postage vendors:

✦ Endicia at

    http://www.endicia.com/

✦ Stamps.com at

    http://www.stamps.com/welcome/custom/home01/index86.
    html

You can buy postage and print your labels directly from eBay. If you have plans to sell on other platforms or your website, it may be best to have your own software on your computer.

Free USPS package pick up

Yes! Some things *are* free! If you print electronic postage for just one Priority Mail or Express Mail package through one of the vendors mentioned in this section, you can request a free pickup for all your packages. Go the post office's website at www.usps.com and type *carrier pickup* in the search box — or go directly to http://carrierpickup. usps.com. You can request a next-day pickup as late as 2:00 a.m. CT.

Okay, I'm a savvy-enough consumer and businesswoman that I don't believe in paying for extras — nor do I believe in being a victim of hidden charges. The online postage arena — while providing helpful tools that make running your eBay business easier — is fraught with bargains, deals, and introductory offers. I urge you to read these offers carefully so you know what you're getting yourself into: Evaluate how much it will cost you to start *and to maintain* an ongoing relationship with the company. Although you may initially get some free hardware and pay a low introductory rate, the fine print might tell you that you've *also* agreed to pay unreasonably high monthly prices six months down the line. I always double-check pricing before getting into anything, and I urge you to do the same.

Endicia

At the beginning of PC graphics in the early '90s, I attended a cutting-edge industry trade show. I had a successful graphics-and-advertising business, so I was interested in the latest and greatest innovations to bring my business off the light table and onto my computer. In a smallish booth were a couple of guys peddling new software that enabled artists to design direct-mail pieces from the desktop. What an innovation! Their inexpensive software even let you produce your own bar coding for the post office. I fell in love with that software and used it throughout my graphics career.

That program, DAZzle, combined with the originators' patented Dial-A-Zip, became the basis for today's software that is distributed to all Endicia customers. There isn't a more robust mailing program on the market.

Endicia has all the features of PayPal shipping and more:

✦ **Buy your postage online:** With a click of your mouse, you can purchase your postage instantly using your credit card or by direct debit from your checking account. You can register your preferences when you sign up with Endicia, and you get a Price Advisor, as shown in Figure 1-6.

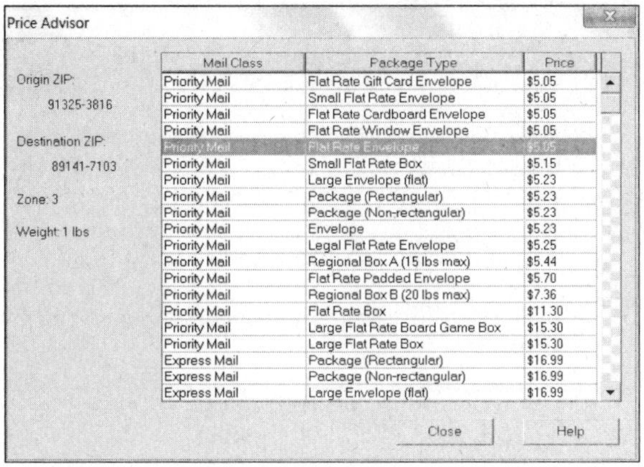

Figure 1-6: Endicia offers a Price Advisor that checks for the lowest shipping rates.

✦ **Print postage for all classes of mail, including international:** From Anniston, Alabama, to Bulawayo, Zimbabwe, the DAZzle software not only prints postage but also lists all your shipping options and applicable rates. For international mailing, it also advises you as to any prohibitions (for example, no prison-made goods can be mailed to Botswana), restrictions, necessary customs forms, and areas served within the country.

✦ **Print customs forms:** You no longer have to go to the post office with your international packages. Just print the customs form from the DAZzle software and give the package to your letter carrier.

✦ **Free tracking numbers on Priority Mail, First Class, and Standard Post:** Delivery confirmations may be printed also for Media Mail for only $.20.

✦ **Mailpiece design:** Endicia Internet postage is based on DAZzle, an award-winning mailpiece design tool that lets you design envelopes, postcards, and labels with color graphics, logos, pictures, text messages, and rubber stamps. You can print your mailing label with postage and delivery confirmation on anything from plain paper (tape it on with clear tape) to fancy 4 x 6 labels in a label printer from an extensive list of label templates.

✦ **Integration with insurance:** If you've saving time and money using U-PIC (a private package insurer — see Chapter 3) or Endicia's own insurance, you can send your monthly insurance logs electronically at the end of the month — a service integrated into the DAZzle software. There's no need to print a hard copy and mail in this information.

✦ **No cut-and-paste necessary:** Endicia software integrates with most common software programs. With the DAZzle software open on your computer, highlight the buyer's address from an e-mail or the PayPal site and then press Ctrl+C. The address automatically appears in the DAZzle postage software. No pasting needed.

Book VII Chapter 1

Organizing Your Merchandise and Shipping Area

Getting the "Commercial Base" discount

Printing your postage electronically (online) gives a real benefit; the Commercial Base Price reduction, which is available for Priority Mail and Express Mail. For Priority Mail packages weighing 10 pounds or less, commercial base prices average 13 percent lower than retail (at the post office) prices, and are based on zone and weight. For Express Mail, the commercial base prices are 3.5 percent lower than the retail prices.

For international shipping, you'll get 5- and 8-percent discounts on Priority Mail International and Express Mail International.

Endicia offers two levels of service. All the features just listed come with the standard plan. Their premium plan adds customizable e-mail, enhanced online transaction reports and statistics, business reply mail, return shipping labels (prepaid so your customer won't have to pay for the return), and stealth indicias.

The *stealth indicia* (also known as the *postage-paid indicia*) can be an awesome tool for the eBay seller. By using this feature, your customer will not see the exact amount of postage you paid. This permits some of your trade secrets to remain . . . um, secret.

With all these features, you'd think that Endicia's service would be expensive, but it's not. The standard plan is $9.95 a month, and the premium plan is $15.95 a month. For a free 60-day trial just for my readers, go to my "friends" page at Endicia (as shown in Figure 1-7) at

www.endicia.com/coolebaytools

eBay and PayPal shipping services

eBay continues to add great features for sellers. Now you cannot only buy postage and ship with USPS through eBay but also print labels on your own printer. If you ship lots of items and use a different service for printing your postage, both eBay and PayPal allow you to input tracking information on the site. Just click the Add Tracking Info link for the transaction on PayPal, as shown in Figure 1-8. Input the USPS, UPS, or other shipping company's tracking or delivery-confirmation information (see Figure 1-9), and PayPal sends an e-mail to your buyer with that information.

Figure 1-7:
My friends get a 60-day free trial. Be my friend and save!

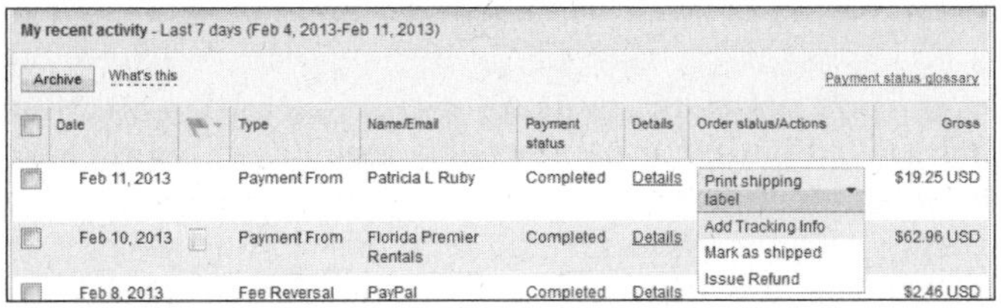

Figure 1-8:
Choosing to add tracking information.

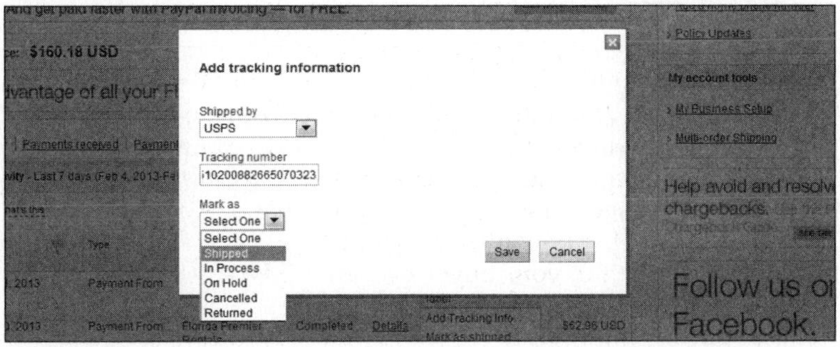

Figure 1-9:
Adding the shipper's tracking number and status.

The information you added appears in both the record of your PayPal transaction and the buyer's record in their account, as shown in Figure 1-10.

Figure 1-10:
Tracking
becomes
part of the
sales record
on your My
eBay page.

> **Sale status & notes**
>
> **Status Summary** (Sale Date: Feb-11-13)
>
> Checkout: Feb-11-13   Payment Date: Feb-11-13   Shipment Date: Feb-11-13
> Last email sent: Feb-11-13 (2)   Feedback sent: Yes   Feedback received: No
>
> **Payment Information**
> ☑ $ Payment received on   Paid with
> 02 / 11 / 2013   PayPal
>   PayPal Transaction Details
>
> **Shipping Information**
> ☑ Shipped on   Shipping via
> 02 / 11 / 2013   Standard Shipping
>
> Tracking # 9405510200882665070323
> USPS
> Edit Tracking Number

eBay shipping services work great when you're just starting out in your business — but after you get rolling, you need a mailing service that includes e-mail and recordkeeping, such as Endicia or Stamps.com. The issue connected with using eBay for shipping is important: When you process your shipping (UPS or USPS), the shipping amount is deducted from your PayPal (sales revenue) balance. I like to keep my expenses separate in my book-keeping process.

If you're starting a business in earnest, you need to keep track of your online expenses separately. Allowing PayPal to deduct your shipping costs from your incoming revenue can create a bookkeeping nightmare. You need to have exact figures for expenses and income — and it helps keep confusion to a minimum when your deposits (withdrawals from your PayPal account to your bank) match your sales receipts. If you want to ship through eBay, be sure you withdraw your sales amount to your checking account *before* you process your shipping. That way your shipping can be charged to your business credit card for easier tracking.

To purchase postage and print your label for a specific purchase, click the Print Shipping Label button next to the payment record in your PayPal account overview. You'll be taken through a step-by-step process for paying for your shipping and printing the appropriate label on your printer.

Stamps.com

Stamps.com purchased 31 Internet postage patents from e-stamp, making its services a combination of the best of both sites. (e-stamp discontinued its online postage service late in 2000; I was a big fan.) Many eBay sellers moved their postage business over to Stamps.com.

Stamps.com works with software that you probably use every day, such as Microsoft Word, Outlook, and Office; Corel WordPerfect; and Intuit. Here are some features you might enjoy:

+ **Use your printer to print postage.** If your printer allows it, you can even print your envelopes along with bar-coded addresses, your return address, and postage. This saves quite a bit in label costs.

  The Stamps.com Envelope Wizard permits you to design your own envelopes, including a logo or graphics. You can purchase a box of 500 #10 envelopes for as little as $4.99 at an office supply store.

+ **Have Stamps.com check that your addresses are valid.** Before printing any postage, the Stamps.com software contacts the USPS database of every valid mailing address in the United States. This Address Matching System (AMS) is updated monthly.

+ **Have Stamps.com add the extra four digits to your addressee's ZIP code.** This nifty feature helps ensure swift delivery while freeing you of the hassle of having to look up the information.

Purchasing postage is as easy as going to the Stamps.com website and clicking your mouse. Your credit card information is kept secure on its site. With Stamps.com, you don't *need* any extra fancy equipment, although most introductory deals come with a free 5-pound-maximum postal scale. The scale also functions on its own. Serious users should get a better-quality postage scale from a seller on eBay or through Office Depot.

Because Office Depot delivers any order more than $50 free the next day, it's a great place to get paper and labels. Better buys on scales, though, can be found on eBay, especially if you search *postage scale*. I use a super-small, 50-pound-maximum scale that I bought on eBay for under $20.

Stamps.com charges a flat rate of $15.99 per month. The site regularly offers sign-up bonuses that include as much as $20.00 free postage or a free 5-pound-maximum digital postage scale. To find the Stamps.com deal of the month, visit its website at

```
http://www.stamps.com/welcome/custom/home01/index86.html
```

**Book VII
Chapter 1**

**Organizing Your
Merchandise and
Shipping Area**

Chapter 2: Shipping without Going Postal

In This Chapter

✓ Understanding the overall shipping process

✓ Checking out different shippers

✓ Signing up with FedEx

✓ The good ol' United States Postal Service

✓ Using UPS

✓ Shipping directly from eBay and PayPal

The best part of an eBay business is making the sale and receiving payment. After that comes the somewhat tedious process of fulfilling your orders. You shouldn't feel bad if this is the point that makes you pause and sigh. Order fulfillment is one of the biggest challenges that face any online enterprise.

But as an eBay entrepreneur, you *must* attend to these tasks, however much you'd rather not. In this chapter, you explore your shipping options. I give you the lowdown on the three major carriers — FedEx, UPS, and the U.S. Postal Service — so you can see who fits your requirements. (For the scoop on insurance coverage, see Chapter 3 in this minibook.)

Shipping: The Heart of Your Business

Shipping can be a make-or-break point for eBay sellers. Being expert at knowing the correct carrier, box size, and packaging will affect your bottom line. Even if the selling portion of your transaction goes flawlessly, the purchased item has to get to the buyer in one piece. If it doesn't, the deal could be ruined — and so could your reputation.

U.S. postage at a big discount!

I just had to share this with you! The figure shows a picture of an envelope I received for an eBay purchase. I had to e-mail the seller to find out how and why she used so many stamps.

The seller is a collector of U.S. postage. She checks out eBay auctions and buys deals on old sheets of mint state stamps. United States stamps, no matter how old, are always good, so she buys these stamps at discount and uses them on her eBay packages. However, she did mention that when she brings her packages to the post office, all the clerks scatter to take a break!

As a footnote, I just checked eBay and found a whole lot of United States postage stamps selling for under face value! Like a *1997 Mars Rover Pathfinder* $3.00 Sheetlet that went for $1.99. The hint to finding these deals is to search for the type of stamp — but don't include the word *stamp* in your keyword search — and then select the Stamps category. Other sellers for this sheetlet grossed as much as $6.00 for the stamp. I guess some sellers will never learn.

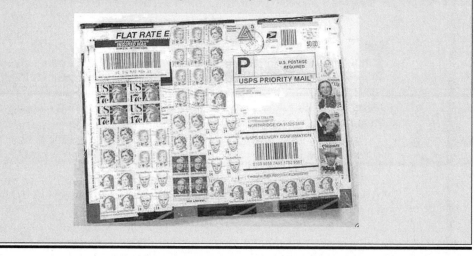

The best way to avoid shipping problems is to do your homework beforehand, determine which method is likely to work best, spell out how you intend to ship the item, and charge accordingly. I offer more than one shipping option — including overnight — to satisfy the buyer who may want a specific method of shipment.

Shipping is the heart of an e-commerce business like yours. Don't even think of selling an item without evaluating your shipping options:

1. **Before listing the item, figure out how the package will ship.**

You don't have to package it up right away, but you should have reviewed your options. The two critical factors in shipping are weight and time. The more a package weighs — and the faster it has to be delivered — may or may not reflect higher costs. The time to think about packing and shipping is *before* you put the item up for sale.

2. **Know your carrier options.**

In the United States, the three main shipping options for most eBay transactions are the U.S. Postal Service, FedEx, and UPS. See the section "Shopping for a Shipper" (try saying *that* five times fast) for information on how you can get rate options from each service, painlessly and online.

3. **Before estimating shipping costs to price your item, make sure that you include all possible fees.**

Keep in mind that if your item will sell for over $250, PayPal will require signature delivery in case the package goes missing and the buyer makes a claim. Paying for this option for United States Postal Service (USPS) packages will set you back $2.70, as opposed to the free (if you use electronic postage) Delivery Confirmation (tracking number).You should also include any insurance costs. (For more on insurance see Chapter 3.)

If you offer free shipping, your item will receive preference in eBay's search. Consider this option by building shipping costs in the item price. This works best when an item is light and can be shipped cheaply — while not sacrificing speed. At the very least, offer a flat rate to all your customers.

eBay's policy reads as follows:

"By providing shipping details in your listing, you can manage buyer expectations from the start. This helps avoid confusion with unexpected shipping costs, and shipping and handling time."

If you offer free shipping in your listing and eBay can confirm that the buyer did not pay extra for shipping, you will automatically receive a 5-star rating on your shipping and handling charges as part of your Detailed Seller Ratings

It's best to post a flat shipping amount (or use the eBay online shipping calculator) to give buyers an idea of how much shipping will cost. This way, buyers can consider the extra cost when comparing different sellers who offer the same item. Figure out what the packed item will weigh and then estimate shipping costs; the online calculators can help.

Keep in mind, though, that if your idea of reasonable shipping costs doesn't jibe with those of your buyers, you may end up with a ding in your DSR feedback rating for shipping fees.

If the item is particularly heavy and you need to use a specialized shipping service, be sure to say in your listing description that you're just giving an estimate and that the final cost will be determined prior to shipping.

Shipping calculations can be off target, and you may not know that until after you take the buyer's money. If the mistake is in your favor and is a biggie, notify the buyer and offer a refund. But if shipping ends up costing you a bit more, take your lumps and pay it. You can always let the buyer know what happened and that you paid the extra cost. Who knows, it may show up on your feedback from the buyer! (Even if it doesn't, spreading goodwill never hurts.)

4. **Ship the item as soon as your receive payment; eBay bases shipping time on your selection of carrier, as in Figure 2-1.**

   Make sure you ship the item to arrive in the time that eBay estimates. Ship that package no more than a day or so after payment (or after the e-check clears). If you can't, immediately e-mail the buyer and explain the delay.

Figure 2-1:
The customer knows up front when the item should arrive.

Shipping:	**FREE** Expedited Shipping | See details
	Item location: **Sag Harbor, New York, United States**
	Ships to: **Worldwide**
Delivery:	On or before **Tue. Feb. 19** to 91325
	Estimated by eBay **FAST 'N FREE** ⓘ
Payments:	*PayPal*, Bill Me Later | See details
Returns:	14 days money back, buyer pays return shipping | Read details

When you input the tracking number into the PayPal transaction detail, a follow-up e-mail will automatically be sent to let the buyer know the item's on the way.

Why not include a thank-you note (a receipt would be a businesslike addition) in each package you send out — I always do. As a customer I also appreciate this courtesy. It always brings a smile to the recipient's face. It never hurts to take every opportunity to promote goodwill (and future business and positive feedback).

Shopping for a Shipping Carrier

When you're considering shipping options, you must first determine what types of packages you'll generally be sending (small packages that weigh less than two pounds or large and bulky packages) and then decide how you'll send your items.

Planning before listing the item is a good idea.

Deciding on your carrier can be the most important decision in your eBay business. You need to figure out which one is more convenient for you (located close to your home base, provides pick up service, gives better customer service) and which is the most economical. Settling on one main shipper to meet most of your needs is important because all your records will be on one statement or in one area. However, you may also need a secondary shipper for other types of packages.

Shipping can make or break your customer service. Whoever delivers the package to the buyer is an extension of your company. Professional labels, clean boxes, nifty packing peanuts — those are the things you control. Safe and timely delivery falls into the hands of complete strangers, but the buyer will blame you for the tardiness or sloppiness of the shipping. Your bottom line isn't the shipper's, and no matter how many refunds they offer when they don't meet their promised schedules, it won't help when you have irate customers. Simple equation: Irate customers = lousy feedback.

So what's a seller to do? Do you use the shipper that other sellers rave about? Perhaps opt for convenience or low price? After you decide on a shipper, how often do you re-evaluate its services?

The rest of the chapter will help you with this decision.

Meeting your front line

Who constitutes the front line of your eBay business? My shipping front line is Scott, the UPS man; George, the Post Office carrier; and Ken, who picks up for FedEx Ground. I know the front-line guys because they help my eBay business run smoothly. They don't leave deliveries outside under a bush, and they deliver packages to my neighbor if I'm not home. They pick up my sundry packages with a smile and a lighthearted "They're sure buying things on eBay, aren't they?" I respond with a smile and a bit of friendly chitchat.

Wait, are you telling me that you don't get the same service? Have you ever taken a moment to chat with your delivery person? When you personalize a business relationship (such as addressing the person by name), you become more than a street address, you become . . . well . . . a *person*. When you're no longer a number, you become a fellow human being with needs and wants. Believe it or not, people *want* to make other people happy.

I leave a signal when there are packages to be picked up, and every one is picked up. When somebody delivers a big box, it goes to the back door near my studio, so I don't have to drag it through the front door and across the house.

Try building a relationship with your shipping front line. I've invited them to company holiday parties and offered them a cool drink on a hot summer day. The result? My shipping is the easiest part of my business.

Location, location, location

What happens if you have to drop off your packages for shipment? It's important to consider the closest local drop-off point for your carrier. Each of the major carriers has a search feature on its website to find the nearest drop-off location. You input your address or ZIP code, and the feature tells you the locations closest to you.

To get the location lowdown quickly, go to the following sites:

✦ **FedEx:** www.fedex.com/us/dropoff

✦ **USPS:** www.usps.com/locator/welcome.htm

✦ **UPS:** www.ups.com/dropoff

Be sure to read the details about each location online. Different fees may be involved in dropping off packages. Some locations may accept certain types of packages and not others. Read the fine print.

Comparing prices

The consensus is that a particular method of shipping is cheaper for large items and another is cheaper for small packages. Each method has its own peculiarities.

Take a look at Table 2-1 and compare the pricing for certain types of packages, the prices are based on your business having an account (or printing USPS postage electronically). Retail counter rates are the highest, and daily pickup rates will be somewhat less. Trying to translate the rate charts for some major carriers can be a real challenge. I recommend you get pricing estimates directly from their websites or software after you open your account.

Know that there are extras for some services, so become familiar with the variations and hidden costs like preferred customer rates and gas fees. Home delivery adds up to $2.75 per package for UPS and FedEx packages. For example, USPS offers regional and flat-rate discounts (see further on).

Table 2-1	Rectangular Package Shipping Times and Costs (NY to LA)		
3-Day Services			
Weight (lbs)	USPS Priority*: 2–3 Days ($)	UPS Select: 3 Business Days ($)	FedEx Express Saver 3 Business Days ($)
1	6.51	18.85	16.50
2	9.88	21.90	19.20
3	13.40	25.20	21.70
4	16.13	28.30	24.80
5	18.70	30.60	27.80
6	21.42	34.40	31.55
7	24.05	37.80	34.65
8	27.01	41.30	37.85
9	30.03	44.45	40.75
10	32.66	47.50	43.95
5-Day or Longer			
Weight (lbs)	USPS Standard Parcel Select ($)	UPS Ground: 5 Business Days ($)	FedEx Home Delivery 5 Business Days ($)
1	5.78	9.76	7.21
2	9.71	11.17	8.27
3	11.69	12.86	9.13
4	13.06	13.75	9.80
5	13.81	14.90	10.32
6	14.67	15.27	10.55
7	15.54	15.78	10.85
8	16.40	16.69	11.38
9	17.27	17.72	12.09
10	18.13	18.89	12.89

Book VII Chapter 2

Shipping without Going Postal

Shipping the BIG stuff

When it comes to shipping heavy or big stuff, you have a few options. Because I like using FedEx, I check with FedEx Freight first. A friend once purchased four large heavy-equipment tires on eBay, and there was no way they could go with a regular carrier. We told the seller to place the tires on a pallet and secure them. They were picked up by FedEx Freight. Shipping was reasonable, but the caveat was that the shipment had to be delivered to a place of business, not a residential location.

The `www.freightquote.com` website negotiates rates with several major freight-forwarders. Before attempting to sell a heavy item, sign on to their website with the weight and dimensions of your shipment, and they'll give you a free quote on the spot.

If you plan on shipping a lot of packages via FedEx or UPS, it would behoove you to contact a representative to find out if they can offer you further discounts.

You, Too, Can Use FedEx

FedEx is world-famous for its reliable service. It's the number-one choice for all major companies who have to get packages on time. In 1978, FedEx introduced the slogan "When it Absolutely, Positively has to be there over-night" and has built its business on that promise. FedEx acquired Roadway Package Service (RPS) and formed FedEx Ground, which has a separate division called FedEx Home Delivery that delivers to residences. For the services they provide, you'll be happy to know they are still devoted to their on-time promise. Read on.

If you ever have an issue or a question about a FedEx shipment, you can reach their award-winning customer service staff on Twitter. Just address your Tweet to @FedEx.

FedEx Ground and Home Delivery

When FedEx's Home Delivery began, their slogan was "The neighborhood-friendly service that fits the way we live, work, and shop today." Although I rarely get warm fuzzies from my package delivery, this slogan brought meaning to the philosophy behind their service: to bring professional shipping to your home residence. Now FedEx Home Delivery is part of FedEx Ground, and offers low rates and high-quality service. They're the only shipper that offers a money-back guarantee on home service. They deliver until 8:00 p.m. *and* on Saturdays, but not on Mondays.

To open an account, visit the FedEx.com site, to learn more about FedEx, visit the Ground website, shown in Figure 2-2, at

```
http://www.fedex.com/us/fedex/shippingservices/
       package/ground.html
```

Figure 2-2: The FedEx Ground home page.

Even if you have a current FedEx, you need to sign on to add the Ground service (which includes Home Delivery). Registering for Ground service is even easier than registering on eBay, so give it a shot. (Check the next section to see how easy it is.)

I opened my FedEx Ground account through a link on the FedEx home page, and got the skinny on how to use the service. FedEx gives you a service schedule to let you know how long it will take your package to arrive at its destination (see Figure 2-3). The online calculator allows you to choose the option of home delivery, so you don't even have to look up alternative rates and charts.

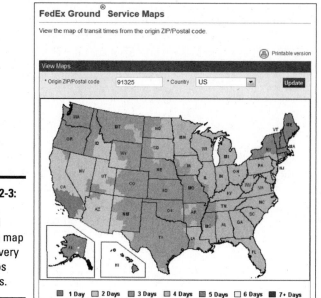

Figure 2-3:
FedEx
Ground
service map
for delivery
from Los
Angeles.

Here are a few fast facts about FedEx Ground services:

✦ You print your own labels and barcodes for your packages and track
them online.

✦ FedEx Ground works on a zone system based on your ZIP code and how
far the package is going. Refer to the FedEx Ground zone chart or get the
cost online through the online calculator.

✦ Each shipment is covered for $100 in declared value. Additional insur-
ance can be purchased (see Chapter 3 of this minibook).

✦ Residential deliveries are limited to 70-pound packages.

✦ Daily pick-up service adds an additional charge.

✦ Dropping off packages at FedEx counters (this includes all those handy
FedEx Kinko's locations) incurs no additional charge.

To find the closest drop-off location for your FedEx packages, go to www.
fedex.com/us/dropoff and type your ZIP code. Check that the location
accepts Ground, and check the cutoff times.

Signing up with FedEx

You sign up for a FedEx account only once, but it's a two-step process. If you just want to log in to the website, you can. At that point, decide whether you want to sign up for an actual, for-real FedEx account. When you have both a login and an account, you'll be able to ship your items quickly from your own private FedEx web space.

To get a FedEx account and be able to ship right away, follow these steps:

1. **Go to** www.fedex.com/us.

2. **On the left side of the screen, click the New Customer? Register Now link.**

   The FedEx registration page appears.

3. **Read the options on the FedEx page and decide how you wish to register online.**

   Click the appropriate link to either open a FedEx account, bring your existing account online, or if you ship only occasionally, get a user ID only.

4. **If you're signing up for a new account, click the Open a FedEx Account link.**

5. **On the resulting registration page, type the following information:**

   • **User ID:** Make up an ID you'll remember. (I tried my eBay user ID and it was already taken — I guess they have lots of customers.)

   • **Password:** Come up with a password you'll remember. For tips on selecting safe passwords, see Book IX, Chapter 4.

   • **Secret Question:** Input your password reminder, secret question, and answer. This way, if you ever forget your password or have to prove your identity to FedEx, you'll have a mind jogger.

   • **Contact information:** Type your name, company name (optional), address, city, state, e-mail address, and phone number.

   • **Agree to the terms of use:** If you want to ship via FedEx, you must agree to their terms. Click the link provided if you want some boring legalese to read. When you decide to play by their rules, click I Accept.

6. **Read the FedEx Terms of Use agreement (I'm sure you'll read every word) and then select the checkbox, indicating that you read and accept the terms.**

**Book VII
Chapter 2**

**Shipping without
Going Postal**

7. **Select the Open a FedEx Account option near the bottom of the registration page (if it's not already selected).**

8. **Click the Continue link.**

9. **Follow the prompts and input your credit card information.**

   Finally, you're presented with your very own nine-digit FedEx account number.

If you want to ship something now, click Start Using FedEx Ship Manager. Otherwise, log in later when you're ready to ship.

FedEx online

FedEx has one of the most intuitive online apps for shipping. The FedEx Ship Manager interface will turn your computer into a one-person shipping machine. You can search for rate quotes, track packages, and use the shipping notification option to send tracking information e-mails to your recipients.

To ship your item from the FedEx website, just Sign In and go to the online Ship Manager by clicking the Ship link. You'll be presented with a simple, all-in-one online waybill. Figure 2-4 shows you what it looks like.

You can copy and paste addresses from your PayPal account into the online form. Just highlight the text you want to copy and press Ctrl+C. To paste the text, place your cursor in the area you want to fill and press Ctrl+V.

When you're filling out the form, note some important entries must be made in Step 3 (not pictured):

✦ **Service type:** If you're shipping to a residence via Ground. Select Ground in the service type and be sure to place a check mark in "This is a Residence Address" in Step 2.

✦ **Dimensions:** Be sure that you know the proper dimensions for the package you're sending.

   If you sell repeat items in your eBay business, why not measure the boxes ahead of time and keep a list near your computer so you'll know the size? (For example: *Light kit 14 x 12 x 26.*)

✦ **FedEx Ship Alert:** Select the e-mail option to send the buyer (and yourself) a notice that the package was shipped and when it is delivered.

After you fill out the form, you can click the Courtesy Rate button at the bottom to get a shipping-cost estimate (not including any special discounts).

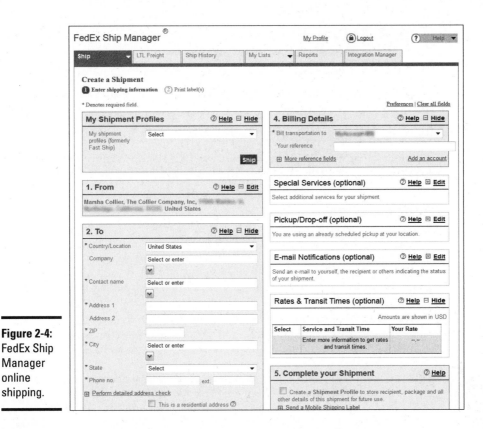

Figure 2-4:
FedEx Ship Manager online shipping.

When shipping with FedEx online, if your package is valued over $100 and you use U-PIC for your insurance (see Chapter 3 in this minibook), put $0 in the Declared Value box. Make note of the package on an insurance log and submit it to U-PIC.

Saving more by paying with American Express

If you have an American Express Business credit card (which also allows you access to the American Express Open Network), you can save even more on your FedEx shipments!

✔ **Save 5 percent** of all FedEx Ground shipments with your Open Savings Discount.

✔ **Save 12 to 21 percent additionally** on your FedEx Express shipments with the

Advantage program. Sign up for this program at `http://www.fedex.com/us/open-savings/index.html`

To be sure your American Express card is officially linked so you get the discount, call the FedEx/Open Network desk at 1-800-231-8636. As a member of the Open Network, you can also save money on other business needs.

Shipping with USPS

I'm a big fan of the U.S. Postal Service. Just ask my wonderful letter (er, multiple parcel) carrier, George. I use the post office for the bulk of my online sales because it's convenient and saves me money. In my 15 years selling items on eBay, they've never lost a package.

The USPS is open to everyone. You don't have to set up an account to use its services. To get a basic idea of what you'll pay to send a package, you can access a rate calculator on the USPS website (www.usps.com), shown in Figure 2-5.

Convenient and fast

The post office has worked hard to keep up with the competition in the parcel business by offering many online features and custom pickup. They also offer many classes of service, with a weight maximum of 70 pounds. Table 2-2 shows the transit times for services that are most popular with eBay sellers. Note that the USPS delivers packages seven days a week, the other major carriers count only five business days.

Figure 2-5: The United States Postal Service website.

Table 2-2		Most Popular USPS Services
Service	*Time to Cross the Country (Days)*	*What You Can Ship*
First Class	3–5	First Class mail can be used to mail anything, as long as it weighs 13 ounces or less. You can send a letter, a large envelope, or a small package.
Priority Mail	2–3	Priority Mail is just First Class mail on steroids (for heavier items).
Standard Post or Parcel Select	2-8	Standard Post is cheaper (and slower) than Priority Mail.
Media Mail	2-8	Media Mail is the least expensive way to mail heavy items. The only caveat is that you can use Media Mail to ship only books, film, manuscripts, printed music, printed test materials, sound recordings, scripts, and computer-recorded media such as CD-ROMs and diskettes.

**Book VII
Chapter 2**

Shipping without
Going Postal

Read on for details on the most popular forms of mail used by eBay sellers.

First Class

Good old regular mail — in particular, First Class — is the way we send bills and letters. It works also as an economical alternative for eBay items weighing up to 13 ounces.

Sending items in bubble-wrap envelopes will often get the shipping weight under the 13-ounce maximum for First Class mail.

Too many sellers make the jump to Priority Mail because they don't take the time to think about the weight of their items. It doesn't have to ship in an envelope to go via First Class mail.

Priority Mail

The two- to three-day Priority Mail service is the most popular form of shipping for eBay packages. There are three price options: Flat Rate. Regional

Rate, and weight/distance. You can get free cartons from the post office. (See Chapter 1 for a complete list of what the USPS supplies for your mailing needs.) You can also print postage online through Endicia (`http://www.endicia.com/`) or Stamps.com at

`www.stamps.com/welcome/custom/home01/index86.html`

See Chapter 1 for more about these postage options.

The Priority Mail rates are perfect for 1-pound packages (starting at $4.90 flat-rate cross-country when printed online) and 2-pound packages (from $5.80, based on distance). They also have a flat-rate Priority envelope in which you can jam in as much as possible (regardless of the package's final weight) for $4.90.

Because USPS rates are based on distance and weight, you can save money by using their new flat-rate Priority Mail boxes. (I've been able to jam quite a bit into them!) The new Regional Rate boxes (sizes A, B, and C) can be a deal with the medium size B box starting at $6.91. Flat-rate boxes ship anywhere in the United States for as little as $12.35 for a medium box.

The Priority Mail rates (including free shipping materials) are attractive until you get into heavier packages.

Standard Post (AKA Parcel Select)

If you want to use the USPS and have a heavy package (up to 70 pounds) that doesn't fit the requirements for Media Mail, use Standard Post (formerly Parcel Post). Even with the latest rate changes, USPS Parcel Post rates can be highly competitive when you compare them to the UPS or FedEx Ground rates.

When you print your postage electronically, this service is called Parcel Select. Standard Post is for those who buy postage at the Post Office.

Media Mail

To stay new and hip, the post office renamed its old Book Rate to Media Mail, causing many eBay sellers to mistakenly miss out on this valuable mailing tool. The savings are immense. The drawback is that you must mail only books, cassettes, videos, or computer-readable media. Transit time on Media Mail is at least 7to 10 days, but the cost savings on heavy packages may be worth it — as long as your customers realize how long transit time can be.

Understanding the costs

The Postal Service levies additional charges for some often-used services but also gives free services to online postage customers:

✦ **Pickup:** If you print your own postage from an online service (see Chapter 1) or print direct from eBay or the PayPal site, the post office offers free pickup, as shown in Figure 2-6. You have to give your packages to your carrier at the time of your regular delivery or schedule a pickup on the USPS site at

```
https://tools.usps.com/go/ScheduleAPickupAction!input.
action
```

✦ **Insurance:** This guarantees that you're covered if your package doesn't arrive safely and will reimburse you up to the value you declare when purchasing the insurance, up to a maximum of $5,000. If your package gets lost or severely mangled in shipping, the Postal Service will, after a thorough investigation (see Chapter 3), pay your claim. Fees start at $1.95 for packages up to $50. For discounted insurance, read Chapter 3.

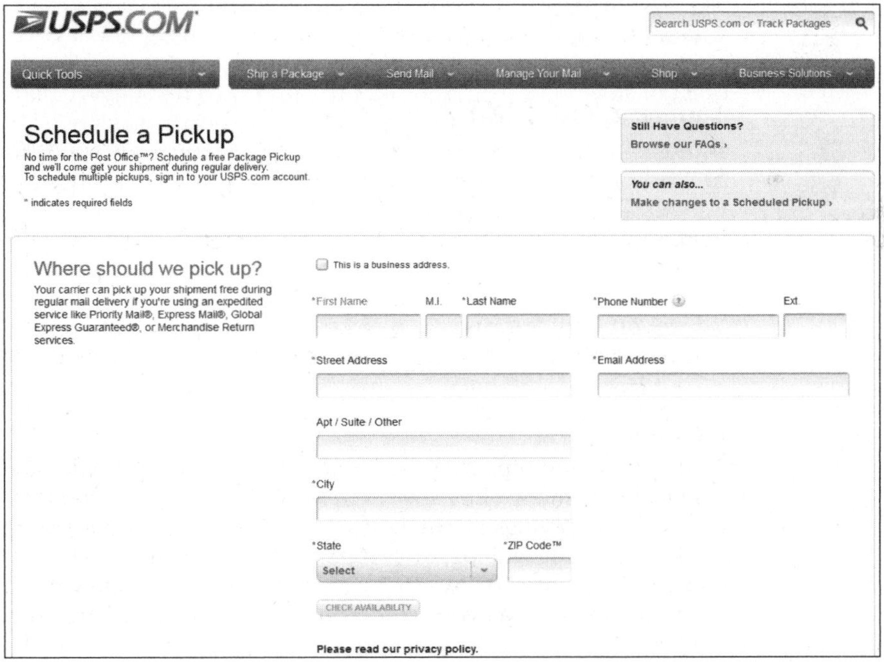

**Book VII
Chapter 2**

**Shipping without
Going Postal**

Figure 2-6:
Put in your request for pickup the day before your pickup day.

✦ **USPS Tracking:** Previously known as Delivery confirmation, USPS Tracking you'll get point-by-point tracking details. It also provides you with proof of delivery or attempted delivery. This number is included free for most postal services when you print your postage electronically. You can check the status of any package by submitting the number online at

```
https://tools.usps.com/go/TrackConfirmAction!input.
action
```

You can also verify a package's delivery by calling a toll-free number, 800-222-1811.

For a quick way to find out postal zones from your place of business, go to

```
http://postcalc.usps.gov/Zonecharts
```

Getting on the UPS Bandwagon

Today's UPS is a $45 billion company focusing on enabling commerce around the world. Every day UPS delivers more than 15.8 million packages and documents — I'm sure much of which represents eBay transactions.

UPS considers neither Saturday nor Sunday to be delivery days. So when your package is quoted for a 5-day delivery and those five days cross over a weekend, add two days to the delivery schedule. (The USPS and FedEx Ground deliver packages on Saturday.)

Here are some quick facts about UPS:

✦ Shipping with UPS requires that you pay a different rate for different zones in the country (zones 1–8). The cost of your package is based on its weight, your ZIP code (where there package ships from), and the addressee's ZIP code (where the package is going). To figure out your cost, use the handy UPS cost calculator shown in Figure 2-7.

✦ UPS offers a chart that defines the shipping time for your ground shipments.

✦ Each package has a tracking number that you can input online to verify location and time of delivery.

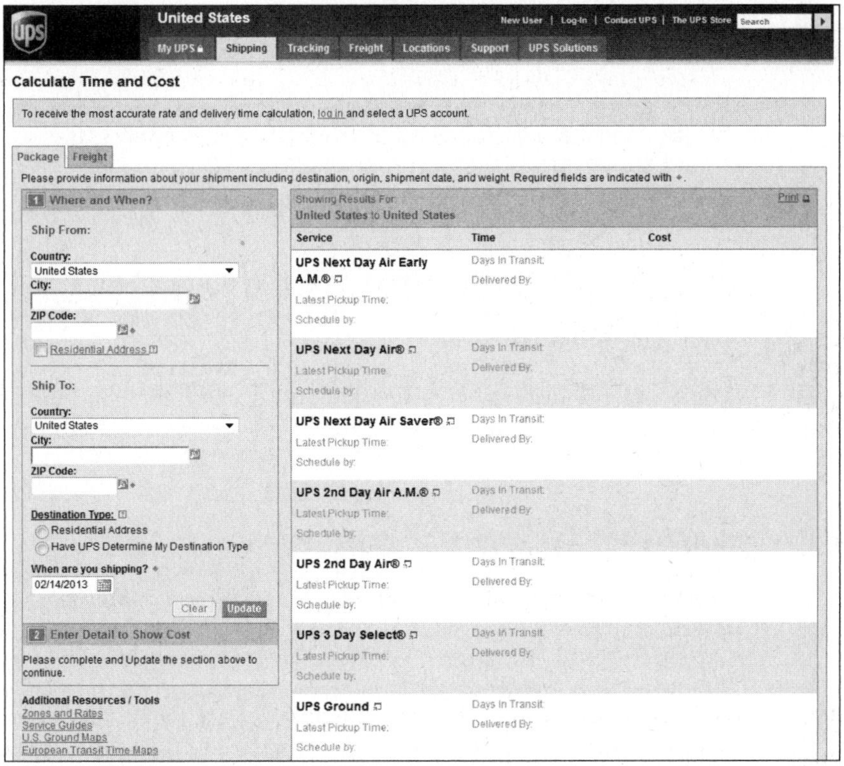

Figure 2-7:
The UPS cost (and transit time) calculator.

- ✦ Ground service delivery to a residence costs $2.80 (3 Day Select an additional $3.20) more than delivery to a commercial location.
- ✦ UPS delivers packages Monday through Friday.

Comparing costs

Although we always complain when the U.S. Postal Service raises their rates, you should know that all other shipping carriers raise their rates every year.

Annual rate increases are why being lulled into complacency can be dangerous. Evaluate your shipping charges and your shipper's fees every year to keep up with the increases and possible cuts into your bottom line.

While we all *think* that UPS Ground is cheaper than the post office, it's not true in every case.

Every UPS package is automatically insured for up to $100, assuming you declare a value. Insurance up to the first $300 is $1.80. After the first $300, it runs $.60 per $100. The post office charges extra for this service, but you can save money either way by using a private insurance policy for your packages (see Chapter 3).

The de-facto standard for eBay shipping is Priority Mail. Compared to UPS 3-Day Select, Priority Mail is the clear cost-saving winner if you must ship packages for swift delivery.

For heavier packages, UPS is considerably cheaper than Parcel Post for packages over 6 pounds. After your packages pass that point, and if time is *not* of the essence, UPS may be the best way to go.

Variable UPS rates

When you ship via UPS and are trying to figure out how to get the best rates, you have quite a conundrum. UPS basically has three rates for small-time shippers:

✦ **Retail rate:** This is the rate you pay when you go to the UPS Customer Center and they create the label for you. It's the most expensive. With the eBay/PayPal solution, you can save yourself some bucks by printing your own bar-coded labels and dropping the packages at the Customer Center or giving the packages to a UPS driver.

✦ **Standard rate:** Use UPS for the rare large box or heavy shipment. An on-demand, or occasional, shipper can call UPS for a next-day pickup. You have to pay an additional $2.75 per package for the driver to pick up from you if you don't feel like bringing the package to the UPS local counter.

✦ **Daily account:** When you hit the big time, you're able to get the lowest UPS rates and have a driver make daily stops to pick up your packages. Are you suffering from the delusion that it costs a bundle to have regular UPS package pickup service? (I was, too.) Surprise — it doesn't really.

Shipping Items through PayPal

I consider PayPal to be *de rigueur* (a *must have,* to all you non-French speakers) for all online sellers. By using PayPal, a seller can streamline the buyer's shopping experience, making it simple to buy, click, and pay. Along with all the timesaving tools PayPal supplies for the seller, they now offer online shipping services for items through the United States Postal Service or UPS at no extra charge. This is a convenient system for those who don't ship many packages each week because there's no need to use additional software or sign up with an additional service.

Sounds good so far, but (I hate the *buts* — don't you?) the PayPal postage system can make bookkeeping a nightmare for large-scale shippers. That's because PayPal withdraws the postage amounts directly from your PayPal account balance. This is problematic because the result is that your books won't balance: Your final deposits won't match your posted eBay or web sales.

You can make this arrangement work more efficiently by posting your PayPal sales to your bookkeeping program and *then* withdrawing your money before processing your shipping. Then you simply charge your shipping to a credit card, which will help you balance your books at month's end.

When you're ready to deal with shipping, you simply sign on to your PayPal account and handle it right on the site. To begin the shipping process, follow these steps:

1. **Log in to your PayPal account page.**
2. **Click the Print Shipping Label button next to the item in the row.**
3. **If this is your first time using PayPal labels setup your printer preferences by clicking in the upper-right corner.**

   Default printing preferences are set for any laser or inkjet printer with an 8.5 x 11 standard paper size.

PayPal shipping with the USPS

If you plan to use the ever-popular United States Postal Service, printing your postage and labels through PayPal gives you a free delivery confirmation with Priority Mail. A delivery confirmation is available also for Media Mail, Parcel Post, and First Class mail for a minimal charge.

After you've chosen USPS as your shipper, you'll see a confirmation page similar to the one shown in Figure 2-8. At the side of the page, your mailing address and the ship-to address are listed. After you've confirmed that this information is correct, fill out the details of the form, including

✦ **Service type:** Choose the level of mailing service you want for your package from this drop-down list. Priority Mail is usually the standard.

✦ **Package size:** From this drop-down list, select the type of package you're sending. Keep the following in mind:

- *Package/thick envelope:* Your package or envelope qualifies for this status if the length and girth (all the way around) is no more than 84 inches.

- *Large package:* Your package is larger than the preceding category, but doesn't exceed 108 inches in combined length and girth.

- *USPS flat-rate envelope:* These are handy Express and Priority Mail envelopes (available free from the USPS; see Chapter 1 for information on how to get them delivered to your door). They allow you to ship whatever fits into the envelopes at a flat rate, no matter how much the package weighs. (If you really stuff them, you can always reinforce your envelope with clear shipping tape — I do!)

✦ **Weight:** Here you enter the weight of your package.

✦ **Tracking Number:** Confirmation and Tracking is free with Priority Mail.

✦ **Signature confirmation:** Signature confirmation provides you a signature and date of delivery and is available for many levels of service. If you'd like a signature confirmation for your package, it will add $2.20 to the postage cost. You can track the progress of your package as it travels through the USPS online.

Don't forget that if you ship an item with a value over $250, PayPal requires signature confirmation for the item to be covered under the PayPal Seller Protection program.

✦ **Display postage value on label:** If you'd prefer not to show the amount of the postage on the label, do not check this box. That way, whatever handling fees you charge your customer are transparent.

On the other side of the coin, if you're trying to be a good seller (so you can receive great DSR ratings), you might not want to hide how much you actually pay for shipping. That way, the customer can see that you haven't padded the shipping fees to pad your wallet.

✦ **Add message to buyer e-mail:** Customer service to the fore! Put a check mark in the box and type a short note to let your customers know you appreciate their business.

✦ **Item(s) purchased by:** In this area you see the name of the item you're shipping and the buyer's eBay ID.

Purchase and print USPS postage

Manage your shipment | Tell us how we can improve this page | Help

Purchase and print USPS postage using PayPal. You can also purchase UPS postage.

First time users: ✕
Please setup your printer preferences here!

🖨 Printer and label receipt preferences

Order details

Item(s) purchased by 4u2buy4me2sell	Item price	Qty.	Shipping service	Expected delivery	Total
eBay for Dummies SIGNED Marsha Collier 2012 Paperback How to Sell on Book NEW	$21.70	1	USPS Media Mail	Feb 26, 2013	$21.70

Total shipping cost paid by buyer   Free

Order total $21.70

Ship from

Marsha Collier   [change]
▓▓▓▓▓▓▓▓▓▓▓
The Collier Company
Northridge, CA 91325-3816
United States

Shipping from:**91325-3816** ?

Ship to

▓▓▓▓▓▓▓▓▓▓   [change]
▓▓▓▓▓▓▓▓▓▓
Las Vegas, NV 89149
United States
Eligible for seller protection

☑ Add message to buyer email
This message will appear in the email with tracking information sent to the buyer.

Thank you for your
purchase!

Package Details ?

Service: [Compare delivery services]

Media Mail™ (2-8 days) - Package/Thick Enve... ▼

Up to 70 pounds and 84 inches in combined length and girth. Girth is the distance around the thickest part of the package. You certify to USPS that the contents of your shipment qualify for the Media Mail postage rate.

Weight: [Change dimensions]

1lb. or less ▼

▼ **Additional Options**

☐ Add Signature Confirmation™ (US $2.20)

☑ Add insurance (Cost varies based on package value)

☐ Print SKU/order number on label

Mailing Date

February 15, 2013 (Today) ▼

Your postage cost

Postage cost:	$2.53
Delivery Confirmation™:	$0.20
Total:	**$2.73**

☑ Display postage value on label

[Purchase postage]   [Review]

☐ Sign up for the Billing Agreement to skip login in the future and automatically use your PayPal balance to pay for shipping labels. See details

Up to 32% off

You're receiving discounted USPS rates
Learn more

Figure 2-8:
Setting up the details of your shipment.

When you've finished filling in the form and everything looks okay, complete your USPS shipping with these steps:

1. **Click Review.**

   The PayPal Shipping Center review page appears. All the information from the previous page is listed. If you've made a mistake at any entry, click Change next to the erroneous entry. Or if you prefer, you may click Cancel and start over.

2. **If everything looks okay, click Purchase Postage.**

   Unless you've agreed to automatic payment, you'll have to sign in to your PayPal account once again.

3. **Select your method of payment by clicking the arrow next to payment methods.**

   If you've withdrawn your PayPal balance to your bank, prior to printing your labels, you may select a credit card or bank account with which to pay for the postage.

4. **Click the Pay Now button.**

   Your preferred payment method is charged for the postage amount, and a new window opens to allow you to print postage on your printer.

5. **Print the label by clicking Print Label.**

   The label will look like the one in Figure 2-9.

Figure 2-9:
The printed label.

You can now request a pickup from the post office by clicking the Request Pickup link, which takes you directly to the USPS site.

PayPal shipping with UPS

Shippers such as UPS charge different rates based on how often you use their services. If you're shipping many packages a week, it might be best if you print your labels directly from the UPS site. All PayPal UPS shipments are charged the Occasional Shipper rate. If you only use UPS once in a while, the PayPal method will work perfectly for you.

If you've selected UPS as your shipper on the PayPal Shipping page, you're brought to a page with these choices:

✦ **UPS account:** You can open a new UPS account immediately online or, if you have an existing UPS account number, you may type the number in this field.

To open a new account, you have to verify your company data (it's already entered here from your PayPal account information) and let UPS know approximately how many packages you ship per week.

✦ **Shipping payment information:** You also have to indicate whether you'd like to pay for your shipping with your PayPal account, or if you'd like the shipping billed to your existing UPS account.

When you've finished filling in the form, finish by following these steps:

1. **Click Continue.**

You'll see a confirmation page.

2. **If the information is correct, click Continue.**

If any of the information is wrong, click Edit and go back and make your corrections.

3. **If the shipping agreement appears, read it and, if you agree, click I Agree.**

Now you're ready to print a label.

4. **Fill out the requested information.**

5. **Print the sample label.**

By printing a sample label, you make sure that your printer is working properly.

6. **Print the label by clicking Print Label.**

When your label has printed, you may elect to go back to your PayPal Overview page to track the package by clicking Check Shipment, as shown in Figure 2-10.

**Book VII
Chapter 2**

**Shipping without
Going Postal**

	Date		Type	Name/Email	Payment status	Details	Order status/Actions	Gross
	My recent activity | Payments received | Payments sent							View all of my transactions
	My recent activity - Last 7 days (Feb 8, 2013-Feb 15, 2013) ⚠							
	Archive What's this							Payment status glossary
☐	⊞ Feb 15, 2013		Payment To	eBay Inc Shipping	Completed	Details		-$2.73 USD
☐	Feb 15, 2013		Transfer To	Bank Account	Pending	Details		-$211.26 USD
☐	Feb 15, 2013		Payment From		Completed	Details	Print shipping label ▾	$72.99 USD
☐	Feb 14, 2013		Payment From		Completed	Details	Shipped, Track ▾	$21.70 USD

Figure 2-10:
Your PayPal
Overview
page after
shipping.

The items you've selected to ship will include a Check Shipment link, and the charges for your shipment will appear in your history log. to track the package's progress and confirm delivery, you may click the Check Shipment button at any time after you've shipped your item.

Chapter 3: Insuring Your Item's Delivery

In This Chapter

✔ Knowing your insurance options

✔ Addressing your packages correctly

✔ Filing a claim with the major carriers

This chapter reveals the practical link between insurance and timely delivery — and how the wise seller can use both to ensure a better experience for both buyer and seller. The key is an assumption: When someone buys an item from you, the buyer assumes that the item will be shipped in 24 to 48 hours (customers prefer a quick 24-hour turnaround). A little-known rule of the online world is the Federal Trade Commission's *30-day mail-order rule* that applies to all online sales, as well as to mail-order businesses.

Unless you (as the seller) state a specific shipping time, all items must be shipped within 30 days.

Adopted in 1975, this FTC rule proclaims these buyer's rights:

✦ The buyer must receive the merchandise when the seller says it will arrive, or earlier.

✦ If delivery is not promised within a certain time period, the seller must ship the merchandise to the buyer no later than 30 days after receiving the order.

✦ If the buyer doesn't receive the merchandise within that 30-day period, the buyer can cancel the order and get his or her money back.

This rule must be part of the reason why eBay won't allow items on the site for presale (or *drop-shipping*, detailed in Book IV, Chapter 4) unless you can guarantee that the item will be shipped within 30 days. In each of those cases, you must indicate in your description that the item is a presale or drop-ship.

Ensuring your peace of mind by insuring your shipment

Sure, "lost in the mail" is an excuse we've all heard hundreds of times, but despite everyone's best efforts, sometimes things do get damaged or misplaced during shipment. The universe is a dangerous place; that's why we have insurance. I usually offer to get insurance from the shipper if the buyer wants to pay for it, and I *always* get it on expensive, one-of-a-kind, or very fragile items. In my item description, I spell out that the buyer pays for insurance.

The major shippers offer insurance that's fairly reasonably priced, so check out their rates at their websites. But don't forget to read the details. For example, many items on eBay are sold MIMB (mint in mint box). True, the condition of the original box often has a bearing on the final value of the item inside, but the U.S.

Postal Service insures only what is *in* the box. So, if you sold a Malibu Barbie mint in a mint box, USPS insures only the doll and not the original box. Pack carefully so your buyer gets what's been paid for. Be mindful that shippers won't make good on insurance claims if they suspect that you caused the damage by doing a lousy job of packing.

Alternatively, when you're selling on eBay in earnest, you can purchase your own parcel-protection policy from a private insurer. When you use this type of insurance, combined with pre-printed electronic postage, you no longer have to stand in line at the post office to have your insured packaged logged in by the clerk at the counter.

Another thing comes to light here. Note that the rule states that the merchandise must be delivered in 30 days. The rule doesn't say "unless the item gets lost in the mail." This means that *you*, the seller, are responsible for your packages arriving at their destinations. This makes insurance more important than ever, especially on expensive items.

Insurance Options

When you're shipping a large amount of merchandise on a regular basis, you're going to have to deal with the issue of whether you buy insurance against damage or loss. You, as the seller, are responsible for getting the product to the buyer. The lost-in-the-mail excuse doesn't cut the mustard, and having a tracking number doesn't guarantee anything, either.

Buyers who don't receive items that they've paid for can file a fraud report against you. Buyers can also have the payment removed from your PayPal account, and you have no defense against this.

Self-insuring your items

Some sellers on eBay self-insure their packages. In other words, they take the risk and use money out of their own pockets if they have to pay a claim. In this sense, *self-insuring* is considered seller's jargon, not an official legal status (only licensed insurance agents can offer insurance).

These sellers are usually careful about packing their items to prevent damage. (Check out Chapter 1 to find out about choosing and finding packing materials.) They also use tracking numbers when using the Postal Service.

Savvy self-insurers usually do *not* self-insure items of high value. If you sell mostly lower-priced items (under $100) and decide to self-insure, consider making an exception when you do occasionally sell an expensive item. Bite the bullet and pay for the shipping insurance; doing so could save you money and hassle in the long run.

Insuring through the major carriers

All the major shippers are in the shipping business (duh), not in the insurance business. Insuring is an annoying — but necessary — sideline to their package-transit businesses.

Most carriers, other than the United States Postal Service, cover all shipments automatically (and at no extra charge) for the first $100 of package value. By the way, the *package value* of an item sold on eBay is the final bid (or Buy It Now) amount. Of course, you can always buy additional package insurance for your shipped items. Should a package get lost or damaged, making a claim opens an entirely new can of worms.

Note that FedEx and UPS clearly state that they offer "Declared Value Liability" instead of "insurance." Declared value indicates the carrier's liability for a shipment. Both carriers only cover up to $100, and you must pay fees shown in Table 3-1 for their additional liability coverage.

Table 3-1	Insurance/Liability Retail Rates for Commercial Carriers
Shipper	*Shipper Rate*
FedEx Declared Value	$0.85 per $100 (after first $100 of value) $2.55 minimum
UPS Declared Value	$100.01 to $50,000.00 (after first $100.00 of value) plus $.90 per each $100.00 (or part of $100.00) up to $50,000.00 $1.80 minimum

(continued)

Table 3-1 *(continued)*

Shipper	Shipper Rate
USPS	$1.95 for $0.01 – up to $50.00 value
	$2..45 for $50.01 – $100.00 value
	$3.05 for $100.01 – $200.00 value
	$5.10 for $200.01 – $300.00 value
	$5.10 for up to $300.00 value plus $1.15 for each additional $100 of value over $300.00

Getting private, discounted shipping insurance

If you think that printing your own postage is slick, you're gonna love electronic insurance. eBay offers insurance through ShipCover when you purchase postage and print labels through eBay. Your insurance value may be declared in any amount from the selling price of the item to a maximum of $1,000.

When you purchase ShipCover insurance to cover your USPS parcels through eBay, you are also charged a surplus line tax and stamping fee, as shown in Table 3-2.

As you know, USPS rates change from time to time, and those changes may not always show up immediately on the eBay site. Check for changes in postal rates at

```
http://pages.ebay.com/help/pay/shipping-insurance.
html#shipcover
```

Table 3-2 — ShipCover Insurance Prices (Domestic and International)

Insured value	Price in Addition to Postage	Surplus Line Tax*	Stamping Fee*
$0.01 to $100.00	$1.65	3%	None
$100.01 to $200.00	$3.30	3%	0.20%
$200.01 to $300.00	$4.95	3%	0.20%
$300.01 to $400.00	$6.60	3%	0.20%
$400.01 to $500.00	$8.25	3%	0.20%
$500.01 to $600.00	$9.90	3%	0.20%
$600.01 to $1,000.00	$9.90, plus $1.65 for every additional $100.00 over $600.00	3%	0.20%

An even less expensive alternative is the very popular Universal Parcel Insurance Coverage (U-PIC) service, which has provided discounted package insurance for over 22 years. U-PIC removes the post-office-insurance hassle because you can handle your insurance electronically. You can insure packages that you send through USPS, UPS, FedEx, and other major carriers. If you use U-PIC insurance on USPS-shipped packages, you can save as much as 80 percent on insurance rates.

U-PIC caters to individual eBay sellers amidst its many big-business clients through its relationship with Endicia. The insurance is built in to the DAZzle postage software.

Here are some great features of the U-PIC service:

✦ **No time wasted standing in line at the post office:** The U-PIC service is integrated into online postage solutions such as Endicia (described in Chapter 1 of this minibook).

✦ **Quick payments on claims:** If you have a claim, U-PIC pays it within 7 days of receiving all required documents from the carrier.

As with any insurance policy, assume that if you have many claims against your packages, you can be dropped from the service. (This thought only gives me more impetus to package my items properly — I never want to be banished back to the counter lines!)

✦ **Blanket approval:** U-PIC is approved by all major carriers. And turnabout is fair play: All carriers covered must be on the U-PIC approved carrier listing.

✦ **Savings:** Again, depending on the quantity and type of items you ship, using U-PIC may save you up to 85 percent on your insurance costs.

FedEx charge $.85 per $100.00 of package value with a $2.55 minimum. And UPS charges $0.90 per $100 with a $1.80 minimum. By using U-PIC, you can insure your FedEx and UPS packages for $.25 to $.40 per $100.00 value with no minimum. Table 3-3 compares U-PIC and USPS insurance rates.

Table 3-3	USPS and U-PIC Domestic Insurance Coverage Rate Comparison	
Coverage	*USPS*	*U-PIC*
$.01 to $50.00	$1.95	
$50.01 to $100	$2.45	$.25 - $.40
$100.01 to $200.00	$3.05	$.50 - $.80
$200.01 to $300.00	$5.10	$.75-$1.20

You can visit the U-PIC website (see Figure 3-1) and poke around, but to get the best information, call U-PIC at the toll-free number. A sales representative will explain to you exactly how to declare value based on your present system. At the end of each shipping month, you fax, e-mail, or snail-mail your shipping reports to U-PIC.

To apply for your own U-PIC policy — with no charge to apply and no minimum premium — go directly to the application on the website at `http://bit.ly/eBayBusiness`.

They're a great bunch of people — tell 'em Marsha sent ya!

To apply for the U-PIC service, you must fill out a Request to Provide (RTP) form. You must answer questions about who you are, how many packages you send, how many insurance claims you've filed in the past two years, and your average value per package. After you fill out the online form and agree to the policy (Evidence of Insurance), a U-PIC representative will contact you within 48 hours.

Figure 3-1: The U-PIC home page.

To place a claim with U-PIC on a USPS shipment, just go to the U-PIC website, click the Claims link, and then choose an option from the File a Claim Online menu. You must supply the following:

✦ A signed letter, stating the loss or damage from the consignee

✦ A completed U-PIC claim form (one claim form per claim)

✦ A copy of the original invoice or the end-of-auction form

If you're a high-volume shipper, you can negotiate an even lower rate with U-PIC. To reach U-PIC, call toll-free at 800-955-4623.

Avoiding Mistyped Addresses

Lost packages are the bane of all carriers. The post office has been dealing with this problem since they opened the Dead Letter Office in 1825. It was renamed as part of the USPS reorganization in 2011 to the MRC, or *Mail Recovery Center*.

The Mail Recovery Center employees (I'll call them MRCs) are the only people legally permitted to open lost mail. When an address label gets smooshed, torn, wet, or otherwise illegible — which means the box can't be delivered — it finds its way into the hands of the folks at the MRC, who open the package with the hope of finding enough information to get it to the rightful owner.

Book VII Chapter 3

Insuring Your Item's Delivery

Make sure that you always include a packing slip — like the kind you print from Selling Manager or My eBay — inside your packages. The packing slip should have both your address and the buyer's address so that if the label is illegible, the packing slip will identify the owner and the package can be delivered.

Of course, having the buyer's address correct on the label is critical to begin with. The following ideas and practices will help you create accurate shipping labels:

✦ **Copy and paste the buyer's address:** The safest way to correct addressing is to cut and paste the buyer's address information from an e-mail or the PayPal payment confirmation or download.

✦ **Don't depend on the carrier to correct an address:** No carrier is going to tell you whether the address you have is incorrect. The only time I've had inaccurate addresses corrected is when I used electronic postage printing.

✦ **Use software or online services to check your buyer's address:** It's good business practice to confirm the viability of an address before you send your item. Software such as DAZzle (from Endicia at www.endicia.com, which I discuss in Chapter 1) corrects most common addressing errors such as misspelled city or street names. If you have a question about a ZIP code, you can check it at the USPS website at www.usps.com/zip4. See how DAZzle verified the address in Figure 3-2?

If you have the Google toolbar (which I highly recommend in Book VIII), or go to www.google.com, you can type any UPS, post office, or FedEx tracking number and find the current tracking information from the carrier's website. Just copy and paste the tracking number into the Google search box and start your search. You'll come to a page that presents a link to track packages — with your number and carrier showing. Click the link and you end up at the carrier's site with all the current tracking information. Nice!

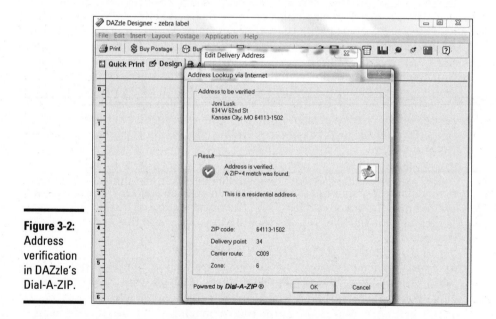

Figure 3-2: Address verification in DAZzle's Dial-A-ZIP.

Making a Claim When Shipping Goes Bad

If you've been selling or buying on eBay for a while, there's a chance that you've made a claim for lost or damaged packages. The process is often grueling — with all the paperwork that's involved — and the decision of the carrier is final. If you don't agree with the carrier, you could try small claims court. But realize that you'll lose a day of work — and when you're in court, you'll face all the legalese you find in the teeny-tiny print on the carrier's terms of service.

A couple of claim stories

Several years ago, I purchased an original-wardrobe uniform tunic from the *Star Trek* series that was framed and autographed by Leonard Nimoy. When it came, in an appropriate large box surrounded with lots of Styrofoam peanuts and bubble wrap, it also sported a 4" x 4" hole in the side, and it looked like someone had taken a sword to the box! Not only that, but there was a sad sound of glass tinkling when I shook the box. Oh, yes — the delivery man had dumped the box, rung the bell, and run.

The carrier couldn't argue about the damage. The claim department tried to give me the line that the item was packed incorrectly. (Does that mean it was sent with a big hole already in the side of the box?) Then they offered me a partial payment. Gee, I really wanted the glass-particle-infested, ripped tunic now. It took a while, but the damages were so obvious that the carrier had to give in and agreed to send a check to the seller. Upon hearing this decision, the seller refunded my payment. (I wonder how long the seller had to wait for *his* payment?)

There was also a dress that I sold and shipped Priority Mail. It never arrived. I had a boiling-hot buyer on the other end, but luckily, I had proof of mailing in the form of a delivery confirmation to show her. I nagged the post office about the package, but as you'll read in the section, "Filing a claim with the post office," you have to wait 30 days for a package to be *officially* declared lost. On the 29th day, the box was returned to me with no explanation or fanfare, and just a return-to-sender stamp on the front.

I understand the hassles because I've had to make several claims myself. I'd like to help you avoid similar unpleasant experiences, or at least make them less unpleasant. I present information about the U.S. Postal Service first because their claim process is more stringent than that of the other carriers. With any carrier, however, you need to gather the same type of backup information before making a claim.

Filing a claim with the post office

Making a claim with the post office: Oh man, talk about a hassle. But making a claim with any carrier isn't a bowl of cherries on any day. Before making a claim with the USPS, check to make sure your package was covered by postal insurance, purchased at the time of mailing. If you use private insurance instead, you make a claim with your insurance carrier, not the post office.

When a package is lost in transit, you must wait a minimum of 21 days after the mailing date before you make the claim. If an item arrives at the buyer's door damaged, you may make a claim with the post office immediately.

There's always a question as to who makes the claim:

+ **Damaged or lost contents:** Either the seller or the buyer can file the claim.

+ **Complete loss:** When a package has not turned up within 30 days, the seller files the claim.

You can file your claim online direct on the USPS site at

> https://www.usps.com/ship/file-insurance-claims.htm

If you want to make your claim at the Post Office, you must get a copy of *PS Form 1000, Domestic Claim or Registered Mail Inquiry*. Go to the post office or download it at

> http://about.usps.com/forms/ps1000.pdf

Fill out the form with all the details required and bring your backup information.

To make a damage claim, you must produce evidence of insurance. This can be either of the following documents:

+ **Original mailing receipt:** The receipt that was stamped at the post-office counter when the item was mailed.

+ **Original box or wrapper:** This must show the addresses of both the sender and the recipient along with whatever tags or stamps the post office put on the package to say it's insured.

You must also produce evidence showing the value of the item *when it was mailed*. The following list shows some of the documents accepted by the post office for damage claims (however, they may ask for more thorough proof):

+ Sales receipt or descriptive invoice

+ Copy of your canceled check or money order receipt

+ Picture and description of a similar item from a catalog if your receipt isn't available

+ A letter from the seller stating the value of the item

+ Your own description of the item, including date and time the item was purchased and whether it's new or vintage

Finding or buying lost packages

When the post office pays your claim, it will usually ask to keep your item. Your item and thousands of others will end up at one of the Mail Recovery Centers across the country. Here it joins the other lost and salvage mail to be sold, usually at auction.

Items valued over $5 are held for three months, and Registered Mail and insured packages are held for six months. Then they're auctioned. Formerly the "Dead Letter Office," the MRC has had several consolidations that have centralized the operation from four centers into one. The post office Mail Recovery Center is in Atlanta, GA.

Now the post office sells the stuff at via online auctions. If you'd like to check them out, go to www.govdeals.com/ and search for *Atlanta Recovery Center*. If you're interested in buying post-office surplus (such as an old truck or supplies), check out eBay seller usps-al-pmsc.

For missing packages, you (the seller) need a letter from the buyer (dated 30 days after the package was mailed) stating that the buyer never received the package.

If your buyer is too cranky to cooperate, go to the actual post office where you mailed the package. Ask for a written statement that there is no record of the delivery being made. Postal employees can look up the insurance or delivery confirmation numbers to find whether the delivery took place, but the post office will charge you $6.60 for their efforts. That amount will be reimbursed *if* the post office decides to pay your claim because it doesn't locate your package under a bale of hay in Indiana. If all goes well and your claim is deemed legit, you should get your payment within 30 days. If you don't hear from the post office within 45 days (maybe the payment got lost in the mail?), you have to submit a duplicate claim using the original claim number.

Note to self (and to you): Always make a copy of any form you give to the government.

Filing a claim with UPS

Whoa! The stories of filing claims with UPS are legendary. Almost any eBay seller can tell you quite a story. I must admit that making a claim with UPS is a good deal easier than making a claim with the post office. After they file and accept your damage claim, you get a check within five days.

For damaged packages, UPS recently streamlined the process, although the buyer must make the claim. You *can* (if you really want to) call 1-800-PICK-UPS (cute, eh?) to file your claim. The better idea is to try the online reporting feature by going to www.ups.com and clicking the File a Claim link. Be sure you make your report to UPS within 48 hours of delivery.

On the online claim form, you'll be asked to input all information about the package and the damage. UPS seems to be familiar with its own handiwork because you get to select your particular type of damage from a menu. After you've filled out and submitted the form, just sit on your haunches and wait for the UPS claims department to contact you.

I recommend that you print your form after filling it out so you can keep all claim reference information in one place.

After the buyer makes the claim, UPS sends a Damage/Loss Notification Letter form to the seller. The seller must fill out the form to state the item's value and attach supporting documentation. The form can then be faxed back to UPS for final verification.

Save the damaged item and all the packaging that it came in. UPS may send an inspector out to look at the package before they approve a claim.

If a UPS shipment appears to be lost, the seller must call UPS to request a package tracer. If UPS is unable to prove delivery, the claim is paid.

Filing a claim with FedEx

Filing a claim with FedEx is similar to the UPS procedure, except FedEx gives you a little more leeway as to time. Instead of the 48-hours-after-delivery deadline, you have 15 business days to make your claim. (This extra time sure helps out when a package is delivered to your house and you're out of town.) FedEx processes all Concealed Loss and Damage claims within five to seven days after receiving all the paperwork and information.

As with UPS, keep all packaging, along with the item, in case FedEx wants to come and inspect the damage.

You can make your FedEx claim in a couple of ways:

✦ **By fax:** You can download a PDF claim form with instructions at

www.fedex.com/us/customer/claims/Claims.pdf

Fill out the form and fax it to the number on the form.

✦ **Online:** Fill out the online claim form on a secure server by going to
www.fedex.com/us/ and clicking the File a Claim on a Package link.

You must have a FedEx login to begin your claim. (See Chapter 2 in this
minibook for instructions on how to get your login.) You still have to
mail or fax your supporting documentation. When you file online, you
can also choose to receive e-mail updates from FedEx regarding your
claim (good idea).

The claim payment will be sent to the seller, so it's up to the seller to make
restitution with the buyer. As the seller, you should refund the money as
soon as the claim is approved.

Power Selling on eBay

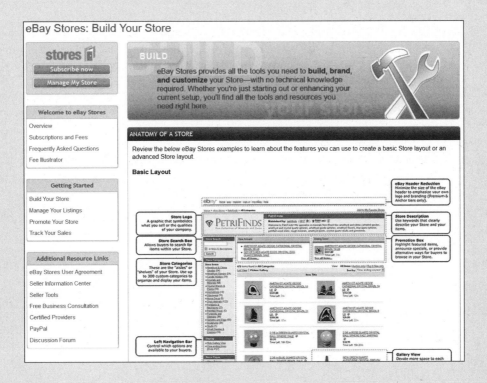

Visit www.dummies.com/extras/ebaybusinessaio and discover great tips for taking your online sales to the next level.

Contents at a Glance

Chapter 1: Going Pro with eBay's Selling Manager

In This Chapter

✔ **Signing up for free**

✔ **Understanding Selling Manager features**

✔ **Sending invoices**

✔ **Tracking your payments**

✔ **Relisting the easy way**

✔ **Downloading reports**

*O*nce the selling bug has bitten you, it's a natural transition to go from listing a few items a month to 50 or more. And that, dear reader, means you are officially running an eBay business. Congratulations! There's a good and a bad side to this increase. The good is that you're making considerably more money than you did before signing up with eBay. The bad? It's time to start investing in some tools to keep your business professional. This chapter gets you started with some of the best available tools.

The first tool that can help smooth your transition makes the process of running eBay sales consistent — Selling Manager. The next step is Selling Manager Pro; I talk about the differences later in this chapter.

Book III gets into eBay's free Turbo Lister program (it gets your items on the site and saves the listings for future use). As with Turbo Lister, Selling Manager and Selling Manager Pro are a suite of tools for managing your selling business from your My eBay page on any device (as long as it is Internet connected). eBay gives you this tool for free, but you've got to request it — and I tell you how to do that in this chapter. I also tell you how to navigate

Selling Manager (as well as the Pro version) to find the tools you need to manage your eBay business.

After you've gotten a taste of Selling Manager, you'll no doubt want to go Pro. The Pro version adds several advanced features such as automatic listing and relisting of items, automated payment, shipping status, and feedback to buyers. It costs $15.99 per month but is free for Premium and Anchored Store subscribers.

 I've run well over 60 listings at a time, successfully managing them with Selling Manager Pro. I use it along with PayPal and QuickBooks (see Book IX for more about this method). This approach provides a one-stop, professional solution for my medium-size eBay business.

Getting Selling Manager

So if you have some sales under your belt, go to the link I've included here to install the Selling Manager tool on your My eBay page. Point your browser to the following web address:

```
http://pages.ebay.com/sellerinformation/selling
resources/sellingmanager.html
```

On the Selling Manager information page, click the Subscribe Now button. After eBay confirms your login information, the system will begin populating your Selling Manager with your information from the My eBay Selling area. And the Selling link on the side navigation area changes to Selling Manager.

You can click the Selling Manager link to view a summary of your sales activities. Figure 1-1 shows a brand new Selling Manager Summary page. (The Selling Manager and Selling Manager Pro pages look very much the same.)

The Summary page lists at-a-glance statistics so you can see what's going on with your sales quickly, at any time. Links to other pages are included at the bottom of the Selling Manager Summary page.

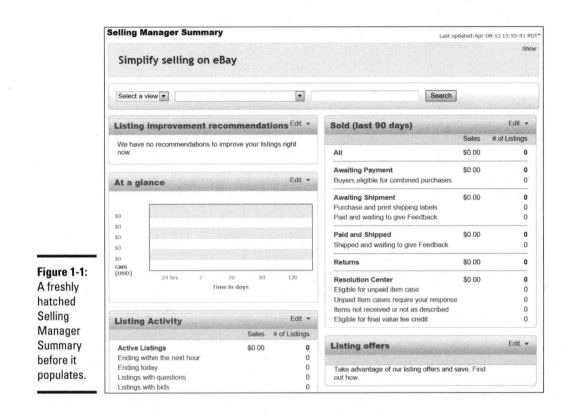

Figure 1-1:
A freshly
hatched
Selling
Manager
Summary
before it
populates.

Selling Manager Features

A versatile program, the standard version of Selling Manager allows you
to monitor or automate many of the more tedious eBay tasks. The page is
broken into several boxes, which I break down here.

At a Glance

We all like to know how we're doing, and the *At a Glance* area allows you to
do just that. A bar chart (see Figure 1-2) that shows a sales summary for the
last 24 hours, last 7 days, 30 days and last 120 days is integrated with eBay
so there's no lag time from selling to viewing.

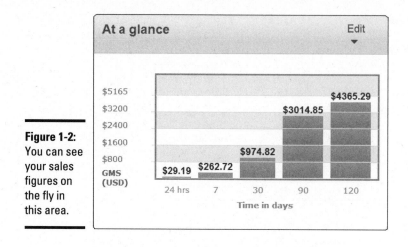

Figure 1-2:
You can see
your sales
figures on
the fly in
this area.

Seller Dashboard Summary box

Available to sellers once they have received ten Detailed Seller Ratings, the Seller Dashboard Summary box gives you a quick way to check your status on eBay. As shown in Figure 1-3, the Dashboard Summary covers the all-important results of the DSR ratings you get from your buyers. (Find more about Detailed Seller Ratings in Book I, Chapter 5.) It also keeps you apprised of whether you're following eBay's policies or, instead, have violated any in the recent past.

If you're a Top Rated Seller Plus, you also see your DSR-based Final Value Fee discount (more on that in Book VIII, Chapter 3) as well as your PowerSeller level (if you have attained such status).

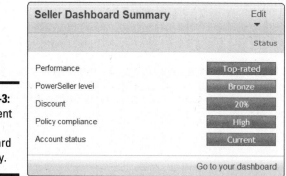

Figure 1-3:
My current
Seller
Dashboard
Summary.

At the bottom of the Seller Dashboard Summary box is a link that will take you to your official dashboard. Click it, and you see a page like the one in Figure 1-4. Here you can find out the details of what makes you a good seller in eBay's eyes — and in your customers' eyes, too.

Don't obsess too much about your dashboard. Okay, I did (and still do sometimes). Check it once a week. Bottom line: If you're doing the best job you can, there's not much more you can do to change things. If your dashboard indicates a problem with your sales performance (as noted in the Listing Improvement Recommendations area), once a week is good enough to evaluate and make the necessary changes to your system.

Listing Activity

An important box on the Selling Manager Summary page is Listing Activity. You'll get some valuable information there. It references what you did — or didn't — sell, along with even more stats on your sales. This section points out the most important activities you will view once you've got some transactions in progress.

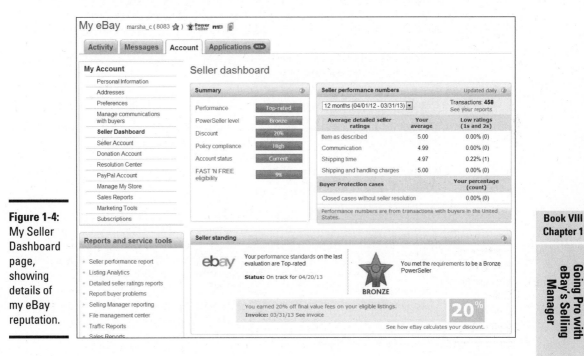

Figure 1-4: My Seller Dashboard page, showing details of my eBay reputation.

Active Listings

Click the Active Listings link on the Summary page, and you can observe the bidding action just as you can from the My eBay Selling page. The color-coding that indicates auction bidding activity is the same as on the My eBay Selling page. (If the current price is in green and bolded, your item has a bid and the number reflects the high bid. The current price is in red if there are no bids.) Your listings are accessible with a click of your mouse.

You have the option to sort and see only auctions or fixed-price listings on the Active Listings page. You can also search your own listings by keyword or item number.

Unsold Listings

You can access your Unsold listings from the links on the left side of the page. But the important link here is the link to items Eligible for Relist Fee Credit. This link will conveniently take you to the listings that you can relist, and if they sell the second time, eBay will refund your initial listings fees.

You need to know that to be eligible for relisting credit (once you have exceeded your free listings and have to pay inserting fees), the item gets only one shot at reselling. If it's been relisted twice, you need to start the listing again by using the Sell Similar link. The Sell Similar link (versus the Relist link) starts the transaction in a new cycle for the sale, thereby making it eligible for the relisting credit if it doesn't sell.

Scheduled Listings

The Scheduled Listings link on the Summary page takes you to any auction or fixed-price listing you've asked eBay to begin at a later time or date (or through Turbo Lister). You can also view these pending (scheduled) listings through links that narrow them to listings that start within the next hour — or start today.

When you enter the Scheduled Listings area (by clicking the Scheduled Listings link), you can go directly to any of your listings. If you want to promote your listing-to-be in a banner ad (or create a link to it from elsewhere on the Internet), you can do so using the URL of the pending listing. (See Book VI for more information on promoting your eBay business.)

From the Scheduled Listings page, you can confirm all information about the sale, as well as make any changes to the listing or to the scheduling time.

Working your Resolution Center

I hate to see items in the Awaiting Payment area of the Summary page, because it means there's a good chance I might not get paid for an item. I always keep an eye on my Sold, Awaiting Payment items and send out a payment reminder after a day has passed. If you haven't received payment for an item that ended at least two days ago, you can open an unpaid item case by clicking the Resolution center link. Here's a description of some options you see once you've opened a case in the Resolution Center:

✔ **Open cases:** This is where the items awaiting payment fall when they become eligible for you to file an Unpaid Item case. This happens when seven days have passed without a payment being received.

✔ **Awaiting other member's response:** After you've filed an unpaid-item case, the item goes into this area. It links to a dispute page that lists all outstanding disputes. The buyer is expected to answer your dispute here — and you can answer that answer.

✔ **Final Value Fee credit:** This is the category where buyers go if, after all your attempts to get action, they haven't responded and haven't sent payment. (If they don't cough up within ten days after you file a case, the listing moves to this category automatically.)

✔ **Items not received or significantly not as described:** Here's where you can see whether a buyer has notified eBay of an item that hasn't shown up when expected or arrived and wasn't what the buyer expected.

In the Resolution Center, you will also be able to handle any cases (cancel transactions when a buyer makes a mistake) that occur during your eBay business.

Sold

The Sold listings on the Summary page, shows you the details of the past 90 days' worth of transactions. You can get to the details by clicking appropriate links in the Sold box (refer to Figure 1-1). This is where Selling Manager really shines. You'll find quite a few links here, including these:

✦ **Awaiting payment:** This is where items that have been won or bought are shown before a payment is made.

✦ **Buyers Eligible for combined purchases:** Here you'll see when a buyer buys more than one item from you (yay!) and you need to combine the items into a single invoice. Otherwise the buyer may pay you once for each transaction — and then you'll incur extra transaction fees from

PayPal. Also, combined purchases help if you want to give your good customers a break on shipping.

✦ **Awaiting Shipment:** When a buyer has sent payment through PayPal, the transaction automatically moves to this category.

✦ **Paid and Shipped:** After an item is paid for, a reference to it appears here so you can keep abreast of the feedback you need to leave. When you've shipped an item and posted your tracking number, you can also check to see when the item is delivered.

✦ **Resolution Center:** This is where you turn in non-paying buyers and see if a buyer has opened a complaint on one of your transactions.

Seller tools links

Scroll down the page and you'll see the Seller Tools box on the left side of the Summary page. It's a powerful group of links that allow you to download and export your sales history to your computer. You also have quick links to PayPal, Multi Variation Merger (see Book III, Chapter 3 for the details), your eBay Store, and to the good old My eBay Selling page — in case you get nostalgic for the old, pre-Selling Manager days.

Manage My Store

If you have an eBay Store, you'll see a box on the Selling Manager Summary page with all the links you need to manage your store, as shown in Figure 1-5. You can access reports, e-mail marketing tools, Markdown Manager, and more. Also here you will find the all-important Vacation Settings to take your listings offline if you need a break. (See Book VIII, Chapter 4 for more on the eBay Store tools.)

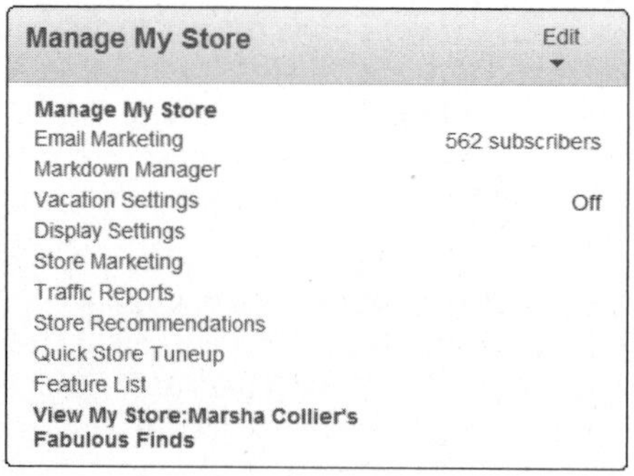

Manage My Store	Edit ▾
Manage My Store	
Email Marketing	562 subscribers
Markdown Manager	
Vacation Settings	Off
Display Settings	
Store Marketing	
Traffic Reports	
Store Recommendations	
Quick Store Tuneup	
Feature List	
View My Store:Marsha Collier's Fabulous Finds	

Figure 1-5: The Manage My Store links box.

Getting More from Selling Manager

Within Selling Manager, you'll find lots of handy tools to run your business more efficiently. In this section, I mention some of the most-used features.

Handling transaction activities

One of my favorite features of Selling Manager is that I can follow the progress of my sales from the Summary page. When an item has been won or paid for using PayPal, I can click the appropriate link to see the list of items ready for an action (such as shipping). Figure 1-6 shows my Sold: Awaiting Shipment area in Selling Manager.

Notice the record number next to the buyer's information. To send an eBay message or combined invoice, follow these steps:

1. **Click the record number to the left of the buyer's User ID and e-mail address.**

   The Transaction Detail record for the sale appears. The Buyer information appears at the top of the page (name, address, phone number) and any items sold to that buyer are below, as in the area shown in Figure 1-7. (If the buyer has made more than one purchase, you'll see a notation stating as much. You then have the option to click the link to combine purchases in the sales record.)

2. **To send an eBay message to the buyer:**

   1. *Click the feedback number next to the buyer's User ID.* This will take you to the buyer's Feedback profile.

   2. *On the Feedback profile click Contact Member.* A window will open, showing the item you have sold to the buyer.

   3. *Click the item. Then click continue.* An eBay Message contact form appears.

   4. *Write your message and click Send the button.*

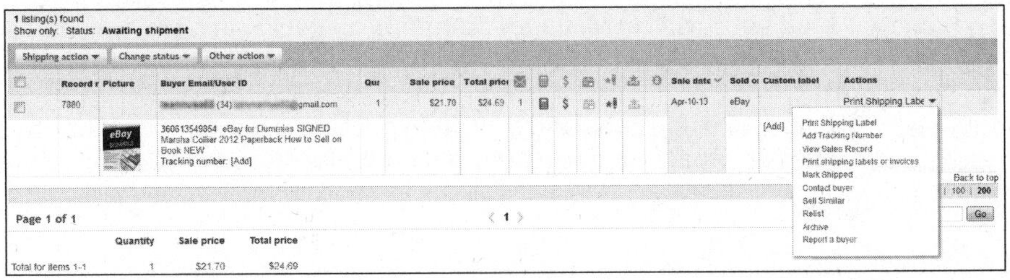

Figure 1-6:
Sold and ready to ship.

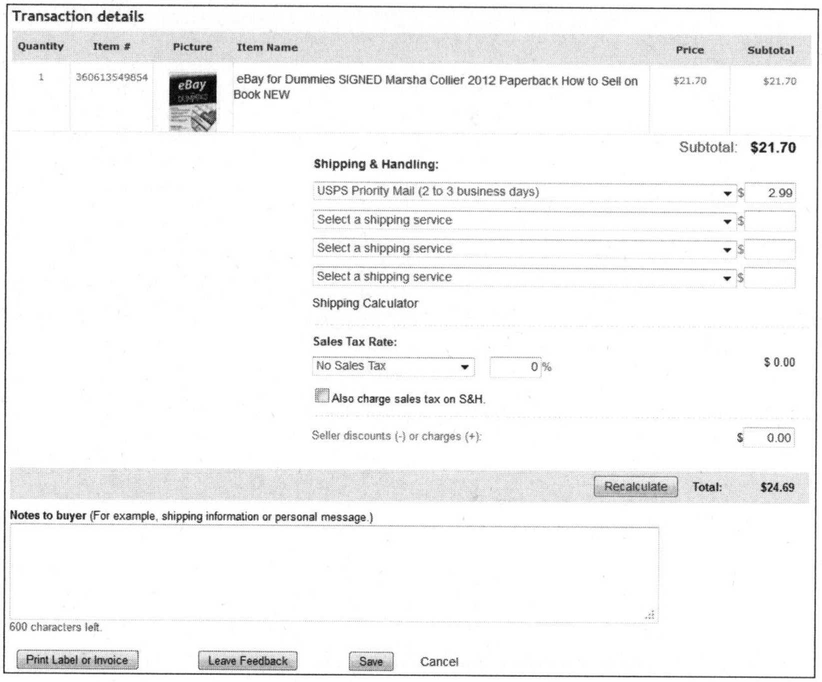

Transaction details

Quantity	Item #	Picture	Item Name	Price	Subtotal
1	360613549854		eBay for Dummies SIGNED Marsha Collier 2012 Paperback How to Sell on Book NEW	$21.70	$21.70

Subtotal: **$21.70**

Shipping & Handling:

USPS Priority Mail (2 to 3 business days)	▾	$ 2.99
Select a shipping service	▾	$
Select a shipping service	▾	$
Select a shipping service	▾	$

Shipping Calculator

Sales Tax Rate:

No Sales Tax ▾   0 % $ 0.00

☐ Also charge sales tax on S&H.

Seller discounts (-) or charges (+): $ 0.00

Recalculate   Total: **$24.69**

Notes to buyer (For example, shipping information or personal message.)

600 characters left.

Print Label or Invoice   Leave Feedback   Save   Cancel

Figure 1-7:
Reviewing
transaction
details.

3. **To send a combined invoice (prior to payment):**

   1. *Click one of the record numbers attributed to the buyer's purchase.*

   2. *Find the combined purchases button and click it.* Purchases are combined into one transaction with each item showing its own record number.

   3. *Return to the Sold: Awaiting Payment area and click Send Invoice next to the transaction.*

Tracking payments and shipping

Selling Manager makes many selling processes considerably easier. Take a look your Selling Manager Summary page. From here, you can see how many buyers have paid for their purchases — and how many haven't.

If you've sold items and you're expecting payments, be sure to check the Summary page several times a day. When a buyer makes his or her payment using PayPal, eBay will update your records. (PayPal also sends you a payment-received e-mail.)

After you ship the item, you can indicate any pertinent information on the Sales Status & Notes screen, shown in Figure 1-8. The transaction information in Figure 1-8 is available when you click the record number next to the item that's been shipped. After you ship the item, select the check box next to Shipped On and the date will appear automatically. Now, type in the tracking number (I do this from PayPal as I double-check for buyers notes before I print a label), and click Save, the record moves from the Sold: Awaiting Shipment page to the Paid and Shipped page. This change is also reflected on the Summary page.

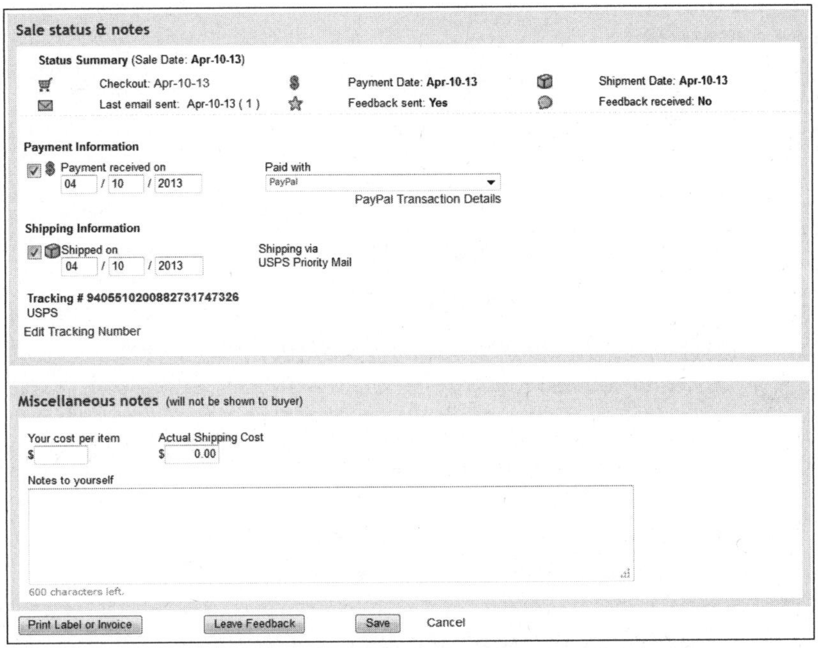

Sale status & notes

Status Summary (Sale Date: **Apr-10-13**)

	Checkout: Apr-10-13		Payment Date: **Apr-10-13**		Shipment Date: **Apr-10-13**
	Last email sent: Apr-10-13 (1)		Feedback sent: **Yes**		Feedback received: **No**

Payment Information

☑ $ Payment received on
04 / 10 / 2013

Paid with
PayPal
PayPal Transaction Details

Shipping Information

☑ Shipped on
04 / 10 / 2013

Shipping via
USPS Priority Mail

Tracking # 9405510200882731747326
USPS

Edit Tracking Number

Miscellaneous notes (will not be shown to buyer)

Your cost per item
$

Actual Shipping Cost
$ 0.00

Notes to yourself

600 characters left.

[Print Label or Invoice]   [Leave Feedback]   [Save]   Cancel

Figure 1-8:
You can edit sales-record information.

Book VIII Chapter 1

Going Pro with eBay's Selling Manager

Relisting and Selling Similar Items

Wouldn't it be better if you could select a whole bunch of items and relist them all together? Step up to Selling Manager for a one-click option. You can access items that have not sold, logically enough, from the Unsold Items area. Relisting is accomplished with a click of the mouse.

To relist an item (or Sell Similar) through Selling Manager, follow these steps:

1. **Go to the Unsold Items listings.**

   To do so, click the appropriate link on the left of the page in Selling Manager (or just link through the Summary page).

2. **Mark the items to relist (or Sell Similar) by selecting the check box next to each item's Title, as shown in Figure 1-9.**

Figure 1-9: Relisting from the Unsold Items page.

You may select any or all of the items listed on the page.

3. **Click the Relist button (or the Sell Similar button).**

   The Relist Multiple Items page appears.

4. **Review all the items listed (along with the fees).**

5. **Submit the items by clicking the Submit All button.**

Figure 1-10 shows a portion of the Relist Multiple Items page that includes a complete review of the details of each item. If you proceed at this point, the items will be relisted exactly as you had them listed before. At the bottom of the list, eBay recaps all relisting fees.

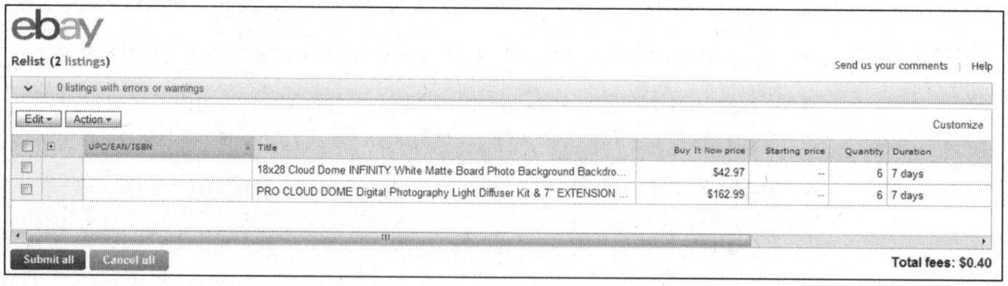

Figure 1-10: Relisting several items at once.

Accessing Selling Manager Reports

I like Selling Manager because it gives you the opportunity to keep all your selling information in one place. It also provides a downloadable report — in spreadsheet format — that you can archive for your records. Here's the information you can expect to find in the report:

✦ **Sales record number:** The number assigned to the transaction by Selling Manager for identification purposes.

✦ **User ID:** The eBay user ID of the person who purchased the item from you.

✦ **Buyer zip:** The buyer's ZIP code.

✦ **State:** The state the buyer resides in.

✦ **Buyer country:** The country your buyer lives in.

✦ **Item number:** The eBay number assigned to the item when you listed it for sale on the site.

✦ **Item title:** The title of the listing as it appeared on eBay.

✦ **Quantity:** The number of items purchased in the transaction.

✦ **Sale price:** The final selling price of the item.

✦ **Shipping amount:** The amount you charged for shipping the item.

✦ **Shipping insurance:** If the buyer paid insurance, it's listed next to his or her sales record.

✦ **State sales tax:** If you've set up Selling Manager to calculate sales tax for your in-state sales, and sales tax was applied to the item when it was sold, that amount is listed here.

✦ **Total price:** The GSA (gross sales amount) for the transaction.

✦ **Payment method:** The method of payment used by the buyer. This is inserted automatically if the item is paid through PayPal, or manually inserted by you into the sales record if paid by another method.

✦ **Sale date:** The date the transaction occurred on eBay.

✦ **Checkout:** The date of checkout. This is usually the same as the transaction date.

✦ **Paid on date:** The date the buyer paid for the item.

✦ **Shipped on date:** The ship date you entered in Selling Manager.

✦ **Feedback left:** Whether you left feedback for the buyer is indicated by a Yes or No in this column.

✦ **Feedback received:** The feedback rating left for you by the buyer (positive, negative, or neutral).

✦ **Notes to yourself:** If you input any personal notes regarding the transaction in the sales record, they appear here.

Keep in mind that Selling Manager reports are available on the site for only four months, so be sure to download your information regularly.

Notice that there is no column reflecting the eBay fees you paid for listing and selling the item. If you have plenty of time on your hands, you can create another column and input the fees from your eBay invoice for each item. Save time by posting the monthly total once a month in your bookkeeping program.

To get the file from eBay to your computer, follow these steps:

1. **Go to your My eBay page.**

The opening page of Selling Manager is your My eBay Summary page.

2. **Under Seller Tools, click the File Management Center link.**

This takes you to the File Management Center.

3. **Click the Create a Download Request link.**

A Create a Download Request page appears, as shown in Figure 1-11.

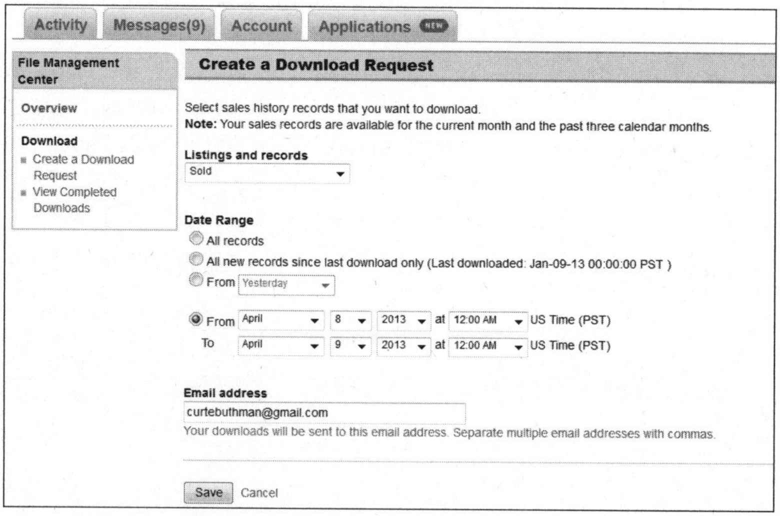

Figure 1-11: Getting the data.

| Activity | Messages(9) | Account | Applications NEW |

File Management Center

Overview

Download
- Create a Download Request
- View Completed Downloads

Create a Download Request

Select sales history records that you want to download.
Note: Your sales records are available for the current month and the past three calendar months.

Listings and records
Sold

Date Range
○ All records
○ All new records since last download only (Last downloaded: Jan-09-13 00:00:00 PST)
○ From Yesterday
● From April 8 2013 at 12:00 AM US Time (PST)
   To April 9 2013 at 12:00 AM US Time (PST)

Email address
curtebuthman@gmail.com
Your downloads will be sent to this email address. Separate multiple email addresses with commas.

Save Cancel

4. **Select the listings and records you want from the drop-down menu.**

   Your e-mail address is already filled in, but you may add another if you want duplicate notifications.

5. **Select the time period you want to include in your report.**

   It's best to generate monthly or quarterly reports, so that your reports coincide with specific tax periods. You can always combine more than one report in your spreadsheet program to show different periods of time.

6. **Click the Save button.**

   You then see a confirmation page and a confirmation number for your request. eBay will send you an e-mail when your report is ready.

7. **You will receive an e-mail (almost immediately).**

   Click the link in the e-mail, and you're taken to the View Completed Downloads page.

8. **Click the link to download the file.**

   The Save As dialog box appears, as shown in Figure 1-12.

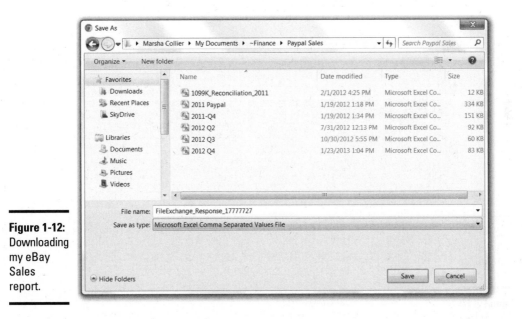

Figure 1-12: Downloading my eBay Sales report.

9. **Rename the file to reflect the sales month and year, and then click Save.**

   After the file is downloaded, you'll see a confirmation with your new filename.

TIP

It's a good idea to create a directory on your computer with a name such as eBay Sales. In this directory, you can store all the reports you download from eBay, PayPal, or any other online service. Be sure to include this directory when you perform regular data backups.

Now you can open the new file in Microsoft Excel. It will look similar to Figure 1-13.

With simple spreadsheet commands, you can customize the look of your report. For example, if the column for Buyer Country is unnecessary for your records (for example, if you ship only within the United States, that information is not useful), you can delete the column in two quick steps:

1. **Highlight the column by clicking the column letter.**

2. **Choose File➪Cells➪Delete.**

   Voilà! The offending column is no more.

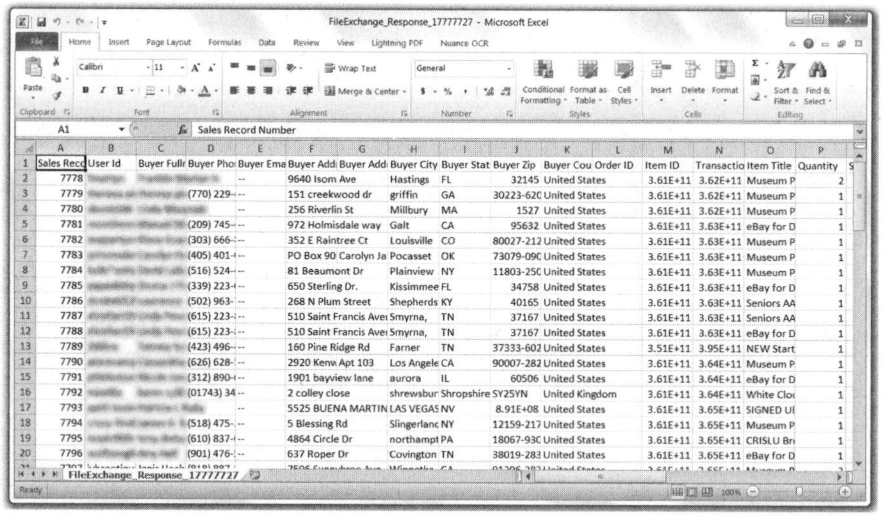

Figure 1-13:
My imported eBay sales report.

| Sales Record Number | | | | | | | | | | | | | | | |

TIP

All spreadsheet tasks mentioned here can be performed in similar fashion in Google Docs.

The spreadsheet generated by Selling Manager is much more useful if you total the columns. That way, you can see your total sales at a glance. To total a spreadsheet column:

1. **Click in the blank cell at the bottom of the column you want to total.**

2. **Click and drag over the cells you want to sum.**

3. **Click the AutoSum (Σ) button (also found under Formulas tab).**

4. **The total appears.**

If you want to total the columns next to the one you just totaled, you don't have to re-input the formula. Just highlight the results cell from your last formula, and highlight cells in the same row that you want to contain totals of the columns. Then under Editing, click below the Σ symbol to fill cells right, as shown in Figure 1-14. This copies the formula to the connecting cells and all the columns are totaled.

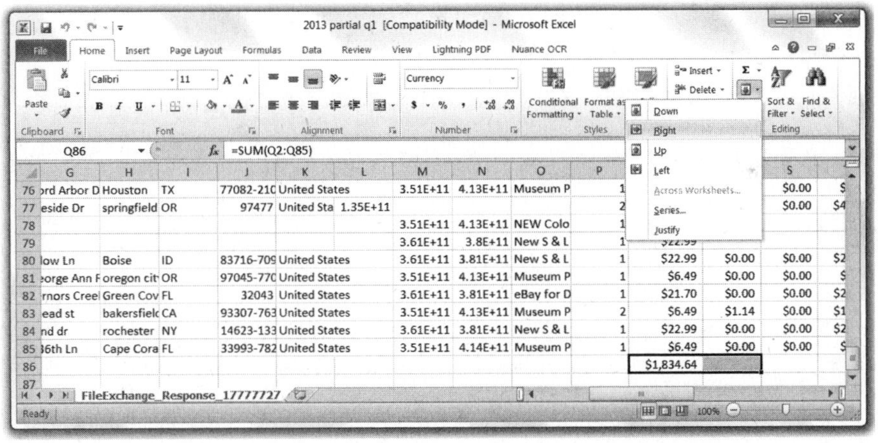

Figure 1-14: Totaling the columns.

Chapter 2: Managing Sales with eBay Apps and Third-Party Tools

In This Chapter

✔ **Checking out the Apps Center**

✔ **Deciding on third-party management services**

✔ **Figuring out what to automate**

✔ **Looking at three third-party options**

*W*hen you get to the point of running up to 20 listings at a time, I highly recommend that you begin to use a management tool. At this level of activity, using eBay's Selling Manager (or Selling Manager Pro) will suit you nicely, and I go over how these tools work in Chapter 1. But when your eBay business begins to push 100 listings a week, I recommend that you get additional help in the form of an app or software.

Whether you use an online service or software residing on your own computer is a personal decision. You may find it easier to use an online system because you can log on to your selling information at any time from any computer. But if you want to archive your work locally, you may prefer an app that does the work on your computer and uploads the final products to eBay.

Most desktop-based software packages have features that enable you to do your work on your computer and then upload (or download) your data when you go online.

In either case, if your business has reached the level where you need a listing or management tool, congratulations! In this chapter, I want to save you some time finding the service or software that's right for you. I outline some of the tasks that a management product would preferably provide, and compare prices of several services.

Finding Function-Specific Apps

A visit to the eBay Apps Center will dazzle you with hundreds of third-party applications that have all been verified by eBay. Such verification means that these apps should always be up to date and ready for any of eBay's changes.

You'll find apps designed for many functions that fall into categories such as checkout, customer support, finance and accounting, inventory listing, marketing and merchandising, research and reporting, shipping and payments, and sourcing. They integrate directly with the eBay.com interface for sellers in the United States.

The apps are the brain-children of developers who have been vetted to join the eBay Developers program, and they're offered in the eBay Apps Center only after rigorous testing. When you visit the Apps Center, you find reviews and ratings from other eBay sellers. Take the time to read these comments to see whether an app is right for you.

Find the eBay Apps Center (shown in Figure 2-1) from your My eBay page by clicking Applications and then the Apps Center link. You can also find it by going directly to

```
http://applications.ebay.com/selling?EAppsHome
```

Although the Apps Center has many choices, you may find that sometimes you need a more robust program to better fit your business style. The remaining sections in this chapter give you tips and ideas on saving time and money by using such software.

Figure 2-1: Hundreds of handy apps are available at the Apps Center.

Choosing Your Management Tools

If you searched the Internet for eBay-management services and software, you'd come up with a bunch. For simplicity's sake, I've chosen to examine just a few of these services in this chapter. After speaking to many sellers, I've found online services that offer two important features:

+ **Uptime reliability:** Uptime is vital here; you don't want the server that holds your photos going down or mislaunching your sales.

+ **Regular updates:** Look for software that's continually updated to match eBay changes.

Using a site or software to run your sales takes practice, so I suggest that you try any that appeal to you and offer free preview trials. As I describe these different applications, I include a link so you can check them out further.

Some software and services work on a monthly fee; others work on a one-time purchase fee. For a one-time-purchase software application to truly benefit you, it must have the reputation for updating its software each time eBay makes a change to its procedures and policies. The programs I discuss in this chapter have been upgraded continually to date.

Most services have a free trial period. Be sure that you don't spend a bunch of your precious time inputting your entire inventory, only to discover you don't like the way the service works. Instead, input a few items to give the service a whirl.

There's a huge difference between auction-*listing* software and sites and auction-*management* products. For many a seller, listing software like eBay's Turbo Lister (see Book III, Chapter 4) may just do the trick. Combine that with eBay's Selling Manager Pro (a *management* program) and your eBay business will be humming along just fine.

When your business activity level increases and you turn to an auction-management solution for your eBay business, you should look for certain standard features (described next). Also consider what information-management features you currently have through your bookkeeping program (see Book IX). You have the data there, regardless of whether you use it in a management solution.

Book VIII
Chapter 2

Managing Sales with eBay Apps and Third-Party Tools

Certifying a Certified Provider

eBay endorsement is a cloudy subject. I get e-mails upon e-mails from people asking about one company or another, telling me a particular company is

- Recommended by eBay
- Endorsed by eBay
- Owned by eBay (because the eBay logo appears in the website)

None of the above is ever true. There is a Certified Provider program from eBay in which eBay qualifies businesses who want to do business with the eBay community. Note that I used the word *qualify.* That does not mean *endorse.*

By having the Certified Provider program, eBay manages the influx of apps, allowing only the best and most compliant apps on to eBay. When the program started in 2004, as stated by eBay, qualifications were "Participants *(in the program)* must have extensive experience with eBay, pass a strict certification exam and provide a number of proven customer references that are checked by eBay."

The program was revamped in 2011, and many providers were removed from the list. The new criteria became:

- **Marketplace Impact:** We select eBay developers who are impacted the most by eBay changes and who can make the most impact on your business.

- **Customer Satisfaction:** Don't take our word for it. We gauge customer satisfaction through annual customer surveys and ongoing product review.

- **Feature Support:** Certified Providers must support the features you need the most to be a part of the program.

If you are considering doing business with someone who provides services for eBay sellers, look for comments by those who have done business with that provider. Whenever I do business with someone who gives eBay (or any web-related) advice, I run a Google search on the company's name (or its eBay User ID) and the word *fraud* to see whether the company has been involved in any fraudulent activities that haven't been made widely public.

Looking for Essential Features

Here are some must-have features to look for when you evaluate the offerings of auction-management services and products:

✦ **Image hosting:** Some hosts dazzle you with gigabytes of image storage. Keep one thing in mind: eBay requires images now to be at least 500 pixels on one side; this means your images will hover around 1MB in size. This means you could store approximately 1,000 pictures in a 1GB storage space Unless you're a big-time seller, you really don't need tons of storage space. (For more about the ins and outs of image hosting, refer to Book V, Chapters 4 and 5.)

Your eBay images should be archived on your computer (how about in a folder called *eBay Images*?). Images for current listings should be on the hosted site — only while the transaction is in progress. After the buyer has the item and all is well, you can remove the images from the remote server.

If you have your own website, there's a good chance you already have free image-hosting space, as noted in Book V.

✦ **Listing design tools:** The basis of most of these products is a good listing function. You'll be able to select from supplied templates or design your own and store them for future use. Be sure to use a spell checker. There's nothing worse than sloppy spelling in a listing.

✦ **Listing uploading tools:** Most products have a feature that launches a group of listings to eBay all at once. They may also allow you to schedule auctions to get underway at a prescribed time.

You can also expect to be able to put together your listings at your leisure offline and upload them to your service. Most products archive your past listings so that you can relist at any time. Many services also offer bulk relisting.

✦ **E-mail management:** You may be provided with sample e-mail letters (templates) that you can customize with your own look and feel. That's a nice touch, or you can just use the e-mail templates described in Book VIII, Chapter 1.

✦ **Feedback automation:** Post feedback in bulk to a number of your buyers, or leave pre-designed feedback for each, one by one. Some products support automatic positive feedback that kicks in when a buyer leaves you positive feedback.

✦ **Sales reports:** Some services (even the least expensive) offer you some sort of sales analysis. Be sure to take into account how much you really need this feature, basing your estimate on data that you may already receive from QuickBooks, PayPal, eBay Stores, or SquareTrade.

Exploring Advanced Features

Depending on the type of business you run, you may need some of the more advanced features offered by management products:

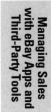

**Book VIII
Chapter 2**

**Managing Sales
with eBay Apps and
Third-Party Tools**

✦ **Inventory tools:** Management products may allow you to create inventory records for your different products, such that you can click a bunch of them to list them automatically. When an item is sold, the tool deducts the item from your inventory automatically.

✦ **Sales-tax tracking and invoicing:** With full management, you can expect your sales tax to be calculated into your invoices and complete line-item invoices to be sent automatically. Multiple items, when purchased by the same buyer, will be combined.

✦ **Consignment tracking:** If you're a Trading Assistant, be sure to look for a product that enables you to separately track the products you sell for different clients. You should also be able to produce reports of consignment sales by customer.

✦ **Shipping:** Most of the services will give you the option of printing your packing lists and shipping labels directly from the product. Some of the larger services integrate with the major shippers, allowing you to go directly to particular shippers' sites and ship your items using their software.

Finding More to Automate

Now that eBay has become a world marketplace, a single-page auction or item listing is becoming an increasingly valuable piece of real estate. Millions may view your sale, and the more auctions and fixed-price items that you can list, the better your chance to make a good living. Time is money: You need to post quickly and accurately.

Posting auctions, keeping records, cataloging inventory, managing photos, and gathering statistics are all tasks that you can automate. The more your business grows, the more confusing details may become. Automated tools can help you keep it all straight.

However, the more paid tools you use, the more expense you may be adding to your business. Always keep your bottom line in mind when evaluating whether to use fee-based software and services — eBay's beginner Selling Manager is free.

You'll have to perform back office tasks, no matter how few (or how many) listings you're running. Depending on your personal business style, you may want to automate any or all of the following tasks. You may choose to use a single program, a manual method, or use some features from one program and some from others. For those who aren't ready for the automated plunge, I offer alternatives here. Where appropriate, I insert references that guide you to places in this book (or on the web) where you can find more information about the automated services I discuss.

Setting up a link to your eBay listings

Until you get your own eBay store, setting up a link to your listings from your website or blog is a great alternative. That way, visitors to your site can browse your listings directly on eBay. You can produce your own listing gallery without any fancy programs or auction-management software, and at no additional cost.

To make a link to your eBay listings without installing fancy scripts, you need to do two things:

1. **Test the following URL in your browser, substituting your own User ID in place of the bold italics:**

   `http://shop.ebay.com/merchant/`***yourUserID***

   Figure 2-2 shows a sample of what you'll see.

2. **After checking your link, insert the following HTML into your site to include a link to your eBay sales:**

   ```
   <a href="http://shop.ebay.com/merchant/yourUserID">
      <b>Click <I>here</I> to view YourUserID Gallery</b>
      </a >
   ```

   You can also use this in your e-mails to customers to show them just what's for sale at any given moment.

Figure 2-2: My eBay listings from the link.

Automating end-of-auction e-mail

If you want to set up e-mails to be sent automatically after an auction ends, you must use a software application. The software should download your final auction results, generate the e-mail, and let you preview the e-mail before sending it out. Many of the online sites discussed later in this chapter send out winner confirmation e-mails automatically when an auction is over.

If you want to use this option, be sure that you set preferences to preview the e-mail before sending.

Keeping inventory

Many eBay sellers depend on the notebook method — crossing off items as they're sold. If that works for you, great. Others prefer to use an Excel spreadsheet to keep track of inventory.

Most of the management packages handle inventory for you. Some automatically deduct an item from inventory when you launch an auction. You have your choice of handling inventory directly on your computer or keeping your inventory online with a service that's accessible from any computer, wherever you are.

I handle my inventory on my desktop through QuickBooks. When I buy merchandise to sell, and I post the bill to QuickBooks, it automatically puts the merchandise into inventory. When I input my sale, it deducts the items sold from standing inventory. I can view a status report whenever I want to see how much I have left — or have to order.

Composing HTML for listings

Fancy descriptions are nice, but fancy doesn't make the item sell any better. Competitive pricing and low (free?) shipping rates work in your favor — especially with Best Match Search. Also, a clean listing with as many photos as necessary goes a long way toward selling your product. Some software and services offer a large selection of templates to gussy up your descriptions.

The use of simple HTML doesn't slow the loading of your page, but the addition of miscellaneous images (decorative backgrounds and animations) can make viewing your item a distasteful chore.

Don't fret; you can make do by repeatedly incorporating two or three simple HTML templates, cutting and pasting new text as necessary. Most listing programs offer you several template choices. I recommend that you stick with a few that are similar, giving a standardized look to your listings — which is just the way major companies give a standardized look to *their* advertising and identity. Your customers will get used to the look of your auctions and feel comfortable each time they see one.

I use SeaMonkey Composer (a free program from the people who brought us the Firefox Internet browser) to generate much of my code for auction descriptions. Visit Book V, Chapter 3 for more information on this handy program.

An important line of code that everyone seems to forget is the one that inserts a picture into your auction description. You need (due to eBay policy) to embed any images that have text you inserted within your description. These types of images are no longer allowed as your main eBay pictures. On the Sell an Item page, click the tab to view in HTML mode, and insert the following line below where you'd like your image to appear in your description:

```
<img src="http://www.yourwebsiteserver.com/imagename.jpg">
```

Be sure to substitute your own server and image name. If you want to put one picture above another, type <p> and then repeat the HTML line with a different image name.

If you're in a rush and need a quick and easy HTML generator, go to my website at www.coolebaytools.com and click Tools. In addition, Book V has sample HTML code for descriptions, as well as a chart of all the code you'll ever need for an eBay auction.

One-click relisting or selling similar

Automating speeds up the process of posting or relisting items. After you input your inventory into the software, posting or relisting your auctions is a mouse click away. All the auction-management software packages that I detail in this chapter include this feature.

If you buy your items in bulk, you might want to take advantage of eBay's free relisting tool. By clicking the Sell a Similar Item link (see Figure 2-3) on any successful listing on your My eBay Sold items, you can automatically relist. The Sell Similar process starts the listing as new, so if it doesn't sell you can avail yourself of the Relist feature. If you've exceeded your free listing amount for the month, if the item sells the second time around, your listing (insertion fee) for the first listing will be credited.

Figure 2-3:
The Relist and Sell Similar links live near the top of your ended listing.

Although Sell Similar is for relisting items, it works also when listing a duplicate of an item that has sold successfully. The only difference is that you aren't credited for the unsold auction listing fee.

One savvy seller I know uses the eBay Sell Similar feature to post new listings. She merely clicks the Sell Similar link, and then cuts and pastes her new information into the existing HTML format. That's why her items all have the same feel and flavor.

Scheduling listings for bulk upload

If you're a store owner and want to schedule a future automated launch of your listings without incurring eBay's $.10 fee, you must use an online management service (check out the "Opting for Third-Party Management" section). If you can be at your computer to send your items to eBay singly or in bulk, you can use the Turbo Lister application, which eBay offers at no charge.

Checking out

When someone wins or buys an item, eBay's checkout integrates directly with PayPal. If you're closing less than 100 sales a day, that's all you need. eBay and PayPal will also send an e-mail to you and the buyer so that you can arrange for payment.

A personalized winner's notification e-mail can easily contain a link to your PayPal payment area, making a checkout service unnecessary.

Printing shipping labels

Printing shipping labels without printing postage can be the beginning of a laborious two-step process. I recommend alternatives: Endicia (for Mac and Windows), Stamps (Windows) and PayPal (eBay) for all operating systems — all of which can print your labels and postage in one step. Check out Book VII, Chapter 1 for information on how this works.

Generating customized reports

Sales reports, ledgers, and tax information are all important reports that you should have in your business. Online services and software supply different flavors of these reports.

PayPal allows you to download your sales data into a format compatible with QuickBooks, a highly respected and popular bookkeeping program. You can also choose to download your data in Excel spreadsheet format. PayPal reports are chock-full of intensely detailed information about your sales and deposits. Putting this information in a standard accounting software program on a regular basis makes your year-end calculations easier to bear.

Submitting feedback

If you're running a lot of listings, leaving feedback can be a chore. One solution is to automate the submission of feedback through the online services of eBay's Selling Manager Pro. But timing the automation of this task can be tricky.

Opting for Third-Party Management

You may want to run your business from any computer, anywhere in the world. If that's the case, you might do best with an online service. Auction-management websites handle almost everything, from inventory management to label printing. Some sellers prefer online (or hosted) management sites because you can access your information from any computer. You might use every feature a site offers, or you might choose a bit from column A and a bit from column B and perform the more personalized tasks manually. Read on to determine what service might best suit your needs.

Although quite a few excellent online services for automating sales are available, I have room here to show you only a few. Many services are similar in format, so in the following sections I point out some of the highlights of a few representative systems.

Vendio

I have fond memories of the early days on AuctionWeb (the forerunner of eBay). Some are especially about the other folks I met when we were all starting out with the online selling experience. The site (originally AuctionWatch), was founded in summer of 1998 as a message board for online sellers. In 1999, when I was struggling to get out the first edition of *eBay For Dummies,* Mark Dodd and Rodrigo Salas were laying hands on multiple millions from venture capitalists to begin a new auction-service site.

Hard work pays off, because today that site is Vendio (`http://www.vendio.com/`, as shown in Figure 2-4) — and it has served more than a million sellers over the years to improve their bottom line.

One of the things that makes Vendio unique is its range of offerings. In addition to auction management, Vendio has a full complement of research tools and other offerings. Each tool, should you choose to use it, is offered *a la carte.*

Here are just a few features of their auction-management suite:

+ **Item and inventory management:** Keep track of your items and launch with a click from their site.

+ **Image hosting:** For eBay auctions, image hosting is based on how much you need at a time. For $2.95 a month, you can store up to 3 MB of pictures.

+ **Auction reporting:** Generates accounts receivable, item history, and post-sales reports from the Reports area. Reports include customizable views of your sales data, item and auction data, accounts receivable, and sales tax.

+ **Templates and listing:** Choose from over 160 very professional listing templates. You can use their predefined color templates or use your own homemade templates.

+ **Post-auction management (included in Basic Sales Manager):** Sends out automated e-mail to your winners, linking them to your own branded checkout page. If customers want to pay with PayPal or your own merchant account, they have to link from there. Vendio combines multiple wins for shipping and invoicing. You have the option to set six different feedback comments, which you choose at the time of posting.

Vendio offers a fully customizable store you can place on your own web space — at no additional charge. When you set up your store, all your listed items are seamlessly integrated. To get current information and sign up for a free trial, go to `http://www.vendio.com/`.

Figure 2-4:
Vendio
offers
multichannel
e-commerce
solutions.

Meridian

Meridian Software was developed by eBay Shooting Star Top Rated Plus seller, Joe Cortese. Through his own experience on eBay, he developed this service to fulfill all the needs of an eBay seller, at a very reasonable price.

As a high-volume eBay seller, he was looking for an easier way to handle his 3,000 unique auctions a month. You can apply the same technology to your auctions. Meridian features enterprise-level listing and more:

✦ **Item and inventory management:** Includes calendar- and time-based scheduling (that is, dates and times for launching auctions), automated auction launching and relisting, the capability to import past or current auctions, and the capability to import auction data from a spreadsheet or database.

✦ **Image hosting:** Offers space for storing pictures. You can upload bulk images to its website or FTP your images directly.

✦ **Auction reporting:** Generates current running auction statistics — the total number and dollars of current and past auctions — and an itemized report of each auction.

✦ **Post-auction management:** Allows you to send (manually or automatically) a variety of customized e-mails to winners and nonpaying bidders. Your invoices can link directly to PayPal.

**Book VIII
Chapter 2**

Managing Sales
with eBay Apps and
Third-Party Tools

✦ **Consignment tools:** For sellers who sell for others (see information on eBay's Trading Assistant program in Book IV, Chapter 3), Meridian offers complete tracking and inventory by consignor.

The post-auction management features also include the ability to send automatic feedback and to create mailing labels for each sale. So that feedback isn't posted until you're sure the transaction is successfully completed, you have the option of disabling the automatic feedback feature. Visit the website (pictured in Figure 2-5) at www.noblespirit.com.

Figure 2-5:
Meridian automates your workflow.

Auction Wizard 2000

Way back in 1999, Standing Wave Software developed a product that would handle large inventories and meet the needs of the growing eBay population. Enter Auction Wizard. In 2000, the company introduced a more robust version, Auction Wizard 2000, to meet the challenges presented by changes on eBay.

This software is a tour-de-force of auction management, whose pieces are integrated into one program. Some of its special features enable you to

✦ **Handle consignment sales.** Keep track of consignment sales by consignees, including all fees.

✦ **Edit your images before uploading.** The software allows you to import your images, and crop, rotate, or resize images for your auctions.

✦ **Upload your pictures with built-in FTP software.** You can do this while you're working on your auctions, eliminating the need for another piece of auction-business software.

The program interface is straightforward. I always plunge into new programs without reading the instructions, and I was able to use the program right off the bat. I'm still not a whiz at it, but that's probably because Auction Wizard 2000 has so many features that I haven't had the time to study them all.

To begin using the software, simply download your current eBay auctions directly into the program. When your auctions close, send customized e-mails (the program fills in the auction information) and manage all your end-of-auction business. Some sellers launch their auctions using Turbo Lister, and then retrieve them and handle the end-of-auction management with Auction Wizard 2000 (see Figure 2-6). For a 60-day free trial, go to their site at

`www.auctionwizard2000.com.`

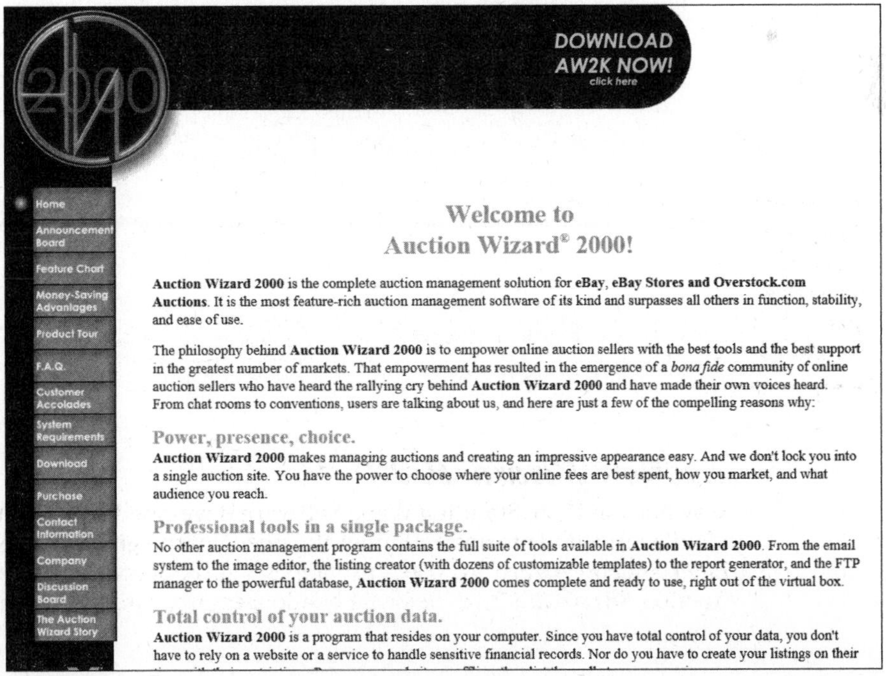

Figure 2-6: You can use Auction Wizard 2000 on your own computer, online or not.

Book VIII Chapter 2

Managing Sales with eBay Apps and Third-Party Tools

Chapter 3: Attaining PowerSeller and Top Rated Seller Status

In This Chapter

↙ **Moving up the tiers**

↙ **Qualifying for PowerSeller status**

↙ **Becoming a Top Rated Seller**

↙ **Understanding the benefits of becoming a recognized seller**

*W*hen you browse through items on eBay, you're bound to notice a Top Rated Plus icon next to a member's User ID. To the uninitiated, this may look like an award given to a seller for selling thousands of items on eBay — but it's not. The eBay Top Rated Plus status is given only to those sellers who uphold the highest levels of professionalism and customer service on the site. Take a look at mine in Figure 3-1.

Figure 3-1:
My proudly
displayed
Top Rated
Seller Plus
badge.

There are three levels of upgraded status for eBay sellers:

✦ **PowerSellers:** These members have to maintain certain monthly levels of gross merchandise sales (total dollar amount of eBay sales — GMS in eBay-speak), and they must get there by providing excellent customer service.

✦ **Top Rated Sellers:** eBay sellers at this level don't have to have as large volume of sales as an eBay PowerSeller, but they face stricter customer service requirements.

✦ **Top Rated Seller Plus:** Only the sellers who fully commit to their businesses get this status. In searches, only Top Rated Plus sellers have badges next to their listings.

eBay community values

The eBay community values aren't taken lightly by the eBay community and eBay employees. The values were set out early on by the company's founder, Pierre Omidyar.

✔ We believe people are basically good.

✔ We believe everyone has something to contribute.

✔ We believe that an honest, open environment can bring out the best in people.

✔ We recognize and respect everyone as a unique individual.

✔ We encourage you to treat others the way that you want to be treated.

All eBay sellers are expected to uphold these tenets in all their dealings on the site. Okay, no snickering from the peanut gallery; we all know that quite a few sellers don't follow these precepts. But then, they're not PowerSellers or Top Rated Sellers, are they?

You may notice that many sellers on the site with feedback ratings in the tens of thousands do not have the Top Rated Plus badge on their listings. That's not because they're not good people; it's just that some of their transactions may have gone not-so-good. In this case, be sure to check the seller's feedback and thoughtfully evaluate it. Many times buyers do not read the seller's policies before they buy — and then give negative feedback (as in the case of buyers not reading the seller's warnings when buying liquidation merchandise).

In this chapter, I tell you what it takes to join these exclusive eBay sellers — and the benefits the status offers. To check for new updates on these seller requirements, visit eBay at

```
http://pages.ebay.com/sellerinformation/sellingresources/
    powerseller_requirements.html
```

Becoming an eBay Elite Seller

Aside from the benefits mentioned throughout this chapter, consider this very important reason to be recognized on eBay: eBay's Best Match search algorithm weighs every item and every seller. Attaining recognition as a seller who is in business seriously makes a difference in how prominently your listings are displayed on eBay.

Joining PowerSeller ranks

The ranks of PowerSellers have five levels of membership, depending on your monthly sales, as shown in Table 3-1. Each PowerSeller tier gives the seller more privileges from eBay. One of the most valuable benefits is that when an issue needs to be addressed with eBay, PowerSellers can access priority customer-service support.

Table 3-1	PowerSeller Tier Sales Volume Requirements	
Tier	*Annual GMS ($)*	*Transactions*
Bronze	$3,000	**AND** 100
Silver	$36,000	or 3,600
Gold	$120,000	or 12,000
Platinum	$300,000	or 30,000 items
Titanium	$1,800,000	or 180,000 items

To become a PowerSeller on eBay, you must fulfill the following requirements:

✦ **Be an active eBay member for at least 90 days.**

✦ **Sell a minimum of $3,000 in sales or 100 items per month, over the past 12 months.**

✦ **Buyer Protection cases must be less than 1 percent of your total number of transactions with U.S. buyers.**

✦ **Maintain at least a 98 feedback percentage.**

✦ **Keep your eBay account current.**

✦ **Comply with all eBay policies.** To obtain or keep PowerSeller status, you must not exceed the following:

 • *Bronze level:* 4 violations in a 90-day period

 • *Silver/Gold levels:* 5 violations in a 90-day period

 • *Platinum level:* 6 violations in a 90-day period

 • *Titanium level:* 7 violations in a 90-day period

✦ **Maintain a minimum rating of 4.6 or higher for the past 12 months in all four Detailed Seller Ratings (DSRs).** Occurrences of 1s and 2s on DSRs with U.S. buyers may not to exceed the following rates and counts:

 • *Items as described:* 1.00 percent and a count of 3

- *Communication:* 2.00 issues and a count of 3

- *Shipping time:* 2.00 percent and a count of 3

- *Shipping & handling charges:* 2.00 percent and a count of 3

✦ **Run your business by upholding eBay's community values (see the earlier sidebar).**

PowerSeller eligibility is reviewed every three months. You can track your progress on your Seller Dashboard. (I tell you more about Seller Dashboard in Book II, Chapter 5.)

Becoming a Top Rated Seller

Becoming a PowerSeller is good, but Top Rated Seller status gives you better ranking in search and more benefits (read on). Top Rated status is reviewed monthly. As a Top Rated Seller, your Feedback profile page will show your ranking (Figure 3-2 shows an example).

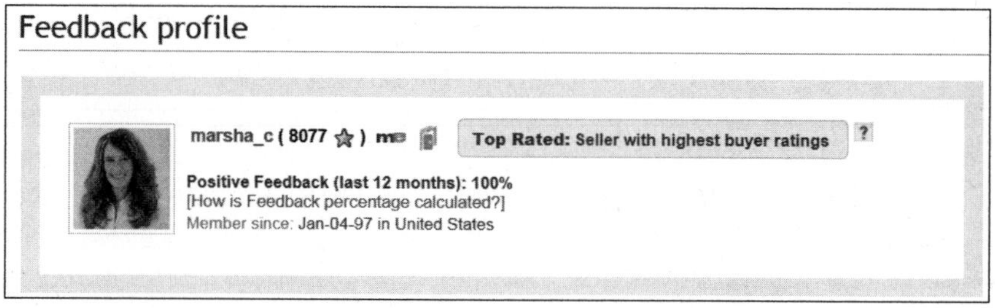

Figure 3-2: Feedback profile page of a Top Rated Seller.

To become a Top Rated Seller on eBay, fulfill the following requirements:

✦ Be an active eBay member for at least 90 days.

✦ 100 or more transactions with U.S. sellers within the past year

✦ Sell a minimum of $1,000 in annual sales to U.S. buyers.

✦ Buyer Protection cases must be less than .5 percent of your total number of transactions with U.S. buyers.

✦ Maintain at least a 98 feedback percentage.

✦ Keep your eBay account current.

✦ Comply with all eBay policies.

✦ Occurrences of 1s and 2s on DSRs with U.S. buyers may not exceed the following rates and counts:

- **Items as described**: .5 percent and a count of 2

- **Communication**: .5 percent and a count of 2

- **Shipping time**: .5 percent and a count of 2

- **Shipping & handling charges**: .5 percent and a count of 2

✦ Tracking numbers must be uploaded to eBay/PayPal for at least 90 percent of your transactions.

PowerSeller eligibility is reviewed every three months. You can track your progress on your Seller Dashboard (more on the Dashboard in Chapter 1).

Getting highlighted on eBay: Top Rated Plus

To align with evolving consumer expectations, eBay updated the Top Rated Seller status to "Plus." These are the only sellers that receive a badge; the Top Rated Plus seal (see Figure 3-3) appears on all these seller's listings.

Figure 3-3:
The eBay Top Rated Seller Plus badge.

Also, on the Feedback profile page of all Top Rated Sellers, this recognition is displayed: "Top Rated: Seller with highest buyer ratings."

It isn't a very big jump to attain "Plus" status after you're a Top Rated Seller. After you meet the Top Rated Seller requirements, you have to meet only these two additional requirements:

✦ **One-day handling:** Include one-day handling in your listings (meaning you ship within one day of purchase) and post the tracking.

✦ **Money-back return policy:** Offer a money back, 14-day (or longer) return policy.

Many sellers find these last two requirements too onerous and don't even attempt Top Rated Plus Status. That's a bit short sighted. Read on to find out about a benefit that affects your bottom line.

The Benefits of Membership

As an eBay recognized seller, you get a few perks that can help you build your business. The efforts you put into servicing your customers and selling on eBay are rewarded through the PowerSeller and Top Rated Seller programs.

PowerSeller perks

As a PowerSeller member, you will have access to some super-secret places on the eBay site reserved for PowerSellers. There's a PowerSeller discussion board, and even special items at the eBay store. All this magic is accessed by the screen shown in Figure 3-4, at

```
http://pages.ebay.com/sellerinformation/sellingresources/
    powerseller.html
```

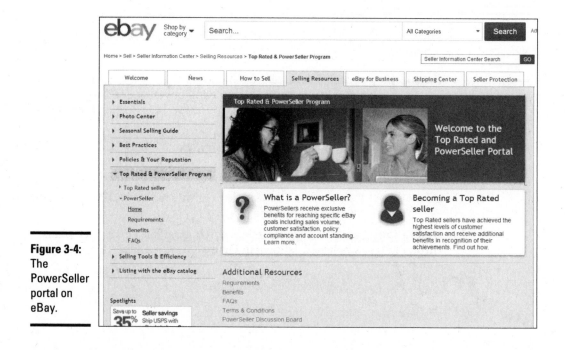

Figure 3-4:
The
PowerSeller
portal on
eBay.

Automatic FIVE-star Detailed Seller Ratings (DSRs)

eBay has come to value that the highest-quality sellers give people the best buying experience on the site. So they've devised a plan (tied into those gnarly Detailed Seller Ratings) to reward those who play by the rules.

A distinct benefit of following good customer service policies is the fact that if you follow the rules given here. (Note that some of the stars in the rating will be grayed out when your buyer goes to leave you feedback.)

✓ **Communication:** If there is no contact between you and your buyer (you provide complete, relevant descriptions — to the point that the buyer gets all the information right from your listing) and you specify one-day handling time, when the buyer leaves you feedback, you will automatically receive a Five-Star rating.

✓ **Shipping Time:** Buyers will not be able to leave a score of less than five stars if you specified one-day handling and upload the tracking numbers by the end of the next business day (11:59 p.m.) Pacific Time after the buyer's payment clears. Also, delivery must be confirmed (via the tracking numbers) within four business days from when the payment clears, or within your shipping mode's estimated delivery time if less than four days.

✓ **Shipping Cost:** If you offer free shipping and the buyer takes advantage of that option, the buyer cannot lower your rating in this category.

In addition to having their own discussion board, eBay PowerSellers get other benefits:

✦ **Unpaid Item Protection:** PowerSellers not only get Final Value Fee and listing credits when faced with a non-paying buyer, they also get a credit for any Listing Upgrade Fees (for example, Buy It Now, Bold, or Subtitle) — you know, all that extra fluff.

✦ **UPS rate discounts:** You can save up to 23 percent off UPS Standard List Rates for Ground Services, based on a 13-week average. See Figure 3-5 for details. To check for any changes to the discount system, visit

```
http://ebay.promotionexpert.com/eBayCarrierDiscount/
    how_much_can_i_save.jsp
```

✦ **Health Care Solutions:** PowerSellers can build health insurance plans through eBay's provider, shown in Figure 3-6. More information can be found at

```
http://www.healthinsureanswers.com/
```

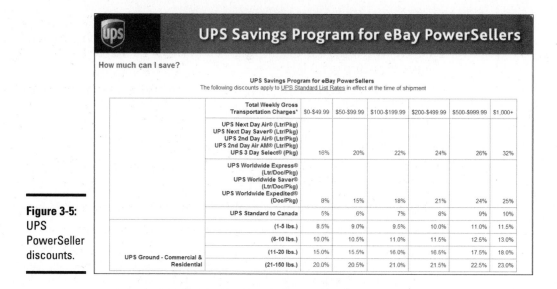

Figure 3-5: UPS PowerSeller discounts.

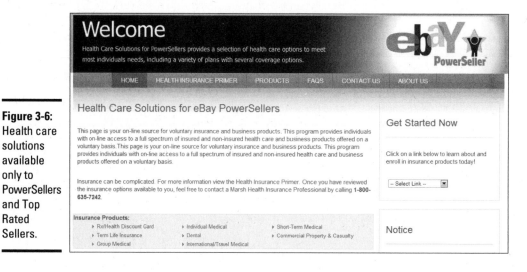

Figure 3-6: Health care solutions available only to PowerSellers and Top Rated Sellers.

Top Rated Seller benefits

The highest levels of benefits go to Top Rated Sellers. They get the Unpaid item protection as PowerSellers do, as well as access to the Discussion Board, the UPS discounts, and access to health care plans. There are added benefits:

+ **Increased visibility in Best Match search:** Now eBay gives the advantage to the listings of the upper half of sellers in terms of buyer satisfaction. Sellers with highest detailed seller ratings within the last 30 days receive more exposure than the average seller.

+ **USPS Commercial Plus pricing:** Platinum or Titanium level PowerSellers get this rate when you print labels on eBay.

Top Rated Seller Plus benefits

When you have met all requirements and attain the Top Rated Seller Plus status you get these additional perks:

+ **Badge:** eBay will display the Top Rated Seller Plus badge on your listings.

+ **Higher search ranking:** You get maximum exposure in search.

+ **20-percent discount on Final Value Fees:** eBay discounts the Final Value Fees on the monthly bill to those who maintain high standards and meet the Top Rated Seller Plus requirements.

Chapter 4: Deciding When You Need an eBay Store

In This Chapter

✓ Understanding the lure of online stores

✓ Counting the costs

✓ Setting up a store

✓ Marketing and making a sale

*I*f you're doing well selling your items on eBay, are you itching to open an eBay Store? Have you used the eBay Buy It Now feature in one of your listings? Have you sold via Fixed Price listings? Did either work for you? An eBay Store is a giant collection of your listings. If you're a highly active seller, having an eBay Store may help your business (plus you get more free listings a month and other benefits).

Opening an eBay Store can expand a successful business. An eBay Store provides you with your own little corner of eBay where you can leverage your good relationships with your customers and sell directly to them. But the eBay Stores platform is not a total solution, and having an eBay Store is no one-way ticket to Easy Street. (There's no such ticket anyway. But you knew that.)

I get e-mails all the time from people who open their own eBay Stores and are still not successful in moving merchandise. Why? Because running an eBay Store is not an instant key to online success. And because you can sell on eBay without having a designated eBay Store. No matter how many money-back guarantees you receive from online gurus promising magical success on eBay, the only magic is putting your shoulder, nose, and whatever else to the grindstone — and exerting the effort necessary to bring customers to your store.

If you're running many listings and your business is doing well, the discounts on fees, upgrades, and more maybe reason enough to open a store. This chapter should give you all the information you need to make a thoughtful decision.

If you're just beginning on eBay, the best advice I can give you is to hold off on opening an eBay Store until your feedback rating is over 100. Participating in transactions on eBay is a natural teacher because you'll see mistakes that sellers make when they sell to you. Some sellers are plain unfriendly, and by buying and selling on eBay you'll have a true understanding of how quality customer service will help you build your business. You'll also learn from your own mistakes and be able to provide better service to your customers.

Locating Your Special Place Online

When you're opening an eBay Store, you have just three main rules to remember and apply: location, location, location. If you were going to open a brick-and-mortar store, you could open it (for example) in the corner strip mall, at a shopping center, or even in a suburb. You'd have to decide in what location your store would do best; that goes for an online store as well. You'll find tons of locations where you can open an online store, including online malls (when you can find them) and sites such as Amazon.com, Etsy, and (of course) eBay.

You have to pay rent for your online store, of course, but opening and running an online store isn't nearly as expensive as doing the same for a tangible store in the real world (where you also have to pay electrical bills, maintenance bills, and more). Plus, the ratio of rent to (hopefully successful) sales makes an online store a much easier financial decision, and your store's exposure to the buying public can be huge.

eBay wants you to succeed as well. After all, the more you sell, the more eBay earns in Final Value Fees. As a seller who delivers good customer service, you're rewarded with discounts.

Checking Out Online Stores Galore

According to comScore Media Metrix, in February 2013, these e-commerce sites garnered an astounding number of *unique* visitors (counting *all* of one person's visits to the sites just *once* a month) from home, work, and university locations:

✦ **WalMart:** 38,854,000

Think about this when you consider whether people are still shopping the web looking for bargains.

✦ **eBay:** 65,754,000

✦ **Craigslist**: 46,380,000

✦ **Apple, Inc**: 75,321,000

✦ **Amazon.com:** 108,140,000 (This total includes all Amazon sites.)

Back in the day, eBay must have felt competition from the Yahoo! Small Business feature and from Amazon.com — and so decided to open its doors (in July 2001) to sellers who wanted their own online stores. Originally, those stores represented fixed-price sales and were a normal progression so eBay could continue as the world's marketplace.

eBay itself is a kind of online store that specializes in selling *your* stuff, not *theirs.* It doesn't stock a stick of merchandise and it isn't in competition with you. In addition to its staggering number of visitors, eBay offers you the most reasonable store rent, as shown in Table 4-1.

Table 4-1	Monthly Costs for an Online Starter Store		
	eBay	*Yahoo! Merchant Solutions*	*Amazon Professional Selling Plan*
Basic rent	$19.95	$39.95	$39.99
Listing fee	150 free/month	0	0
Highest final value/ transaction fee	Tiered, up to 9%	1.5%	Referral fees up to 25%

Amazon ended reasonably-priced Shops in 2006, to move sellers to their more expensive plans. It doesn't take a rocket scientist to convince you that having an eBay Store is an excellent bargain. Keep in mind that eBay is based on merchandise sales, and the public actively shops eBay Stores. Now, I know that many online stores aren't based on auctions, but eBay Stores can feature both auctions and fixed-price listings — happily, the Buy It Now items you list are as easy to handle as auctions. To review the prices and rules before you open your eBay Store, go to

```
http://pages.ebay.com/storefronts/start.html
```

When you're ready to get down to virtual brass tacks, the details of setting up your eBay Store are available on the web page shown in Figure 4-1, at `http://pages.ebay.com/storefronts/building.html`.

Book VIII
Chapter 4

Deciding When You
Need an eBay Store

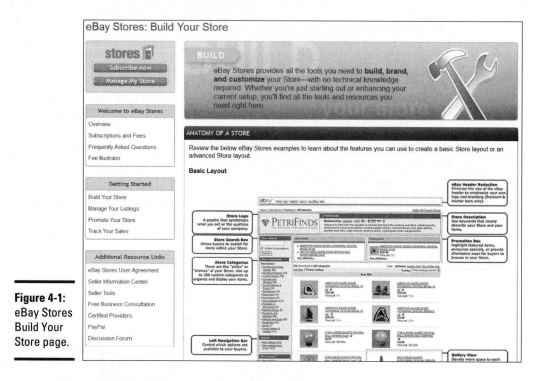

Figure 4-1:
eBay Stores
Build Your
Store page.

Deciding to Open an eBay Store

So you think it's time to open an online store, eh? And eBay looks like the place to do it? Well, if you feel it in your gut and you're ready to take the leap, here's what you need to know. eBay has few requirements when it comes to opening an eBay Store:

+ **Registered user:** You need to be a registered seller on the eBay site with a credit card on file.

+ **PayPal account:** You need to have a Verified PayPal account; better yet, at the Business or Premier level. Accepting credit cards is a necessity for building sales, and PayPal is integrated into the site, as well as being widely accepted by buyers.

Be sure you understand how a PayPal account works so you can decide on the types of payments you will accept — and with which countries you intend to do business.

When you're ready to get started, you can find the eBay Store hub at `http://stores.ebay.com/` (as shown in Figure 4-2). It doesn't get much easier than that! Personally, I like to add these additional prerequisites to back you up for success:

✦ **Sales experience:** Having selling (and buying) experience over and above eBay's meager prerequisite is a big plus. The best teacher (aside from this book) is the school of hard knocks.

✦ **Merchandise:** Opening an eBay Store with only one each of ten items isn't a good idea. You need to have some quantifiable stock of merchandise to support consistent sales.

✦ **Devotion:** You need to have the time to check into your eBay business at *least* once a day, and the time to ship the purchased merchandise in a prompt manner.

Figure 4-2:
The eBay Stores hub.

Choosing Between Store Types

All eBay Stores are on a level playing field. All your items are equally searchable on eBay, so you can be right up there with the big guys and compete. The first cost differential is the type of store you want to open.

Even the basic ($19.95) eBay Store gives you a lot of options; higher level stores build on these. Here are my favorite highlights:

+ **Listings:** All your eBay listings, whether auction or fixed-price, will appear in your eBay Store.

+ **Custom URL (web address):** Your eBay Store will have its own Internet address that you can use in links in promotional material — even to promote your store on the Internet. (My eBay Store address is `http://stores.ebay.com/Marsha-Colliers-Fabulous-Finds`)

+ **Store search:** When customers visit your eBay Store, they will be able to search within your listings for their desired item — with your own personal search engine.

+ **Selling Manager:** This is the super eBay software that replaces your All Selling page in My eBay. If you have a Premium-level eBay Store, you get Selling Manager Pro for free, the $15.99 a month fee is waived. I use it and love it. Basic eBay Stores get Selling Manager as part of the package.

+ **Cross-Promotion boxes:** By editing the promotion boxes, you can highlight which items are displayed on your Item, Bid Confirm, and Purchase Confirm pages.

+ **Three hundred store categories:** You can sell (say) sporting goods in one category, women's fashion in another, fine art in one more. . . . you have up to 300 custom categories for your varied merchandise.

+ **Fifteen custom pages:** You can use custom pages to customize the look of your eBay Store, make different landing pages, list your store policies, and make the store your own. (I use only a few custom pages and it suits me fine!)

+ **Custom store header:** Get your own brand by designing a graphic store header.

+ **Markdown Manager:** Hold a sale in your store! Select items to discount for a period of time and offer discounted pricing. You can run sales on up to 250 listings a day in a Basic Store and Anchor stores up to 5,000.

+ **Vacation hold:** Ever wish you could make your listings temporarily unavailable, or let your customers know you'll be out of town? This great feature allows you to do just that.

+ **Stores To Go**: Get a widget to share on your blog or social network (see Figure 4-3) that highlights your eBay items. Find this hidden treasure at `http://togo.ebay.com/`.

+ **Create Promotional Flyers:** Online tool to help you design a flyer to promote other items and include in your shipments.

+ **Search engine keyword management:** You may customize search engine keywords in Manage My Store to improve your store's page rankings in the search engines to which eBay feeds.

+ **Traffic Reports**: Page Views, Daily Unique Visitors, referring domains (are other websites pointing to your listings?), most popular pages, and more are available for all store owners. Premium and Anchor eBay Stores get even more in-depth data.

+ **Sales Reports Plus:** You'll have access to monthly in depth reports on your sales (sample shown in Figure 4-4). And you'll get an e-mail from eBay each month to remind you to check them out.

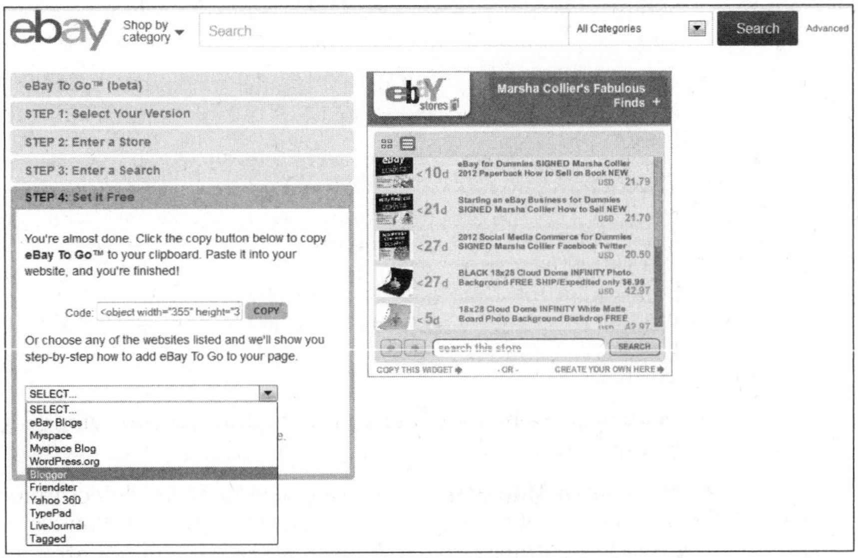

Figure 4-3: Get a widget for your store!

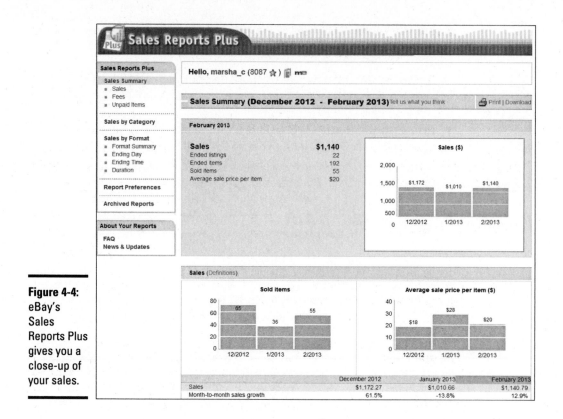

Figure 4-4: eBay's Sales Reports Plus gives you a close-up of your sales.

eBay Stores are available on three levels:

✦ **Basic Store:** For $19.95 a month ($15.95 when paid annually), you get your own eBay Store with all the benefits. A Basic Store entitles you to 150 free listings (auction or fixed-price) a month. If you use all your free listings, each auction will cost $.25 and fixed price will be $.20 (Media, Books, DVDs, movies. music and video games $.05).

✦ **Premium Store:** You get all the benefits of a Basic Store, plus more advanced sales and traffic reports. Your first 500 listings are free. After that, auctions will run $.15 and fixed-price listings, $.10.This type of Store will set you back $59.95 per month, or $49.95 when you pay the bill annually.

✦ **Anchor Store:** This is a top-of-the-line Store on eBay. For as low as $179.95 a month (when you pay annually) or $199.95 a month (month by month), you may list up to 2,500 items for fees (additional auctions are $.10, fixed-price listings are $.05).

There is no limit to the number of items you put up for sale in the Basic Store. An Anchor Store can have as few or as many items as the Basic Store. Many high-level Power and Top Rated Sellers find that the Basic eBay Store fulfills their needs.

When people visit your eBay Store, they have no way of knowing whether you have a Basic, Featured, or Anchor Store. The design of your Store is up to you — you can make it as fancy as you want.

Knowing the Fee Structure

When you have an eBay Store, other fees are involved (are you surprised?) in addition to the monthly fee, you'll have to take note of, options fees, and Final Value Fees. These fees are different for eBay Store sellers than for those selling on eBay without a Store.

Items sold by eBay Store owners carry a similar fee structure as items listed on the eBay site, but the actual numbers and percentages are different. The difference in cost helps you decide which items to put in your store, your auctions, or on your website. Knowing the prices in Tables 4-2 and 4-3 upfront helps you to decide what you need to get for each item in the different sales formats.

Table 4-2	Store Inventory Listing Upgrades		
Upgrade	*Auctions (All durations ($)*	*Fixed Price 3, 5, 7 and 10 day*	*Fixed Price 30 days and Good Till cancelled*
Gallery Plus	0.35	0.35	1.00
Item subtitle	0.50	0.50	1.50
Listing Designer	0.10	0.10	0.10
Bold	2.00	2.00	2.00
Value Pack (Gallery Plus, Listing Designer, and Subtitle)	0.65	0.65	2.00

Table 4-3	Store Final Value Fees
Categories	*Final Value Fee (Maximum $250)*
Computers/Tablets & Networking Video Game Consoles	4%
Consumer Electronics Cameras & Photos	6%
Coins & Paper Money Stamps	6%
Musical Instruments & Gear	7%
Motors Parts & Accessories	8%
Clothing, Shoes & Accessories	9%
Collectibles	9%
Home & Garden	9%
Camera & Photo Accessories	9%
Cell Phone Accessories	9%
All Other Categories	9%

Upper-level eBay Stores get Selling Manager Pro for free. The Basic eBay Store gives you free use of Selling Manager. You have to go to the Selling Manager sign-up page and sign up. As a Store owner, you won't be charged, but you must go through the sign-up process to avail yourself of these great tools.

Selecting Your eBay Store Name

You've decided to take the plunge and open an eBay Store. Have you thought of a good name for your Store? The name doesn't have to match your eBay user ID, but both names are more recognizable if they relate clearly to each other. You can use your company name, your business name, or a name that describes your business. I recommend that you use the same name for your eBay Store that you plan to use in all your online businesses. By doing so, you begin to create an identity (or, as the pros call it, a *brand*) that customers will come to recognize and trust.

Your online eBay Store should not replace your e-commerce enabled website (see Book VI) but, instead, should be an extension of it. When people shop your eBay Store, take the opportunity to make them customers of your website through your package inserts. Good deal!

Setting Up Shop

It's time to get down to business. You get to the eBay Stores hub page as follows: At the bottom of the Home page, you'll find a pop-up menu. Click the Stores link from the Buy area of this menu, and on the right side of the resulting page, click the Open a Store link on the right (refer to Figure 4-2). This takes you to the Seller's hub of eBay Stores. If you click all the links you see here, you get the eBay company line about how good an eBay Store can be for your business. Okay, you already *know* how good an eBay Store can be for your business, so skip the propaganda and get right down to business (but don't forget to check for any policy changes that may affect your Store's operations).

Before you click that link to open your eBay Store, ask yourself two questions:

✦ **Can I make a serious commitment to my eBay Store?** Any store — especially this one — is a commitment; it won't work for you unless you work for it. You have to have the merchandise to fill it and the discipline to continue listing your fixed-price *and* auction items. Your store is a daily, monthly, and yearly obligation.

When you go on vacation, you can use the eBay Store's Vacation Feature and eBay will either close your item listings or put up a notification letting your customers know that you're on vacation until a specified date.

You can close your eBay Store temporarily, but eBay will reserve your store name for only 30 days. After that, you have to come up with a new name (and your competition may have taken over your old store name, especially if it's famous).

✦ **Will I work for my eBay Store even when I don't feel like it?** You have to be prepared for the times when you're sick or just don't feel like shipping but orders are waiting to be shipped. You have to do the work anyway; it's all part of the commitment.

eBay gives you the venue, but it's in your own hands to make your mercantile efforts a success. If you can handle these responsibilities, read on!

Subscribing to eBay Stores

If you're serious and ready to move on, assuming you're already using Selling Manager, look for the box of Seller tools and click the Open an eBay Store link. You can also go to the page at `http://pages.ebay.com/ storefronts/building.html` and click the Subscribe Now button in the upper-left corner of the page. You're taken to subscription page.

eBay wants to ease you into this eBay Store thing. Make you feel comfortable, so you'll get the easy stuff first. Figure 4-5 shows you the initial sign-up screen, where you get to select the level of Store you want. It's an easy choice, start small with the $15.95 version. Come to think of it, many sellers have been running the Basic version for years and have been very happy with it.

After you've clicked the page's proverbial *Continue* button, eBay has a little page to show you a couple of benefits of opening your Store. With the Basic Store, you get Selling Manager and Sales Reports Plus for free. You don't have to do anything but click Continue because eBay already inserted the check marks in the selection boxes for you. If, for some reason, they don't appear, put a check in each box by clicking it, and then click Continue.

The resulting page is where eBay starts to get serious. It shows your monthly charges and the User Agreement (see Figure 4-6). Here eBay changes the friendly *Continue* button to the businesslike *Subscribe*. That's to let you know that this is serious. When you click Subscribe, the clock starts to tick on your monthly fees.

Don't subscribe to an eBay Store unless you're ready to get started immediately. Fees start the day you sign up, so why not read this chapter first and get centered on what you want to do? While you're thinking, the next section offers some pointers.

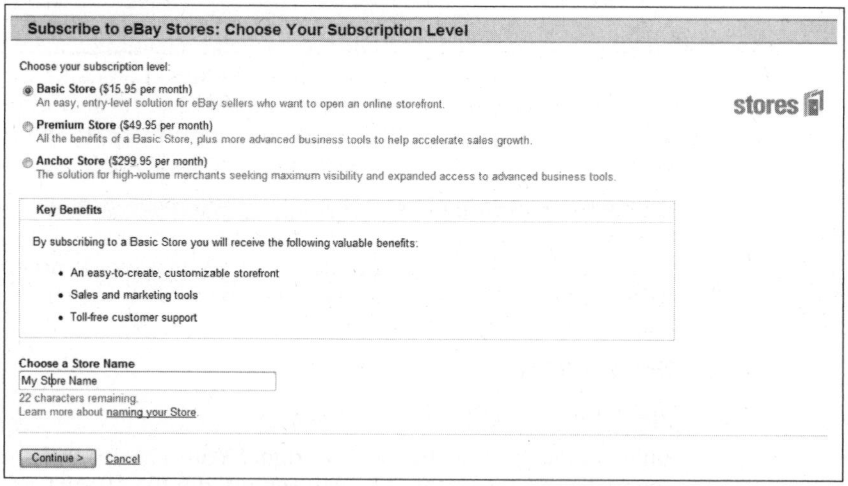

Subscribe to eBay Stores: Choose Your Subscription Level

Choose your subscription level:

◉ **Basic Store** ($15.95 per month)
An easy, entry-level solution for eBay sellers who want to open an online storefront.

○ **Premium Store** ($49.95 per month)
All the benefits of a Basic Store, plus more advanced business tools to help accelerate sales growth.

○ **Anchor Store** ($299.95 per month)
The solution for high-volume merchants seeking maximum visibility and expanded access to advanced business tools.

stores 🏬

Key Benefits

By subscribing to a Basic Store you will receive the following valuable benefits:

- An easy-to-create, customizable storefront
- Sales and marketing tools
- Toll-free customer support

Choose a Store Name

My Store Name

22 characters remaining.
Learn more about naming your Store.

[Continue >]   Cancel

Figure 4-5:
Taking the big step — go ahead and just do it.

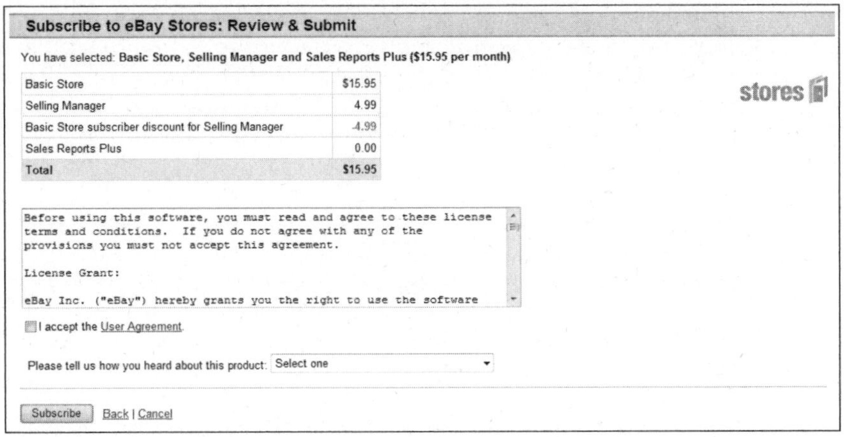

Subscribe to eBay Stores: Review & Submit

You have selected: **Basic Store, Selling Manager and Sales Reports Plus ($15.95 per month)**

Basic Store	$15.95
Selling Manager	4.99
Basic Store subscriber discount for Selling Manager	-4.99
Sales Reports Plus	0.00
Total	$15.95

stores

> Before using this software, you must read and agree to these license terms and conditions. If you do not agree with any of these provisions you must not accept this agreement.
>
> License Grant:
>
> eBay Inc. ("eBay") hereby grants you the right to use the software

☐ I accept the User Agreement.

Please tell us how you heard about this product: Select one ▼

[Subscribe] Back | Cancel

Figure 4-6:
Why not give the User Agreement a read before checking the box?

Making the required decisions

You need to make a few decisions to create a good store. So before building your eBay Store, read the following sections. Depending on the whims and changes that move through eBay, the order in which you have to implement these decisions can vary, but these are choices that you must make:

1. **Choose a color theme.**

eBay provides some elegant color and graphics themes (see Figure 4-7). Until you have the time to go hog-wild and design a custom masterpiece, you can choose one of the clearly organized layouts, either pre-designed ones or based on easily customizable themes. You can always change the color scheme or layout for your eBay Store later. Don't select something overly bright and vibrant; you want something that's easy on the eyes, which is more conducive to a comfortable selling environment.

You have the option of selecting a store theme that doesn't require you to insert a custom logo or banner. I strongly recommend *against* skipping the logo or banner. You need to establish a unifying brand for your online business. You might want to work one up well before you get to the point of selecting a store theme.

2. **Click Continue.**

3. **Type your new eBay Store's name.**

You've decided on a store name, right? Your eBay Store's name can't exceed 35 characters. Before you type it, double-check that you aren't infringing on anyone's copyrights or trademarks. You also can't use any permutation of eBay trademarks in your store's name.

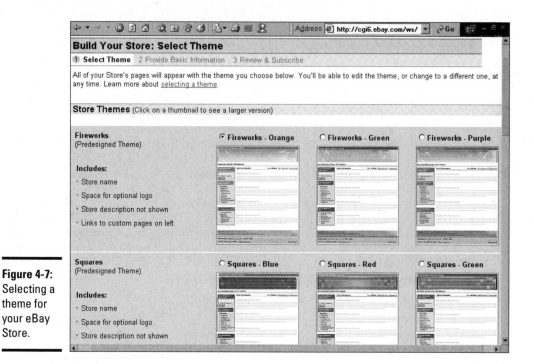

Figure 4-7:
Selecting a
theme for
your eBay
Store.

4. Type a short description of your store.

When I say short, I mean *short*. You have only 300 characters to give a keyword filled description of your store and merchandise. You can't use HTML coding to doll up the description, and you can't use links. Just the facts please, and a *little* bit of dazzle.

The importance of this description is huge. When people use search engines such as Google and Bing, this is the area where they look to find keywords to classify and list your store.

Consider writing your copy ahead of time in Word. Then, still in Word, highlight the text and choose Tools➪Word Count. Word gives you the word count of the highlighted text. Check the character count with spaces, to be sure your text fits.

5. Select a graphic to jazz up the look of your store.

You can use one of eBay's clip-art-style banners or create a custom 310-x-90-pixel banner of your own. If you use one of eBay's graphics, you must promise (hand over heart) that you won't keep it there for long. (See the text after this set of steps for info on designing your own graphics — or hiring someone to do it.)

Now you're getting somewhere. At this point, your eBay Store is just about ready to roll.

6. **Click Continue.**

   Now you should have an idea of what your store will look like. You're about to open an eBay Store, complete with storefront (drumroll, please).

7. **Sign up for the Basic Store ($15.95 a month), and click the Start My Subscription Now button.**

8. **Click the supplied link to get in the trenches and customize your Store further.**

If you're wondering in which category your Store will be listed on the eBay Stores home page, it's up to you to make that choice. eBay checks the items as you list them in the standard eBay category format. For example, if you have six books listed in the Books: Fiction and Nonfiction category and five items in the Cameras & Photo category, you'll be in the listings for both categories. Your custom Store categories (read on) are used to classify items only in your Store.

Designing an eBay Store logo

If you use one of eBay's prefab graphics and just leave it there, people shopping your eBay Store will know that you aren't serious enough about your business to design a simple and basic logo. I've had many years of experience in advertising and marketing, and I must tell you that a custom look will beat clip art any day. Your store is special — put forth the effort to make it shine.

If you have a graphics program, design a graphic with your store's name. Start with something simple; you can always change it later when you have more time. Save the image as a GIF or JPG file, and upload it as you would any other image.

A bunch of talented graphic artists make their living selling custom web graphics on eBay. If you aren't comfortable designing, search eBay for *ebay store banner* or *ebay store design*. Graphic banners on eBay sell for about $5 to $150 — certainly worth the price in the time you'll save.

Running Your Store

You can customize your store at any time by clicking Manage My Store, which is a link on your Selling Manager page or, at the bottom of your eBay Store's home page, the Seller, Manage Store link.

**Book VIII
Chapter 4**

**Deciding When You
Need an eBay Store**

Create an About the Seller page

If you haven't already created an eBay About Me page, do it now! The About Me page becomes the About the Seller page in your store. This page is a primary tool for promoting sales. (See Book I, Chapter 8 for more on the About Me page.) You can put this page together in about ten minutes, max, with eBay's handy and easy-to-use templates.

The page shown in Figure 4-8 appears, with headings describing important tasks for your Store.

Store design

In the Store Design area (see the screen shot of mine in Figure 4-9), you can perform major tasks required for your store.

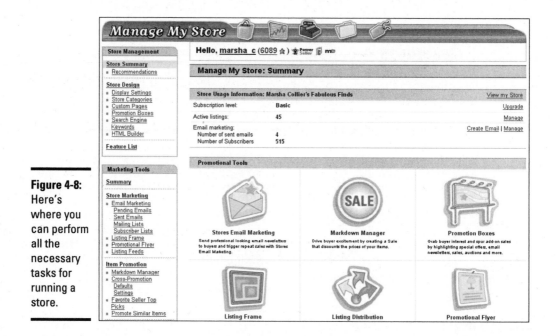

Figure 4-8: Here's where you can perform all the necessary tasks for running a store.

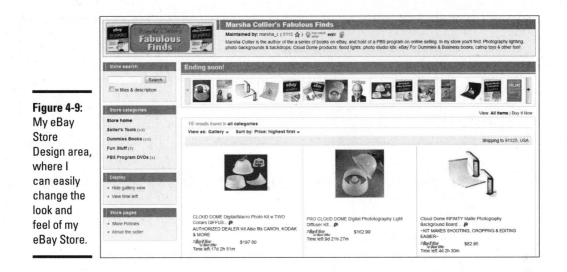

Figure 4-9:
My eBay
Store
Design area,
where I
can easily
change the
look and
feel of my
eBay Store.

Here are a just few of the tasks you should consider revisiting:

✦ **Store design:** You can always go back to the design area and change the name of your Store or the theme of your pages. You can also change the way your store items are displayed: Gallery View (as shown in Figure 4-10) or List View. Neither view is inherently better, but I like the Gallery View because it shows the thumbnail gallery pictures of my items.

You should also select the order in which your items will sort. Highest Priced First, Lowest Priced First, Items Ending First, or Newly Listed First. I like Items Ending First as my sort, so buyers can get the chance to swoop in on items closing soon.

✦ **Custom pages:** Most successful eBay sellers have (at the very least) a Store Policies page. Figure 4-11 shows you the one for my store. When you set up a policies page, eBay supplies you with a choice of layouts. Just click the Create New Page link to select the template that you want to use. Don't freak out if you don't know HTML; eBay helps you out with an easy-to-use HTML generator, as found in the Sell an Item form.

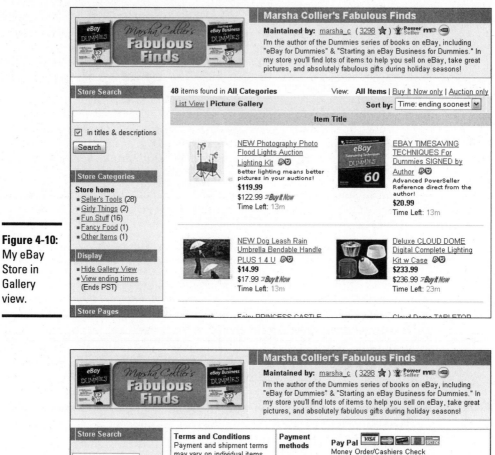

Figure 4-10:
My eBay
Store in
Gallery
view.

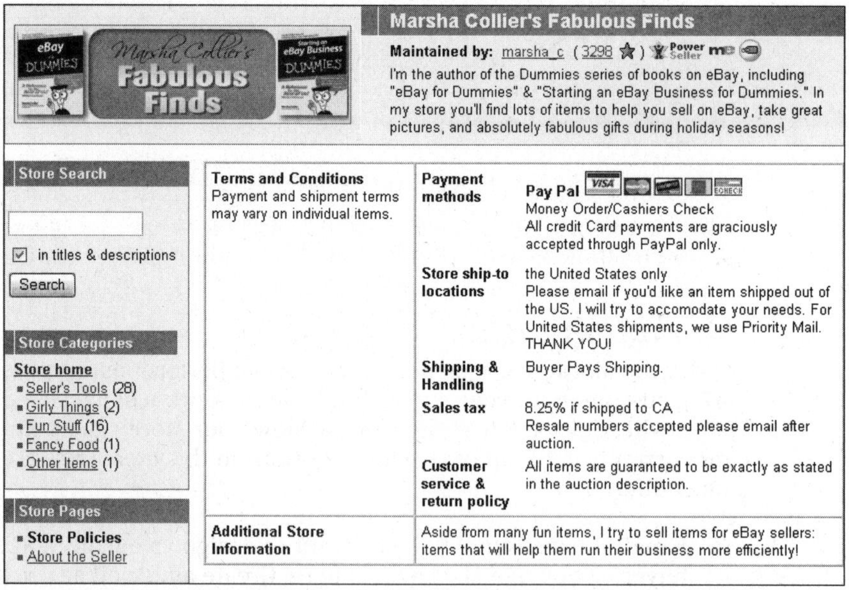

Figure 4-11:
My eBay
Store's
policies
page.

Following are some important policies to include:

- *Indicate to what locations you'll ship.* If you don't ship overseas or outside the United States., make that clear. Ditto if you do. Just make sure you know what's required to ship internationally before you promise to do it.

- *Specify the sales tax you plan to collect.* If your state doesn't require you to collect sales tax, leave the area blank. If it does, select your state and indicate the proper sales tax. Most states won't require you to collect sales tax unless the sale is shipped to your home state. Check the links in Book IX, Chapter 2 to verify your state's sales tax regulations.

- *State your customer service and return policy.* Fill in the information regarding how you handle refunds, exchanges, and so on. Be sure to include whatever additional store information you think is pertinent.

You can also set up a custom home page for your Store, but it's not a popular option. Most sellers feel it's best to let visitors go right to the listings of what's for sale.

✦ **Custom categories:** Here's where you really make your eBay Store your own. You may name up to 300 custom categories that relate to the varied items you sell in your store.

✦ **Promotion boxes:** Set up some promotion boxes and change them every month or so to keep your store's look fresh. Select items for promotion that work well with the particular selling season. You have the option of inserting a filmstrip of your items, as I do on my Store's home page. When your prospective buyer mouses over one of the photos, it expands. (Take a look at Figure 4-12.)

✦ **Search engine keywords:** Check out this area to see the keywords that eBay forwards to the major web shopping and search feeds. If you think there are better keywords, be sure to add them.

Marketing tools

Under the Marketing tools heading, you can perform many tasks that help bring customers to your store. You have the option of clicking a Summary page, which gives you a quick look at how your store's marketing features are currently set. You have a lot of options in this area. Here are a few of the many offered:

✦ **E-mail marketing:** When you want to design an e-mail campaign to your buyers, you have all the tools here. Create an e-mail newsletter, create one for sending later, and manage your subscriber lists — all from one convenient area.

Figure 4-12:
Mousing over an image on my eBay Store home page brings up an enlarged quick view.

✦ **Listing frame:** Select this option after you set up an eBay Store. Don't ask questions, just do it. The custom listing-header display is one of the best tools you can use to bring people into your eBay Store. Since I don't believe in cluttering up my listing pages with a lot of graphics, I use the option to have a store invitation message appear above the description in my item listings. Click the link and select the option to Show Your Custom Listing Header on all your eBay auctions and fixed-price sales. This custom header encourages shoppers to visit your eBay Store when they browse your eBay listings. When customizing, you may include your store logo, as well as a search box specific to your eBay Store.

Item promotions

eBay has added some excellent ways to promote your Store. As an eBay Store owner, you have access to promotional tools that other sellers can't use. One of the most valuable of these is cross-promotions — there's no charge to use it, either!

✦ **Cross-promotions:** The cross-promotion box appears after a buyer places a bid on or purchases an item from an eBay seller. The beauty of having an eBay Store is that the cross-promotion box appears *twice:* once with your regular listings and again with a different assortment of items (if you want), after someone buys an item. Best of all? You get to select which categories' items are selected from to display with your individual auctions. Figure 4-13 shows a cross-promotion box that appears when someone views one of my auctions.

Figure 4-13: A cross-promotion in one of my eBay auctions.

You can set up the promotions so that they default to show other items from related store categories. Again, every listing has two sets of options: one for when a user views your listings and the other for when someone bids or wins your item.

✦ **Markdown Manager:** So you say you have to raise some cash to buy new merchandise? Why not run a sale? By clicking here, you can select items to put on sale. After they've been marked down, they'll appear as "On Sale."

Making a sale

From the buyer's point of view, shopping an eBay Store is not much different from buying items on the core site. eBay Stores feature fixed-price sales (as well as auctions); buyers will get the merchandise as soon as you can ship it (preferably the day after they pay). When a buyer makes a purchase from an eBay Store, here's what happens:

1. The buyer clicks the Buy It Now button on the listing page. The Review Payments page appears, where the buyer can review the purchase. This page contains the shipping amount that you specified when you listed the item.

2. The buyer reviews shipping information, and may select from options. When eBay notifies you that a sale has been made, you have all the information you need.

3. The buyer reviews the transaction and then clicks the Confirm button. The information about the sale is e-mailed to you, and the buyer receives confirmation of the sale.

Your eBay Store is an essential backup to your auctions. It's a great place to put out-of-season items, accessories for the items you sell actively, and even consignment items between re-listings. Considering the very affordable price of an eBay Store, you have to make only a few sales per month to pay for it. And when your sales start to build, your efforts will be greatly rewarded!

Book IX

Office and Legal

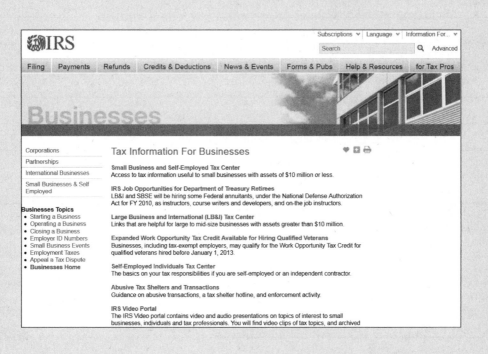

Visit www.dummies.com to find inspiration and how-to information on a wide range of subjects.

Contents at a Glance

Chapter 1: Getting Legal with the State and the Feds

In This Chapter

✔ Filing a fictitious name statement (for real)

✔ Getting a business license and other regulatory details

✔ Choosing a legal business format

*I*f you've played around on eBay, had some fun, and made a few dollars, good for you — enjoy yourself! When you start making serious money, however, the government no longer considers your business to be a hobby. It's time to consider some issues such as business structure, tax planning, and licenses; this chapter offers as painless an entrée as possible.

When you're concentrating on fulfilling multiple orders and keeping your customers happy, the last thing you need is a G-man breathing down your neck. Worst-case scenario: How about getting audited in December when you haven't been keeping up-to-date records all year? I know this sounds like stripping the fun out of doing business on eBay, but taking a bit of time and effort now can save you a ton of trouble later on (and will save you money in penalties).

Giving Your Business an Official Name

In most states in the United States, you can find funny liner ads in the classified section of the local newspaper. They're called *fictitious name statements*. No, the statements aren't fictitious, but in effect, the names are — and as such, they need to be registered with your state before you can open a bank account in a business's name. This is also referred to as your DBA (or Doing Business As) name. They let the state know who owns and operates a business. In California, you must file a fictitious name statement within 40 days of the commencement of your business. (Other state laws vary, so check the websites listed later in this chapter for more information on your state's requirements.) Your statement must also include a physical address where the business is operated — not a post office box address.

Don't waste your money online!

All kinds of expensive services on the Internet are more than willing to handle the work for you for a fat fee. Don't spend too much of your money if you don't have to. If newspaper publication is required, look for a small community newspaper or business journal (if they still exist in your part of the world) and call them to see whether they handle this type of legal ad. Most small publications are 90 percent supported by the money they make on filing legal ads. They're the experts on this type of filing. Plus, you get to help out another small business in your community. Every five years, it's a good thing to file your company's DBA (Doing Business As) with the nice lady at the local newspaper office.

When my DBA came up for renewal I noticed that my state had a $26 renewal fee which was about one-fifth of what an online legal site wanted to charge me. I couldn't believe they were charging so much; I figured I must be missing something, so I called my State office. The lady who answered was actually grateful that I called; she said it was a shame that businesses mark up the cost of this service so much. So, when it comes to renewals, consider going to your state's website (you can find it in the state links listed in Table 1-1) and you may be able to renew for a small fee online or through the mail.

Before you assume that registering a name isn't required in your state, check with your state's business code. (Links to all 50 states are presented later in the chapter.) Some states, such as Indiana, require that you register the assumed name of your business with the Secretary of State.

In the states requiring publication, your fictitious name statement must be published in an adjudicated (officially approved) newspaper for a certain amount of time. Ostensibly, this is to let the community know that a business is starting and who owns it. The newspaper supplies you with a proof of publication, which you keep in your files as a record of your filing. You generally have to renew the statement after a prescribed number of years.

After you have your officially stamped proof of publication, you can bring that to the bank and open an account in your business name, which is an important step in separating your personal living expenses from the business.

Taking Care of Regulatory Details

Let me give you some important advice to make your life easier in the long run: Don't ignore city, county, state, and federal regulatory details. Doing so may seem to make life easier at the get-go, but if your business is successful,

Book IX
Chapter 1

Getting Legal
with the State
and the Feds

one day your casual attitude will catch up with you. The usual attitude of government is that "Ignorance of the law is no excuse." You must comply with all the rules and regulations that are set up for your protection and benefit.

Business license or city tax certificate

Business licenses are the official-looking pieces of paper you see behind the register at brick-and-mortar businesses. Every business must have one, and depending on your local laws, you may have to have a *city license* or a *city tax registration certificate.* Yes, even if you're running a business out of your home and have no one coming to do business at your home, you may still need this. If you don't have one, the authorities may charge you a bunch of penalties if they ever find out. Avoiding this step isn't worth that risk.

To save you hanging on the phone, listening to elevator music, and being transferred and disconnected ad nauseam, I supply you with the direct links to apply for your licenses in Table 1-1. These URLs are accurate at the time of this writing, but as everybody knows, URLs change frequently. Check the following for updates:

```
http://www.sba.gov/content/what-state-licenses-and-
    permits-does-your-business-need
```

Table 1-1	Websites for Business License Information
State	*Link*
Alabama	http://revenue.alabama.gov/licenses/munbuslic.cfm
Alaska	http://commerce.alaska.gov/dnn/cbpl/Home.aspx
Arizona	http://www.azdor.gov/Business/LicensingGuide.aspx
Arkansas	http://asbdc.ualr.edu/business-information/1006-business-licenses-taxes-permits.asp
California	www.calgold.ca.gov/
Colorado	http://www.sos.state.co.us/pubs/business/main.htm
Connecticut	www.ct-clic.com/Content/Smart_Start_for_Business.asp
Delaware	https://onestop.delaware.gov/osbrlpublic/Home.jsp

(continued)

Table 1-1 *(continued)*

State	Link
District of Columbia	`http://brc.dc.gov/licenses/licenses.asp`
Florida	`www.myflorida.com/dbpr/`
Georgia	`www.sos.state.ga.us/firststop/`
Hawaii	`http://hawaii.gov/dcca/areas/breg`
Idaho	`http://www.state.id.us/business/licensing.html`
Illinois	`http://www.illinois.gov/business/Pages/default.aspx`
Indiana	`www.in.gov/business_guide.htm`
Iowa	`www.iowalifechanging.com/business/blic.html`
Kansas	`www.accesskansas.org/businesscenter/index.html?link=start`
Kentucky	`http://onestop.ky.gov/start/Pages/occupational.aspx`
Louisiana	`http://geauxBiz.com`
Maine	`http://www.maine.gov/portal/business/licensing.html`
Maryland	`http://www.dat.state.md.us/sdatweb/tralicen.html`
Massachusetts	`http://www.mass.gov/dor/businesses/help-and-resources/licensing-and-regulation.html`
Michigan	`http://www.michigan.gov/statelicensesearch`
Minnesota	`www.positivelyminnesota.com/Business/`
Mississippi	`https://www.mssbdc.org/Documentmaster.aspx?doc=1002`
Missouri	`http://www.business.mo.gov/register.asp`
Montana	`http://revenue.mt.gov/forbusinesses/one-stop_licensing/default.mcpx`
Nebraska	`https://www.nebraska.gov/osbr/cgi/domestic.cgi?/OSBRApplication/init/init/None`
Nevada	`http://www.nvsos.gov/index.aspx?page=419`

**Book IX
Chapter 1**

**Getting Legal
with the State
and the Feds**

State	Link
New Hampshire	www.nh.gov/revenue/business/dra_licenses.htm
New Jersey	www.state.nj.us/njbusiness/starting/
New Mexico	http://www.businesslicenses.com/Licenses/NM/
New York	http://www.nys-permits.org/
North Carolina	http://www.blnc.gov/start-your-business/business-licenses-permits
North Dakota	www.nd.gov/businessreg/license/index.html
Ohio	http://development.ohio.gov/business services.htm
Oklahoma	http://okcommerce.gov/new-and-existing-business/starting-a-new-business/startup-guide/
Oregon	http://www.bizcenter.org/
Pennsylvania	http://www.pabizonline.com/Pages/default.aspx
Rhode Island	https://www.ri.gov/taxation/BAR/
South Carolina	http://sc.gov/Business/Pages/license PermitsAndRegistration.aspx
South Dakota	http://www.sdreadytowork.com/economic-development.aspx
Tennessee	http://www.tn.gov/topics/Business
Texas	http://www.texas.gov/en/discover/Pages/topic.aspx?topicid=/business
Utah	http://www.utah.gov/business/starting.html
Vermont	http://www.vermont.gov/portal/business/
Virginia	https://apps.cao.virginia.gov/IDC/index.html
Washington	www.dol.wa.gov/business/
West Virginia	http://www.business4wv.com
Wisconsin	www.wisconsin.gov/state/byb/
Wyoming	http://soswy.state.wy.us/Business/Business.aspx

State sales tax number

If your state has a sales tax, a *sales tax number* (the number you use when you file your sales tax statement with your state) is required before you officially sell anything. If sales tax applies, you may have to collect the appropriate sales tax for every sale that ships within the state that your business is in.

Some people also call this a *resale certificate* because when you want to purchase goods from a wholesaler within your state, you must produce this number (thereby certifying your legitimacy as a seller) so the dealer can sell you the merchandise without charging you sales tax.

To find the regulations for your state, if you can't find the information on the web pages listed in Table 1-1, try the following site that supplies links to every state's tax board, which should have the answers to your questions (look for a link to sales and excise taxes):

www.taxadmin.org/fta/link/forms.html

Don't withhold the withholding forms

If you're going to be paying anyone a salary, you'll need an *employer identification number* (EIN), also known as a *federal tax identification number*. Every business has one. It's like a Social Security Number for a business, identifying your business on all government forms: a nine-digit number assigned to all businesses for tax filing and reporting. You may also need one for your state.

If you have regular employees, you need to file *withholding forms* to collect the necessary taxes, along with Social Security taxes, that you must send to the state and the IRS on behalf of your employees. You're also expected to deposit those tax dollars with the IRS and your state on the date required, which may vary from business to business. Many enterprises go down because the owners just can't seem to keep their fingers out of withheld taxes — which means the money isn't available to turn in when the taxes are due. (This is another reason you should have a separate bank account for your business.)

No need to dawdle. Why not get the number while you have the time:

✦ There's no charge to get your employer ID number (EIN).

✦ An employer ID number can be assigned by filing IRS form SS-4. Go to the IRS website to apply online:

www.irs.gov/businesses/small/article/0,,id=102767,00.
html

Book IX
Chapter 1

Getting Legal
with the State
and the Feds

Or if you'd rather mail in the form, the details and downloadable form are available as a PDF file.

✦ State employer ID numbers for taxes may depend on your state's requirements. Visit the following for an overview of the requirements for every state in the country:

`http://www.taxadmin.org/fta/link/default.php?lnk=10`

Selecting a Business Format

After you've fulfilled all the regulatory details, you need to formally decide how you want to run your company. You need to set up a legal format and you need to make a merchandise plan. (For more on merchandise planning, visit Book IV, Chapter 2.)

When you have a business, any type of business, it has to have a legal format for licensing and tax purposes. Businesses come in several forms, from a sole proprietorship all the way to a corporation. A "corporation" designation isn't as scary as it sounds. Yes, Microsoft, IBM, and eBay are corporations, but so too are many businesses run by individuals.

Each form of business has its pluses and minuses — and costs. I go over some of the fees involved in incorporating later in this chapter. For now, I detail the most common types of businesses, which I encourage you to weigh carefully.

I'm not a lawyer, so be sure to consult with a professional in the legal and financial fields to get the latest legal and tax ramifications of the various business formats.

Sole proprietorship

If you're running your business by yourself part-time or full-time, your business is a *sole proprietorship*. Yep, doesn't that sound official? A sole proprietorship is the simplest form of business; you don't need a lawyer to set it up. Nothing is easier or cheaper. Most people use this form of business when they're starting out. Many people often graduate to a more formal type of business as things get bigger.

If a husband and wife file a joint tax return, they *can* run a business as a sole proprietorship (but only one of you can be the proprietor). However, if both you and your spouse work equally in the business, then running it as a partnership — with a written partnership agreement — is a much better idea. (See the next section, "Partnership," for more information.) A partnership protects you in case of your partner's death. In a sole proprietorship, the business ends with the death of the proprietor. If the business has been a sole proprietorship in your late spouse's name, you may be left out in the cold.

Being in business adds a few expenses, but many things that you spend money on now (relating to your business) can be deducted from your state and federal taxes. The profits of your business are taxed directly as part of your own income tax, and the profits and expenses are reported on Schedule C of your 1040 tax package. As a sole proprietor, you're at risk for the business liabilities. All outstanding debts are yours, and you could lose personal assets if you default. Also, as your business becomes profitable, this business format forces you to pay an additional self-employment tax.

Also, you must consider the liability of the products you sell on eBay. If you sell foodstuffs, vitamins, or nutraceuticals (new-age food supplements) that make someone ill, you may be personally liable for any court-awarded damages. If someone is hurt by something you sell, you may also be personally liable as the seller of the product.

In a sole proprietorship, as with any form of home-based business, you may be able to get an insurance rider to your homeowner's insurance policy to cover you against some liabilities. Check with your insurance agent.

Partnership

When two or more people are involved in a business, it can be a *partnership*. A general partnership can be formed by an oral agreement. Each person in the partnership contributes capital or services and both share in the partnership's profits and losses. The income of a partnership is taxed to both partners, based on the percentage of the business that they own or upon the terms of a written agreement. Any losses are also split. The partnership must file its own tax return (Form 1065) reporting the business financials to the IRS.

You'd better be sure that you can have a good working relationship with your partner: This type of business relationship has broken up many a friendship. Writing up a formal agreement when forming your business partnership is an excellent idea. This agreement is useful in solving any disputes that may occur over time.

Book IX
Chapter 1

Getting Legal
with the State
and the Feds

Getting legal documents prepared

Many of the required business documents do not require a lawyer, but some do, depending on the complexity (and size) or your business situation. I have set up a folder with some free sample documents that you can print or download from my collection of Small Business Forms at `http://www.scribd.com/marsha__collier`

If you're thinking of setting up one of the business formats described in this chapter, you may also be interested in organizing things online. Visit `www.legalzoom.com`; this company handles legal document preparation for business incorporation, partnerships, and more for reasonable prices. Documents are prepared according to how you answer online questionnaires. LegalZoom checks your work, and e-mails your documents or mails them printed on quality acid-free paper for your signature.

When it comes to setting up an official company format with your state, you may just want to (at the very least) consult with an attorney. Perhaps you can find one who is also a member of your local Chamber of Commerce.

In your agreement, be sure to outline things such as

+ How to divide the profits and losses
+ Compensation to each partner
+ Duties and responsibilities of each partner
+ Restrictions of authority and spending
+ How disputes should be settled
+ What happens if the partnership dissolves
+ What happens to the partnership in case of death or disability

One more important thing to remember: As a partner, you're jointly and severally responsible for the business liabilities and actions of the other person or people in your partnership — as well as for your own. Again, this is a personal liability arrangement. You are both personally open to any lawsuits that come your way through the business.

The partnership has to file an informational return with the IRS and the state, but the profits of the partnership are taxed to the partners on their personal individual returns.

LLC (limited liability company)

A *limited liability company,* or LLC, is similar to a partnership but also has many of the characteristics of a corporation. An LLC differs from a partnership mainly in that the liabilities of the company are not passed on to the members (owners). Unless you sign a personal guarantee for debt incurred, the members are responsible only to the total amount they have invested into the company. But all members *do* have liability for the company's taxes.

A limited liability company doesn't require all of the legal red tape and obsessive-compulsive bureaucracy that a regular corporation requires. For example, while a corporation will require a board of directors, board meetings, an annual stockholders' meeting, and meeting minutes of all these events, a limited liability company won't.

You'll need to put together an operating agreement, similar to the partnership agreement. Doing so also helps establish which members own what percentage of the company for tax purposes. Most states will require you to file Articles of Organization forms to start this type of business.

An LLC is taxed like a sole proprietorship, with the profits and losses passed on to the members' personal tax returns. An LLC may opt to pay taxes like a corporation and keep some of the profits in the company, thereby reducing the tax burden to individual members. Although members pay the LLC's taxes, the LLC must still file Form 1065 with the IRS at the end of the year. This gives the IRS extra data to be sure that the individual members properly report their income.

Some states levy additional special or minimum taxes on an LLC. Be sure to check with your state's business department.

Corporation

A corporation has a life of its own: its own name, its own bank account, and its own tax return. A *corporation* is a legal entity created for the sole purpose of doing business. If you're a sole proprietor and you're incorporating, one of the main problems you face is realizing that you can't just help yourself to the assets of the business. Yes, a corporation can have only one owner — but that owner is the shareholder(s). If you can't accept that you can't write yourself a check from your corporation — unless it's for a specified salary or for the reimbursement of legitimate expenses — then you may not be cut out to face the responsibility of running your own corporation.

There are two types of corporations; it's best that you consult your accountant or lawyer to decide which is best for you.

Book IX
Chapter 1

Getting Legal
with the State
and the Feds

+ **C corporations** are what we normally consider as corporations. This is the business format of the big guys. It is taxed as a separate entity and subject to the corporate income tax shown in Table 1-2.

+ **S corporations** are corporations that have filed a special election with the IRS. They are not subject to corporate income tax. But are treated similarly (not identically) to partnerships for tax purposes.

The state in which you run your business sets up the rules for the corporations operating within its borders. You must apply to the Secretary of State of the state in which you want to incorporate. Federal taxes for corporations presently range from 15 to 35 percent, and they're generally based on your net profits.

Table 1-2	2013 Federal Tax Rates for Corporations
Taxable Income ($)	*Tax Due*
0 to 50,000	15%
50,001 to 75,000	$7,500 plus 25% on amount over $50,000
75,001 to 100,000	$13,750 plus 34% on amount over $75,0004
100,001 to 335,000	$22,250 plus 39% on amount over $100,000
335,001 to 10,000,000	$113,900 plus 34% of amount over $335,000
10,000,001 to 15,000,000	$3,400,000 plus 35% of amount over $10,000,000
15,000,001 to 18,333,333	$5,150,000 plus 38% of amount over $15,000,000
18,333,334 and more	35%

Employee owners of corporations can use the company to shelter income from being taxed by dividing the income between their personal and corporate tax returns. This is frequently called *income splitting;* it involves setting salaries and bonuses so that any profits left in the company at the end of its tax year will be taxed at only the 15 percent rate.

To compare what you pay and how much you'd pay in taxes if you left profits in a small corporation — important to know if you're going that route — see Table 1-2.

Considering that the individual Federal tax-rate percentages for incomes up to $75,000 annually can go as high as 28 percent, the trouble of keeping a corporation for your business may be a huge money-saver.

The Tax Foundation (http://taxfoundation.org/) offers its 2013 State Business Tax Climate Index that lists the ten highest- and ten lowest-ranked states:

✦ **Ten best states** in this year's Index are Wyoming, South Dakota, Nevada, Alaska, Florida, Washington, New Hampshire, Montana, Texas, and Utah. Many of these states do not have one or more of the major taxes, and thus do not have the associated complexity and distortions.

✦ **Ten lowest-ranked, or worst, states** are Maryland, Iowa, Wisconsin, North Carolina, Minnesota, Rhode Island, Vermont, California, New Jersey, and New York.

The full index report and state-by-state ranking can be found at

http://taxfoundation.org/article/2013-state-business-tax-climate-index

Most states also have their own taxes for corporations. In Table 1-3, you see the basic tax for C Corporations (assuming your corporation makes money after payroll and other expenses). Please check with your tax professional; many states have franchise taxes, inventory taxes — and goodness knows what else — as well.

Table 1-3	2013 State Corporate Income Tax Rates	
State	*Tax Rates and Brackets*	*Note This . . .*
Alabama	6.5%	Federally deductible.
Alaska	1.0% > $0	
	2.0 > 10K	
	3.0 > 20K	
	4.0 > 30K	
	5.0 > 40K	
	6.0 > 50K	
	7.0 > 60K	
	8.0 > 70K	
	9.0 > 80K	
	9.4 > 90K	
Arizona	6.968%	Minimum tax $50.

State	Tax Rates and Brackets	Note This . . .
Arkansas	1.0%	> $0
	2.0 > 3K	
	3.0 > 6K	
	5.0 > 11K	
	6.0 > 25K	
	6.5 > 100K	
California	10.84%	Minimum tax $800.
Colorado	4.63%	
Connecticut	7.5% or higher (income tax or tax on capital)	Minimum capital $250; additional 20% surtax applies for tax years 2012 and 2013.
Delaware	8.7% on the first $20 million	
District Of Columbia	9.975%	Minimum tax $100.
Florida	5.5%	
Georgia	6%	
Hawaii	4.4% > $0	
	5.4 > 25K	
	6.4 > 100K	
Idaho	7.6%	Minimum tax $20.
Illinois	9.5%	Sum of corporate income tax rate of 7.0% plus a replacement tax of 2.5%.
Indiana	8%	Indiana tax rate is scheduled to decrease to 7.5% on July 1, 2013.
Iowa	6.0% > $0	50% of federal income tax is deductible.
	8.0 > 25K	
	10.0 > 100K	
	12.0 > 250K	

(continued)

Table 1-3 *(continued)*

State	Tax Rates and Brackets	Note This . . .
Kansas	4% > $0	In addition to the flat 4% corporate income tax, Kansas levies a 3.0% surtax on taxable income over $50,000.
Kentucky	4.% > $0	Plus the larger of a gross receipts tax equal to 0.095% of gross sales or 0.75% of gross profits, or a minimum tax of $175.
	5.0 > 50K	
	6.0 > 100K	
Louisiana	4.0% > $0	Federally deductible.
	5.0 > 25K	
	6.0 > 50K	
	7.0 > 100K	
	8.0 > 200K	
Maine	3.5% > $0	
	7.93 > 25K	
	8.33 > 75K	
	8.93 > 250K	
Maryland	8.25%	
Massachusetts	8%	Minimum tax of $456.
Michigan	6%	
Minnesota	9.8%	
Mississippi	3.0% > $0	
	4.0 > 5K	
	5.0 > 10K	
Missouri	6.25%	50% is deductible.
Montana	6.75%	Minimum tax is $50.
Nebraska	5.58% > $0	
	7.81 > 50K	
Nevada	None	
New Hampshire	8.5% > $50K	

**Book IX
Chapter 1**

**Getting Legal
with the State
and the Feds**

State	Tax Rates and Brackets	Note This . . .
	9.25 > 150K	
New Jersey	6.5% > 50K	
	7.5 > 100K	
	9.0 > 100K	
New Mexico	4.8% > $0	
	6.4 > 500K	
	7.6 > 1,000,000	
New York	7.1%	Small business taxpayers in New York pay rates of 6.5%, 7.1%, and 4.35% on three brackets of entire net income up to $390,000 .
North Carolina	6.9%	
North Dakota	1.68% - 5.15%	Federally deductible.
Ohio		Ohio no longer levies a tax based on income, but instead imposes a Commercial Activity Tax (CAT) equal to $150 for gross receipts sitused to Ohio of between $150,000 and $1 million, plus 0.26% of gross receipts over $1 million. (The *situs* is the place to which, for purposes of legal jurisdiction or taxation, a property belongs.)
	8.5 > 50K	
Oklahoma	6.0%	
Oregon	6.6%	Minimum tax $10.
Pennsylvania	9.99%	
Rhode Island	9.0%	
South Carolina	5.0%	
South Dakota	None	

(continued)

Table 1-3 *(continued)*

State	Tax Rates and Brackets	Note This . . .
Tennessee	6.5%	
Texas	1.0%	
Utah	5.0%	Minimum tax $100.
Vermont	6.0% > $0	Minimum tax $250.
	7.0 > 10K	
	8.5 > 25K	
Virginia	6.0%	
Washington	Varies	
West Virginia	7%	Corporate rate is scheduled to decline to 6.5% after 2013.
Wisconsin	7.9%	
Wyoming	None	

Often, in small corporations, most of the profits are paid out in tax-deductible salaries and benefits. The most important benefit for a business is that *any liabilities belong to the corporation*. Your personal assets remain your own, because they have no part in the corporation.

Chapter 2: The Joys of Taxes and Business Reporting

In This Chapter

✔ Finding a tax professional

✔ Understanding first things first: Bookkeeping basics

✔ Saving your records to save your bacon

✔ Letting your reports talk to you

✔ Keeping your company records organized and safe

You'll get no argument from me that bookkeeping can be the most boring and time-consuming part of your job. You may feel that you just need to add your product costs, add your gross sales, and bada-bing, you know where your business is. Sorry, not true. Did you add that roll of tape you picked up at the supermarket today? Although it cost only $1.29, it's a business expense. How about the mileage driving back and forth from suppliers, garage sales, and flea markets? Those are expenses, too. I suspect that you're not counting quite a few other "small" items just like these in your expense column.

I must confess that I enjoy posting my expenses and sales after I actually get into the task. It gives me the opportunity to know exactly where my business is in its course at any given moment. Understand, I'm not using a pencil-entered ledger system to do that; my tool of choice is a software program that's fairly easy to use. But the concepts behind the tools matter too. In this chapter, I give you the lowdown on the basics of bookkeeping — and emphasize the importance of keeping records in case Uncle Sam comes calling. Keep reading: This chapter is *required*.

Dealing with a Professional

Have you ever wondered why big businesses have CFOs (chief financial officers), vice presidents of finance, CPAs (certified public accountants), and bookkeepers? It's because keeping the books is the backbone of a company's business.

Do you have a professional going over your books at least once a year? You should. A paid professional experienced in business knows what to do when it comes to your taxes. Due to the complexity of the tax code, not just any paid preparer will suffice when it comes to preparing your business taxes. Here's a list of possible people who can prepare your tax returns.

✦ **Tax preparer (or consultant):** This is the person you visit at the local we-file-for-you tax office. Did you know that a tax preparer could be anybody? There is no licensing involved. H&R Block hires as many as 100,000 seasonal workers as tax preparers each year. Where do these people come from? I'm sure that some may be experts on the tax code, but the sheer number of tax preparers and the lack of regulation can make using a we-file-for-you tax office a risky proposition for business-people who want to minimize their tax liability.

According to a recent United States General Accounting Office report estimated that 2.2 American citizens overpaid their taxes by an average of $610 per year because they claimed the standard deduction when it would have been more beneficial to itemize. Half of those taxpayers used a paid preparer who clearly was not cognizant of the full tax law as it applied to these individuals. Scary, huh?

✦ **Volunteer IRS-certified preparers:** The AARP (American Association of Retired Persons) does an outstanding job of assembling nearly 35,000 tax preparers to serve the needs of low-to-middle-income taxpayers (special attention going to those over 60). Their goal is to maximize legal deductions and credits, resulting in "tangible economic benefits" for their clients. These volunteers have to study, take a test, and become *certified by the IRS* before they can lend their services to the cause.

In recent years, AARP volunteers served a total of 2.6 million seniors in the United States. My mother was a retired corporate comptroller, and she volunteered in this program for many years. (She was disappointed when she made her lowest score on the IRS test — a 94 percent!) They staff nearly 6,000 sites nationwide. To find the one near you, call 1-888-227-7669 and select Tax-Aide Information or go to the AARP Foundation tax-aide locator at

```
http://www.aarp.org/applications/VMISLocator/
    searchTaxAideLocations.action
```

✦ **Public accountant:** A public accountant, or PA, must fulfill educational, testing, and experience requirements and obtain a state license. PAs must take an annual course to maintain their status.

✦ **Enrolled agent:** Often called one of the best-kept secrets in accounting, an enrolled agent is federally licensed by the IRS. (CPAs and attorneys are licensed by the state.) EAs must pass an extensive annual test on tax law and tax-return preparation every year to maintain their status. (They also have to pass annual background checks.) Enrolled agents are authorized to appear in place of a taxpayer before the IRS.

Many EAs are former IRS employees. To find an enrolled agent near you, go to the www.naea.org website and enter the Find an EA area.

✦ **Certified public accountant:** Certified public accountants (CPAs) must complete rigorous testing and fulfill experience requirements as prescribed by the state in which they practice. Most states require every CPA to obtain a state license.

CPAs are accountants. They specialize in recordkeeping and reporting financial matters. Their important position is as an advisor regarding financial decisions for both individuals and businesses. CPAs must take an annual course to maintain their status.

Keeping the Books: Basics to Get You Started

Although posting bookkeeping entries can be boring, clicking a button to generate your tax information is a lot easier than manually going over pages of sales information on a pad of paper. That's why I like to use a software program, particularly QuickBooks (more about that program later).

I suppose that you *could* use plain ol' paper and a pencil to keep your books; if that works for you, great. But even though that might work for you now, it definitely won't in the future. Entering all your information into a software program now — while your books may still be fairly simple to handle — can save you a lot of time and frustration in the future, when your eBay business has grown beyond your wildest dreams and no amount of paper can keep it all straight and organized. I discuss alternative methods of bookkeeping in Chapter 3 in this minibook. For now, I focus on the basics of bookkeeping.

Tracking everything in and out

To effectively manage your business, you must keep track of *all* your expenses — down to the last roll of tape. You need to keep track of your inventory, how much you paid for the items, how much you paid in shipping, and how much you profited from your sales. If you use a van or the family car to pick up or deliver merchandise to the post office (I can load eight of the light kits that I sell on eBay into our car), you should keep track of this mileage as well. When you're running a business, you should account for every penny that goes in and out.

Bookkeeping has irrefutable standards called GAAP (Generally Accepted Accounting Principles) that are set by the Financial Accounting Standards Advisory Board. (It sounds scary to me, too.) *Assets, liabilities, owner's equity, income,* and *expenses* are standard terms used in all forms of accounting to define profit, loss, and the fiscal health of your business.

Accounting for everything — twice

Every time you process a transaction, two things happen: One account is credited while another receives a debit (kind of like yin and yang). To get more familiar with these terms (and those in the following list), see the definitions in the chart of accounts in Chapter 3 in this minibook. Depending on the type of account, the account's balance either increases or decreases. One account that increases while another decreases is called *double-entry accounting:*

✦ When you post an expense, the debit *increases* your expenses and *decreases* your bank account.

✦ When you purchase furniture or other assets, it *increases* your asset account and *decreases* your bank account.

✦ When you make a sale and make the deposit, it *increases* your bank account and *decreases* your accounts receivable.

✦ When you purchase inventory, it *increases* your inventory and *decreases* your bank account.

✦ When a portion of a sale includes sales tax, it *decreases* your sales and *increases* your sales tax account.

Manually performing double-entry accounting can be a bit taxing (no pun intended). A software program, however, will automatically adjust the accounts when you input a transaction.

Separating business and personal records

As a business owner, even if you're a sole proprietor (see Chapter 1 in this minibook for information on business types), you should keep your business books separate from your personal expenses. By isolating your business records from your personal records, you can get a snapshot of which areas of your sales are doing well and which ones aren't carrying their weight. But that isn't the only reason keeping accurate records is smart; there's the IRS to think about, too. In the next section, I explain Uncle Sam's interest in your books.

REMEMBER

Okay, posting bookkeeping can be boring. But at the end of the fiscal year, when you have a professional do your taxes, you'll be a lot happier — and your tax preparation will cost you less — if you've posted your information cleanly and in the proper order. That's why using a program such as QuickBooks (see Chapter 3 in this minibook) is essential to running your business.

Records Uncle Sam May Want to See

One of the reasons we can have a great business environment in the United States is because we all have a partner, Uncle Sam. Our government regulates business and sets the rules for us to transact our operations. To help you get started with your business, the IRS maintains a small-business website (shown in Figure 2-1) at the following address:

```
www.irs.gov/businesses/small
```

In this section, I highlight what information you need to keep and how long you should keep it (just in case you're chosen for an audit).

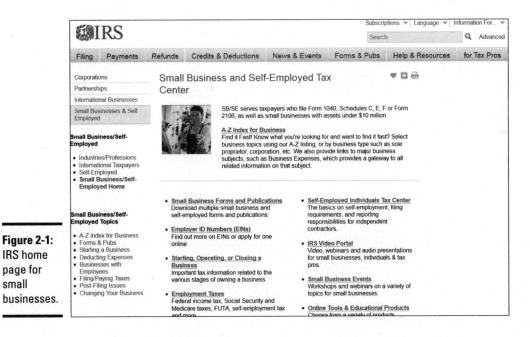

Figure 2-1:
IRS home page for small businesses.

Supporting information

Aside from needing to know how your business is going (which is really important), the main reason to keep clear and concise records is because Uncle Sam may come knocking one day. You never know when the IRS will choose *your* number and want to examine your records. In the following list, I highlight some of the important pieces of supporting information (things that support your expenses on your end-of-year tax return):

+ **Receipts:** Please heed this advice: *Save every receipt you get.* If you're out of town on a buying trip and have coffee at the airport, save that receipt — it's a deduction from your profits. Everything related to your business may be deductible, so you must save airport parking receipts, taxi receipts, receipts for a pen that you picked up on your way to a meeting, *everything.* If you don't have a receipt, you can't prove the write-off.

+ **Merchandise invoices:** Saving all merchandise invoices is as important as saving all your receipts. If you want to prove that you paid $400 and not the $299 retail price for that PlayStation 2 that you sold online for $500, you'd *better* have an invoice of some kind. The same idea applies to most collectibles, in which case a retail price can't be fixed. Save all invoices!

+ **Outside contractor invoices:** If you use outside contractors — even if you pay the college kid next door to go to the post office and the bank for you — you should get an invoice from them to document exactly what service you paid for and how much you paid. This is supporting information that will save your bacon, should it ever need saving.

+ **Business cards:** It may sound like I'm stretching things a bit, but if you use your car to look at some merchandise, pick up a business card from the vendor. If you're out of town and have a meeting with someone, take a card. Having these business cards can help substantiate your deductible comings and goings.

+ **A daily calendar:** This is where your smartphone or tablet comes in. Every time you leave your house or office on a business-related task, make note of it either on the website that hosts your calendar (Google Calendar syncs easily) or on your mobile devices. Keep as detailed a hoard of minutiae as you can stand. At the end of the year, I print out my Google calendar by month for tax backup. Staple the pages together and include the hard copies in your files with your substantiating information.

+ **Credit card statements:** You're already collecting credit card receipts, right? It's not a bad idea to scan these before they fade or get lost — but it isn't crucial if time is an issue. If you have your statements, you have a monthly proof of expenses. When you get your statement each month, post it into your bookkeeping program and itemize each and every charge, detailing where you spent the money and what for. (QuickBooks has a split feature that accommodates all your categories.) File these statements with your tax return at the end of the year in your year-end envelope.

I know that all this stuff will pile up, but that's when you go to the store and buy some plastic file-storage containers to organize it all. To check for new information and the lowdown on what you can and can't do, ask an accountant or a CPA. Also visit the IRS Tax Information for Businesses site (they even have videos), shown in Figure 2-2, at

www.irs.ustreas.gov/businesses

How long should you keep your records?

How long do you have to keep all this supporting information? I hate to tell you, but I think I've saved it all. I must have at least ten years of paperwork in big plastic boxes and old files in the garage. But you know, I'm not too extreme; the period in which you can amend a return or in which the IRS can assess more tax is never less than three years from the date of filing — and can be even longer.

Figure 2-2:
Get tax
information
from the
horse's
mouth here.

The IRS wants you to save anything related to your tax return for three years. But if you take a look at Table 2-1, the IRS may want backup documentation for up to six years. So for safety's sake, keep things for six years, if only to prove you're innocent. (As an aside, because I'm paranoid, I still keep everything for the maximum mentioned by the IRS: seven years.)

Table 2-1	Keep Records for This Length of Time
Circumstance	*Keep Records This Long*
You owe additional tax (if the following three points don't apply)	3 years
You don't report all your income and what you don't report is more than 25% of the gross income shown on your return	6 years
You file a fraudulent tax return	Forever
You don't bother to file a return	Forever
You file a claim of refund or credit after you've filed	3 years or 2 years after the tax was paid (whichever is longer)
Your claim is due to a bad debt deduction or worthless securities	7years
Employment Tax records	At least 4 years after the date that the tax becomes due or is paid, whichever is later
You have information on assets	Life of the asset

Even though I got the information in Table 2-1 directly from the IRS website and literature (Publication 583, "Starting a Business and Keeping Records"), it may change in the future. You can download a PDF copy of the booklet by going to the following address:

www.irs.gov/pub/irs-pdf/p583.pdf

It doesn't hurt to store your information for as long as you can stand it and stay on top of any changes the IRS may implement.

Getting the Most from Your Reports

After you're up and running with your eBay business, you can look forward to having lots of reports to evaluate. Of course, you get a plethora of reports from PayPal, eBay, and so on, but the most important reports are those you generate from your bookkeeping program (software such as QuickBooks or an online service such as Outright). I use the QuickBooks software package to manage my business records, and it keeps several common reports (Balance Sheet, Accounts Payable, P&L, and so on) in an easily accessible area. If you check out the Reports tab in your bookkeeping program, I'll bet you find similar items. Before your eyes glaze over, though, check out this section for straightforward descriptions of these reports and the information they provide.

Similar sales and financial reports are common to all businesses, and reviewing them on a monthly basis can help you stay on top of yours.

To get your business reports when you need them, you must post your sales receipts regularly — and thereby update the "money in" and "inventory out" figures. Post your payments at least weekly (especially on your company credit card — post those transactions the minute you make purchases) — and reconcile your checkbook the moment your bank statement arrives.

What does posting and reconciling tasks get you? The opportunity to press a button and get a complete picture of your business. From the reports you generate, you find out whether your business is profitable, what products are selling, and if you're spending too much money in a particular area. Keeping your books up to date allows you to find problems before they become unmanageable.

If you run your sales and financial reports only quarterly rather than monthly, a problem — such as not pricing your items high enough — could be mushrooming out of control before you can detect and correct it.

Understanding the balance sheet

Your balance sheet provides the best information on your business. It pulls data from all the other reports and gives you a complete look at the financial condition of your business.

Your balance sheet shows all your assets:

✦ **Cash in bank:** The money in your business bank account.

✦ **Accounts receivable:** If you've invoiced anyone and not received payment as yet, that amount is reflected here.

✦ **Inventory assets:** This is the value of the merchandise you've purchased for resale but have not sold yet.

✦ **Other assets:** Things owned by your business (not by you), such as furniture and vehicles. These are long-term assets that build accumulated depreciation. They're not considered in the current asset figure.

✦ **Accumulated depreciation:** This is depreciation, over time, of your long-term assets. This is either calculated by your accounting program or given to you by your accountant.

Your balance sheet also shows your liabilities:

✦ **Accounts payable:** Money you owe vendors and money due on unpaid credit cards show up here.

✦ **Sales tax:** The money you've collected on sales tax (that is due to your state) is a liability.

✦ **Payroll liabilities:** If you haven't made a bank deposit (it's faster to make payment on the Federal online payment system at www.eftps. gov).covering the money you've withdrawn from employees (withholding taxes, Social Security, Medicare, and so on), it shows up here.

Your equity shows up in the (literal and figurative) bottom line. It will include the initial investment in your business and the net income total from your profit-and-loss statement.

An important business ratio — the *net working capital ratio* — is drawn from your balance sheet. Subtracting your current liabilities from your current assets gets you the *net* dollar amount of your *working capital* (that is, how much capital you have left to work with). But to get the net working capital *ratio*, divide your current assets by your current liabilities. Any value over 1.1 means you have a positive net working capital. If you need a loan from a bank, this is the first figure the loan office will look for.

Tracking your accounts payable

When bills come in, post them in your accounting program. This will generate the *accounts payable* report. Accounts payable is the area that shows how much you owe and when it's due. This is crucial information for meeting your obligations on time.

When you pay an outstanding bill, the bookkeeping program deducts the money from your checking account and marks the bill as paid. That bill will no longer appear on this report.

Knowing your sales-tax liability

One of the vendors you'll owe money to is your state. (In California, the State Board of Equalization collects such debts.) Every time you post an invoice or sales receipt that charges sales tax, that amount shows up in the *sales-tax liability report*. You run this report on a timeframe determined by the state; you may be required to report monthly, quarterly, or yearly. Also, how often you report may depend on your total in-state sales. Just make sure you match your reporting with your state's requirements.

COGS — the cost of merchandise sold — is a separate consideration from sales tax. For a closer look at COGS, see *Intermediate Accounting For Dummies* by Marie Loughran (Wiley), available at www.dummies.com.

Analyzing your profit and loss statement

If your accountant asks for your income statement, he or she is asking for your *profit-and-loss statement*, or *P&L*. This report lays out clearly every penny you've spent and brought in. You can set these reports to generate by any period of time; usually eBay sellers produce them by calendar month.

A summary P&L itemizes all your income and expense accounts individually and totals them by category. This way, you'll be able to isolate individual areas where you may notice a problem, such as spending too much in shipping supplies.

Please use the following list of income and expense accounts as a guide, and not as gospel. I am not a tax professional, and I suggest that when you set up your own income and (especially) expense accounts, you go over them with a licensed tax expert. Here's a glimpse at the kinds of accounts and categories you see on a P&L statement:

✦ **Income:** Every dollar you bring in is itemized as income. For many sellers, this can break down into several individual accounts. These figures are automatically generated by your bookkeeping program from the sales receipts you input. The total of all these income areas is subtotaled at the bottom of this area as total income.

   • **Sales:** This totals eBay sales and shipping income in separate totals. These figures subtotal as total sales.

   • **Website advertising:** If you're a member of any affiliate programs (Google Ads on your site count here too) or have a newsletter that takes advertising, this income posts here.

   • **Consulting:** Income from providing consulting services or teaching others.

✦ **Cost of goods sold (COGS):** This area itemizes by category all the costs involved in your eBay (and website) sales only. None of your business operating expenses, such as your telephone bill, show up here; they're farther down on the report. Your eBay COGS may subtotal in different accounts, such as

- **Merchandise:** The cost of merchandise that you bought to resell.

- **eBay fees:** Here's where you post your eBay fees from your credit card statement.

- **PayPal fees:** This figure is automatically generated from your sales receipts.

- **Shipping postage:** The totals of the amounts you spend for shipping your eBay items.

- **Shipping supplies:** The costs of padded mailers, bubble wrap, tape, and boxes. When those items are paid for, the bookkeeping program inserts the totals here.

- **Outside service fees:** If you pay for photo hosting or third-party management tools, they appear here.

Cross-reference your cost of goods sold to your sales reports. You've expensed inventory bought, but your merchandise may be sitting idle in your storage area. The COGS report works with other reports, such as inventory reports (also generated by QuickBooks), sales reports, and P&Ls, to give you a solid picture of where your business is going.

Your cost of goods sold is subtotaled under the heading total COGS.

✦ **Gross profit:** Your bookkeeping program magically does all the calculations — and you'll be able to see in a snapshot whether your eBay business is in good, profitable health. This particular figure is the gross profit *before* you figure in your company expenses (often called G&A, for *general and administrative costs*).

Now come your expenses. Listed in individual accounts, you have subtotals for your various business operating expenses, as follows:

✦ **Payroll expenses:** The total amounts you pay your employees.

✦ **Taxes:** Broken out by state and federal, the taxes you've paid to the regulating agencies for running your business.

✦ **Supplies:** Computer and office supplies. How much paper goes through your printer? Not to mention those inkjet cartridges, pens, computers, telephones, copiers, and network equipment. All those expenses appear here.

✦ **Seminars and education:** Did you buy this book to educate yourself on your eBay business? It counts. Have you attended a seminar to educate yourself on eBay? Going to a business conference? Those count too.

✦ **Contract labor:** This is the money you pay to anyone who is not an employee of your company, such as an off-site bookkeeper or a company that comes in to clean your office. The federal government has stringent rules as to who classifies as an independent contractor. Check this website for the official rules:

```
http://www.irs.gov/Businesses/Small-Businesses-&-
    Self-Employed/Small-Business-and-Self-Employed-
    Tax-Center-1
```

✦ **Automobile expenses:** This is where you post expenses, such as parking, gas, and repairs for an automobile used for your eBay business. If you have only one vehicle that you also use for personal transportation, your tax person may have you post a percentage of its use in this area.

✦ **Telephone:** Do you have a separate phone line for your business?

✦ **Advertising:** Expenses you incur when running advertising campaigns, such as in Google AdWords or in your eBay banner program.

Your expenses will come to a whopping total at the bottom. Then, at the very bottom of the page, will be your net income. This is your *bottom-line profit*. I wish you all a very positive bottom line!

Keeping Your Records and Data Safe

If the hazard of not backing up your computer isn't a tired subject, I don't know what is. Whenever you hear someone talking about their latest computer crash, all the person can do is stare blankly into the distance and say, "I lost everything!" I admit it's happened to me — and I'm sure that you've heard this cry from others (if you've not uttered it yourself): "If only I'd backed up my files!"

What about a natural disaster? It can happen, you know. When I went to sleep on January 16, 1994, I didn't know that the next day, when I attempted to enter my office, everything would be in shambles. My monitors had flown across the room, filing cabinets turned over, and oh, did I mention the ceiling had collapsed? The Northridge earthquake taught me some solid lessons about keeping duplicate records and backed-up data copies *in an offsite location*.

 Reasonably priced, secure backup can be accomplished in the cloud these days through SkyDrive, Google, Amazon, or any one of a group of providers for a reasonable cost. Consider these — along with a backup drive on premises — for your own peace of mind.

If a computer crash or natural disaster has happened to you, you have my deepest and most sincere sympathy. It's a horrible thing to go through.

What's another horrible thing? A tax audit: It can make you feel like jumping off a cliff if you've been filing your hard documentation with the shoebox method. (You know, one box for 2011, one for 2012, and so on.) Filing or scanning your receipts and PDF backup documentation in an organized easy-to-find format can pay off in future savings of time (and nerves). (Again: Back up these PDFs to the cloud.)

I want to tell you up front that I don't always practice what I preach. I don't always back up my stuff on time. I do make an attempt to back up to SkyDrive every time I remember. Following best practices for backing up your computer data and safeguarding the hardcopy documents that you inevitably will have just makes life easier.

Taking the time to organize and safeguard your data and records now may save you days, weeks, or months of work and frustration later.

Backing Up Your Data

I'm not specifically suggesting that you go out and buy backup software (though I think it's a good idea). I *am* suggesting that you back up the eBay transaction records and other data on your computer *somehow*. Consider the following points when choosing how to back up the data you can't afford to lose:

+ Regularly back up at least your data folder onto an external hard drive.

+ Backup software can make your backup chores less *chorelike*. Most packages enable you to run backups unattended and automatically, so you don't have to remember anything. (External hard drives come with their own sync software to handle this for you.)

+ Backup software doesn't have to be expensive; System Image is included in Windows 7 and 8 and will back up your entire hard drive. If you really need software, search Google with the term *backup Windows.* This query returned more results than I could ever need!

For peace of mind, save these backups as well to a cloud drive of your choice. You'll feel much safer.

+ Consider making monthly backups of the info from your PayPal account. You can download the data directly from the site and can archive several years' worth on the drive.

Saving Your Backup Paperwork

Business records are still mostly paper, and until such time as the entire world is electronic, you'll have some paperwork to store unless you scan in every document. You can buy manila file folders almost anywhere. A box of 100 costs less than $10, so expense is no excuse for lack of organization. If you don't have filing cabinets, office supply stores sell collapsible cardboard boxes that are the perfect size to hold file folders. You can buy six of these for around $8. An external hard drive is a must for backup documentation as well.

And just what do you need to file in your new organized office? Here are a few important suggestions:

✦ **Equipment receipts and warranties:** You never know when some important piece of your office hardware will go on the fritz, and you'll need the receipt and warranty information so you can get it fixed. Also, the receipts are backup documentation for your bookkeeping program's data.

✦ **Automobile expenses:** Gasoline receipts, parking receipts, repairs — anything and everything to do with your car. You use your car in your eBay business (for example, to deliver packages to the post office for shipping), don't you?

✦ **Postal receipts:** Little slips of paper that you get from the post office. If you use an online postage service, print a postage report once a month and file it in your filing cabinets or boxes as well.

✦ **Credit card statements:** Here in one location can be documentation on your purchases for your business. Make a folder for each credit card; file every month after you pay the bill and post the data.

✦ **Merchandise receipts:** Merchandise purchased for resale on eBay. Documentation of all the money you spend.

✦ **Licenses and legal stuff:** Important! Keep an active file of anything legal; you will no doubt have to lay hands on this information at the oddest moment. It's reassuring to know where it is.

✦ **Payroll paperwork:** Even if you print your checks and such on the computer, you should organize state and federal filing information in one place.

✦ **Canceled checks and bank statements:** The only ways to prove you've paid for something.

✦ **Insurance information:** Policies and insurance proposals should all be kept close by.

I'm sure you can think of some more things that can benefit from a little bit of organization. When you need the information quickly, and you can find it without breaking a sweat, you'll be glad you kept things organized.

Chapter 3: Taking Care of Your Finances

In This Chapter

✔ **Understanding bookkeeping**

✔ **Using accounting software efficiently**

*W*hen you meet with one of the professionals described in Chapter 2 in this minibook, you'll need to bring a complete and accurate set of books. To prepare accurate books, you can hire a bookkeeper (who will use accounting software) or you can learn how to use accounting software yourself. Don't shy away; you *can* do this. Lots of folks who are successfully using bookkeeping software today knew nothing about bookkeeping before they set up their own accounts. I'm one of them. This chapter paves the way into effective and relatively painless bookkeeping.

Keeping an accurate accounting of your business gives you one major benefit: You can, at any time, look at your bookkeeping and have an idea of how well (or not) your business is doing.

When your business gets so busy that you have no time to post your bookkeeping, you can hire a part-time bookkeeper to come in and do your posting for you. Sites like Elance (`https://www.elance.com/`) or even Twitter can help.

I researched to find which software was the best selling and easiest to use. I had many discussions with CPAs, enrolled agents, and bookkeepers. The software that these professionals most recommend for business — generally considered the best, which is why I devote so much of this chapter to it — is Intuit's QuickBooks. For those just starting out, Outright, a bookkeeping app found at `http://outright.com`, integrates directly is a good place to start for your newly hatched businesses. A good idea might be to start with Outright and later move to QuickBooks when your business really starts making money.

What? Double-Entry Accounting?

You already understand double-entry accounting if you keep your checkbook up to date. Professional-level business bookkeeping is quite similar, done through a similar double-entry system.

Double-entry accounting requires each transaction to be recorded in two accounts. From one account there is a debit (minus) and the other gets a credit (plus), as shown in Table 3-1. When the books are reconciled, this method minimizes errors as the sum of the accounts with debit balances should equal the sum of credit balance accounts.

Table 3-1	Double-Entry Bookkeeping Transactions	
Account	*Debit*	*Credit*
Assets	Increase	Decrease
Expenses	Increase	Decrease
Liabilities	Decrease	Increase
Owner's Equity	Decrease	Increase
Revenues	Decrease	Increase

Stephen L. Nelson, the author of *QuickBooks 2013 All-in-One For Dummies* (John Wiley & Sons, Inc.), describes it this way: "The formula [behind double-entry accounting] says that a business owns stuff and that the money or the funds for that stuff come either from creditors (such as the bank or some vendor) or the owners (either in the form of original contributed capital or perhaps in reinvested profits)."

To be honest, this whole double-entry bookkeeping makes my head spin and makes me a little sick to my stomach. That's why I use QuickBooks software to do the work of debiting and crediting for me automatically. If you really want to understand in depth how this all works, I recommend you read Stephen's book; you can find the latest edition at www.dummies.com.

Starting Out Right with Outright

If you're just starting out as a sole proprietor, you will probably file a Schedule C on your Federal 1040 form to cover your business. While a bit less complex, a service that is not a full-fledged double-entry accounting program may be just what you need.

Outright is an example of web-based *SaaS (software as a service)* that integrates directly into your eBay account. It's a simple online solution for sole proprietors that automatically pulls in PayPal data and categorizes it so that taxes and reporting become far less onerous.

The simplicity of Outright will make the process a straightforward proposition to help you to get into the habit of keeping accurate books. There's no need for you to set up an official chart of accounts (Table 3-2 further on) when you're starting out. Plus, it will pull together all the pieces when it comes to tax time.

To sign up with Outright for free, you can go to the eBay App center at `http://applications.ebay.com/` and type **Outright** into the search text box (as I've done in Figure 3-1) or visit their website at `http://outright.com/`.

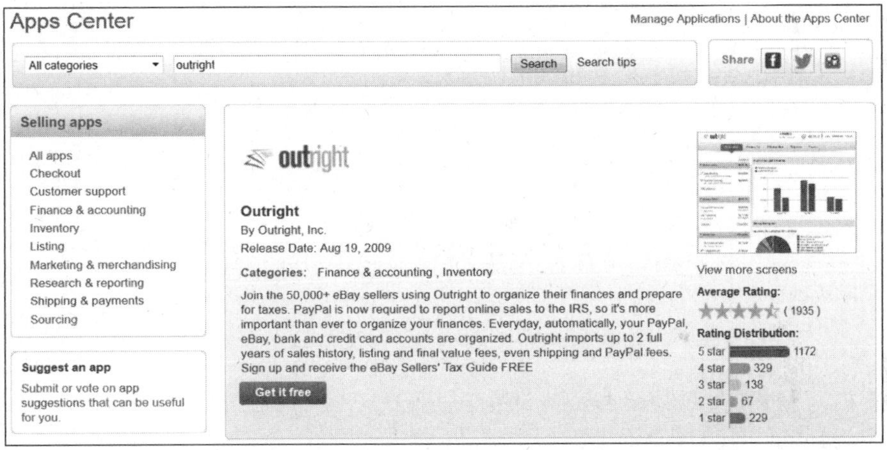

Figure 3-1: The eBay App Center search for Outright.

The minute you sign up for the free version, the Outright app begins to populate with your eBay sales history and PayPal transactions. The app prepares an area (accessed from your Selling Manager page) that will give you full access to your sales data. If you want to use Outright as your complete bookkeeping system, the paid version — Outright Plus — is what you need. The cost is $9.95 per month (or $99 a year) and you get more features — including importing bank accounts and tracking/reporting your Annual, Quarterly, and Sales Tax figures.

Again, there's no need for you to set up an official chart of accounts when you're starting out. If you're going to use Outright to compile all your tax data for your business, however, you had better use their paid account — and input each and every expense, down to the last paper clip. This due diligence will populate the Outright Schedule C worksheet (see Figure 3-2) for tax-filing time.

TIP

Even though I use QuickBooks for my company accounts, I use the free version of Outright to get my data for my PayPal sales receipts (shown in Figure 3-3). It's much easier than using the PayPal site. See "Posting Sales from PayPal My Way," further along in this chapter, for the lowdown.

Part II	Expenses	
8	⊕ Advertising	$0.00
9	⊕ Car and truck expenses	$0.00
10	Commissions and fees	$0.00
11	⊕ Contract labor	$0.00
12	Depletion	$0.00
13	Depreciation and section 179 expense deduction	$0.00
14	Employee benefit programs	$0.00
15	Insurance (other than health)	$0.00
16a	Interest: Mortgage (paid to banks, etc.)	$0.00
16b	Interest: Other	$0.00
17	Legal and professional services	$0.00
18	⊕ Office expense	$0.00
19	Pension and profit-sharing plans	$0.00
20a	Rent or lease: Vehicles, machinery, and equipment	$0.00
20b	Rent or lease: Other business property	$0.00
21	Repairs and maintenance	$0.00
22	⊕ Supplies	$0.00
23	⊕ Taxes and licenses	$0.00
24a	⊕ Travel, meals, and entertainment: Travel	$0.00
24b	⊕ Travel, meals, and entertainment: Deductible meals and entertainment	$0.00
25	⊕ Utilities	$0.00
26	Wages (less employment credits)	$0.00

Figure 3-2: Outright's Schedule C chart is where you track expenses.

Figure 3-3: A single transaction detail from PayPal looks like this in Outright.

	Transaction from: PayPal		✕
Date	**Name**	**Category**	**Amount ($)**
FEB 22			**$160.21**
	~~ – PRO CLOUD DOME Digital Photo .	Sales	$152.00
	~~ – SALESTAX: 6EF49245RV861322Y	Sales Tax Collected	$13.30
	PayPal – PayPal Fee: 6EF49245RV861322Y	PayPal Fees	-$5.09

QuickBooks: Professional Bookkeeping

QuickBooks offers several versions, from basic to enterprise (company-size) solutions tailored to different types of businesses. The various versions have a few significant differences. QuickBooks Pro adds job costing and expensing — and the capability to design your own forms. QuickBooks online does a darn good job, too, so check out the comparison at

```
http://quickbooks.intuit.com/product/accounting-software/
     quickbooks-comparison-chart.jsp
```

and see which version is best for you. I use QuickBooks Pro (the least expensive desktop edition), so that's the version I describe in the rest of this section. If you're just purchasing QuickBooks Pro, you may have an updated version that works a bit differently. But the accounting basics that the software provides for your business don't change.

I update my QuickBooks software every few years, and the product improvements continue to save me time in performing my bookkeeping tasks. If you find that you don't have time to input your bookkeeping data, you may have to hire a part-time bookkeeper. The bonus is that professional bookkeepers probably already know QuickBooks. Also, at the end of each year, the QuickBooks program will supply you with all the official reports your enrolled agent (EA) or certified public accountant (CPA) will need to do your taxes. (Yes, you really *do* need an EA or a CPA.) You can even send your preparer a backup on a flash drive or a CD. See how simple bookkeeping can be?

QuickBooks Pro

When you first fire up QuickBooks Pro, you must answer a few questions to set up your account. Among the few things you need to have ready — before you even begin to mess with the software — are the following starting figures:

✦ **Cash balance:** This may be the amount in your checking account (no personal money, please!) or the amount of money deposited from your eBay profits. Put these profits into a separate checking account to use for your business.

✦ **Accounts receivable balance:** Does anyone owe you money for some auctions? Outstanding payments make up this total.

✦ **Account liability balance:** Do you owe some money? Are you being invoiced for some merchandise that you haven't paid for? Total it and enter it when QuickBooks prompts you.

If you're starting your business in the middle of the year, gather any previous profits and expenses that you want to include because you'll have to input this information for a complete annual set of diligently recorded books. I can guarantee that this is going to take a while. But you'll be thanking me for insisting that you get organized. It just makes everything work smoother in the long run.

QuickBooks EasyStep Interview

After you've organized your finances, you can proceed with the QuickBooks EasyStep Interview, which is shown in Figure 3-4. The EasyStep Interview is designed to provide a comfort level for those with accounting-phobia and those using a bookkeeping program for the first time. If you mess things up, you can always use the Back arrow and change what you've input. If you need help, simply click the Help button and the program will answer many of your questions. Hey, if worst comes to worst, you can always delete the company file (including your erroneous inputs) and start over.

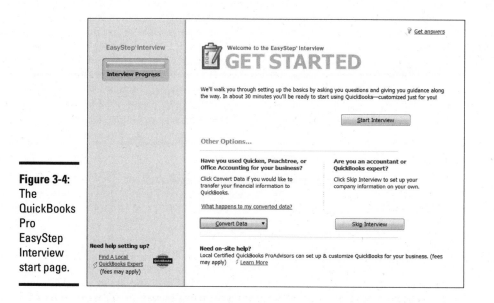

Figure 3-4:
The
QuickBooks
Pro
EasyStep
Interview
start page.

For the whirlwind tour through the QuickBooks EasyStep Interview, just follow these steps (which are only a general guideline):

1. **Start QuickBooks, and choose the Create a New Company option.**

You're now at the EasyStep Interview.

2. **On the first page of the interactive portion of the interview, type your company name (this becomes the filename in your computer) and the legal name of your company.**

   If you've filed a fictitious name statement (see Chapter 1 in this mini-book), the fictitious name is the legal name of your company.

3. **Continue to follow the steps, answering other questions about your business, such as the address and the type of tax form you use.**

4. **When QuickBooks asks what type of business you want to use, choose Retail Shop or Online Commerce (as I did in Figure 3-5).**

   If you have a business other than your eBay sales — perhaps consulting or teaching others — you may want to just leave the Company box blank in QuickBooks, specify no business option, and build your own chart of accounts from the one they give you — that's what I did.

Figure 3-5:
Selecting
your
company
type.

[screenshot: EasyStep Interview — Select your industry]

Tell us your industry and we'll customize QuickBooks to work best for you.

You will be able to review our recommendations and change them in this interview. And, you can always change each of these settings later. Explain

Note: Don't see your industry? Choose an industry that is similar to yours. Examples

Select an industry from the list

Industry
Legal Services
Lodging (Hotel, Motel)
Manufacturer Representative or Agent
Manufacturing
Medical, Dental, or Health Service
Non-Profit
Professional Consulting
Property Management or Home Association
Real Estate Brokerage or Developer
Rental
Repair and Maintenance
Restaurant, Caterer, or Bar
Retail Shop or Online Commerce
Sales: Independent Agent
Transportation, Trucking, or Delivery

Need help setting up?

Find A Local
QuickBooks Expert
(fees may apply)

How does QuickBooks use my industry selection?

Leave...   < Back   Next >

5. **When QuickBooks asks whether you want to use its chosen chart of accounts, choose Yes.**

   You can always change the accounts later. If you want to spend the time, you can input your entire custom chart of accounts — more about that in the next section — manually (but I *really* don't recommend it, since the generated chart is easily edited).

6. **Answer some more general questions, which I'm sure you can handle with the aid of the intuitive QuickBooks help feature.**

7. **When the preferences pages appear, I recommend that you select the option that says, "Enter the bills first and then enter the payments later."**

This is a handy option; if you input your bills as they come in, you can get an exact idea of how much money you owe at any time by just starting the program.

8. **Click the box to indicate that you collect sales tax.**

9. **On the Sales Tax preferences page, indicate the agencies for which you collect sales tax, and then set up the tax-collecting information.**

10. **Decide whether you want to use QuickBooks to process your payroll.**

Even if you're the only employee, using QuickBooks payroll information makes things much easier when it comes to required deductions and filling out your payroll deposits. I subscribe additionally to QuickBooks Enhanced Payroll — which files reports and sends my business' Federal and State payments for me, electronically and automatically. This saves hours of labor and pays for itself over a year's time.

11. **Answer a few more questions, including whether you want to use the cash basis or accrual basis of accounting.**

The *accrual* basis posts sales the minute you write an invoice or post a sales receipt, and posts your expenses as soon as you post the bills into the computer. Accrual basis accounting gives you a clearer picture of where your company is financially than cash-basis accounting does. The *cash basis* is when you record bills by writing checks — expenses are posted only when you write the checks. This way of doing business may be simpler, but the only way you'll know how much money you owe is by looking at the pile of bills on your desk.

12. **If you're comfortable, just click Leave and then input the balance of your required information directly into the program without using the Interview feature.**

Setting Up a Chart of Accounts

After you've finished the EasyStep Interview and have successfully set up your business in QuickBooks, the program presents a *chart of accounts* — essentially an organization system, rather like file folders, that keeps all related data in the proper area. When you write a check to pay a bill, it deducts the amount from your checking account, reduces your accounts payable, and increases your asset or expense account if that's appropriate.

You have a choice of giving each account a number. These numbers, a kind of bookkeeping shorthand, are standardized throughout bookkeeping. Believe it or not, everybody in the industry seems to know what number goes with what item. To keep things less confusing, I like to use titles as well as numbers.

To customize your chart of accounts, follow these steps:

1. **Choose Edit⇨Preferences.**

2. **Click the Accounting icon (on the left).**

3. **Click the Company preferences tab and indicate that you'd like to use account numbers.**

An editable chart of accounts appears, as shown in Figure 3-6. Because QuickBooks doesn't assign account numbers by default, you'll need to edit the chart to create them.

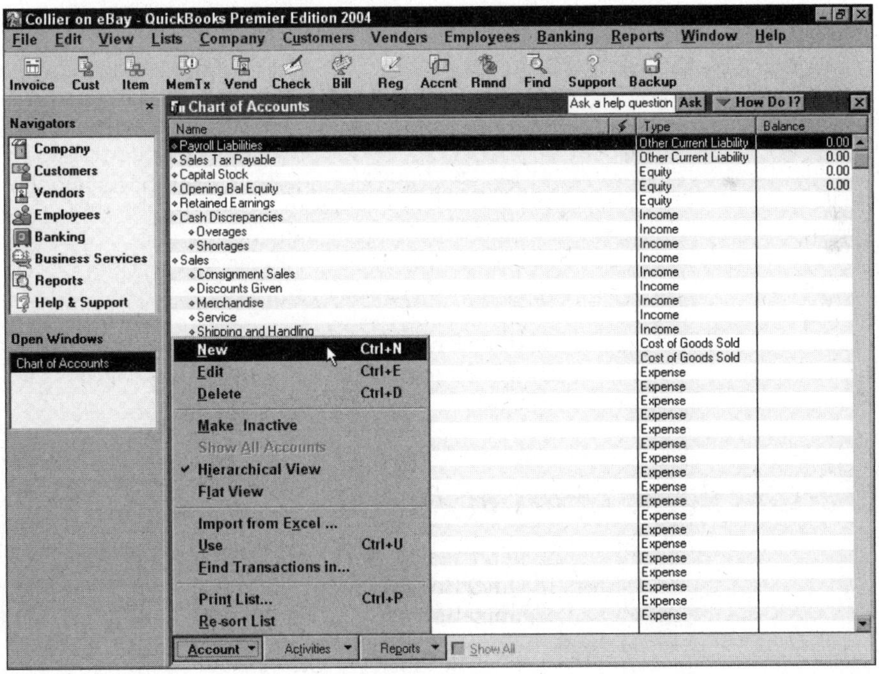

Figure 3-6:
Your chart of accounts now has numbers generated by QuickBooks.

4. **Go through your QuickBooks chart of accounts and add any missing categories.**

   You may not need all these categories — and you can always add more later. In Table 3-2, I show you a chart of accounts that a CPA wrote for an eBay business. To get an idea of how you can customize the chart of accounts, also look at Figure 3-7, which shows you the chart of accounts from my own business.

Table 3-2	**eBay Business Chart of Accounts**	
Account Number	*Account Name*	*What It Represents*
1001	Checking	All revenue deposited here and all checks drawn upon this account.
1002	Money market account	Company savings account.
1100	Accounts receivable	For customers to whom you extend credit.
1201	Merchandise inventory	Charge to cost of sales as used, or take periodic inventories and adjust at that time.
1202	Shipping supplies	Boxes, tape, labels, and so forth; charge these to cost as used, or take an inventory at the end of the period and adjust to cost of sales.
1401	Office furniture and equipment	Desk, computer, telephone.
1402	Shipping equipment	Scales, tape dispensers.
1403	Vehicles	Your vehicle if it's owned by the company.
1501	Accumulated depreciation	For your accountant's use.
1601	Deposits	Security deposits on leases.
2001	Accounts payable	Amounts owed for the stuff you sell, or charged expenses.
2100	Payroll liabilities	Taxes deducted from employees' checks and taxes paid by company on employee earnings.
2200	Sales tax payable	Sales tax collected at time of sale and owed to the state.
2501	Equipment loans	Money borrowed to buy a computer or other equipment.

Account Number	Account Name	What It Represents
2502	Auto loans	This is for when you get that hot new van for visiting your consignment clients.
3000	Owner's capital	Your opening balance.
3902	Owner's draw	Your withdrawals for the current year.
4001	Merchandise sales	Revenue from sales of your products.
4002	Shipping and handling	Paid by the customer.
4009	Returns	Total dollar amount of returned merchandise.
4101	Interest income	From your investments.
4201	Other income	Income not otherwise classified.
5001	Merchandise purchases	All the merchandise you buy for eBay; you'll probably use subaccounts for individual items.
5002	Freight in	Freight and shipping charges you pay for your inventory, not for shipments to customers.
5003	Shipping	Shipping to your customers: USPS, FedEx, UPS, and so on.
5004	Shipping supplies	Boxes, labels, tape, bubble wrap, and so on.
6110	Automobile expense	When you use your car for work.
6111	Gas and oil	Filling up the tank.
6112	Automobile repairs	When your business owns the car.
6120	Bank service charges	Monthly service charges, NSF charges, and so forth.
6140	Contributions	Charity.
6142	Data services	Does an outside firm process your payroll?
6143	Internet service provider	What you pay to your Internet provider.
6144	Website hosting fees	Fees paid to your hosting company.
6150	Depreciation expense	For your accountant's use.
6151	eBay fees	What you pay eBay every month to stay in business, based on your sales.

(continued)

Table 3-2 *(continued)*

Account Number	Account Name	What It Represents
6152	Discounts	Fees you're charged for using eBay and accepting credit card payments; deducted from your revenue and reported to you on your eBay statement.
6153	Other auction site fees	You may want to set up subcategories for each site where you do business, such as Yahoo! or Amazon.
6156	PayPal fees	Processing fees paid to PayPal.
6158	Credit card or merchant-account fees	If you have a separate merchant account, post those fees here.
6160	Dues	Membership fees you pay if you join an organization (relating to your business) that charges them.
6161	Magazines and periodicals	Books and magazines that help you run and expand your business.
6170	Equipment rental	Postage meter, occasional van.
6180	Insurance	Policies that cover your merchandise or your office.
6185	Liability insurance	Insurance that covers you if (for example) someone slips and falls at your place of business (can also be put under Insurance).
6190	Disability insurance	Insurance that will pay you if you become temporarily or permanently disabled and can't perform your work.
6191	Health insurance	If you provide it for yourself, you may be required to provide it to employees.
6200	Interest expense	Credit interest and interest on loans.
6220	Loan interest	When you borrow from the bank.
6230	Licenses	State and city licenses.
6240	Miscellaneous	Whatever doesn't go anyplace else in these categories.
6250	Postage and delivery	Stamps used in your regular business.

Account Number	Account Name	What It Represents
6251	Endicia.com fees	Fees for your eBay business postage service.
6260	Printing	Your business cards, correspondence stationery, and so on.
6265	Filing fees	Fees paid to file legal documents.
6270	Professional fees	Fees paid to consultants.
6280	Legal fees	If you have to pay a lawyer.
6650	Accounting and bookkeeping	Bookkeeper, CPA ,or EA.
6290	Rent	Office, warehouse, and so on.
6300	Repairs	Can be the main category for the following subcategories.
6310	Building repairs	Repair to the building you operate your business in.
6320	Computer repairs	What you pay the person to set up your wireless network.
6330	Equipment repairs	When (say) the copier or the phone needs fixing.
6340	Telephone	Regular telephone, fax lines.
6350	Travel and	Business-related travel, business meals.
6360	Entertainment	When you take eBay's CEO out to dinner to benefit your eBay business (don't forget to invite me too).
6370	Meals	Meals while traveling for your business.
6390	Utilities	Major heading for subcategories that follow.
6391	Electricity and gas	Electricity and gas.
6392	Water	Water.
6560	Payroll expenses	Wages paid to others.
6770	Supplies	Office supplies.
6772	Computer	Computer, tablets, software, and supplies.
6780	Marketing	Advertising or items you purchase to give out that promote your business.
6790	Office	Miscellaneous office expense, such as bottled water delivery?

(continued)

Table 3-2 *(continued)*

Account Number	Account Name	What It Represents
6820	Taxes	Major category for the following subcategories below.
6830	Federal	Federal taxes.
6840	Local	Local (city, county) taxes.
6850	Property	Property taxes.
6860	State	State taxes.

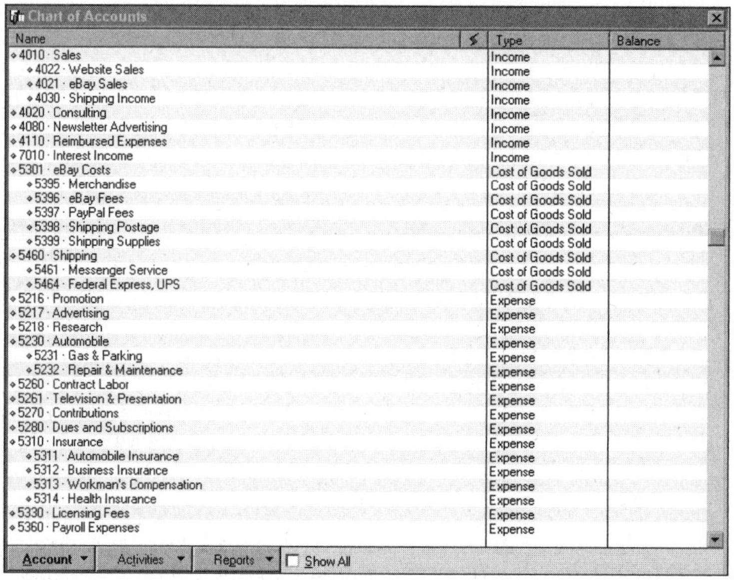

Figure 3-7:
The chart
of accounts
from my
eBay
business.

Having QuickBooks Report on Your eBay Business

QuickBooks can give you up-to-the-minute reports about the status of your eBay business and keep track of everything — including payroll and sales-tax liability — in the background. Here are a few things that I like about using QuickBooks to streamline an online business:

✦ **Inventory reports:** As you purchase inventory, aside from deducting the money from your checking account and expensing your merchandise account, QuickBooks adds the purchased merchandise to your inventory. Every time you sell an item, QuickBooks deducts the item from your inventory.

Figure 3-8 shows you a part of an inventory report that I pulled out of the program. You can see how valuable the data is. With a click of my mouse, I can see how much I have left in stock and the average number of items I've sold per week.

Figure 3-8: A portion of my inventory-tracking report.

The Collier Company, Inc.
Inventory Stock Status by Item
April 2012 through March 2013

	Item Description	Pref Vendor	Reorder Pt	On Hand	Order
Inventory					
Cloud Dome Angle	Cloud Dome Angled collar	Cloud Dome, Inc		1	
Cloud Dome 7 collar	Cloud Dome 7 collar	Cloud Dome, Inc		7	
Cloud Dome	Cloud Dome NO COLLAR	Cloud Dome, Inc		7	
Brush Set	Pur Minerals Brush Set	Santa fe Produc...		7	
Ossential	Obagi Ossential	Santa fe Produc...		9	
Obagi	Obagi Kit			1	
Black SY lamp	True color sy			3	
Singelringen	Singelringen			0	
QVC xmas	QVC Christmas Jewlery			6	
5550 Bulb	Full SPectrum Bulb			14	
PBS					
Online Business	Your Online Business Plan			11	
MYFOL	▶ Making Your Fortune Online			24	
PBS - Other				0	
Total PBS				13	
Calendar	Fraggle Rock			-9	
20" Tent	20" Photo Tent			1	
28" Tent	28" Photo Tent			9	
Angled Collar	Cloud Dome Angled Collar	Cloud Dome, Inc		34	
Black Infiniti	Black Infiniti Board	Cloud Dome, Inc		9	

5:48 PM
03/01/13

✦ **Sales-tax tracking:** Depending on how the program is set up (based on your own state sales tax laws), you can request a report that has all your taxable and nontaxable sales. The report calculates the amount of sales tax you owe. You can print this report for backup information of your sales-tax payments to the state.

✦ **Payroll:** Whether you use the Enhanced Payroll Service to prepare your payroll or input the deductions yourself, QuickBooks posts the appropriate withholdings to their own accounts. When it comes time to pay your employees' withholding taxes, QuickBooks can generate the federal reporting form (all filled in) for submitting with your payment.

✦ **Sales reports:** QuickBooks gives you a plethora of reports with which you can analyze your sales professionally. One of my favorite reports is the Sales by Item Summary. This report gives you the following information for every inventoried item you sell, in whatever time period you choose:

  • Quantity sold

  • Total dollar amount sold

- Percentage of sales represented by each item
- The average price the item sold for
- COGS (cost of goods sold) by item
- Average cost of goods sold by total sales per item
- Gross profit margin in dollar amounts
- Gross profit margin expressed as percentage

Depending on how you post your transactions, you can analyze your eBay sales, website sales, and brick-and-mortar sales (individually or together). You can also select *any* date range for your reports.

Posting Sales from PayPal My Way

Some sellers import PayPal data into QuickBooks; I don't. The problem with the import is that a new customer file is set up for each of your sales.

Saving each sale as a new customer will make your database huge in no time. Last time I checked, the maximum number of names (employees, customers, vendors) for QuickBooks Pro is 14,500. QuickBooks is a large program to begin with, and if you're going to use it (and update it) for several years, the database might explode.

If you've ever worked with large files, you know that the larger the data file, the more chance there is for the data to become corrupt. That's the last thing you want. Besides, a successful online business can max out QuickBooks with over 14,000 customers in just a few years.

To keep track of your customers, you download a PayPal monthly report and import it into an Excel spreadsheet to build your customer database.

Posting sales to match deposits

In this section, I show you a procedure I developed to process my PayPal sales. I've run it past several accountants and QuickBooks experts, and it's garnered rave reviews. I'm sharing it with you because I want you to be able to run your business smoothly. Lots of sellers use this method. It shortens your inputting time.

Rather than posting an invoice for every customer I input my sales into a customer sales receipt as shown in Figure 3-9. Whenever I make a PayPal deposit into my business checking account — which is every few days, depending on how busy sales are — I post my sales into QuickBooks. This way, the total of my sales receipt equals the amount of my PayPal deposit. (If you've ever tried to reconcile your PayPal deposits with your sales *and* your checking account, you know how frustrating it can be.)

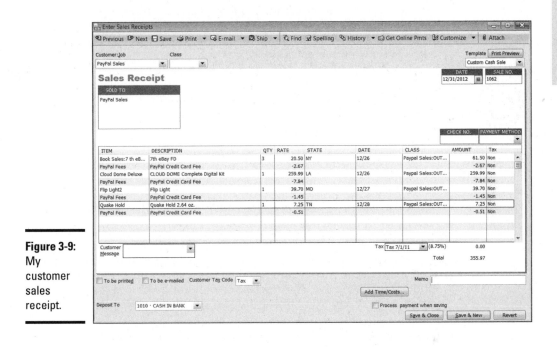

Figure 3-9:
My
customer
sales
receipt.

In my QuickBooks, I designate PayPal as the customer. It makes no difference who bought what; the only thing that matters is which item sold (to deduct from inventory) and for how much (to post to my financial data).

Customizing the sales data

The program gives you the flexibility to customize forms, and Figure 3-9 shows my customized sales receipt for PayPal sales. PayPal is a taxable customer when sales are made in the State of California, and the appropriate sales tax is applied automatically. I added the following when I customized the form:

✦ **PayPal fees:** I set up PayPal fees as a credit against sales. (In Figure 3-9, you can see they are applied as a negative.) This helps me match the total amount of the sales receipt to my PayPal deposit. It also gives me a discount line in my sales reports that tracks my total paid in PayPal fees. The PayPal fees line appears also in the cost of goods sold area of my financial statements.

In case you're wondering about eBay fees, they have their own line in my chart of accounts. I charge eBay fees to my company credit card. When the credit card expenses are posted, eBay fees post as an expense to the eBay fees account.

✦ **State:** I type the two-letter state abbreviation of the shipping location with each item. This serves as backup information for my State Board of Equalization (the California sales tax board) and also allows me to run reports on what has sold in which states.

✦ **Date:** The date at the top of the sales receipt is the posting date. The date in the product posting indicates the date the PayPal payment was posted.

✦ **Class:** Every item posted in QuickBooks can be part of a defined class to make it easier for you to isolate certain types of transactions. I set up two classes of PayPal sales: California sales and out-of-state sales. California sales are classified as taxable; out-of-state sales are classified as nontaxable. QuickBooks calculates the tax liability automatically.

Although PayPal does send a Form 1099 at the end of the year, it does not break out sales tax.

✦ **Tax classification:** When I type the first two letters into the class area (OU for out-of-state sales and CA for in-state sales), the tax line changes automatically to Tax or Non-Tax. QuickBooks would do this whether I show this field in the sales receipt or not, but by having it appear, I can use it as a secondary reminder to post the taxable class properly.

By inputting my eBay sales data in this way, I streamline the process in several ways. I post data to only one program once. From this sales receipt I get updated inventory reports, accurate sales tax data, and accurate expense and income tracking. It also eases the process of reconciling my checking account.

Chapter 4: Keeping You and Your Business Secure Online

In This Chapter

✔ **Fighting spam and scams**

✔ **Choosing a good secret question and password**

✔ **Reporting hijacked accounts to eBay**

*O*nline security is something everybody worries about, but few people do anything about it. When people's accounts are hacked, they whine and moan about online security, but they don't give a moment's thought as to why using a user ID as a password (tell me you didn't do that) *wasn't* the best choice.

Even if you avoid such classic blunders, you have to keep your wits about you online. Sad to say, some people out there *are* trying to dupe you; it's time to take charge of our own security and fight back in the best ways we can. Some scams pretend to be from eBay, PayPal, Citibank, and others — and try to bilk you out of your personal information. I show you a fairly foolproof way to recognize those. I also show you how spammers get your e-mail address. Even if you never give it out, they have ways of getting it from you. In this chapter, I hope to teach you how to be a little more savvy about which e-mails you open — and how to fight back.

Staying Away from Spam

Every morning when I get to my computer, I have to allow about five minutes to clear the spam out of my e-mail. It used to take up to half an hour, considering that I turn on my computer and am greeted by close to 200 e-mails every day. Read on to see how I've cut my spam-scanning time!

Spam has become so sneaky. Everyone is scurrying to get the latest in antispam software, but I've found that antispam software was causing me to lose e-mail that I needed, because it seems that the word *eBay* is a favorite of spammers. I want *news* on eBay, but I don't want to get those make-a-fortune-on-eBay e-mails.

I also would rather not hear from Mr. Felix Kamala, son of the late Mr. A.Y. Kamala. It seems his family lost millions in Zimbabwe to a scammer in the government, and he wants me to help him get his secret stash of "Fifteen million five hundred thousand united state dollars." He was going to give me 20 percent just for helping him — how thoughtful! (In case you didn't know, this e-mail is part of what the FBI calls the *Nigerian e-mail scam* — also called the 419 scam — named after the African penal code violated with this crime.)

An interesting site — FraudGallery.com (at `www.potifos.com/fraud`) — collects these e-mails and posts them fairly regularly. Check out the page when you have a minute — it's amusing!

Know that most e-mail providers; your ISP and the free providers like Outlook, Hotmail and Gmail, install spam filters so we are not quite as exposed as much as we were in the past. I have found that the free providers actually do a better job than one might expect.

Keeping your e-mail address quiet

Have you ever signed up for anything on the Internet? Before you signed up, did you check to see whether the site had a posted privacy-policy page? Did you notice a tiny check box surreptitiously placed at the bottom of the page that says you agree to receive e-mails from the site? You probably didn't.

After you type your name in a box on the Internet agreeing to accept e-mail, expect to receive a *lot* of mail. Check any site for a Privacy Policy and read how they treat e-mail addresses. Many sites openly admit that they share your address. You are now an opt-in customer. *Opt in* means that you *asked* to be on a list, and a site with a loose Privacy Policy can even sell your address to spammers.

Take a look at Figure 4-1. It's a description from an eBay listing for a CD containing 93,000,000 opt-in e-mail addresses. Yes, you can buy access to all those potential suckers for only $9.99.

Figure 4-1:
A tempting offer to violate people's privacy.

> ## For sale: 93,000 opt-in gaming email addresses
>
> **Other email lists are available - please see our other listings**
>
> This list was validated on 16th September 2012
>
> - All addresses are from opt-in gamers.
> - All addresses have been checked with our verification software.
> - All false / invalid email addresses have been removed.
> - The list has been cleaned to remove duplicate addresses.

Just opening your e-mail and loading images can give you away as well. Spammers will often make up return e-mail addresses to mask their true locations (as you can tell by some of the "From" addresses). If you open and view their e-mail, the e-mail sends a notice to the spammers' server, and then they know that the e-mail address is valid. This practice can also be masked in the HTML to occur when the e-mail consists of merely a picture — when it goes back to grab the picture for your e-mail, it reports that your e-mail address is good.

Recognizing Spam

Much of the spam you get can be recognized by the subject line. I used to check my e-mail after I downloaded it to my computer. That's a dangerous procedure, though, considering that some e-mails do their real job by delivering malware that's set up to self-install if the attachment — or even the e-mail itself — is opened.

Finding spam before it finds you

When using a web-based e-mail service, you are often comfortably shielded from spam. My Gmail account, for example, automatically sends suspicious-looking e-mails to the spam folder. (Hotmail — now Outlook — labels that folder Junk.) I need to check this folder regularly, because I don't always *white-list* (that is, give the platform permission to accept e-mails from specific parties) everyone in advance. Many times e-mail I want to see falls through the cracks so I check the spam folder about once a month. But I am protected from the many spammers by Gmail or Hotmail (now Outlook) filters.

When you are using a company server or an Internet service provider (ISP) for your e-mail, the filters may not be as strong. To prevent spam and the possibility of downloading dangerous e-mails (which may include malware) to my own computer, I suggest the program MailWasher (available free at http://www.mailwasher.net/). Figure 4-2 shows my mailbox, ready to de-spam.

MailWasher lists your e-mail directly from your ISP's server. It does not download the e-mail to your computer. By using MailWasher, you can delete the offending e-mails from your mailbox, and then bring only the ones you want into your e-mail program.

Delete	Bounce	Blackli	Status	Size	From	Subject	Sen ▽	To	Attac
✓	✓	✓	Possible	2.7KB	dale halverson (astyllan@mail.bulgaria.com)	Cgllesiotv Re: Your H_y_d_r_0_c_0_d_0_	15 Mar	hans da	none
			Normal	4.3KB	Gordon Boucher (yipe23@tourspain.es)	Fw: Fw: Upt0 50% off on Prescr1pt1on DF	15 Mar	marshac	none
			Normal	3.0KB	Raphael Swanson (vgpfqvj44@wanadoo.fr)	Re:crewel INdian generic Citratemorgen	15 Mar	marshac	none
			Normal	3.2KB	tiana peele (peele8384@proxad.net)	Fwd: Full Meds Here. Fwd: Xanlalx ~ Vali	15 Mar	marshac	yes
			Normal	3.6KB	pqplylqvntzh@mail2rusty.com	Start saving now	15 Mar	marshac	none
			Normal	3.2KB	alysha rosenberg (jp.rosenberg@interbusiness	Fwd: Have Pills x/ana/x < Valiu/m/ % vK	14 Mar	dummies	yes
			Normal	2.2KB	Trina Garrison (umedriband@velnet.co.uk)	The NEW ISSUE STOCK I was telling you	14 Mar	marshac	none
			Normal	3.9KB	apjfbpb@attglobal.net	Re: ti Over Due wj Account	14 Mar	marshac	none
			Normal	3.3KB	Jeffery Haskins (jefferyhaskinshj@translate.ru	Spring time!	14 Mar	marshac	none
			Normal	8.0KB	velma_ewing@yahoo.com breeders	You Will Enjoy This	14 Mar	Marshac	none
			Normal	2.2KB	Lavonne N. Bingham (lbinghamcw@tvh.be)	06-Refinance as low as 2.90%	14 Mar	dummies	none
			Normal	2.9KB	roniemvafofbo@baguda.com	dummies Boost Your Cable Modem Speec	14 Mar	Yvette L	none
			Normal	5.8KB	Viola Cantu (jsavcxy@yahoo.com)		14 Mar	marshac	none
			Normal	5.7KB	chun-she (carrie@t-online.de)	Ïíñâôëòà ñäìèíàð	14 Mar	marshac	
			Normal	4.4KB	reports-headers (reports-response@habeas.c	[habeas.com #240754] AutoReply: Spam	14 Mar	marshac	none
			Normal	7.6KB	apxbdnfp@germany.net	Be All You Can Be.d k o	14 Mar	dummies	none
			Normal	4.3KB	Leigh Callahan (x505bli@150mail.com)	Re: Get it in the convenience of your hom	14 Mar	marshac	none
✓	✓	✓	Possible	4.2KB	Jarvis Sykes (sbyl9cz@aloha.net)	unhappy about the size of your love tool.	14 Mar	marshac	none
			Normal	2.7KB	rudy cato (gc7347@telesp.net.br)	Many On Stocks. Fwd: Vcod1n > X/A/VA	14 Mar	marshac	yes
			Normal	2.5KB	houston.christian@yahoo.com	With this simple patch I became bigger an	10 Mar	marshac	none

Figure 4-2: The free version of Mail-Washer.

As you can see from Figure 4-2, I can find out the following:

✦ **Who supposedly sent the e-mail, and from where:** I'm not really acquainted with (for instance) Lavonne N. Bingham (note that her e-mail address ends in .be — that's Belgium). I'm also not familiar with Viola Cantu, who strangely has jsavcxy as her e-mail ID at Yahoo. Not to mention my ol' buddy chun-she, otherwise known as carrie@t-online.de. (Hmmm, Germany? Don't know anyone there either.)

✦ **E-mail subject:** Just in case chun-she really does know me, he or she should know that I can't read the Cyrillic subject line (see the high-lighted row in Figure 4-2). I'm pretty sure I can delete that one. And although Velma sent me an e-mail letting me know how much I'd "enjoy" some unspecified thing, I'm really too busy to enjoy anything arriving from out of the blue just now, so I guess I'll delete that e-mail too.

✦ **To:** The To line can be a definite tip-off that an e-mail is spam. If some-one has e-mailed to a name other than my own or to an e-mail box at my website (with news about mortgages), I can assume that the e-mail wasn't sent by someone I know. For example, one e-mail was sent to Yvette. I have no Yvette at this e-mail address. (No naïfs here, either.)

✦ **Attachments:** If there's an attachment from someone I don't know, I delete the entire e-mail. As a matter of fact, I delete most e-mails with attachments. If a friend wants to send me something, they can always resend it.

By using MailWasher, you can delete the offending e-mails from your mail-box on the server, and then bring only the ones you want into your e-mail program.

MailWasher allows you to put check marks next to suspect e-mails. You can merely delete them, or you can bounce them back to whence they came and blacklist them (so they'll always be marked for deletion if they e-mail you again).

My e-mail program is set to get e-mail from the server only when I ask it to, so after I delete all the spam, I can click Send/Receive and feel considerably safer.

I've used the Pro version of MailWasher (see my website for details), which can scan more than one e-mail account. However, I suggest that you down-load the free version for one e-mail account and see whether you like it before paying $39.95 for the Pro version. You can download the free version at `www.mailwasher.net`.

Checking out nefarious e-mail

What? It seems I've received an e-mail from PayPal. They say my account needs to be renewed. Oh my! I certainly don't want to lose my PayPal account.

Or how about an e-mail from PayPal that says:

> *We recently reviewed your account and suspect that your PayPal account may have been accessed by an unauthorized third party. Protecting the security of your account and of the PayPal network is our primary concern. Therefore, as a preventative measure, we have temporarily limited access to sensitive PayPal account features.*

> *Click below in order to regain access to your account:*

Uh-huh. Right. As in, STOP RIGHT THERE!

Take a good look at the e-mail. Who is it addressed to? When PayPal sends you an e-mail, the opening line says "Dear (*your registered name*)." In my case, a real e-mail from PayPal read, "Dear Marsha Collier." Spam e-mails are usually more generic, addressed to "Dear Valued User" or "Dear *youremailaddress*.com." PayPal will *never* address an e-mail to your e-mail address.

Responding to these e-mails is tantamount to giving away your information to a stranger. Don't do it. I did some very careful investigating so I could show you how the scam works. Please read about what I found, but please read this first:

DO NOT TRY THIS AT HOME. If you suspect a message is spam, delete it.

I did open the e-mail shown in Figure 4-3, very carefully. It was an HTML message, and the trick I used works *only* with HTML e-mail: I right-clicked it and found (as expected) a View Source option.

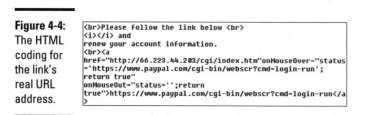

From: PayPal Service [service@paypal.com]   Sent: Sun 3/14/2004 2:36 PM
To: marshac@collierad.com
Cc:
Subject: Account issue

Dear PayPal valued member,

Due to concerns, for the safety and integrity of the PayPal
community we have issued this warning message.

It has come to our attention that your account information needs to be renew due to
inactive members, spoof reports and frauds.
If you could please take 5-10 minutes out of your online experience and renew your
records you will not run into any future problems with the online service.
However, failure to update your records will result in account deletion.
This notification expires on March 17,

Once you have updated your account
interrupted and will continue as normal

Please follow the link below
and renew your account information.
https://www.paypal.com/cgi-bin/websc

PayPal®

PayPal Service Department

Copy
Save Picture As...
Save Background As...
Select All
View Source
Edit Message
Properties

Figure 4-3:
Viewing the
source on
an e-mail.

The Notepad program opened, and I saw the e-mail in HTML text. I scrolled to the bottom, finding the line that said *Please follow the link below* (followed by a URL, as shown in Figure 4-4).

Figure 4-4:
The HTML
coding for
the link's
real URL
address.

```
<br>Please follow the link below <br>
<i></i> and
renew your account information.
<br><a
href="http://66.223.44.203/cgi/index.htm"onMouseOver="status
='https://www.paypal.com/cgi-bin/webscr?cmd=login-run';
return true"
onMouseOut="status='';return
true">https://www.paypal.com/cgi-bin/webscr?cmd=login-run</a
>
```

Take a good long look at the link, and at the URL embedded in the e-mail. Look just before it in the source code and you can see that the link *really* redirects whoever clicks it to `http://66.223.44.203/cgi/index.htm` — *not* to the PayPal secure URL! Liar, liar, pants on fire.

Okay, I investigated so I could show you what's going on (but again, *don't try this at home, friends* — it's risky). When I clicked the link, I came to a duplicate of the PayPal Log In page — or is it? A quick glance at the address bar of my browser confirmed I'd been misdirected. If I were really on PayPal, the URL address would have read like this:

```
https://www.paypal.com/cgi-bin/webscr?cmd=_login-run
```

Note that the real PayPal URL begins with `https`, not `http`. The s in `https` stands for *secure*.

If you want to find out for sure whether your PayPal or eBay (or bank account) account has a problem or suggests you view a recent charge, close the e-mail, go directly to the site and log in at the *real* URL. If your account does have a problem, you'll know right away.

Fighting Back!

There's quite a bit that you can do to help stop spam. According to Federal law, every e-mail should have an Unsubscribe link that does not require you to enter your e-mail address to stop getting the e-mails. Sound good? Well, there's a nasty catch. Read on.

Often the link that says "Click here to have your name removed from the list" goes directly to a site where the spammers actually collect e-mails from people and then exploit them. Have you ever clicked one of those? I have. I found out that those links are the gold standard for collecting valid e-mail addresses! If you respond to the spam in any way, shape, or form, they know they've reached a valid address — and watch the spam (or worse) to your mailbox increase!

When signing up for some sort of newsletter with an organization you're new to or unsure of, use an anonymous Yahoo!, Gmail, Outlook or Live address. It's easy enough to sign up for one, and if spammers get hold of that address, they will not be privy to your private address.

Also, no matter how curious you are about enlarging certain parts of your anatomy, don't even open the e-mails you receive on those topics. And certainly don't respond.

Last, report spammers. Several legitimate sites take reports and forward them to the appropriate authorities. Don't bother trying to forward the spam to the sender's ISP. These days they're mostly forged with aliases, and all you'll do is succeed in clogging up the e-mail system. Here are a couple of places you can go to report spammers:

✦ **Federal Trade Commission:** Yes, your tax dollars are at work. The FTC would like you to forward unwanted or deceptive messages to

`http://www.ftc.gov/opa/2004/07/newspamemail.shtm`

There the message becomes available to law enforcement (especially vital if the e-mail is trying to get your personal information).

✦ **SpamCop.net:** This outfit's been around since 1998 and reports spam e-mails to ISPs and mailers. A Report Spam tab appears on the home page (`http://www.spamcop.net/`) and these folks work hard to get spammers out of the loop.

Keeping Your Password (and Accounts) Secure

When was the last time you changed your passwords? I mean the whole enchilada: eBay, PayPal, your online bank account? Hey, I'm not the keeper of the *shoulds,* but you *should* change your critical passwords every 30 days — rain or shine. That's not just me saying that. It's all the security experts who know this kind of stuff. The world is full of bad-deed-doers just waiting to get their hands on your precious personal information. Password theft can lead to your bank account being emptied, your credit cards being pushed to the max, and worst of all, someone unsavory out there posing as you.

You've probably seen commercials on TV poking fun at the very real problem of identity theft. If you ask around your circle of friends, no doubt you'll find someone who knows someone who's been in this pickle. It can take years to undo the damage caused by identity theft, so a better plan is to stay vigilant and protect yourself from becoming a victim. It can also take a lot of money — a Utica College study found that it costs the average victim of identity theft an actual dollar loss of $31,356.

In this section, I give you some tips for selecting good passwords and other personal security information. I also show you the type of passwords to stay away from and what to do if (heaven forbid!) your personal information is compromised.

Reporting hijacked accounts

If someone gets hold of your personal information, the most important thing to do is report it immediately. If you see any items that aren't yours on the Items I'm Bidding On or the Items I'm Selling area of your My eBay page, it's time to make a report — and *fast!*

Okay, you know that something hinky is going on with your eBay account because *you* never placed a bid on the Britney Spears stage-worn T-shirt. (Did you? Let's say you didn't.) And you can't imagine that your spouse did, either (but double-check just to be sure). Here's what to do immediately:

✦ **Change your personal e-mail account password with your ISP.** Go to your ISP's home page and look for an area called Member Center or something similar. In the Member Center, access your personal account information — probably through a link called something like My Account. You should be able to change your password there.

✦ **Change the e-mail account password on your home computer.** Don't forget to change the password on your computer's e-mail software as well (Outlook, Firefox, and the like), so you can continue to download your e-mail from the server.

Perhaps you discover that your private information has been compromised when you suddenly can't log in to your eBay or PayPal account. If this happens on eBay, follow these steps to request a new password:

1. **Go to the eBay Sign In page.**

Don't type your password. You just tried that and it doesn't work.

2. **Click the *Forgot your password* link, as shown in Figure 4-5.**

Figure 4-5:
The Forgot your password link on the Sign In page.

eBay Welcome to eBay

Sign in

User ID

Password

Forgot your user ID or password?

☑ Stay signed in (Uncheck if you're on a shared computer)

Sign in

New to eBay?

Register

Doing this takes you to a page (shown in Figure 4-6) where you're prompted to type in your user ID. Those silly security questions that you answered when you registered for eBay become very important now.

3. **Answer at least one of the questions you see on the page, and then provide your registered phone number and ZIP code.**

4. **Click Continue.**

   eBay will e-mail you instructions for resetting your password.

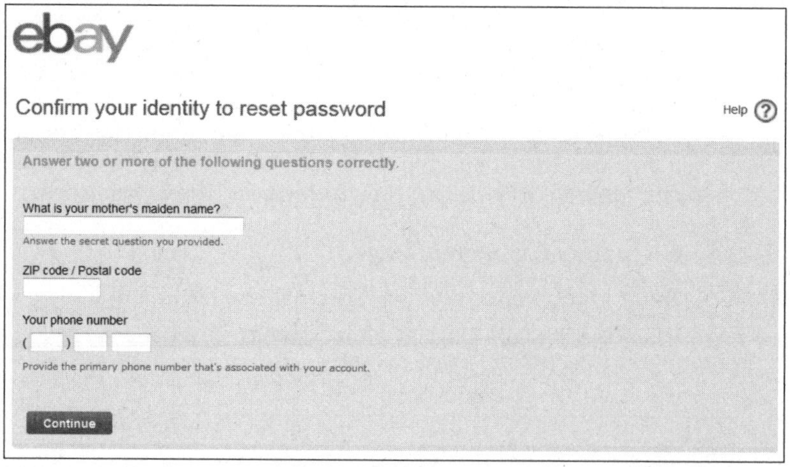

Figure 4-6:
Answer
two or
more of the
following
questions
correctly.

> # ebay
>
> Confirm your identity to reset password   Help (?)
>
> Answer two or more of the following questions correctly.
>
> What is your mother's maiden name?
> [   ]
> Answer the secret question you provided.
>
> ZIP code / Postal code
> [   ]
>
> Your phone number
> (   ) [   ] [   ]
> Provide the primary phone number that's associated with your account.
>
> [Continue]

5. **When the e-mail arrives, follow the steps and change your password.**

   If you *don't* get eBay's e-mail telling you how to change your password, it means some fraudster may have changed the contact information in your eBay account. See the sidebar "Act quickly but don't freak out" for instructions on what to do.

6. **If all goes well and you can change your password, go to the link pictured in Figure 4-7 to change your password hint (that's the secret question that lets the system know you're you).**

Choosing a good secret question

If you read the harrowing procedure in the "Act quickly but don't freak out" sidebar, you know that having someone sabotage your eBay account is something you never want to go through. But if your secret question is easy to figure out, someone with bad intentions can wreak havoc on your account even more easily.

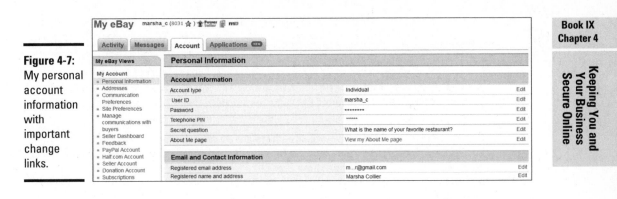

Figure 4-7:
My personal
account
information
with
important
change
links.

Your password is only as secure as the secret question, so *don't relate your password and secret question to each other in any way.* For example, do not make your secret question a clue to your password — and *especially* don't make your password answer the secret question. Better yet, think of your secret question as a separate, auxiliary security device for your account.

Figure 4-8 shows eBay's Create a Secret Question and Answer page, which you can access from your My eBay Preferences page. It shows several suggested questions.

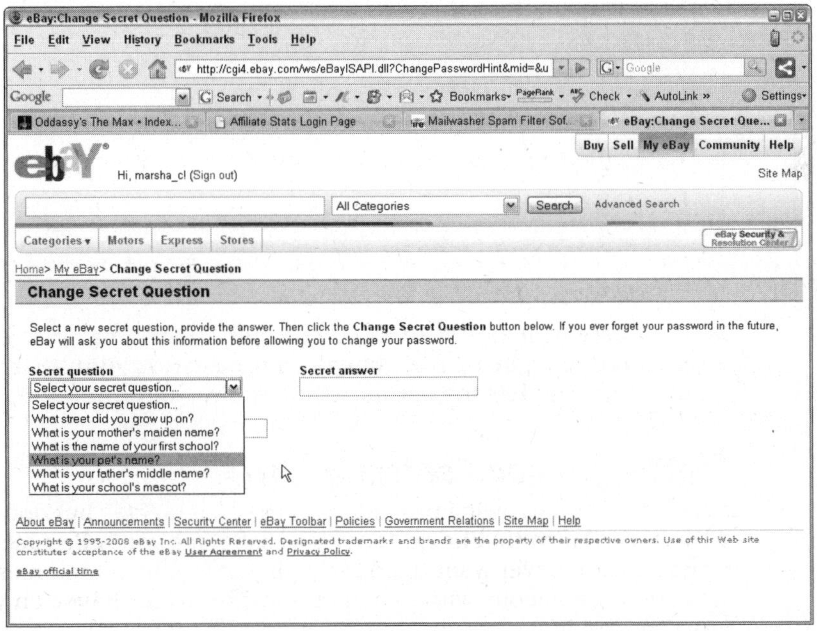

Figure 4-8:
Create
your secret
question.

REMEMBER

Act quickly but don't freak out

If you can't seem to get a new password for your eBay account, and you're unsuccessful at contacting eBay, there's still hope. Remain calm, follow these steps, and take notes as you go:

1. **Since the redesign of the eBay website, there are no more bottom links on the home page. Scroll all the way to the bottom, and on the left side of the page you will see a light-colored tab labeled** *Legal & more*. **Click there and links to all eBay interior pages appear (see the figure).**

   Alternatively, you can go to any eBay item page (or any page on the site) and find a link at the very bottom to the Security Center. Whichever set of links you go to, click the link to the Security Center.

2. **When you get to the Security Center, find the Report Problem category.**

3. **Under the Report Problem headline click** *Report an Account Theft*.

4. **On the following page, find the boldface headline that reads** *If you can't sign in, contact us immediately*. **Click the link to contact eBay immediately.**

   The page that appears has a link you can use to call eBay.

5. **Click the** *Call us* **link (they are on duty 24/7).**

   You will be presented with a number to call and a customer service representative will help you sort things out.

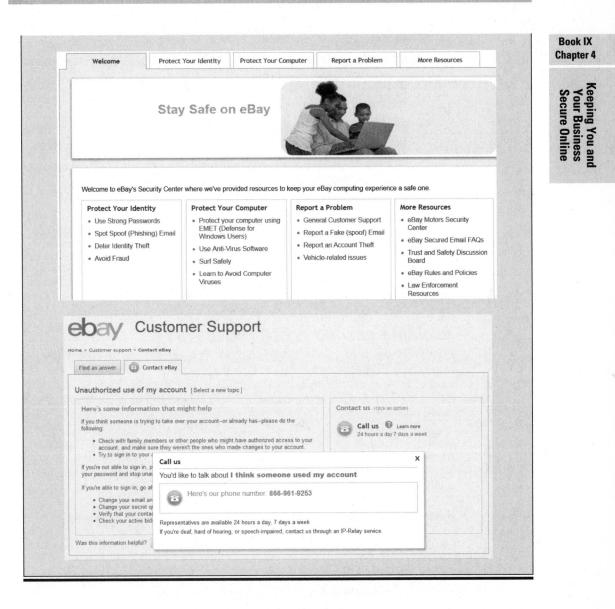

Here are some tips for setting a secure secret question:

✦ **Never use your mother's maiden name.** That is most likely the *secret* that your bank uses as your challenge question. (They usually ask when you open the account.) So that is definitely out — you don't want to give *anybody* that word.

✦ **Select a question and provide a** *creative* **answer:**

- **What is your pet's name?** Give an answer such as Ralph the Rhino or Graak the Pterodactyl or something a bit more wildly creative. Don't give your actual pet's name (or species). Anyone who knows you is likely to know your pet's name.

- **What street did you grow up on?** Name an unusual landmark from your hometown. Don't use a street name.

- **What is the name of your first school?** Make up a good one — perhaps Elementary Penguin Academy? School of Hard Knox?

- **What is your father's middle name?** Make up a goodie or skip it.

- **What is your school's mascot?** There's a lot of creativity that can go on here. How about red-and-white-striped zebra? Pink elephant?

Your bylaws for selecting answers to a secret question are two: Be creative, *and* be sure you remember the darned thing! (And here's one more: Don't use any of the examples I just used. Make up your own.)

Avoiding easily hacked passwords

Poorly chosen passwords are the number-one loophole for hackers. If you think that hackers are just a small group of hypercaffeinated teenagers, think again. It's now also the domain of small- and big-time crooks who hack into an account, spend a few thousand dollars that belong to someone else, and move on.

I searched Google for hacking software and came up with over 2 million matches. Many of these websites offer an arsenal of free hacking tools. They also provide step-by-step instructions for beginners on how to crack passwords. The Internet can be its own worst enemy.

Here are some industrial-strength tips for setting a secure password:

✦ **Number of characters:** Compose your password of more than eight characters.

✦ **Case sensitivity:** Because passwords are case-sensitive, take advantage of the feature. Mix lowercase and uppercase in your passwords.

✦ **Letters and numbers:** Combine letters and numbers to make your passwords harder to crack.

✦ **Proper words:** Don't use proper words that appear in the dictionary. Think of the title of your favorite book. Make your password the first two letters of each word with numbers in the middle (*not* sequential).

Stay smart: Don't be a make-it-easy!

Any beginning hacker (or tech-smart teenager) can figure out your password if it falls into the following categories. Don't use 'em! They are pathetically easy!

✔ **The obvious:** The word *Password*. D'oh!

✔ **Birthdays:** Don't use your birthday, your friend's birthday, or John F. Kennedy's birthday. Not only are these dates common knowledge, but so is this truism: A series of numbers is easy to crack.

✔ **Names:** Don't use your first name, last name, your dog's name, or anyone's name. Again, it's common knowledge and easy to find out. (Most people know my husband's name; it's been in many of my books!)

✔ **Contact numbers:** Nix on *any* Social Security Number (if they get hold of *that* one — watch out!), phone numbers, your e-mail address, or street address. For classic phone-book information, try sites like Spokeo (`http://www.spokeo.com/`), pipl (`https://pipl.com/`), or PeekYou (`http://www.peekyou.com/`).

✔ **Any of the lousy (easily cracked and most frequently used) passwords in the table:** The words in this table have been gleaned from password dictionaries available from hackers. Note that this is *not* a complete list by any means; there are thousands of common (lousy) passwords, and "unprintable" ones are a lot more common than you may think. If you really care to scare yourself, Google the phrase *common passwords*.

!@#$%	!@#$%^&	!@#$%^&*(	0	0000	00000000	0007
007	01234	123456	02468	24680	1	1101
111	11111	111111	1234	12345	1234qwer	123abc
123go	12	131313	212	310	2003	2004
54321	654321	888888	a	aaa	abc	abc123
action	absolut	access	admin	admin123	access	administrator
alpha	asdf	animal	biteme	computer	eBay	enable
foobar	home	Internet	login	love	mypass	mypc
owner	pass	password	passwrd	papa	peace	penny
pepsi	qwerty	secret	superman	temp	temp123	test
test123	whatever	whatnot	winter	windows	xp	xxx
yoda	mypc123	powerseller	sexy			

It should go without saying, but what the heck: Don't use any of the sample passwords shown here. It's safe to say that lots of people will be reading this book, and anything seen by lots of people isn't secret. (I know you know that, but still.)

Chapter 5: Networking Your Office

In This Chapter

✔ **Setting up your network**

✔ **Getting secure, Internet style**

The first time I spoke to my editors about putting information in my books about networking a home business, they scoffed at me. People who worked at home in the early days didn't need computer networks (as if networks were solely for big companies with lots of cubicles). The more I spoke to the eBay community, however, the more I saw the need for home networks — and the more people asked me about them.

I started writing about eBay in 1998, and now it's more than ten years later. A lot of technology has washed under the bridge, and many advances have been made. Setting up a network in 1999 meant spending hours (maybe days) changing settings, testing, checking computers, and cursing. That was if you were lucky enough to finally get it right. Otherwise — as was the case for most home users, including me — you'd give up, take the whole thing as a loss, and go on with your life.

Luckily for us non-techie types, networks are considerably more home-network-friendly than in the old days. Also, more pleasant modes of networking (other than having miles of Ethernet cables snaking around the walls of your house) came to the fore of technology.

By networking your home (or office) you'll save time by having the flexibility to work from different rooms or locations. You can also list items out by the pool (or in your backyard) in summer!

This chapter is a quick-and-dirty discussion of home networks installed on Windows-based PCs. Happily, since I have a Mac user in my home, I've found that networking is pretty universal. In this chapter, I give you a lesson on what I know works for most people. (Hey, if it doesn't work, don't e-mail me — head back to the store and get your money back!)

At this point, I want to remind you that I'm not a super techno-whiz, even though I do host a *Computer and Technology Radio* show (just like I'm not a lawyer or an accountant). Ping me on Twitter (@marshacollier) if you're having trouble — I'll try to help.

The What and Why of Networks

What is a network? Well, these days it doesn't mean a TV channel: A *network* is a way to connect computers so that they can communicate with each other — as if they were one giant computer with different terminals. The best part is that a network enables all those computers to share a single high-speed Internet connection, as well as the sharing of printers and other peripherals. When you set up a network, you can give Internet access to several appropriately equipped devices — computers, tablets, smartphones, or TVs. From each networked device, it's possible to access other networked devices.

You can connect as many devices as you like and run your business from anywhere in your home — you can even hook up your laptop, tablet, or smartphone from the bedroom if you don't feel like getting out of bed.

Now for the *whys* of a home network. A network is a convenient way to run a business. All businesses use them, and so should you. You can extend your DSL line, fiber-optic, or Internet cable connection so that you can access it anywhere in your home — as well as in your office.

In networked computers, you can set directories in each computer to be *shared.* That way, other computers on the network can access those directories. You can also password-protect specific files and directories to prevent others (your children or your employees) from accessing them.

Variations of a Home Network

You have a choice of three types of home networks: Ethernet, powerline, and wireless. See Table 5-1 for a quick rundown of some pros and cons of each.

Table 5-1	**Network Pros and Cons**	
Network Type	*Pros*	*Cons*
Traditional Ethernet*	Fast, cheap, and easy to set up	Computers and printers must be hardwired; cables run everywhere
Powerline	Fast; your home is prewired with outlets	Electrical interference may degrade the signal
Wireless network**	Pretty fast; wireless (no ugly cords to deal with)	May not be reliable because of interference from home electrical devices

*Connects computers over a maximum of 328 feet of cabling.

**Several flavors of wireless are available. See "Hooking up with wireless," later in this chapter.

So many networks, so little time

The best part of networking today is that you can combine more than one type of network to form a fully functional, professional data-transfer medium with Internet access — throughout the house. In my house, I used to have an Ethernet/home phoneline/wireless combination. Home phoneline networks (10 Mbps networks that operate over existing phone lines without the need for additional wiring, routers, or hubs) aren't popular with consumers. It's not that they didn't work flawlessly; they did. It just seems that I'm the only one in the United States with enough otherwise-unused phone jacks in my home and office to make it work.

After the downfall of phoneline networking, the geniuses began to think, "What does the average home have lots of outlets for?" Hmmmm, how about electricity? Duh, how about running the network through a home's electric outlets? And behold, the powerline network was born.

Now we have wireless networks too — and they're life-changing when they work. It's funny to see a whole new generation of people moving around tweaking antennas to try to get a good signal. It reminds me of television when I was a kid. (Maybe I should put some tinfoil around the wireless antenna? Naw. People might look at me funny.)

Many people still use an Ethernet connection to hardwire the network's main (desktop) computer to connect to a wireless router. If you have an office, it's nice to know that Ethernet cabling will work over 300-foot distances. You can then connect laptops (and desktops) throughout the house via wireless and powerline.

The wireless network is the hot ticket — highly touted by the technorati, and, er, assimilating more households all the time. However, in a home office setting, the wireless signal may experience interference because many networks run with the same 2.4GHz technology as some home wireless telephones. I have a wireless network and it works great. My primary network hookup is via Ethernet. But it's actually a hybrid, combining Ethernet, powerline, and wireless

With broadband over powerline, you get high-speed Internet directly into your home electrical system. Just plug in your powerline boxes (more on that later) and you're up and running.

All networks need the following two devices:

✦ **Router:** A router allows you to share a single Internet IP address among multiple computers. A router does exactly what its name implies; it routes signals and data to and from the different computers on your network.

If you have one computer, the router can act as a firewall or even a network device leading to a wireless print or media server.

✦ **Modem:** You need a modem for an Internet connection. You get one from your cable or phone company and plug it into an outlet with cable (just like your TV) or into a phone jack if you have DSL. The modem connects to your router with an Ethernet cable.

If you have broadband, you don't need to have a main computer powered on to access the connection anywhere in the house. If you keep a wireless-enabled printer turned on, you can also connect to that and print from your laptop in another room — right through the wireless network.

Extending wireless with powerline

An ingenious invention, a *powerline wireless extender* uses your existing home powerlines to carry your network and your high-speed Internet connection. You access the network by plugging a powerline adapter wired to your router into an electrical outlet on the wall. Then another little box can be placed farther away in your home to broadcast an additional wireless signal. Standard powerline networks have been around for a while; this is the second round of technological advances for them.

I have used a powerline wireless extender so I can bring my network out to the garage and to far points in my home.

Hooking up a powerline network or extender is so easy that it's a bit disappointing — you'll wonder why it isn't more complicated. Most installations work immediately right out of the box. Figure 5-1 shows you the base setup. Other rooms need only a powerline wireless adapter.

Hooking up the wireless/powerline network goes like this:

1. **The high-speed connection comes in through your DSL or cable line.**

2. **Plug the cable line (or phoneline for DSL) into your modem.**

3. **Connect one "in" Ethernet cable from your modem to a router.**

4. **Connect the "out" Ethernet cable to the wireless powerline extender.**

5. **Plug the wireless powerline extender into a convenient wall outlet.**

6. **Plug the wireless powerline receiver box into a convenient wall outlet wherever you want to extend the signal.**

That's it!

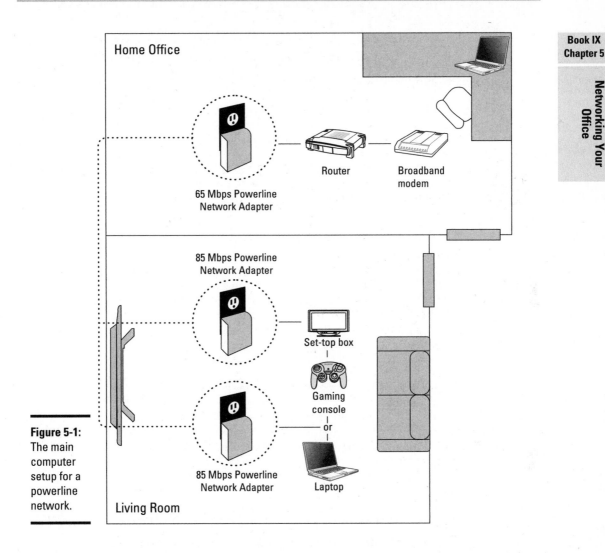

Figure 5-1:
The main
computer
setup for a
powerline
network.

The benefits of using powerline as a Wi-Fi network *or* as a network extender
are as follows:

✦ **It's fairly inexpensive.** The requisite powerline magic box costs around
$50, but you'll need one for each computer you connect.

✦ **It's fast — as fast as (or faster than) other network connections.** You
could stream DVD movies from one room to another.

✦ **The networking connection is made through your existing electrical
wiring.** It doesn't consume extra electricity.

✦ **Installation is easy.** Just plug a cable into your computer, and connect
the cable to the powerline box. Plug in the powerline box.

If you have a high-speed Internet connection, no doubt you received a modem when you signed up. Because it's not common to connect the modem directly to your computer (a router does the network routing for you), you may already have a router.

The network integration works like this:

✦ The high-speed connection comes in through your DSL or cable line.

✦ The cable (or DSL) line plugs into your modem.

✦ An Ethernet cable goes from your modem into a router.

✦ One "out" Ethernet cable connection from the router goes to a local computer.

✦ Another "out" Ethernet cable goes to the powerline adapter.

✦ The powerline box plugs into a convenient wall outlet.

When you want to connect the computers in other rooms to the network, just plug in a magic powerline box.

Hooking up with wireless

Wireless networking — Wi-Fi (or, to the more technically inclined, IEEE 802.11) — is the go-to technology for all kinds of networks. It's an impressive system when it works, with no cables or connectors to bog you down.

If you're worried about your next-door neighbor hacking into your computer through your wireless connection, stop worrying. Wireless networks are protected by their own brand of security, called WPA (Wi-Fi Protected Access). Although super-hackers have cracked this system, it's the best currently available for the home office user.

WPA utilizes a *pre-shared key* (PSK) mode, where every user on the network is given the same passphrase. In the PSK mode, security depends on the strength and secrecy of the passphrase. So, to link your laptop or desktop to a wireless network with WPA encryption, you need the pre-determined passphrase. Just enter it during setup — on every computer that uses the network — and you should be good to go.

Most free Wi-Fi hotspots you come across may have no encryption, so never send personal information in such an environment.

The different flavors of wireless

If you've ever used a wireless telephone at home, you've used a technology similar to a wireless network. Most home wireless phones transmit on the radio frequency band of 2.4 GHz and have the option to choose from several channels automatically to give you the best connection.

You may get confused when you see the different types of wireless available. Here's the lowdown on the variations:

✦ **802.11a:** This is a wireless format that works really well — fast with good connectivity. It's used when you have to serve up a wireless connection to a large group of people, as in a convention center or a dormitory. It delivers data at speeds as high as 54 Mbps (megabits per second). It also runs at the 5 GHz band, so it doesn't compete with wireless phones or microwave ovens for bandwidth

✦ **802.11b:** My laptop has a built-in 802.11b card, so I can connect to the ever popular hotspots in Starbucks and airports. It's a fairly common wireless type and is used on the most platforms. It travels over the 2.4 GHz band. The 802.11b version is slower than the 802.11a version, transferring data at only 11 Mbps.

The lower frequency of 2.4 GHz drains less power from laptops and other portable devices. Also, 2.4 GHz signals travel farther, and can penetrate walls and floors more effectively than 5 GHz signals.

✦ **802.11g:** This flavor is based on the 2.4 GHz band. It speeds data up to a possible 54 Mbps, and it's backward-compatible with 802.11b service.

✦ **802.11n:** The newest mode builds on the previous standards by adding multiple-input multiple-output (MIMO). MIMO is a technology that uses multiple antennas (usually built into the router) to carry more information than previously with a single antenna. It uses the 5 GHz band (versus the 2.4 it used previously). It can increases speed through your TCP/IP connection to 450 Mbps.

✦ **802.11ac**: The very latest iteration comes in two speeds: 867 Mbps and 1300 Mbps. It also works only on the 5 GHz band and dual-band routers can only operate on 2.4 GHz band at speeds of 802.11n. Theoretically, 802.11ac can go up to speeds of 6.93 Gbps and beyond, but since it's so new, we'll have to wait and see. For a peek at what's coming, go to

```
http://blogs.cisco.com/wireless/cisco-will-ride-the-
   802-11ac-wave2/
```

For maximum speed at this time, your entire network needs to be an 802.11n 5 GHz network. Some of my legacy devices only work at 2.4 GHz, so I run a dual system and let the device make its own choice of connection speed.

Setting up your wireless network

Installing your wireless network isn't a gut-wrenching experience either (although it can be if the signal doesn't reach where you want it). You hook up your computer (a laptop works best) to the wireless access point (the gizmo with the antenna that broadcasts your signal throughout your home or office) to perform some setup tasks such as choosing your channel and setting up the WPA code. (The wireless access point often comes with a preset WPA code).

After you complete the setup and turn on your wireless access point, you have a Wi-Fi hotspot in your home or office. Typically, a hotspot provides coverage for about 100 feet in all directions, although walls and floors cut down on the range.

Here are some simplified steps on configuring your network:

1. **Run a cable from your DSL or cable line to your modem.**
2. **Connect an Ethernet cable from your modem to your router.**
3. **Connect another Ethernet cable to your wireless access point.**
4. **Type in the passphrase to all computers on the network.**

Take a look at the network diagram in Figure 5-2.

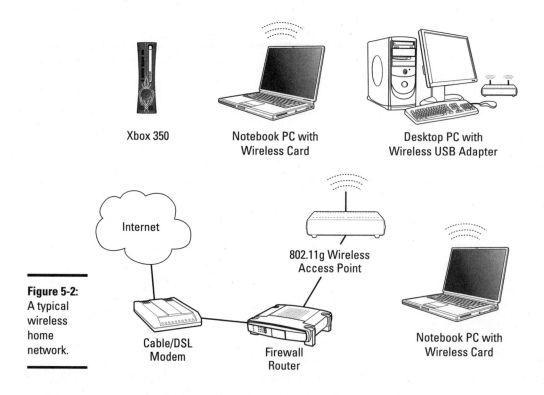

Xbox 350

Notebook PC with Wireless Card

Desktop PC with Wireless USB Adapter

Internet

802.11g Wireless Access Point

Figure 5-2: A typical wireless home network.

Cable/DSL Modem

Firewall Router

Notebook PC with Wireless Card

Internet Security and Your Home Network

Broadband Internet connections are always on — which means your computer is exposed to possible invaders. You should shield your computer with a strong firewall and an antivirus program.

When you're connected to the Internet, you're exposed not only to hackers but also to threats such as *Trojan horses,* programs that can get into your computer when you innocently view an infected website. Once inside your computer, the Trojan horse, like ET, phones home. From there, an evil-deed-doer, who now has a direct line to your computer, may be able to wreak havoc with your precious data.

Visit the website for Gibson Research Corporation at www.grc.com. Gibson Research is the brainchild of an early PC pioneer, Steve Gibson, who's renowned in the world of codes and programming. Steve is *the* expert when it comes to exposing the vulnerabilities of systems over the Internet. A few free diagnostic programs on this site will check your computer's vulnerability to Internet threats.

Shields UP! (at https://www.grc.com/faq-shieldsup.htm) and LeakTest (https://www.grc.com/lt/leaktest.htm) test your computer for vulnerabilities — and terrify you with results that expose the your Internet connection as a sitting duck. Which is an excellent reason to use them — and then get to fixing the holes.

Index

S

Notes

Notes

Notes

About the Author

Marsha Collier, one of the world's foremost experts and educators in the fields of eBay and e-commerce, is also a top-selling eBay author with over 1 million copies of her books in print (including special editions for the UK, Germany, France, Canada, Australia, China, and an edition in Spanish). And her name frequently crops up in the same breath as e-commerce and customer service; no surprise there. She's the author of the *For Dummies* series on eBay (*eBay For Dummies, Starting an eBay Business For Dummies, eBay Business All-in-One For Dummies*) plus many other related, best-selling titles.

Marsha is especially proud of two books: *eBay For Dummies,* the bestselling book for eBay beginners, and *eBay Business All-in-One For Dummies,* the bestselling title on operating an eBay business. She intermixes her writing about eBay with her role as experienced spokesperson. While traveling across the United States and around the world, she makes regular appearances on television, radio, and in print to discuss online commerce and customer service. In her spare time, Marsha co-hosts the *Computer and Technology Radio* on wsradio.com (http://www.wsradio.com/wsradio/show_details/52).

Marsha earned her eBay stripes as a longtime seller on the site. She began her eBay selling career in 1996 to earn extra money for her daughter's education (and eventually paid for university with her eBay earnings). She grew her business to a full-time venture and was one of the first eBay PowerSellers. Nowadays, you can find everything from autographed copies of her books to photo supplies, pet toys, and DVDs in her eBay Store ("Marsha Collier's Fabulous Finds") at http://stores.ebay.com/Marsha-Colliers-Fabulous-Finds and on her website, www.coolebaytools.com.

In 2004, Marsha began publishing a blog, Marsha Collier's Musings http://mcollier.blogspot.com to talk about timely topics she thinks her readers will enjoy. An early innovator in social media, Marsha penned several books, two of her favorites are *The Ultimate Online Customer Service Guide* and *Social Media Commerce For Dummies*. Her online brand has grown as she shares her thoughts on how businesses can make the most of the Internet. She has recently been awarded several honors:

> 2013 Forbes: *Top 20 Women Social Media Influencers*
>
> 2013 Forbes: *Top 50 Social Media Power Influencers*
>
> Edelman Tweetlevel: *Top Media 100 Users by Influence*
>
> 2012 Forbes: *Top 50 Social Media Power Influencers*
>
> 2012: *30 Best Female Bloggers*

2012 Small Business Book Awards, Startup Book Category: *Starting an eBay Business For Dummies*

2012: *The 100 Most Powerful Women On Twitter*

2011 Forbes: *Top 10 Women Social Media Influencers*

2011 PeerIndex: *#1 Customer Experience Online Influencers*

Marsha currently resides in Los Angeles, CA. You can contact Marsha via her website, `coolebaytools.com`.

Dedication

This book is dedicated to all you prospective eBay and online sellers who have the dream and the drive to succeed. I wrote this book for you, and I share my expertise and research so you can skip the trial-and-error and go straight to work gaining the most profits. Those who succeed join me in knowing that hard work and loving what you do get the job done — and lead you to financial achievement and contentment.

Good luck in your endeavors. I know this book will help you get to the next level.

Acknowledgments

Writing a book is a monumental task. Lots of people have helped, but the lion's share of assistance comes from the encouragement that I receive from social media friends and the eBay community.

I've had unending support from my fiancé, Curt Buthman. We've had to put our lives on hold while I've been writing this book, and he's been really swell (yes, I said swell) putting up with my crazy writing schedule. I am ever grateful for his love and understanding.

If it weren't for Patti "Louise" Ruby's friendship and support as the tech editor for this book, I think I might have lost my mind. She helped me keep on top of the many changes on the eBay site and never said no to my seemingly endless requests.

Once again, I was blessed with Leah Michael and Barry Childs-Helton who were my editors on this book. Working with Leah is a dream. She's there to lend her unique style of smart savvyness to my words. She truly "gets it" like no one else. And Barry cleans up after us both. You'd almost think there's no one on earth with such vast experience with the English language. I'm honored to have them as my editors; they help create the very best in the *For Dummies* series. Thank you, Leah and Barry.

Then, of course, I thank the management at John Wiley & Sons, Inc., my publisher, Andy Cummings, and my acquisitions editor, Steven Hayes, both work hard to fill the world with instructional and entertaining books.

Publisher's Acknowledgments

Executive Editor: Steven Hayes

Senior Editors: Leah Michael,
    Barry Childs-Helton

Technical Editor: Patti Louise Ruby

Editorial Assistant: Annie Sullivan

Sr. Editorial Assistant: Cherie Case

Project Coordinator: Sheree Montgomery

Cover Image: Laptop and cart:
    © Henrik Jonsson / iStockphoto;
    Background: © Jelena Veskovic /
    iStockphoto; Shopping icons:
    © Elena Genova / iStockphoto

Apple & Mac

iPad For Dummies,
5th Edition
978-1-118-49823-1

iPhone 5 For Dummies,
6th Edition
978-1-118-35201-4

MacBook For Dummies,
4th Edition
978-1-118-20920-2

OS X Mountain Lion
For Dummies
978-1-118-39418-2

Blogging & Social Media

Facebook For Dummies,
4th Edition
978-1-118-09562-1

Mom Blogging
For Dummies
978-1-118-03843-7

Pinterest For Dummies
978-1-118-32800-2

WordPress For Dummies,
5th Edition
978-1-118-38318-6

Business

Commodities For Dummies,
2nd Edition
978-1-118-01687-9

Investing For Dummies,
6th Edition
978-0-470-90545-6

Personal Finance
For Dummies,
7th Edition
978-1-118-11785-9

QuickBooks 2013
For Dummies
978-1-118-35641-8

Small Business Marketing Kit
For Dummies,
3rd Edition
978-1-118-31183-7

Careers

Job Interviews
For Dummies,
4th Edition
978-1-118-11290-8

Job Searching with
Social Media
For Dummies
978-0-470-93072-4

Personal Branding
For Dummies
978-1-118-11792-7

Resumes For Dummies,
6th Edition
978-0-470-87361-8

Success as a Mediator
For Dummies
978-1-118-07862-4

Diet & Nutrition

Belly Fat Diet For Dummies
978-1-118-34585-6

Eating Clean For Dummies
978-1-118-00013-7

Nutrition For Dummies,
5th Edition
978-0-470-93231-5

Digital Photography

Digital Photography
For Dummies,
7th Edition
978-1-118-09203-3

Digital SLR Cameras &
Photography For Dummies,
4th Edition
978-1-118-14489-3

Photoshop Elements 11
For Dummies
978-1-118-40821-6

Gardening

Herb Gardening
For Dummies,
2nd Edition
978-0-470-61778-6

Vegetable Gardening
For Dummies,
2nd Edition
978-0-470-49870-5

Health

Anti-Inflammation Diet
For Dummies
978-1-118-02381-5

Diabetes For Dummies,
3rd Edition
978-0-470-27086-8

Living Paleo For Dummies
978-1-118-29405-5

Hobbies

Beekeeping
For Dummies
978-0-470-43065-1

eBay For Dummies,
7th Edition
978-1-118-09806-6

Raising Chickens
For Dummies
978-0-470-46544-8

Wine For Dummies,
5th Edition
978-1-118-28872-6

Writing Young Adult Fiction
For Dummies
978-0-470-94954-2

Language &
Foreign Language

500 Spanish Verbs
For Dummies
978-1-118-02382-2

English Grammar
For Dummies,
2nd Edition
978-0-470-54664-2

French All-in One
For Dummies
978-1-118-22815-9

German Essentials
For Dummies
978-1-118-18422-6

Italian For Dummies
2nd Edition
978-1-118-00465-4

e **Available in print and e-book formats.**

Math & Science

Algebra I For Dummies,
2nd Edition
978-0-470-55964-2

Anatomy and Physiology
For Dummies,
2nd Edition
978-0-470-92326-9

Astronomy For Dummies,
3rd Edition
978-1-118-37697-3

Biology For Dummies,
2nd Edition
978-0-470-59875-7

Chemistry For Dummies,
2nd Edition
978-1-1180-0730-3

Pre-Algebra Essentials
For Dummies
978-0-470-61838-7

Microsoft Office

Excel 2013 For Dummies
978-1-118-51012-4

Office 2013 All-in-One
For Dummies
978-1-118-51636-2

PowerPoint 2013
For Dummies
978-1-118-50253-2

Word 2013 For Dummies
978-1-118-49123-2

Music

Blues Harmonica
For Dummies
978-1-118-25269-7

Guitar For Dummies,
3rd Edition
978-1-118-11554-1

iPod & iTunes
For Dummies,
10th Edition
978-1-118-50864-0

Programming

Android Application
Development For
Dummies, 2nd Edition
978-1-118-38710-8

iOS 6 Application
Development For Dummies
978-1-118-50880-0

Java For Dummies,
5th Edition
978-0-470-37173-2

Religion & Inspiration

The Bible For Dummies
978-0-7645-5296-0

Buddhism For Dummies,
2nd Edition
978-1-118-02379-2

Catholicism For Dummies,
2nd Edition
978-1-118-07778-8

Self-Help & Relationships

Bipolar Disorder
For Dummies,
2nd Edition
978-1-118-33882-7

Meditation For Dummies,
3rd Edition
978-1-118-29144-3

Seniors

Computers For Seniors
For Dummies,
3rd Edition
978-1-118-11553-4

iPad For Seniors
For Dummies,
5th Edition
978-1-118-49708-1

Social Security
For Dummies
978-1-118-20573-0

Smartphones & Tablets

Android Phones
For Dummies
978-1-118-16952-0

Kindle Fire HD
For Dummies
978-1-118-42223-6

NOOK HD For Dummies,
Portable Edition
978-1-118-39498-4

Surface For Dummies
978-1-118-49634-3

Test Prep

ACT For Dummies,
5th Edition
978-1-118-01259-8

ASVAB For Dummies,
3rd Edition
978-0-470-63760-9

GRE For Dummies,
7th Edition
978-0-470-88921-3

Officer Candidate Tests,
For Dummies
978-0-470-59876-4

Physician's Assistant Exam
For Dummies
978-1-118-11556-5

Series 7 Exam
For Dummies
978-0-470-09932-2

Windows 8

Windows 8 For Dummies
978-1-118-13461-0

Windows 8 For Dummies,
Book + DVD Bundle
978-1-118-27167-4

Windows 8 All-in-One
For Dummies
978-1-118-11920-4

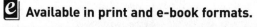 **Available in print and e-book formats.**

Take Dummies with you everywhere you go!

Whether you're excited about e-books, want more from the web, must have your mobile apps, or swept up in social media, Dummies makes everything easier .

Dummies products make life easier!

- DIY
- Consumer Electronics
- Crafts

- Software
- Cookware
- Hobbies

- Videos
- Music
- Games
- and More!

For more information, go to **Dummies.com®** and search the store by category.

FOR **DUMMIES**

A Wiley Brand